Lecture Notes in Computer Science 15891

Founding Editors

Gerhard Goos
Juris Hartmanis

The series Lecture Notes in Computer Science (LNCS), including its subseries Lecture Notes in Artificial Intelligence (LNAI) and Lecture Notes in Bioinformatics (LNBI), has established itself as a medium for the publication of new developments in computer science and information technology research, teaching, and education.

LNCS enjoys close cooperation with the computer science R & D community, the series counts many renowned academics among its volume editors and paper authors, and collaborates with prestigious societies. Its mission is to serve this international community by providing an invaluable service, mainly focused on the publication of conference and workshop proceedings and postproceedings. LNCS commenced publication in 1973.

Osvaldo Gervasi · Beniamino Murgante ·
Chiara Garau · Yeliz Karaca ·
Maria Noelia Faginas Lago · Francesco Scorza ·
Ana Cristina Braga

Editors

Computational Science and Its Applications – ICCSA 2025 Workshops

Istanbul, Turkey, June 30 – July 3, 2025
Proceedings, Part VI

 Springer

Editors
Osvaldo Gervasi 🆔
University of Perugia
Perugia, Italy

Beniamino Murgante 🆔
University of Basilicata
Potenza, Italy

Chiara Garau 🆔
University of Cagliari
Cagliari, Italy

Yeliz Karaca 🆔
University of Massachusetts
Worcester, MA, USA

Maria Noelia Faginas Lago 🆔
University of Perugia
Perugia, Italy

Francesco Scorza 🆔
University of Basilicata
Potenza, Italy

Ana Cristina Braga 🆔
University of Minho
Braga, Portugal

ISSN 0302-9743   ISSN 1611-3349 (electronic)
Lecture Notes in Computer Science
ISBN 978-3-031-97616-2   ISBN 978-3-031-97617-9 (eBook)
https://doi.org/10.1007/978-3-031-97617-9

Preface

The compiled 14 volumes (LNCS volumes 15886–15899) consist of the peer-reviewed papers from the 68 Workshops of the 2025 International Conference on Computational Science and Its Applications (ICCSA 2025), which was held between June 30 – July 3, 2025 in Istanbul (Türkiye). The peer-reviewed papers of the main conference tracks are published in a separate set made up of three volumes (LNCS 15648–15650).

The conference was held in a hybrid form, with the large majority of participants in presence, hosted by Galatasaray University, Istanbul, Türkiye. We enabled virtual participation for those who did not attend the event in person due to logistical, political and economic problems, by adopting a technological infrastructure via open-source software (jitsi + riot) and a commercial Cloud infrastructure.

With the 2025 edition, ICCSA celebrated its 25th anniversary, a quarter of a century as a memorable moment that is harmoniously aligned with Istanbul, an extraordinary city located at the crossroads and acting as a bridge connecting Asia and Europe, representing different cultures, beliefs as well as lifestyles, which highlights its intercultural fabric.

ICCSA 2025 marked another fruitful and thought-provoking academic event in the International Conferences on Computational Science and Its Applications (ICCSA) conference series, previously held in Hanoi, Vietnam (2024), Athens, Greece (2023), Málaga, Spain (2022), Cagliari, Italy (hybrid with a few participants in presence in 2021 and completely online in 2020), whilst earlier editions took place in Saint Petersburg, Russia (2019), Melbourne, Australia (2018), Trieste, Italy (2017), Beijing, China (2016), Banff, Canada (2015), Guimaraes, Portugal (2014), Ho Chi Minh City, Vietnam (2013), Salvador, Brazil (2012), Santander, Spain (2011), Fukuoka, Japan (2010), Suwon, South Korea (2009), Perugia, Italy (2008), Kuala Lumpur, Malaysia (2007), Glasgow, UK (2006), Singapore (2005), Assisi, Italy (2004), Montreal, Canada (2003), and (as ICCS) Amsterdam, the Netherlands (2002) and San Francisco, USA (2001).

Computational Science constitutes the main pillar of most present research, industrial and commercial applications, and plays a unique role in exploiting ICT innovative technologies, and the ICCSA conference series has, accordingly, provided ample opportunities to researchers and industry practitioners to discuss new ideas, to share complex problems and their solutions, and to shape new trends in Computational Science. As the conference mirrors society from a scientific point of view, this year's undoubtedly dominant theme was large language models, machine learning and Artificial Intelligence (AI) and their applications in the most diverse technological, economic and industrial fields, amongst the others.

The ICCSA 2025 conference was structured in six general tracks covering the fields of computational science and its applications: Computational Methods, Algorithms and Scientific Applications – High Performance Computing and Networks – Geometric Modeling, Graphics and Visualization – Advanced and Emerging Applications – Information Systems and Technologies – Urban and Regional Planning. In addition, the conference consisted of 68 workshops, focusing on topical issues of utmost importance to science, technology and society: from new computational approaches for earth science, to mathematical methods for image processing, new statistical and optimization methods, several Artificial Intelligence approaches, sustainability issues, smart cities and related technologies, to name some.

In the Workshops' proceedings, we accepted 362 full papers, 37 short papers and 2 Ph.D. Showcase papers from total of 1043 submissions (Acceptance rate 38.4%). In the Main Conference Proceedings, we accepted 71 full papers, 6 short papers and 1 Ph.D. Showcase paper from 269 submissions to the General Tracks of the Conference (with an acceptance rate of 29.9%). We would like to convey our sincere appreciation to the workshops' chairs and co-chairs and program committee members for their diligent work, commitment and dedication.

The success and consistent maintenance of the ICCSA conference series in general, and of ICCSA 2025 in particular, rely upon the support of many people: authors, presenters, participants, keynote speakers, workshop chairs, session chairs, organizing committee members, student volunteers, Program Committee members, Advisory Committee members, International Liaison chairs, reviewers and other individuals in various roles. Thus, we take this opportunity to wholehartedly thank each and everyone.

We additionally wish to thank publisher Springer for their agreement to publish the proceedings, besides sponsoring part of the best papers awards and for their kind assistance and cooperation during the editing process.

We would cordially like to invite you to refer to the ICCSA website https://iccsa.org, where you can find the relevant details regarding this academic endeavor and event of ours.

June 2025

Osvaldo Gervasi
Yeliz Karaca
Beniamino Murgante
Chiara Garau

A Welcome Message from the Organizers

The International Conference on Computational Science and Its Applications (ICCSA) reflects a culmination of meticulous and dedicated efforts and academic endeavors toward the progress of science and technology.

One of the most noteworthy aspects of ICCSA is its fostering of a collective spirit, bringing together a plethora of participants from all over the world. Correspondingly, this merging power manifests itself in the 25th anniversary of ICCSA, which is a quarter of a century, in Istanbul, Türkiye, which connects and acts as a bridge between two continents, namely Asia and Europe. This unique location in the world hosts the 25th year of ICCSA at Galatasaray University, located on Çırağan Avenue by Istanbul's Bosphorus, which is an established international university bestowed with a distinctive past of teaching tradition, research and education exceeding five centuries.

Istanbul, having served as the capital city of four empires, namely the Roman Empire (330–395), the Byzantine Empire (395–1204 and 1261–1453), the Latin Empire (1204–1261) and the Ottoman Empire (1453–1922), is an exceptional city of the Republic of Türkiye founded by Mustafa Kemal Atatürk.

Situated at a strategic location along the historic Silk Road, Istanbul is at the core of extending rail networks which span across Europe and West Asia along with the only sea route between the Black Sea and the Mediterranean.

The cultural, historical and economic pulses of the country are evident in Istanbul whose rooted origins have embraced varying beliefs, lifestyles and populace, which highlights the city's mosaic quality with blended fabric in a constant harmonious flow. This has enabled cultures to grow and be nurtured, which is profoundly rooted in its urban culture.

Computational Science constitutes the main pillar of most present research, industrial and commercial activities besides manifesting a unique role in exploiting and addressing innovative Information and Communication Technologies. Thus, the 25-year-old ICCSA conference series provides remarkable opportunities to get acquainted with leading researchers, scientists, scholars, practitioners and many more while exchanging innovative ideas and initiating new partnerships, associations and bonds.

With the hosting of Galatasaray University, I would personally and on behalf of the Local Organizing Committee, with the members Emre Alptekin, Gülfem Işıklar Alptekin, Cengiz Kahraman, Abdullah Çağrı Tolga and Ayberk Zeytin, like to convey our sincere gratitude and thanks to everyone who exerted their efforts in and contributed to the realization of ICCSA 2025. With these notes and remarks, welcome to Istanbul!

Cordially yours,

On behalf of the Local Organizing Committee.

June 2025   Yeliz Karaca

Organization

Honorary General Chairs

Bernady O. Apduhan   Kyushu Sangyo University, Japan
Kenneth C. J. Tan   Sardina Systems, UK

General Chairs

Yeliz Karaca   University of Massachusetts, USA
Osvaldo Gervasi   University of Perugia, Italy
David Taniar   Monash University, Australia

Program Committee Chairs

Beniamino Murgante   University of Basilicata, Italy
Chiara Garau   University of Cagliari, Italy
Ana Maria A. C. Rocha   University of Minho, Portugal
A. Çağrı Tolga   Galatasaray University, Turkey

International Advisory Committee

Jemal Abawajy   Deakin University, Australia
Dharma P. Agarwal   University of Cincinnati, USA
Rajkumar Buyya   Melbourne University, Australia
Claudia Bauzer Medeiros   University of Campinas, Brazil
Manfred M. Fisher   Vienna University of Economics and Business, Austria
Pierre Frankhauser   University of Franche-Comté/CNRS, France
Marina L. Gavrilova   University of Calgary, Canada
Sumi Helal   University of Florida, USA & Lancaster University, UK
Bin Jiang   University of Gävle, Sweden
Yee Leung   Chinese University of Hong Kong, China

International Liaison Chairs

Ivan Blečić	University of Cagliari, Italy
Giuseppe Borruso	University of Trieste, Italy
Elise De Donker	Western Michigan University, USA
Maria Noelia Faginas Lago	University of Perugia, Italy
Maria Irene Falcão	University of Minho, Portugal
Robert C. H. Hsu	Chung Hua University, Taiwan
Yeliz Karaca	University of Massachusetts Chan Medical School, USA
Tae-Hoon Kim	Zhejiang University of Science and Technology, China
Vladimir Korkhov	Saint Petersburg University, Russia
Takashi Naka	Kyushu Sangyo University, Japan
Rafael D. C. Santos	National Institute for Space Research, Brazil
Maribel Yasmina Santos	University of Minho, Portugal
Anastasia Stratigea	National Technical University of Athens, Greece

Workshop and Session Organizing Chairs

Beniamino Murgante	University of Basilicata, Italy
Chiara Garau	University of Cagliari, Italy

Award Chair

Wenny Rahayu	La Trobe University, Australia

Publicity Committee Chairs

Elmer Dadios	De La Salle University, Philippines
Nataliia Kulabukhova	Saint Petersburg University, Russia
Daisuke Takahashi	Tsukuba University, Japan
Shangwang Wang	Beijing University of Posts and Telecommunications, China

Local Organizing Committee Chairs

Emre Alptekin	Galatasaray University, Turkey
Gülfem Işıklar Alptekin	Galatasaray University, Turkey
Cengiz Kahraman	İstanbul Technical University, Turkey
A. Çağrı Tolga	Galatasaray University, Turkey
Ayberk Zeytin	Galatasaray University, Turkey

Technology Chair

Damiano Perri	University of Perugia, Italy

Program Committee

Vera Afreixo	University of Aveiro, Portugal
Vladimir Alarcon	Northern Gulf Institute, USA
Filipe Alvelos	University of Minho, Portugal
Debora Anelli	Polytechnic University of Bari, Italy
Hartmut Asche	Hasso-Plattner-Institut für Digital Engineering Ggmbh, Germany
Nizamettin Aydın	İstanbul Technical University, Turkey
Ginevra Balletto	University of Cagliari, Italy
Nadia Balucani	University of Perugia, Italy
Socrates Basbas	Aristotle University of Thessaloniki, Greece
David Berti	ART SpA, Italy
Michela Bertolotto	University College Dublin, Ireland
Sandro Bimonte	CEMAGREF, TSCF, France
Ana Cristina Braga	University of Minho, Portugal
Tiziana Campisi	Kore University of Enna, Italy
Yves Caniou	Université Claude Bernard Lyon 1, France
Alessandra Capolupo	Polytechnic University of Bari, Italy
José A. Cardoso e Cunha	Universidade Nova de Lisboa, Portugal
Rui Cardoso	University of Beira Interior, Portugal
Leocadio G. Casado	University of Almería, Spain
Mete Celik	Erciyes University, Turkey
Maria Cerreta	University of Naples Federico II, Italy
Ta Quang Chieu	Thuyloi University, Vietnam
Rachel Chien-Sing Lee	Sunway University, Malaysia
Birol Ciloglugil	Ege University, Turkey
Mauro Coni	University of Cagliari, Italy

Florbela Maria da Cruz Domingues Correia	Polytechnic Institute of Viana do Castelo, Portugal
Alessandro Costantini	INFN, Italy
Roberto De Lotto	University of Pavia, Italy
Luiza De Macedo Mourelle	State University of Rio De Janeiro, Brazil
Marcelo De Paiva Guimaraes	Federal University of Sao Paulo, Brazil
Frank Devai	London South Bank University, UK
Joana Matos Dias	University of Coimbra, Portugal
Aziz Dursun	Virginia Tech University, USA
Laila El Ghandour	Heriot-Watt University, UK
Rafida M. Elobaid	Canadian University Dubai, United Arab Emirates
Maria Irene Falcao	University of Minho, Portugal
Florbela P. Fernandes	Polytechnic Institute of Bragança, Portugal
Paula Odete Fernandes	Polytechnic Institute of Bragança, Portugal
Adelaide de Fátima Baptista Valente Freitas	University of Aveiro, Portugal
Valentina Franzoni	University of Perugia, Italy
Andreas Fricke	University of Potsdam, Germany
Raffaele Garrisi	Centro Operativo per la Sicurezza Cibernetica, Italy
Ivan Gerace	University of Perugia, Italy
Maria Giaoutzi	National Technical University of Athens, Greece
Salvatore Giuffrida	University of Catania, Italy
Teresa Guarda	Universidad Estatal Peninsula de Santa Elena, Ecuador
Sevin Gümgüm	Izmir University of Economics, Turkey
Malgorzata Hanzl	Technical University of Lodz, Poland
Maulana Adhinugraha Kiki	Telkom University, Indonesia
Clement Ho Cheung Leung	Chinese University of Hong Kong, China
Andrea Lombardi	University of Perugia, Italy
Marcos Mandado Alonso	University of Vigo, Spain
Ernesto Marcheggiani	Katholieke Universiteit Leuven, Belgium
Antonino Marvuglia	Luxembourg Institute of Science and Technology, Luxembourg
Michele Mastroianni	University of Salerno, Italy
Hideo Matsufuru	High Energy Accelerator Research Organization, Japan
Fernando Miranda	Universidade do Minho, Portugal
Giuseppe Modica	University of Reggio Calabria, Italy
Majaz Moonis	University of Massachusetts, USA
Nadia Nedjah	State University of Rio de Janeiro, Brazil
Paolo Nesi	University of Florence, Italy

Suzan Obaiys — University of Malaya, Malaysia
Marcin Paprzycki — Polish Academy of Sciences, Poland
Eric Pardede — La Trobe University, Australia
Ana Isabel Pereira — Polytechnic Institute of Bragança, Portugal
Damiano Perri — University of Perugia, Italy
Massimiliano Petri — University of Pisa, Italy
Telmo Pinto — University of Coimbra, Portugal
Alessandro Plaisant — University of Sassari, Italy
Maurizio Pollino — ENEA, Italy
Alenka Poplin — Iowa State University, USA
Marcos Quiles — Federal University of São Paulo, Brazil
Nguyen Huu Quynh — Thuyloi University, Vietnam
Albert Rimola — Universitat Autònoma de Barcelona, Spain
Humberto Rocha — University of Coimbra, Portugal
Marzio Rosi — University of Perugia, Italy
Lucia Saganeiti — University of L'Aquila, Italy
Francesco Scorza — University of Basilicata, Italy
Marco Paulo Seabra dos Reis — University of Coimbra, Portugal
Jie Shen — University of Michigan, USA
Francesco Tajani — Sapienza University of Rome, Italy
Rodrigo Tapia Mcclung — Centro de Investigación en Ciencias de Información Geoespacial, Mexico
Eufemia Tarantino — Polytechnic University of Bari, Italy
Sergio Tasso — University of Perugia, Italy
Ana Paula Teixeira — Universidade do Minho, Portugal
Yiota Theodora — National Technical University of Athens, Greece
Giuseppe A. Trunfio — University of Sassari, Italy
Toshihiro Uchibayashi — Kyushu University, Japan
Marco Vizzari — University of Perugia, Italy
Frank Westad — Norwegian University of Science and Technology, Norway
Fukuko Yuasa — High Energy Accelerator Research Organization, Japan
Ljiljana Zivkovic — Republic Geodetic Authority, Serbia

Workshops

Workshop on Advancements in Applied Machine-Learning and Data Analytics (AAMDA 2025)

Workshop Organizers

Alessandro Costantini	INFN, Italy
Daniele Cesini	INFN, Italy
Elisabetta Ronchieri	INFN, Italy
Barbara Martelli	INFN, Italy

Workshop Program Committee Members

Alessandro Costantini	Istituto Nazionale di Fisica Nucleare (INFN), Italy
Daniele Cesini	Istituto Nazionale di Fisica Nucleare (INFN), Italy
Elisabetta Ronchieri	Istituto Nazionale di Fisica Nucleare (INFN), Italy
Barbara Martelli	Istituto Nazionale di Fisica Nucleare (INFN), Italy
Luca Dell'Agnello	Istituto Nazionale di Fisica Nucleare (INFN), Italy

Advanced and Innovative Web Apps 2025 (AIWA 2025)

Workshop Organizers

Damiano Perri	University of Perugia, Italy
Osvaldo Gervasi	University of Perugia, Italy
Stelios Kouzeleas	International Hellenic University, Greece
Sergio Tasso	University of Perugia, Italy

Workshop Program Committee Members

David Berti	ART SpA, Italy
JungYoon Kim	Gachon University, South Korea
TaiHoon Kim	Zhejiang University of Science and Technology, China

Advanced Processes of Mathematics and Computing Models in Complex Data-Intensive Computational Systems (AMCM 2025)

Workshop Organizers

Yeliz Karaca	University of Massachusetts Chan Medical School and Massachusetts Institute of Technology, USA
Dumitru Baleanu	Lebanese American University, Lebanon
Osvaldo Gervasi	University of Perugia, Italy
Yudong Zhang	University of Leicester, UK
Majaz Moonis	University of Massachusetts Chan Medical School and Massachusetts Institute of Technology, USA

Workshop Program Committee Members

TaeHoon Kim	Zhejiang University of Science and Technology, China
Martin Bohner	Missouri University of Science and Technology, USA
Shuihua Wang	University of Leicester, UK
Khan Muhammad	Sungkyunkwan University, South Korea
Mahmoud Abdel-Aty	Sohag University, Egypt
Aziz Dursun	Virginia Polytechnic Institute and State University, USA
Kemal Güven Gülen	Namık Kemal University, Turkey
Akif Akgül	Hitit Üniversitesi, Turkey

Advanced Numerical Approaches for Assessment and Design of No-Tension Masonry Structures (ANAMS 2025)

Workshop Organizers

Antonino Iannuzzo	Universitá degli studi del Sannio, Italy
Carlo Olivieri	Universitá Telematica Pegaso, Italy
Andrea Montanino	CIMNE, Spain
Elham Mousavian	University of Edinburgh, UK

Workshop Program Committee Members

Pietro Meriggi	Roma Tre University, Italy
Francesca Perelli	University of Naples Federico II, Italy
Marialuigia Sangirardi	University of Oxford, UK
Sam Cocking	University of Cambridge, UK

Matteo Salvalaggio	University of Minho, Portugal
Vittorio Paris	University of Bergamo, Italy
Luigi Sibille	Norwegian University of Science and Technology, Norway
Natalia Pingaro	Politecnico di Milano, Italy
Martina Buzzetti	Politecnico di Milano, Italy
Generoso Vaiano	Pegaso Telematic University, Italy
Alessandra Capolupo	Politecnico di Bari, Italy
Amal Gerges	Università degli Studi di Cagliari, Italy
Fabian Orozco	National Autonomous University of Mexico, Mexico
Nathanael Savalle	Polytech Clermont and Université Clermont Auvergne, France
Luca Umberto Argiento	University of Naples Federico II, Italy
Bartolomeo Pantó	Durham University, UK

Unveiling the Synergies Between Air Quality and Climate PlAnning (AQCliPA 2025)

Workshop Organizers

Angela Pilogallo	University of L'Aquila, Italy
Luigi Santopietro	University of Basilicata, Italy
Filomena Pietrapertosa	IMAA CNR, Italy
Monica Salvia	IMAA CNR, Italy
Carlo Trozzi	IMAA CNR, Italy
Valeria Scapini	Central University of Chile, Chile

Workshop Program Committee Members

Lucia Saganeiti	IMAA-CNR, Italy
Lorena Fiorini	University of L'Aquila, Italy
Antonio Mazza	IMAA-CNR, Italy
Gabriele Nolè	IMAA-CNR, Italy
Carmen Guida	University of Naples "Federico II", Italy
Floriana Zucaro	University of Naples "Federico II", Italy
Sabrina Lai	University of Cagliari, Italy
Chiara Garau	University of Cagliari, Italy

Advancements in Spatial assessment of Socio-Ecological SystemS (ASSESS 2025)

Workshop Organizers

Daniele Cannatella	TU Delft, The Netherlands
Giuliano Poli	University of Naples Federico II, Italy
Eugenio Muccio	TU Delft, The Netherlands
Claudiu Forgaci	TU Delft, The Netherlands

Workshop Program Committee Members

Daniele Cannatella	TU Delft, The Netherlands
Giuliano Poli	University of Naples Federico II, Italy
Eugenio Muccio	University of Naples Federico II, Italy
Claudiu Forgaci	TU Delft, The Netherlands
Maria Cerreta	University of Naples Federico II, Italy
Maria Somma	University of Naples Federico II, Italy
Laura Di Tommaso	University of Naples Federico II, Italy
Sabrina Sacco	Politecnico di Milano, Italy
Piero Zizzania	University of Naples Federico II, Italy
Gaia Daldanise	CNR IRISS, Italy
Benedetta Grieco	University of Naples Federico II, Italy
Giuseppe Ciciriello	University of Naples Federico II, Italy
Marta Dell'Ovo	Politecnico di Milano, Italy
Francesco Piras	University of Cagliari, Italy
Diana Rolando	Politecnico di Torino, Italy
Stefano Cuntò	University of Naples Federico II, Italy
Ludovica La Rocca	University of Naples Federico II, Italy

Blockchain and Distributed Ledgers: Technologies and Applications (BDLTA 2025)

Workshop Organizers

Vladimir Korkhov	Saint Petersburg State University, Russia
Elena Stankova	Saint Petersburg State University, Russia
Nataliia Kulabukhova	Saint Petersburg State University, Russia

Workshop Program Committee Members

Adam Belloum	University of Amsterdam, the Netherlands
Dmitrii Vasiunin	Deutsche Telekom Cloud Services E.P.E., Greece
Serob Balyan	Osensus Arm LLC, Armenia
Suren Abrahamyan	Osensus Arm LLC, Armenia
Ashot Sergey Gevorkyan	NAS of Armenia, Armenia

Michal Hnatic	Univerzita Pavla Jozefa Šafárika v Košiciach, Slovakia
Michail Panteleyev	Saint Petersburg Electrotecnical University, Russia
Martin Vala	Univerzita Pavla Jozefa Šafárika v Košiciach, Slovakia
Nodir Zaynalov	Tashkent University of Information Technologies named after Muhammad al Khwarizmi, Uzbekistan
Michail Panteleyev	Saint Petersburg Electrotecnical University, Russia
Alexander Degtyarev	Saint Petersburg University, Russia
Alexander Bogdanov	St. Petersburg State University, Russia

Bio and Neuro Inspired Computing and Applications (BIONCA 2025)

Workshop Organizers

| Nadia Nedjah | State University of Rio de Janeiro, Brazil |
| Luiza de Macedo Mourelle | State University of Rio de Janeiro, Brazil |

Workshop Program Committee Members

Nadia Nedjha	State University of Rio de Janeiro, Brazil
Luiza de Macedo Mourelle	State University of Rio de Janeiro, Brazil
Luigi Maciel Ribeiro	State University of Rio de Janeiro, Brazil
Joelmir Ramos	Federal University of Rio de Janeiro, Brazil
Rogério Moraes	Brazilian Navy, Brazil
Marcos Santana Farias	Institute of Nuclear Energy, Brazil
Luneque Silva Jr.	Federal University of ABC, Brazil
Alan Oliveira	University of Lisboa, Portugal
Brij Bhooshan Gupta	Asia University, Taiwan

Computational and Applied Mathematics (CAM 2025)

Workshop Organizers

| Maria Irene Falcão | University of Minho, Portugal |
| Fernando Miranda | University of Minho, Portugal |

Workshop Program Committee Members

Fernando Miranda	University of Minho, Portugal
Graça Tomaz	Polytechnic of Guarda, Portugal
Helmuth Malonek	University of Aveiro, Portugal

Isabel Cacao	University of Aveiro, Portugal
João Morais	Autonomous Technological Institute of Mexico, Mexico
Lidia Aceto	University of Eastern Piedmont, Italy
Luís Ferrás	University of Porto, Portugal
M. Irene Falcão	University of Minho, Portugal
Patrícia Beites	University of Beira Interior, Portugal
Paulo Amorim	FGV EMAp, Brazil
Regina de Almeida	University of Trás-os-Montes e Alto Douro, Portugal
Ricardo Severino	University of Minho, Portugal

Computational and Applied Statistics (CAS 2025)

Workshop Organizer

| Ana Cristina Braga | ALGORITMI Research Centre, LASI, University of Minho, Portugal |

Workshop Program Committee Members

Adelaide Freitas	University of Aveiro, Portugal
Andreas Futschik	Johannes Kepler University Linz, Austria
Ana Cristina Braga	University of Minho, Portugal
Ângela Silva	University of Minho, Portugal
Arminda Manuela Gonçalves	University of Minho, Portugal
Carina Silva	Polytechnic Intitute of Lisbon, Portugal
Elisete Correia	University of Trás-os-Montes e Alto Douro, Portugal
Frank Westad	Norwegian University of Science and Technology, Norway
Isabel Natario	New University of Lisbon, Portugal
Irene Oliveira	University of Trás-os-Montes e Alto Douro, Portugal
Ivan Rodriguez Conde	University of Vigo, Spain
Joaquim Gonçalves	Instituto Politécnico do Cávado e do Ave, Portugal
Lino Costa	University of Minho, Portugal
Marco Reis	University of Coimbra, Portugal
Maria Filipa Mourão	Polytechnic Institute of Viana do Castelo, Portugal
Maria João Polidoro	Polytechnic Institute of Porto, Portugal
Martin Perez Perez	University of Vigo, Spain
Michal Abrahamowicz	McGill University, Canada
Vera Afreixo	University of Aveiro, Portugal

Werner G. Müller	Johannes Kepler University Linz, Austria
Bruna Silva Ramos	University Lusiada de Famalicão, Portugal
Inês Sousa	University of Minho, Portugal
Luís Miguel Rocha Matos	University of Minho, Portugal
Manuel Carlos Figueiredo	University of Minho, Portugal

Cyber Intelligence and Applications (CIA 2025)

Workshop Organizer

| Gianni D'Angelo | University of Salerno, Italy |

Workshop Program Committee Members

Gianni D'Angelo	University of Salerno, Italy
Francesco Palmieri	University of Salerno, Italy
Massimo Ficco	University of Salerno, Italy
Arcangelo Castiglione	University of Salerno, Italy

Computational Methods for Business Analytics (CMBA 2025)

Workshop Organizers

| Cláudio Alves | Universidade do Minho, Portugal |
| Telmo Pinto | Universidade do Minho, Portugal |

Workshop Program Committee Members

Abdulrahim Shamayleh	American University of Sharjah, United Arab Emirates
Ana Rocha	University of Minho, Portugal
Angelo Sifaleras	University of Macedonia, Greece
Cristóvão Silva	University of Coimbra, Portugal
José Valério de Carvalho	University of Minho, Portugal
Miguel Vieira	Universidade Lusófona, Portugal
Rita Macedo	Université de Lille, France
Ana Moura	Universidade de Aveiro, Portugal
Cristina Lopes	ISCAP, Portugal
Eliana Costa e Silva	Instituto Politécnico do Porto, Portugal

Computational Methods, Statistics and Industrial Mathematics (CMSIM 2025)

Workshop Organizers

Maria Filomena Teodoro	IST ID, Instituto Superior Técnico, Portugal
Marina Alexandra Pedro Andrade	ISCTE – Lisbon University Institute, Portugal
Paula Simões	University of Lisbon, Portugal
Teresa A. Oliveira	IST ID, Instituto Superior Técnico, Portugal

Workshop Program Committee Members

Amilcar Oliveira	Universidade Aberta and Universidade de Lisboa, Portugal
Victor Lobo	Escola Naval and NOVA IMS Almada, Portugal
António Pacheco	IST Universidade de Lisboa, Portugal
Eliana Costa	Escola Superior de Tecnologia e Gestão IPPorto, Portugal
Aldina Correia	Escola Superior de Tecnologia e Gestão IPPorto, Portugal
Fernando Carapau	University of Évora, Portugal
Ricardo Moura	Portuguese Naval Academy, Portugal
Ana Borges	Escola Superior de Tecnologia e Gestão IPPorto, Portugal
Cristina Lopes	ISCAP IPPorto, Portugal
Fernanda Costa	University of Minho, Portugal
Cabrita Carlos	IPBeja, Portugal
Maria Luísa Morgado	University of Trás os Montes e Alto Douro and University of Lisbon, Portugal
Rosário Ramos	Universidade Aberta, Portugal
Sofia Rézio	Iscal, Instituto Politécnico de Lisboa, Portugal
Matteo Sacchet	University of Turin, Italy
Marina Marchisio Conte	University of Turin, Italy
António Seijas-Macias	University of Coruña, Spain
Luís F. A. Teodoro	University of Glasgow, UK and University of Oslo, Norway
Christos Kitsos	University of West Attica, Greece
M. Filomena Teodoro	Universidade de Lisboa, Portugal
Marina A. P. Andrade	Instituto Universitário de Lisboa, Portugal
Paula Simões	Military Academy and Universidade Nova de Lisboa, Portugal
Teresa Oliveira	Universidade Aberta and Universidade de Lisboa, Portugal

Computational Optimization and Applications (COA 2025)

Workshop Organizers

Ana Rocha	ALGORITMI Research Centre, LASI, University of Minho, Portugal, Portugal
Humberto Rocha	ALGORITMI Research Centre, LASI, University of Minho, Portugal, Portugal

Workshop Program Committee Members

Florbela Fernandes	Polytechnic Institute of Bragança, Portugal
Clara Vaz	Polytechnic Institute of Bragança, Portugal
Ana Pereira	Polytechnic Institute of Bragança, Portugal
Filipe Alvelos	University of Minho, Portugal
Joana Dias	University of Coimbra, Portugal
Eligius M. T. Hendrix	University of Málaga, Spain
Emerson José de Paiva	Federal University of Itajubá, Brazil
Ana Paula Teixeira	University of Trás-os-Montes and Alto Douro, Portugal
Lino Costa	Universidade do Minho, Portugal

Coastal Cities Versus Inland Areas. Hypotheses for Sustainable Regeneration Through Ecosystem Services of 'Hooking' and Rehabilitation of Brownfield Sites (CoastalCities_VS_InlandAreas 2025)

Workshop Organizers

Celestina Fazia	Università di Enna Kore, Italy
Angrilli Massimo	University of Chieti-Pescara, Italy
Valentina Ciuffreda	University of Chieti-Pescara, Italy
Maurizio Oddo	Università di Enna Kore, Italy
Marcello Sestito	Università di Enna Kore, Italy
Clara Stella Vicari Aversa	University of Reggio Calabria, Italy

Workshop Program Committee Members

Alessandro Camiz	Università d'Annunzio, Italy
Thowayeb Hassan	King Faisal University, Saudi Arabia
Alessandro Barracco	Università Kore di Enna, Italy
Mario Morrica	University of Urbino, Italy
Mariana Ratiu	University of Oradea, Romania
Alanda Akamana	Mohammed VI Polytechnic University, Morocco
Kaoutare Amini Alaoui	Mohammed VI Polytechnic University, Morocco

Computational Astrochemistry 2025 (CompAstro 2025)

Workshop Organizers

Marzio Rosi	University of Perugia, Italy
Daniela Ascenzi	University of Trento, Italy
Nadia Balucani	University of Perugia, Italy
Stefano Falcinelli	University of Perugia, Italy

Workshop Program Committee Members

Dario Campisi	Università degli Studi di Perugia, Italy
Giacomo Giorgi	Università degli Studi di Perugia, Italy
Andrea Giustini	Università degli Studi di Perugia, Italy
Luca Mancini	Università degli Studi di Perugia, Italy
Albert Rimola	Universitat Autònoma de Barcelona, Spain
Gianmarco Vanuzzo	Università degli Studi di Perugia, Italy
Dimitrios Skouteris	Master-Tec, Italy
Piero Ugliengo	Università degli Studi di Torino, Italy
Franco Vecchiocattivi	Università degli Sudi di Perugia, Italy
Giacomo Pannacci	Università degli Studi di Perugia, Italy
Costanza Borghesi	Università degli Studi di Perugia, Italy
Marco Parriani	Università degli Studi di Perugia, Italy
Marta Loletti	Università degli Studi di Perugia, Italy
Fernando Pirani	Università degli Studi di Perugia, Italy
Andrea Lombardi	Università degli Studi di Perugia, Italy
Noelia Faginas Lago	Università degli Studi di Perugia, Italy
Paolo Tosi	Università di Trento, Italy
Cecilia Coletti	Università degli Studi Chieti-Pescara, Italy
Nazzareno Re	Università degli Studi Chieti-Pescara, Italy
Linda Podio	Osservatorio Astrofisico di Arcetri INAF, Italy
Claudio Codella	Osservatorio Astrofisico di Arcetri INAF, Italy
Gabriella Di Genova	Università degli Studi di Perugia, Italy

Computational Methods for Porous Geomaterials (CompPor 2025)

Workshop Organizers

Vadim Lisitsa	IPGG SB RAS, Russia
Evgeniy Romenski	IPGG SB RAS, Russia

Workshop Program Committee Members

Vadim Lisitsa	Institute of Petroleum Geology and Geophysics SB RAS, Russia
Evgeniy Romenski	Sobolev Institute of Mathematics SB RAS, Russia
Vladimir Cheverda	Sobolev Institute of Mathematics SB RAS, Russia
Tatyana Khachkova	IPGG SB RAS, Russia
Dmitry Prokhorov	IPGG SB RAS, Russia
Mikhail Novikov	Sobolev Institute of Mathematics SB RAS, Russia
Sergey Solovyev	Sobolev Institute of Mathematics SB RAS, Russia
Kirill Gadylshin	LLC RNBashNIPIneft, Russia
Olga Stoyanovskaya	Lavrentev Institute of Hydrodynamics SB RAS, Russia
Yerlan Amanbek	Nazarbaev University, Kazakstan

Workshop on Computational Science and HPC (CSHPC 2025)

Workshop Organizers

Elise de Doncker	Western Michigan University, USA
Hideo Matsufuru	High Energy Accelerator Research Organization, Japan

Workshop Program Committee Members

Elise de Doncker	Western Michigan University, USA
Hideo Matsufuru	High Energy Accelerator Research Organization (KEK), Japan
Fukuko Yuasa	KEK, Japan
Issaku Kanamori	RIKEN, Japan
Hiroshi Daisaka	Hitotsubashi University, Japan
Norikazu Yamada	KEK, Japan
Naohito Nakasato	University of Aizu, Japan
Robert Makin	Western Michigan University, USA

Cities, Technologies and Planning 2025 (CTP 2025)

Workshop Organizers

Giuseppe Borruso	University of Trieste, Italy
Beniamino Murgante	University of Basilicata, Italy
Malgorzata Hanzl	Lodz University of Technology, Poland
Anastasia Stratigea	National Technical University of Athens, Greece
Ljiljana Zivkovic	Republic Geodetic Authority, Serbia
Ginevra Balletto	University of Trieste, Italy

Workshop Program Committee Members

Giuseppe Borruso	University of Trieste, Italy
Beniamino Murgante	University of Basilicata, Italy
Malgorzata Hanzl	Lodz University of Technology, Poland
Anastasia Stratigea	National Technical University of Athens, Greece
Ljiljiana Zivkovic	Republic Geodetic Authority of Serbia, Serbia
Ginevra Balletto	University of Cagliari, Italy
Silvia Battino	University of Sassari, Italy
Mara Ladu	University of Cagliari, Italy
Maria del Mar Munoz Leonisio	University of Cádiz, Spain
Ahinoa Amaro Garcia	University of Las Palmas of Gran Canaria, Spain
Maria Attard	University of Malta, Malta
Enrico D'agostini	World Maritime University, Sweden
Francesca Krasna	University of Trieste, Italy
Brisol Garcia Garcia	Polytechnic University of Quintana Roo, Mexico
Tu Anh Trinh	UEH University, Vietnam
Giovanni Mauro	Università degli Studi della Campania, Italy
Maria Ronza	University of Naples Federico II, Italy
Massimiliano Bencardino	University of Salerno, Italy
Tomasz Bradecki	Silesian University of Technology, Poland
Dorota Kamrowska-Załuska	Gdańsk University of Technology, Poland
Iwona Jażdżewska	University of Lodz, Poland
Yiota Theodora	National Technical University of Athens, Greece
Apostolos Lagarias	University of Thessaly, Greece
George Tsilimigkas	University of the Aegean, Greece
Akrivi Leka	National Technical University of Athens, Greece
Maria Panagiotopoulou	National Technical University of Athens, Greece
Andrea Gallo	Ca' Foscari University of Venice, Italy
Francesca Sinatra	University of Trieste, Italy

Digital Transition: Effects on Housing Mobility, Market, Land Governance (DIGITRANS 2025)

Workshop Organizers

Fabrizio Battisti	University of Florence, Italy
Fabiana Forte	University of Campania, Italy
Orazio Campo	Sapienza University of Rome, Italy
Alessio Pino	Kore University of Enna, Italy
Carlo Pisano	University of Florence, Italy
Mariolina Grasso	Kore University of Enna, Italy

Workshop Program Committee Members

Fabrizio Battisti	University of Florence, Italy
Fabiana Forte	Università della Campania Luigi Vanvitelli, Italy
Orazio Campo	University of Rome "La Sapienza", Italy
Alessio Pino	Kore University of Enna, Italy
Carlo Pisano	University of Florence, Italy
Mariolina Grasso	Università Kore di Enna, Italy

Evaluating Inner Areas Potentials (EIAP 2025)

Workshop Organizers

Diana Rolando	Politecnico di Torino, Italy
Alice Barreca	Politecnico di Torino, Italy
Manuela Rebaudengo	Politecnico di Torino, Italy
Giorgia Malavasi	Politecnico di Torino, Italy

Workshop Program Committee Members

John Accordino	Virginia Commonwealth University, USA
Francesco Bruzzone	Università Iuav di Venezia, Italy
Maria Cerreta	Università degli Studi di Napoli Federico II, Italy
Maddalena Chimisso	Università degli Studi del Molise, Italy
Chiara Chioni	Università degli Studi di Trento, Italy
Annalisa Contato	Università degli Studi di Palermo, Italy
Cristina Coscia	Politecnico di Torino, Italy
Marta Dell'Ovo	Politecnico di Milano, Italy
Benedetta Di Leo	Università Politecnica delle Marche, Italy
Sara Favargiotti	Università degli Studi di Trento, Italy
Maddalena Ferretti	Università Politecnica delle Marche, Italy
Salvo Giuffrida	Università degli Studi di Palermo, Italy
Barbara Lino	Università degli Studi di Palermo, Italy
Umberto Mecca	Politecnico di Torino, Italy
Beatrice Mecca	Politecnico di Torino, Italy
Giuliano Poli	Università degli Studi di Napoli Federico II, Italy
Marco Rossitti	Politecnico di Milano, Italy
Alexandra Stankulova	Politecnico di Torino, Italy
Elena Todella	Politecnico di Torino, Italy
Asja Aulisio	Politecnico di Torino, Italy
Giulia Datola	Politecnico di Milano, Italy

Francesco Calabrò	Università degli Studi Mediterranea di Reggio Calabria, Italy
Valeria Saiu	Università degli Studi di Cagliari, Italy
Maria Rosa Trovato	Università di Catania, Italy

Econometric and Multidimensional Evaluation in Urban Environment (EMEUE 2025)

Workshop Organizers

Maria Cerreta	University of Naples Federico II, Italy
Carmelo Maria Torre	Polytechnic University of Bari, Italy
Pierluigi Morano	Polytechnic University of Bari, Italy
Simona Panaro	University of Naples Federico II, Italy
Felicia Di Liddo	University of Naples Federico II, Italy
Debora Anelli	University of Naples Federico II, Italy

Workshop Program Committee Members

Carmelo Maria Torre	Polytechnic University of Bari, Italy
Maria Cerreta	University of Naples Federico II, Italy
Pierluigi Morano	Polytechnic University of Bari, Italy
Francesco Tajani	Sapienza University of Rome, Italy
Simona Panaro	University of Naples Federico II, Italy
Felicia di Liddo	Polytechnic University of Bari, Italy
Debora Anelli	Sapienza University of Rome, Italy
Giuliano Poli	University of Naples Federico II, Italy
Maria Somma	University of Naples Federico II, Italy
Simona Panaro	University of Campania Luigi Vanvitelli, Italy
Laura Di Tommaso	University of Naples Federico II, Italy
Caterina Loffredo	University of Naples Federico II, Italy
Ludovica La Rocca	University of Naples Federico II, Italy
Sabrina Sacco	Politecnico di Milano, Italy
Piero Zizzania	University of Naples Federico II, Italy
Gaia Daldanise	CNR IRISS, Italy
Benedetta Grieco	University of Naples Federico II, Italy
Giuseppe Ciciriello	University of Naples Federico II, Italy
Marta Dell'Ovo	Politecnico di Milano, Italy
Daniele Cannatella	TU Delft University, The Netherlands
Eugenio Muccio	University of Naples Federico II, Italy
Sveva Ventre	University of Naples Federico II, Italy

Governance of Energy Transition: Environmental, Landscape, Social and Spatial Planning (ENERGY_PLANNING 2025)

Workshop Organizers

Mara Ladu	University of Cagliari, Italy
Ginevra Balletto	University of Cagliari, Italy
Emilio Ghiani	University of Cagliari, Italy
Alessandra Marra	University of Salerno, Italy
Roberto De Lotto	University of Pavia, Italy
Balázs Kulcsár	Chalmers University of Technology, Sweden

Workshop Program Committee Members

Riccardo Trevisan	University of Cagliari, Italy
Marco Naseddu	University of Cagliari, Italy
Giuseppe Borruso	University of Trieste, Italy
Andrea Gallo	University of Trieste, Italy
Francesca Sinatra	University of Trieste, Italy
Maria Attard	University of Malta, Malta
Tu Anh Trinh	UEH University Ho Chi Minh City, Vietnam
Marcello Tadini	University of Eastern Piedmont, Italy
Luigi Mundula	University for Foreigners of Perugia, Italy
Silvia Battino	University of Sassari, Italy
Maria del Mar Munoz Leonisio	University of Cádiz, Spain
Anna Richiedei	University of Brescia, Italy
Michele Pezzagno	University of Brescia, Italy
Federico Mertellozzo	University of Firenze, Italy
Marco Mazzarino	IUAV University Venice, Italy

Ecosystem Services in Spatial Planning for Climate Neutral Urban and Rural Areas (ESSP 2025)

Workshop Organizers

Sabrina Lai	University of Cagliari, Italy
Francesco Scorza	University of Basilicata, Italy
Corrado Zoppi	University of Cagliari, Italy
Beniamino Murgante	University of Basilicata, Italy
Carmela Gargiulo	University of Naples Federico II, Italy
Floriana Zucaro	University of Naples Federico II, Italy

Workshop Program Committee Members

Alfonso Annunziata	University of Basilicata, Italy
Ginevra Balletto	University of Cagliari, Italy
Ivan Blečić	University of Cagliari, Italy
Giuseppe Borruso	University of Trieste, Italy
Barbara Caselli	University of Parma, Italy
Maria Cerreta	University of Naples Federico II, Italy
Chiara Garau	University of Cagliari, Italy
Carmen Guida	University of Naples Federico II, Italy
Federica Isola	University of Cagliari, Italy
Francesca Leccis	University of Cagliari, Italy
Federica Leone	University of Cagliari, Italy
Silvia Rossetti	University of Parma, Italy
Luigi Santopietro	University of Basilicata, Italy
Carmelo Torre	Polytechnic of Bari, Italy

The 15th International Workshop on Future Information System Technologies and Applications (FiSTA 2025)

Workshop Organizers

Bernady O. Apduhan	Kyushu Sangyo University, Japan
Rafael Santos	Brazilian National Institute for Space Research, Brazil

Workshop Program Committee Members

Agustinus Borgy Waluyo	Monash University, Australia
Andre Ricardo Abed Grégio	Federal University of Paraná, Brazil
Eric Pardede	La Trobe University, Australia
Kai Cheng	Kyushu Sangyo University, Japan
Ching-Hsien Hsu	Asia University, Taiwan
Fenghui Yao	Tennessee State University, USA
Yusuke Gotoh	Okayama University, Japan
Alvaro Fazenda	Federal University of São Paulo, Brazil
Kazuaki Tanaka	Kyushu Institute of Technology, Japan
Tengku Adil	MARA Technological University, Malaysia
Toshihiro Yamauchi	Okayama University, Japan
Yasuaki Sumida	Kyushu Sangyo University, Japan
Earl Ryan Aleluya	MSU-Iligan Institute of Technology, Philippines
Cherry Mae G. Villame	MSU-Iligan Institute of Technology, Philippines
Anton Louise De Ocampo	Batangas State University, Philippines
Krishnamoorthy Ranganthan	Chennai Institute of Technology, India

Flow Management in Urban Contexts (FMUC 2025)

Workshop Organizers

Alessio Pino	Kore University of Enna, Italy
Giovanna Acampa	Kore University of Enna, Italy

Workshop Program Committee Members

Giovanna Acampa	University of Florence, Italy
Alessio Pino	Kore University of Enna, Italy
Mariolina Grasso	Università Kore di Enna, Italy
Fabrizio Battisti	University of Florence, Italy
Fabrizio Finucci	Roma Tre University, Italy
Antonella G. Masanotti	Roma Tre University, Italy
Daniele Mazzoni	Roma Tre University, Italy

Geographical Analysis, Urban Modeling, Spatial Statistics 2025 (Geog-And-Mod 2025)

Workshop Organizers

Beniamino Murgante	University of Basilicata, Italy
Giuseppe Borruso	University of Trieste, Italy
Hartmut Asche	University of Potsdam, Germany
Rodrigo Tapia McClung	CentroGeo, Mexico
Andreas Fricke	University of Potsdam, Germany

Workshop Program Committee Members

Giuseppe Borruso	University of Trieste, Italy
Beniamino Murgante	University of Basilicata, Italy
Hartmut Asche	University of Potsdam, Germany
Rodrigo Tapia-McClung	Centro de Investigación en Ciencias de Información Geoespacial (CentroGeo), Mexico
Andreas Fricke	University of Potsdam, Germany
Malgorzata Hanzl	Lodz University of Technology, Poland
Anastasia Stratigea	National Technical University of Athens, Greece
Ljiljiana Zivkovic	Republic Geodetic Authority of Serbia, Serbia
Ginevra Balletto	University of Cagliari, Italy
Silvia Battino	University of Sassari, Italy
Mara Ladu	University of Cagliari, Italy
Maria del Mar Munoz Leonisio	University of Cádiz, Spain
Ahinoa Amaro Garcia	University of Las Palmas of Gran Canaria, Spain
Maria Attard	University of Malta, Malta

Enrico D'agostini	World Maritime University, Sweden
Francesca Krasna	University of Trieste, Italy
Brisol García García	Polytechnic University of Quintana Roo, Mexico
Tu Anh Trinh	UEH University, Vietnam
Giovanni Mauro	Università degli Studi della Campania, Italy
Maria Ronza	University of Naples Federico II, Italy
Massimiliano Bencardino	University of Salerno, Italy
Andrea Gallo	Ca' Foscari University of Venice, Italy
Francesca Sinatra	University of Trieste, Italy
Salvatore Dore	University of Trieste, Italy

Geogames for Sustainable Development (Geogames 2025)

Workshop Organizer

Alenka Poplin	Iowa State University, USA

Workshop Program Committee Members

Alenka Poplin	Iowa State University, USA
Bruno Amaral de Andrade	Portucalense University, Portugal
Brian Tomaszewski	Rochester Institute of Technology, USA
Deepak Marhatta	Tribhuvan University, Nepal
Alessandro Plaisant	University of Sassari, Italy
David Schwartz	Rochester Institute of Technology, USA
Silvia Rossetti	University of Parma, Italy
Floriana Zucaro	University of Naples Federico II, Italy
Alfonso Annunziata	University of Basilicata, Italy
Reza Askarizad	University of Cagliari, Italy
Chiara Garau	University of Cagliari, Italy
Tanja Congiu	University of Sassari, Italy

Geomatics for Resource Monitoring and Management (GRMM 2025)

Workshop Organizers

Alberico Sonnessa	Politecnico di Bari, Italy
Eufemia Tarantino	Politecnico di Bari, Italy
Alessandra Capolupo	Politecnico di Bari, Italy

Workshop Program Committee Members

Umberto Fratino	Politecnico di Bari, Italy
Valeria Monno	Politecnico di Bari, Italy

Antonino Maltese	Università degli studi di Palermo, Italy
Athos Agapiou	Cyprus University of Technology, Cyprus
Michele Mangiameli	Università di Catania, Italy
Angela Gorgoglione	Universidad de la República de Uruguay, Uruguay
Roberta Ravanelli	University of Liège, Belgium
Ester Scotto di Perta	Università degli studi di Napoli Federico II, Italy
Giacomo Caporusso	CNR, Italy
Andrea Montanino	International Centre for Numerical Methods in Engineering of Barcelona, Spain
Antonino Iannuzzo	Università degli studi del Sannio, Italy
Alessandro Pagano	Politecnico di Bari, Italy
Francesco Di Capua	Università degli Studi della Basilicata, Italy
Albertini Cinzia	CNR-IREA, Italy
Alessandra Saponieri	Università degli studi del Salento, Italy
PierFrancesco Recchi	Università degli studi di Napoli Federico II, Italy
Vincenzo Totaro	Politecnico di Bari, Italy
Stefania Santoro	CNR Water Research Institute, Italy
Francesco Bimbo	University of Foggia, Italy
Cristina Proietti	Istituto Nazionale di Geofisica e Vulcanologia, Italy
Carla Cavallo	University of Salerno, Italy
Gaetano Falcone	Università degli Studi di Napoli Federico II, Italy
Valeria Belloni	Sapienza University of Rome, Italy
Alessandra Mascitelli	University of Chieti-Pescara, Italy

HERitage and CLIMAte neutrality. Resilient approach for nature centered/based sustainable cities (HERCLIMA 2025)

Workshop Organizers

Celestina Fazia	Università di Enna Kore, Italy
Angrilli Massimo	University of Chieti-Pescara, Italy
Clara Stella Vicari Aversa	University of Reggio Calabria, Italy
Dorina Camelia Ilies	University of Oradea, Romania
Mariana Ratiu	University of Oradea, Romania

Workshop Program Committee Members

Alessandro Camiz	Università d'Annunzio, Italy
Mario Morrica	University of Urbino, Italy
Thowayeb Hassan	King Faisal University, Saudi Arabia
Alessandro Barracco	Università Kore di Enna, Italy
Kaoutare Amini Alaoui	Mohammed VI Polytechnic University (UM6P), Morocco

| Mariana Ratiu | University of Oradea, Romania |
| Valentina Ciuffreda | Università Chieti-Pescara, Italy |

International Workshop on Information and Knowledge in the Internet of Things (IKIT 2025)

Workshop Organizers

Teresa Guarda	Universidad Estatal Península de Santa Elena, Ecuador
Luis Enrique Chuquimarca Jimenez	Universidad Estatal Península de Santa Elena, Ecuador
Gustavo Gatica	Universidad Andrés Bello, Chile
Filipe Mota Pinto	Polytechnic Institute of Leiria, Portugal
Arnulfo Alanis	Instituto Tecnológico de Tijuana, Mexico
Luis Mazon	Universidad Estatal Península de Santa Elena, Spain

Workshop Program Committee Members

Arnulfo Alanis	Instituto Tecnológico de Tijuana, Mexico
Bruno Sousa	University of Coimbra, Portugal
Carlos Balsa	Instituto Politécnico de Bragança, Portugal
Filipe Mota Pinto	Instituto Politécnico de Leiria, Portugal
Gustavo Gatica	Universidad Andrés Bello, Chile
Isabel Lopes	Instituto Politécnico de Bragança, Portugal
José-María Díaz-Nafría	Universidad a Distancia, Spain
Maria Fernanda Augusto	BiTrum Research Group, Spain
Maria Isabel Ribeiro	Instituto Politécnico Bragança, Portugal
Modestos Stavrakis	University of the Aegean, Greece
Simone Belli	Universidad Complutense de Madrid, Spain
Walter Lopes Neto	Instituto Federal de Educação, Brazil

International Workshop on territorial Planning to integrate Risk prevention and urban Ontologies (IWPRO 2025)

Workshop Organizers

Beniamino Murgante	University of Basilicata, Italy
Roberto De Lotto	University of Pavia, Italy
Elisabetta Maria Venco	University of Pavia, Italy
Caterina Pietra	University of Pavia, Italy

Workshop Program Committee Members

Stefano Borgo	Consiglio Nazionale delle Ricerche ISTC, Italy
Valentina Costa	Università di Genova, Italy
Hamid Danesh Pajouh	Middle East Technical University, Turkey
Ilaria Delponte	Università di Genova, Italy
Lorena Fiorini	Università de L'Aquila, Italy
Veronica Gazzola	Politecnico di Milano, Italy
Ghazaleh Goodarzi	Islamic Azad University, Iran
Michele Grimaldi	Università degli Studi di Salerno, Italy
Alessandra Marra	Università degli Studi di Salerno, Italy
Naghmeh Mohammadpourlima	Åbo Akademi University, Finland
Francesca Pirlone	Università di Genova, Italy
Silvia Rossetti	Università di Parma, Italy
Bahareh Shahsavari	University of Minnesota, USA
Ilenia Spadaro	Università di Genova, Italy
Maria Rosaria Stufano Melone	Politecnico di Bari, Italy

Regional Connectivity, Spatial Accessibility and MaaS for Social Inclusion (MaaS 2025)

Workshop Organizers

Mara Ladu	University of Cagliari, Italy
Ginevra Balletto	University of Cagliari, Italy
Gianfranco Fancello	University of Cagliari, Italy
Tanja Congiu	University of Sassari, Italy
Patrizia Serra	University of Cagliari, Italy
Francesco Piras	University of Cagliari, Italy

Workshop Program Committee Members

Marco Naseddu	University of Cagliari, Italy
Italo Meloni	University of Cagliari, Italy
Giuseppe Borruso	University of Trieste, Italy
Andrea Gallo	University of Trieste, Italy
Francesca Sinatra	University of Trieste, Italy
Maria Attard	University of Malta, Malta
Tu Anh Trinh	UEH University, Vietnam
Marcello Tadini	University of Eastern Piedmont, Italy
Luigi Mundula	University for Foreigners of Perugia, Italy
Silvia Battino	University of Sassari, Italy
Brunella Brundu	University of Sassari, Italy
Veronica Camerada	University of Sassari, Italy

Maria del Mar Munoz Leonisio	University of Cádiz, Spain
Anna Richiedei	University of Brescia, Italy
Michele Pezzagno	University of Brescia, Italy
Marco Mazzarino	IUAV University Venice, Italy

The Development of Urban Mobility Management, Road Safety and Risk Assessment (MANTAIN 2025)

Workshop Organizers

Antonio Russo	Università degli Studi di Enna, Italy
Corrado Rindone	University of Reggio Calabria, Italy
Antonio Polimeni	University of Messina, Italy
Florin Rusca	Politehnica University of Bucharest, Romania
Grigorios Fountas	Aristotle University of Thessaloniki, Greece
Antonio Comi	University of Rome Tor Vergata, Italy

Workshop Program Committee Members

Massimo Di Gangi	University of Messina, Italy
Orlando Marco Belcore	University of Messina, Italy
Antonio Polimeni	University of Messina, Italy
Socrates Basbas	Aristotle University of Thessaloniki, Greece
Claudia Caballini	Polytechnic of Torino, Italy
Efstathios Bouhouras	Aristotle University of Thessaloniki, Greece
Stefano Ricci	Sapienza University of Rome, Italy
Marina Zanne	University of Lubljana, Slovenia
Kh Md Nahiduzzaman	Mohammed VI Polytechnic University, Morocco
Alexsandra Deluka Tibljaš	University of Rijeka, Croatia
Guilhermina Torrao	Aston University, UK

Multidimensional Evolutionary Evaluations for Transformative Approaches (MEETA 2025)

Workshop Organizers

Maria Cerreta	University of Naples Federico II, Italy
Giuliano Poli	University of Naples Federico II, Italy
Maria Somma	University of Naples Federico II, Italy
Gaia Daldanise	CNR IRISS, Italy
Ludovica La Rocca	University of Naples Federico II, Italy

Workshop Program Committee Members

Maria Cerreta	University of Naples Federico II, Italy
Giuliano Poli	University of Naples Federico II, Italy
Maria Somma	University of Naples Federico II, Italy
Laura Di Tommaso	University of Naples Federico II, Italy
Sabrina Sacco	Politecnico di Milano, Italy
Piero Zizzania	University of Naples Federico II, Italy
Gaia Daldanise	CNR IRISS, Italy
Benedetta Grieco	University of Naples Federico II, Italy
Giuseppe Ciciriello	University of Naples Federico II, Italy
Marta Dell'Ovo	Politecnico di Milano, Italy
Daniele Cannatella	TU Delft, The Netherlands
Eugenio Muccio	University of Naples Federico II, Italy
Francesco Piras	University of Cagliari, Italy
Diana Rolando	Politecnico di Torino, Italy
Sveva Ventre	University of Naples Federico II, Italy
Caterina Loffredo	University of Naples Federico II, Italy
Ludovica La Rocca	University of Naples Federico II, Italy
Simona Panaro	University of Campania Luigi Vanvitelli, Italy

Building Multi-dimensional Models for Assessing Complex Environmental Systems (MES 2025)

Workshop Organizers

Vanessa Assumma	University of Bologna, Italy
Caterina Caprioli	Politecnico di Torino, Italy
Giulia Datola	Politecnico di Milano, Italy
Federico Dell'Anna	University of Bologna, Italy
Marta Dell'Ovo	Politecnico di Milano, Italy
Marco Rossitti	Politecnico di Milano, Italy

Workshop Program Committee Members

Vanessa Assumma	Università di Bologna, Bologna
Caterina Caprioli	Politecnico di Torino, Italy
Giulia Datola	DAStU Politecnico di Milano, Italy
Federico Dell'Anna	Politecnico di Torino, Italy
Marta Dell'Ovo	Politecnico di Milano, Italy
Marco Rossitti	Politecnico di Milano, Italy
Francesca Torrieri	Politecnico di Milano, Italy
Mariarosaria Angrisano	Università Telematica Pegaso, Italy
Maksims Feofilovs	Riga Technical University, Latvia

Danny Caprini	Politecnico di Milano, Italy
Giulio Cavana	Politecnico di Torino, Italy
Sebastiano Barbieri	Politecnico di Torino, Italy
Marta Bottero	Politecnico di Torino, Italy
Francesco Cosentino	Politecnico di Milano, Italy
Silvia Ronchi	Politecnico di Milano, Italy
Chiara Mazzarella	TU Delft, Netherlands
Marco Volpatti	Politecnico di Torino, Italy
Chiara D'Alpaos	Università degli Studi di Padova, Italy
Alessandra Oppio	Politecnico di Milano, Italy
Alessia Crisopulli	Politecnico di Milano, Italy
Domenico D'Uva	Politecnico di Milano, Italy
Giorgia Malavasi	Politecnico di Torino, Italy
Rubina Canesi	Università degli Studi di Padova, Italy
Elena Todella	Politecnico di Torino, Italy
Beatrice Mecca	Politecnico di Torino, Italy
Giulia Marzani	University of Bologna, Italy
Isabella Giovanetti	University of Bologna, Italy
Lucia Petronio	University of Bologna, Italy
Franco Corti	University of Padova, Italy
Salvatore De Pascalis	Politecnico di Milano, Italy
Valeria Vitulano	Politecnico di Torino, Italy
Lorenzo Diana	Università degli studi di Napoli Federico II, Italy
Maksims Feofilovs	Riga Technical University, Latvia
Marco De Luca	Politecnico di Torino, Italy
Ilaria Cazzola	Politecnico di Torino, Italy
Andrea De Toni	Politecnico di Milano, Italy
Eugenio Muccio	University of Naples Federico II, Italy
Giuliano Poli	University of Naples Federico II, Italy
Francesco Sica	University "La Sapienza" of Rome, Italy
Elena Di Pirro	Università degli Studi del Molise, Italy
Riccardo Alba	Università di Torino, Italy
Irene Regaiolo	Università di Torino, Italy
Francesca Cochis	Università di Torino, Italy

Modelling Liveable Cities: Techniques, Methods, Challenges, and Perspectives Behind the 'X-Minute' City (MLC 2025)

Workshop Organizers

Federico Mara	University of Pisa, Italy
Valerio Cutini	University of Pisa, Italy
Alessandro Araldi	Université Côte d'Azur, France

| Flávia Lopes | Chalmers University of Technology, Sweden |
| Giovanni Fusco | Université Côte d'Azur, France |

Workshop Program Committee Members

Simone Rusci	University of Pisa, Italy
Lorena Fiorini	University of L'Aquila, Italy
Chiara Di Dato	University of L'Aquila, Italy
Francesco Zullo	University of L'Aquila, Italy
Alfonso Annunziata	University of Basilicata, Italy
Beniamino Murgante	University of Basilicata, Italy
Alessandro Araldi	Universitè Côte d'Azur, France
Chiara Garau	University of Cagliari, Italy
Giampiero Lombardini	Università di Genova, Italy
Flavia Lopes	Chalmers University of Technology, Sweden
Giovanni Fusco	Universitè Côte d'Azur, France

Mathematical Methods for Image Processing and Understanding 2025 (MMIPU 2025)

Workshop Organizers

Ivan Gerace	Università degli Studi di Perugia, Italy
Gianluca Vinti	Università degli Studi di Perugia, Italy
Arianna Travaglini	Università degli Studi della Basilicata, Italy

Workshop Program Committee Members

Ivan Gerace	University of Perugia, Italy
Gianluca Vinti	University of Perugia, Italy
Arianna Travaglini	University of Basilicata, Italy
Marco Baioletti	University of Perugia, Italy
Marco Donatelli	University of Insubria, Italy
Anna Tonazzini	C.N.R. Pisa, Italy
Muhammad Hanif	Ghulam Ishaq Khan Institute of Engineering Sciences and Technology, Pakistan
Francesco Marchetti	University of Padua, Italy
Wolfgang Erb	University of Padua, Italy
Danilo Costarelli	University of Perugia, Italy
Francesco Santini	University of Perugia, Italy
Valentina Giorgetti	University of Perugia, Italy

Mobility Opportunities Bridging Inequalities: Social Inclusion and Gender Equity Initiatives Strategies Against Fragmentation and Complexity of Mobility (MOBIL-EGI 2025)

Workshop Organizers

Tiziana Campisi	University of Enna Kore, Italy
Guilhermina Torrao	Aston University, UK
Socrates Basbas	Aristotle University of Thessaloniki, Greece
Tanja Congiu	University of Sassari, Italy
Stefanos Tsigdinos	National Technical University of Athens, Greece
Florin Nemtanu	Politehnica University of Bucharest, Romania

Workshop Program Committee Members

Massimo Di Gangi	University of Messina, Italy
Orlando Marco Belcore	University of Messina, Italy
Francesco Russo	Mediterranean University of Reggio Calabria, Italy
Alexandros Nikitas	University of Huddersfield, UK
Marilisa Nigro	Rome Tre University, Italy
Kh Md Nahiduzzaman	Mohammed VI Polytechnic University, Morocco
Efstathios Bouhouras	Aristotle University of Thessaloniki, Greece
Antonio Comi	University of Rome Tor Vergata, Italy
Edouard Ivanjko	University of Zagreb, Slovenia
Osvaldo Gervasi	University of Perugia, Italy
Beniamino Murgante	University of Basilicata, Italy
Chiara Garau	University of Cagliari, Italy

MOdels and indicators for assessing and measuring the urban settlement deVElopment in the view of NET ZERO by 2050 (MOVEto0 2025)

Workshop Organizers

Lorena Fiorini	University of L'Aquila, Italy
Lucia Saganeiti	CNR-IMAA, Italy
Angela Pilogallo	CNR-IMAA, Italy
Alessandro Marucci	University of L'Aquila, Italy
Francesco Zullo	University of L'Aquila, Italy

Workshop Program Committee Members

Ginevra Balletto	University of Cagliari, Italy
Giuseppe Borruso	University of Trieste, Italy
Chiara Garau	University of Cagliari, Italy

Beniamino Murgante	University of Basilicata, Italy
Giulia Desogus	University of Cagliari, Italy
Ljiljana Zivkovic	Republic Geodetic Authority, Serbia
Luigi Santopietro	University of Basilicata, Italy
Ilaria Delponte	University of Genoa, Italy
Carmen Guida	University of Naples Federico II, Italy
Chiara Di Dato	University of L'Aquila, Italy

5th Workshop on Privacy in the Cloud/Edge/IoT World (PCEIoT 2025)

Workshop Organizers

Lelio Campanile	Università degli Studi della Campania Luigi Vanvitelli, Italy
Mauro Iacono	Università degli Studi della Campania Luigi Vanvitelli, Italy
Michele Mastroianni	Università degli Studi di Foggia, Italy

Workshop Program Committee Members

Arcangelo Castiglione	Università degli Studi di Salerno, Italy
Maria Ganzha	Warsaw University of Technology, Poland
Daniel Grzonka	Cracow University of Technology, Poland
Antonio Iannuzzi	Università degli Studi Roma Tre, Italy
Armando Tacchella	Università degli Studi di Genova, Italy
Biagio Boi	University of Salerno, Italy
Marco De Santis	University of Salerno, Italy
Fiammetta Marulli	Università degli Studi della Campania "L. Vanvitelli", Italy
Christian Riccio	Università degli Studi della Campania "L. Vanvitelli", Italy
Luigi Piero Di Bonito	Università degli Studi di Napoli Federico II, Italy

Preserving Our Past: Spatial and Remote Sensing Technologies for Cultural Heritage in a Changing Climate (POP 2025)

Workshop Organizers

Maria Danese	CNR-ISPC, Italy
Nicola Masini	CNR-ISPC, Italy
Rosa Lasaponara	CNR-IMAA, Italy

Workshop Program Committee Members

Maria Danese	CNR-ISPC, Italy
Nicola Masini	CNR-ISPC, Italy
Rosa Lasaponara	CNR-IMAA, Italy
Dario Gioia	CNR-ISPC, Italy
Giuseppe Corrado	Università degli Studi della Basilicata, Italy
Canio Sabia	CNR-ISPC, Italy

Processes, methods and tools towards RESilient cities and cultural and historic sites prone to SOD and ROD disasters (RES 2025)

Workshop Organizers

Elena Cantatore	Polytechnic University of Bari, Italy
Dario Esposito	Polytechnic University of Bari, Italy
Alberico Sonnessa	Polytechnic University of Bari, Italy

Workshop Program Committee Members

Elena Cantatore	Politecnico di Bari, Italy
Dario Esposito	Politecnico di Bari, Italy
Alberico Sonnessa	Politecnico di Bari, Italy
Valeria Belloni	Sapienza University of Rome, Italy
Michela Ravanelli	Sapienza University of Rome, Italy
Silvano Dal Sasso	University of Basilicata, Italy
Francesco Chiaravalloti	CNR - IRPI, Italy
Roberta Ravanelli	University of Liège, Belgium
Alessandra Mascitelli	University of Chieti-Pescara, Italy
Francesco Di Capua	University of Basilicata, Italy
Gabriele Bernardini	Università Politecnica delle Marche, Italy
Vito Domenico Porcari	University of Basilicata, Italy
Carmen Rosa Fattore	University of Basilicata, Italy
Stefania Santoro	Water Research Institute, Italy

Scientific Computing Infrastructure (SCI 2025)

Workshop Organizers

Vladimir Korkhov	Saint Petersburg State University, Russia
Elena Stankova	Saint Petersburg State University, Russia
Nataliia Kulabukhova	Saint Petersburg State University, Russia

Workshop Program Committee Members

Adam Belloum	University of Amsterdam, the Netherlands
Dmitrii Vasiunin	Deutsche Telekom Cloud Services E.P.E., Greece
Serob Balyan	Osensus Arm LLC, Armenia
Suren Abrahamyan	Osensus Arm LLC, Armenia
Ashot Sergey Gevorkyan	NAS of Armenia, Armenia
Michal Hnatic	Univerzita Pavla Jozefa Šafárika v Košiciach, Slovakia
Michail Panteleyev	Saint Petersburg Electrotecnical University, Russia
Martin Vala	Univerzita Pavla Jozefa Šafárika v Košiciach, Slovakia
Nodir Zaynalov	Tashkent University of Information Technologies named after Muhammad al Khwarizmi, Uzbekistan
Michail Panteleyev	Saint Petersburg Electrotecnical University, Russia
Alexander Degtyarev	Saint Petersburg University, Russia
Alexander Bogdanov	St. Petersburg State University, Russia

Ports and Logistics of the Future - Smartness and Sustainability (SmartPorts 2025)

Workshop Organizers

Andrea Gallo	Università degli Studi di Trieste, Italy
Gianfranco Fancello	University of Cagliari, Italy
Giuseppe Borruso	Università degli Studi di Trieste, Italy
Enrico D'agostini	World Maritime University, Sweden
Silvia Battino	Università degli Studi di Sassari, Italy
Veronica Camerada	Università degli Studi di Sassari, Italy

Workshop Program Committee Members

Giuseppe Borruso	University of Trieste, Italy
Beniamino Murgante	University of Basilicata, Italy
Ginevra Balletto	University of Cagliari, Italy
Silvia Battino	University of Sassari, Italy
Mara Ladu	University of Cagliari, Italy
Maria del Mar Munoz Leonisio	University of Cádiz, Spain
Ahinoa Amaro Garcia	University of Las Palmas of Gran Canaria, Spain
Maria Attard	University of Malta, Malta
Enrico D'agostini	World Maritime University, Sweden
Francesca Krasna	University of Trieste, Italy

Tu Anh Trinh	UEH University - Ho Chi Minh City, Vietnam
Giovanni Mauro	Università degli Studi della Campania, Italy
Maria Ronza	University of Naples Federico II, Italy
Massimiliano Bencardino	University of Salerno, Italy
Andrea Gallo	Ca' Foscari University of Venice, Italy
Francesca Sinatra	University of Trieste, Italy
Salvatore Dore	University of Trieste, Italy
Veronica Camerada	University of Sassari, Italy
Brunella Brundu	University of Sassari, Italy
Gianfranco Fancello	University of Cagliari, Italy
Marcello Tadini	University of Eastern Piedmont, Italy
Marco Mazzarino	IUAV University Venice
José Ángel Hernández Luis	University of Las Palmas de Gran Canaria, Spain
Marco Naseddu	University of Cagliari, Italy
Maurizio Cociancich	Adriafer, Italy
Giovanni Longo	University of Trieste, Italy
Luca Toneatti	University of Trieste, Italy
Martina Sinatra	University of Cagliari, Italy
Enrico Vanino	University of Sheffield, UK
Patrizia Serra	University of Cagliari, Italy
Agostino Bruzzone	University of Genoa, Italy
Marco Petrelli	University of Roma 3, Italy

Smart Transport and Logistics - Smart Supply Chains (SmarTransLog 2025)

Workshop Organizers

Francesca Sinatra	University of Trieste, Italy
Maria del Mar Munoz	Universidad de Cádiz, Spain
Brunella Brundu	University of Sassari, Italy
Patrizia Serra	University of Cagliari, Italy
Salvatore Dore	University of Trieste, Italy
Marco Naseddu	University of Cagliari, Italy

Workshop Program Committee Members

Giuseppe Borruso	University of Trieste, Italy
Beniamino Murgante	University of Basilicata, Italy
Ginevra Balletto	University of Cagliari, Italy
Silvia Battino	University of Sassari, Italy
Mara Ladu	University of Cagliari, Italy
Maria del Mar Munoz Leonisio	University of Cádiz, Spain
Ahinoa Amaro Garcia	University of Las Palmas of Gran Canaria, Spain

Maria Attard	University of Malta, Malta
Enrico D'agostini	World Maritime University, Sweden
Francesca Krasna	University of Trieste, Italy
Tu Anh Trinh	UEH University, Vietnam
Giovanni Mauro	Università degli Studi della Campania, Italy
Maria Ronza	University of Naples Federico II, Italy
Massimiliano Bencardino	University of Salerno, Italy
Andrea Gallo	Ca' Foscari University of Venice, Italy
Francesca Sinatra	University of Trieste, Italy
Salvatore Dore	University of Trieste, Italy
Veronica Camerada	University of Sassari, Italy
Brunella Brundu	University of Sassari, Italy
Gianfranco Fancello	University of Cagliari, Italy
Marcello Tadini	University of Eastern Piedmont, Italy
Marco Mazzarino	IUAV University Venice
José Ángel Hernández Luis	University of Las Palmas de Gran Canaria, Spain
Marco Naseddu	University of Cagliari, Italy
Maurizio Cociancich	Adriafer, Italy
Giovanni Longo	University of Trieste, Italy
Luca Toneatti	University of Trieste, Italy
Martina Sinatra	University of Cagliari, Italy
Enrico Vanino	University of Sheffield, UK
Patrizia Serra	University of Cagliari, Italy
Agostino Bruzzone	University of Genoa, Italy
Marco Petrelli	University of Roma 3, Italy

Smart Tourism (SmartTourism 2025)

Workshop Organizers

Silvia Battino	University of Sassari, Italy
Francesca Krasna	University of Trieste, Italy
Ainhoa Amaro	University of Las Palmas de Gran Canaria, Spain
Maria del Mar Munoz	University of Cádiz, Spain
Brisol García García	Polytechnic University of Quintana Roo, Mexico
Marta Meleddu	University of Sassari, Italy

Workshop Program Committee Members

Giuseppe Borruso	University of Trieste, Italy
Beniamino Murgante	University of Basilicata, Italy
Gianfranco Fancello	University of Cagliari, Italy
Mara Ladu	University of Cagliari, Italy

Martina Sinatra	University of Cagliari, Italy
Salvatore Dore	University of Trieste, Italy
Marco Mazzarino	IUAV University Venice, Italy
Veronica Camerada	University of Sassari, Italy
Brunella Brundu	University of Sassari, Italy
Maria Attard	University of Malta, Malta
Ginevra Balletto	University of Cagliari, Italy
Giovanni Mauro	University degli Studi della Campania, Italy
Salvatore Lampreu	University of Sassari, Italy
Maria Ronza	University of Naples, Italy
Massimiliano Bencardino	University of Salerno, Italy

Sustainable evolution of long-Distance frEight and paSsenger Transport (SOLIDEST 2025)

Workshop Organizers

Francesco Russo	University of Reggio Calabria, Italy
Andreas Nikiforiadis	Democritus University of Thrace, Greece
Orlando Marco Belcore	University of Messina, Italy
Antonio Comi	University of Rome Tor Vergata, Italy
Tiziana Campisi	Kore University of Enna, Italy
Aura Rusca	Politehnica University of Bucharest, Romania

Workshop Program Committee Members

Massimo Di Gangi	University of Messina, Italy
Orlando Marco Belcore	University of Messina, Italy
Antonio Polimeni	University of Messina, Italy
Socrates Basbas	Aristotle University of Thessaloniki, Greece
Efstathios Bouhouras	Aristotle University of Thessaloniki, Greece
Marina Zanne	University of Ljubljana, Slovenia
Marilisa Nigro	Rome Tre University, Italy
Edoardo Marcucci	Molde University College, Norway
Eugen Rosca	Polytechnic University of Bucharest, Romania
Kh Md Nahiduzzaman	Mohammed VI Polytechnic University, Morocco
Beniamino Murgante	University of Basilicata, Italy
Chiara Garau	University of Cagliari, Italy

Sustainability Performance Assessment: Models, Approaches, and Applications Toward Interdisciplinary and Integrated Solutions (SPA 2025)

Workshop Organizers

Francesco Scorza	University of Basilicata, Italy
Sabrina Lai	University of Cagliari, Italy
Francesco Rotondo	Università Politecnica delle Marche, Italy
Jolanta Dvarioniene	Kaunas University of Technology, Lithuania
Michele Campagna	University of Cagliari, Italy
Corrado Zoppi	University of Cagliari, Italy

Workshop Program Committee Members

Federico Amato	University of Lausanne, Switzerland
Ferdinando Di Carlo	University of Basilicata, Italy
Maddalena Floris	University of Cagliari, Italy
Federica Isola	University of Cagliari, Italy
Giuseppe Las Casas	University of Basilicata, Italy
Federica Leone	University of Cagliari, Italy
Giampiero Lombardini	University of Genoa, Italy
Federico Martellozzo	University of Florence, Italy
Alessandro Marucci	University of L'Aquila, Italy
Ana Clara Moura	Universidade Federal de Minas Gerais, Brazil
Beniamino Murgante	University of Basilicata, Italy
Silviu Nate	Lucian Blaga University of Sibiu, Romania
Anastasia Stratigea	National Technical University of Athens, Greece
Francesco Zullo	University of L'Aquila, Italy
Luigi Santopietro	University of Basilicata, Italy
Benedetto Manganelli	University of Basilicata, Italy

Specifics of Smart Cities Development in Europe (SPEED 2025)

Workshop Organizers

Chiara Garau	University of Cagliari, Italy
Katarína Vitálišová	Matej Bel University, Slovak Republic
Marco Fanfani	University of Florence, Italy
Anna Vaňová	Matej Bel University, Slovak Republic
Kamila Borsekova	Matej Bel University, Slovak Republic
Paola Zamperlin	University of Florence, Italy

Workshop Program Committee Members

Claudia Loggia	University of KwaZulu-Natal, South Africa
Francesca Maltinti	University of Cagliari, Italy
Alessandro Plaisant	University of Sassari, Italy
Alenka Poplin	Iowa State University, USA
Silvia Rossetti	University of Parma, Italy
Gerardo Carpentieri	University of Naples Federico II, Italy
Carmen Guida	University of Naples Federico II, Italy
Floriana Zucaro	University of Naples Federico II, Italy
Anastasia Stratigea	National Technical University of Athens, Greece
Yiota Theodora	National Technical University of Athens, Greece
Giovanna Concu	University of Cagliari, Italy
Paolo Nesi	University of Florence, Italy
Emanuele Bellini	University of Roma Tre, Italy
Mana Dastoum	Polytechnic University of Madrid, Spain
Barbara Caselli	University of Parma, Italy
Martina Carra	University of Brescia, Italy
Alfonso Annunziata	University of Basilicata, Italy
Elisabetta Venco	University of Pavia, Italy
Caterina Pietra	University of Pavia, Italy
Enrico Collini	University of Florence, Italy
Luciano Alessandro Ipsaro Palesi	University of Florence, Italy

Smart, Safe, and Healthy Cities (SSHC 2025)

Workshop Organizers

Chiara Garau	University of Cagliari, Italy
Gerardo Carpentieri	University of Naples Federico II, Italy
Carmen Guida	University of Naples Federico II, Italy
Tanja Congiu	University of Sassari, Italy
Martina Carra	University of Brescia, Italy
Alenka Poplin	Iowa State University, USA

Workshop Program Committee Members

Rosaria Battarra	Istituto di Studi sul Mediterraneo, Italy
Barbara Caselli	University of Parma, Italy
Francesca Maltinti	University of Cagliari, Italy
Romano Fistola	Università degli Studi di Napoli Federico II, Italy
Alessandro Plaisant	University of Sassari, Italy
Silvia Rossetti	University of Parma, Italy
Marco Fanfani	University of Florence, Italy
Reza Askarizad	University of Cagliari, Italy

Floriana Zucaro	University of Naples Federico II, Italy
Anastasia Stratigea	National Technical University of Athens, Greece
Yiota Theodora	National Technical University of Athens, Greece
Giovanna Concu	University of Cagliari, Italy
Francesco Zullo	University of L'Aquila, Italy
Paola Zamperlin	University of Florence, Italy
Vincenza Torrisi	University of Catania, Italy
Tiziana Campisi	University of Enna Kore, Italy
Katarína Vitálišová	Matej Bel University, Slovakia
Tazyeen Alam	University of Cagliari, Italy
Mana Dastoum	Polytechnic University of Madrid, Spain
Martina Carra	University of Brescia, Italy
Alfonso Annunziata	University of Basilicata, Italy
Elisabetta Venco	University of Pavia, Italy
Caterina Pietra	University of Pavia, Italy

Smart and Sustainable Island Communities (SSIC 2025)

Workshop Organizers

Chiara Garau	University of Cagliari, Italy
Anastasia Stratigea	National Technical University of Athens, Greece
Yiota Theodora	National Technical University of Athens, Greece
Giovanna Concu	University of Cagliari, Italy

Workshop Program Committee Members

Milena Metalkova-Markova	University of Portsmouth, UK
Tarek Teba	University of Portsmouth, UK
Alenka Poplin	Iowa State University, USA
Gerardo Carpentieri	University of Naples Federico II, Italy
Carmen Guida	University of Naples Federico II, Italy
Floriana Zucaro	University of Naples Federico II, Italy
Silvia Rossetti	University of Parma, Italy
Barbara Caselli	University of Parma, Italy
Martina Carra	University of Brescia, Italy
Alfonso Annunziata	University of Basilicata, Italy
Maria Panagiotopoulou	National Technical University of Athens, Greece
Apostolos Lagarias	University of Thessaly, Greece
Paola Zamperlin	University of Florence, Italy
Vincenza Torrisi	University of Catania, Italy
Giuseppina Vacca	University of Cagliari, Italy
Roberto Minunno	Curtin University, Australia
Marco Zucca	University of Cagliari, Italy

Elisabetta Venco	University of Pavia, Italy
Caterina Pietra	University of Pavia, Italy
Pietro Crespi	Politecnico di Milano, Italy

From STreet Experiments to Planned Solutions (STEPS 2025)

Workshop Organizers

Silvia Rossetti	Università degli Studi di Parma, Italy
Angela Ricciardello	Kore University of Enna, Italy
Francesco Pinna	Università degli Studi di Cagliari, Italy
Chiara Garau	Università degli Studi di Cagliari, Italy
Tiziana Campisi	Kore University of Enna, Italy
Vincenza Torrisi	University of Catania, Italy

Workshop Program Committee Members

Martina Carra	University of Brescia, Italy
Barbara Caselli	University of Parma, Italy
Tanja Congiu	University of Sassari, Italy
Gabriele D'Orso	University of Palermo, Italy
Matteo Ignaccolo	University of Catania, Italy
Md Kh Nahiduzzaman	Mohammed VI Polytechnic University, Morocco
Muhammad Ahmad Al-Rashid	University of Malaya, Malaysia
Alessandro Plaisant	University of Sassari, Italy
Marianna Ruggieri	University of Enna Kore, Italy
Michele Zazzi	University of Parma, Italy

Sustainable Tourism Evaluations: approaches, methods and indicators (STEva 2025)

Workshop Organizers

Mariolina Grasso	Università Kore di Enna, Italy
Fabrizio Finucci	Roma Tre University, Italy
Daniele Mazzoni	Roma Tre University, Italy
Antonella G. Masanotti	Roma Tre University, Italy
Giovanna Acampa	University of Florence, Italy

Workshop Program Committee Members

Giovanna Acampa	University of Florence, Italy
Fabrizio Finucci	Roma Tre University, Italy
Mariolina Grasso	"Kore" University of Enna, Italy

Alberto Marzo	Ministero della Cultura, Italy
Antonella G. Masanotti	Roma Tre University, Italy
Daniele Mazzoni	Roma Tre University, Italy
Rocco Murro	Sapienza University of Rome, Italy
Claudio Piferi	University of Florence, Italy
Alessio Pino	"Kore" University of Enna, Italy
Nicoletta Setola	University of Florence, Italy
Laura Calcagnini	Roma Tre University, Italy
Antonio Magarò	Roma Tre University, Italy
Janos Ghyerghyak	University of Pécs, Hungary
Ágnes Borsos	University of Pécs, Hungary
Fabrizio Battisti	University of Florence, Italy

Sustainable Development of Ports (SUSTAINABLEPORTS 2025)

Workshop Organizers

Tiziana Campisi	University of Enna KORE, Italy
Giuseppe Musolino	University of Reggio Calabria, Italy
Efstathios Bouhouras	Aristotle University of Thessaloniki, Greece
Elen Twrdy	University of Ljubljana, Slovenia
Elena Cocuzza	University of Catania, Italy
Aura Rusca	Politehnica University of Bucharest, Romania

Workshop Program Committee Members

Massimo Di Gangi	University of Messina, Italy
Orlando Marco Belcore	University of Messina, Italy
Antonio Polimeni	University of Messina, Italy
Claudia Caballini	Polytechnic of Torino, Italy
Gianfranco Fancello	University of Cagliari, Italy
Marina Zanne	University of Lubljana, Slovenia
Stefano Ricci	Sapienza University of Rome, Italy
Beniamino Murgante	University of Basilicata, Italy
Chiara Garau	University of Cagliari, Italy

Theoretical and Computational Chemistry and Its Applications (TCCMA 2025)

Workshop Organizers

Noelia Faginas Lago	Università di Perugia, Italy
Andrea Lombardi	Università di Perugia, Italy
Marcos Mandado Alonso	University of Vigo, Spain

Workshop Program Committee Members

Noelia Faginas-Lago	University of Perugia, Italy
Andrea Lombardi	University of Perugia, Italy
Marcos Mandado	University of Vigo, Spain
Angeles Peña	University of Vigo, Spain
Luca Mancini	Universiy of Perugia, Italy
Massimiliano Bartolomei	CSIC, Spain
Cecilia Coletti	University of Chieti-Pescara, Italy
Iñaki Tuñón	Universidad de Valencia, Spain
Albert Rimola Gilbert	Universitat Autònoma de Barcelona, Spain
Stefano Falcinelli	University of Perugia, Italy
Dario Campisi	University of Perugia, Italy
Ernesto García Para	University of the Basque Country, Spain
Giacomo Giorgi	University of Perugia, Italy
Tomás González Lezana	IFF CSIC, Spain
Enrique M. Cabaleiro Lago	Universidade de Santiago de Compostela, Spain
Aurora Costales	Universidad de Oviedo, Spain
Angel Martin	Universidad de Oviedo, Spain
Jose Manuel	University of Vigo, Spain
Annarita Laricchiuta	CNR ISTP Bari, Italy
Fernando Pirani	University of Perugia, Italy

Transport Infrastructures for Smart Cities (TISC 2025)

Workshop Organizers

Francesca Maltinti	University of Cagliari, Italy
Mauro Coni	University of Cagliari, Italy
Benedetto Barabino	University of Brescia, Italy
Nicoletta Rassu	University of Cagliari, Italy
James Rombi	University of Cagliari, Italy

Workshop Program Committee Members

Francesco Pinna	University of Cagliari, Italy
Chiara Garau	University of Cagliari, Italy
Mauro D'Apuzzo	University of Cassino, Italy
Roberto Minunno	Curtin University, Australia
Tiziana Campisi	University of Enna Kore, Italy
Roberto Ventura	University of Brescia, Italy
Alessandro Plaisant	University of Sassari, Italy
Massimo Di Francesco	University of Cagliari, Italy

Vincenza Torrisi   University of Catania, Italy
Paola Zamperlin   University of Florence, Italy

Transforming Urban Analytics: The Impact of Crowdsourced Mapping and Advanced AI Techniques on Future Cities (Tr-UrbAna 2025)

Workshop Organizers
Ayse Giz Gulnerman Gengec   Ankara Hacı Bayram Veli University, Turkey
Müslüm Hacar   Tildiz Technical University, Turkey
Himmet Karaman   Istanbul Technical University, Turkey

Workshop Program Committee Members
Beniamino Murgante   University of Basilicata, Italy
Abdulkadir Memduhoğlu   Harran University, Turkey
Zeynel Abidin Polat   İzmir Katip Çelebi University, Turkey
Güzide Miray Perihanoğlu   Van Yüzüncü Yıl University, Turkey
Tugba Memisoglu Baykal   Ankara Hacı Bayram Veli University, Turkey

From structural to TRAnsformative-change of City Environment: challenges and solutions and perspectives (TRACE 2025)

Workshop Organizers
Pierluigi Morano   Polytechnic University of Bari, Italy
Maria Rosaria Guarini   Sapienza University of Rome, Italy
Francesco Sica   Sapienza University of Rome, Italy
Francesco Tajani   Sapienza University of Rome, Italy
Marco Locurcio   Polytechnic University of Bari, Italy
Debora Anelli   Polytechnic University of Bari, Italy

Workshop Program Committee Members
Felicia di Liddo   Politecnico di Bari, Italia
Valeria Saiu   Università di Cagliari, Italia
Emma Sabatelli   Sapienza Università di Roma, Italia
Antonella Roma   Sapienza Università di Roma, Italia
Giuseppe Cerullo   Sapienza Università di Roma, Italia
Lucia della Spina   Università di Reggio Calabria, Italia
Alejandro Segura de la Cal   Politecnico di Madrid, Spain
Yilsy Nuñez   Politecnico di Madrid, Spain
Gabriella Maselli   Università di Salerno, Italy
Maria Rosa Trovato   Università di Catania, Italy

Manuela Rebaudengo	Politecnico di Torino, Italy
Pierfrancesco De Paola	Università di Napoli Federico II, Italy
Daniela Tavano	Università della Calabria, Italy
Maria Saez	University of Granada, Spain
Paola Amoruso	LUM "Giuseppe Degennaro" University, Italy

Temporary Real Estate management: Approaches and methods for Time-integrated impact assessments and evaluations (TREAT 2025)

Workshop Organizers

Chiara Mazzarella	TUDelft, The Netherlands
Hilde Remoy	TUDelft, The Netherlands
Maria Cerreta	University of Naples Federico II, Italy

Workshop Program Committee Members

Chiara Mazzarella	TU Delft, The Netherlands
Hilde Remoy	TU Delft, The Netherlands
Maria Cerreta	University of Naples Federico II, Italy
Maria Somma	University of Naples Federico II, Italy
Simona Panaro	University of Campania Luigi Vanvitelli, Italy
Laura Di Tommaso	University of Naples Federico II, Italy
Caterina Loffredo	University of Naples Federico II, Italy
Ludovica La Rocca	University of Naples Federico II, Italy
Sabrina Sacco	Politecnico di Milano, Italy
Piero Zizzania	University of Naples Federico II, Italy
Gaia Daldanise	CNR IRISS, Italy
Benedetta Grieco	University of Naples Federico II, Italy
Giuseppe Ciciriello	University of Naples Federico II, Italy
Marta Dell'Ovo	Politecnico di Milano, Italy
Daniele Cannatella	TU Delft, The Netherlands
Eugenio Muccio	University of Naples Federico II, Italy
Sveva Ventre	University of Naples Federico II, Italy

Supporting the Transition to Ecological Economy in Cities Regeneration: Circular Model Tools for Reusing Architecture and Infrastructures (TReE 2025)

Workshop Organizers

Mariarosaria Angrisano	Pegaso University, Italy
Giulio Cavana	Politecnico di Torino, Italy
Francesca Buglione	CNR-ISPC, Italy

| Antonia Gravagnuolo | CNR-ISPC, Italy |
| Piera Della Morte | Pegaso University, Italy |

Workshop Program Committee Members

Giulia Datola	Politecnico di Milano, Italy
Vanessa Assumma	University of Bologna, Italy
Marco Volpatti	Politecnico di Torino, Italy
Sebastiano Barbieri	Politecnico di Torino, Italy
Caterina Caprioli	Politecnico di Torino, Italy
Marta Dell'Ovo	Politecnico di Milano, Italy
Federico Dell'Anna	Politecnico di Torino, Italy
Elena Todella	Politecnico di Torino, Italy
Danny Casprini	Politecnico di Milano, Italy
Grazia Neglia	Università Telematica Pegaso, Italy
Francesca Nocca	Università degli Studi di Napoli Federico II, Italy
Giulio Cavana	Politecnico di Torino, Italy
Francesca Buglione	CNR-IPSC, Italy
Marco Rossitti	Politecnico di Milano, Italy
Jhon Escorcia	Politecnico di Torino, Italy
Beatrice Mecca	Politecnico di Torino, Italy
Sara Biancifiori	Politecnico di Torino, Italy

Urban Digital Twins and Data Spaces: Shaping the Future of Sustainable Cities (TwinAbleCities 2025)

Workshop Organizers

Dessislava Petrova Antonova	Sofia University, GATE Institute, Bulgaria
Beniamino Murgante	University of Basilicata, Italy
Senthil Rajendran	RMSI, Bahrain
Tiziana Campisi	Kore University of Enna, Italy
Mila Koeva	University of Twente, The Netherlands

Workshop Program Committee Members

Dessislava Petrova-Antonova	Sofia University, Bulgaria
Mila Koeva	The University of Twente, The Netherlands
Beniamino Murgante	University of Basilicata, Italy
Senthil Rajendran	RMSI, Bahrain
Tiziana Campisi	Kore University of Enna, Italy

Urban Regeneration: Innovative Tools and Evaluation Model (URITEM 2025)

Workshop Organizers

Fabrizio Battisti	University of Florence, Italy
Giovanna Acampa	University of Florence, Italy
Orazio Campo	Sapienza University of Rome, Italy
Melania Perdonò	University of Florence, Italy

Workshop Program Committee Members

Fabrizio Battisti	University of Florence, Italy
Giovanna Acampa	University of Florence, Italy
Orazio Campo	University of Rome "La Sapienza", Italy
Melania Perdonò	Università degli Studi di Firenze, Italy

Urban Space Accessibility and Mobilities (USAM 2025)

Workshop Organizers

Chiara Garau	DICAAR, University of Cagliari, Italy
Alessandro Plaisant	University of Sassari, Italy
Barbara Caselli	University of Parma, Italy
Mauro D'Apuzzo	University of Cassino and Southern Lazio, Italy
Gabriele D'Orso	University of Palermo, Italy
Matteo Ignaccolo	University of Catania, Italy

Workshop Program Committee Members

Mauro Coni	University of Cagliari, Italy
Martina Carra	University of Brescia, Italy
Tiziana Campisi	University of Enna Kore, Italy
Tanja Congiu	University of Sassari, Italy
Francesca Maltinti	University of Cagliari, Italy
Silvia Rossetti	University of Parma, Italy
Barbara Caselli	University of Parma, Italy
Angela Pilogallo	University of L'Aquila, Italy
Lorena Fiorini	University of L'Aquila, Italy
Reza Askarizad	University of Cagliari, Italy
Francesco Pinna	University of Cagliari, Italy
Aime Tsinda	University of Rwanda, Rwanda
Youssef El Ganadi	International University of Rabat, Morocco
Marco Migliore	University of Palermo, Italy
Alessio Salvatore	Italian National Research Council, Italy
Giuseppe Stecca	Italian National Research Council, Italy

Paola Zamperlin	University of Florence, Italy
Vincenza Torrisi	University of Catania, Italy
Gerardo Carpentieri	University of Naples Federico II, Italy
Carmen Guida	University of Naples Federico II, Italy
Floriana Zucaro	University of Naples Federico II, Italy
Alfonso Annunziata	University of Basilicata, Italy
Elisabetta Venco	University of Pavia, Italy
Caterina Pietra	University of Pavia, Italy
Tazyeen Alam	University of Cagliari, Italy
Valerio Cutini	University of Pisa, Italy

UX Mobility 2025: Placing User Experience at the Center of Urban Mobility: Methods and Frameworks (UXM 2025)

Workshop Organizers

Carmen Guida	Università degli Studi di Napoli Federico II, Italy
Gerardo Carpentieri	Università degli Studi di Napoli Federico II, Italy
Federico Messa	Systematica srl, Italy
Lamia Abdelfattah	Systematica srl, Italy

Workshop Program Committee Members

Rosaria Battarra	Istituto di Studi sul Mediterraneo CNR, Italy
Romano Fistola	Università degli Studi di Napoli Federico II, Italy
Lucia Saganeiti	IMAA-CNR, Italy

Virtual Reality and Augmented reality and applications (VRA 2025)

Workshop Organizers

Damiano Perri	University of Perugia, Italy
Osvaldo Gervasi	University of Perugia, Italy
Chau Ma Thi	University of Engineering and Technology, Vietnam National University, Hanoi, Vietnam
Paolo Nesi	University of Florence, Italy
Pierfrancesco Bellini	University of Florence, Italy

Workshop Program Committee Members

| David Berti | ART SpA, Italy |
| JungYoon Kim | Gachon University, South Korea |

TaiHoon Kim	Zhejiang University of Science and Technology, China
Marcelo de Paiva Guimares	Federal University of São Paulo, Brazil
Sergio Tasso	University of Perugia, Italy

Workshop on Advanced and Computational Methods for Earth Science Applications (WACM4ES 2025)

Workshop Organizers

Luca Piroddi	University of Cagliari, Italy
Patrizia Capizzi	University of Palermo, Italy
Marilena Cozzolino	University of Molise, Italy
Sebastiano D'Amico	University of Malta, Malta
Chiara Garau	University of Cagliari, Italy
Giuseppina Vacca	University of Cagliari, Italy

Workshop Program Committee Members

Andrea Angelini	CNR ISPC, Italy
Ilaria Barone	Università degli Studi di Padova, Italy
Patrizia Capizzi	University of Palermo, Italy
Luigi Capozzoli	CNR, Italy
Alberto Carletti	University of Cagliari, Italy
Emanuele Colica	University of Malta, Malta
Marilena Cozzolino	Università del Molise, Italy
Sebastiano D'Amico	University of Malta, Malta
Chiara Garau	University of Cagliari, Italy
Luciano Galone	University of Malta, Malta
Peter Iregbeyen	University of Malta, Malta
Mariano Lisi	Basilicata Aerospace Cluster CLAS, Italy
Raffaele Martorana	Università di Palermo, Italy
Paolo Mauriello	Università del Molise, Italy
Veronica Pazzi	University of Florence, Italy
Raffaele Persico	Università della Calabria, Italy
Luca Piroddi	University of Cagliari, Italy
Sina Saneiyan	Binghamton University, USA
Mercedes Solla	Universidade de Vigo, Spain
Deodato Tapete	ASI, Italy
Giuseppina Vacca	University of Cagliari, Italy
Enrica Vecchi	University of Cagliari, Italy

Sponsoring Organizations

ICCSA 2025 would not have been possible without the tremendous support of many organizations and institutions, for which all organizers and participants of ICCSA 2025 express their sincere gratitude:

Galatasaray University, Istanbul, Türkiye
(https://gsu.edu.tr/en)

African Mathematical Union
(https://www.africanmathunion.org/)

Springer Nature Switzerland AG, Switzerland
(https://www.springer.com)

The University of Massachusetts, USA
(https://www.umass.edu/)

University of Perugia, Italy
(https://www.unipg.it)

University of Basilicata, Italy (http://www.unibas.it)

Monash University, Australia
(https://www.monash.edu/)

Kyushu Sangyo University, Japan
(https://www.kyusan-u.ac.jp/)

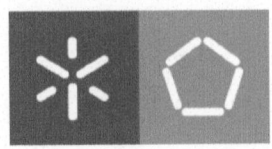

Universidade do Minho
Escola de Engenharia

University of Minho, Portugal
(https://www.uminho.pt/)
Venue
ICCSA 2025 took place in: **Galatasaray University, Istanbul, Türkiye**

Additional Reviewers

Reviewers
The review tasks for each workshop have been carried out by the workshop Organizers
and the members of the workshop Program Committee.

Plenary Lectures

Sky Safe with GAI and Post-quantum Computing

Elizabeth Chang

Professor of Cyber Security and Head of Discipline, University of the Sunshine Coast, Australia

Abstract. Professor Chang's talk in this presentation has two distinct parts. To start, she will introduce the landscape of cybersecurity development, attacks, threats, and vulnerabilities, as well as state-of-the-art cyber protection, cyber defence, and cyber incident prevention. This is followed by a discussion of the impact of Generative AI (GAI) and quantum-safe cryptographic computing, highlighting the major issues and challenges in research, education, and training. In conclusion, she will present a vision for Sky Safe solutions, aiming to achieve cyber resilience that supports business and economic stability, enhances human capabilities, and promotes environmental sustainability.

Disaster Preparedness and Risk Profiling in the Digital Era from Earth Observation Lens

Jagannath Aryal

Department of Infrastructure Engineering, University of Melbourne, Australia

Abstract. Natural hazards which turn into disasters result in severe losses of lives, infrastructure, and property. Disasters such as earthquakes and landslides and their impacts on transportation safety, infrastructure resilience, and displacement of people to new places are challenges. To address such challenges, earth observation data and intelligent methods can provide potential solutions in developing decision support systems. This talk will present the state of the art in Earth observation for disaster resilience using intelligent methods. In the Earth observation space, digitalisation has revolutionised the way we map, monitor, and develop decision support systems. Global case study examples covering earthquake-induced landslides from the Himalayan region will cover the digital capabilities. The digital capabilities will embrace object recognition, interpretation, and their accurate and precise capture to integrate into digital models. The developed digital models from representative case studies can be leveraged in other jurisdictions in profiling risks to protect lives and infrastructure and creating disaster preparedness in the era of digital age and digital economy.

Intelligent Image Enhancement for Real-World Applications in Adverse Atmospheric Conditions

Khan Muhammad

Department of Global Convergence, Sungkyunkwan University, South Korea

Abstract. The adverse impacts of atmospheric conditions such as haze, fog, and low-light environments pose significant challenges for real-world applications reliant on computer vision, including autonomous driving, surveillance, and remote sensing. This keynote explores cutting-edge advancements in intelligent image enhancement, drawing insights from two pivotal studies. The first introduces HazeSpace2M, a comprehensive dataset and novel classification-guided dehazing framework that improves image clarity across diverse atmospheric conditions, addressing the gap between synthetic and real-world dehazing performance. The second focuses on LoLI-Street, a benchmark for low-light image enhancement tailored to urban environments, extending beyond enhancement to enable robust object detection and scene understanding. Taken together, these contributions demonstrate how integrating domain-specific datasets, advanced algorithms, and performance benchmarks can significantly elevate the reliability of computer vision systems under challenging weather and lighting conditions. Attendees will gain valuable insights into the methodologies, datasets, and practical applications driving innovation in this field, with implications for research and industry alike.

In Memory of Carmelo Torre

Unfortunately, Professor Carmelo Torre, one of the cornerstones of the ICCSA Conference, passed away last December, leaving everyone stunned and deeply saddened. His loss has created a profound void within our academic community. Carmelo was not only a respected scholar and dedicated contributor to the success and growth of ICCSA, but also a generous colleague, mentor, and friend to many. His intellectual rigor, warm personality, and unwavering commitment to advancing research will be remembered with great admiration. As we continue the work he helped shape, we honor his legacy and the indelible mark he left on all of us. Carmelo Torre graduated in engineering at the Polytechnic of Bari with a thesis on urban planning under Dino Borri's guidance. He began his research career by collaborating with Franco Selicato. During his PhD at the University of Naples Federico II under Luigi Fusco Girard, he specialized in real estate market analysis and multi-criteria evaluation methods. He explored the social impacts of urban transformations with his lifelong friend Maria Cerreta. His first ICCSA participation was in Perugia in 2008, in the session Geographical Analysis, Urban Modeling, Spatial Statistics. Instantly captivated by the conference, his charisma enabled him to involve various Italian scientific communities, including those in real estate and statistics. ICCSA became a yearly commitment for him, where he valued the high editorial quality of the proceedings and the dynamic post-presentation discussions and debates he passionately and expertly enriched. In 2012, alongside Maria Cerreta and Paola Perchinunno, he organized the workshop Econometrics and Multidimensional Evaluation in the Urban Environment (EMEUE), fostering dialogue on critical topics. His influence steadily grew, drawing numerous research groups to ICCSA and establishing real estate and assessment as one of the conference's leading fields. A pillar of ICCSA, he was involved across all facets of the event. Torre's contributions to academic discourse were marked by intellectual rigor and innovative thinking. His conference interventions consistently challenged conventional wisdom, offering insights transcending disciplinary boundaries. Beyond the conference, he passionately advocated for equity and social justice. His left-leaning ideology, though firm, earned respect from those with differing views, thanks to his sincerity and loyalty. He was creative, generous, and always willing to help, even at a personal cost. Despite battling illness, he maintained his characteristic optimism, warmth, cheerfulness, and commitment, supported by his partner, Caterina Rinaldo. His legacy lives on in his ideas, dedication, and unmatched generosity.

Contents – Part VI

Geomatics for Resource Monitoring and Management (GRMM 2025)

Advanced and Innovative Web Apps 2025 (AIWA 2025)

B2B Service for Tracking User Behavior

Bui Ngoc Son[1], Vu Thu Diep[2], and Phan Duy Hung[1(✉)] (iD)

[1] FPT University, Hanoi, Vietnam
{sonbn7,hungpd2}@fe.edu.vn
[2] HaNoi University of Science and Technology, Hanoi, Vietnam
diep.vuthu@hust.edu.vn

Abstract. This paper presents a solution for collecting user action data for the B2B model. Collecting user data plays an important role in personalized experience, product improvement and business strategy optimization. Data helps Internet platforms publish personalized content and products, and helps businesses optimize subsequent campaigns and improve advertising performance. In addition, data also helps improve customer service, detect errors and prioritize user interfaces. In the field of AI and Machine Learning, data is an important foundation for training models, making the system smarter and more automated. By effectively exploiting user data, businesses can make accurate decisions, optimize operating processes and anticipate market trends, thereby improving performance and quality services. Collecting user data not only helps individuals experience and optimize business strategies, but also opens up opportunities for businesses to provide data collection and analysis services in a B2B (Business to Business) model. Many companies do not have the ability to automatically collect and process big data, so they turn to third-party data aggregation services from various sources. These businesses use the data to optimize subsequent campaigns, anticipate consumer trends, and improve products. The approach and results of this discussion can be fully applied to other types of user data.

Keywords: B2B Service · Data Collection · User Tracking · User Behavior

1 Introduction

1.1 Problem and Motivation

Currently, the demand for B2B (business-to-business) is growing strongly in the era of technology 4.0, especially in many fields when businesses increasingly focus on digital transformation and optimizing work processes.

In software services and digital platforms (SaaS), businesses are looking for technology solutions to help manage data, automate processes using platforms such as customer relationship management (CRM), supply chain management (SCM), data analysis tools, etc. In particular, the analysis tools of these platforms often collect information about user behavior such as activity history, usage habits to optimize the experience as well as predict needs.

© The Author(s), under exclusive license to Springer Nature Switzerland AG 2026
O. Gervasi et al. (Eds.): ICCSA 2025 Workshops, LNCS 15891, pp. 3–16, 2026.
https://doi.org/10.1007/978-3-031-97617-9_1

With digital marketing for B2B, not only stopping at traditional surveys, many businesses have applied digital marketing strategies such as SEO, digital content, and advertising on online platforms. And on these platforms, collecting user data is also very popular, however, the collected data is somewhat different from management platforms such as: collecting emails, clicks, website behavior, personal information, etc. to be able to deploy personalized campaigns, display ads suitable for each audience. Not only that, more and more businesses also customize according to customer needs according to industry, product or business model characteristics. The data collected from these models is quite diverse so that businesses can personalize experiences or create unique products and services.

One type of user website data collection is gathering user location data. When collecting the location of many users in a certain number, analysts can determine the number of customers interested in which products, thereby developing reasonable strategies with stores at the counter as well as suggesting reasonable products. Another example of data collection is collecting personal information of users when they register to use website features, valuable information such as age, address or transaction history can help analysts have a deeper insight into the level of interest of users in products depending on age or geography. Not only that, some websites and apps such as TikTok, Reddit also create surveys about interests, things that users are interested in, thereby displaying content, products or creating features with the lowest risk while still optimizing profits. In addition, some large e-commerce websites such as Amazon and eBay also collect users' product clicks for analysis, and when the number of clicks on a product reaches the threshold where the AI knows what product the user is interested in, the website display that product along with countless related products to retain users as well as increase the conversion rate much higher than displaying products on the website randomly and illogically.

Collecting e-commerce web user behavioral data through computer mouse information is part of analyzing user habits. Computer mouse information not only tells analysts about user behavior and habits on the website, but also helps them understand user emotions as mentioned [1]. Not only that, this is an easy-to-collect type of data that also has many meanings. In addition to expressing emotions, computer mouse information also shows analysts all user activities on the website based on the path of the mouse, products of interest based on clicks, click density or movement on the website.

Computer mouse information can include many factors such as mouse coordinates, click coordinates, mouse scrolling, etc. and when these data are large enough, they can let analysts know whether the website's UI is good or not. For example, the rate of missing a button click or areas on the website that are less interested. From there, the user experience can be optimized. In addition, the data also shows which products users are interested in based on how long their mouse lingers on that product. So that businesses can optimize advertising, display products that meet user needs, thereby increasing conversion rates as well as traffic. However, collecting computer mouse information is still very difficult to implement for many small and medium-sized businesses. The first problem is the huge amount of data because the mouse can move very quickly as well as perform countless other actions in a moment, thereby creating a lot of data in a short period of time. Second, the storage capacity and understanding of big data technologies of many businesses or digital transformation companies are still limited when they only collect simple information such as button clicks, visits, and that data is not good enough to be used to truly analyze user behavior. Third, many businesses that want to collect and analyze this data need the support of third parties at a high cost and can be blocked by the user's own extensions. And finally, compliance with ethics and privacy regulations such as the General Data Protection Regulation (GDPR) in Europe or the California Consumer Privacy Act (CCPA) in the US must also be a top priority.

1.2 Related Work

The results of some studies have been found, for example: In [2], the author presented an advanced website analysis support tool that focuses on tracking mouse behavior and processing real-time data to optimize the efficiency of data collection on the website. This tool uses the mouse path vectorization technique, which significantly reduces the amount of data transmitted through the JavaScript library but still ensures high accuracy. The system includes a vectorizer to optimize and compress data, a log tracker to track, and also supports session storage and playback of user sessions. The tests have shown amazing results when it can reduce up to 85% of the transmitted data size and 84% of the number of requests. And the tool still works well under limited network conditions. The tool not only supports user experience analysis but also has the ability to expand when integrated with large data analysis systems such as Google Analytics. In [3], a method combining user modeling, mouse behavior tracking and recommendation system is presented to enhance user experience on e-commerce platforms. The study has built a recommendation algorithm based on user interaction data, including click events, mouse movements and mouse hover time. The results show that the system achieves 87.50% accuracy in recommending suitable products and received positive reviews from 40 survey participants. AIMT-UXT mentioned in [4] is an open tool that supports the collection, storage and analysis of computer mouse information on the web, integrating many analytical modules such as single-view, heatmap and fuzzy logic to evaluate UX and t-SNE clustering algorithm to group users according to behavioral characteristics. The goal is to introduce a method for evaluating user experience through mouse tracking data and artificial intelligence (AI). The system with high reliability when compared with the traditional method based on questionnaire (SUS), UX classification assessment makes it a potential tool for low-cost UX assessment without depending on any commercial solutions.

During the research, real-time processing systems all apply Socket.IO[1] so that the Client can communicate with the Backend in the most efficient and optimal way. Some systems proposed in [5–7] all apply it and achieve high efficiency. Therefore, this study also apply it in this system.

In paper [8] it is concluded that HDFS is a powerful distributed file system that plays a core role in big data processing applications. It is designed to provide efficient and reliable data storage and processing, meeting the needs of large-scale systems. From there, this paper decided to implement it in this paper.

---

[1] https://socket.io/.

Spark Streaming[2] processes data continuously, meaningful data is processed and analyzed as it is generated. This is useful for applications that require real-time feedback or continuous data analysis such as financial transactions, monitoring systems, and social media stream processing. Spark Streaming is applied in many fields such as [9–12]. Therefore, it also be implemented in this research. In [13–15], very promising results have been achieved using Apache Kafka[3], which is an open-source distributed event streaming platform used by thousands of companies for high-performance data pipelines, streaming analytics, data integration, and mission-critical applications. On the other hand, in paper [16], combining Kafka and Spark Streaming to build a system that delivers high performance. So Kafka also be used here along with Spark Streaming.

This paper takes a different approach, this work focuses on collecting user computer mouse information and transmitting this data accurately and minimizing loss as much as possible with the big data processing technologies mentioned above but still ensuring simplicity in deployment and integration into the system without changing the current structure of the website.

2   Contribution

The main contribution of this paper is to propose a service to collect user behavior through computer mouse information. Each step has been studied and evaluated to find a suitable processing method for automatic data collection. The service is implemented with 3 simple steps: Collect data, send data, stream data and store. In which, data collection includes data preprocessing. This work also tested the results and performance when deploying the system on the test environment which is mentioned in the results section of this thesis. The rest of the thesis is organized as follows. Section 2 describes the system architecture, the implementation method is analyzed in Sect. 3. Finally, the implementation results and conclusions are discussed in Sect. 4.

3   System Architecture

3.1   Architecture Overview

In general, the model this paper propose is deployed for businesses that provide data collection services (Service Provider) to other businesses in need (Business Partner). Through the Internet, businesses in need of data collection will connect with the service provider. And businesses can collect user data, analyze website data after deploying additional functions and functions according to the provider's API description. The basic system architecture is shown in Fig. 1.

Going into Business Partner, the website of businesses that want to track user computer mouse information, JavaScript is the best choice because of the language's ability to access the Document Object Model (DOM). Then, the data collected from JavaScript can be sent to the server in many different ways. However, sending a huge amount

---

[2] https://spark.apache.org/.

[3] https://kafka.apache.org/.

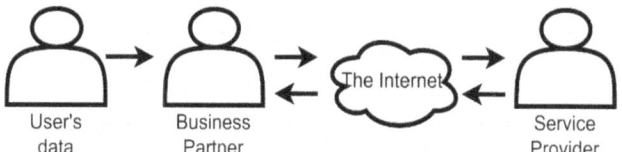

Fig. 1. Architecture overview of B2B Service

of data from the user's mouse to the web server does not have many options. Therefore, Socket.IO will be deployed into the website system to bridge the communication between the layers. As for the web server, the website will have to add some functions according to the API description to be able to encrypt and send the collected data to the Service Provider. The data sent from Business Partner must ensure security standards such as HTTPS or TLS to ensure that the data is not attacked. The system architecture of Business Partner is shown in Fig. 2.

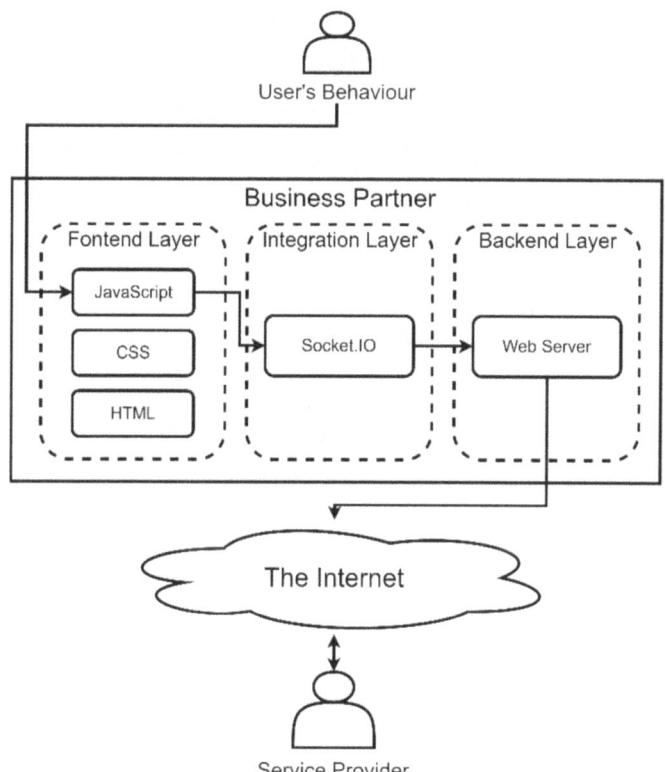

Fig. 2. Architecture of Business Partner

As for the Service Provider, the system has an API gateway that ensures the use of necessary security to ensure that it is not attacked, as well as authenticating and authorize requests from Business Partners using security methods such as OAuth, API Key, etc. And the API Gateway also coordinates requests to other components in the system. Data after authentication via the API gateway is uploaded to Kafka and then stored in HDFS through Spark. Data in HDFS is processed by Spark and sent to Business Partner or displayed directly on the system dashboard depending on the needs. The system architecture of the Service Provider is shown in Fig. 3 and the service of the proposed system includes the following subcomponents are listed in detail in Table 1.

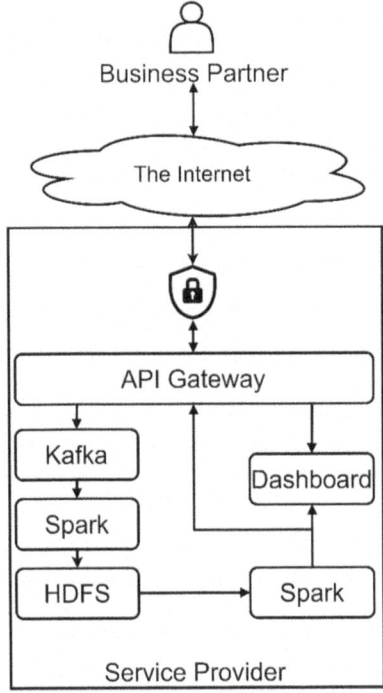

Fig. 3. Architecture of Service Provider

Table 1. Subcomponents included in proposed system

Component	Description
Kafka	Kafka creates topics, each topic can represent a user, and with the strength of receiving and distributing data, Kafka takes on the role of continuously receiving data from the server into the specified topic and distributing them efficiently into HDFS through Spark
Spark Streaming	Spark with the strength of processing and analyzing big data, will be used to analyze continuously updated data in HDFS to visualize data for analysts, as well as taking on the task of broadcasting data from Kafka and saving to HDFS
HDFS	Data received from Kafka will be distributed into blocks, along with creating and distributing data copies on Data nodes to increase retrieval speed, ensure availability and reliability, load balancing as well as better scalability

3.2 System Requirements

To meet the needs of the experiment, a website in Python with Flask Framework is created. This website is deployed on the test platform. The test platform here includes a physical machine with Intel I5-13600KF 3.50 GHz chip, 8GB RAM, Windows 11 64 bit, and a virtualization platform Oracle VirtualBox Version 7.1.0 r164728, 4GB RAM, 2 CPUs, PIIX3 chipset, Ubuntu 22.04 LTS operating system. And the software's versions are listed in detail in Table 2.

Table 2. Version of software and systems be used

Name	Version
Python	3.10.12
Flask	3.0.3
Socket.IO	4.1.2
Hadoop	3.4.0
Kafka	3.8.0
Scala	2.13
Zookeeper	3.8.4
Spark	3.5.3

Python, Flask, and Socket.io are used with the most popular versions to create a Business Partner test environment. The same applies to Hadoop, Spark, and Kafka as their versions are well compatible with each other. Zookeeper and Scala are installed alongside the Kafka installation.

4 System Design and Implementation

4.1 Business Partner Layer

Client

In this system, Python and Flask are used to create a sample website to serve as a testing environment. First, the Frontend is embedded with a JavaScript code consisting of the following components listed in Table 3:

Table 3. Components included in the Frontend of the Client

Component	Description
socket	Connects to the server to receive data from the frontend
port	The port of the server
Mouse_Coordinate	The name of the event that receives mouse coordinate
Clicked_Coordinate	The name of the event that receives mouse's clicked coordinate

(*continued*)

Table 3. (*continued*)

Component	Description
document	An object that represents the entire HTML in the browser, allowing JavaScript to interact and manipulate the content of the website
X-coordinate	The horizontal coordinate of the mouse
Y-coordinate	The vertical coordinate of the mouse
Button clicked	Parameter that determines whether the mouse is being clicked
Mouse_Event	Name of channel on socket

Process 1 presents the process of collecting data using script and sending collected data to socket's channel. Line 1 initializes socket on specified port. Line 2–9 presents the process of handling "Mouse_Coordinate" event. When document detects the changing of mouse movement, retrieves X-coordinate and Y Coordinate from web page and create an object to store it (Line 3–7). Then send it's coordinate to channel on socket (Line 8). In addition, the process of handling "Clicked_Coordinate" event (Line 10–19) has the same structure as "Mouse_Coordinate" but with the addition of retrieving button clicked.

Process 1: Collecting data using script and sending collected data to socket's channel

1. **INITIALIZE** socketConnection **TO CONNECT TO** specifiedPort
2. **WHEN** document **DETECTS** 'Mouse_Coordinate' event:
3.   **SET** mouseX **TO RETRIEVE** X-coordinate **FROM** web page
4.   **SET** mouseY **TO RETRIEVE** Y-coordinate **FROM** web page
5.   **CREATE** moveData **OBJECT WITH**:
6.   **PROPERTY** x = mouseX
7.   **PROPERTY** y = mouseY
8.   **SEND** moveData **TO** 'Mouse_Event'
9. **END WHEN**
10. **WHEN** document **DETECTS** 'Clicked_Coordinate' event:
11.   **SET** mouseX **TO RETRIEVE** X-coordinate **FROM** web page
12.   **SET** mouseY **TO RETRIEVE** Y-coordinate **FROM** web page
13.   **SET** mouse_clicked **TO RETRIEVE** button clicked **FROM** web page
14.   **CREATE** clickedData **OBJECT WITH**:
15.   **PROPERTY** x = mouseX
16.   **PROPERTY** y = mouseY
17.   **PROPERTY** clicked = mouse_clicked
18.   **SEND** clickedData **TO** 'Mouse_Event'
19. **END WHEN**

And from there, both the mouse path and the location where the user's mouse clicks are collected. Each user activity is collected through the script and saved on the socket. From there, the web server will collect and process for the next steps.

Web Server

In addition to operating the website, the Web Server also takes on two other tasks: processing data from the client and pushing processed data to Kafka. In this part, the components for operation include in Table 4:

Table 4. Subcomponents included in the Web Server

Components	Description
producer	Used to send data to the specified topics of Kafka
Kafka producer	Is a class provided by the Kafka library
Bootstrap servers	Parameter used to assign the address of the Kafka broker
Value serializer	Parameter used to serialize data before sending it to Kafka

Process 2 presents Kafka's producer, which is used to send data from business partner to service provider. The producer configuration has 2 parts. First is setting the bootstrap server with the address that is provided by the service provider (Line 2). And the second is the data sent by the producer is guaranteed to be serialized before sending (Line 3).

Process 2: Kafka producer Configuration

1. **INITIALIZE** Kafka producer **WITH CONFIGURATIONS**:
2.   **SET** bootstrap servers **TO** Kafka broker address
3.   **SET** value serializer **TO** Json Serializer

The process 3 below extract data when received it on socket's channel (Line 1). After extracting X value, Y value and clicked from data to x, y, clicked (Line 3–5), create structureData with extracted value (Line 6), then use initialized producer in process 2 to send it to service provider's Kafka's topic (Line 7).

Process 3: Extracting data on Socket's channel and using Producer to send data

1. **WHEN** 'Mouse_Event' on socket **IS RECEIVED**:
2.   **FUNCTION** handleMouseEvent(data):
3.   **SET** x **TO EXTRACT** 'X value' **FROM** data
4.   **SET** y **TO EXTRACT** 'Y value' **FROM** data
5.   **SET** clicked **TO EXTRACT** 'clicked' **FROM** data
6.   **CREATE** structuredData **WITH** x, y, clicked
7.   **USE** producer **TO SEND** structuredData **TO** Kafka's topic **IN** Kafka Broker
8.   **FLUSH ALL** messages **TO ENSURE IMMEDIATE SENDING**
9. **END FUNCTION**
10. **END WHEN**

After performing the above processes, the data from here is transferred to the Service Provider for processing for the next steps. This issue is presented in the section below.

4.2 Service Provider Layer

Kafka, Spark and HDFS

Producer from Business Partner after sending data to the pre-designated topic on Kafka is backed up to ensure reliability as well as prevent data loss. Then ready for Consumers to subscribe and read data from the partition of that topic.

Process 4 shows the process of initializing Spark Consumer to subscribing the topic on Kafka Broker to DataFrame. From the beginning, data source format set as Kafka's format (Line 2), then define the address of Kafka Broker and the topic which is the target of subscribing (Line 3 – 4). In addition, the message should be set to read from earliest to ensure the correctness (Line 5). After those setup steps, the data will be streamed.

Process 4: Initialize Consumer and read data from Kafka using Spark to DataFrame

1. **INITIALIZE** DataFrame **TO READ** and **LOAD FROM** Kafka **USING** Spark **WITH CONFIGURATIONS**:
2.   **WITH FORMAT** 'kafka'
3.   **WITH OPTION** 'bootstrap.servers' **SET TO** 'Kafka broker address'
4.   **WITH OPTION** 'subscribe' **SET TO** 'Kafka's topic'
5.   **WITH OPTION** 'startingOffsets' **SET TO** 'earliest'

In process 5, DataFrame must pre-process before writing into HDFS. First, define schema for DataFrame with "x", "y", "clicked" as integer, integer, string (Line 1 – 4).

Then parse DataFrame with steps: Convert "value" column to string and set to json (Line 6). After setting json, parse json use defined schema and set to parsedData. Then extract and select all fields from parsedData (Line 7 - 8).

Process 5: Pre-Processing data

---

1. **DEFINE** schema **FOR** DataFrame **WITH FIELDS**:

2.   'x' **AS INTEGER**

3.   'y' **AS INTEGER**

4.   'clicked' **AS STRING**

5. **PARSE** DataFrame:

6.   **SET** json **TO CONVERT** 'value' **COLUMN TO STRING**

7.   **SET** parsedData **TO PARSE** json **USING** schema

8.   **EXTRACT** and **SELECT** all fields **FROM** parsedData

---

Process 6 presents the process of writing prased DataFrame into HDFS. Strating write data from parsed DataFrame into HDFS with configurations. First, set "outputMode" to "append" (Line 2), which defines how it interacts with HDFS. Second is setting format when appending (Line 3), "json" here is selected format. Finally, set the save location and checkpoint location in HDFS (Line 4 – 5).

Process 6: Write parsed DataFrame to HDFS

---

1. **START WRITING** data **FROM** parsed DataFrame **WITH CONFIGURATIONS**:

2.   **SET** outputMode **TO** 'append'

3.   **SET** format **TO** 'json'

4.   **SET** outputLocation **TO** 'HDFS folder location'

5.   **SET** checkpointLocation **TO** 'HDFS checkpoint location'

6. **WAIT INDEFINITELY FOR** streaming query **TO TERMINATE**

Visualize with Spark and HDFS

User mouse data stored in HDFS is continuously uploaded by Spark via Kafka and is also continuously streamed by another Spark session for analysis and visualization purposes. Here, Spark data fetched from HDFS is divided into two separate sets called dataMove and dataClicked. With dataMove, the data only has the mouse coordinates, used to get the user's movement data on the website. Meanwhile, dataClicked has an additional mouse click attribute to determine the location on the page where the user has clicked. Both data types are shown in Table 5:

Table 5. Structure of data's mouse information

	X coordinate	X coordinate	Clicked
dataMove	O	O	–
dataClicked	O	O	O

Both data sets, when displayed together on a graph on the dashboard, provide the clearest view for analysts when studying user behavior. This data can also be exported in Json or csv format if desired.

4.3 Implementation

A simulated E-commerce website using Flask has been deployed. The front end of the website has been embedded with JavaScript code to collect mouse information as mentioned in Process 1, and the backend has also been added with a function to send data to the Service Provider as shown in Process 2 and 3. The sample web page is shown in Fig. 4.

Fig. 4. Experimental Website

To simulate a user using and interacting with the website, the computer mouse has been used to interact with the website for a while. When moving the mouse, all mouse information is sent to the socket to communicate with the server. Through the processing steps from Process 4 to 6, Service Provider obtain the user's behavior when interacting with the mouse on the Web page. The results are presented in Fig. 5.

The test results show us which products are of interest even without any analysis tools based on click density as well as customer activity area in a short time. This information when extracted is in Json format as shown in Fig. 6.

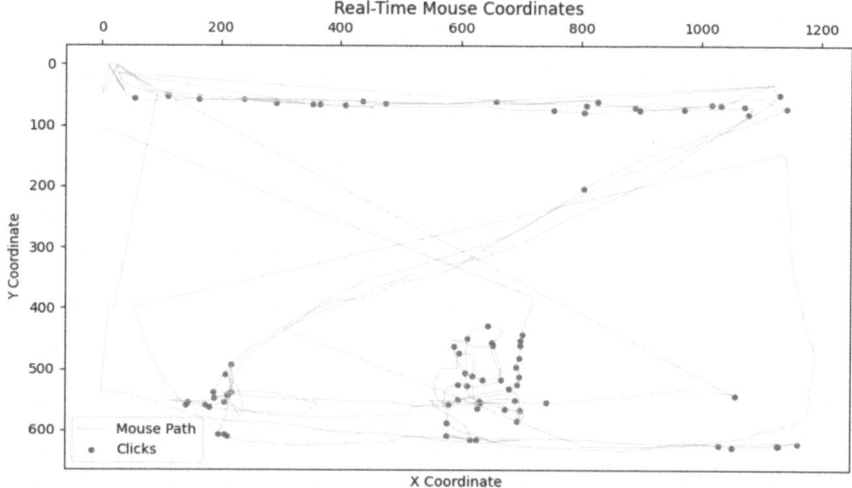

Fig. 5. Experiment Result

```
{"x":578,"y":557}
{"x":580,"y":557}
{"x":581,"y":557}
{"x":581,"y":557,"clicked":"0"}
{"x":582,"y":557}
{"x":583,"y":557}
{"x":584,"y":557}
{"x":586,"y":556}
{"x":587,"y":556}
{"x":588,"y":556}
```

Fig. 6. An example of the exported data in Json format

From the exported data, the results shown that the information above is simple and convenient enough to be used for other analytical tasks. Moreover, with the amount of information extracted, providing data for machine learning tasks is completely simple.

5 Conclusion and Perspective

In conclusion, this paper introduces a method to deploy a B2B service that collects user data. It is worth noting that this method is very flexible and effective when it is extremely easy to deploy for both Business Partners and Service Providers. In particular, Business Partners do not need to intervene too deeply in their systems when applying this method. In addition, the method is also very scalable when adding parameters to the code is also extremely simple, thereby helping Service Providers customize the code to create different services based on this study's method.

In this work, this paper focuses on implementing mouse data collection in an easy and efficient way. In the future, this study aims to extend this method and map it to other collection scenarios while still ensuring user data privacy laws. This work is designed with concurrency and scalability in mind and considers improving performance and data collection in more complex scenarios.

References

1. Lali, P., Naghizadeh, M., Nasrollahi, H., Moradi, H., Mirian, M.S.: Your mouse can tell about your emotions. In: 4th International Conference on Computer and Knowledge Engineering (ICCKE), pp. 47–51. IEEE, Mashhad (2014)
2. Čegan, L., Filip, P.: Advanced web analytics tool for mouse tracking and real-time data processing. In: 14th International Scientific Conference on Informatics, pp. 431–435. IEEE, Poprad, Slovakia (2017)
3. Tanjim-Al-Akib, M., Ashik, L.K., Walid, H.-A., Chowdhury, K.: User-modeling and recommendation based on mouse-tracking for e-commerce websites. In: Computer and Information Technology (ICCIT), pp. 517–523. (2016)
4. Souza, K.E.S., Seruffo, M.C.R., De Mello, H.D. Souza, D.D.S., Vellasco, M.M.B.R.: User experience evaluation using mouse tracking and artificial intelligence. IEEE Access 7, 96506–96515 (2019)
5. Josh, Godwin Sam. Asynchronous Wi-Fi Control Interface (AWCI) Using Socket IO Technology. arXiv preprint arXiv:1810.05502 (2018)
6. Singh, Y.V., Singh, H., Chauhan, J.K.: Online collaborative text editor using socket.IO. In: 2021 3rd International Conference on Advances in Computing, Communication Control and Networking (ICAC3N), pp. 1251–1253. Greater Noida, India (2021)
7. Rajarajeswari, P.L., et al.: Reach—a chat application. In: 2024 10th International Conference on Advanced Computing and Communication Systems (ICACCS), pp. 1961–1966. Coimbatore, India (2024)
8. Shvachko, K., Kuang, H., Radia, S., Chansler, R.: The hadoop distributed file system. In: 2010 IEEE 26th Symposium on Mass Storage Systems and Technologies (MSST), pp. 1–10. Incline Village, NV, USA (2010)
9. Chung, N.N., Hung, P.D.: Logging and monitoring system for streaming data. In: Luo, Y. (eds.) Cooperative Design, Visualization, and Engineering. CDVE 2020. LNCS, vol. 12341. Springer, Cham (2020). https://doi.org/10.1007/978-3-030-60816-3_21
10. Hung, P.D., Hanh, T.D., Tung, T.D.: Term deposit subscription prediction using spark MLlib and ML packages. In Proceedings of the 2019 5th International Conference on E-Business and Applications (ICEBA 2019), pp. 88–93. Association for Computing Machinery, New York, NY, USA (2019)
11. Dat, D.Q., Hung, P.D.: Clustering of time-series balance history data streams using apache spark. In: Luo, Y. (eds.) Cooperative Design, Visualization, and Engineering. CDVE 2020. LNCS, vol. 12341. Springer, Cham (2020). https://doi.org/10.1007/978-3-030-60816-3_13
12. Nam, L.H., Hung, P.D.: Building a big data oriented architecture for enterprise integration. In: Luo, Y. (eds.) Cooperative Design, Visualization, and Engineering. CDVE 2021. LNCS, vol. 12983. Springer, Cham (2021). https://doi.org/10.1007/978-3-030-88207-5_17
13. Alothali, E., Alashwal, H., Salih, M., Hayawi, K.: Real time detection of social bots on twitter using machine learning and apache kafka. In: 2021 5th Cyber Security in Networking Conference (CSNet), pp. 98–102. Abu Dhabi, United Arab Emirates (2021)
14. Ilasariya, S., Patel, P., Patel, V., Gharat, S.: Image steganography using blowfish algorithm and transmission via apache kafka. In: 2022 4th International Conference on Smart Systems and Inventive Technology (ICSSIT), pp. 1320–1325. Tirunelveli, India (2022)
15. Phan, T.-C., Phan, A.-C., Trieu, T.-N.: Real-time opinion extraction and classification for vietnamese posts on social networks. In: 2020 12th International Conference on Knowledge and Systems Engineering (KSE), pp. 19–24. Can Tho, Vietnam (2020)
16. Le Noac'h, P., Costan, A., Bougé, L.: A performance evaluation of apache kafka in support of big data streaming applications. In: 2017 IEEE International Conference on Big Data (Big Data), pp. 4803–4806. Boston, MA, USA (2017)

Contribution to Nosocomial Infections Detection via Biosensors Particles Spatial Simulation in Mixed Reality Environment

Stelios Kouzeleas[1](✉) and Ioannis Tsolakidis[2]

[1] Department of Interior Architecture, International Hellenic University, Serres, Greece
stelios_kouzeleas@yahoo.fr
[2] Natural Environment and Climate Change Agency, Serres, Greece
i.tsolakidis@necca.gov.gr

Abstract. Nowadays, various studies show that many millions of patients globally are affected by healthcare-associated infections (HAIs) or nosocomial infections each year, causing hundreds of thousands direct deaths, presenting a crucial public health problem with serious social and economic implications with a predicted increasing tendency. Biosensor systems propose today a realizable way face to standard methods for detecting bacterial infections in clinical environments, as these standard methods are time-consuming and costly, presenting many limitations. This study involves interdisciplinary scientific areas to describe a theoretical frame of a real-time digital multi-system simulation of nosocomial infections in Mixed Reality environment. The theoretical description of the technical conditions and requirements of such a system will contribute to a future implementation of a real-time 3D spatial detection, quantification and simulation with future data monitoring of nosocomial bacteria rates. The proposed simulation system is based on combined simulation methods and mainly on voxels/point clouds technology with a potential comparison and evaluation with ideal rates in a comprehensible way. This will allow healthcare specialists and political decision makers to evaluate a hospital environment sanitary by taking suitable measures.

Keywords: Nosocomial infections simulation · AR 3D spatial simulation of nosocomial bacteria · Mixed Reality · Nosocomial bacteria detection with biosensors · 3D voxel simulation

1 Introduction

Nowadays, infectious diseases is a very serious healthcare problem as they are responsible for about 15% of all deaths worldwide [1]. In the last years, various studies show that almost 4 million patients in Europe are affected by healthcare-associated infections (HAIs) or nosocomial infections each year, causing approximately 37,000 direct deaths. By 2050, these deaths are expected to reach 10 million worldwide, presenting a crucial public health problem with serious social and economic implications [2].

© The Author(s), under exclusive license to Springer Nature Switzerland AG 2026
O. Gervasi et al. (Eds.): ICCSA 2025 Workshops, LNCS 15891, pp. 17–32, 2026.
https://doi.org/10.1007/978-3-031-97617-9_2

Some of the most serious public health problems causing hospital stays, higher medical expenses, and greater rates of death are indeed nosocomial infections and bacterial resistance [3]. Recent studies have also indicated that surgical and nosocomial infections may increase about 8 extra hospital days for patients with approximately $15 billion in additional expenses annually only in USA and $4.5 billion in the UK for 4 extra hospital days [4, 5]. Nosocomial infections affect between 5% and 20% of hospital patients worldwide while only in Europe the corresponding costs are estimated at almost € 7 billion per year [6].

According to the World Health Organization (WHO), Anti-Microbial Resistance (AMR) of bacteria, viruses and many parasites no longer respond effectively to medicines with traditional methods. So, AMR could lead almost 30 million people globally into extreme poverty [7].

Today, the traditional diagnostic methods of nosocomial infections have limitations because they rely on time-consuming laboratory procedures of 1–5 days [8] with significant delays in diagnosis and treatment process [1]. While new advanced microbiological techniques with molecular and nonmolecular methods reduce the time of bacteria detection [9], these traditional methods of detection and identify nosocomial bacteria still present limitations on their reliability, sensitivity, efficiency and range of applications [10]. They use PCR-based techniques, or mass spectrometry techniques, as Matrix-assisted laser desorption-ionization time of flight mass spectrometry (MALDI-TOF) [11], intricate and time-consuming techniques with no sufficient acid amplification and sample preparation at once, which is still remains a challenge [7].

On the other hand, at the new age of technology, biosensor systems that record biological parameters propose today a realizable way to traditional methods for detecting bacterial infections in clinical environments. Biosensors based on different materials develop new reliable methods to detect pathogens in many areas and they seem to offer greater stability and sensitivity [12]. They identify different infections quickly with accuracy, in real time and on-site [1]. In the past 10 years ASSURED criteria gave guidelines and the framework in order to develop numerous Point-of-Care (PoC) biosensors devices [13].

Studies in disease infections detection simulation have been undertaken by dynamic, complex and hybrid simulation models. These simulation models and surveillance systems focus, among others, to 2D diagrams for synthetic data generation, statistic comparison in 2D line charts, using developed data structures and data location, programming algorithms with 2D spatial distributions results, indoor location-based services for more efficient representation and management of indoor spatial data, etc. [14].

Thus, an effective and comprehensive bacterial infections simulation is significant factor to the contribution of the HAIs problem solution. This study is in the first phase of theoretical development and focuses on a technical preparation of future spatial simulation of nosocomial infections. The proposed methodology takes into account state-of-the-art spatial simulation techniques in 3D Mixed Reality (MR) environment (and no linear diagrams) by quoting related studies, technology of biosensors and their adaptation to the proposed simulation system by contributing to a hospital environment sanitarian evaluation by healthcare specialists and political decision makers.

2 Objectives and Innovation

2.1 Objectives of the Research Proposal

This research addresses the technical requirements of spatial simulation proposal of nosocomial infections particles of hospital rooms via biosensors technology in order to contribute to a hospital environment sanitarian assessment. The proposed simulation system/methodology objectives are quite similar with a previous study of the same authors on Air Quality emissions from biosensors inside buildings [15] regarding, among others, the:

(1) detection and management of nosocomial infections particles inside a hospital environment via an adapted semi automatic biosensors network, with the use of trained personnel,
(2) representation of nosocomial infections particles in 3D VR spatial simulation environment based either on real or render images virtual tours with superimposed gradient spatial simulation [15],
(3) simulation of nosocomial infections particles in 3D volumetric point cloud/voxel simulation with spatial reference in AR environment [15],
(4) contribution to a wireless biosensors grid system creation adapted for infections particles measurement,
(5) theoretical description of an adapted methodology of 2D/3D effective spatial modelling for various simulation environments with the use of infections particles representation system [15],

2.2 Innovation of the Research Proposal

As this research is the extension of a previous study on Air Quality emissions from biosensors inside buildings [15], the innovation of this research proposal focuses on interdisciplinarity various simulation & modelling approaches and techniques to represent nosocomial infections particles from biosensors in a hospital environment. In particular, the innovation concerns, among others:

(1) a simultaneous 3D spatial structure modelling with nosocomial infections particles rates nebula representation in 3D point clouds/voxels either in immersive VR/AR environment as almost all studies simulate these rates only in 2D/3D linear diagrams or 2D spatial format [15],
(2) a method to obtain accurate measurements by improving a connection biosensors system to a network and the corresponding transferring data,
(3) a volumetric building modelling methodology for AR simulation,
(4) provide to any user the ability to real-time immersive experience, via VR/AR environment,
(5) a significant contribution to health experts or political decision-makers for (a) better understanding nosocomial infections behavior and (b) deliberating over the same understandable spatial simulation in order to take appropriate actions,
(6) ensure an immersive pedagogical experience of an academic student on nosocomial infections behavior via an interactive volumetric simulation.

3   BioSensors for Infections Detection

3.1   Types of Biosensors

The biosensors addressed to infections are classified in terms of pathogens detection and in terms of technical detection. In terms of pathogens detection, the biosensors are classified in three main categories [1]:

(a) immunosensors, which pose the potential to improve the pathogen and toxin diagnostic-processes, regarding pathogens, such as Leishmania, SARS-CoV-2, H1N1, Gram-positive bacteria, etc.,

(b) aptasensors, which detect target (bio) markers as biorecognition elements [16], regarding pathogens, such as S. aureus, E. coli, etc., and

(c) genosensors, which detect the hybridization reactions of target nucleic acids, either DNA or RNA [17], regarding pathogens, such as Human serum samples, DNA sample, Saliva sample, etc.

In terms of technical detection there are many biosensors based on several detection techniques, such as [18]:

(a) interferometric biosensor, which is a label-free sensitive biosensor with interference of two light waves [7],

(b) photonic biosensor, based on evanescent wave detection for point-of-care analysis which is the practice of diagnosing patients at the point of need [18],

(c) electrochemical biosensor, which is the most employed transducer including amperometric, potentiometric, conductometric & impedimetric techniques [19–21],

(d) piezoelectric biosensor, which is quartz crystal microbalance biosensor detecting resonance frequency changes of bacteria on the sensor surface) [18],

(e) optical biosensor, which is electromagnetic radiation that interacts with the analyte, [18], (see Fig. 1).

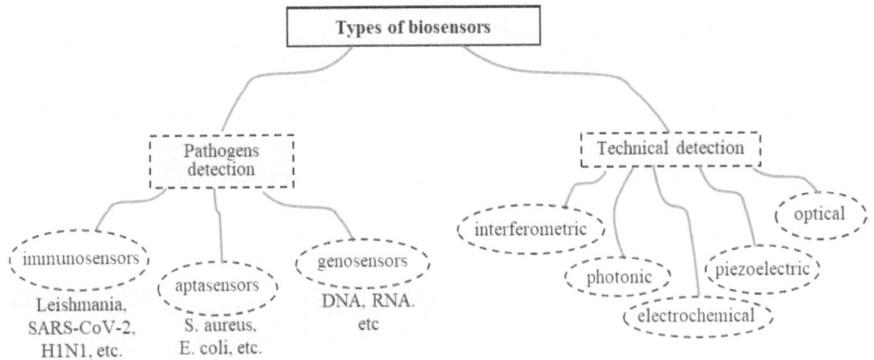

Fig. 1. Types of biosensors in terms of pathogens & technical detection

Certain low-cost biosensors produced by inject-printed techniques and exhibited better sensitivity in biosensor performance [22–24].

3.2   Advantages and Limits of Biosensors

Traditional diagnostic methods have disadvantages, such as:

(a) increased costs, longer diagnostic times,
(b) specialized equipment and trained personnel,
(c) greater sample volumes and sample handling protocols,
(d) increasing the possibility of contamination and human error [25].

On the other hand, biosensors present many advantages, such as

(a) quick analysis times and high loading capacity [26],
(b) great sensitivity [27],
(c) selectivity, which is the capacity to interact with a particular target analyte (molecule) [28],
(d) reproducibility by performing under difficult conditions [29],
(e) response time, which is the duration to read and generate a signal [25],
(f) distinguish between different strains of pathogens within a single sample and
(g) conditions requiring continuous monitoring.

However, the bigger limit of biosensors is the high cost [30] while scalability presents financial and logistical difficulties, although using cost-effective materials and promoting open-source designs can reduce overall costs [31]. In addition, no biosensor currently in use can perform real-time quantitative testing for huge arrays.

4   Infections Detection and Simulation Studies–Discussions

Researches in disease infection detection and simulation are based on 2D statistic charts using mainly structure and location data with algorithms of 2D spatial distribution results.

Agent-Based Model (ABM) is a bottom-up simulation method for dynamic modelling with autonomous entities called agents. This method is often use in disease infection simulation in order to discover spatial and temporal patterns analysis via 2D diagrams for synthetic data generation, while other microscale simulation with surveillance system on hospital-acquired infection prevention and control use comparison in 2D line charts simulation [32].

Agent based modelling is an effective simulation method to simulate the spread of infection via interactions of agents which are individual and/or collective entities. In GAMA platform which is an open-source development environment for an agent-based modelling language (GAML) a simulator was created in order to simulate infection spread, infected people and the level of infectivity in QGIS, an open-source GIS environment [33].

System Dynamics (SD) is a top-down continuous simulation modelling method capable to simulate non-linear relationships using differential equations [34].

Discrete Event Simulation (DES) models the sequence of activities and events in time of a detection system operation [32]. DES captures the variability and the randomness of multiple elements (e.g. individual objects behavior, age, health status, etc.) within a detection system [35].

Hybrid Simulation Models (HSM is a simulation modelling method combining at least 2 different simulation modelling methods [36].

Another method called LAMP has been integrated into a specific biosensor surface (Surface Plasmon Resonance – SPR) in order to detect S. aureus and methicillin-resistant genes [37]. Similar studies use LAMP method with a nucleic acid biosensor (LFNAB) in order to identify the amplification products via immunoreactions and visual detection [38] while other study use LAMP with integrating DNA extraction and colorimetric detection in order to identify E. faecium gene by even naked eye in 1 h [39].

Another simulation model called Montel Carlo simulates antibiotic-resistant bacteria in hospital units. It represents patients and staff members and their interactions, such as handwashing compliance, via colonization curves by allowing to study the impact of infection control measures and being a precious educational tool for staff [40].

An infectious disease simulator is based on contact network generator using techniques from location-aware search into the hospital environment by processing millions of locations and structures data in order to simulate spatial distributions [41].

Several infectious disease simulators, represent only parameter variation with calibration results [42], parameters values by estimating the transmission dynamics [43] or surveillance systems for infection prevention and control by 2D statistics data comparison [44].

5   Research Methodology

5.1   Introduction

The research methodology of the present study is based on a previous study of the same authors on Air Quality emissions from biosensors inside buildings [15]. It takes into account modelling and simulation techniques, communication and connection specifications affection the research organization. The methodological steps consist in (1) BioSensors implementation and measurements of nosocomial infections parameters (2) Geometry modelling (3) Simulation techniques (4) Spatial 3D representation in VR/AR environment (see Fig. 2).

5.2   Biosensors Implementation & Nosocomial Infections Measurements

A biosensor is an analytical device composed of a biological sensing element (antibody, enzyme, DNA) in close contact with a physical transducer (converts bio-recognition event into a measurable signal) which together relate the concentration of an analyte (substance of interest that needs detection) to a measurable electrical signal with the aid of an amplifier (signal amplification), a biocomponent (target analyte) and a bioreceptor (molecule that specifically recognizes the analyte) [25]; the schematic representation of the biosensor (see Fig. 3).

The biosensor implementation is a process with many problems that principally have to do with the biosensor transitioning from the lab to the clinic 45]. In real, only a few biosensors, such as glycose sensor have been successfully translated from research labs to clinical settings [45].

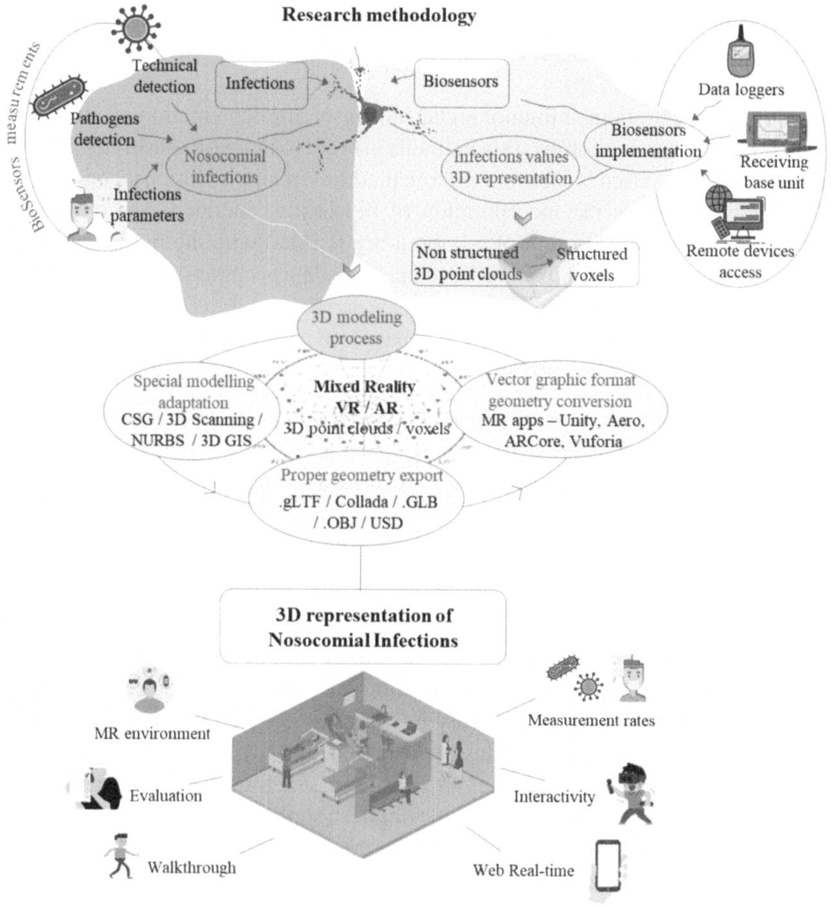

Research methodology

Technical detection

Infections

Biosensors

Data loggers

Pathogens detection

Nosocomial infections

Infections values 3D representation

Biosensors implementation

Receiving base unit

Infections parameters

Non structured 3D point clouds

Structured voxels

Remote devices access

3D modeling process

Special modelling adaptation CSG / 3D Scanning / NURBS / 3D GIS

Mixed Reality VR / AR 3D point clouds / voxels

Vector graphic format geometry conversion MR apps – Unity, Aero, ARCore, Vuforia

Proper geometry export .gLTF / Collada / .GLB / .OBJ / USD

3D representation of Nosocomial Infections

MR environment

Measurement rates

Evaluation

Interactivity

Walkthrough

Web Real-time

Fig. 2. Research schematic methodology

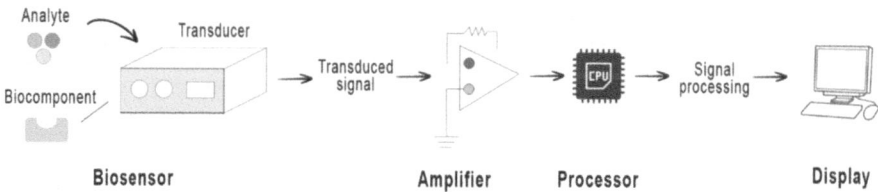

Analyte

Transducer

Biocomponent

Transduced signal

CPU

Signal processing

Biosensor

Amplifier

Processor

Display

Fig. 3. Schematic representation of a typical biosensor [25]

Today, many implementation methods are being actively researched aiming to novel fabrication procedures, lower costs, accessibility increase, incompatibilities resolution, standardization data formats, data management platforms and biosensors connection, etc. [25]. Another research area is the buildup of organic material on the biosensor surface ("biofouling") in order to increase performance [46].

A main biosensor implementation problem, is also to guarantee the reproducibility of experiments and diagnostic procedures and not only to ensure the accuracy of results via adequate adjustments [25].

Another research about immunological biosensor implementation focuses on the improvement antibody immobilization methods in order to increase sensitivity [47] while research about DNA-based biosensors explore methods of amplification techniques [48].

Another challenge is the incorporation of biosensor-generated data into existing Information Management System of a Laboratory (LIMS) with the implementation of open-source biosensor platforms in order to enhance data accessibility and facilitate the real-time diagnostic process [49].

The proposed implementation process is based on a data recording system which is generally made of 3 components [50]:

(a) a network of biosensors at the measuring points converting nosocomial diseases values into electrical analog or digital signals
(b) an acquisition system (digital or analog) reading and logging electrical signals from biosensors
(c) a computer allowing the storage, the processing and the analysis of the acquired values.

The connection of the 3 components can be implemented via (a) wired connection and (b) wireless connection by radio frequency transmission. Each type of connection present advantages/disadvantages depending on the components distance, the ease and the cost of installation and finally the potentiality to modify the system with electromagnetic interferences. In case of radio wireless connection, the acquisition system positions the transmitting part close to the biosensor facilitating the transmission of the measured values to the receiving part. At the same time, modern sophisticated systems integrate the transmitting part and the biosensor in the measuring instrument by placing the receiving part near to the computer in order to facilitate the values transmission [1].

The proposed system, running in web environment, requires the creation of recording stations (Stations) of the biosensor results in special data loggers which are located appropriately in the hospital area. The data is then sent to the central base unit and then stored, processed and visualized, according to what was mentioned in the technical part of the data transfer. The entries will be made by trained hospital personnel (see Fig. 4).

5.3 Simulation System and Techniques

Simulations of spatial elements and descriptive forms with interdisciplinary approaches [51] is almost an inevitable way with an added value for particles spatial simulation.

This study is based on a state-of-the-art 3D spatial simulation system in either a modern 3D point cloud/voxels nebula surround environment or an immersive VR/AR evolving environment [15]. The proposed system can be transformed in a power educational tool contributing either to medicine students or to a common language creation between medicine experts and political decision makers for a social policy.

Today, several interdisciplinary simulation techniques are used in complex spatial simulation issues providing access to complex databases [52], 3D modelling based

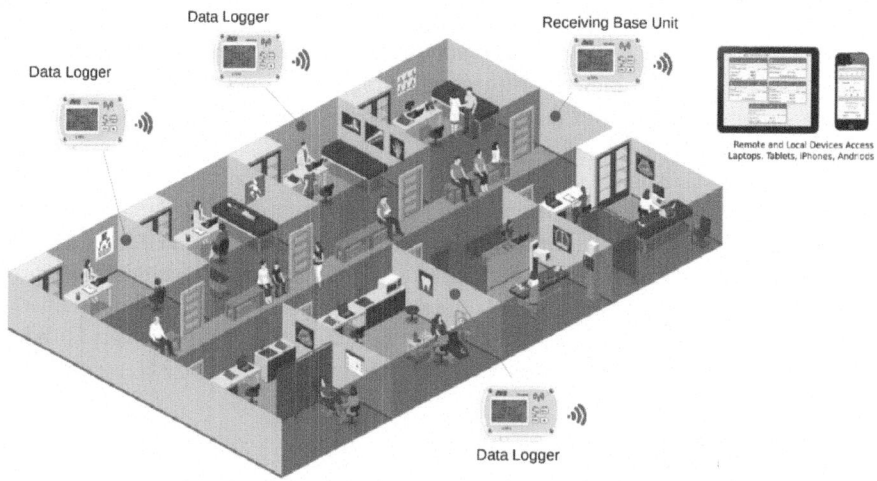

Fig. 4. Schematic 3D diagram of sensor installation and data transmission [50, 74]

either on VRML programming or even on modern CAD systems integrating Building Information Modelling (BIM) procedures, displays interpolation technology, etc.

The two most prevailing particle methods of "Smooth Particle Hydrodynamics - (SPH)" and "Moving Particle Semi-implicit (MPS)" allowing integral representation of quantities and spatial derivatives and incompressible fluid flow are used today for fluid mechanics [53]. Thus, particles spatial simulation techniques, such as infection and comfort conditions can be supported by VR/AR techniques for volumetric representation [15] dealing with OpenGL techniques, other approaches that convert particles to volumetric data representing point density and texture-mapping [54], image overlay, telecommunications and wireless, etc. However, points cloud/Voxel simulation method is a sophisticated and optimal way to represent this kind of particles as this method segments the space into cubes of precise dimensions and structure with a 3D cube table [55]. This method exploits the screen technology and energy visualization, such as Cave Automatic Virtual Environment [15], as well as special devices capable to see superimposed rendering images over the real word, such as Head Mounted Displays (HMD) and See-through Displays by using Tracking and Client-Server Network Architecture technology [56], etc.

5.4 3D Spatial Geometry Modelling Process

A lot of 3D complex spatial modelling methods and techniques are implementing in volumetric visualization such as Grid Mapping and voxels [57], point clouds [58], Constructive Solid Geometry – CSG, NURBS surfaces [59], 3D scanning and object's recognition [60] 3D GIS topology elements [61], Boundary Representations, Spatial subdivision representations, etc. The 3D spatial modelling and representation of nosocomial infections is a technically painful procedure due to the Mixed Reality communication protocols and the complex connection of special devices [15].

These 3D model's creation methods [62] representing the spatial surrounds in AR environment need to be converted into appropriate formats such as OBJect format, Collada, etc. [63] by specific AR software allowing create interactive experiences by blending virtual elements with the real world, such as, Unity platform, Adobe Aero, ARCore, Vuforia, etc.

In addition to standard CAD software, many software using photogrammetric methods with multiple angles, extract 3D geometry and texture data that need to be converted in proper format such as GL Transmission Format (gLTF), gLB format, USDZ format or Universal Scene Description (USD) format, etc. [64]. The necessary technical synchronization and adaptation between the plethora of formats/protocols and the biosensors implementation requirements in practice from the lab to the clinic is a very difficult interdisciplinary challenge that many researchers are working on [15, 31].

5.5 Nosocomial Infections Values 3D Representation

VR Simulation. Architectural and urban spatial digital simulations [65], as well as many CAD and rendering environments create 3D models with solids, surfaces, meshes, NURBS and Bezier polygons tools [51]. These 3D models have to be converted into appropriate VR 360° scene format based on

(a) directly 3D vector models,
(b) 360° bitmaps from 3D models or
(c) 360° real photos superposition (see Fig. 5).

User-friendly digital tools and visualization methods [66] are adapted to the final VR 360° scene into multimedia elements, such as interactive superimposed areas, 360° panoramas et video, block of images, popup information, interactive HTML5 or JAVAScript programming elements, etc. [67].

Other different interpolation techniques and algorithms in 2D within GIS systems, such as Inverse Distance Weighting (IDW) and radial basis function (RBF) contribute to infection modelling and simulation by grouping points with similar characteristics. The GIS "nebula" simulation results can be also used as a superimposed multimedia element in the final VR 360° environment [15].

AR 3D Cloud/Voxel Simulation

The modelling/simulation of the space (e.g. hospital room, etc.) will be implemented either in VR and/or AR environment [15]. This simulation will be supported by specifics techniques, such as point cloud data, CSG, Boundary and Spatial sub-division simulation [62] generated from CAD/GIS software, taking into account specific requirements of biosensors integration, geometry modelling, 3D clouds points, etc.

The Lidar technique will convert spatial 3D model of points cloud into an appropriate file (CSV) with geometry definition (OBJ) [68] and finally into a voxel model based on voxel-algorithm from points cloud [15, 69]. It is crucial to say that point cloud representation nowadays is cheaper and easiest to generate, due to low cost lidar systems with SLAM technology [70].

More specifically voxelization is a process of transferring vector data into a structure that represents discretely geometry and semantics. Three are the main components of

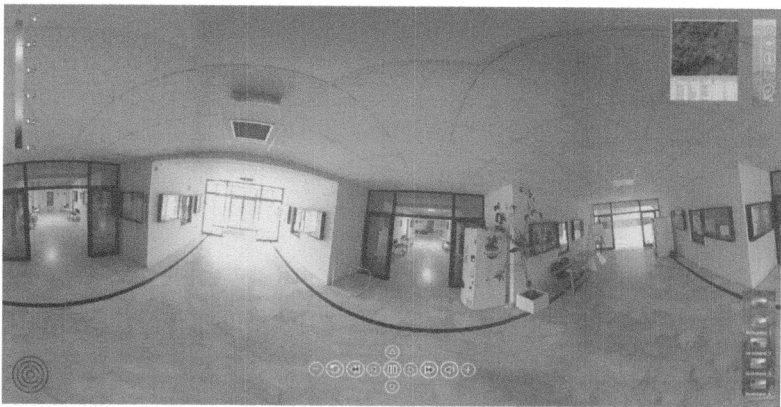

Fig. 5. VR 360° "nebula" simulation results with superimposed multimedia elements

the procedure starting a) with the input geometry, b) the voxelization and c) the data storage, visualization and export [71]. Although, is extremely important the choice of certain criteria in the voxelization procedure such as voxelization algorithms that will be implemented, the availability of common software that will be used, different libraries (Open3D, Unity Point Cloud Viewer etc.), the compression and decompression method that will be selected, the testing platform and other [71].

While VR representation needs either specific VR head glasses, the AR representation needs a specific tablet/smartphone with integrated sensors that track movements and objects position. Theoretically the nosocomial infections rates in form of interpolated 3D voxels will be transparent allowing visual and spatial perception of the user (see Fig. 6).

The above system which consists of many individual functions that have to be performed, the integration of different data (biosensors, etc.), the implementation of communications between the various sub-systems, the visualization products for end users and much more, requires the adoption of modern frameworks or architectures such as a Service-Oriented System [72].

5.6 Advantages/Limitations of Simulation and Modelling Processes

The processes of modelling and representation have many advantages but also present a lot of limitations.

The main advantage of the simulation process is the use of voxels which allows accurate particles volumetric simulation of complex objects, almost impossible to be simulated with other methods.

The main advantage of the modelling process is the implementation and the complementarity of interdisciplinary spatial modelling methods such as grid mapping & voxels, point clouds, 3D scanning, CSG, etc.

On the other hand, the main limitation of the simulation process is the complexity of the biosensor's implementation in relation to the values extraction and representation with a multitude of devices and software.

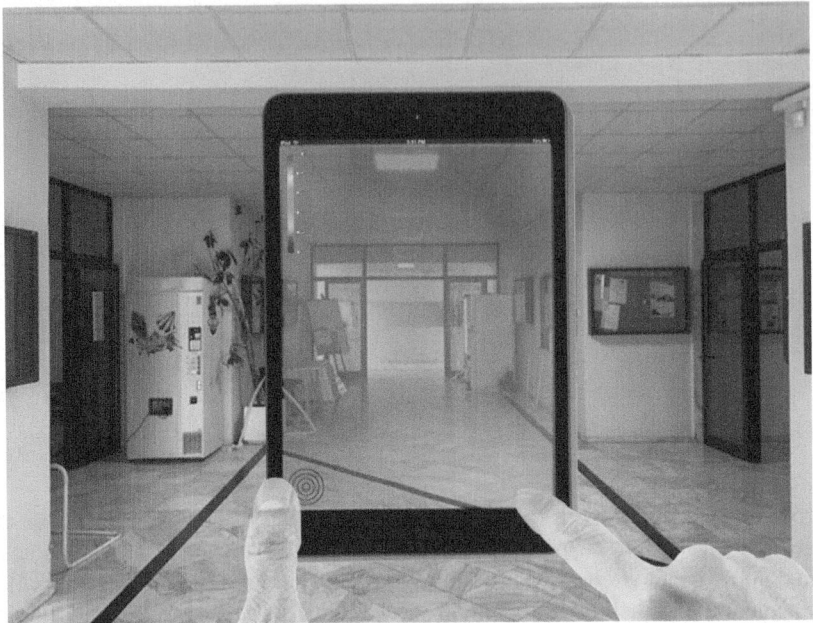

Fig. 6. Theoretical representative simulation results of the proposed pilot representation system in AR environment after future implementation

The main limitation of the modelling process is the exhaustive technical requirements due mainly to the format incompatibilities resolution and standardization data of the different modelling software and the specific MR devices communication protocols.

6 Conclusions

The infectious diseases are considered as a major global health challenge. Current diagnostic methods present a lot of limitations related to time-consuming laboratory procedures, while biosensors facilitate with accuracy the on-site detection of various pathogens.

The theoretical development of the proposed nosocomial infections particles rates spatial simulation allows an understandable and accurate 3D representation via modern point clouds/voxel techniques. This simulation allows a real-time VR/AR immersive walkthrough with significant scientific and social impact [73], while current systems offer 2D/3D charts statistics [15].

The use of 3D point clouds/voxels technique allows an accurate particles volumetric simulation in relation with interdisciplinary spatial modelling methods. However, these simulation and modelling techniques present implementation and incompatibilities limitations.

The proposed spatial simulation could facilitate the communication between a medicine experts and non-expert users, such as clients, hospital staff, even public authorities in social health plans discussion.

The biosensor chip technology progress and the biosensing systems with artificial intelligence (AI) and machine learning (ML) for huge amounts and high-quality representative datasets management is an imminent perspective [7]. The involvement of modern technologies, such as Internet of Things and 5G network's fast transmission rate will increase the effectiveness of detection and simulation methods of infectious diseases or even chronic ailments [25].

References

1. Nakhjavani, S.A., Mirzajani, H., Carrara, S., Onbasli, M.: Advances in biosensor technologies for infectious diseases detection. Trends Anal. Chem. **180** (2024)
2. HospiMedica International staff: Portable Biosensor Platform to Reduce Hospital-Acquired Infections (2024). https://www.hospimedica.com/patient-care/articles/294802722/portable-biosensor-platform-to-reduce-hospital-acquired-infections.html. Accessed 28 Feb 2025
3. Xiao, Y.: Nosocomial infections and bacterial resistance. In: Li, L. (eds.) Infectious Microecology. Theory and Applications, in book series: Advanced Topics in Science and Technology in China, Springer (2014)
4. McFee, R.B.: Nosocomial or hospital-acquired infections: an overview. Disease-a-Month **55**, 422–438 (2009)
5. National Nosocomial Infections Surveillance System: National Nosocomial Infections Surveillance (NNIS) System Report, data summary from January 1992 through June 2004, issued October 2004. Am. J. Infect. Control **32**, 470–485 (2004)
6. World Health Organization: Report on the Burden of Endemic Health Care-Associated Infection Worldwide (2011). https://apps.who.int/iris/bitstream/handle/10665/80135/9789241501507_eng.pdf. Accessed 12 Mar 2025
7. De Felice, M., et al.: Fighting nosocomial antibiotic-resistant infections through rapid and sensitive isothermal amplification-powered point-of-care (POC) diagnostics. Trends Anal. Chem. **165** (2023)
8. Harbarth, S., Hawkey, P.M., Tenover, F., Stefani, S., Pantosti, A., Struelens, M.J.: Update on screening and clinical diagnosis of meticillin-resistant staphylococcus aureus (MRSA). Int. J. Antimicrob. Agents **37**, 110–117 (2011)
9. Hassoun, A., Linden, P.K., Friedman, B.: Incidence, prevalence, and management of MRSA bacteremia across patient populations-a review of recent developments in MRSA management and treatment. Crit. Care **21**, 211 (2017)
10. Ferone, M., Gowen, A., Fanning, S., Scannell, A.: Microbial detection and identification methods: bench top assays to omics approaches. Comprehen. Rev. Food Sci. Food Safety **19**, 3106–3129 (2020)
11. Rychert, J.: Commentary: benefits and limitations of MALDI-TOF mass spectrometry for the identification of microorganisms. J. Infectiol. 2(4), 1–5 (2019)
12. Koçak, E., Ozkul, C., Bozal-Palabiyik, B., Süslü, İ, Uslu, B.: Electrochemical biosensors for rapid diagnosis of bacterial infections: design, targets and applications in clinical setting. Electroanalysis **35**, 11 (2023)
13. Land, K.J., Boeras, D.I., Chen, X.S., Ramsay, A.R., Peeling, R.: REASSURED diagnostics to inform disease control strategies, strengthen health systems and improve patient outcomes. Nat. Microbiol. **4**, 46–54 (2019)
14. Claridades, A.R.C., Lee, J.: Developing a data model of indoor points of interest to support location-based services. J. Sens. **8885384**, 16 (2020). https://doi.org/10.1155/2020/8885384
15. Kouzeleas, S., Tsolakidis, I.: Assessment contribution of an architectural indoor healthy status via biosensors particles spatial simulation. Lect. Notes Comput. Sci. **14825**, 168–183 (2024)

16. Wu, D., et al.: Pt/Zn-TCPP nanozyme-based flexible immunoassay for dual-mode pressure–temperature monitoring of low-abundance proteins. Anal. Chem. **96**, 21 (2024)
17. Manzanares-Palenzuela, C.L., Martín-Fernández, B., Sánchez-Paniagua López, M., López-Ruiz, B.: Electrochemical genosensors as innovative tools for detection of genetically modified organisms. TrAC, Trends Anal. Chem. **66**, 19–31 (2015)
18. Vazquez, J-M-M.: interferometric biosensors for rapid identification of nosocomial infections. Doctoral thesis, University autonome of Barcelona, (2017)
19. Wang, Y., et al.: Bimetallic single-atom nanozyme-based electrochemical photothermal dual-function portable immunoassay with smartphone imaging. Anal. Chem. **96**, 33 (2024)
20. Braz, B., et al.: Disposable electrochemical platform based on solid-binding peptides and carbon nanomaterials: an alternative device for leishmaniasis detection. Mikrochim. Acta **190**, 8 (2023)
21. Yadav, S., Abubakar Sadique, M., Ranjan, P., Khan, R.: Synergistically functionalized molybdenum disulfide-reduced graphene oxide nanohybrid based ultrasensitive electrochemical immunosensor for real sample analysis of COVID-19. Anal. Chim. Acta **1265** (2023)
22. Carota, A.G., et al.: Low-cost inkjet-printed nanostructured biosensor based on CRISPR/Cas12a system for pathogen detection. Biosens. Bioelectron. **258** (2024)
23. De Araujo, W.R., Lukas, H., Torres, M.D.T., Gao, W., De la Fuente-Nunez, C.: Low-cost biosensor technologies for rapid detection of COVID-19 and future pandemics. ACS Nano J. **18**(3), 1757–1777 (2024)
24. De Oliveira, P.R., et al.: Low-cost, facile droplet modification of screen-printed arrays for internally validated electrochem-ical detection of serum procalcitonin. Biosens. Bioelectron. **228** (2023)
25. Scott, G.Y., et al.: Transforming early microbial detection: Investigating innovative biosensors for emerging infectious diseases. Adv. Biomark. Sci. Technol. **6**, 59–71 (2024)
26. Quazi, M.Z., Hwang, J., Song, Y., Park, N.: Hydrogel-based biosensors for effective therapeutics. Gels **9**, 7 (2023)
27. Kim, Y., Gonzales, J., Zheng, Y.: Sensitivity-enhancing strategies in optical biosensing. Small Weinheim an der Bergstrasse Germany **17**, 4 (2021)
28. Hammond, J.-L., Formisano, N., Estrela, P., Carrara, S., Tkac, J.: Electrochemical biosensors and nanobiosensors. Essays Biochem. **60**(1), 69–80 (2016)
29. Kano, S., Jarulertwathana, N., Mohd-Noor, S., Hyun, J.K., Asahara, R., Mekaru, H.: Respiratory monitoring by ultrafast humidity sensors with nanomaterials: a review. Sensors **22**, 3 (2022)
30. Pires, N.M.M., Dong, T., Hanke, U., Hoivik, N.: Recent developments in optical detection technologies in lab-on-a-chip devices for biosensing applications. Sensors **14**, 8 (2014)
31. Zucolotto, V.: Specialty grand challenges in biosensors. Front. Sens. **1** (2020)
32. Nguyen, L.K.N., Megiddo, I., Howick, S.: Simulation models for transmission of health care–associated infection: a systematic review. Am. J. Infect. Control **48**, 810–821 (2020)
33. McElwee, F.: Healthcare Associated Infection Simulator (2022). https://healthdatainsight.org.uk/project/healthcare-associated-infection-simulator/. Accessed 12 Feb 2025
34. Roy, M.A., May, R.M.: Infectious diseases of humans: dynamics and control. Oxford University Press (1991). https://doi.org/10.1093/oso/9780198545996.001.0001
35. Morgan, J.S., Howick, S., Belton, V.: A toolkit of designs for mixing discrete event simulation and system dynamics. Eur. J. Oper. Res. **257**, 907–918 (2017)
36. Mustafee, N., Powell, J., Brailsford, S.C., Diallo, S., Padilla, J., Tolk, A.: Hybrid simulation studies and hybrid simulation systems: definitions, challenges, and benefits. In: Proceedings of the 2015 Winter Simulation Conference, pp. 1678–1692 (2015) https://ieeexplore.ieee.org/document/7408287

37. Nawattanapaiboon, K., et al.: SPR-DNA array for detection of methicillin-resistant Staphylococcus aureus (MRSA) in combination with loop-mediated isothermal amplification. Biosens. Bioelectron. **74** (2015)

38. Chen, Y., Cheng, N., Xu, Y., Huang, K., Luo, Y., Xu, W.: Point-of-care and visual detection of P. aeruginosa and its toxin genes by multiple LAMP and lateral flow nucleic acid biosensor. Biosens. Bioelectron. **81** (2016)

39. Dinh, V.P., Lee, N.Y.: Fabrication of a fully integrated paper microdevice for point-of-care testing of infectious disease using Safranin O dye coupled with loop-mediated isothermal amplification. Biosens. Bioelectron. **204** (2022)

40. Sébille, V., Valleron, A.-J.: A computer simulation model for the spread of nosocomial infections caused by multidrug-resistant pathogens. Comput. Biomed. Res. **30**, 4 (1997)

41. Hlady, C.S.: Nosocomial infection modeling and simulation using fine-grained healthcare data (2011). https://iro.uiowa.edu/esploro/outputs/doctoral/Nosocomial-infection-modeling-and-simulation-using/9983777110102771. Accessed 10 Jan 2025

42. Elliott, T.M., Lee, X.J., Foeglein, A., Harris, P.N., Gordon, L.G.: A hybrid simulation model approach to examine bacterial genome sequencing during a hospital outbreak. BMC Infect. Dis. **20**, 72 (2020)

43. Wang, L., Ruan, S.: Modeling nosocomial infections of methicillin-resistant staphylococcus aureus with environment contamination. Sci. Report. **7** (2017)

44. Wen, R., Li, X., Liu, T., Lin, G.: Effect of a real-time automatic nosocomial infection surveillance system on hospital-acquired infection prevention and control. BMC Infect. Diseases **22** (2022)

45. Sin, M.L.Y., Mach, K.E., Wong, P.K., Liao, J.C.: Advances and challenges in biosensor-based diagnosis of infectious diseases. Expert Rev. Mol. Diagn. **14**, 2 (2014)

46. Xu, J., Lee, H.: Anti-biofouling strategies for long-term continuous use of implantable biosensors. Chemosensors **8**, 3 (2020)

47. Ross, G.M.S., Bremer, M.G.E.G., Wichers, J.H., Van Amerongen, A., Nielen, M.W.F.: Rapid antibody selection using surface plasmon resonance for high-speed and sensitive hazelnut lateral flow prototypes. Biosensors **8**, 4 (2018)

48. Feng, X., et al.: Recombinase polymerase amplification-based biosensors for rapid zoonoses screening. Int. J. Nanomed. **18** (2023)

49. Zheng, X., Miao, F., Udomwong, P., Chakpitak, N.: Registered data-centered lab management system based on data ownership safety architecture. Electronics **12**, 8 (2023)

50. DeltaOHM: HD35 Wireless data logger (2024). https://www.google.com/url?sa=t&source=web&rct=j&opi=89978449&url=https://www.otm.sg/wp-content/uploads/DeltaOHM-HD35-wireless-datalogger-datasheet-en.pdf&ved=2ahUKEwjjw4PHg6qMAxV3SfEDHbyVNj0QFnoECBYQAQ&usg=AOvVaw08yavpXmr3-iNC9lGhrsJm

51. Kouzeleas, S.: Processes aspects of modelling, interactive digital visualization and multimedia representation of architectural and urban area. In: 11th International Conference on Computer Graphics and Artificial Intelligence (3IA2008), pp. 205–210. Athens, Greece (2008)

52. Walczak, K., Cellary, W.: Building database applications of virtual reality with X-VRML. In: 7th international conference on 3D Web technology (Web3D '02). USA (2002)

53. Li, G., et al.: A review on MPS method developments and applications in nuclear engineering. Comput. Meth. Appl. Mech. Eng. **367** (2020)

54. Ma, K.-L., Schussman, G., Wilson, B.: Visualization for computational accelerator physics. Hansen, C., Johnson, C. (eds.) Visualization Handbook, pp. 919–935 (2005)

55. Goldstein, R., Breslav, S., Khan, A.: Towards voxel-based algorithms for building performance simulation. In: IBPSA-Canada eSim Conference. Canada (2014)

56. Li, W., Nee, A., Ong, S.K.: A state-of-the-art review of augmented reality in engineering analysis and simulation. Multimodal Technol. Interact. **1**(3), 17 (2017)

57. Elfes, A.: Using occupancy grids for mobile robot perception and navigation. Computer **22**, 46–57 (1989)
58. Qu, T., Sun, W.: Usage of 3d point cloud data in bim (building information modelling): current applications and challenges. J. Civil Eng. Architect. **9**(11), 1269–1278 (2015)
59. The Apple Technical Journal Homepage. https://download.blender.org/source/chest/blender_2.03_tree/docs/nurbs.html. Accessed 31 Jan 2024
60. Russell, S.J., Norvig: artificial intelligence: a modern approach, 2nd edn. Prentice Hall (2003)
61. Zlatanova, S.: 3D Modelling for Augmented Reality. Int. Arch. Photogram. Remote Sens. **34**(2W2) (2001)
62. Hinks, T., Carr, H., Truong-Hong, L., Laefer, D.F.: Point cloud data conversion into solid models via point-based voxelization. J. Surv. Eng. **139**(2), 72–83 (2013)
63. Barazzetti, L., Banfi, F.: Historic BIM for mobile VR/AR applications. In: Ioannides, M., Magnenat-Thalmann, N., Papagiannakis, G. (eds) Mixed Reality and Gamification for Cultural Heritage, 1st edn. pp. 271–290, Springer Cham (2017). https://doi.org/10.1007/978-3-319-49607-8_10
64. Di Giulio, M., Grande, R., Di Campli, E., et al.: Indoor air quality in university environments. Environ. Monit. Assess. **170**(1), 509–517 (2010)
65. Kouzeleas, S.: Architectural and urban spatial digital simulations. Int. J. Eng. Model. **36**(2), 95–118 (2023)
66. Kouzeleas, S., Mammou, O.: Architectural, urban digital design and spatial simulation tools in digital cities cartography: contribution in spatial design and perception. Int. Am. J. Contemp. Res. **2**(8), 237–256 (2012)
67. Kouzeleas, S., Nikolaidou, S., Goussios, D., Goulas, A.: Pilot interactive visualization tool of a Participatory Guarantee System: the case of 'Terra Thessalia''s PGS. Int. J. Eng. Innov. Technol. **9**(9), 1–17 (2020)
68. Shahrin, M.R., Hashim, F.H., Zaki, W.M.D.W., Hussain, A., Raj, T.: 3D indoor mapping system using 2D LiDAR sensor for drones. Int. J. Eng. Technol. **7**(4), 179–183 (2018)
69. Huang, M., Wei P., Liu, X.: An efficient encoding voxel-based segmentation (EVBS) algorithm based on fast adjacent voxel search for point cloud plane segmentation. Remote Sens. **11**(23) (2019)
70. Trybała, P., Kujawa, P., Romańczukiewicz, K., Szrek, A., Remondino, F.: Designing and evaluating a portable lidar-based slam system. Int. Arch. Photogramm. Remote. Sens. Spat. Inf. Sci. **48–1**(W3), 191–198 (2023)
71. Aleksandrov, M., Zlatanova, S., Heslop, D.J.: Voxelisation and voxel management options in Unity3D. ISPRS Ann. Photogram. Remote Sens. Spatial Inform. Sci. **10–4**(W2), 13–20 (2022)
72. Stojanovic, V., Trapp, M., Hagedorn, B., Klimke, J., Richter, R., Döllner, J.: Sensor data visualization for indoor point clouds. Adv. Cartography GISci. ICA **2**, 1–8 (2019)
73. Kouzeleas, S.: Scientific impact of architectural indoor augmented reality 3D digital representa-tions. Int. J. Adv. Res. **10**(02), 425–432 (2022)
74. Icograms designer: Templates - hospital (2025). https://icograms.com/templates/all/hospital. Accessed 1 Mar 2025

Dockerized Architecture for a Progressive Web App: An Italian Collocations Dictionary

Damiano Perri[1]([📧])([ID]), Osvaldo Gervasi[1]([ID]), Sergio Tasso[1]([ID]), Irene Fioravanti[2]([ID]), Fabio Zanda[2]([ID]), Stefania Spina[2]([ID]), and Luciana Forti[2]([ID])

[1] Department of Mathematics and Computer Science, University of Perugia, Perugia, Italy
{damiano.perri,osvaldo.gervasi,sergio.tasso}@unipg.it
[2] University for Foreigners of Perugia, Perugia, Italy
{irene.fioravanti,fabio.zanda,stefania.spina,luciana.forti}@unistrapg.it

Abstract. The aim of this work is to realise a scalable architecture for the provision of certain services to students and learners. During the course of a PRIN research project, an IT infrastructure is being set up for the consultation of Italian lexical combinations by students and learners interested in studying Italian. The system is proposed on an experimental basis, by means of a Progressive Web App that allows users to access and consult the developed contents independently of the operating system they use, without necessarily requiring the installation of an application developed in the native machine language of the operating system. This article explains in detail how the backend of the system is realised, with a focus on the development and testing phase. All the services that will be explained have been containerised via Docker, in order to guarantee portability, scalability of the system and future improvements.

Keywords: Mobile Developing · Artificial Intelligence · Progressive Web App

1 Introduction

The realisation of a computer architecture always requires a preliminary study, an analysis of the requirements, an estimate of the costs that will have to be borne in order to calibrate the initial investment and the implementation time with the expectations of those requiring the service and the final result to be obtained. This article presents a development methodology for the realisation of an infrastructure capable of scaling the computational power that can be delivered in order to guarantee the proper functioning of the service even with a high number of users that varies dynamically throughout the day, while maintaining a low cost.

O. Gervasi et al. (Eds.): ICCSA 2025 Workshops, LNCS 15891, pp. 33–43, 2026.
https://doi.org/10.1007/978-3-031-97617-9_3

The proposed infrastructure has the task of managing the operation of an Italian lexical collocation dictionary [1] that must be used by students or language learners belonging to various levels of competence, and that can allow these people to consult in a simple and fast way without necessarily installing a native application on their device.

To achieve this result, it was first necessary to decide what type of product to create, in particular the choice fell on Progressive Web Apps (PWA). PWAs are web applications that offer a user experience similar to that of native applications, but are accessible via a browser and do not require separate installation. Developing using a technology of this type allows to drastically reduce the time necessary to create the application, since instead of referring to multiple programming languages, such as Java for Android and Swift for iOS, it is possible to use a single programming language, JavaScript, which allows to create multi-platform applications, simultaneously supporting Android, iOS, Windows, MacOS and Linux.

Furthermore, there are also other advantages related to the use of PWAs, such as being free from the policies of the official smartphone Stores, not necessarily having to go through an approval process for the publication of the application and the possibility of updating the application in real time without having to wait for users to install the new version. Costs are further reduced by the fact that it is not necessary to purchase the license for the publication of the application, which is instead mandatory for native applications. The article is organized as follows: Sect. 2 presents an analysis of the current scientific literature that addresses similar topics to the one proposed in this article, Sect. 3 describes the architecture of the system, within it you can find SubSect. 3.1 describes the proposed development environment, SubSect. 3.2 describes the backend for managing user requests. Section 4 summarizes the conclusions and future developments.

2   Related Works

The use of Docker is now considered a standard for the creation of applications to be delivered via cloud infrastructures [2,3]. Its characteristic is that it allows the creation of microservices, or small containers within which one or more processes are running. Even if containerized, experimental results show that applications such as Apache, nginx or MySQL maintain very high performance [4,5] and are perfectly comparable to the performance they would have if they were run natively on the machine. This is because Docker does not use complete virtualization but isolates at the namespace level to keep the applications' workspaces separate. This allows you to run multiple instances of the same container without necessarily having to create a virtual machine for each of them.

Furthermore, using Docker allows developers to create a scalable system, as it is possible to increase or decrease the number of containers running based on the number of requests that the system must handle [6–8].

Developing an application that can run on modern smartphones is a complex operation that can be done by following two main paths. The first is to create the application natively, that is, using the specific programming languages of each operating system, such as Java or Kotlin for Android and Swift for iOS [9,10]. This first phase requires a considerable amount of time, as it is necessary to create two separate applications and the code that can be reused is very limited. Unless developers have very specific needs, such as the needs of using high computational power from the GPU, or access to particular sensors, it is possible to create a cross-platform application using a single programming language like as JavaScript [11,12]. In fact, there are frameworks, i.e. Ionic[1], React Native[2], Flutter[3] that allow you to write an application and see it running in real time within your browser [18,19].

Ionic for example allows Capacitor[4] or Cordova[5] integration. These two tools provide the capability to produce Hybrid Apps: in case a native application is needed, Cordova exports the HTML and JavaScript code into two separate projects, Android and iOS, all starting from a web application [22,23]. What must be taken into account is the publication phase of the applications, which takes a considerable amount of time, as the code submission phase, the review phase, and the cost of the licence to publish on the store must be considered.

3   Discussion

In this section, the system architecture is presented, which has been designed to be scalable and easily upgradable.

The infrastructure utilises the potential of the cloud, which allows you to pay a monthly fee based on the use of the provider's services. The formula is that of pay-per-use, i.e. you pay according to the services you use, and it is not necessary to buy a physical server, but you can use the virtual servers made available by the provider. Based on this, it appears essential to organise the system in such a way as to avoid waste and at the same time guarantee a quality service for end users. First of all, two subnets were created, the first being used for the development and testing of the application, the second being dedicated to production, i.e. the management of users accessing the service. Access to the network must take place via the infrastructure's central gateway, which not only sorts requests towards the production backend, but also implements appropriate firewall rules to guarantee network security.

The architecture that is described is represented in Fig. 1.

The description of the development environment is given in SubSect. 3.1, while SubSect. 3.2 describes the backend that handles user requests. All servers and services that will be described are based on Docker containers.

---

[1] https://ionicframework.com/.
[2] https://reactnative.dev/.
[3] https://flutter.dev/.
[4] https://capacitorjs.com/.
[5] https://cordova.apache.org/.

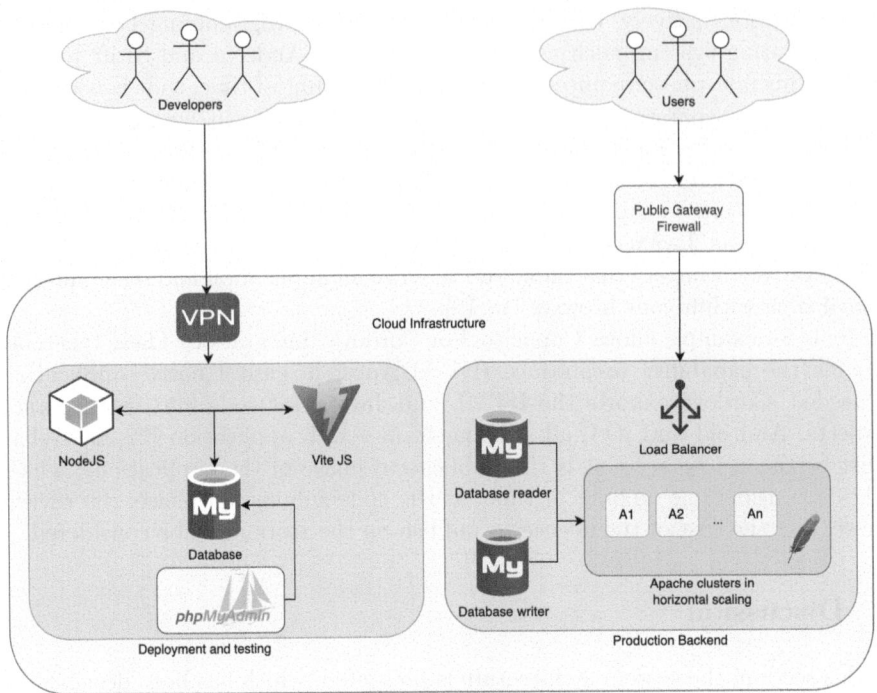

Fig. 1. System Architecture.

3.1 Development Environment

The test environment is fundamental to the realisation of an application, it must be separate from the production environment and in general must not be accessible to end users. Its purpose is to enable the development of applications and their testing in order to guarantee the absence of problems and malfunctions. The application envisages the creation of a dictionary that can be consulted via a web browser, The user connecting to the page must be able to type a word and will receive in output a list of lexical combinations that contain the word typed in, selecting the one of interest the user will have to obtain the information he or she requires. To solve this problem, first of all a database is required, in our case a MySQL relational database was selected, which by design guarantees a very high speed in the consultation phase and the possibility of making useful queries using SQL syntax.

The container containing the database was built using the official MySQL image[6] [24]. Among the precautions necessary for its realisation, we mention the fact of not exposing port 3306, which is the default port for the MySQL database, outside of the test network, as it is not necessary for users to be able to access the database directly, in order to improve the security of the system.

---

[6] https://hub.docker.com/_/mysql.

A second container based on a phpMyAdmin[7] image had to be created to manage the database [25]. The functionalities provided by this container allow the database to be easily managed via a web page. In fact, developers can connect via a browser to the database administration platform and, after authenticating themselves with their credentials, will have access to the tables and contents of the database itself. To guarantee maximum system security, the connection is only made via VPN.

As far as the code development environment is concerned, a solution based on two docker containers was chosen, the first containing Node.js[8], Ionic and Ionic Capacitor, and the second containing the web server[9].

The first container aims to provide a development environment containing all the necessary packages for building JavaScript-based web applications that are also graphically faithful to the native design of the devices. This is ensured by the use of IONIC, which provides a series of graphical components, such as buttons, table styles, text styles, and many others, realised in such a way as to adapt dynamically to the device that is using the application. In this way, a user using an Android smartphone will have a different graphic appearance to a user using an iPhone, but the source code will remain the same. The implementation of this first container was carried out using a custom image. This was made possible by defining a Dockerfile containing the instructions needed to install the basic packages of NodeJS, Ionic and Capacitor; in addition to the basic libraries needed to run these applications.

The second container was realised using the official Vite[10] image. The use of a Vite server allows the development phase of the application to be greatly facilitated, since changes to the code are reported in real time on all devices that are connected to the server. Suppose we have an Android smartphone and a laptop and we connect both to the web page containing the code we are developing to create our application. As soon as we make a change to the source code, this will be reflected in real time on both devices, which will automatically reload the page and immediately show the new code. Thanks to this functionality, it is possible to test changes on several devices at the same time in a very short time.

The development environment, realised with the technologies described, allows services to be easily encapsulated, packages and libraries used by the applications to be easily updated, allows easy backup and roll back of the images that manage the containers, and allows deployment to be performed quickly and easily. In addition, the possible addition of further docker containers, e.g. for testing a possible web server, does not require any substantial changes to the infrastructure, as docker containers are by nature independent of each other.

---

[7] https://hub.docker.com/r/phpmyadmin/phpmyadmin.
[8] https://hub.docker.com/_/node.
[9] https://vitejs.dev/.
[10] https://hub.docker.com/r/vitejs/vite.

3.2   The Backend

The purpose of the production environment is to handle the requests of users connecting to the service. It is crucial that this portion of the infrastructure is able to deliver the required services quickly and without errors. The realisation of the production infrastructure adopts an approach derived from the High Availability theory, which involves the creation of several instances of the same service, so as to guarantee continuity of service even in the event of failure of one of them.

As for the database, this was configured using a MySQL cluster [26,27]. A cluster is composed of several nodes, in the case presented here we have a total of two nodes of which one will have the task of performing reads and writes, while the other will only have the task of performing reads. In other words, two identical MySQL containers are created, and they are put in communication and synchronisation with each other. This means that when data is updated on the main node, it is replicated in real time on the secondary node. The primary node is the one that can perform the writes, while the secondary node is the one that can only perform the reads. Such an infrastructure is robust in that a failure of one of the two nodes does not compromise the service, as the other node is able to continue providing the required services. In the event of a failure of the primary node, the secondary node can be promoted to the primary node and thus be able to perform both writes and reads to the database. This type of approach also allows upgrades to be performed safely without compromising service delivery, since in the event that there is a need to shut down the main node to upgrade libraries and packages, the secondary node will continue to provide the services required by users. Having multiple nodes also allows user requests to be distributed, so since the workload related to readings is distributed between the two nodes, there is an improvement in overall system performance.

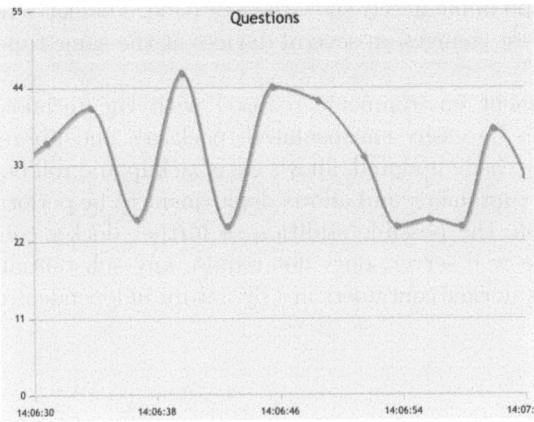

Fig. 2. Graph of queries received by the database cluster in real time.

As far as the web page accessed by users is concerned, this is managed by a cluster of Apache containers [28]. The Apache containers are all identical to each other, as they are generated from the same docker image. The cluster can dynamically adapt the number of containers according to the number of requests the cluster receives. The greater the number of user requests, the greater the number of nodes. This ensures that low running costs are maintained at times of low load. For example, at night, when there are few users connecting to the system, the number of Apache containers will be reduced to a minimum, while during daylight hours, when there are many users connecting to the system, the number of Apache containers can be increased to ensure a fast and error-free service. This technique, also known as horizontal scalability, can be performed while the system is switched on and is completely transparent to users.

Access to the data contained in the apache cluster is via a server a load balancer [29] whose task is to sort requests evenly distributed among the various nodes using the Round Robin algorithm [30,31].

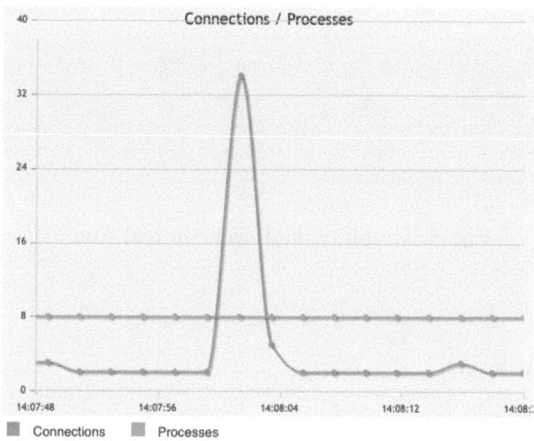

Fig. 3. Graph of connections received by the database cluster in real time.

Upstream of the infrastructure is the gateway, which not only provides the access port to the system, but also manages the firewall rules to guarantee network security. These rules include, for example, those for denying connections to unauthorised ports. This infrastructure is capable of delivering user services and also allows it to be further expanded should the numbers of those who wish to use the dictionary increase as it will always be possible to increase the number of nodes within the Apache cluster and the MySQL cluster. In addition, if the dictionary and its functionalities were to become extremely more complex in the future, it might also be possible to implement vertical scalability, i.e. to increase the hardware resources of the already existing nodes in order to guarantee ever higher performance.

Figures 2, 3 and 4 show the graphs of the queries, connections and data usage received by the database cluster in real time. The graphs were obtained by means of phpmyadmin, which provides many functionalities: in addition to managing the contents of the database, it is also possible to monitor its utilisation in real time and to obtain vital statistics to understand whether there are user peaks or problems to be analysed. It is also important to note that PhpMyAdmin is a free and open source software maintained by an active user community on GitHub[11].

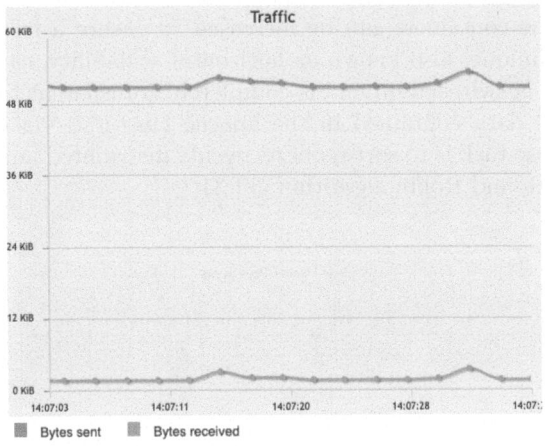

Fig. 4. Graph of data usage in real time.

4   Conclusions

This article presents a scalable architecture for developing and hosting a dictionary of Italian lexical collocations, which can be provided to Italian language students and learners.

Scalable architecture is now essential to reduce management costs and guarantee a correct user experience. It allows the computational power made available by the IT infrastructure that manages the service to be dynamically adapted based on the number of users connected to the system at the same time, thus avoiding a waste of resources. Using Docker both for the development phase and the creation of the backend was fundamental: from the point of view of IT security, it allowed the application to be broken down into multiple microservices, each of which was containerized and, therefore, isolated from the others, preventing a possible cyber attack from compromising the entire system. Furthermore, the use of docker allows updates and improvements to be made to the system by creating new images, which, in the circumstance that these have problems, can be replaced by restoring the previous images.

---

[11] https://github.com/phpmyadmin/phpmyadmin.

The testing, experimentation and improvement phase is still in progress; future improvements may be integrated into the system, also analyzing the user feedback that will arrive over the next few months, but for the moment it is possible to affirm that the first version of the proposed infrastructure described in this article is able to provide the requested service and thanks to its structure it is easily expandable and improvable.

Acknowledgements. The research has been funded by PRIN 2022 - PNNR M4.C2.1.1. - ERC secotr SH4, title *"DICI-A Dizionario delle Collocazioni Italiane per Apprendenti A Learner Dictionary of Italian Collocations"*. Financed by the European Union NextGenerationEU. CUP J53D23008060006.

The authors thank Grammarly Inc., Quillbot Inc., Deepl SE, and Google LLC for using their platforms to improve the concepts they wanted to formulate in English.

References

1. Perri, D., Fioravanti, I., Gervasi, O., Spina, S.: Combining Grammatical and Relational Approaches. A Hybrid Method for the Identification of Candidate Collocations from Corpora, pp. 138–146 (2024). https://aclanthology.org/2024.mwe-1.18/

2. Garg, S., Garg, S.: Automated cloud infrastructure, continuous integration and continuous delivery using docker with robust container security. In: 2019 IEEE Conference on Multimedia Information Processing and Retrieval (MIPR), pp. 467–470 (2019). https://doi.org/10.1109/MIPR.2019.00094

3. Antonova, V.M., Egorov, M.A., Blinov, V.P., Malikova, E.E., Malikov, A.Y.: Studying the principles of infocommunication network virtualisation using the docker platform. In: 2024 Systems of Signals Generating and Processing in the Field of on Board Communications, pp. 1–5 (2024). https://doi.org/10.1109/IEEECONF60226.2024.10496739.

4. Kithulwatta, W.M.C.J.T., Jayasena, K.P.N., Kumara, B.T.G.S., Rathnayaka, R.M.K.T.: Performance evaluation of docker-based apache and nginx web server. In: 2022 3rd International Conference for Emerging Technology (INCET), pp. 1–6 (2022). https://doi.org/10.1109/INCET54531.2022.9824303

5. Perri, D., Simonetti, M., Tasso, S., Ragni, F., Gervasi, O.: Implementing a scalable and elastic computing environment based on cloud containers. In: Lecture Notes in Computer Science (including subseries Lecture Notes in Artificial Intelligence and Lecture Notes in Bioinformatics), vol. 12949, pp. 676–689 (2021). https://doi.org/10.1007/978-3-030-86653-249

6. Wang, W.: Research on using docker container technology to realize rapid deployment environment on virtual machine. In: 2022 8th Annual International Conference on Network and Information Systems for Computers (ICNISC), pp. 541–544 (2022). https://doi.org/10.1109/ICNISC57059.2022.00112

7. Nurwarsito, H., Sejahtera, V.B.: Implementation of dynamic web server based on operating system-level virtualization using docker stack. In: 2020 12th International Conference on Information Technology and Electrical Engineering (ICITEE), pp. 33–38 (2020). https://doi.org/10.1109/ICITEE49829.2020.9271710

8. Kumar, K., Kurhekar, M.: Economically efficient virtualization over cloud using docker containers. In: 2016 IEEE International Conference on Cloud Computing in Emerging Markets (CCEM), pp. 95–100 (2016). https://doi.org/10.1109/CCEM.2016.025

9. Golhar, R.V., Vyawahare, P.A., Borghare, P.H., Manusmare, A.: Design and implementation of android base mobile app for an institute. In: 2016 International Conference on Electrical, Electronics, and Optimization Techniques (ICEEOT), pp. 3660–3663 (2016). https://doi.org/10.1109/ICEEOT.2016.7755391

10. Hauser, D.: Test-Driven iOS Development with Swift: Write Maintainable, Flexible, and Extensible Code Using the Power of TDD with Swift 5.5. Packt Publishing (2022). ISBN 180323248X

11. Koram, N., Garg, R.: Review on mobile app development: tools and techniques. In: 2023 IEEE World Conference on Applied Intelligence and Computing (AIC), pp. 260–266 (2023). https://doi.org/10.1109/AIC57670.2023.10263908

12. Pinto, C.M., Coutinho, C.: From native to cross-platform hybrid development. In: 2018 International Conference on Intelligent Systems (IS), pp. 669–676 (2018). https://doi.org/10.1109/IS.2018.8710545.

13. Babich, L.V., Svalov, D.A., Smirnov, A.L., Babich, M.V.: Neurorehabilitation control application: development using ionic framework. In: 2018 26th Telecommunications Forum (TELFOR), pp. 420–425 (2018). https://doi.org/10.1109/TELFOR.2018.8611880

14. Yang, Y., Zhang, Y., Xia, P., Li, B., Ren, Z.: Mobile terminal development plan of cross-platform mobile application service platform based on ionic and cordova. In: 2017 International Conference on Industrial Informatics - Computing Technology, Intelligent Technology, Industrial Information Integration (ICIICII), pp. 100–103 (2017). https://doi.org/10.1109/ICIICII.2017.28

15. Dabit, N.: React Native in Action: Developing iOS and Android Apps with JavaScript (2019). ISBN 1617294055

16. Novac, O.C., Novac, C.M., Ciora, B., Gordan, C.E., Gordan, M.I., Bujdos'o, G.: The rise of mobile development: a comparison between Ionic and Flutter. In: 2022 14th International Conference on Electronics, Computers and Artificial Intelligence (ECAI), pp. 1–10 (2022). https://doi.org/10.1109/ECAI54874.2022.9847460

17. Lohani, D.: Taking Flutter to the Web: Learn how to build crossplatform UIs for web and mobile platforms using Flutter for Web (2022)

18. Behl, K., Raj, G.: Architectural pattern of progressive web and background synchronization. In: 2018 International Conference on Advances in Computing and Communication Engineering (ICACCE), pp. 366–371 (2018). https://doi.org/10.1109/ICACCE.2018.8441701

19. Gowri, S., Pappa, C.K., Tamilvizhi, T., Nelson, L., Surendran, R.: Intelligent analysis on frameworks for mobile app development. In: 2023 5th International Conference on Smart Systems and Inventive Technology (ICSSIT), pp. 1506–1512 (2023). https://doi.org/10.1109/ICSSIT55814.2023.10060902

20. Bosnic, S., Papp, I., Novak, S.: The development of hybrid mobile applications with Apache Cordova. In: 2016 24th Telecommunications Forum (TELFOR), pp. 1–4 (2016). https://doi.org/10.1109/TELFOR.2016.7818919

21. Vladimirovich, B.M., Andreyevich, S.D., Vladimirovna, B.L., Leonidovich, S.A.: Development of the mobile application for control of the neuro-electrostimulator of type 'SYMPATHOCOR-01' using apache cordova. In: Ural Symposium on Biomedical Engineering. Radioelectronics and Information Technology (USBEREIT), 2018, pp. 72–75 (2018). https://doi.org/10.1109/USBEREIT.2018.8384553

22. Malavolta, I.: Web-based hybrid mobile apps: state of the practice and research opportunities. In: 2016 IEEE/ACM International Conference on Mobile Software Engineering and Systems (MOBILESoft), pp. 241–242 (2016). https://doi.org/10.1145/2897073.2897133

23. Uniyal, S.P., Joshi, K., Singh, V.K., Aggarwal, A., Chhabra, G., Kumar, A.: Comparative analysis of app size variations between react native and apache cordova powered android applications. In: 2023 Second International Conference on Augmented Intelligence and Sustainable Systems (ICAISS), pp. 1697–1702 (2023). https://doi.org/10.1109/ICAISS58487.2023.10250551

24. Malhotra, R., Bansal, A., Kessentini, M.: Vulnerability analysis of docker hub official images and verified images. In: 2023 IEEE International Conference on Service-Oriented System Engineering (SOSE), pp. 150–155 (2023). https://doi.org/10.1109/SOSE58276.2023.00025

25. Gabarro, S.A.: Using PhpMyAdmin. In: Web Application Design and Implementation: Apache 2, PHP5, MySQL, JavaScript, and Linux/UNIX, pp. 151–158 (2007). https://doi.org/10.1109/9780470083963.ch12

26. Tummalapalli, S., Machavarapu, V.R.: Managing MySQL cluster data using Cloudera impala. Procedia Comput. Sci. **85** (2016). International Conference on Computational Modelling and Security (CMS 2016), pp. 463–474. ISSN 1877-0509. https://doi.org/10.1016/j.procs.2016.05.193

27. Perri, D., Simonetti, M., Gervasi, O.: Deploying efficiently modern applications on cloud. In: Electronics (Switzerland) **11**(3) (2022). All Open Access, Gold Open Access, Green Open Access. https://doi.org/10.3390/electronics11030450, https://www.scopus.com/inward/record.uri?eid=2-s2.0-85123753434&doi=10.3390%2felectronics11030450&partnerID=40&md5=48cb887b0ef5347839dfea38121158df

28. Tasso, S., Cal'o, S., Gervasi, O., Perri, D.: Integration of an artificial intelligence model into a smartphone flutter application to solve a live image classification problem. In: Lecture Notes in Computer Science (including subseries Lecture Notes in Artificial Intelligence and Lecture Notes in Bioinformatics), vol. 14815, pp. 39–55 (2024). https://doi.org/10.1007/978-3-031-65154-03, https://www.scopus.com/inward/record.uri?eid=2-s2.0-85200998470&doi=10.1007%2f978-3-031-65154-03&partnerID=40&md5=4ee5be56b8dcb78d8ebf534f6ad4b9cd

29. Rahman, M., Iqbal, S., Gao, J.: Load balancer as a service in cloud computing. In: 2014 IEEE 8th International Symposium on Service Oriented System Engineering, pp. 204–211 (2014). https://doi.org/10.1109/SOSE.2014.31

30. Pramono, L.H., Buwono, R.C., Waskito, Y.G.: Round-Robin algorithm in HAProxy and Nginx load balancing performance evaluation: a review. In: 2018 International Seminar on Research of Information Technology and Intelligent Systems (ISRITI), pp. 367–372 (2018). https://doi.org/10.1109/ISRITI.2018.8864455

31. Kaur, S., Kumar, K., Singh, J., Ghumman, N.S.: Round-robin based load balancing in software defined networking. In: 2015 2nd International Conference on Computing for Sustainable Global Development (INDIACom), pp. 2136–2139 (2015). https://ieeexplore.ieee.org/document/7100616

Automated Generation of Web Resources for the Locative Web

Rui José[✉][iD]

Algoritmi Research Centre, University of Minho, Braga, Portugal
rui@dsi.uminho.pt

Abstract. The concept of the locative web has been around for a while. We should expect the web principles of openness and uniform access to provide a solid alternative for developing locative systems, but the locative web has never succeeded. In this study, we extend the original concept of locative web with a conceptual framework to support the large-scale publication of locative web content by many independent publishers. To pursue this vision, we explore the concept of a locative resource as a small, data-centric web resource that represents the information and actions meaningful for a specific locative situation. These resources can be automatically generated in large numbers from datasets, and each can serve a very concrete situation. Our research aims to study the tools and processes that could support the convenient and cost-effective transformation of locative datasets owned by multiple independent entities into a global web of locative resources. As part of the experimental work, we developed a prototype implementation of a locative sites toolkit. We also developed four deployment case studies, in which we used that toolkit to generate locative resources from diverse types of datasets. The key contributions are a set of novel concepts for locative web systems and a set of guidelines for dealing with data heterogeneity and allow many independent entities, all of them with their particular datasets and publication goals, to conveniently publish their data as locative resources while promoting their convergence as part of a global locative web.

Keywords: locative web · data-centric · linked-data

1 Introduction

Locative media is a familiar presence in our lives nowadays. We have diverse systems that seek to explore the blending between the physical and the digital worlds. Location-based applications are now a given, allowing us to find our way in an unknown territory, make a more engaging visit to an art museum, or remember where we parked our car. Millions of users are constantly producing geo-tagged or place-based content by taking photos, following routes, publishing tweets, and making restaurant reviews.

© The Author(s), under exclusive license to Springer Nature Switzerland AG 2026
O. Gervasi et al. (Eds.): ICCSA 2025 Workshops, LNCS 15891, pp. 44–60, 2026.
https://doi.org/10.1007/978-3-031-97617-9_4

However, most of these services are delivered as custom mobile applications. Each of those applications packages the information, usage contexts and interactive features needed to offer a particular locative experience. This strong coupling between a mobile application and a specific locative situation allows the application to be designed to match precisely its target usage context. Ideally, this would offer the best possible user experience, but in reality, it becomes a fundamental limitation to a broader deployment of locative services.

The first problem is that embedding this association directly into the application design is not scalable for either service creators or users. For service creators, this custom development can be costly and limited budgets commonly result in low-quality applications that fail to meet user expectations or produce the intended engagement. For service users, an extensive application offer is also not the answer. Each application serves only a tiny fraction of potential usage situations. Any person would need to install endless applications and constantly switch between them to match the multiple, diverse, highly dynamic and often overlapping activities that compose daily life. Not only will no one ever be able to do that, but people rarely even become aware of applications created only for less frequent or unexpected situations. The consequences are high development costs and a small user base.

The second problem is how this development paradigm leads to extreme conceptual, technical, and administrative fragmentation, making it hard to create locative systems beyond a single management domain. Each application becomes a usage and data silo, and even if multiple applications serve the same physical space, they cannot combine their service value, as there are no easy paths for integration. This fragmentation is particularly harmful in urban contexts, where many independent information layers might be needed to serve diverse personal interests, immediate needs, or thematic perspectives. This fragmentation is a serious obstacle to convergence and generativity, two fundamental enablers for the disruptive nature of digital innovation [18].

These limitations have been highly detrimental to the open and widespread deployment of locative services. Even though we are witnessing a significant trend towards many new forms of locative data across public and private entities, there are no convenient and effective ways to deliver such data as part of genuinely locative experiences. We have many open data repositories, mapping systems, location-based APIs and web portals making locative data available on the web, but the value of this data is never truly realised until it is placed in those contexts where it would be more meaningful. We can thus conclude that many potentially valuable locative services are never created because of the high entry barrier associated with the custom mobile application paradigm. This represents a significant missed opportunity and a massive waste of potential value for data owners and for those who would benefit from those services.

1.1   The Locative Web

A fascinating aspect of web technology is how it can be appropriated for endless purposes. The basic principles of openness, scalability and uniform access [1] have allowed the frontiers of web development to expand continuously through creativity and ingenuity more than by cutting-edge technologies. These basic principles should also provide an obvious and sound alternative for developing locative systems. However, the concept of a locative web [17] has never produced any meaningful impact. Locative services remain one of the few areas where web technologies have not yet been able to deliver the same level of openness and interoperability that has entirely reshaped other domains. Even though the potential for a locative web is everywhere, it also remains beyond reach.

In this study, we extend the original concept of locative web with a conceptual framework to support the large-scale deployment of locative web content by many independent publishers. We build on the vision that locative services should aspire to the same universality and openness principles of the web. To pursue this vision, we explore the concept of a locative resource as a small, data-centric, web-based resource that represents only the information and actions considered meaningful for a specific locative situation. The core idea is that these resources might be automatically generated from datasets so that they can be produced in large numbers, and each can serve a very concrete situation. These resources can then be linked through a variety of semantic connections. With this design, we can attain all common web capabilities while also supporting multiple situated information-finding practices.

This solution may represent a breakthrough for locative services. Firstly, it offers a low entry barrier for the creation of locative services, allowing any entity to conveniently publish its locative data and make it readily available for anyone to use in the proper contexts and for any purpose. Secondly, links between resources provide an open model for the interoperability between many heterogeneous and independent systems, bringing them together into a coherent whole composed of the autonomous and open contributions of many independent entities. Thirdly, a web representation of locative resources allows any system resource to be addressed in a unified way by any web browser. It also paves the way for a new generation of universal locative applications supporting interaction across any locative resource, anywhere, and for diverse and possibly unforeseen purposes.

1.2   Research Goals

Our research goal is to produce new knowledge about tools and processes to support the convenient and cost-effective transformation of locative datasets owned by multiple independent entities into a global web of locative resources. From a technical perspective, we will repurpose, as much as possible, the plethora of technologies, standards and best practices at the core of the success of the Web. The key challenge, however, is how to empower many independent entities with very different datasets and publication goals to freely create their own publication processes while promoting convergence between their independent operations. The key contributions of this work are a novel locative resource concept that connects the Web to concrete situational contexts, a locative site toolkit designed to support the transformation of source data into collections of locative web resources, and a set of guidelines for dealing with data heterogeneity.

2   Related Work

Many cities have experimented with various technologies for locative services. Examples include mobile applications, augmented reality, digital twins or even common websites. Digital Twins [13] provide a joint digital model combining many layers of services. They are proposed as a data-centric platform for smart city practitioners to conduct simulations and demonstrate alternative urban development scenarios [8]. Likewise, 3D city models [2] are also becoming increasingly common and benefiting from 3D spatial data standards, such as CityGML [12] or BIM [15]. These systems may support a broad range of tasks beyond visualisation, but they are primarily meant for simulation, predictive maintenance and applications that require geometric models. OGC standards aim to guarantee interoperability and maximise the value of geospatial data. This allows OGC-compliant software, e.g. GeoCloud4SDI [16], to be interoperable and ready for adoption across multiple cities, but the focus is on providing complex geoprocessing capabilities [10]. They do not represent an alternative to the generic and widespread publication of locative services.

Web technologies can offer a powerful foundation for openness in geospatial efforts [11]. The Locative Web initiative [17] aimed to leverage web technologies as the content model while adding locative properties to link web resources to specific locations. However, simply embedding locative data into web pages does not support the integration of locative resources from many domains into a coherently locative web that people can easily discover, access and navigate for their own purposes. Openness in locative systems has also been addressed in the context of public display networks [6] as a model where the roles of display owners and content creators could be separated. Data Spaces [4] is a major initiative to promote the potential of the emerging data-driven economy. Their primary purpose is to create a context where multiple entities in a target domain may agree about which data they are willing to share under what conditions and for what purposes. Data spaces may become a significant source of domain-specific quality data for locative web resources, for example, in the areas of cultural heritage [14] and urban data [5].

The novelty in our work emerges from the unique combination of simple, tested and well-known web technologies and a data-driven content generation process that enables a systematic approach to the representation of locative web resources. This is unique in the way it can bring together the many layers of endless urban stakeholders into a coherent web of locative data and services. It is also unique in how it may offer a consistent interface to the digital features associated with any place, point, object, service, event or street in the city.

3   Conceptual Model

This section describes our initial efforts to conceptualize a novel locative web system. We introduce two key concepts that may help materialize web support for locative systems: locative resources and locative sites.

3.1   Locative Resources

The locative web resource is the core concept and the unifying abstraction in our vision for a locative web. A locative resource represents a small content unit associated with a physical or abstract context. As web resources, they are identifiable entities that can be accessed over the web via a URI (Uniform Resource Identifier). They represent a locative entity of a specific type, and they contain a structured data payload representing that entity. These resources are locative primarily because they contain contextual properties describing their target situation, e.g. a place name, a set of coordinates, an area served or some abstract usage context. Their content should correspond to the information and actions meaningful for that situation.

In line with the vision of a device-independent Web [3], locative resources should be ready to be delivered via many different web-connectable access mechanisms. Their primary representation is in the form of a linked data object [7] in json-ld. All resources share the same general structure, even though their data payload will be specific to each resource type. This structured representation is essential for broad interoperability and to facilitate agents' interpretation of locative resources. It is also the core data from which multiple other representations can be created for specific presentation channels, such as custom mobile applications, augmented reality or public displays.

The assumption is that these structured resources are generated through automated processes directly from data sources. This is essential for publishing them in large numbers and matching each with a very specific usage micro-context. To ensure universal access by humans, locative resources should also have an HTML representation. The generation of the web representation should also be automated and entirely based on the respective json-ld representation. This model shields the web generation process from any dependencies on source data, publication context or navigation structures other than settings related explicitly to HTML content, such as web presentation frameworks or visual presentation settings.

The structure of a json-ld representation of a locative resource is represented in Fig. 1. It comprises five major sections: Resource Header, Master Data Entity, Related Data Entities, Relationships and Imported Elements.

Resource Header. The Resource Header section provides a set of generic properties for describing any locative resource. This common schema is key in the unified model for locative resources. Clients can always expect to find subsets of these properties, and they will be able to interpret them across any type of

JSON-LD Resource

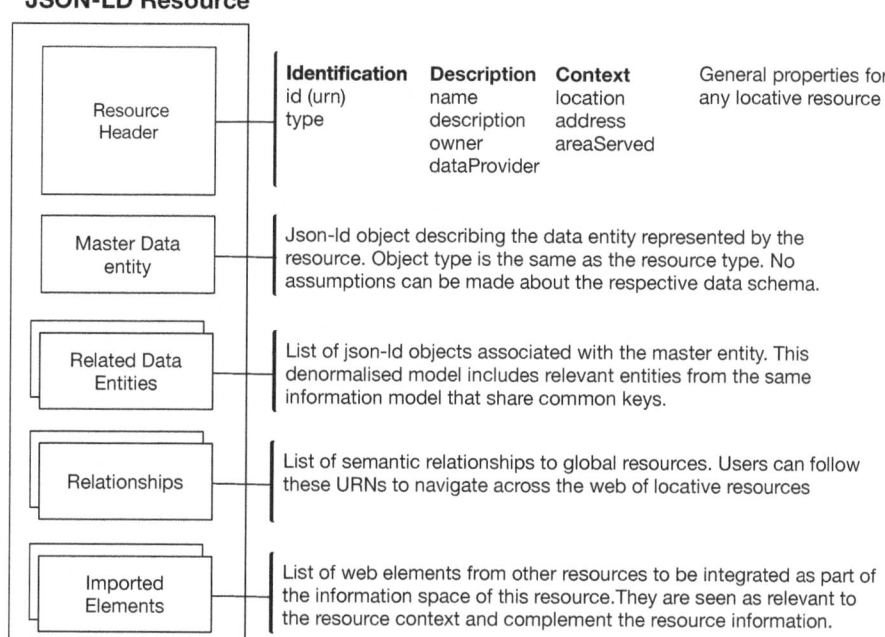

	Identification	Description	Context	General properties for
Resource Header	id (urn) type	name description owner dataProvider	location address areaServed	any locative resource

Master Data entity — Json-Id object describing the data entity represented by the resource. Object type is the same as the resource type. No assumptions can be made about the respective data schema.

Related Data Entities — List of json-Id objects associated with the master entity. This denormalised model includes relevant entities from the same information model that share common keys.

Relationships — List of semantic relationships to global resources. Users can follow these URNs to navigate across the web of locative resources

Imported Elements — List of web elements from other resources to be integrated as part of the information space of this resource.They are seen as relevant to the resource context and complement the resource information.

Fig. 1. The structure of a locative resource.

locative resource, regardless of its data payload. This guarantees interoperability, universality of resource access and navigability across the entire web of locative resources. Some of these properties, e.g. the domain name, will be based on attributes from the publication context. Others, e.g., the title, will be based on attributes from the data payload of the resource, particularly in the master entity.

The id attribute provides a unique ID for resource identification. These identifiers for locative resources follow NGSI-LD entity naming rules, with some adjustments to make them more aligned with the requirements of a federated system, where URNs need to be globally unique, resolvable, and interoperable across different organizations. Further generic attributes include the resource type, name, title, description, data provider, and other metadata properties that help to provide a multidimensional resource description.

Another set of Resource Header properties supports the association between the resource and specific locative situations. We consider diverse types of situational properties, such as geographic coordinates, address, place IDs, a symbolic location name, a served area, an activity type, or any other property that may help to characterize the context to which the respective content is associated. As shown by previous locative web efforts [17], simply adding coordinates to web resources is not enough to create locative experiences. However, this is still an essential element for linking resources to contexts in a way that is valuable for both Humans and machines. These properties can be globally unique identifiers, but they can also be local references within a specific domain. This allows the system to repurpose many types of situated context hints, such as a street name, an office number or an image of an artwork.

Master Data Entity. The Master Data Entity section is the main data payload in a locative resource. It contains a linked-data object with the core data associated with the entity represented by the locative resource. If the locative resource represents a bus stop, this entity might be a GtfsStop object with the key information about the bus stop itself. While any schema can be used in this master data entity, ideally, it should be based on standard data models many third parties can interpret.

Related Data Entities. The Related Data Entities section contains complementary data related to the entity represented by the master data entity. For example, a resource representing a bus stop should include information about the stop itself (id, name, location). However, it should also include information about which bus routes stop there and when. This information is not directly about the stop itself but will be critically relevant for most people at that stop.

This resource section addresses a core challenge associated with the mapping between the information model of the source data and the information model represented by locative resources. Locative resources are not abstract data entities within a more extensive data model, at least not in the traditional sense of an entity-relationships model. Their purpose is to serve as a focal point for all the relevant information and services about a specified context and offer Human users a valuable locative experience. Therefore, each locative resource should be conceived as an independent physical or abstract entity that is meaningful for users in a given situation and encapsulates all the relevant data from that perspective.

Mapping these two perspectives requires a suitable balance between what should be provided at a single resource and what should be available by switching to another resource. Interpreting information in the proper context can provide locative meaning to that information, which is a key goal of this model. However, too many small resources associated with very small contexts may lead to excessive context changes, hindering user experience. Information should thus be provided in contexts that are relevant and meaningful to users, and it should include enough related information to support the most common needs and avoid an excessive number of context changes.

To serve this purpose, locative resources need to support some level of denormalization that combines the representation of a master or parent object with the representation of key-related entities as nested data. This may result in data duplication across locative resources, but it helps them serve their role as aggregating contexts for information related to a given situation.

Relationships. The Relationships section represents connections to other related resources. Like on the web, links represent interactive jumps to a different resource with a different context based on the semantics of a relationship between both resources. These connections form the edges of a global locative data graph, where locative resources are the nodes. These relationships play an important role in defining the situated context of resources. We can expect many of these relationships, especially those within a single information model, to be primarily derived from data relationships. However, many others, especially those between different data domains, can be expected to be primarily based on the proximity of their situational contexts. These relationships provide navigation possibilities that help people reach the most relevant resource in a given situation, even if they start from another situationally proximate resource, possibly from another information domain. This ability to move between related contexts until reaching the most suitable one is essential because situated information-seeking strategies can be much more meaningful when they include the users' ability to interpret their current situation. They can navigate a situated information space and "tune in" to any content relevant to the current situation without relying on complex personalisation mechanisms. Therefore, these relationships can also be seen as another element, in addition to contextual properties, that can help establish the situational relevance of locative resources. They offer a more flexible and crowdsourced model for extending the semantics of their situational relevance.

Imported Elements. The Imported Elements section supports data sharing between resources. It enables a presentation unit from one resource to be included as a presentation unit at another resource. For example, elements from nearby bus stops, showing the next departures at each stop, might be included in a campus resource describing travel alternatives from the Campus to the City Centre. This is a fundamental flexibility mechanism of the system, enabling data from one resource to be included as relevant information within the context of many other resources. To be more effective, this is something that should occur primarily in the web representation of resources. This way, the mapping between a particular data entity and a web component that can present it is a problem that only needs to be addressed once, at the source resource where the element was originally published. Importing elements from other resources does not necessarily establish any relationship between those resources. It is just about sharing content across many contexts where it might be relevant.

3.2   Locative Sites

We introduce the concept of a locative site as a publication context for locative resources in a single information model. Resources in the same locative site will share a common domain name and will be part of the same administrative domain managed by a single publisher entity. One can imagine a locative site corresponding to what is normally expected as the scope of a simple themed mobile application for an event, a museum, an urban tour or an urban resource directory.

A locative site consumes several data sources to generate and publish locative resources based on that data. We envision that publishers may choose diverse tools and practices to publish their locative sites, mainly depending on the nature of their source data. These could range from interactively editing their data on a dedicated platform to importing and transforming large datasets. Regardless of these many possible tools, locative sites are always expected to be generated by automated processes. This automation empowers publishers to create rich locative experiences directly from their data. It is also the enabler for some of the core properties of the concept, such as: the ability to publish large numbers of small and unique resources, each targeting only a specific locative context; promoting a common structure across all resources; and generating multiple coherent representations of the same resource, e.g. JSON or HTML.

Unlike common websites, which are mainly conceived from top to bottom, locative sites are mainly about the specific data elements they publish and not so much about their aggregate perspective or navigation structures. The publication of a locative site is structured around resource bundles. Each bundle constitutes a publication unit within that locative site and supports the transformation and publication of a specific type of resource from a specific data source. All the resources in the same bundle will thus represent the same entity type and be based on the same data model, with each resource corresponding to an item in the source dataset. Examples of resource bundles may include the list of bus stops of a bus operator, the list of exhibition rooms in a museum or the list of bike racks in a city.

Locative sites can be published independently; therefore, each site may have its own data model. Still, resources can have any type and number of connections to other resources outside the respective locative site. This allows locative sites published by many autonomous entities to converge into a single and continuous locative web without enforcing any centralized solution.

4   Experimental Work

To assess the potential of this novel locative web approach and uncover possible limitations, we conducted an experimental work that combined the implementation of a locative sites toolkit, the development of four case studies involving diverse locative datasets and the progressive optimization of a data transformation workflow to support the publication of the respective locative resources.

4.1   Locative Sites Toolkit

The concept of locative resources does not involve any assumptions about how they are published. Like on the web, we envision many publication practices, from individual interactive publications to automated large-scale generation processes. Our initial implementation of a tool for generating locative sites from locative datasets was mainly driven by the need to experiment with publication processes and allow tools and practices to evolve side-by-side. As part of our effort to identify and characterize publication tools for locative resources, we have implemented a development library and a set of data models and templates to support the efficient and reliable transformation of source data into locative websites representing specific information domains. This development was made progressively and alongside the development of the four case studies. The diverse requirements emerging from those four studies have been instrumental in the toolkit's design, and the toolkit was at the core of all four case studies. At a conceptual level, this toolkit helps to accomplish the following tasks:

- Publication of a locative web domain comprising various interconnected collections of data entities and their respective web representations
- Methods to streamline the transformation of various data sources into json-ld while validating and adjusting data according to standard data models.
- A common web publication model that offers a familiar interface across resources and supports core navigation features between resources.
- The ability to generate web representations for the various types of data models present in the resource data.
- A set of relationship management techniques to support the flexible integration of various types of resources, possibly published by many independent stakeholders

4.2   Case Studies

To improve the validity of the process and broaden the range of requirements, we selected a diverse set of case studies, specifically the four case studies described in Table 1.

Table 1. Summary of the four case studies

Case Study	Description	Source Data
City Statues	Inventory of all urban statues	Spreadsheets + Images
Bus Information	GTFS data about local bus system	GTFS data
Christmas Fair	Stages, events and timetables	WebSite + PDF
Department	Department offices and their usage	Spreadsheets + Images

These case studies are diverse regarding their application domains, the nature of their source data or the complexity of their information models. Together, they pose diverse challenges and appeal to different sets of features. They are all real use cases for which other alternatives to provide the same information have already been tried, either as mobile applications, websites or paper leaflets. This confirms the relevance of the case studies and provides a strong background for comparing approaches.

The City Statues case study provides information about the statues in the city of Braga. This data was only being used internally by the Municipality services as an inventory of local patrimony. The service comprises locative resources describing each of the statues, including information about the author, the type of work, a description, the location and photos. The source data is structured as spreadsheets, along with image files of the statues. The Bus Information case study was entirely based on standard GTFS data from the local operator. This case study is more complex regarding the information model, with various types of data entities, but it leverages the benefits of a standard data model. The Christmas Fair case study is the program for Christmas events in Braga. This data was available as a PDF document and also as a website. This is the most challenging case regarding the information format because there are many potential data entities and many alternative ways to design the information model. The Department case study involves information about our University Department, combining different layers of information related to rooms, people, events and activities.

4.3   Development Workflow

The development of the four case studies involved starting with basic, custom workflows and then progressively introducing new abstractions and convergence mechanisms that could generalize the custom strategies emerging from each workflow. The goal was to identify the most relevant abstractions and practices for the large-scale semi-automated generation of locative web resources from datasets. Figure 2 represents the generic structure of the process, which comprises three main steps: data modelling, generation of the json-ld representation of each locative resource and generation of its web representation.

Data Modeling. The initial data modelling step is the identification of the entities represented by the data, with their properties and relationships. At this stage, this is mostly a logical data model, which is expected to be detailed in terms of specific attributes and relationships but makes no assumptions about concrete types or representations. The source data may then undergo multiple data transformation processes before it can be used as input to generate locative sites. These transformations may involve procedures to adjust, combine, merge, estimate or complete the source data. The most common examples may include the combination of data from multiple datasets, the adjustment of data field names and values, the generation of metadata, the categorization of data items and the association of external media, such as images. This is a common ETL (Extract, Transform, Load) process for which data processing tools already exist. The problem is that, without concrete expectations about the source data, there is not much that can be generalized. However, we can design the process to mitigate the complexity associated with heterogeneous data sources and promote convergence mechanisms. Our first convergence mechanism was to define the output of this process as a list of JSON objects, all with the same data schema and

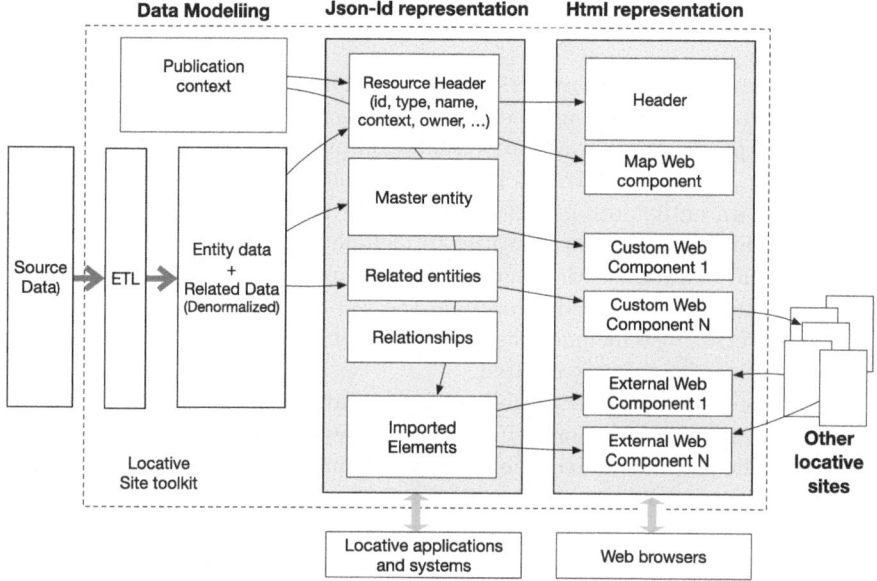

Fig. 2. Workflow for resource generation.

each corresponding to the data of one locative resource. This assumption isolates subsequent process phases from the inherent complexity associated with highly heterogeneous data sources. The second convergence mechanism uses data models to define how data is organized, stored, and managed. Data models provide a fundamental interoperability mechanism to promote convergence among diverse data sources, content types and presentation alternatives. More specifically, they should play a key role in the following features:

– Validation of data sources or data produced during transformation and export processes.
– Specification of the structure of locative resources in the core json-ld representation.
– Defining the types of entities represented by locative resources.
– Associating specific HTML representations with specific types of resources, thus promoting the reusability of development components.
– Automatic generation of UI interfaces for locative resources and services

Considering the key role that interoperability plays in these systems, locative resources should be, as much as possible, based on standard data models that can be interpreted unambiguously by any third party. In our implementation, we mainly used data models based on the NGSI-LD specifications [9].

Json-ld Representations. This step is where the locative resources are generated and published as JSON-LD objects. This publication occurs as part of locative sites that represent a common publication domain by a specific publisher.

The generation process involves going through each of the data entities in the source data and combining its data with the general bundle and locative site properties to produce the json-ld representation of that resource. An important part of this mapping is the transformation of some of the specific data fields in the master data entity into generic properties of the resource header. Another is deciding which Related Data Entities to include in the locative resource. This decision should be linked with some level of anticipation about the nature of the data that should be presented to users in the web representation. The resource generation process also includes the integration of relationships within and outside the locative site being generated.

From the perspective of the publication of locative resources, it is relevant to distinguish between connections within a single locative site scope and those that span across the global locative web and involve multiple locative sites managed by autonomous entities. In the former case, there is complete knowledge and control over the data entities involved. In the latter case, these relationships must be explicitly defined as part of the publication specifications. The same is true for Imported Elements, which also need to be defined explicitly based on some interpretation of relevance.

Web Representation. In our toolkit, the json-ld representation is generated first, and the web representation is generated afterwards and is entirely based on the json-ld data. There are two main challenges involved.

The first is to transform the resource data into a unified web interface for any locative resource. Web interfaces provide a simple but universal channel to deliver the value of locative information. They should identify the resource, display data elements that can represent the resource data and leverage relationships to offer navigability opportunities to other resources. Depending on their semantics, some relationships can be presented as navigation menus. Others might be presented as data elements with a link for more advanced interactions with the target resource. In this study, we have not made significant advances in the design of this generic interface.

The second challenge is to create web representations for data schemas that can be very diverse. Regarding this challenge, we explored a solution based on web components. This involves creating the web components according to specific guidelines and then registering them to be associated with a specific data schema. This association only means that the web component was conceived for that specific data schema and does not imply any assumptions about what will be presented. The expectation is that for a single data schema, many different visualisations may be created to embrace creativity and present very diverse perspectives about that data. In our implementation, we explored this approach and developed several web components for the schemas in our case studies.

5   Discussion

The implementation of the locative sites toolkit and the development of the four case studies described in the previous section were instrumental in assessing the various dimensions involved in transforming data into locative resources. In particular, they have provided us with relevant findings about the challenges raised by data heterogeneity and different strategies for dealing with it. Each case study faced its own small obstacles, but the real challenge was their diversity and the ability of the system to handle those heterogeneous datasets and publication goals. Addressing this challenge involves a delicate balance between openness and convergence. On the one hand, we need openness to embrace the inherent heterogeneity stemming from a vast diversity of endless data sources managed by multiple autonomous entities. On the other hand, we need convergence to ensure that the output of all those transformations is consistent and ready to integrate a global web of locative resources. When developing these case studies, we identified four general guidelines that may help to manage this trade-off.

Avoid Heterogeneity. The most impactful way to address heterogeneity is to avoid the problem altogether. We cannot impose our own standards, but we can acknowledge that many de facto standards are widely used across many domains. They are well-tested, they have formal specifications, and some of them can be very relevant to society in general. For example, the General Transit Feed Specification (GTFS) is used by transit agencies across the world to publish up-to-date transit information. Because of GTFS, we could easily reproduce our Bus Information case study in many cities worldwide. Recent trends towards dataspaces might help many more domain-specific standards to emerge as clear winners in those domains.

Divide the Problem. The second strategy is to decompose the resource generation process into key functional scopes, each addressing only one specific part of the problem and its input assumptions. We did this when we defined the input for generating locative resources as a list of JSON objects of the same schema. We can extract two significant benefits by breaking the larger problem into smaller ones. The first is that well-defined boundaries between different parts of the problem help to limit the propagation of the complexities caused by heterogeneity. The other is that having smaller and simpler parts will significantly help find similarities between independent transformation processes. This should promote the emergence of common abstractions and tools that may hinder heterogeneity within that particular context.

Absorb Heterogeneity. Assuming we will always have to deal with heterogeneity, the following guideline is to absorb the impacts of heterogeneity. We have used three primary techniques that fit this concept: smaller schemas, avoidance of type proliferation and repurposing custom data fields as generic resource properties. Smaller schemas are a valuable practice because a larger schema is never a perfect match when we try to repurpose it across different domains or datasets in the same domain. Smaller schemas are much more reusable than larger ones because they can be recombined to form larger concepts. For example, contextual properties in our locative resources are small and widely used schemas to represent addresses, locations, service areas or places. Even if some parts of a locative resource are not known to a client, these smaller and highly recognisable schemas will ensure that key parts of the resource can be interpreted appropriately. Another technique is to avoid type proliferation, i.e. the excessive creation of distinct data types to represent variations of similar entities. This proliferation can lead to unnecessary complexity, maintenance challenges, and reduced code readability. In our model, resource types describe the type of entity represented by the resource but do not mandate any data schemas. By separating resource types from rigid expectations about the data in those resources, we avoid the traps of type explosion. Finally, we also designed the transformation process in a way that many specific properties of the master data representing the resource are mapped into generic properties of the resource header, making sure that even if a particular client cannot interpret the master data, the fundamental properties of that resource will still be able to provide key information about that resource. This creates alternative, partially redundant representations of the same data on the same resource. However, it introduces another layer of flexibility for addressing distinct usage contexts based on that data.

Drive Convergence. The final insight is about promoting convergence. Developing our four case studies involved many micro-design decisions, most of which were not particularly relevant to the outcome of any process. However, when we consider the development of multiple locative sites, it becomes evident that many similar problems are being addressed separately as site-specific problems. Consequently, we end up with many separate, slightly different, incompatible solutions to similar problems. Most of those solutions will be perfectly reasonable, and it will even be hard to claim that any of them might be better or worse. The problem, however, is how everyone will be repeating the same effort over and over again. Still, we do not wish to hinder innovation. On the contrary, we would like a thriving community where new solutions may continuously emerge to complement or replace previous ones. From this perspective, what is essential is the ability to drive convergence by progressively promoting shared reusable elements. This is a form of nudging developers to convergence by giving them the alternative to reuse what has already been developed instead of spending their effort creating another solution to a solved problem. Schemas can also become a key driver for the convergence and reuse of components. On the input side, they can allow data transformation processes to be replicated across many data sources. They should also enable simple, guided, assisted processes for locative content generation. On the output side, they can support the development of web components that present specific data elements anywhere such data may exist.

6 Conclusions and Future Work

This paper presents a novel locative resource concept that may help create a new generation of web-based locative services. We describe the concept and early implementation of a locative site toolkit designed to support the transformation of source data into locative web resources. A key challenge in this approach is generalising those data processing activities. Based on the results of four case studies, we identified four general guidelines that may help mitigate the consequences of heterogeneity and contribute to the viability of more generic locative resource generation procedures. In future work, we aim to explore how artificial intelligence techniques may help to understand the data entities composing any information model and assist with the mapping to specific types of locative resources.

Acknowledgments. We acknowledge the contribution of Braga Municipality in providing the statues data used in this study.

Disclosure of Interests. The authors have no competing interests to declare that are relevant to the content of this article.

References

1. Berners-lee, B.T.: Long live the web. Sci. Am. 80–85 (2010)
2. Biljecki, F., Stoter, J., Ledoux, H., Zlatanova, S., Çöltekin, A.: Applications of 3d city models: state of the art review. ISPRS Int. J. Geo Inf. **4**, 2842–2889 (2015). https://doi.org/10.3390/ijgi4042842
3. Butler, M., Giannetti, F., Gimson, R., Wiley, T.: Device independence and the web. IEEE Internet Comput. **6** (2002). https://doi.org/10.1109/MIC.2002.1036042
4. Commission, E.: Commission staff working document - on common European data spaces (2022)
5. Cuno, S., Bruns, L., Tcholtchev, N., Lämmel, P., Schieferdecker, I.: Data governance and sovereignty in urban data spaces based on standardized ICT reference architectures. Data **4** (2019). https://doi.org/10.3390/data4010016
6. Davies, N., Langheinrich, M., Jose, R., Schmidt, A.: Open display networks: a communications medium for the 21st century. Computer **45**, 58–64 (3 2012). https://doi.org/10.1109/MC.2012.114
7. Heath, T., Bizer, C.: Linked data: evolving the web into a global data space. Synth. Lect. Semant. Web: Theory Technol. **1**, 1–121 (2011). https://doi.org/10.2200/S00334ED1V01Y201102WBE001
8. Hämäläinen, M.: Urban development with dynamic digital twins in Helsinki city. IET Smart Cities **3**, 201–210 (2021). https://doi.org/10.1049/smc2.12015
9. (ISG), C.I.M.C.E.I.S.G.: Context information management (CIM); OpenAPI specification for ngsi-ld api (2024)
10. Kiehle, C., Greve, K., Heier, C.: Requirements for next generation spatial data infrastructures-standardized web based geoprocessing and web service orchestration. Trans. GIS **11** (2007). https://doi.org/10.1111/j.1467-9671.2007.01076.x
11. Kolas, D., Dean, M., Hebeler, J.: Geospatial semantic web: architecture of ontologies. In: IEEE Aerospace Conference Proceedings 2006 (2006). https://doi.org/10.1109/aero.2006.1656068

12. Kutzner, T., Chaturvedi, K., Kolbe, T.H.: CityGML 3.0: new functions open up new applications. PFG – J. Photogram. Remote Sens. Geoinf. Sci. **88**(1), 43–61 (2020). https://doi.org/10.1007/s41064-020-00095-z

13. Lehtola, V.V., et al.: Digital twin of a city: review of technology serving city needs. Int. J. Appl. Earth Obs. Geoinf. **114**, 102915 (2022). https://doi.org/10.1016/j.jag.2022.102915

14. Niccolucci, F., Felicetti, A., Hermon, S.: Populating the data space for cultural heritage with heritage digital twins. Data **7** (2022). https://doi.org/10.3390/data7080105

15. Oulidi, H.J., Hajji, R.: Open BIM Standards (2021). https://doi.org/10.1002/9781119885474.ch4

16. Tripathi, A.K., Agrawal, S., Gupta, R.D.: Geocloud4sdi: a cloud enabled open framework for development of spatial data infrastructure at city level. Earth Sci. Inform. **16** (2023). https://doi.org/10.1007/s12145-022-00893-6

17. Wilde, E., Kofahl, M.: The locative web. In: Proceedings of the First International Workshop on Location and the Web - LOCWEB '08, vol. 300, pp. 1–8 (2008). https://doi.org/10.1016/S1071-5819(02)00127-1

18. Yoo, Y., Boland, R.J., Lyytinen, K., Majchrzak, A.: Organizing for innovation in the digitized world. Organ. Sci. **23**, 1398–1408 (2012). https://doi.org/10.1287/orsc.1120.0771

Flow Management in Urban Contexts (FMUC 2025)

Synergy Between BIM and e-Procurement: A New Paradigm for Digital Procurement Management

Enrico Pasquale Zitiello$^{(\boxtimes)}$, Francesca Porcellini, Eliana Basile, Antonio Salzano, and Maurizio Nicolella

Department of Civil, Architectural and Environmental Engineering, University of Naples Federico II, 80125 Naples, Italy
enricopasquale.zitiello@unia.it

Abstract. The Architecture, Engineering and Construction (AEC) sector is undergoing a digital transformation thanks to Construction 4.0 technologies. Among these, e-procurement represents a key element for the optimisation of tendering procedures and the improvement of administrative transparency, through the dematerialisation of documents and the rationalisation of workflows, resulting in time and cost reductions in procurement. In parallel, Building Information Modeling (BIM), stimulated by national and international regulations, allows a more integrated management of design information, improving the quality of decisions and reducing errors and inefficiencies. However, the integration between BIM and e-procurement is still limited, as e-procurement mainly focuses on document digitisation without fully exploiting the potential of BIM for advanced data management. With this in mind, this research aims to analyse the state of the art regarding the joint application of BIM and e-procurement in the public procurement sector. Through an in-depth bibliographical analysis, the main scientific studies and existing application experiences will be examined in order to identify best practices, still existing criticalities and phases of tendering procedures where BIM can bring the greatest added value. Furthermore, in order to concretely understand the potential and limits of this integration, an application to a case study will be developed, analysing in detail the achievable advantages and the problems encountered in the operational implementation. The analysis conducted also aims to outline possible evolutionary scenarios and strategies to overcome the technological, organisational and regulatory barriers that currently hinder full interoperability between these two technologies. The final objective is to provide a comprehensive picture of the opportunities arising from the joint adoption of BIM and e-procurement, highlighting how this synergy can improve efficiency, transparency and economic sustainability in public procurement.

Keywords: e-procurment · BIM · Construction 4.0 · Digital Procurement Management

O. Gervasi et al. (Eds.): ICCSA 2025 Workshops, LNCS 15891, pp. 63–77, 2026.
https://doi.org/10.1007/978-3-031-97617-9_5

1 Introduction

Public procurement management is a complex process involving various actors such as contracting entities, economic operators and control authorities, and consists of several phases each of which plays a crucial role in ensuring transparency and fairness in the assignment of tasks. In particular the procurement phase plays a key role as it identifies the economic operator to be entrusted with the execution of works or the supply of goods or the provision of services. European public procurement law regulates two main criteria for the selection of the successful tenderer the lowest price criterion and the most economically advantageous tender (MEAT). This criterion appears to be more preferred as it allows the procuring entity to assess, in addition to the economic component, a multitude of parameters which may include technical, functional and innovative features, Criteria of environmental and social sustainability, as well as the assessment of costs throughout the life cycle (Life Cycle Costing - LCC) of the work, service or supply, thus generating a multidimensional evaluation approach.

The adoption of the MEAT criterion thus allows a comprehensive evaluation of the offer, through a single criterion it is possible to evaluate the offer on the basis of price, or cost, using a cost-effectiveness approach such as life-cycle cost, or best value for money (Forum on the Competitiveness of the European Rail Supply Industry, European Commission, October 2017). However, the effective implementation of the MEAT criterion requires the ex-ante definition of evaluation criteria (and related sub-criteria, indicators and weighting methodologies) that meet the requirements defined as fundamental principles by the 2014 European Directive such as transparency, objectivity and equal treatment, verifiability and measurability. The correct formulation of these elements is essential to ensure a fair and impartial competitive comparison between the tenders submitted by economic operators. The main challenge facing contracting authorities is precisely the definition of these criteria, which must not compromise, as highlighted by the European directive, the transparency and efficiency of the tender award process. To meet these needs, technological tools such as e-procurement platforms have emerged, which digitise the entire procurement process and minimise human interaction in order to optimise the traceability of operations and guarantee a reduction in time and greater transparency of the tender process.

Another technology that is gaining increasing importance is Building Information Modeling (BIM), thanks also to European and national regulations that require its use in public procurement; these regulations, however, incentivise the use of BIM only as a tool necessary to build the model but not as a process management tool. The objective of this paper is to highlight the potential of the combined use of e-procurement and BIM platforms in the tendering process.

In fact, BIM offers a digital and parametric representation of every aspect of a construction project and presents itself as a valuable tool for the definition and management of the bidding phase due to its ability to represent objective and quantifiable parameters, BIM allows for a more precise and automated evaluation of bids, thus simplifying the selection process, reducing time and costs, and increasing transparency in the evaluation of bids. Furthermore, the use of BIM to check compliance with tender requirements and to score bids according to defined parameters minimises the risk of errors and subjectivity, ensuring a more objective selection. In this context, the authors present a methodological proposal that integrates BIM technology into the public procurement process using the MEAT criterion. The suggested methodology is designed to optimise the efficiency and transparency of the tendering process by reducing error margins and minimising subjectivity in tender evaluation. The authors also plan to test the proposed methodology through the analysis of case studies in order to validate it and refine the automated analysis techniques. Particular focus will be placed on the identification of parameterisable criteria - i.e. those parameters that can be translated into objective data within the BIM model - and on automated bid evaluation techniques. The ultimate goal is to develop a system that, through e-procurement platforms and BIM, allows to significantly reduce the time of procedures and the risks related to human errors or decisions influenced by subjective factors, leading to faster and more transparent public procurement management.

2   State of Art

The construction sector, globally, is known for its resistance to the adoption of new technologies. This conservative tendency is also clearly manifested in the implementation of e-procurement [1], despite the fact that procurement activities are particularly frequent and relevant in this field [2]. The concept of procurement supports a delivery relationship between buyers and sellers and can be defined as the search for information on requirements for goods/services, and the willingness to promise, i.e. the flow of information within the quotation and negotiation functions [2]. The traditional process that serves as the basis for today's e-procurement is composed of a series of well-defined activities that, although autonomous, are interconnected and organised according to a logic determined by the specific procurement strategy or procedure adopted [3]. The study [2] divides procurement into two phases: contracting and settlement. Contracting includes supplier search, supply promise and definition of goods/services requirements, managing the information flow (availability, dispatch) for quotations and negotiations. Settlement includes payment (transaction) and the physical transfer of goods/services (delivery). Other studies [4, 5] group procurement activities into four main contractual phases: the pre-contractual phase, the contractual phase, the administrative management phase of the contract and the post-contractual phase. Procurement can also be classified into two main types: structured and unstructured [6]. Structured procurement processes are highly automated in terms of requirements identification, ordering and fulfilment. In fact, if demand is regular and product specifications do not change over time, transition costs can be reduced by creating an automated order with minimal human interference [2]. Unstructured procurement occurs when products or services are not suitable for predefined automated procedures. In this case, human intervention is required to search, request, match suppliers and create the order by exploiting the best available offers, thus not constraining the procurement [2]. In summary, when discussing structured procurement, reference is made to goods with well-defined characteristics, since the delivery of such goods is faster and easier. This is due to the clarity of the technical specifications and the ease of evaluation of tenders, which reduce decision and implementation times. On the other hand, for unstructured goods, we observe an evolution that is closer to the construction sector, it is difficult to parametrize goods and services because they are too variable.

As defined by Chan, A.P.C; Owusu, E.K e-procurement is the business-to-consumer (B2C), business-to-business (B2B) or business-to-government (B2IG) purchase, as well as the sale of goods, services, works or supplies via the Internet and other information and network systems.

The conceptual and technological origin of eprocument dates back to the 70s and 80s, that is to say the birth of EDI (Electronic Data Interchange) technologies. EDI enabled the structured exchange of standardised business documents between trading partners via dedicated networks, representing a first significant form of digitisation of B2B transactions, albeit characterised by high implementation complexity and significant costs. However, e-procurement in its modern sense, understood as the pervasive application of technologies based on Internet protocols and web interfaces for the management of purchasing processes, saw its actual genesis and diffusion from the second half of the 1990s, coinciding with the commercial expansion of the World Wide Web. This period marked a shift from closed, two-sided systems to more open, accessible and interoperable solutions (often based on client-server or web-based architectures), fostering the development of B2B marketplaces and software platforms dedicated to automating the corporate purchasing cycle. The next phase, post dot-com speculative bubble (early 2000s), saw a technological consolidation and a more mature and strategically oriented adoption of such solutions by organisations globally. The development process of e-procurement technologies over time is presented in Fig. 1 [3].

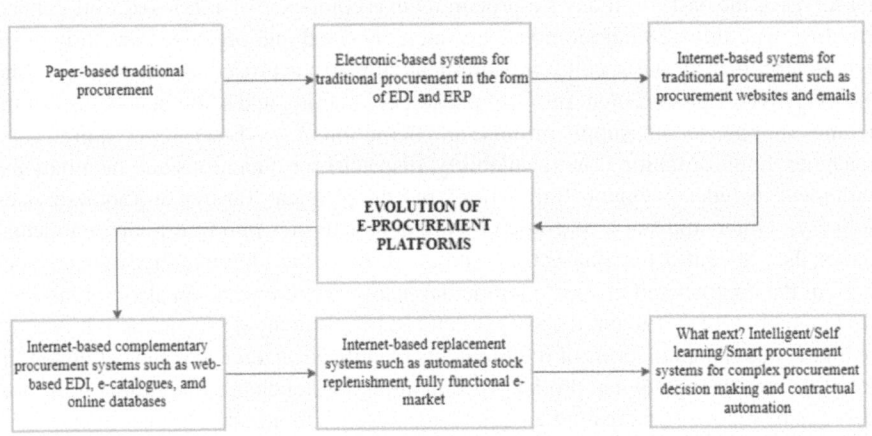

Fig. 1. Evolution of e-procurement [3]

In conclusion, the progressive technological advancement of digital tools has been the driving force behind the transformation of procurement processes. This has enabled the overcoming of manual methodologies and led to a radical digitisation of procurement activities both within the public administration and in the private business context.

According to some studies [7, 8] the e-procurement process can be described in six different phases.

- e-sourcing: this process involves the search for new potential suppliers via the Internet, either in general or through specific B2B marketplaces. It takes place in the information-gathering phase of the procurement process;
- e-tendering: it consists of sending requests for information (RFIs), requests for prices (RFPs) and other enquiries to suppliers, receiving responses via Internet technologies. The data involved are focused on the product or service. In this phase, an initial screening can be carried out to qualify a selected number of suppliers for the negotiation phase (a process generated in the supplier contact phase);
- e-informing: handles supplier information, such as quality certifications, financial status and unique capabilities, without involving transactions. Information may come from third-party suppliers or from internal company investigations;
- e-reverse auctions: e-reverse auctions allow the purchasing company to obtain goods and services at the lowest price or a combination of price and other conditions via Internet technologies. Auctions are negotiated in real time and result in a final offer between buyer and supplier. (This is how the negotiation phase is characterised);
- e-MRO and Web-based ERP (Enterprise Resource Planning): focus on the creation and approval of purchase requests. E-MRO deals with indirect items (maintenance, repair and operational materials), while the Web-based ERP deals with product-related items (order fulfilment phase);
- e-collaboration: manages the collection and dissemination of purchasing-related information, such as product versions, designs and sales forecasts, available on the purchasing company's website or extranet. This reduces errors and synchronises suppliers with the buyer.

There are, however, several variants of electronic models. According to Costa and Grilo [9], the e-procurement process consists of ten sequential activities covering the entire procurement cycle.

- ex-ante e-evaluation: i.e. the multi-criteria assessment of procurement needs and strategies;
- e-notice: the electronic publication of procurement notices;
- e-submission: the electronic submission of proposals;
- e-decision: the electronic evaluation of proposals, the subsequent communication of the evaluation results with discussion and analysis of the results;
- e-award: the electronic awarding of contracts to suppliers with the best proposals;
- e-ordering: concerning activities that include sending an order document from public buyers to suppliers and the transmission of delivery instructions for ordered goods and services;
- e-invoicing: i.e. the request for payment for goods and services ordered and delivered on agreed terms;
- e-payment: the agreed management of electronic payments and their execution;
- e-contract management: i.e. the use of electronic contract management tools to monitor and improve contract performance and document management;
- ex-post e-evaluation: multi-criteria evaluation of contract performance and generation of KPIs to support future tendering processes.

All these processes should be combined and all relevant information should be available electronically. Only in this way can a reduction of administrative work and the automation of operational processes be achieved [9]. The lack of a standardised or universally recognised framework that brings together all e-procurement variants under one source often makes it difficult to accurately identify all the different types of e-procurement actually used to support the activities of the entire e-procurement process [3]. Despite this, e-procurement can be regarded as a complete "end-to-end" solution that integrates and optimises numerous procurement processes within an organisation [10] in a way that integrates and optimises the numerous procurement-related activities within the organisation [3, 9].

In the AEC sector, e-procurement constitutes a significant innovation that, together with the development of other technologies such as BIM, contributes significantly to the ongoing digitisation process in public procurement. In particular, e-procurement, through the use of telematic platforms and dedicated information systems, enables the dematerialisation and optimisation of transactions related to the acquisition of goods and services. This approach induces the automation of operational workflows and the rationalisation of administrative processes, increasing management efficiency. In parallel, BIM, the use of which is regulated and incentivised both nationally and internationally, is increasingly integrated into public procurement procedures. It should be noted, that in the context of procurement, the use of BIM is currently focused on the creation and management of the digital "model" of the work, rather than as an integrated process management methodology. However, the operational integration between e-procurement platforms and the potential offered by the BIM model opens up new perspectives for the optimisation of procurement processes in the AEC sector. The synergetic integration of these two technological domains can evolve the role of BIM from a simple information support to a dynamic and central management tool in procurement procedures. However, an analysis of the literature and current operational practices in the AEC sector reveals a clear dichotomy in the integration of BIM within public procurement processes. On the one hand, in fact, there is an increasing adoption of the model as an integral component of tender documentation for which contracting authorities define the Employer's Information Requirements (EIR) and modelling criteria that economic operators must comply with (Geometric and Information Development Level, data structuring, to exchange formats); on the other hand, a significant gap emerges in the definition of standardised and integrated operating procedures for the effective use of the BIM model during the course of the procurement process itself. While requirements on the model are specified, there is a lack of established methodological frameworks governing how this model should be actively employed by the parties (contracting authority and bidders) within e-procurement platforms. Consequently, although BIM is present as an information artefact in tenders, its transformative potential on the procurement process remains largely unexpressed often relegating the model to an information support role rather than a central and dynamic tool of the procurement process. A factual response to the above is provided by the 'Report on Digitisation and BIM Tenders 2023' [11]. This document, now in its seventh analytical edition and edited by OICE, censuses the public tenders for Architectural and Engineering Services launched in the period between 1 January and 31 December 2023. The analysis focuses on tenders in which the use of BIM methodologies is envisaged, aimed at the digital management of all the information related to a project, in the various phases of its life cycle. The processing of the report is based on the data collected by the OICE Tenders Office as part of its daily market monitoring activities, the results of which are published monthly in the OICE/Informatel Observatory. In the years under analysis (2015–2023), the number of tenders for Architectural and Engineering Services referring to BIM showed an overall growing trend. The tenders analysed, in the year 2023, are classified according to the four main modes of reference to BIM, two of which are related to the tender access phase and two to the tender evaluation phase.

With regard to the tender access phase.

- BIM is referred to as part of the evaluation of technical capacity and linked to the tenderer's previous experience;
- BIM is requested as a professional suitability requirement (often under penalty of exclusion), with regard to individual professional figures and linked to the possession of organisational capacities, tools necessary to carry out the required activity and possible BIM certifications.
- While for the tender evaluation phase with MEAT:
- BIM is evaluated as a sub-criterion of the 'professionalism and adequacy of the offer';
- BIM is evaluated as a sub-criterion of the 'methodological characteristics of the offer'.

In addition to these four ways of referring to BIM, a certain number of tenders can be found that refer to a generic request for design in BIM; in these cases BIM is mentioned in generic terms, i.e. as a way of carrying out the service, but without this profile being the subject of a specific score when evaluating the offer, or qualification, as a minimum level for access to the tender [11] (Fig. 2).

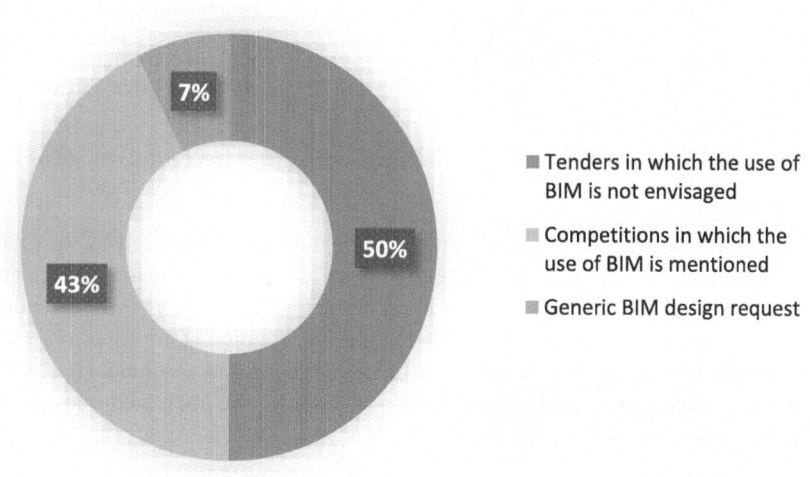

Fig. 2. Graph identifying the percentage of BIM use in tenders carried out in 2023 [11]

As can be seen from the graph, in 2023 only 14.8% of the total mention the use of BIM as a generic way, i.e. without attributing specific scores, but only considering it as a contractual element of the service, registering a decrease compared to 2022. The decrease in the percentage of the total number of notices with 'generic request for design in BIM' shows how contracting authorities are maturing, albeit slowly, a real awareness of the use of BIM, publishing, as a result, detailed notices and comprehensive annexes; in fact, in 29.4% of cases contracting authorities attached the specifications to the notice. Entering more specifically and considering, therefore, what is reported in the tender specifications, sub-classes were identified depending on the type of citation adopted that can be subdivided into two macro-categories: specific reference to BIM (BIM is cited independently regardless of the criteria), non-specific reference to BIM (BIM is cited together with other criteria). These sub-categories are: BIM process management, BIM software, experience of other projects already realised in BIM, and presence of BIM experts in the working group (Fig. 3).

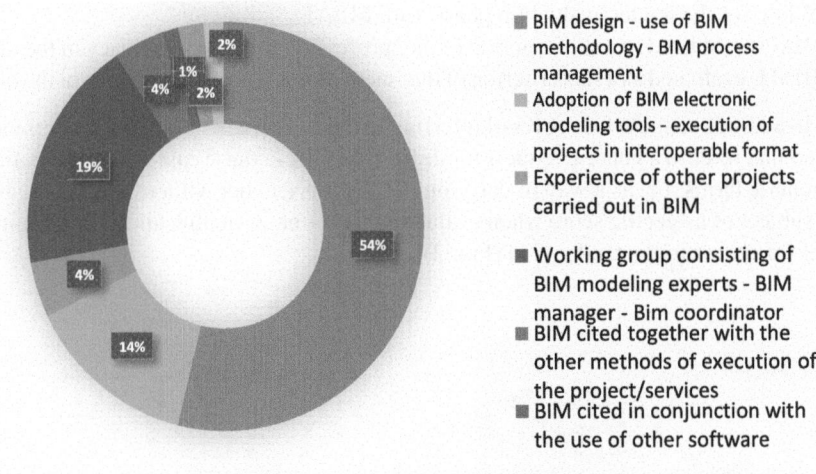

Fig. 3. Identification of subclasses in percentage of use in tenders carried out in 2023 [11]

At the conclusion of the analysis, the empirical evidence provided by the graphical representation below indicates that, although a real awareness of the importance and key role that BIM could play within public procurement is maturing, it is still evident that a proportion of public procurements retain the misconception that the adoption of BIM is merely the use of application tools or is primarily configured as a technical scoring factor in tenders, rather than as a methodological paradigm for the integrated management of the information life cycle of the work (Fig. 4).

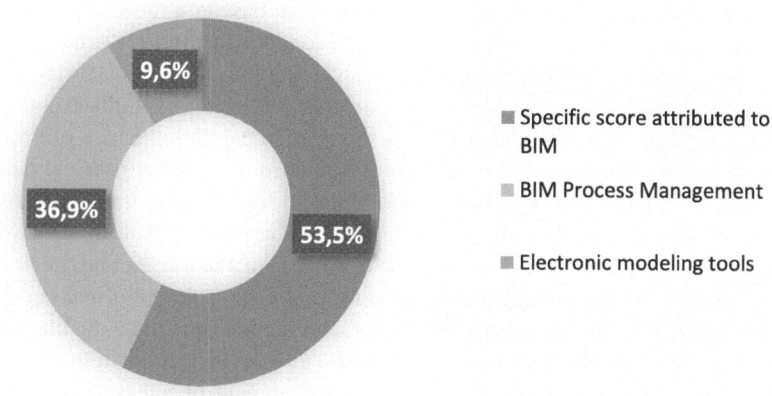

Fig. 4. Graph identifying in percentage the ways of using BIM in the tenders carried out in 2023 [11]

3 State of Art Analysis

The literature review reveals that eProcurement offers several advantages, including process automation that minimises the likelihood of human error, ensures faster delivery times and optimises overall operational efficiency. There is also increased competition among suppliers, as eProcurement systems provide a transparent platform that fosters competition for the award of contracts. Finally, eProcurement enables data-driven decision-making processes, allowing available information to be exploited to improve strategic choices. However, despite these obvious benefits, there are still significant difficulties related to the effective implementation of such procedures within public administrations. These problems are mainly related to inadequate infrastructure, insufficient staff training and resistance to change [13]. Furthermore, as discussed in the previous section, there is a lack of a real link between e-procurement procedures and BIM; although the latter is used as an information artefact in tenders, its transformative potential in the procurement process remains largely unexpressed, often relegating the model to a role of mere information support rather than a central and dynamic tool in the procurement process. As argued by Costa and Grilo [9], the application of BIM in the context of e-procurement is an enabling factor for the optimisation of e-procurement systems, allowing the adoption of more advanced approaches. Moreover, this synergy promotes the development of large electronic and interoperable networks that interact dynamically, enhancing the automation of many operational activities and improving information and knowledge management. In fact, BIM brings to e-procurement the possibility to build, within the various process activities, a more cooperative work between all specialities allowing a more efficient use of resources, a consequent decrease in time and errors due to lack of information and communication [9, 12] and an increase in transparency. With BIM-based e-procurement, information can actually travel more fluidly through the application of the various agents within procurement processes [9]. The synergy between e-procurement and BIM is, therefore, a strategic solution to address the main issues in public procurement. ANAC data, based on the European TED platform, show, in fact, that Italy has significantly longer procurement times than France, Germany and Spain, both for MEAT (279 days) and lowest price (195 days) contracts [14]. This slowness leads to high costs for both the public administration and businesses, negatively affecting the quality of services. In parallel, the lack of transparency in the procurement system fosters corruption, undermines competition and public trust. E-procurement supported by BIM methodologies digitises and traces the entire procurement lifecycle and, thus, thanks to the increased accessibility of information and the strengthening of stakeholder control, it can contribute to a more efficient, fairer and more accountable system by reducing time and ensuring clearer decision-making processes. In conclusion, the integration of BIM in e-procurement represents a qualitative leap for e-procurement in the AEC sector. It shifts the focus from the simple digital management of documents and procedures to the digital management of integrated and structured project information, thus achieving a more intelligent, accurate, transparent and collaborative procurement process, capable not only of optimising the tendering phase, but also of laying the foundations for a more efficient management of the entire life cycle of the built work.

4 Methodological Proposal and Case Study

In the context of a public procurement procedure aimed at awarding a contract for the provision of services and/or the execution of works for the realisation of a construction project, the award phase represents a crucial moment. In particular, the choice of the winning economic operator is based on the evaluation of the tenders submitted, through which the participants propose solutions to meet the needs expressed by the public administration. In the European context, public procurement legal regimes allow for two basic types of tender selection criteria, namely the lowest price criterion and the MEAT. In particular, according to the provisions of the 2014 EU Public Procurement Directives, the MEAT is the overriding criterion, although it should be noted that it is often possible to select the tender based on its price alone [15]. The decision to make MEAT the priority criterion is linked to the fact that it does not evaluate the offer only on the basis of its price, but emphasises best value for money by taking into account different aspects, such as quality, environmental and social factors, life-cycle costs and innovation [16]. MEAT, therefore, does not only consider price, but takes into account a plurality of elements, shifting the focus from mere cost minimisation to a broader and more articulated evaluation, which allows for an analysis of the economic operator's ability to meet the entity's specific needs. Given its characteristics, the MEAT requires an evaluation process that is based on clear, transparent and objective criteria, allowing for an objective comparison between the different offers and the selection of the one that offers the best overall value. In this regard, the precise definition of evaluation criteria and their weighting is a crucial aspect for the success of the MEAT: these criteria must be relevant to the subject matter of the contract, measurable and verifiable in order to ensure a transparent and objective evaluation. Consequently, the public authority is obliged to specify the evaluation criteria in detail in the tender notice, together with the method of tender evaluation based on these criteria. Otherwise, the lack of clear and precise criteria risks undermining the validity of the entire selection process, opening the way to possible disputes by economic operators participating in the tender procedure. Therefore, a correct application of the MEAT requires a strong commitment on the part of contracting authorities to define transparent and objective evaluation criteria and to conduct a rigorous and impartial evaluation process that is able to ensure that the final choice of tender is indeed the economically most advantageous one. In this context, BIM fits in as a potentially very useful tool to make this procedure faster and more transparent. By exploiting the parametric nature of BIM, the authors of this study identify the possibility of implementing the MEAT tender procedure in an automated manner. In particular, the parametric nature of BIM would allow the criteria defined by the contracting authority to be translated into parameters that can be modified and managed directly within the BIM model. To this end, a methodological proposal has been developed and is currently being validated through a case study simulating an "integrated tender" procedure (joint awarding of executive design and works), as defined by Italian law. The objective of this methodology is to parameterise those criteria that are objective and quantifiable, allowing the management of tender evaluation to be increasingly automated and transparent. However, it is emphasised that at this stage there is still the possibility of attaching supplementary supporting documentation through which the economic operator can submit its offer relating to those criteria that cannot be parameterised and which therefore still require an ad hoc evaluation by the examining commission. By way of example, the performance of systems or even thermal, acoustic and energy performance of the building envelope can be counted among the parameterisable criteria (Table 1.). On the contrary, solutions proposed by tradesmen to deal with the logistical criticalities inherent in site management, particularly in complex and constrained urban contexts such as historic city centres, are examples of evaluation elements which, at present, hardly lend themselves to parameterisation.

The proposed methodological framework, which entails the integration of Building Information Modelling (BIM) within the public procurement process, is structured according to a workflow illustrated in Fig. 5. Specifically, the methodology is articulated into five phases and involves two categories of stakeholders: the contracting authority, responsible for drafting and publishing the tender notice as well as evaluating the submitted proposals, and the economic operators, who participate in the tender by submitting their bids.

Phase I: Creation of the BIM Model. This phase, entirely under the responsibility of the contracting authority, entails the digitalisation of the procurement object. The public administration undertakes the development of a parametric BIM model of the building, consistent with the content of the previously developed technical and economic feasibility project. The BIM model must be produced or converted into an open format such as IFC, in order to ensure interoperability with various BIM software solutions. This facilitates communication within the design team and enables a broad range of economic operators to participate, regardless of the technological tools they employ. It is important to highlight that this digitalisation phase includes the translation of evaluation criteria and sub-criteria—intended for use in the tendering process—into parameters and properties of the BIM model elements.

Table 1. Example of parameterizable criteria.

Criterion	Description	Translation of the criterion into parameters
Technological solutions for windows and doors	Improvement proposals aimed at improving window and door frames, with reference to thermal-acoustic and environmental characteristics	Thermal transmittance of glass Thermal transmittance of the frame Thermal transmittance of the window Solar factor Air permeability Sound absorbing power
Technological solutions for insulating materials and wall finishes	Proposals aimed at improving insulating and finishing materials, in relation to their technical, energy and environmental characteristics	Thermal conductivity Thermal transmittance Phase shift and attenuation factor Sound absorbing power

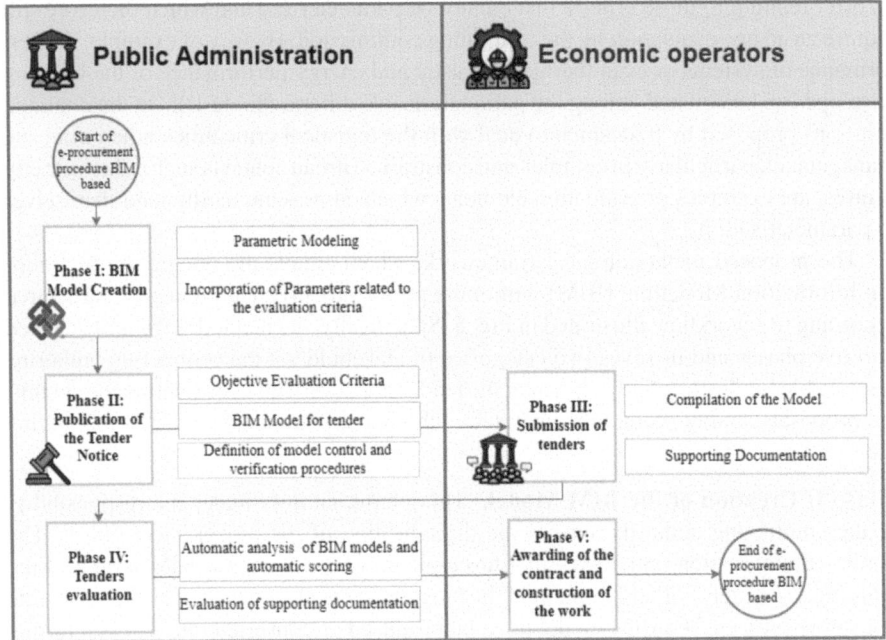

Fig. 5. Workflow of the methodological proposal – public e-procurement with MEAT award criterion, BIM-supported procedure.

Phase II: Drafting and Publication of the Tender Notice. In this phase, the public administration formalises and publishes the requirements and procedures governing the procurement process. Among the documents provided to the economic operators are: the information specification, the bid evaluation matrix, and the BIM model. The information specification outlines the information requirements of the BIM model and defines the methodologies that the contracting authority intends to employ to verify the compliance and quality of the models submitted by the bidders.

The evaluation matrix must include the criteria and sub-criteria, along with the corresponding scores, that the contracting authority plans to adopt for assessing the bids. It is essential that the selection of these criteria prioritises quantifiable and measurable aspects, avoiding subjective or ambiguous elements. An innovative aspect of this methodological proposal lies in the use of the BIM model as part of the tender documentation: the model created by the contracting authority is provided to all competitors, ensuring that all economic operators begin with the same level of information and allowing each to develop their proposals based on a shared reference model.

Phase III: Submission of Bids. In this phase, economic operators translate their proposals into data within the provided BIM model. Participating firms complete the editable parameters within the model, entering information related to their technical offers. It is crucial at this stage to ensure that the model is completed in accordance with the standards set out in the information specification. Moreover, bidders are required to supplement the BIM model with supporting technical documentation. This documentation serves both to justify and explain the proposed technical solutions implemented within the model, and to provide information related to aspects of the proposal that, by their nature, cannot be directly parameterised within the BIM environment.

Phase IV: Evaluation of Bids. This phase—traditionally time-consuming and resource-intensive, and often subject to the subjectivity of the evaluation committee—is significantly simplified and made more transparent through the use of BIM. The evaluation committee is tasked with verifying that the BIM models submitted by the bidders comply with the requirements outlined in the information specification, ensuring adherence to the standards defined by the contracting authority. In particular, using specific tools with Model Checking capabilities, the committee assesses the consistency and completeness of the information contained in the BIM models, identifying any errors, inconsistencies or omissions. At this stage, dedicated software is employed to automatically assign scores based on the values of predefined parameters, thereby ensuring an objective and transparent evaluation process and reducing the risk of errors or partiality. In this way, the BIM model becomes a key instrument in the tender procedure for the assessment of bids.

Phase V: Contract Award and Execution of the Works. The award of the contract to the economic operator achieving the highest score marks the beginning of the execution phase. In the case of integrated procurement, this includes both the detailed design and the actual construction of the project. It is important to note that the BIM methodology continues to play a crucial role during the construction phase, serving as a tool for the management of monitoring information. It allows for the tracking of changes, the management of design variations, and the monitoring of costs and timelines.

5   Conclusions and Future Development

The public procurement sector is faced with significant challenges such as excessively long procurement times and lack of transparency in decision-making processes, therefore, a change is needed to modify the current instruments and push towards the adoption of innovative technologies and methodologies. The methodological proposal presented here, which sees the interaction between BIM and e-procurement, stands as a concrete answer to the problems encountered. However, the success of this integration depends on accurate implementation and a deep understanding of the potential offered by each technology; it is essential to precisely identify the evaluation criteria, which can be very variable and range from purely technical aspects (such as the building's energy performance and the characteristics of the materials used) to more complex elements (such as environmental sustainability and technological innovation), and parameterise them so that they can be managed within the model. Once parameterisable criteria have been defined, it is necessary to develop automated techniques for reading, checking and scoring them. In this context, current traditional Model Checking systems, while remaining useful for verifying the conformity of the BIM model, may prove insufficient to handle the complexity and variety of information to be evaluated. This may require the use of advanced programming tools, such as Python, which, due to its flexibility and powerful data analysis libraries, can be used to automatically extract relevant information from the BIM model and transform it into structured data, and artificial intelligence and machine learning techniques, which allow for analysing large amounts of data from tenders by identifying significant anomalies potentially invisible to traditional manual analysis. Furthermore, machine learning algorithms could be trained to automatically evaluate bids by reducing the risk of errors and subjective influences. Therefore, in order to validate the methodological proposal and demonstrate its effectiveness, the authors of the article propose to develop a series of case studies on real projects in order to test the integration of BIM, e-procurement and advanced analysis technologies in real-life contexts, so as to identify strengths and weaknesses of the methodology. Particular attention will be paid to the identification of the most suitable parameterizable criteria for the automated evaluation of tenders and to the development of automated analysis and scoring techniques. The expected impact is a reduction in awarding times, an increase in transparency and the guarantee of higher quality of works and services, thus offering concrete benefits for public administration and thus, demonstrating a transformation in public procurement with this methodology.

References

1. Issa, R.R.A., Flood, I., Caglasin, G.: A survey of e-business implementation in the US construction industry. ITcon 8, 15–28 (2003). https://www.itcon.org/2003/2
2. Grilo, A., Jardim-Goncalves, R.: Challenging electronic procurement in the AEC sector: BIM-based integrated perspective. Autom. Constr. 20, 107–114 (2011). https://doi.org/10.1016/j.autcon.2010.09.008
3. Chan, A.P.C., Owusu, E.K.: Evolution of electronic procurement: contemporary review of adoption and implementation strategies. Buildings 12, 198 (2022). https://doi.org/10.3390/buildings12020198

4. Owusu, E.K., Chan, A.P., Ameyaw, E.: Toward a cleaner project procurement: Evaluation of construction projects' vulnerability to corruption in developing countries. J. Clean. Prod. **216**, 394–407 (2019). https://doi.org/10.1016/j.jclepro.2019.01.124
5. Ruparathna, R., Hewage, K.: Sustainable procurement in the Canadian construction industry: current practices, drivers and opportunities. J. Clean. Prod. **109**, 305–314 (2015). https://doi.org/10.1016/j.jclepro.2015.07.007
6. Subramaniam, C., Shaw, M.: The effects of process characteristics on the value of B2B e-procurement, Information Technology and Management, pp. 161–180. Khuver Academic Publishers (2004). https://doi.org/10.1023/B:ITEM.0000008080.17926.2b
7. de Boer, L., Harink, J.H.A. Heijboer, G.J.: A model for assessing the impact of electronic procurement forms. In: Proceedings of the 10th International Annual IPSERA Conference, 8 - 11 April 2001, pp. 119–130. Jonkoping, Sweden (2001)
8. Knudsen, D.: Aligning corporate strategy, procurement strategy and e-procurement tools. Int. J. Phys. Distrib. Logist. Manag. **33**, 720–734 (2003)
9. Costa, A.A.; Grilo, A.: BIM-based e-procurement: An innovative approach to construction e-procurement. Sci. World J. 1–15 (2015)
10. Vaidya, K., Sajeev, A.M., Callendar, G.: Critical factors that influence e-procurement implementation success in the public sector. J. Public Procure. **6**, 70–99 (2006)
11. Report OICE sulla digitalizzazione e sulle gare BIM 2023, OICE. https://www.oice.it/849794/2024-oice-7-rapporto-sulla-digitalizzazione-e-gare-bim
12. Grilo, A., Jardim-Goncalves, R.: Value proposition on interoperability of BIM and collaborative working environments. Autom. Construct. **19**(5), 522–530 (2010). https://doi.org/10.1016/j.autcon.2009.11.003
13. Egwim, P., Dike, B., Nmecha, M.: Adapting the e-procurement process from the private and public sector: a comprehensive overview, vol. 1, pp. 1–15. https://doi.org/10.5281/zenodo.13929696
14. Analisi dei tempi di aggiudicazione degli appalti in Italia e in Europa sulla base dei dati TED, ANAC. https://www.anticorruzione.it/-/analisi-dei-tempi-di-aggiudicazione-degli-appalti-in-italia-e-in-europa-sulla-base-dei-dati-ted-1-ottobre-2024
15. Sebastian, B., Jan, G., Monika, P., Wojciech, S.: The most economically advantageous tender in the public procurement system in the european union. In: Bilgin, M., Danis, H., Karabulut, G., Gözgor, G. (eds.) Eurasian Economic Perspectives. Eurasian Studies in Business and Economics, vol. 12/1. Springer, Cham (2020). https://doi.org/10.1007/978-3-030-35040-6_26
16. PUBLIC PROCUREMENT CONTRACTS. Fact Sheets on the European Union (2025). www.europarl.europa.eu/factsheets/en

A Place-Based Multi-sectoral Project for the Definition of Indicators and Thresholds to Support Sustainable Mobility Policies in Italian Cities

Francesco Alberti[1] ⓘ, Giacomo Rossi[1] ⓘ, Giovanna Acampa[1] ⓘ,
and Alessio Pino[2](✉) ⓘ

[1] University of Florence, Via P.A. Micheli 2, 50129 Florence, Italy
[2] University of Enna "Kore", Cittadella Universitaria, 94100 Enna, Italy
alessio.pino@unikorestudent.it

Abstract. This paper describes the background, methodology, and expected outcomes of the URGET VADEMECUM 2030–2050 Research Project of National Interest (PRIN, Progetto di Ricerca di Interesse Nazionale), funded by the Italian Ministry of University and Research in the framework of the Italian National Recovery and Resilience Plan (NRRP) and the Next Generation Europe fund. The project addresses the issue of urban transition towards carbon neutrality, the pivot of the European Green Deal program, by proposing an innovative assessment procedure to support sustainable urban mobility policies in Italy, which is characterized by the highest car-dependency rate among major European countries, following a place-based approach. The proposed step-by-step procedure combines different analysis and evaluation methodologies, i.e., Threshold Theory, Cluster Analysis, and Multi-Criteria Analysis, re-interpreted in an up-to-date way to provide structured guidance for public authorities to select the most efficient and cost-effective measure packages in terms of suitable technologies, transport policies, urban planning, and regulatory issues, fitting to places' peculiar characteristics.

As the first step of the procedure, a set of indicators and related thresholds, processed using GIS tools, are meant to define the spatial variables that can affect urban mobility in that specific context, narrowing down the number of viable transport modes, innovative technologies and services, to be subjected to the subsequent evaluation steps.

Keywords: sustainable mobility · indicators · threshold theory

1 Introduction

Mobility is one of the fields of technological innovation that have most affected the evolution of settlement systems in close relation to the availability of low-cost energy sources. From the mid-19th century to the end of the 20th, the two great revolutions in the field of transportation - the rail-transit revolution and the automobile revolution – have allowed a seemingly limitless process of urban growth in most industrialized regions.

O. Gervasi et al. (Eds.): ICCSA 2025 Workshops, LNCS 15891, pp. 78–89, 2026.
https://doi.org/10.1007/978-3-031-97617-9_6

In recent decades, the process has expanded at an increasingly frantic pace in emerging countries. The figures of global urbanization are well-known: the rate of urban population will reach approx. 70% of 9,2 billion people in 2050; it was 36% of 3,7 billion in 1970 and 46,5% of 6,1 billion in 2000 [1].

In the meantime, a new "wave of innovation" [2] has taken off, pushed by the need for sustainability and the double sword of Damocles of climate change and oil depletion. In detail, they derive from opposite trends related to the use of fossil fuels, which still cover more than 90% of the total energy needs in the transport sector: on the one hand, the risk of natural disasters due to the concentration of greenhouse gases (GHGs) in the atmosphere; on the other hand, that of a global recession, due to the rising cost of fuels as the joint effect of a steady increase in demand and the depletion of primary source [3]. In the fight against global threats, which require energy diversification and the search for a balance between consumption and resources, the questions raised by the issue of transport in cities differ from the past. Now, we are trying to understand whether and how leveraging mobility governance through the combination of technological innovation, planning, and management can allow for meeting the objective set by the Paris Agreement (2015): that is, to limit the global temperature increase at the end of this century "well below" 2 °C above pre-industrial levels (and preferably restrict the rise to 1.5 °C), shorting the 23% of global CO2 emissions from fuel combustion accounted for by the transportation sector (74% of which generated by road transport).

From this perspective, mobility planning appears to be one of the main tools available to the public sector to set up urban sustainability policies, opposite to how traffic congestion caused by unrestrained development of private motorization at the detriment of other transport modes has been a source of functional imbalance and environmental degradation in urban areas in all industrialized regions of the planet.

This issue significantly affects all three "pillars" of sustainable development – Environment, Economy, and Social cohesion [4]. Moreover, it shows most evidently their mutual conflict potential within urban and metropolitan contexts, as shown in Table 1.

Table 1. Transportation Impacts on Sustainability [4]

Economic	Social	Environmental
Traffic congestion	Inequity of impacts	Air pollution
Mobility barriers	Disadvantages in mobility	Climate change
Vehicular accidents	Impacts on human health	Loss of habitats
Transportation facility costs	Community cohesion	Water pollution
Consumer transportation costs	Community livability	Hydrologic impacts
Depletion of non-renewable resources	Aesthetics	Noise pollution

Moreover, the role of transport is implied in the achievement of most of the 17 Sustainable Development Goals of the UN Agenda 2030 and directly or indirectly mainstreamed into 12 targets of 8 SDGs (Fig. 1), as expressly specified by the High-level

Political Forum on Sustainable Development (HLPF), the UN central platform for the follow-up of the Agenda [5].

The European Union addresses the aim to turn mobility into a lever of urban sustainability in many documents, directives, and funding programs (e.g., Horizon 2020 Work program "Mobility for Growth" and Horizon Europe's Cluster 5 "Climate, Energy, and Mobility) and initiatives (e.g., URBACT, CIVITAS, ELTIS, EPOMM, etc.).

In 2011, with the publication of the White Paper *Roadmap to a Single European Transport Area. Towards a competitive and resource-efficient transport system*, the European Commission set the goal for the Member Countries to halve the use of conventionally fuelled cars in cities by 2030 and phase them out by 2050.

Two years later, the *Urban Mobility Package* was adopted by the EU to stimulate a shift towards sustainable transport modes, such as walking, cycling, and public transport, and new patterns for car use and ownership, using Sustainable Urban Mobility Plans (SUMP) as a tool for addressing significant issues such as congestion, air/noise pollution, climate change, road accidents, waste of public space and the integration of new mobility services [6].

The transition of urban mobility from the car-dominant model to a multimodal and innovative model is also one of the priorities set by the European Urban Agenda (2016).

The aim of achieving net-zero GHG emissions from human activities in the EU by 2050 was first envisaged in the EC Communication *A clean planet for all: strategic long-term vision for a prosperous, modern, competitive and climate-neutral economy by 2050* (2018) and finally established as a pivot of the European Green Deal, launched in December 2019 by the Von der Layen Commission. For the transport field, it implies a reduction of 90% of emissions by 2050.

In this framework, in December 2020, the EC adopted the *Sustainable and Smart Mobility Strategy – putting European transport on track for the future* (SSMS), calling for an acceleration of the processes already underway, so far in a piecemeal fashion, for "the decarbonization and modernization of the entire transport and mobility system."

Consistently, sustainable mobility is one of the assets of the *Next Generation Europe* program for the allocation of 'recovery and resilience' funding in response to the crisis caused by the COVID-19 pandemic.

2   The Research Project: URGET VADEMECUM 2030–50

2.1   A Support to Italy's "Mobility Shift"

Among the major European countries, Italy has the highest motorization rate (62 vehicles per 100 inhabitants, 20% more than the EU average). 44 Mio of the 50 Mio vehicles in circulation are cars and motorbikes, and only 100,000 (i.e., less than 1% of the total amount) are buses [7].

In 2019, 22 million people traveled to work and 11 million to school daily. Data on Italy's 14 metropolitan cities show that during the pandemic, the rate of trips made by public transport halved compared to the previous period (from 10.8% to 5.4%); the car fell just a few points short (from 62.5% to 59%), while soft mobility (including micro-electric mobility) rose from 24.1% to 32.7% [8]. The pandemic also highlighted the limits and alternatives of urban mobility, showing the well-being potential of less urbanized areas [9], characterized by fewer flows and narrow-scope mobility [10].

Since 2011, when national guidelines for the development of SUMPs (Sustainable Urban Mobility Plans) were introduced following the European guidelines, 196 SUMPs have been initiated by individual Municipalities above 100,000 inhabitants, Unions of Municipalities, Provinces, and Metropolitan Cities, financed mainly by a specific state fund. However, only 79 are already operational.

The UE policies to support the transition to cleaner, greener and smarter mobility, which have a cornerstone in the "SUMP concept," as stressed in The New EU Urban Mobility Framework adopted in 2021 following the SSMS, are the references of a research project led by an interdisciplinary pool from the Universities of Florence, Naples "Federico II," and Enna "Kore" (Sicily) and the Polytechnic University of Turin, namely URGET VADEMECUM 2030–50 ("URban de-pollution and de-carbonisation from emissions GEnerated by Transport systems: eVAluation of DEdicated Methodologies, technologies and EConomic thresholds for an Unprecedented Mobility at 2030–50", here shortened to UV30–50). The project was acknowledged as a Research Project of National Interest (PRIN, Progetto di Ricerca di Interesse Nazionale) by the Italian Ministry of University and Research and funded with NRRP (National Recovery and Resilience Plan from the Next Generation EU program.

The outcomes of the project, currently in the middle of its overall development, are intended to influence and support decision-making as far as urban transport and related urban planning choices are concerned, allowing for the selection of the most efficient and cost-effective urban mobility scenarios tailored to the specific urban context, among the different available combinations of policies and measures aimed at reducing transport-related environmental and climate impacts.

2.2 Research Background

A further reference point of the UV30-50 project is the *Global Macro-Roadmap to Decarbonise the Transport Sector*, launched at the 22nd Conference of Parties in Marrakech (2016) by the platform Paris Process on Mobility and Climate. The roadmap identifies a balanced package of actions according to the so-called A-S-I approach, which combines Avoid (reduce unnecessary travel, e.g., through land use planning, logistics redesign, and remote services), Shift (shift goods and people to the most efficient and sustainable modes), and Improve (improve the environmental performance of energy fuels and vehicles, co-modality, and transport management) [11].

A significant precedent of the approach underlying the research project is represented by the study conducted by VIBAT (Visioning and Backcasting for Transport Policy) in London in 2007–2009. The study reviewed about 150 policy interventions for reducing transport-related CO_2 emissions. It grouped them into 12 policy packages (including Low-emission vehicles, Alternative fuels, Pricing regimes, Public transport, Walking and cycling, Urban planning, ICT, etc.). The study assumes that applying a range of policy packages, clustered as scenarios, can meet the gap between business-as-usual projections and strategic targets [12].

A preliminary task of the UV30-50 project is to define a package of A-S-I policy interventions compliant with the Italian context. The ordered checklist of the key items to be considered is reported below.

1) To reduce the dependence on transport to meet people's everyday needs (work, education, healthcare, shopping, recreation, etc.).
   Fields of action:

   – Development of motionless communication and smart working to a reasonable extent; provision of public remote and home services.
   – Balanced land-use planning aimed at reducing people's mobility due to the lack of basic services and facilities, incl. leisure opportunities, close to the residence.

2) To reduce the strong dependence on private motorized transport for traveling within the urban/metropolitan area by promoting the shift to soft mobility (walking and cycling, guaranteeing safety).
   Fields of action:

   – Creating safe pedestrian networks within and among the urban neighborhoods and districts, including sidewalk improvements, increased road crossings, walkable public spaces, parks, greenways, etc.
   – Creation of hierarchical, well-equipped cycling networks to effectively connect the main urban zones and magnets, incl. fast inter-municipal links.

3) To reduce car dependence on motorized displacements.
   Fields of action:

   – Provision of efficient and cost-effective modal alternatives to meet different mobility-related needs, including commuting and random mobility, such as:
     i. Alternative options to private vehicles: rail, metro, and road public transport; shared mobility; park & plug (in/out) & ride solutions; MaaS.
     ii. Alternative options for private vehicles: micro-and light-mobility vehicles.
   – Provision of widespread and user-friendly points of interchange between different transport modes.
   – Measures to limit car use (e.g., traffic-restricted zones, parking, road pricing, etc.)

4) To reduce the dependence on crude oil for the propulsion of transport systems.
   Fields of action:

   – Migration toward the electrification of presently un-electrified transport modes and vehicles (using as much electricity from renewable sources as possible), including:
     i. Public road transport
     ii. Private road transport
     iii. Urban logistics
   – Fostering the take-up of further alternative fuels and energy carriers (e.g., fuel cells).

5) Mitigate/compensate for the local pollution and GHG emissions generated by transport systems at the different stages of the transition, including residual non-compressible emissions.

Fields of action:

- Monitoring and management of the local aspects of transport-related emissions - i.e.
  i. Combustion emissions by motor vehicles.
  ii. Further emissions derived from the wear of brakes and tires, as well as from the dust raised by rolling and given the wear of paving.
- Monitoring and management of the local aspects of transport-related pollution - i.e.,
  i. Temperature inversion and stack effects in urban environments concerning the pollution of the surrounding areas.
  ii. Pollutants' accumulation from motorways, urban rings, roads, etc.
- Creation or improvement of green infrastructures aimed at CO_2 sequestration and air purification.

The analysis must also consider the forthcoming EU initiatives announced in the SSMS, including a strategic roll-out plan for deploying alternative fuel infrastructure and subsidies for users to make more sustainable transport choices.

In the dynamic context of global change, it is also essential to record in real-time post-pandemic implications for mobility in European urban areas. The infection acted as an accelerator for many processes, like the diffusion of smart working, e-commerce, and other digital services, which can result in, or be addressed to, a permanent reduction of daily transport demand. Moreover, while public transport demonstrated its lack of resilience in the face of the crisis, other modes, like cycling and light electric vehicles, have made progress, along with the concept of the "15-min city" [13], which is expected to have a significant influence on urban and mobility planning in the next future. The sudden outbreak of the Russian-Ukrainian crisis, with its immediate repercussions on energy costs, has been a further factor of uncertainty; similar geopolitical situations can shape the context of mobility.

2.3 Essential Methodological Structure of UV30–50

The research project will develop an innovative assessment methodology aimed at defining tailor-made, place-based, as well as technologically oriented solutions to foster the transition to sustainable mobility in Italian cities and towns.

A novel approach to the Threshold Theory [14] and a modern application of Multi-Criteria Analysis (MCA) [15, 16] will be put in sequence for analyzing and assessing alternative scenarios, integrating modal and technological options.

A further step is to join the concept of threshold with the clustering methodology [17]. Cluster analysis is adopted for processing data when no assumption is made about their mutual relationships. In this case, clusters refer to possible combinations of strategic actions in the field of urban mobility to achieve the goal of de-carbonization and de-pollution while optimizing costs.

2.4 Indicators and Thresholds

The research's core is identifying significant indicators and thresholds to be applied in the construction of transitional and/or alternative climate-neutral and clean mobility scenarios. The wide range of options theoretically available to promote transition according to the A-S-I framework has to pass the scrutiny of actual operating conditions, which depend on a) spatial settings, b) the limits, both operational and economic, of the various transport options, along with the market take-up and implementation of new technologies and innovative solutions in the transport sector, and c) the costs and availability of resources.

a) The first selection of all potential policy packages depends on the structural features of the site, among which morphological features (i.e., size, form, and structure of the urban area) and land-use-related parameters (e.g., population, density, and distribution of land use) are those that most affect mobility. By further developing GIS-based applications, already tested by the research unit of the University of Florence, spatial thresholds will be derived from the analysis of both physical (e.g., road widths) and accessibility parameters (e.g., network distances from urban attractors) that condition the use of transport infrastructure.

   Furthermore, threshold values for ecosystem services will be explored to assess the potential of green areas within and around the urban area to compensate for residual CO_2 emissions from different urban transport scenarios.

b) The second level of selection will depend on transport issues, to which thresholds can be related, on the one hand, to the viable transport modes and, on the other hand, to the performances of new transport technologies and solutions, with particular regard to the transition to electric vehicles.

   After that, different scenarios addressed to achieve carbon neutrality in urban mobility will be obtained by clustering data from real travels, the implementation of new ITS (e.g., electrical geofencing, MaaS), and reinterpreted random utility models.

c) The range of urban mobility scenarios compliant with the place, resulting from the previous assessing stages, will pass through the further sieve of cost analysis. Thresholds will refer to the additional costs (per user) needed for implementing each alternative scenario, which must either be spent before the interventions or be spread over a period.

   After a test phase of the procedure in selected cities representative of different sizes and complexity levels of Italian urban settlements, the final stage of the proposed methodology focuses on Multicriteria Analysis. This is structured in the following steps: i) selection of the alternative sustainable mobility scenarios (resulting from thresholds and cluster analysis); ii) definition of judgment criteria; iii) analysis of the impacts on the alternative mobility scenarios; iv) assessment of the actions' impacts on each selected criteria; v) aggregation of judgments; 6) choice of the preferred/optimal sustainable mobility scenario(s) to orient administrations' choices in achieving the best results with the minimal resource allocation [18].

A Focus on Spatial Indicators. One of the most innovative aspects of the methodology delivered by UV30–50 is the importance acknowledged of spatial variables, usually overlooked by transport planning, in selecting alternative options to be considered in building local strategies for decarbonized and unpolluted urban mobility.

The specific objective of the research for the first stage of the proposed selective procedure is to articulate, within a nested structure, a set of indicators and related thresholds, both by systemizing indicators already used in urban studies and spatial planning and by defining new ones, to assess the propensity and potential of a given urban system to meet the targets of overall decrease, modal differentiation, and improved environmental performance of internal motorized mobility, consistent with the aforementioned A-S-I framework.

There is empirical and scientific evidence that low-density dispersed urban patterns and rigid land-use zoning generate car dependency, higher energy consumption, and emissions from transport. In contrast, compact mixed-use urban patterns are more likely to reduce people's dependence on transport for their daily needs and encourage sustainable mobility [19, 20]. Monocentric or polycentric settlement patterns may also influence the choice of different public transport systems according to the geometric features of the road network. Instead, the presence of blue-green corridors may favor or discourage, depending on the acclivity of the terrain or the availability of crossing points, the creation of bicycle routes, whether isolated or integrated into a network. In turn, the connectivity and attractiveness of pedestrian systems are strongly conditioned by the characteristics of urban fabrics and streets, the location of public spaces and facilities, the urban landscape, the microclimate of streets, etc.

A non-exhaustive list of spatial variables to be included in the assessment is given below in Table 2. The definition of relevant indicators, significant combinations, and threshold values is one of the expected outcomes of UV30-50.

a) The first selection of all potential policy packages depends on the structural features of the site, among which morphological features (i.e., size, form, and structure of the urban area) and land-use-related parameters (e.g., population, density, and distribution of land use) are those that most affect mobility. By further developing GIS-based applications, already tested by the research unit of the University of Florence, spatial thresholds will be derived from the analysis of both physical (e.g., road widths) and accessibility parameters (e.g., network distances from urban attractors) that condition the use of transport infrastructure.

   Furthermore, threshold values for ecosystem services will be explored to assess the potential of green areas within and around the urban area to compensate for residual CO_2 emissions from different urban transport scenarios.

b) The second level of selection will depend on transport issues, to which thresholds can be related, on the one hand, to the viable transport modes and, on the other hand, to the performances of new transport technologies and solutions, with particular regard to the transition to electric vehicles.

   After that, different scenarios addressed to achieve carbon neutrality in urban mobility will be obtained by clustering data from real travels, the implementation of new ITS (e.g., electrical geofencing, MaaS), and reinterpreted random utility models.

c) The range of urban mobility scenarios compliant with the place, resulting from the previous assessing stages, will pass through the further sieve of cost analysis. Thresholds will refer to the additional costs (per user) needed for implementing each alternative scenario, which must either be spent before the interventions or be spread over a period.

The procedure will be tested in selected cities with different sizes and complexity levels to represent the whole range of Italian urban settlements. Then, the final stage of the proposed methodology focuses on Multicriteria Analysis. This is structured into the following steps: i) selection of the alternative sustainable mobility scenarios (resulting from thresholds and cluster analysis); ii) definition of judgment criteria; iii) analysis of the impacts on the alternative mobility scenarios; iv) assessment of the actions' impacts on each selected criteria; v) aggregation of judgments; 6) choice of the preferred/optimal sustainable mobility scenario(s).

Table 2. Spatial variables in cities affecting urban mobility and possible indicators.

City form, demography and density	Land features	Urban fabric features
Population density and level of urbanization	Land morphology (acclivity)	Building and population density
Settlement's monocentric or polycentric pattern	Presence of natural barriers and characteristics of crossing points	Classification of specialized (non-residential) fabrics and monofunctional compounds
Compactness/fragmentation/urban sprawl	Agricultural and natural areas	Size and morphology of urban blocks
Demography dynamics		Building coverage
		Mixed uses
		Historic urban fabric
Land use	Transport network geometry	Urban microclimate
Land use and urban land use	Existing road and transport infrastructure density and classification	Building dimensional ratio (between buildings' height and street width)
Classification and distribution of public open space	Street density	Location of urban heat islands
Classification of urban attractors and centralities	Variability of road cross-sections	Urban green areas (for climate mitigation and CO_2 sequestration)
Multimodal accessibility to urban attractors	Space-syntax analysis [21] (integration and connectivity of street and road networks)	

Further indicators refer to topical concepts in urban studies focusing on public transport and soft mobility as the keys to a paradigm shift in spatial planning to achieve sustainable and resilient cities: Transit-oriented development [22], Urban walkability [23, 24] and bikeability [25] and the City of Proximity [26], as synthesized in Table 3.

Table 3. New urban concept pivoted on sustainable mobility and related indicators

Transit-oriented development	Walkability/bikeability	City of proximity
Multimodal accessibility of railway nodes	Pedestrian and bicycle accessibility to places and facilities	Urban and neighborhood centralities
Place/Node Analysis [27]	Continuity/legibility of networks	Classification and mapping of local facilities
TOD Index [28]	Integration of paths / public spaces	Accessibility to public spaces and facilities within a 15-min walk or 5-min bike ride
	Presence of traffic-restricted / pedestrian areas	
	Greenways	

GIS platforms and plug-ins are the tools for mapping, analyzing, and visualizing all indicators, the complexity of which is closely related to the availability and quality of geospatial data.

3   Conclusions

The methodology addressed by the UV30-50 research project, based on the combination of consolidated evaluation tools that are re-interpreted in an up-to-date way, is intended to support decision-making and fund-raising by selecting and calibrating different measures and policy packages to reduce/eliminate transport-related pollution and GHG emissions.

The research will be carried out with the involvement of four Municipalities, representative of different sizes and complexity levels of Italian urban areas, as testing benches of the proposed methodology: namely, Turin, Siena, Catania, and Giugliano in the Metropolitan City of Naples. For each of them, example evaluations will be carried out concerning spatial, transport, and economic aspects by applying the thresholds previously defined. The application of the procedure will provide different alternative/transitional scenarios to be subjected to a Multi-Criteria Analysis to select the optimal one. The outcomes from the test phase will be analyzed and integrated to readjust and optimize the methodology, also considering external factors that could positively or negatively affect its application (regulations, socio-economic aspects, possible future crises, etc.). The completion of the research is expected by the end of 2025.

References

1. United Nations, World Urbanization Prospects: the 2009 Revision. http://esa.un.org/unpd/wup/index.htm. Accessed 7 Feb 2024
2. Hargroves, K., Smith, M.: The Natural Advantages of Nations: Business Opportunities, Innovation and Governance in the 21st Century. Earthscan (2005)

3. Newman, P., Beatley, T., Boyer, H.: Resilient cities: responding to peak oil and climate change. Island Press, Washington (2009)
4. VTPI, Victoria Transport Policy Institute: Online Transport Demand Management (TDM) Encyclopedia (2017). http://www.vtpi.org/tdm/tdm67.htm. Accessed 7 Feb 2024
5. You, A., Peet, K., Medimorec, N., Dalkmann, H.: Showcasing the critical role of the transport sector to achieve the Sustainable Development Goals. UN, High-level Political Forum on Sustainable Development (2018)
6. Rupprecht Consult (ed.): Guidelines for Developing and Implementing a Sustainable Urban Mobility Plan, Second Edition. https://urban-mobility-observatory.transport.ec.europa.eu/document/download/87adaa0c-cd13-4ce0-9a15-d138ea31bb2c_en?filename=sump_guidelines_2019_second%20edition.pdf. Accessed 2 Feb 2024
7. ISTAT Database on Italian Vehicle Fleet. http://dati.istat.it/Index.aspx?DataSetCode=DCIS_VEICOLIPRA. Accessed 7 Feb 2024
8. ISFORT: 19° rapporto sulla mobilità degli italiani, CNEL (2022)
9. Acampa, G., Pino, A.: Village repopulation: analysis of extra-economic indicators to evaluate and valorise social generativity in ecovillages. In: Gervasi, O., Murgante, B., Misra, S., et al. (eds.) Networks, Markets, and People: Proceedings of the 2024 International Conference on Computational Science and Its Applications – ICCSA 2024, LNCS, vol. 14300, pp. 376–385. Springer, Cham (2024). https://doi.org/10.1007/978-3-031-74679-6_25
10. Acampa, G., Pino, A.: Filling the old with new life. Application of original indicators for evaluating ecovillages as village repopulation initiatives. Aestimum **85**, 73–86 (2024)
11. Dalkmann, H., Brannigan, C.: Transport and climate change, module 5e, sustainable transport, a sourcebook for policy-makers in developing cities. GTZ global. Ministry for Economic Cooperation and Development, Federal Eschborn, Germany (2007)
12. Hickman, R., Banister, D.: Transport, climate change and the city. Routledge (2015).
13. Moreno, C., Allam, Z., Chabaud, D., Gall, C., Pratlong, F.: Introducing the "15-Minute City": sustainability, resilience and place identity in future post-pandemic cities. Smart Cities **4**(1), 93–111 (2021)
14. Malisz, B.: Teoria Progow (Threshold Theory). Biuletyn IUA, 16 (1963)
15. Beria, P., Maltese, I., Mariotti, I.: Multicriteria versus Cost Benefit Analysis: a comparative perspective in the assessment of sustainable mobility. Eur. Transp. Res. Rev. **4**, 137–152 (2012)
16. Battisti, F.: ELECTRE III for strategic environmental assessment: a "phantom" approach. Sustainability **14**(10), 6221 (2022)
17. Zhang, G., Wang, Z.: Correlation degree and clustering analysis-based alarm threshold optimization. Processes **10**(2), 224 (2022)
18. Acampa, G., Pino, A.: Optimal computing budget allocation for urban regeneration: an unprecedented match between economic/extra-economic evaluations and urban planning. In: Gervasi, O., Murgante, B., Misra, S., et al. (eds.) Computational Science and Its Applications – ICCSA 2023 Workshops, LNCS, vol. 14300, pp. 69–79. Springer, Cham (2023)
19. Newman, P.W., Kenworthy, J.R.: The land use—transport connection: an overview. Land Use Policy **13**(1), 1–22 (1996)
20. Newman, P., Kenworthy, J.: Urban design to reduce automobile dependence. Opolis **2**(1) (2006)
21. Desyllas, J., Duxbury, E., Ward, J., Smith A.: Pedestrian demand modellling of large cities: an applied example from London. UCL Working Paper Series - Paper 62 (2003)
22. Calthorpe, P.: The next american metropolis. Community and the American Dream. Princeton Architectural Press, New York, Ecology (1993)
23. Ewing, R., Handy, S.: Measuring the unmeasurable: urban design qualities related to walkability. J. Urban Des. **14**(1), 65–84 (2009)

24. Maghelal, P.K., Capp, C.J.: Walkability: a review of existing pedestrian indices. J. Urban Region. Inform. Syst. Assoc. **23**(2) (2011)
25. Kellstedt, D.K., Spengler, J.O., Foster, M., Lee, C., Maddock, J.E.: A scoping review of bikeability assessment methods. J. Commun. Health **46**, 211–224 (2021)
26. Alberti, F., Radicchi, A.: From the neighbourhood unit to the 15-minute city. past and recent urban models for post-COVID cities. In: Alberti, F., Matamanda, A.R., He, BJ., Galderisi, A., Smol, M., Gallo, P. (eds.) Urban and Transit Planning. ASTI. Springer, Cham (2023). https://doi.org/10.1007/978-3-031-20995-6_15
27. Bertolini, L.: Spatial development patterns and public transport: the application of an analytical model in the Netherlands". Plan. Pract. Res. **14**(2), 199–210 (1999)
28. Evans, J.E., Pratt, R.H.: Transit Oriented Development, TCRP's Traveler Response to Transportation System Changes Handbook series. Transport Research Board, USA (2007)

A Co-design and Co-evaluation Model for the Reconversion of Dismissed Railways to Greenways: The Case of Misterbianco

Giovanna Acampa[1] ⓘ, Alessio Pino[2](✉) ⓘ, and Mariolina Grasso[2] ⓘ

[1] University of Florence, Via della Mattonaia 8, 50122 Florence, Italy
[2] University of Enna "Kore", Cittadella Universitaria, 94100 Enna, Italy
alessio.pino@unikorestudent.it

Abstract. The conversion of dismissed railway infrastructure into greenways has emerged as a sustainable strategy for enhancing mobility, fostering social interaction, and promoting environmental resilience. This study focuses on the transformation of a segment of the former Circumetnea railway in Misterbianco, a key urban center in the Metropolitan City of Catania. Using a participatory co-design and Social Multi-Criteria Evaluation (SMCE) approach, the research aimed to integrate community needs into the planning and design process.

Through stakeholder engagement, focus groups, and co-evaluation workshops, the study identified mobility patterns, safety concerns, and recreational preferences among Misterbianco's residents. Key findings indicate that the greenway must prioritize accessibility, security, and social value by incorporating dedicated cycling and walking paths, enhanced lighting, and bike-sharing facilities. The SMCE framework allowed for an objective assessment of design alternatives, balancing technical feasibility with community expectations.

The results underscore the importance of participatory planning in infrastructure projects, ensuring that redevelopment efforts align with local needs. The Misterbianco case serves as a model for similar railway-to-greenway conversions, demonstrating how co-evaluation methodologies can optimize functionality, social cohesion, and environmental sustainability. Future research should assess long-term usage patterns and economic impacts to refine planning strategies for green mobility networks.

Keywords: dismissed railways · greenways · SMCE · co-evaluation

1 Introduction

The emergence of railways in 19th-century Europe revolutionized transportation, facilitating economic growth, urban expansion, and cultural exchange [1]. The 1825 launch of the Stockton & Darlington Railway in England showcased the potential of steam locomotives, prompting rapid railway expansion across Europe. Nations like Belgium, France, and Italy invested heavily in railway networks, linking cities, industrial hubs, and ports. This infrastructure enhanced trade, encouraged migration, and required synchronized timekeeping, contributing to standardized time zones. Railways became a symbol of progress, central to the industrial revolution and urban modernization [2].

O. Gervasi et al. (Eds.): ICCSA 2025 Workshops, LNCS 15891, pp. 90–106, 2026.
https://doi.org/10.1007/978-3-031-97617-9_7

By the 20th century, the rise of automobiles and aviation reshaped transportation. Affordable cars, like the Ford Model T, provided individual mobility, while air travel facilitated rapid long-distance connections. Governments prioritized road and airport expansion, diminishing the role of railways in passenger transport [3]. This transition exacerbated urban congestion, pollution, and carbon emissions. Recognizing rail efficiency and sustainability, recent efforts have focused on reintegrating rail into modern mobility systems, particularly through high-speed networks and green transit solutions [4].

Mid-century railway closures disrupted regional transport networks. In the UK, the Beeching cuts of the 1960s led to the closure of over 4,000 miles of railways and 2,000 stations, isolating rural communities [5]. Italy abandoned over 7,000 km of railway, due to economic inefficiency. Across Europe, over 50,000 km of railway tracks have been decommissioned, resulting in economic stagnation, social isolation, and declining accessibility in affected regions [6].

The abandonment of railway infrastructure represents significant economic and environmental loss. The high costs of railway construction and maintenance - including land acquisition, track development, and station building - have gone to waste. Many structures of historical and cultural value have deteriorated rather than being repurposed. The environmental impact is equally severe: without rail options, dependence on high-emission road and air travel has intensified, contributing to climate change and habitat disruption. Instead of becoming green spaces, unused railway corridors have turned into neglected wastelands [7].

The social consequences of railway closures are profound. Many communities have lost access to essential services, education, and employment opportunities, widening disparities between urban and rural areas and displaying damaged heritage [8]. Without intervention, these trends risk entrenching long-term socio-economic inequalities [9].

A potential solution lies in transforming dismissed railways into greenways – linear routes designed for cycling, walking, and ecological conservation. [10] Greenways reconnect fragmented regions and play a key role in the regeneration of territories [11]. Moreover, unused railways often cross marginal areas with an overall complex heritage context [12]. Marginal and inner areas are a critical theme [13]: on the one hand, they are in a state of lack of resources and objective difficulties [14], but their peculiar condition offers possibilities for experimenting with new redevelopment horizons [15]. Their revitalization can improve resilience [16], benefit the local economy and real estate market [17], and align with sustainability goals by promoting green mobility and active lifestyles. This shift reflects a broader urban mobility paradigm, emphasizing reduced car dependency and enhanced public spaces [18]. It should also be considered that shared infrastructures bring social valuation in their design and use [19].

However, effective greenway planning requires community participation and adaptive design strategies, in addition to evaluating its costs and benefits [20, 21], and project feasibility and economic optimization [22]. Successful projects must balance connectivity with local lifestyle integration, ensuring that infrastructure aligns with user needs. A co-design and co-evaluation approach is crucial, engaging stakeholders in decision-making and functional assessment. This will produce a new generation of expanded urban areas, more internally integrated [23].

This paper explores a structured methodology for greenway development, tested through a case study on the dismissed Circumetnea railway in Sicily. A multi-criteria co-design and co-evaluation process was conducted in collaboration with three municipalities, generating data-driven design strategies for specific greenway segments.

The paper is structured as follows:

- Section 2 outlines the concept of greenways and methodologies for co-evaluation.
- Section 3 presents the Circumetnea railway case study, detailing historical evolution and territorial impact, then describes the methodological application, with the co-design and co-evaluation process, analyzing stakeholder engagement and design outputs.
- Section 4 provides conclusions, emphasizing the applicability of participatory models in greenway planning.

2 Materials and Methods

2.1 Greenways

Greenways have been defined in various ways over time, reflecting their evolving functions and applications. Horte and Eisemann describe them as "linear public parks and places that facilitate active travel and recreation in urban areas" [24], emphasizing their role in urban planning and sustainable mobility. Earlier, Little defined a greenway as a "linear open space established along either a natural corridor, such as a riverfront, stream valley, or ridgeline, or overland along a railroad right-of-way converted to recreational use, a canal, scenic road, or other route" [25]. The connection between dismissed railways and greenways dates back to the 1980s with the establishment of the Rails-to-Trails Conservancy, a pioneering initiative that repurposed abandoned rail corridors into multi-use trails. These rail-to-trail conversions have since been implemented in many countries, providing cycling and walking paths that link urban and rural areas, fostering local economic development through increased tourism and business opportunities. Similar initiatives in Germany and France have revitalized disused rail networks, repurposing them for regional transport and active mobility, reducing traffic congestion and urban sprawl [26].

Greenways can be categorized into five primary types based on their function and location [27]:

- Waterfront and riverside greenways – Developed along rivers, lakes, or coastlines, these serve both ecological and recreational purposes.
- Rail-to-trail greenways – Created by repurposing dismissed railway corridors, these provide active mobility routes while preserving historic infrastructure.
- Natural trails – Found in forests, rural areas, and protected landscapes, these trails are primarily leisure-oriented rather than for daily commuting.
- Active Travel Corridors (ATCs) – Explicitly designed for non-motorized transportation, these are integrated with transit hubs and public transport systems.
- Multitype greenways – Combining two or more categories, these maximize accessibility, connectivity, and ecological benefits.

This research focuses on the rail-to-trail and multitype greenways, as they are most relevant to the transformation of the dismissed Circumetnea railway. Rail-to-trail projects directly address the issue of railway abandonment, while multitype greenways offer greater functional diversity, accommodating both active mobility and recreational use [28].

Several successful rail-to-trail conversions demonstrate the social, economic, and environmental benefits of such projects:

- Rail Trail Cycleway (Western Sydney, Australia) – A 16.5-km path created in 2000, designed to promote physical activity in adults aged 18 to 55 [29];
- The 606 (Chicago, USA) – A 2.7-mile (4.35 km) elevated trail repurposed from the Bloomingdale railway line, connecting diverse neighborhoods and supporting urban regeneration [30];
- High Bridge Trail State Park (Virginia, USA) – Originally a railway bridge built in 1854, this was converted into a multi-use trail after its decommissioning, preserving historic infrastructure while promoting recreational use.

Beyond their physical categorization, greenways serve two main purposes [31]:

- Active Mobility (AM) – Facilitating daily commuting and transport via walking and cycling.
- Physical Activity (PA) – Supporting recreational exercise such as jogging and leisure cycling.

Although both functions involve similar infrastructural elements, they differ in user behavior and design requirements. Studies show that PA users typically travel up to 4.2 km, while AM users are conventionally limited to 3 km, though some empirical evidence suggests a threshold of 3.2 km [32].

To maximize functionality, greenway design must consider specific user needs. Research has identified key perceptual and physical factors that influence jogging-friendly environments, which can be applied to both PA and AM-oriented greenways.

For physical activity-focused (PA) greenways, effective design strategies include [33]:

- Minimizing intersections and road crossings to ensure uninterrupted movement.
- Providing essential amenities such as benches, hydration stations, and lighting.
- Using soft but durable surfaces like asphalt or specialized running tracks.
- Integrating natural elements (greenery, water features) while maintaining adequate openness.
- Enhancing cultural identity by incorporating local design elements.

For active mobility (AM) greenways, the literature identifies key infrastructural, environmental, and behavioral considerations [34]:

- Infrastructural characteristics:

  - Flat or gently sloped paths encourage frequent use.
  - Wide, well-paved surfaces (asphalt or compacted gravel) accommodate both pedestrians and cyclists.

– Clearly marked lanes reduce user conflicts and improve safety.

• Environmental and aesthetic factors:

  – Trees and vegetation provide shade and wind protection, making greenways usable in all seasons.
  – Proximity to forests, riversides, or historic landmarks enhances psychological well-being, encouraging longer use.

• Accessibility and connectivity:

  – Greenways should link to public transport (bus stops, train stations, bike-sharing points).
  – Multiple access points ensure usability across different neighborhoods.
  – Behavioral and safety aspects:
  – Solar-powered lighting and emergency call stations improve security, making greenways safer for evening and early morning use.
  – Avoiding intersections with car traffic enhances safety for children, elderly pedestrians, and casual cyclists.

This classification framework provides the basis for analyzing how rail-to-trail greenways, such as the one planned for the Circumetnea railway in Misterbianco, can be designed and optimized. The next section will delve into the historical context and territorial characteristics of the Circumetnea railway, highlighting the factors that have shaped its conversion into a greenway.

2.2 Social Multi-criteria Evaluation (SMCE)

Social Multi-Criteria Evaluation (SMCE) [35] has gained prominence in decision-making processes that involve multiple stakeholders, competing interests, and complex socio-ecological dynamics. Unlike traditional frameworks that prioritize economic or technical factors, SMCE integrates social values, participatory mechanisms, and deliberative processes to improve the legitimacy and effectiveness of policy decisions [36]. It extends Multi-Criteria Decision Analysis (MCDA) by placing greater emphasis on social engagement and conflict resolution, with respect to traditional multi-criteria analyses and comparative evaluations [37]. Proposed by Munda [38], SMCE addresses the limitations of cost-benefit analysis and conventional multi-criteria methods in handling social equity and incommensurable values. Its key features include the integration of quantitative and qualitative evaluation criteria, consideration of stakeholder preferences, the use of non-compensatory aggregation techniques (e.g., ELECTRE [39], NAIADE [40]) to avoid trade-offs that could disregard minority viewpoints, and a focus on sustainability-oriented decision-making [41], particularly in environmental, urban, and rural planning. Preliminary evaluation is indeed relevant to produce a suitable place-based design [42]. In addition to the resolution of decisional conflicts, one key aspect of this typology of decision-making procedures is to accentuate the perception of the economic-civic value of space for inhabitants and users [43]. SMCE has been applied in territorial planning, environmental governance, energy policy, and urban regeneration. In the Basque Country, Spain, Garmendia and Gamboa used SMCE to assess management strategies for the Urdaibai Estuary [44], a UNESCO Biosphere Reserve. The process included stakeholder identification through a snowball method, representation of environmental NGOs, fisheries, tourism operators, and public authorities, and the selection of evaluation criteria such as ecological sustainability, economic viability, and social acceptance. A Multi-Criteria Impact Matrix quantified trade-off, while non-compensatory aggregation techniques (PROMETHEE and NAIADE) ranked alternatives. A deliberative workshop allowed stakeholders to assign weights to different criteria and conduct a sensitivity analysis. This approach ensured that conservation priorities were not overruled by economic interests. Similarly, an SMCE process in Mutriku, Basque Country, helped balance competing land-use demands, revealing conflicts between economic efficiency and environmental sustainability [45].

SMCE has also been used in urban regeneration, where social sustainability – equity, inclusivity, and cultural preservation – must be considered alongside economic and physical transformation, also as an alternative to traditional value-based estimations [46]. A study in Northern Italy applied SMCE to evaluate six social housing strategies, combining stakeholder analysis, economic feasibility assessments, and social cohesion indicators [47]. Using NAIADE, researchers found that high-density social housing, while technically efficient, disrupted community networks. Instead, mixed-use, incremental development models received greater support, highlighting the importance of integrating community perspectives into urban planning.

Co-design and co-evaluation play a fundamental role in SMCE by ensuring that infrastructure projects align with community needs. These participatory approaches allow designers to refine proposals based on real user feedback while fostering transparency and trust. In greenway planning, SMCE supports the evaluation of design alternatives, helping balance transportation efficiency, environmental conservation, and social inclusivity [48].

Several multi-criteria evaluation methodologies are commonly used within SMCE. NAIADE (Novel Approach to Imprecise Assessment and Decision Environments) applies pairwise comparisons to balance technical and social criteria, often used in urban and environmental planning [40]. ELECTRE (Elimination and Choice Translating Reality) ranks alternatives based on threshold-based comparisons, making it suitable for land-use and infrastructure planning. [49] PROMETHEE (Preference Ranking Organization Method for Enrichment Evaluations) orders alternatives according to stakeholder preferences and is widely applied in conservation planning [50]. The Multi-Criteria Impact Matrix (MCIM) allows direct trade-off comparisons and is used in participatory governance [51]. Fuzzy Multi-Criteria Decision-Making (Fuzzy-MCDM) incorporates uncertainty and subjective stakeholder preferences, making it useful in climate adaptation and water resource management [52]. Each method offers specific advantages depending on project goals, stakeholder complexity, and data availability.

3 Case Study Application: The Circumetnea Dismissed Railway

3.1 The Context: History of Circumetnea and Misterbianco

The Ferrovia Circumetnea (FCE) is a historic narrow-gauge railway that encircles Mount Etna, connecting Catania to Riposto along a 110 km route that passes through various towns in the province of Catania [53]. The railway was constructed in phases, with the Catania-Adernò (now Adrano) section opening in 1895, followed by an extension to Bronte in 1897, and completion to Riposto in 1898, enabling connectivity between the Etnean hinterland, the national railway network, and Ionian coast ports.

Throughout the early 20th century, the Circumetnea railway became a crucial freight and passenger transport system, supporting local industries and connecting rural settlements to urban centers. However, after World War II, declining freight traffic, driven by the rise of road transport, significantly impacted railway operations. In response, modernization efforts in the 1950s and 1960s introduced diesel railcars to replace steam locomotives, but competition from automobiles and buses continued to weaken rail-based mobility [54].

Since the 1990s, FCE has focused on passenger transport revitalization and integration with the Catania Metro, which launched in 1999 with an initial segment between Borgo and Porto stations. Over the years, the metro system expanded, replacing certain Circumetnea sections with underground routes and modernized infrastructure. Today, the Ferrovia Circumetnea remains an essential mobility corridor, serving both local commuters and tourists, offering scenic rail journeys through Etna's volcanic landscape and historic settlements.

The Circumetnea railway has undergone numerous route modifications, reflecting shifts in mobility demand and urban expansion. A major transformation occurred in 1999, when the Catania Metro absorbed portions of the surface railway, leading to the decommissioning of the original Catania Porto–Catania Borgo section. The former railway terminus near the port was demolished, and the Galatea metro station replaced a key surface segment. Additionally, sections connecting Catania Borgo to Nesima were abandoned in 2017, as the metro expanded underground, further reducing the Circumetnea's surface presence [55].

The most recent and impactful decommissioning occurred in 2024, with the closure of the Catania Borgo–Paternò railway segment to accommodate new underground metro construction. This decision, which ended over a century of railway service along this stretch, generated significant public debate, as it marked the removal of a historic transportation link. While these modernization efforts have enhanced public transport efficiency, they have also resulted in the loss of original railway corridors, raising questions about alternative uses for abandoned infrastructure.

One of the most relevant transformations concerns the Misterbianco area, a key urban center along the dismissed railway route. The repurposing of the former railway track into a greenway has been proposed as a sustainable urban strategy, integrating non-motorized transport and public space improvements into local planning. This approach is guided by two key objectives: first, to understand how the greenway can meet the mobility and recreational needs of the local community; second, to explore design strategies that maximize usability, safety, and environmental benefits.

To achieve these goals, a co-design and Social Multi-Criteria Evaluation (SMCE) approach was implemented, involving Misterbianco's residents, stakeholders, and planners. The participatory process allowed for a detailed assessment of local needs and expectations, ensuring that the greenway transformation aligns with mobility patterns, environmental considerations, and social dynamics. The next sections will outline the specific methodology adopted, the results of the evaluation, and the final design proposals for the greenway in Misterbianco.

Misterbianco is a municipality in the Metropolitan City of Catania, located 6 km west of Catania. It has a population of approximately 49,000 and covers 37 square kilometers. Originally destroyed by the 1669 Etna eruption, it was rebuilt in the Milicia area. While historically agricultural, Misterbianco has expanded into industrial and commercial sectors, with major landmarks such as the Scavi Archeologici di Campanarazzu, Cattedrale Santa Maria delle Grazie, and Centro Sicilia shopping mall. Its residential growth has been influenced by its proximity to Catania and favored by the employment of national and local incentives [56], making it an important suburban hub.

3.2 Co-design and Co-evaluation Methodology

A co-design and co-evaluation methodology was implemented in Misterbianco from January to June 2024 to plan the conversion of a dismissed railway into a greenway. The process included:

1. Institutional analysis, identifying key stakeholders.
2. Focus groups, gathering community insights.
3. Definition of design perimeters and concepts.
4. Co-design workshops, developing alternatives.
5. Co-evaluation workshops, selecting the best option.
6. Presentation of results to the public.

This participatory approach ensured that the greenway design aligned with local needs, supporting sustainable mobility, recreation, and connectivity. Moreover, this approach falls into the design methodologies based on multi-criteria evaluations [57]. Design-oriented evaluation is being increasingly used, especially for projects involving sustainability [58]. The following sections will describe the methodology and findings in detail.

The first phase involved identifying stakeholders and representatives of different social groups in Misterbianco through web-based searches and place-based investigations. The goal was to engage diverse community actors without filtering by purpose. The analysis identified:

- 4 volunteering associations;
- 1 cultural foundation;
- 10 sports associations;
- 1 theatrical association;
- 15 religious groups;
- 1 tourist association;
- 2 local TV networks;

- 52 food businesses;
- 38 shops.

This mapping ensured broad community representation, forming the basis for co-design and co-evaluation activities in the greenway planning process.

A focus group is a qualitative research method used to gather insights from a diverse group of participants about a specific topic. Guided by a moderator, discussions encourage participants to share opinions, preferences, and expectations, revealing perspectives that may not emerge in structured surveys or individual interviews. In this study, the focus group aimed to identify the primary needs and expected uses of the greenway, along with its role in local mobility and recreational activities.

In Misterbianco, eight participants were selected, ensuring equal gender representation and coverage of all age groups. The survey items in Table 1 were used to guide discussions, beginning with individual opinions before including general perceptions and mobility habits. They followed a funnel approach, in which wider discussions were opened after starting from individual standpoints.

Table 1. Focus Group questions

Code	Questions	Alternatives
FG1	What is your main connection to the area?	Resident/Business owner/Commuter/Worker
FG2	Which is your age group?	18–25/26–40/41–65/66+
FG3	What should be the main purpose of the greenway?	Transportation/Physical activity/Social gathering/Recreational space/Other
FG4	What activity would you engage in on the greenway?	Walking/Running/jogging/Cycling/Socializing/Attending community events/Other
FG5	Which destination would you likely reach through the greenway?	Open question
FG6	What would encourage you to use the greenway more frequently?	Safety measures/Seating areas/Clear signage/Community events/Public transport integration
FG7	What is your bicycle usage preference?	Own bike/Prefer bike-sharing/No bike and would not use bike-sharing/No bike but would use bike-sharing

Table 2 provides an outline of the provenience and institutional relationships of the members of the focus group.

Table 2. Focus Group participants

Participant	Age Group	Connection to the Area	Institutional Affiliation (if any)
P1	18–25	Resident	Local sports association
P2	18–25	Worker	No formal affiliation
P3	26–40	Resident	Business owner (food sector)
P4	26–40	Commuter	Member of a local volunteering group
P5	41–65	Resident	Religious group representative
P6	41–65	Business Owner	Local commerce association
P7	66+	Resident	Cultural foundation member
P8	66+	Resident	No formal affiliation

The following elements emerged:

- several inhabitants of the city work in the industrial area north-west of Piano Tavola and could presumably use the greenway for daily commuting, considering the short extra-urban distance;
- several inhabitants regularly visit the natural area of Oasi di Ponte Barca for recreational purposes, though it is located at 20 km, and this function could be performed at a closer distance if there were equipped green areas in the city's proximity;
- inhabitants frequently go to Catania (5 km from Misterbianco) for various purposes, as it represents a major center;
- inhabitants would be generally more inclined to use the greenway for cycling rather than for jogging, due to the presence of several sports facilities within the city;
- inhabitants perceive a general lack of community events;
- in Misterbianco, it is not common to have private bicycles due to frequent thefts, and this led to the recent closure of two bike shops;
- the introduction of a bike-sharing service would be perceived positively by the population.

Thus, it results that the segment of the greenway within Misterbianco's scope will extend 5 km westward to the industrial area near Piano Tavola and 8 km eastward to Catania, improving connectivity and recreational accessibility. The design prioritizes cycling safety, green areas, interchange stations, a bike-sharing service, and recreational spaces to promote both mobility and social engagement.

In March 2024, a co-design workshop was held, engaging residents and stakeholders in defining the aesthetic and functional aspects of the greenway. Participants provided input on materials, lighting, seating, vegetation, and trail layout, ensuring the design aligns with community expectations. Three alternative road plan models were developed, each adjusting elements such as surface texture, pathway width, and landscaping features to balance safety and usability. The resulting concepts had the following characteristics:

- the first one (Concept 1) appears as a mobility-oriented corridor designed to facilitate efficient cycling and walking connections between Misterbianco and key destinations.

It presents direct, uninterrupted routes with a bidirectional asphalt bike lane and a separate pedestrian path, ensuring smooth, high-speed commuting. A low vegetative buffer provides minimal separation between cyclists and pedestrians, optimizing space efficiency. Street lighting is strategically positioned for safety, and bike parking facilities are integrated at key junctions to enhance multimodal transport connectivity;

– the second one (Concept 2) emphasizes recreational and ecological functions, providing an alternative to the Oasi di Ponte Barca by offering accessible natural spaces closer to Misterbianco. The design incorporates a meandering soft-surfaced pedestrian trail and a permeable paved cycling path, promoting low-impact, leisure-oriented movement. The surrounding environment is characterized by dense vegetation, native tree canopies, and biodiversity-enhancing green buffers, fostering ecological restoration and climate resilience. Seating areas, drinking fountains, and educational signage are distributed along the route, encouraging interaction with the natural surroundings;

– the third concept (Concept 3) represents a hybrid model, balancing mobility, social engagement, and multi-functional public space. This alternative incorporates a dedicated bike lane, a pedestrian promenade, and a multimodal hub, supporting both cycling and alternative transport options such as bike-sharing. The inclusion of small plazas, seating areas, and shaded gathering spaces fosters informal social interactions, while public art, murals, and interactive installations enhance the sense of place. The design also features a flexible-use area, adaptable for community events, pop-up markets, or educational activities. Smart lighting poles with motion sensors ensure safety while minimizing energy consumption. This alternative differs from the others by serving as a socially vibrant corridor, not only facilitating movement but also creating public spaces for engagement and cultural activation.

Following the three concepts developed in the Co-Design Workshop, 3 projects were developed, identified as "The Commuter Greenway", "The Urban Nature Greenway" and "The Community Mobility Greenway". The Commuter Greenway is designed for daily travel, featuring high-speed bike lanes, secure parking, and well-lit paths, ensuring safety for early and late commuters. It connects Misterbianco to the industrial area and Catania, integrating with public transport. The Urban Nature Greenway focuses on recreation and environmental benefits, with green spaces, pedestrian-friendly trails, biodiversity areas, and event spaces for markets and performances. It enhances local access to nature. The Community Mobility Greenway combines bike-sharing stations, smart infrastructure, multimodal hubs, and social spaces, offering a balanced approach to mobility, safety, sustainability, and community engagement, making it the most versatile option.

In the Co-Evaluation Workshop, held in May 2024, participants assessed three preliminary design proposals using Social Multi-Criteria Evaluation (SMCE) supported by the ELECTRE II method, functional for ranking design alternatives in a multi-group perspective. Table 3 reports the weights given to the criteria, chosen by the workshop participants.

The ELECTRE II method was applied to rank three greenway design alternatives – The Commuter Greenway, The Urban Nature Greenway, and The Community Mobility Greenway – based on multiple stakeholder perspectives. The evaluation used five criteria: Accessibility & Connectivity (0.30), Safety & Security (0.25), Environmental Sustainability (0.15), Social & Recreational Value (0.20), and Economic Impact & Feasibility

Table 3. SMCE Criteria and Weights

Criteria	Weight
Accessibility & Connectivity	0.30
Safety & Security	0.25
Environmental Sustainability	0.15
Social & Recreational Value	0.20
Economic Impact & Maintenance Feasibility	0.10

(0.10), with adjusted weight distributions for three groups: commuters, local residents, and policymakers. A decision matrix was built, rating each alternative from 1 to 10. The Commuter Greenway excelled in accessibility but was weaker in environmental and social aspects. The Urban Nature Greenway performed best in sustainability and recreation but was less suitable for commuting. The Community Mobility Greenway achieved balanced scores across all criteria. In the following, the implementation of the ELECTRE II methodology is outlined.

The first step was to compute the Concordance Index. For each pair (A_i, A_j), it is equal to:

$$C\left(A_i, A_j\right) = \sum_{k \in G(A_i, A_j)} W_k \qquad (1)$$

where $G(A_i, A_j)$ is the set of criteria where $A_i \geq A_j$.

For example, $C(A_1, A_2)$ included Accessibility & Connectivity (0.30) and Economic Feasibility (0.10), totaling 0.40. Repeating this for all pairwise comparisons, the concordance matrix is reported in Table 4.

Table 4. Concordance matrix for the ELECTRE II methodology, calculated for the three design alternatives of the greenway's Misterbianco scope.

C(Ai, Aj)	A1 (Commuter)	A2 (Urban Nature)	A3 (Community Mobility)
A1→	–	0.40	0.55
A2→	0.60	–	0.45
A3→	0.45	0.55	–

Then, the discordance index was calculated as:

$$D\left(A_i, A_j\right) = max_{k \in B(A_i, A_j)} \frac{\left|a_{ik} - a_{jk}\right|}{max_k \left|a_{ik} - a_{jk}\right|} \qquad (2)$$

where $B(A_i, A_j)$ is the set of criteria where $A_i < A_j$.

Table 5. Discordance matrix for the ELECTRE II methodology, calculated for the three design alternatives of the greenway's Misterbianco scope.

D(Ai, Aj)	A1 (Commuter)	A2 (Urban Nature)	A3 (Community Mobility)
A1→	–	1.00	0.75
A2→	0.80	–	0.65
A3→	0.60	0.70	–

For instance, $D(A_1, A_2) = 1.00$ due to a significant difference in Environmental Sustainability (A1 = 5, A2 = 9). The final discordance matrix is reported in Table 5.

Finally, outranking relations were established. Using thresholds $\lambda_c = 0.50$, $\lambda_d = 0.75$, an alternative A_i outranks A_j if:

$$C(A_i, A_j) \geq \lambda_c \; AND \; D(A_i, A_j) \leq \lambda_d \tag{3}$$

Applying descending and ascending distillation, A3: The Community Mobility Greenway emerged as the top-ranked option, balancing mobility, security, sustainability, and social engagement. The Commuter Greenway ranked second due to its mobility advantages but weaker environmental and social performance. The Urban Nature Greenway ranked last due to low transportation benefits despite high sustainability scores. This ranking suggests that a mobility-integrated greenway best suits Misterbianco's needs.

4 Conclusions

This study demonstrates the effectiveness of integrating Social Multi-Criteria Evaluation (SMCE) and participatory co-design in greenway planning, ensuring alignment between technical feasibility and local preferences. While greenways are often perceived as a standardized intervention, this research highlights how community engagement reveals differentiated stakeholder responses to various design alternatives. The participatory process, which included focus groups and co-design workshops, identified three conceptually distinct alternatives - the Commuter Greenway, the Urban Nature Greenway, and the Community Mobility Greenway - each addressing specific mobility, recreational, and social needs.

The application of ELECTRE II allowed for a structured ranking of these alternatives based on accessibility, safety, environmental sustainability, social value, and economic feasibility. The results indicate that the Community Mobility Greenway emerged as the most balanced solution, offering bike-sharing, multimodal integration, and community-oriented spaces, which best address the diverse mobility patterns and social needs of Misterbianco's population. The Commuter Greenway ranked second, primarily excelling in connectivity and transport efficiency but receiving lower scores in environmental and social aspects. The Urban Nature Greenway, while valued for its ecological and recreational benefits, ranked lowest due to its limited accessibility for daily mobility.

These findings underscore the context-dependent nature of greenway interventions, challenging the assumption that a single model can universally satisfy diverse urban populations. Instead, this study confirms that different community groups prioritize distinct functional aspects, reinforcing the need for adaptive, participatory approaches in greenway planning. The Misterbianco case exemplifies how co-evaluation methodologies can enhance infrastructure usability, social cohesion, and sustainability. Future research should explore long-term behavioral shifts, economic impacts, and the effectiveness of participatory strategies in green mobility planning, ensuring that greenways remain responsive to evolving community needs. Moreover, precise indicators could be integrated with the bottom-up participatory approach to improve design quality [59].

Acknowledgments. The Municipality of Misterbianco is acknowledged for its involvement in the implementation of the methodological application of this research work.

References

1. Hornung, E., Ostler, M.: Railroads and growth in prussia. J. Eur. Econ. Assoc. **13**(4), 699–736 (2015)
2. Veenendaal, A.J.: European Railways 1825–2001: An Overview. Research Memorandum GD-54, Groningen Growth and Development Centre (2002)
3. Launius, R.: Planes, trains, and automobiles - Choosing transportation modes in the twentieth century. 38th Aerospace Sciences Meeting and Exhibit (2000)
4. Zhang, X., Li, H., Li, Y.: The impacts of high-speed railway on environmental sustainability. Hum. Soc. Sci. Commun. **10**, 21 (2023)
5. Gibbons, S., Heblich, S., Pinchbeck, E.W.: The spatial impacts of a massive rail disinvestment program: the Beeching Axe. J. Urban Econ. **143**, 103691 (2024)
6. Bianchi, A., De Medici, S.: A sustainable adaptive reuse management model for disused railway cultural heritage to boost local and regional competitiveness. Sustainability **15**(6), 5127 (2023)
7. Jasper, S.: Abandoned infrastructures and nonhuman life. Society & Space (2020)
8. Torrieri, F., Oppio, A., Rossitti, M.: Damage assessment for architectural heritage: the Cavallerizza Reale complex in Turin. Valori e Valutazioni **30**, 71–84 (2022)
9. Taylor, Z.: Railway closures to passenger traffic in Poland and their social consequences. J. Transp. Geogr. **14**(2), 135–151 (2005)
10. Acampa, G., Grasso, M., Pino, A.: An MCA proposal with ANP and veto thresholds to support decision-making in former railway track regeneration initiatives. In: Gervasi, O., Murgante, B., Misra, S., et al. (eds.) Computational Science and Its Applications – ICCSA 2024, LNCS, vol. 14300, pp. 376–385. Springer, Cham (2024)
11. Stanganelli, M., Torrieri, F., Gerundo, C., Rossitti, M.: A strategic performance-based planning methodology to promote the regeneration of fragile territories. Lect. Notes Civil Eng. **146**, 149–157 (2021)
12. Rossitti, M., Torrieri, F.: Action research for the conservation of architectural heritage in marginal areas: the role of evaluation. Valori e Valutazioni **30**, 3–42 (2022)
13. Rossitti, M., Torrieri, F.: The THEMA tool to support heritage-based development strategies for marginal areas: evidence from an Italian inner area in Campania Region. Region **9**(2), 109–129 (2022)
14. Acampa, G., Pino, A.: Village repopulation: analysis of extra-economic indicators to evaluate and valorise social generativity in ecovillages. In: Gervasi, O., Murgante, B., Misra, S., et al. (eds.) Networks, Markets, and People: Proceedings of the 2024 International Conference on Computational Science and Its Applications – ICCSA 2024, LNCS, vol. 14300, pp. 376–385. Springer, Cham (2024)

15. Acampa, G., Pino, A.: Filling the old with new life. Application of original indicators for evaluating ecovillages as village repopulation initiatives. Aestimum **85**, 73–86 (2024)

16. Rossitti, M., Torrieri, F.: Circular economy as 'catalyst' for resilience in inner areas. Sustain. Mediterran. Construct. **5**, 64–67 (2021)

17. Oppio, A., Torrieri, F., Dell'Oca, E.: Land value in urban development agreements: methodological perspectives and operational recommendations. Valori e Valutazioni **21**, 87–96 (2018)

18. Acampa, G., Pino, A., Alberti, F.: The URGET VADEMECUM 2030–2050 project: applying threshold theory to sustainable urban mobility. In: Gervasi, O., Murgante, B., Misra, S., et al. (eds.) Computational Science and Its Applications – ICCSA 2024, LNCS, vol. 14300, pp. 233–245. Springer, Cham (2024)

19. Miccoli, S., Finucci, F., Murro, R.: Shared infrastructures: Technique and method for an inclusive social valuation. In: Transport Infrastructure and Systems, pp. 759–768. CRC Press (2017)

20. Del Giudice, V., Passeri, A., Torrieri, F., De Paola, P.: Risk analysis within feasibility studies: an application to cost-benefit analysis for the construction of a new road. Appl. Mech. Mater. **651–653**, 1249–1254 (2014)

21. Acampa, G., Finucci, F., Grasso, M., Magarò, A.: Preliminary approach for the cost-benefit analysis in the building envelope: study and comparison of actions. In: Calabrò, F., Della Spina, L., Bevilacqua, C. (eds.) New Metropolitan Perspectives – NMP 2022, LNCS, vol. 100, pp. 786–794. Springer, Cham (2022)

22. Acampa, G., Pino, A.: Optimal computing budget allocation for urban regeneration: an unprecedented match between economic/extra-economic evaluations and urban planning. In: Gervasi, O., Murgante, B., Misra, S., et al. (eds.) Computational Science and Its Applications – ICCSA 2023 Workshops, LNCS, vol. 14300, pp. 69–79. Springer, Cham (2023)

23. Miccoli, S., Fabrizio, F., Murro, R.: A new generation of urban areas. Feasibility elements. In: Advances in Energy Science and Equipment Engineering, pp. 1146–1149. Taylor & Francis Group (2015)

24. Horte, S.A., Eisemann, E.: Urban greenways: a systematic review and typology. Land **9**(2), 40 (2020)

25. Little, C.E.: Greenways for america. Johns Hopkins University Press (1990)

26. Bartoschek, A.: The unexploited potential of converting rail tracks to greenways. Sustainability **12**(3), 881 (2020)

27. Turner, T.: Greenways, blueways, skyways and other ways to a better London. Landsc. Urban Plan. **33**, 269–282 (1995)

28. Zuniga-Teran, A.A., Orr, B.J., Gimblett, R.H., et al.: Influences on greenways usage for active transportation: a systematic review. Sustainability **15**(13), 10695 (2023)

29. Merom, D., Bauman, A., Vita, P., Close, G.: An environmental intervention to promote walking and cycling - the impact of a newly constructed Rail Trail in Western Sydney. Prev. Med. **36**(2), 235–242 (2003)

30. Gobster, P.H., Rigolon, A.: Up on The 606: understanding the use of a new elevated pedestrian and bicycle trail in Chicago. Transport. Res. Rec.: J. Transport. Res. Board **2644**(1), 83–91 (2003)

31. Chen, X., Wang, S., Liu, X., Wang, X., Huang, Z.: Greenway interventions and physical activity levels: a systematic review and meta-analysis. Int. J. Environ. Res. Public Health **21**(2), 567 (2024)

32. Zhao, J., Zhang, T., Zhao, P., et al.: Exploring restrictions to use of community greenways for physical activity in china: a mixed-methods study. Int. J. Environ. Res. Public Health **20**(14), 6210 (2023)

33. Deng, Y., Liang, J., Chen, Q.: Greenway interventions effectively enhance physical activity levels - A systematic review with meta-analysis. Front. Public Health **11**, 1268502 (2023)
34. Hunter, R.F., et al.: Investigating the physical activity, health, wellbeing, social and environmental impact of a greenway in a deprived community: a longitudinal study. Int. J. Behav. Nutr. Phys. Act. **18**, 155 (2021)
35. Munda, G.: A conflict analysis approach for illuminating distributional issues in sustainability policy. Eur. J. Oper. Res. **194**(1), 307–322 (2009)
36. Saarikoski, H., Mustajoki, J., Barton, D.N., et al.: Multi-criteria decision analysis and environmental decision making. Environ. Sci. Policy **55**, 87–98 (2016)
37. Nicolella, M., Landolfi, R., Pino, A., Scognamillo, C.: Comparative evaluations of sustainability, durability and resilience of external envelopes for environmentally efficient buildings. IOP Conf. Series: Earth Environ. Sci. **296**(1), 012023 (2019)
38. Munda, G.: Social multi-criteria evaluation: Methodological foundations and operational consequences. Eur. J. Oper. Res. **158**(3), 662–677 (2004)
39. Battisti, F.: ELECTRE III for strategic environmental assessment: a "phantom" approach. Sustainability **14**(10), 6221 (2022)
40. Munda, G.: A NAIADE based approach for sustainability benchmarking. Int. J. Environ. Technol. Manage. **6**(1/2), 65–78 (2006)
41. Battisti, F.: SDGs and ESG criteria in housing: defining local evaluation criteria and indicators for verifying project sustainability using florence metropolitan area as a case study. Sustainability **15**(12), 9372 (2023)
42. Finucci, F., Masanotti, A.G., Mazzoni, D.: Preliminary evaluation approaches in the urban regeneration of Corviale in Rome. Lect. Notes Networks Syst. **1186**, 128–141 (2024)
43. Battisti, F., Pisano, C.: Common property in Italy. Unresolved issues and an appraisal approach: towards a definition of environmental-economic civic value. Land **11**(11), 1927 (2022)
44. Garmendia, E., Gamboa, G.: Weighting social preferences in participatory multi-criteria evaluations: a case study on sustainable natural resource management. Ecol. Econ. **84**, 110–120 (2012)
45. Etxano, I., Villalba-Eguiluz, U.: Conflicting values in rural planning: a multifunctionality approach to conflicts in the Basque Country. Sustainability **10**(5), 1431 (2018)
46. Fattinnanzi, E., Acampa, G., Battisti, F., Campo, O., Forte, F.: Applying the depreciated replacement cost method when assessing the market value of public property lacking comparables and income data. Sustainability **12**(21), 8993 (2020)
47. Bottero, M., Datola, G.: Addressing social sustainability in urban regeneration processes: an application of the social multi-criteria evaluation. Sustainability **12**(18), 7579 (2020)
48. Yildirim, V., Yildiz, N.D.: Multi-criteria decision making methods for urban greenway: the case of Aksaray, Turkey. Int. J. Eng. Geosci. **4**(3), 131–138 (2019)
49. Roy, B.: The outranking approach and the foundations of ELECTRE methods. Theor. Decis. **31**(1), 49–73 (1991)
50. Brans, J.P., Vincke, P.: A preference ranking organisation method: the PROMETHEE method for MCDM. Manage. Sci. **31**(6), 647–656 (1985)
51. Kiker, G.A., Bridges, T.S., Varghese, A., Seager, T.P., Linkov, I.: Application of multicriteria decision analysis in environmental decision making. Integr. Environ. Assess. Manag. **1**(2), 95–108 (2005)
52. Zimmermann, H.J.: Fuzzy set theory - and its applications. Springer, Boston (2001)
53. Cinelli, I., Anfuso, G., Privitera, S., Pranzini, E.: An overview on railway impacts on coastal environment and beach tourism in sicily (Italy). Sustainability **13**(13), 7068 (2021)
54. Petino, G., Wilson, J., Knudsen, D.C.: Slow tourism in the ETNA meso region: discovering the rural space with the circumetnea railway. Almatour.: J. Tour. Cult. Territor. Develop. **9**(17) (2018)

55. Pigorini, A., Sciotti, A., Corbo, A., Quarzicci, G., Romualdi, A.: The new major railway lines in Southern Italy: planning and design approaches towards sustainable solutions. In: Expanding Underground - Knowledge and Passion to Make a Positive Impact on the World, pp. 852–860. CRC Press (2023)
56. Battisti, F., Campo, O.: The assessment of density bonus in building renovation interventions. The Case of the City of Florence in Italy. Land **10**(12), 1391 (2021)
57. Baratta, A.F.L., Finucci, F., Magarò, A.: Generative design process: multi-criteria evaluation and multidisciplinary approach. TECHNE – J. Technol. Architect. Environ. 304–314 (2021)
58. Borsos, Á., Finucci, F., Gyergyák, J., Masanotti, A.G.: Evaluation in green building design for conversion projects: case studies and comparative approaches. E3S Web Conf. **436**, 01008 (2023)
59. Baratta, A.F.L., Mariani, M., Mazzoni, D.: The National Innovative Program for Housing Quality (PINQuA). Strategies and Indicators for Design Quality. Lecture Notes in Computer Science (LNCS), vol. 14104, pp. 635–646 (2023)

Evaluation of the Impact of Tourism Flows on the Urban Food Service Industry. A Sensitivity Analysis on the City of Rome

Giovanna Acampa[1] , Alessio Pino[2] , and Alberto Pino[3] (✉)

[1] University of Florence, Via P.A. Micheli 2, 50129 Florence, Italy
[2] University of Enna "Kore", Cittadella Universitaria, 94100 Enna, Italy
[3] Sapienza University of Rome, Via del Castro Laurenziano 9, 00161 Rome, Italy
albertopinonicolella@gmail.com

Abstract. Following the end of the pandemic in 2022, habits regarding leisure, tourism, and dining have been subjected to several changes and oscillations. As proven by several sources, such as the FIPE report and the ISFORT report on citizens' expenses, dining out has become slightly more frequent for residents. At the same time, tourist flows have increased, reaching new records for several European cities, especially in Italy. This latter phenomenon appears to be predominant compared to the former. This variation of flows has also produced variations in urban morphology, with a marked increase in the number of restaurants, especially with an increase in the number of restaurants, yet dependent on tourism oscillations.

By focusing on the city of Rome, this paper evaluates the dependency of the food service industry on tourist flows: this is performed through a quantitative survey of the number and typology of restaurants, a financial analysis to assess the economic flows related to tourism, a break-even analysis to determine the inflection points of this phenomenon, and finally the simulation of decreasing tourism scenarios – made realistic by the current geopolitical situation – complemented by a sensitivity analysis. A 5% tourism drop results in a loss of ~16.5 million meals annually, pushing 450–600 additional restaurants below BEP, while a 10% decline results in 33 million lost meals, increasing failures to 900–1,200 businesses. The historical center is the most vulnerable, potentially losing up to 600 restaurants, while peripheral areas are less affected due to their reliance on local customers.

Keywords: evaluation · sensitivity analysis · food service industry

1 Introduction

In the aftermath of the COVID-19 pandemic, the global tourism and hospitality sectors have entered a phase of accelerated transformation [1]. Following the severe contraction of international mobility in 2020 and 2021, the industry rebounded sharply: according to the United Nations World Tourism Organization [2], international tourist arrivals grew by 30% in 2023 compared to the previous year, with several countries exceeding

O. Gervasi et al. (Eds.): ICCSA 2025 Workshops, LNCS 15891, pp. 107–121, 2026.
https://doi.org/10.1007/978-3-031-97617-9_8

pre-pandemic levels. Italy, in particular, has reasserted its centrality as a global tourist destination, registering over 440 million overnight stays in 2023, a 6.5% increase over 2019 figures. Cities like Rome, Florence, and Venice have seen the return of mass tourism, often referred to as "over-tourism", with visible impacts on urban space, local services, and economic structures [3].

One of the most significantly affected sectors is the food service industry, which has responded to increased tourist flows with a marked proliferation of restaurants, especially in urban historic centers [4]. This dynamic is coupled with evolving local consumption patterns. As reported by the 2023 FIPE and ISFORT reports, Italians are dining out more frequently, particularly in metropolitan contexts such as Rome, where residents consume an estimated 160 meals per year outside the home [5] – 30% higher than the national average. Nevertheless, while local and international consumption is growing, tourism is the predominant force shaping the current urban food economy [6].

This increased reliance on fluctuating tourist flows introduces new vulnerabilities into the urban restaurant ecosystem. Restaurants, particularly those in highly touristic areas, have structured their business models around international demand, raising concerns about financial resilience [7]. External shocks – such as geopolitical crises, changes in visa policy, or future pandemics – could reduce visitor flows and threaten business sustainability. Yet, the financial equilibrium of the restaurant sector is rarely examined in direct relation to its dependency on tourism [8].

This study focuses on Rome as a case study to investigate the structural dependency of the urban restaurant sector on tourism. Through a mixed-method approach involving a quantitative survey of the number and typology of restaurants, a financial analysis and break-even model, and a sensitivity analysis simulating a 5% and 10% drop in tourist flows, the paper seeks to answer the following research question: "to what extent is the economic viability of restaurants in Rome dependent on tourism flows, and what are the potential consequences of moderate declines in international visitors?".

The findings aim to inform not only academic debates on urban tourism and service economies but also policy strategies for urban resilience and sectoral support. Indeed, preliminary evaluations in such a complex context are always crucial and required to make decisions in urban regeneration [9].

2 Materials and Methods

2.1 Break-Even Analysis

Break-even analysis is a fundamental instrument in managerial accounting and operational planning, used to determine the level of output or sales at which total revenues equal total costs. It identifies the point at which an enterprise shifts from loss to profit, thereby offering a quantitative basis for evaluating financial sustainability [10]. The origins of break-even analysis lie in early 20th-century cost-volume-profit (CVP) modeling, which remains foundational in assessing business feasibility under varying economic conditions [11].

The basic formulation of the break-even point (BEP) can be expressed as [12]:

$$BEP = \frac{F}{P - V} \tag{1}$$

where:

- BEP = Break-Even Point;
- F = Fixed costs;
- P = Price per unit;
- V = Variable cost per unit.

This relationship determines the number of units that must be sold to cover all fixed and variable costs. Fixed costs are the expenses that do not change with output volume – such as rent, salaries, or insurance – while variable costs fluctuate with each unit of production or service provided. The denominator, often referred to as the contribution margin per unit, captures the portion of revenue that contributes to covering fixed costs after accounting for variable expenses [13].

The utility of break-even analysis lies in its simplicity and adaptability across sectors. In strategic planning, it is widely used to assess the viability of new ventures, pricing strategies, or market entry decisions [14]. It is particularly valuable in industries with high fixed costs and variable demand, such as manufacturing, hospitality, or transportation, where operational thresholds can critically affect profitability [15].

However, break-even analysis is also subject to limitations. Its underlying assumptions – including constant unit price, linear cost behavior, and stable market conditions – may not hold in real-world contexts marked by volatility, competition, and customer heterogeneity. Additionally, it typically does not account for capital expenditures, inflation, or non-monetary value considerations, and therefore requires integration with broader financial tools such as discounted cash flow analysis, margin of safety, and scenario planning [16].

In urban economies, break-even analysis has been applied to assess small business resilience, especially in sectors sensitive to external shocks – such as tourism-dependent enterprises in city centers, often together with other financial tools, such as Optimal Computing Budget Allocation [17], cost-benefit evaluations [18, 19] or real options analysis [20], supported by Multi-Criteria Decision-Making [21–23] and comparative evaluations [24]. When adapted to spatial and sectoral heterogeneity, the model offers useful insights into the conditions under which businesses maintain economic viability and how variations in cost or demand structures may alter survival thresholds.

2.2 Sensitivity Analysis

Sensitivity analysis is a widely adopted analytical technique used to assess the degree to which the output of a model or system is affected by variations in its input parameters. Its fundamental aim is to evaluate how uncertainty in individual factors – such as prices, costs, or demand – translates into variability in key performance indicators, including profit, break-even thresholds, or return on investment [25]. Originating in systems analysis and managerial economics, sensitivity analysis has become integral in financial modeling, risk assessment, and operational planning, [26] and is often used in combination with multi-criteria analyses [27] to quantify alternatives' inherent risks.

The classical structure of sensitivity analysis involves a base-case scenario derived from deterministic inputs, followed by systematic perturbations of one or more variables to evaluate the resulting change in outcomes [28]. This may be carried out one-factor-at-a-time (OAT) – where a single parameter is varied while others are held constant – or through multi-factor analysis, which evaluates the interaction of simultaneous changes. Formally, for a function $f(x_1,x_2,\ldots,x_n)$, the method assesses the responsiveness of f to partial changes in each x_i [29].

Several modeling approaches support sensitivity analysis. Scenario analysis constructs alternative futures – commonly best-case, base-case, and worst-case scenarios – based on expert judgment or historical data. More advanced frameworks include Monte Carlo simulations, which use stochastic sampling to estimate a probability distribution of outcomes under defined assumptions [30]. These methods are particularly useful in environments characterized by high volatility and exogenous risk factors, such as geopolitical crises, pandemics, or market disruptions.

In business applications, sensitivity analysis is frequently integrated with cost-volume-profit (CVP) models, break-even analysis, and budget forecasting [31]. It enables firms to identify critical thresholds beyond which operational or financial sustainability is compromised. For instance, businesses can test how different levels of fixed cost, price elasticity, or customer churn affect their ability to remain profitable. In sectors with high fixed costs and fluctuating demand – such as hospitality, transportation, or manufacturing – this type of analysis is indispensable for assessing resilience and defining contingency strategies [32].

The interpretive value of sensitivity analysis lies not only in identifying how much an outcome changes, but also in pinpointing which variables have the greatest influence on that change. This supports targeted interventions – such as cost containment, price adjustments, or diversification of revenue streams – focused on the most impactful parameters. Additionally, sensitivity analysis contributes to the evaluation of the margin of safety, or the degree of variation that can be absorbed before a business falls below a critical threshold of viability [33].

The approach plays a central role in strategic decision-making under uncertainty. Clarifying the range and severity of potential deviations from projected outcomes helps both private actors and policymakers to prioritize risks, allocate resources, and design more adaptive and robust operational models in contexts of systemic uncertainty.

3   Case Study: The Food Service Industry in the City of Rome

3.1   Rome and Over-Tourism

In recent years, Rome has become one of the most visited cities in Europe, with tourism playing a central role in its urban economy and morphology. Following the COVID-19 downturn, visitor flows have not only recovered but surpassed pre-pandemic levels [34]. The city recorded approximately 60 million tourist presences in 2023, marking a 9% increase over 2019 [35]. This phenomenon, often described as "over-tourism," manifests in the physical concentration of visitors in specific zones, the saturation of infrastructure, and the reconfiguration of commercial activity around international demand [36]. It also produces a different functionalism within the city, leading to a new generation of urban areas, [37] while subtracting them from the public and social use [38] to turn them into commercial districts, where tourism serves as a private good. Moreover, urban transportation flows are strongly altered and congested [39].

Over-tourism in Rome has produced significant spatial imbalances, with the historic center and a handful of adjoining districts absorbing the majority of tourist flows. Despite bringing short-term economic benefits, a tourism-focused model conflicts with other more structured territorial models [40] [41]. Even outside major cities, where tourism was long conceived as a path for the enhancement of small towns [42], its role is being rethought [43] in favor of more place-based approaches.

This intensification of short-term visits has led to the proliferation of restaurants, short-term rentals, and leisure services, often at the expense of residential and traditional commercial uses, and critically affecting the real estate market and property-related issues [44]. At the same time, peripheral areas remain largely oriented toward local consumption, displaying divergent patterns of economic and spatial development [45] and frequent material decay [46–48], with a negative effect on land value [49] unless targeted initiatives are launched specifically for them [50]. Moreover, the fluctuations in property values (in their economic and environmental dimensions [51] hinder long-term strategies regarding housing and its enhancement [52].

The administrative structure of Rome consists of 15 Municipios, each with distinct demographic, territorial, and socio-economic features. These subdivisions offer a valuable framework for analyzing how tourism and related economic transformations distribute unevenly across urban space (Table 1).

3.2 Quantitative Survey of Restaurants in Rome

The structure and expansion of Rome's restaurant sector have been profoundly shaped by both tourism dynamics and changing patterns in local consumption. In order to assess the extent and typology of food service establishments in the city, a comprehensive quantitative survey was conducted, integrating data from multiple sources, including the FIPE Annual Report (2023), the Registro delle Imprese (Chamber of Commerce), and Google Maps API (for restaurant reviews and categorization). Moreover, some previous crowdmapping and mapping research works were referred to. [53, 54].

As of 2024, the city of Rome hosts approximately 24,000 restaurants, distributed unevenly across the 15 Municipios. Their typological composition reflects varying price points, customer volumes, space requirements, and degrees of dependency on tourist flows. For analytical purposes, four main categories were established [55], drawing from FIPE classifications and adjusted for the urban context:

- Fine Dining – High-end establishments with high average prices, limited capacity, and a strong dependence on international clientele.
- Trattorias – Traditional Italian eateries, moderate in price and volume, often located in tourist-heavy or culturally significant zones.
- Fast Casual/Pizzerias – Medium- to low-cost restaurants focused on high turnover and affordability.

- Street Food/Takeaway – Small footprint businesses relying on high volume, often informal or semi-formal in structure.
- Neighborhood Restaurants – Local-serving establishments embedded in residential areas, with lower prices and limited exposure to tourist demand.

The distribution of these restaurants throughout the Municipios is shown in Table 2.

Table 1. Subdivision and characterization of the 15 Municipios in Rome.

Municipio	Population (2024)	Area (km^2)	Characterization
I	196,000	19.9	Historic core, high tourism, dense restaurant and accommodation presence
II	168,000	13.4	Affluent, semi-central, mixed residential and cultural zones
III	220,000	25.7	Residential, middle-class, low tourism exposure
IV	185,000	32.6	Transitional, with industrial and emerging cultural spaces
V	245,000	27.7	High-density, diverse, gentrifying areas (e.g., Pigneto)
VI	260,000	113.0	Peripheral, low-income, suburban sprawl
VII	310,000	73.0	Densely populated, residential, some tourist corridors (Appian Way)
VIII	150,000	17.5	Regenerating, alternative cultural districts (Ostiense, Garbatella)
IX	195,000	183.0	Business and residential (EUR), low tourism outside central hub
X	235,000	150.0	Coastal, seasonal tourism (Ostia), suburban areas inland
XI	160,000	13.7	Working-class, residential, limited tourism
XII	150,000	20.2	Residential, green areas, low visitor density
XIII	140,000	32.6	Suburban, mixed use, low tourist appeal
XIV	130,000	41.9	Peripheral, mostly residential, very low tourism
XV	155,000	186.0	Affluent suburban zones, low to moderate tourism (e.g., Ponte Milvio)

3.3 Financial Analysis

The financial analysis aims to estimate the cost structures, revenue potential, and viability thresholds of restaurant operations in Rome across the four primary typologies: Fine Dining, Trattorias, Fast Casual / Pizzerias, and Street Food/Takeaway. The analysis integrates publicly available economic data with typology-specific modeling assumptions to construct a framework for break-even evaluation.

Table 2. Definition of restaurant typologies and quantitative survey in each Municipio.

Municipio	Fine Dining	Trattorias	Fast Casual	Street Food	Total
I	723	2,288	2,092	3,412	**8,515**
II	227	843	659	768	**2,497**
III	87	493	471	415	**1,466**
IV	74	407	463	296	**1,240**
V	104	626	618	554	**1,902**
VI	31	456	377	87	**951**
VII	112	758	712	543	**2,125**
VIII	118	774	671	628	**2,191**
IX	83	534	506	373	**1,496**
X	109	719	641	402	**1,871**
XI	48	445	412	309	**1,214**
XII	64	519	392	380	**1,355**
XIII	53	509	418	256	**1,236**
XIV	49	463	397	237	**1,146**
XV	189	695	538	178	**1,600**

Table 3. Generalized calculation of the Break-Even Point for each restaurant typology (in meals/year)

Typology	Avg. Price/Meal (€)	Fixed Costs (€/year)	Variable Cost/Meal (€)	Contribution Margin (€)	BEP (Meals/year)
Fine Dining	120	€220,000 – €370,000	~€40	€80	**~2,750 – 4,625**
Trattorias	50	€180,000 – €300,000	~€18	€32	**~5,600 – 9,400**
Fast Casual/Pizzerias	20	€120,000 – €220,000	~€8	€12	**~10,000 – 18,300**
Street Food/Takeaway	10	€70,000 – €160,000	~€4	€6	**~11,600 – 26,600**

Key input data were sourced from the following:

- FIPE (2023): Average revenues, wage structures, and profitability margins by business type.
- ISTAT (2023) and INPS: Labor cost benchmarks and national averages for food service wages.
- OMI (Osservatorio del Mercato Immobiliare): Municipal-level rental prices for commercial spaces.

- Google Maps Reviews (2024): Used for estimating foot traffic, seating capacity, and price tier distribution across typologies.

  For each restaurant type, the model calculates:

- Fixed costs: Rent, salaries, insurance, taxes, utilities.
- Variable costs: Food and beverage inputs, consumables, cleaning, per-customer utilities.
- Revenue assumptions: Based on average meal prices, table turnover, and seating capacity.

  The assumed average meal prices by typology are the following [56]:

- Fine Dining: €120
- Trattorias: €50
- Fast Casual/Pizzerias: €20
- Street Food/Takeaway: €10.

Fixed costs vary widely by Municipio due to rent differentials. For instance, average rents range from €50–€70/m^2/month in Municipio I to €10–€20/m^2/month in outer districts (OMI, 2023). The average restaurant size was assumed to be 100 m^2 for full-service establishments and 30–50 m^2 for takeaway models. Labor assumptions include 3–12 employees depending on typology, with wage levels estimated using national food service averages (~€21,000/year per FTE) [57].

3.4 Break-Even Analysis

The break-even analysis evaluates the minimum revenue thresholds required for restaurants to remain financially viable, by comparing total costs against projected income per unit sold. It provides a basis for assessing economic vulnerability in the food service sector, particularly under conditions of demand fluctuation or cost volatility. Using data from FIPE (2023), OMI (2023), and INPS wage benchmarks, break-even points (BEP) were calculated for four restaurant typologies, based on fixed costs, variable costs, and average revenue per customer.

Fixed costs included rental expenses, salaries, utilities, and taxes, while variable costs covered food ingredients, consumables, and per-customer overhead. Rent values were derived from the Osservatorio del Mercato Immobiliare (OMI) for Rome's 15 Municipios, with commercial rent ranging from €10/m^2/month in peripheral areas to €70/m^2/month in the historic center. Labor costs reflected staffing needs specific to each typology (from small 3-person teams in takeaway outlets to 10–12 in fine dining) and national wage averages (Table 3).

The BEP values clearly reflect the divergent business models of each typology. High-margin establishments like Fine Dining require fewer customers to break even, while lower-margin models like Street Food depend on high volume. These thresholds become critical when analyzing potential disruptions to demand, as explored in the following sensitivity analysis.

A comparison between the theoretical number of meals required for break-even and the actual number of meals consumed annually in Rome reveals a structural imbalance in the city's food service economy. The aggregate number of meals required to sustain all 23,961 restaurants, based on typology-specific break-even thresholds, amounts to approximately 1.32 billion meals per year. However, estimated total demand – accounting for both residents and tourists – reaches only ~880 million meals per year. This results in a supply-demand gap of approximately 440 million meals annually, indicating that a significant portion of restaurants operate below their financial viability threshold.

Despite this apparent oversupply, the sector does not collapse due to heterogeneous performance across establishments. Industry data and business census reports suggest that typically only 35–40% of restaurants maintain stable financial performance, while the remainder operate either at marginal profitability or sustained deficit, often supported by seasonal spikes, informal labor, or supplementary revenue streams (FIPE 2023; KPMG 2021). This structural fragility underscores the importance of scenario-based risk assessments, particularly in contexts vulnerable to external shocks such as tourism fluctuations.

3.5 Sensitivity Analysis with Scenario Simulation

Given the ongoing geopolitical uncertainty, climate instability, and increasing debate over mass tourism regulation, two realistic tourism decline scenarios were constructed:

- Scenario A: 5% drop in annual tourist arrivals over five years;
- Scenario B: 10% drop in annual tourist arrivals over five years.

Rome currently receives approximately 60 million tourist presences annually (ISTAT 2024), with each tourist consuming an average of 5.5 meals during their stay.

First, the number of tourist meals lost was estimated according to (2).

$$\Delta M = T \cdot r \cdot m \qquad (2)$$

ΔM is the change in total meals consumed by tourists (meals/year), while T is the annual tourist presence in Rome (baseline = 60,000,000), r is the reduction rate in tourist arrivals (e.g., 5% or 10%), and m is the average number of meals per tourist. A 5% decline results in a loss of 16.5 million meals/year, while a 10% decline corresponds to 33 million lost meals/year. These were distributed across Municipios according to (3).

$$\Delta M_i = s_i \cdot \Delta M \qquad (3)$$

s_i is the share of total tourist meals consumed in Municipio i, while ΔM_i is the meals lost in Municipio i. Municipio shares s_i are derived from the proportional tourist distribution (based on hotel beds, Airbnb listings, and tourist density indicators).

Then, the number of restaurants at risk was calculated through (4).

$$F_{i,j} = \frac{\delta_{i,j}}{b_j} \qquad (4)$$

$F_{i,j}$ is the estimated number of additional restaurants falling below BEP, $\delta_{i,j}$ is the decline in meals for restaurants of type j of Municipio i, and finally b_j represents the break-even meals required for restaurant typology j.

Table 4. Number of restaurants falling below BEP in the two scenarios with tourism drops.

Municipio	Scenario A (5% Drop)	Scenario B (10% Drop)
I	250–300	500–600
II	25–40	50–80
III	5–15	10–30
IV	5–10	10–25
V	15–30	30–60
VI	5–10	10–20
VII	20–35	40–70
VIII	20–35	40–70
IX	10–20	20–40
X	15–30	30–60
XI	5–10	10–25
XII	10–15	20–35
XIII	10–15	20–35
XIV	5–10	10–25
XV	15–20	30–40
Total	**450–600**	**900–1,200**

This was then aggregated to evaluate the citywide impact by summating the restaurants falling below BEP throughout the 15 Municipios, as shown in Table 4.

Then, through sensitivity analysis, the Vulnerability was calculated for each Municipio in the two scenarios.

$$V_i = \frac{F_i}{R_i} \tag{5}$$

The results are shown in Table 5.

Table 5. Calculation of the Vulnerability Index for each Municipio through the sensitivity analysis.

Municipio	Restaurants (R_i)	$F_i(A)$	$V_i(A)$	$F_i(B)$	$V_i(B)$
I	8,515	275	0.0323 → **3.2%**	550	0.0646 → **6.5%**
II	2,497	32.5	0.0130 → **1.3%**	65	0.0260 → **2.6%**
III	1,466	10	0.0068 → **0.7%**	20	0.0136 → **1.4%**
IV	1,240	7.5	0.0060 → **0.6%**	17.5	0.0141 → **1.4%**

(*continued*)

Table 5. (*continued*)

Municipio	Restaurants (R$_i$)	F$_i$(A)	V$_i$(A)	F$_i$(B)	V$_i$(B)
V	1,902	22.5	0.0118 → **1.2%**	45	0.0237 → **2.4%**
VI	951	7.5	0.0079 → **0.8%**	15	0.0158 → **1.6%**
VII	2,125	27.5	0.0129 → **1.3%**	55	0.0259 → **2.6%**
VIII	2,191	27.5	0.0125 → **1.3%**	55	0.0251 → **2.5%**
IX	1,496	15	0.0100 → **1.0%**	30	0.0201 → **2.0%**
X	1,871	22.5	0.0120 → **1.2%**	45	0.0240 → **2.4%**
XI	1,214	7.5	0.0062 → **0.6%**	17.5	0.0144 → **1.4%**
XII	1,355	12.5	0.0092 → **0.9%**	27.5	0.0203 → **2.0%**
XIII	1,236	12.5	0.0101 → **1.0%**	27.5	0.0222 → **2.2%**
XIV	1,146	7.5	0.0065 → **0.7%**	17.5	0.0153 → **1.5%**
XV	1,600	17.5	0.0109 → **1.1%**	35	0.0219 → **2.2%**

Municipio I stands out as the vulnerability is more than double the citywide average in Scenario B (6.5%), due to its concentration of tourist-reliant restaurants and high operating costs. Peripheral Municipios (III, IV, VI, XIV) consistently show $V_i < 1.5\%$, even in Scenario B, indicating stronger insulation from tourism shocks.

4   Conclusions

This study has examined the structural dependency of Rome's restaurant sector on international tourism, revealing a condition of systemic economic imbalance and territorial vulnerability. Through a comprehensive analysis of restaurant typologies, financial viability thresholds, and simulated demand shocks, the research demonstrates that a significant portion of food service establishments in the city operate below sustainability thresholds, even under current conditions.

The city's restaurant ecosystem is oversupplied relative to its consumption base. While the break-even distribution of restaurants would require approximately 1.32 billion meals per year, current estimates suggest actual consumption – by both residents and tourists – reaches only ~880 million meals. This structural gap implies that only 35–40% of restaurants are consistently financially viable, while the rest rely on seasonal peaks, informal labor structures, or operate at chronic underperformance.

This fragility is spatially concentrated. The analysis shows that central Municipios, particularly Municipio I, II, and VIII, account for the majority of tourism-dependent restaurants and would bear the greatest losses in the event of a tourism downturn. Under a plausible 10% decline in tourist arrivals, up to 1,450 additional establishments would fall below break-even, with central zones alone accounting for nearly half of these. By contrast, more residential districts such as Municipio VI and XIV demonstrate significantly lower exposure.

These patterns point to a broader economic threat: the over-concentration of restaurant activity in tourism-driven districts, and the city's growing dependence on international visitation, create a form of economic monoculture. This dependency not only amplifies the effects of exogenous shocks but also distorts real estate markets and labor dynamics, undermining the long-term sustainability of the sector.

These findings call for a shift in the criteria used to evaluate urban vitality and commercial health. Indicators of growth in restaurant numbers should be critically reassessed in light of their underlying financial sustainability. For policymakers, this implies the need to reframe support measures, moving beyond sectoral expansion and toward stabilization, diversification, and territorial equity. Urban planning instruments should account for demand thresholds, discourage speculative saturation in central areas, and foster mixed-use ecosystems that blend resident-driven services with tourism infrastructures. In doing so, Rome can begin to transition from a model of intensive exploitation of visitor flows to a more resilient [58] and balanced urban economy.

References

1. Della Corte, V., Doria, C., Oddo, G.: The impact of COVID-19 on international tourism flows to Italy: evidence from mobile phone data. The World Econ. **46**(2), 488–512 (2023)
2. Pinate, A.C., Faggian, A., Brandano, M.G.: The impact of COVID-19 on the tourism sector in Italy: a regional spatial perspective. Tour. Econ. **29**(3), 655–679 (2023)
3. Corbisiero, F., Monaco, S.: Post-pandemic tourism resilience: changes in Italians' travel behavior and the possible responses of tourist cities. Worldwide Hosp. Tourism Themes **13**(3), 369–382 (2021)
4. Cellini, R., Torre, L.: History to eat. The foodification of the historic centre of Florence. Cities **99**, 102607 (2020)
5. Esposito, A.: Tourism-driven displacement in Naples. Italy. Land Use Policy **134**, 106919 (2023)
6. Mascarello, G., Pinto, A., Rizzoli, V., Tiozzo, B., Crovato, S., Ravarotto, L.: Ethnic food consumption in Italy: the role of food neophobia and openness to different cultures. Foods **9**(2), 112 (2020)
7. Madanoglu, M., Ozdemir, O.: Tourism firms' vulnerability to risk: the role of organizational resilience, firm orientation, and industry context. J. Travel Res. **61**(5), 1021–1036 (2022)
8. Parlak, V., Salinas, G., Vargas, M.: Estimating the impact of external shocks on the ECCU: Application to the COVID shock. IMF Working Papers 2021/218, International Monetary Fund (2021)
9. Finucci, F., Masanotti, A.G., Mazzoni, D.: Preliminary evaluation approaches in the urban regeneration of Corviale in Rome. Lect. Notes Netw. Syst. **1186**, 128–141 (2023)
10. Jamaludin, A.: Analysis of break-even point in Cv. Bata Cikarang Indonesia. Int. J. Res. - Granthaalayah **7**(9), 259–267 (2019)
11. Abdullahi, S.R., Bello, S.B., Mukhtar, I.S., Musa, M.H.: Cost-volume-profit analysis as a management tool for decision making in small business enterprise within Bayero University, Kano. IOSR J. Bus. Manag. **19**(2), 40–45 (2017)
12. Kavitha, R.: Cost volume profitability analysis—an empirical study with reference to Salem Steel Authority of India Limited (SAIL), Tamilnadu. Int. J. Bus. Manage. Invent. **7**(5), 46–51 (2018)
13. Alnasser, N., Shaban, O.S., Shaban, Z.: The effect of using break-even-point in planning controlling, and decision making in the industrial Jordanian companies. Int. J. Acad. Res. Bus. Soc. Sci. **4**(5), 626–637 (2014)

14. Dubas, K.M., Hershey, L., Nijhawan, I.P., Mehta, R.: Breakeven and profitability analyses in marketing management using R software. Innov. Mark. **7**(3), 45–78 (2011)
15. Tui, R.N.S., Anas, A.V., Fitriani, N.: Breakeven point and incremental analysis in decision making of lease-purchase option of heavy equipment at nickel lateritic ore mining. ARPN J. Eng. Appl. Sci. **12**(13), 4084–4088 (2017)
16. Kumar, N.C.: Break-even analysis in healthcare setup. J. Res. Finan. Healthcare Administ. (2013)
17. Acampa, G., Pino, A.: Optimal computing budget allocation for urban regeneration: an unprecedented match between economic/extra-economic evaluations and urban planning. In: Gervasi, O., Murgante, B., Misra, S., et al. (eds.) Computational Science and Its Applications – ICCSA 2023 Workshops, LNCS, vol. 14300, pp. 69–79. Springer, Cham (2023)
18. Acampa, G., Finucci, F., Grasso, M., Magarò, A.: Preliminary approach for the cost-benefit analysis in the building envelope: study and comparison of actions. In: Calabrò, F., Della Spina, L., Piñeira Mantiñán, M.J. (eds.) New Metropolitan Perspectives. NMP 2022. LNNS, vol. 482. Springer, Cham (2022). https://doi.org/10.1007/978-3-031-06825-6_74
19. Del Giudice, V., Passeri, A., Torrieri, F., De Paola, P.: Risk analysis within feasibility studies: an application to cost-benefit analysis for the construction of a new road. Appl. Mech. Mater. **651–653**, 1249–1254 (2014)
20. Del Giudice, V., Passeri, A., De Paola, P., Torrieri, F.: Estimation of risk-return for real estate investments by applying Ellwood's model and real options analysis: an application to the residential real estate market of Naples. Appl. Mech. Mater. **651–653**, 1570–1575 (2014)
21. Baratta, A.F.L., Finucci, F., Magarò, A.: Generative design process: multi-criteria evaluation and multidisciplinary approach. TECHNE – J. Technol. Architect. Environ. 304–314 (2021)
22. Acampa, G., Grasso, M., Pino, A.: An MCA proposal with ANP and veto thresholds to support decision-making in former railway track regeneration initiatives. In: Gervasi, O., Murgante, B., Misra, S., et al. (eds.) Computational Science and Its Applications – ICCSA 2024 Workshops, LNCS, vol. 14300, pp. 376–385. Springer, Cham (2024)
23. Acampa, G., Grasso, M.: Heritage evaluation: restoration plan through HBIM and MCDA. IOP Conf. Ser. Mater. Sci. Eng. **949**(1), 012061 (2020)
24. Nicolella, M., Landolfi, R., Pino, A., Scognamillo, C.: Comparative evaluations of sustainability, durability and resilience of external envelopes for environmentally efficient buildings. IOP Conf. Ser. Earth Environ. Sci. **296**, 012023 (2019)
25. Mowbray, F.I., Manlongat, D., Shukla, M.: Sensitivity analysis: a method to promote certainty and validity in nursing research. Can. J. Nurs. Res. **54**(1), 5–7 (2022)
26. Thabane, L., Mbuagbaw, L., Zhang, S., et al.: A tutorial on sensitivity analyses in clinical trials: the what, why, when and how. BMC Med. Res. Methodol. **13**, 92 (2013)
27. Battisti, F.: ELECTRE III for strategic environmental assessment: a "phantom" approach. Sustainability **14**(10), 6221 (2022)
28. Razavi, S., Gupta, H.V.: A new framework for comprehensive, robust, and efficient global sensitivity analysis: 1. Theory. Water Resour. Res. **52**(1), 423–439 (2016)
29. Saltelli, A., Tarantola, S., Chan, K.: A quantitative, model independent method for global sensitivity analysis of model output. Technometrics **41**(1), 39–56 (1999)
30. Ratto, M., Tarantola, S., Saltelli, A.: Sensitivity analysis in model calibration: GSAGLUE approach. Comput. Phys. Commun. **136**(3), 212–224 (2001)
31. Krykacz-Hausmann, B.: Epistemic sensitivity analysis based on the concept of entropy. In: Prado, P., Bolado, R. (eds.) Proceedings of SAMO2001, pp. 31–35. CIEMAT, Madrid (2001)
32. Archer, G., Saltelli, A., Sobol', I.M.: Sensitivity measures, ANOVA like techniques and the use of bootstrap. J. Stat. Comput. Simul. **58**, 99–120 (1997)
33. Fürbinger, J.M.: Sensitivity analysis for modellers. Air Infiltrat. Rev. 17(4) (1996)

34. Testa, F., Galanti, M.T.: Culture & tourism in Rome: what is the future of the Eternal City? A new storytelling to save the old history. AlmaTourism **9**(7), 99–113 (2018)
35. ISTAT: Tourist flows - Fourth quarter 2023. Istituto Nazionale di Statistica (ISTAT) (2024)
36. Vagena, A.: Overtourism: definition and impact. Academia Letters (2021)
37. Miccoli, S., Fabrizio, F., Murro, R.: A new generation of urban areas. Feasibility elements. In: Advances in Energy Science and Equipment Engineering, pp. 1146–1149. Taylor & Francis Group (2015)
38. Miccoli, S., Finucci, F., Murro, R.: Shared infrastructures: technique and method for an inclusive social valuation. In: Transport Infrastructure and Systems, pp. 759–768. CRC Press (2017)
39. Acampa, G., Pino, A., Alberti, F., Rossi, G.: The URGET VADEMECUM 2030–2050 project: applying threshold theory to sustainable urban mobility. In: Calabrò, F., Madureira, L., Morabito, F.C., Piñeira Mantiñán, M.J. (eds.) Networks, Markets & People, LNNS, vol. 1186, pp. 172–181. Springer, Cham (2024)
40. Rossitti, M., Torrieri, F.: The THEMA tool to support heritage-based development strategies for marginal areas: evidence from an Italian inner area in Campania Region. Region **9**(2), 109–129 (2022)
41. Stanganelli, M., Torrieri, F., Gerundo, C., Rossitti, M.: A strategic performance-based planning methodology to promote the regeneration of fragile territories. Lect. Notes Civil Eng. **146**, 149–157 (2021)
42. Acampa, G., Pino, A.: Village repopulation: analysis of extra-economic indicators to evaluate and valorise social generativity in ecovillages. In: Calabrò, F., Madureira, L., Morabito, F.C., Piñeira Mantiñán, M.J. (eds.) Networks, Markets & People, LNNS, vol. 1186, pp. 257–266. Springer, Cham (2024)
43. Acampa, G., Pino, A.: Filling the old with new life: application of original indicators for evaluating ecovillages as village repopulation initiatives. Aestimum **85**, 73–86 (2024)
44. Miccoli, S., Finucci, F., Murro, R.: Integrating stated preference methods for property valuations in housing markets: an experimental case study in Italy. Int. J. Housing Markets Anal. **12**(3), 474–486 (2019)
45. Rossitti, M., Torrieri, F.: Action research for the conservation of architectural heritage in marginal areas: the role of evaluation. Valori e Valutazioni **30**, 3–42 (2022)
46. Torrieri, F., Oppio, A., Rossitti, M.: Damage assessment for architectural heritage: the Cavallerizza Reale complex in Turin. Valori e Valutazioni **30**, 71–84 (2022)
47. Acampa, G., Diana, L., Marino, G., Marmo, R.: Assessing the transformability of public housing through BIM. Sustainability (Switzerland) **13**(10), 5431 (2021)
48. Diana, L., D'Auria, S., Acampa, G., Marino, G.: Assessment of disused public buildings: strategies and tools for reuse of healthcare structures. Sustainability (Switzerland) **14**(4), 2361 (2022)
49. Oppio, A., Torrieri, F., Dell'Oca, E.: Land value in urban development agreements: methodological perspectives and operational recommendations. Valori e Valutazioni **21**, 87–96 (2018)
50. Battisti, F., Campo, O.: The assessment of density bonus in building renovation interventions. The Case of the City of Florence in Italy. Land **10**(12), 1391 (2021)
51. Battisti, F., Pisano, C.: Common property in italy. unresolved issues and an appraisal approach: towards a definition of environmental-economic civic value. Land **11**(11), 1927 (2022)
52. Battisti, F.: SDGs and ESG criteria in housing: defining local evaluation criteria and indicators for verifying project sustainability using florence metropolitan area as a case study. Sustainability **15**(12), 9372 (2023)
53. Finucci, F., Masanotti, A.G.: Crowdmapping: inclusive cities and evaluation. Lect. Notes Comput. Sci. **14112**, 80–90 (2023)

54. Torrieri, F., Oppio, A., Rossitti, M.: Cultural heritage social value and community mapping. Smart Innov. Syst. Technol. **178**, 1786–1795 (2021)
55. Longart, P., Wickens, E., Bakir, A.: An investigation into restaurant attributes: a basis for a typology. Int. J. Hosp. Tour. Adm. **18**(4), 385–411 (2017)
56. Mun, S.G., Jang, S.S.: Restaurant operating expenses and their effects on profitability enhancement. Int. J. Hosp. Manag. **71**, 68–76 (2018)
57. Tyagi, M., Bolia, N.: Approaches for restaurant revenue management. J. Revenue Pricing Manag. **21**(2), 123–134 (2022)
58. Rossitti, M., Torrieri, F.: Circular economy as 'catalyst' for resilience in inner areas. Sustain. Mediterran. Construct **5**, 64–67 (2021)

Ecologica. Urban Regeneration of Buildings of Worship. Cultural and Associative Dynamics in Northern and Southern Europe

Donatella Scatena[1]([✉]) [ID], Marcello Valerio Cadorin[1] [ID], Sergio Amedeo Terracina[1], and Zeynep Gulel[2] [ID]

[1] Sapienza University of Rome, piazzale Aldo Moro, 5, 00185 Rome, Italy
{donatella.scatena,marcellovalerio.cadorin}@uniroma1.it
[2] Mimar Sinan Fine Arts University, Pürtelas Hasan Efendi, Meclis -i Medusan, 24, 34427 Istanbul, Türkiye

Abstract. In its etymological meaning, ecology proposes and argues the theme of home and habitat as an interactive situation of living species. The distinctive features of the urban landscape refer here to the cultural and material heritage and use codes to interpret and assess the characteristics of the cities: historic, suburb or sprawling cities. This analysis does not focus on individual architectural objects, but looks at urban spaces and their relationships between them. The urban regeneration of squares with buildings of worship of this article requires a multidisciplinary approach: to integrate architectural, urbanistic and sociological skills; to understand the cultural and associative dynamics of different communities and the stratification of places. The interactions and flows between the different components of community life are intended for urban textures of public spaces and buildings. Computer science can aid the design process. They are used in computer programs for electronic design and augmented or virtual reality, but their contribution to the analysis of datas in the urban project is still to be developed and implemented. Cases studio are largo Spartaco at Tuscolano in Rome, the Great Mosque of Rome, the Church of SS. Cipriano Cornelio in Calcata, the Catholic Church of SS. Patrizio Giacomo and the Lukiškės square in Vilnius and, Şakirin Mosque and Courtyard in Istanbul.

Keywords: urban regeneration · urban design · public spaces · places of worship · squares · heritages · technologies · ecological · memories

1 *Ecologica* Premise

In 1866 the German doctor and biologist Ernest Haeckel defined the term ecology in his paper *Generelle Morphologie des Organismen*, designating it as "conditions of possibility" (according to I. Kant's expression) the physical, chemical and biological life of humans, animals and plants. In its etymological meaning, ecology proposes and argues the theme of home and habitat as an interactive situation of living species. In the cultural traditions of Europe, it was effectively explained by Aristotle, who regarded the city-state

O. Gervasi et al. (Eds.): ICCSA 2025 Workshops, LNCS 15891, pp. 122–140, 2026.
https://doi.org/10.1007/978-3-031-97617-9_9

as an institution of a political body in which common interests and common reasons of the social corpus converge. Such an order should lead to ways of civil life, which recognize a valid foundation for friendship and the striving towards good. The house as a small town, the city as a great house. In XV century in Italy this principle was affirmed by L. B. Alberti in his "De re aedificatoria" and taken up in the following centuries by other authors such as Palladio, Aldo Van Eyck, Aldo Rossi. In our historical time, ecology suggests searches and paths of dynamic balance (therefore, never solved), from which parameters and elements of a holistic layout of fertile concerns can be defined. To decline the motive of the house as much at the small scale as at the large one: isolated, cities and territories in order to try better prospections of future for men in their environments. To draw profitable tension from *natura naturata* and *natura naturans* according to the happy interpretation of Spinoza. The article, which presents research of the four authors[1], focuses on some key words: Ecological, Memory, Heritage, Urban Regeneration. The contribution aims to relate areas of Europe, from North to South, which extend to the East, places that have as a recurring character both the value assigned to the material and intangible cultural heritage, and a privileged relationship with the sea (Mediteranno, Baltic, Bosphorus) and examined the cities of: Istanbul, Rome, Vilnius. In an age that sees the weight of the spiritual wane in favor of a secularization, the article asks how places of worship, and their public spaces still produce communities and urban regeneration. The reconfiguration of public space, increasingly rapid to cope with social changes dictated by technological progress, can be facilitated by the exploitation of the heritage of places of worship and the adjacent square. These places of the collective insert in the hectic daily life of the metropolis spaces of rest, physical and intellectual, that well lend themselves to be a flywheel for urban regeneration thanks precisely to their ability to aggregate, due not only to religious functions; They create a collective and social virtual and cultural space that today is also fed by new technologies. Our places of worship, as indicated in this article, also benefit from contributions from computer science. The latter can be a useful means both in the project process, to promote participation from below by citizens, and in the expectation of results on an urban scale, through the analysis of flows, perceptions and increased graphic representation. Finally, they can be used for the creation of so-called virtual squares at the service of culture, education and use of the spaces themselves.

2   The Plural Identity of the Collective Open Space

The distinctive features of the urban landscape refer here to the tangible and intangible cultural heritage and use specific codes to interpret and assess the characteristics of the physical city (whether it is a historic city, a suburb or a sprawling city). The analysis does not focus on individual architectural objects but looks at urban spaces as areas of relationship and the relationships between them. This leads to the reading of an even more complex text, where the narrative structure (represented by the urban structure), intertwine and overlap the plots of individuals and social groups. Next to the objective

---

[1] The research bearing the same title of the article is composed by Donatella Scatena (chapters: 2, 7), Marcello Valerio Cadorin (chapters: 3, 4, 5), Sergio Amedeo Terracina (chapter: 1), Zeynep Guel (chapter: 6), coordinated by Professor Donatella Scatena;

city, based on the physicality of hard matter, there is therefore a parallel world made up of subjective cities, represented in (and by) each individual, who not only inhabits the physical space of the city, but also lives simultaneously in the affective spaces, aesthetic and symbolic, of the personal mental city.

Since the contemporary city has difficulty in characterizing itself through open space, what interests us in this article is the meaning of new codes of interpretation of the sense of place; a relationship that combines subjective city and objective city, a cultural and physical path that transforms the concept of unique identity into that of plural identity, an experience of participation between those who inhabit the space and those who must "foresee" and design it. To do this, the research uses readings and interpretations not only of architectural theorists, but especially of Nobel prize winner Amartya Sen[2] and sociologist and anthropologist Richard Sennett. The public spaces given as an example will be a small taxonomy of the participation process in place in the transformation of urban characters of open spaces.

2.1 Urban Landscape Theories

Research on the subjective representation of the environment, which has given rise to a wide literature in the international field, have shown how it is possible to distinguish between an architectural space, understood as objective and physical reality of the territory, and a personal space, understood as individual ways of using and imagining the environmental reality.

2.2 Gordon Cullen Townscape

Theories based on perceptual analysis begin with Gordon Cullen, who in 1961 published the book *Townscape* (literally "urban landscape") text-manifesto in which the author immediately introduces an innovative postulate according to which the city is a particular form of landscape, linked to the persistence of the urban image - here understood as a metaphorical extension of the physical meaning of the laws of optics and biometrics. Cullen also uses a problematic assumption: the "perception" of the urban image is used as a tool for reading and designing space. Exploring the evocative potential and aesthetic characteristics of urban spaces, the book thus identifies the vocabulary and syntax for the description and assessment of the context, using representation techniques consistent with the priority given to visual perception and the daily experience of the city. Cullen develops a vision of urban design through visual education aimed at the construction of a new urban landscape.

2.3 Kevin Lynch Concept of «*Figurability*»

Other important scholars, such as Kevin Lynch, and Steen Eiler Rasmussen, and in Italy Ludovico Quaroni, elaborated almost simultaneously in the 50s and 60s of the last

---

[2] Amartya Kumar Sen is an Indian economist and philosopher, Nobel Prize for economics in 1998, Lamont University Professor at Harvard University, author of "*Identity and Violence*" (2006);

century some fundamental theories on urban perception. In particular, the studies conducted by Lynch, born from the meeting with one of the initiators of the *Gestaltpsycology* Gyorgy Kepes, have always moved in an attempt to remove the theme of the perceptual form of the city from the uncertainty of the individual interpretation, and therefore not codable, introducing the fundamental concept of "figurability". It can be said that this concept is the core of all the research conducted by Lynch, as it points towards a possible objectification, in psychological terms, of the perception of the city, as a result of a relationship between the cognitive structure of and that of the urban environment lived by the inhabitants themselves, in order to a clear "recognizability" of the parties. With his notion of "figurability" of the urban image, Lynch contributed to the birth of a real "cognitive theory of the city", confirming at the same time the considerable distance from the idea of "figure" as matured in the European iconography. Lynch's fame is mainly linked to his 1960's The Image of the City, in which he proposed a perceptive approach to the theme of form and urban landscape. For Lynch, the urban image is structured in a number of recurring elements which he analyses and describes and whose recurrence he tends to verify in his interviews: paths (paths), boundaries (edges), reference points (landmarks), nodes (nodes) and districts (districts). On the basis of this anthropological-perceptive paradigm it is possible to draw a kind of mental topographic map, the so-called mental map, which represents a real visual description of the city. The urban object to acquire significance must become memorizable. Every time a subject occupies an urban space, he has to decipher this enormous complex text that is the city, recognizing in it topological objects useful for his daily action: "living (walking, shopping, parking, etc.) is first and foremost a cognitive or semiotic performance; it requires deciphering the urban text in search of warning signs, possibilities, prohibitions, permission, enjoyment, convenience, etc. This competence is first of all morphological, it consists in recognizing forms and attributing them a meaning connected to the practices of everyday life". In this context, the concept of sense of place is absolutely central: "The sense, or spirit of place, it corresponds to a very complex concept and difficult to reconcile with a linear concept in that it depends both on the features of a territory which together constitute what is defined as the identity of the place, and from the connotation that these features assume in the experience of each individual" [1]. The difficulty of trying to delineate this sense of belonging to a place, understood as meaning for the individual after he has intellectually appropriated it, is evident, being an ambiguous conception, which unites "objectivity and subjectivity, factual geographical reality and inner experience".

2.4 Ludovico Quaroni, Image as Knowledge of Reality

One of the first architects to talk about the perception of personal space in Italy was Ludovico Quaroni, who wrote *Immagine di Roma* in 1969. The innovative choice to talk about Rome, not focusing on structure but image, is conscious for Quaroni because the image is emotionally dirty, passionately addressed, ambiguous for construction, it accompanies and overlaps with the rationality of the language of form, of the project.

Today, the image is the obligatory door of knowledge of reality. More than Urbs, the city of stone, Quaroni is attracted and intrigued by civitas, the population that lives in it and its habits. Habits which, taken as a whole, describe and define the culture of the city, its mentality. The Roman population, proud and contradictory together, is the guarantee that the city is not rigid in its own simulacrum but is always immersed in the flow of transformations. More than the city that is supposed to be completed, the city designed integrally, Quaroni is attracted by the wonder that the city generates continuously in those who inhabit it, the wonderful city.

The city of Rome is seen by Quaroni as "a figurative whole" where the relationship between history and project is expressed and where architecture, contaminating itself with ancient finds, recognizes the legitimacy of its own tradition; those finds can use the "new" as a litmus paper, as a mirror to be questioned and from which to draw a *principium individutionis*.

The contamination that comes from history, from the existing heritage, allows tradition to express itself even if in a confused way. The same "dirty" way that uses memory, both the private of the Intellectual, considered by election depository of values (Manfredo Tafuri), and the collective one that interests in this article and that is used to create an authentic image of the place-city.

Memory produces the image from which the wonderful daily descends: it includes the contaminations of society, the underhanded, the chaotic, the richness of diversity and leads to the creation of a "difficult unity" (Robert Venturi), typical of poetry. Robert Venturi has made much reference to the difficult unity and inclusive process to explain the beauty of the contradiction and complexity of the urban design: easy unity is achieved through the exclusive process of separation, On the contrary, the inclusive process is achieved through the inclusivity of an urban project made of opposite elements, "good ambiguity" and "confusion of experience" that are typical of the poetic process. In fact, Venturi always tells us, the poet does not separate but includes.

2.5   Unification of the Experience Poetic Background of the Mind

The unification of experience, which is typical of the poetic process, was also a great achievement of science, which through Bateson, reveals the relationship between mind and nature and declares that the poetic background of mind is at the basis of the process of biological evolution.

The unification of experience, also read as a network of relationships that connects us to each other, is the great discovery of the new scientific paradigm, which wants to reveal the new and different order that is at the base of dissipative and chaotic phenomena, but above all it wants to reveal the creative capacity of open systems. The unification of experience, also called the structure that connects, through a new covenant between man and nature, helps us to overcome the architectural nihilism of the *Nonplace*, where the excess of space, of time and ego, together with the spectacularized history and the place as loss of identity and sense).

2.6   The Wonderful Everyday

In this contemporary city, like the Rome of Quaroni and the New Jersey of Lynch, which is mostly identified with the physical "periphery", a meaning of public space must be reconstructed, through the wonderful daily life.

To recover the popular sense of the lost place, it is possible replacing the unique identity with a plural identity, through a work of collaboration and participation that starts from the bottom.

This means clearly addressing the problems posed by globalization, compared to being together, which is the primary foundation of the birth of the city and public space. In the projects we must claim substantial aspects of collaboration, we must understand that it is necessary to think in a new way, that it is necessary to trust in the expression of differences and experiences, to think in plural, claiming diversity. To the "miniaturization of individuals" and to the conflictuality that we find in our time, caused by the crisis of values of the West and which finds exegetes in the theory of the conflict of civilizations, it is necessary to answer with the words of Amartya Sen: "The prospects for peace in the contemporary world may arise perhaps from the recognition of the plural nature of our affiliations, and from recourse to reasoned discussion as mere inhabitants of a vast world, Instead of making of ourselves so many prisoners rigidly imprisoned in narrow containers". Going out in the open air, in open public spaces, because, always quoting Sen, "for democracy (we) mean to discuss it publicly". Plural identity versus single identity: "the polis is composed of men of different types; similar populations cannot give rise to the polis". Therefore, the city obliges people to take into account others who have different identities from their own and to relate to them".

It is not a question of suggesting a way of designing or an architecture of trend, but to propose an experience, convinced that the "theories" at the base of this proposed experience "can influence social thought, political action and public policies". This experience is a difficult collaboration because it requires expertise. Aristotle calls it techne, the technical ability to make a thing be, doing it well.

"The positive alternative (to cynicism, nihilism and collusion of unique identity) is a type of collaboration challenging and difficult: that which tries to bring together people who have different or conflicting interests, who do not have mutual sympathy, that they are not equal or simply do not understand each other. The challenge is to respond to the other or start from his point of view. That is the challenge in all cases of conflict management".

2.7 Single Identity Plural Identity for Urban Design

Bruno Zevi has written in a provocative way: «to do architecture means to visualize the genius loci», it is an «absurdity aimed at passivating the project with respect to its surroundings, instead of pushing to create or at least renew it. If Wright, in the innocuous forest of Bear Run, had proposed to mirror the genius loci, instead of the legendary House on the Waterfall he would have built a dirty shack».

The identity of a place must therefore be understood as an uninterrupted succession of evolutionary characteristics.

To give an example, we think of a place familiar to us and in which one recognizes a strong architectural, cultural, social peculiarity: the Mediterranean. To the question: «what is the Mediterranean?» the historian and geographer Fernand Braudel replied: «A thousand things together. Not a landscape, but countless landscapes. Not a sea, but a succession of seas. Not one civilization, but a series of civilizations stacked on top of each other. (…) In the physical landscape as in the human one, the Mediterranean is a cross-roads, the heterodox Mediterranean presents itself to our memory as a coherent image, a system in which everything merges and recomposes into an original unity». On the other hand, the identity of the Mediterranean, in which material and immaterial relations converge into a «space-movement» that has historically created a very strong unitary imaginary, has not remained unchanged over the centuries. In fact, as Lucien Febvre, quoted by Braudel, reminds us, if Herodotus were to mingle with contemporary tourists, he would not recognize any of those that for us are undoubtedly constituent components of the Mediterranean landscape: oranges, lemons, tomatoes, cypresses, chestnuts, peppers, eggplants. Yet both - the landscape coeval with Herodotus and ours - are original landscapes, endowed with their own unmistakable identity. In both, in fact, the sense of belonging of a community to its own environment finds dwelling and expression, understood as «value continuously built by the will of those who inhabit and use the territory». The identity of a landscape is therefore not a fixed and immutable product, but it is an evolutionary concept, insofar as there exists a two-way link of continuous feedback and active interferences between settled communities and territories. Identity, then, turns out to be the result - historical and geographical - of a process of differentiation of one community from others. Identity must therefore be understood as an uninterrupted succession of evolutionary characteristics. This implies first of all to recognize the dynamic character - for its continuous change over time - and paradoxical - for the ability to offer us new objects and symbolic permanence - of the identity of the urban landscape. This procedural definition of the landscape is perfectly consistent with the definition of «identity», which, referring to mathematics, indicates «an equation that continues to be true whatever the value of the symbols of which it is composed». It is a definition that does not deny but rather implies the continuous change of the symbols that enter the equation.

3 Meeting Places. The Collective Spaces of Four Buildings of Worship, to Live Together

The urban regeneration of squares with buildings of worship of this article therefore requires a multidisciplinary approach that integrates, in unison, architectural, urbanistic and sociological skills, because only by understanding the cultural and associative dynamics of the different communities and the stratification of places, it is possible to achieve satisfactory results from the point of view of design and consequences on citizenship. It is only through a deep understanding of a place and the analysis of its aggregative potential that public spaces are created that are inclusive, functional and representative. The urban regeneration of the squares that house places of worship, such as churches and mosques, represents a potential for the contemporary city, also by virtue of the international scenarios of the beginning of the millennium: religious conflict and interfaith dialogue. The squares and buildings of worship are traditionally places of assembly, that is social aggregation, where lay and religious practices are intertwined, daily and extraordinary, such as celebrations of festivals or various events. The regeneration of these spaces requires a deep understanding of the interactions between the different components of community life, as the public space in front of it links the building to the city. It makes not only a facade to admire, isolated monument but place of standing and meeting. Place of reflection, of expectation but also of social contamination.

4   Places in the Mediterranean

4.1   Largo Spartaco al Tuscolano: Saverio Muratori, Paolo Portoghesi and a Smart Square that Incorporates Mixed Land Uses[3]

In the 50's of the second post-war period in the city of Rome, as well as in other Italian cities, there was a program of economic housing: the well-known "Piano INA casa". The plan included, among others, a building expansion of the Tuscolano district by a group of architects headed by Mario De Renzi and Saverio Muratori. In the 1960s, the latter also designed the parish of the district equipped with an oratory, the church of the Mary's Assumption, remained unfinished at the top, especially in the ambitious dome roof in reinforced concrete. The complex is now underground and, therefore, the square in front of it consists of a rhomboid square, Largo Spartaco, located on the country floor and delimited by an inline building of houses with shops, also work of Muratori. The unfinished of the church and the fact that the square is separated from the cult building by a driveway with parking, has caused in the 90s the City of Rome, through the office of the *"Centopiazze"* and the Department of Architecture and Analysis of the City of the Sapienza University, studied a proposal to reorganize the public space in front of it in order to reconnect the parish to the city (in Donatella Scatena, 2008) [2]. The project intervention, coordinated by Paolo Portoghesi[4] has drawn several proposals for integral remaking of the square, which descends towards the hypogeous church with a series of steps and terraces. They have experimented with different solutions, with and without the introduction of tree essences, but what unites all the solutions is the rhombus motif of the pavement of the square that comes from the "boomerang" outfit of the building. Two fountains were inserted in the square, which descend from listening to residents who wish to live the collective space, and that expressed themselves at the time in a kind of participatory design event. For the church, it was planned to replace the original dome with ribs and add a bell tower, where the sculptor Paolo Borghi thought of the statue of an angel, the same artist who will be, together with the same architect Portoghesi, protagonist in the construction of the church of Calcata Nuova. On the design of this space, Portoghesi and Scatena then involved the students of the then architectural design laboratory of the faculty of architecture of Sapienza given by the same designers, another example of bottom-up involvement of third parties, or in any case outsiders to the group of insiders (in Donatella Scatena 2008). Years later, this experience is still valid because the square is yet to regenerate and the principles that inspire the intervention are still valid despite technological evolution. In the second half of the 1990s, virtual reality was still in its infancy, from electronic design to the use of three-dimensional models and rendering programs, which have now become a practice, almost obvious, in design, Reversing

---

[3] Piazza al Tuscolano with the church of the Assumption of Mary, designed by Saverio Muratori and remained unfinished;

[4] Centopiazze group: coordination by P. Portoghesi, with the collaboration of V. G. Berti, C. Del Maro, L. Di Lucchio, M. Pisani, F. Rosa, D. Scatena;

the paradigm of exceptionality as a novelty. A further development of the research project could be the application of models for calculating flows throughout the day of citizens who frequent that square, the place of worship and the oratory, together with a sample of interviews well representative of the uses and functions required, broken down by age groups. The combination of the data obtained, together with the manipulations required by computer science, could confirm, or suggest changes to, the design solutions previously proposed. The words reconnection and connection are currently very popular, if not even abused, in different fields of knowledge, from architectural to computer science, and then go to everyday jargon, but the anthropological and biological vision of Portugal's design science par excellence, architecture, is such that we can understand the insistent use of lozenge in the compositional theme of the pavement of Tuscolano square, If we believe that the urban form of the square is also the result of a: "investigation on the structure that connects all living creatures" [3].

4.2 The Great Mosque of Rome Designed by Paolo Portoghesi. The Use of Technology and Computing Capacity for Effective Help in Managing Urban, Landscape and Cultural Heritage Variables

The Great Mosque of Rome, the best-known project of Paolo Portoghesi, is a place of prayer, with cultural center that promotes interreligious and intercultural dialogue. This building, it should be remembered, is also a destination for tourist visits and not only the Muslim faithful: architecture as a means of social inclusion and amalgamation of different flows, that of the faithful and that of visitors or frequenters the cultural center. Placed in a residual space, adjacent to a railway connecting the capital to the north of Lazio, an infrastructure of speed, a furrow, a divisive sign, commonly perceived as a barrier, thanks to urban design strategies has transformed the place into a hinge between two worlds, the everyday metropolitan and the static calm of spirituality. On the cross-cultural issue of building a place of worship for a religious minority, Portuguese argues that he wants to: "to arrive, in the historical exploration of two architectural civilizations up to identify where they touch; or because they participate of common roots or because in the past grafts have been possible between the two species" [3]. The work is emblematic, above all, for the way in which the architect manages the meeting of the two cultures, the Western Christian and the Eastern Muslim with the place. It is clear what he meant by "poetically dwelling the earth" [2], for the fact that the mighty mole of the built fits into the surrounding hilly panorama, not only respecting the orientation dictated by the Islamic religion, but also the site, that is the major dome insists where there was a "small hill", the architectural elements and finishes, in detail the tree-shaped pillars and materials, marble and brick, are inspired by the surrounding woods and the "archaeological stratification of the place" (in Donatella Scatena 2024) [5]. From the point of view of the city, in summary, Portoghesi states that the urban structure of the project tends to interpret the landscape values of the place according to the visual directions suggested by the shape of the lot, almost coinciding with the cardinal points.

"In the mosque" says Portuguese "listening to the place takes place in different directions: as listening to the physical place (a lot defined geometrically at the foot of two hills on the edge of the Tiber floodplain area); the anthropological place: the city of Rome, and a system of places" (n.d.r. Mecca) [4]. In fact, paraphrasing the symbolism of the decumanico cardo plant of Roman civilization, there is a dialectic, not only horizontal on the ground from the orientation of the building according to the conformation of the lot and territory, but also an ancestral zenith relationship between heaven and earth. Land understood as: "richness of meanings, [...]that the primitive civilizations have assigned to a composite reality [...], the reality of the ground, which is trampled on, of what differs and contrasts with the mobility and transparency of the sea, and the immateriality and depth of the sky. [...] We can therefore say that architecture has learned from the earth plasticity" [5].

The urban and architectural reasoning behind this project makes it clear that there is a connection between the different disciplines and factors involved when talking about urban regeneration, in particular those of memory, culture and landscape: "The 'road' with houses - objects arranged marginally, reacquires, together with the square, the continuity between building and urban fabric. In this respect, based on the observation of the city, there are many examples of continuous connection both in the Islamic tradition and in the Roman one. Isphahan or Cairo have an uninterrupted sequence of public spaces, closed and open, in an almost labyrinthine tangle: market, promenade, place of prayer. In Rome, which has not produced large porches, there is a tendency to reabsorb the monumental emergencies as privileged parts of the fifth street, through the mediation of the great 'facades' [...] in the project of the Islamic Center a road, flanked by semi-pathsopen, mediates between the prayer hall and the city'" (in Donatella Scatena 2024; Portoghesi 1974) [4]. The relationship with the city, even in marginal contexts or in frayed suburbs, is important and delicate when to regenerate a work stimulating community life, in religious cultural field, Because it is necessary to avoid building mega-structures in the desert, thus ends themselves, but that can instead develop an area depressed or forgotten by public policies, a "morphogenetic field", which absorbs, with its "resonances", the testimonies of the past, the Mosque stands at the foot of the ancient settlement of Mount Antenna, is inserted in the landscape, but favors the development of the present and future. Using the expedient of perspective, Portoghesi[5] suggests that the data processing capabilities of current and new technological means should orient the gaze, widening the perspective cone, from architecture - building to architecture - cities, in the direction of the vast area and territory of different scale to ensure that the risks of failure or futility are avoided [6]. The computer sciences are currently used mainly in the contribution to architectural design in the strict sense, think of the reality of BIM, now required by European legislation for certain projects and construction sites, but, in the future, it is foreseeable that they must also provide the necessary interpretation of the copious number of data for a correct geomorphological and anthropological reading of the territory, understood as land, For example, in investigating the presence of

---

[5] Portoghesi Paolo, *Geomorphism, archetypes and symbols in architecture*, in "Agathón", n. 2, 2017, pp. 11–24: "*[...] The category of perspective (risk), linked in painting to the opening of the landscape towards infinity, to the evocation of distance and the wealth of information about the practicability and habitability of the earth, has a strong architectural value, not only because the presence of architecture often accentuates in the views the sense of depth and habitability but because the architecture itself, especially within the urban context, lends itself to be read and interpreted in terms of perspective depth, of an illusionary suggestion of an ideal percorribility of spaces that only the eye can really travel, but which give the observer the impression of being dragged into a journey [...]*";

archaeological ruins or aquifers, but also anthropogenic, not only at the service of new technologies with zero environmental impact for the construction of buildings and how they are lived, both in the occupation of the internal space and in the consumption for their functioning, but also to investigate the perceived interest and well-being on the part of the population to have in suburban or disadvantaged areas of mega-facilities or large projects of urban relevance, with the consequent expenditure of economic resources, but by the result, many times, unfortunately uncertain. The Mosque of Rome seems to be a winning bet in this regard.

4.3   The Church of SS. Cipriano e Cornelio Designed by Paolo Portoghesi in Calcata: The Physical Layout of Small City that Influences Flow Patterns.

North of Rome, but already in the province of Viterbo, you reach the ancient village of Calcata. Here the Portuguese lived in recent decades and here he left a large literary garden and the Church of Saints Cornelius and Cyprian, located in the new part of the country. Calcata nuova is a chaotic urban aggregate, the result of the depopulation of the historic core of the country where the town hall square was lacking a place of worship and was also missing a side that encloses public space.

The intention of Portoghesi was to: "[…] compensate the broken memory, of the old town, with its beautiful church that the inhabitants were forced to leave" [7].

At the small church of Calcata Nuova the traveller arrives climbing a grassy ridge. The church looks back and to enter you have to go around the building, discover it as you go.

While walking around the tufa base of the building we read the ribs of the envelope that close the inner sacred space and act as a structure and want to remember the cliff on which stands Calcata. From the base rises a large star-shaped block that explodes upwards, representing the metaphor of the star being: "absolute centrality but it is not, like the circle, delimitation, closure, but synthesis of opening, irradiation, path, explosion and at the same time recall and concentration. […] symbolic form similar to that of the human eye with the pupil and the radiant iris, which guides the soul upwards"[3].

The silence of the place emphasizes the relationship with nature: "Having identified the symbolic root in reference to the star, the next step could only be a typological investigation, which would bring back to memory the previous experiences of that geometric model. […]" [3], while the symbolic reference to number 7 emancipates architecture from functionalism, in the principle of a parallelism marked by homology between the natural structure and that of the architectural organism, with an "abstract interpretation" [6], which also embodies the concepts of identity and beauty, so that the facade of the church, which completes the urban fifth of the town hall square of Calcata Nuova: "represents the way, of a certain architectural unit, to 'feel' the influence and the call of the urban organism through the logic of its parts as the street and the square" [6].

The cult building brought sociality, sense of community and beauty to a square that was devoid of identity. The cultural heritage of the old town of Calcata, a tuff rock in the middle of the woods, is found in local materials: the massive use of tuff and wood. On the point, the architect clarifies the argument by sharing: "the theory of the setting wants a building to rise in harmony with what is around it" [6]. In his reflections on the current trends of the world of architecture, Portoghesi indicated a possible way to follow in the category of "geomorphism", the model of: "'assonant fragment' […], a point of structural contact between nature and work" [6]. Which led Portuguese to stigmatize: "But isn't the separation between nature and spirit responsible for the promethean attitude of technology that promised salvation in exchange for the defeat and enslavement of nature and makes us feel today the foreboding of ecological catastrophe?" The church of Calcata, completed in 2009, has used modern technologies, such as software for structural modeling, rendering for representation and prefabrication for the supporting elements and completion of the tiburio, but it has declined in a careful regeneration of the urban agricultural space. The virtual is a powerful tool and at the same time an illusion that must be controlled. The architecture under consideration emphasizes the figure of the designer who is aware of the potential of the new technology instrumentation and uses it, without being exploited or deceived. The computer sciences at the service of the project are mature and almost completely assimilated in the design process, while they still have a "blue ocean" to investigate in the field of social sciences for design purposes.

5 Places of the Baltic

5.1 Vilnius, The Catholic Church of SS. Patrizio e Giacomo and the Lukiškės Square: A Memory as Promoter of Seamless Movement

The Mediterranean and the Baltic, linked by a millenary route, the "amber route", are also linked here by a series of university and academic exchanges that the authors have long started between the Lithuanian universities and Sapienza. This gave way to know the approach to the Lithuanian heritage and to understand that the valorization of the heritage is also very much felt in the Baltic countries, eager to recover their historical memory together with the creation of a democratic political reality. Emblematic is the case study of the Catholic church of SS. Patrick and James together with the Lukiškės square in Vilnius (Lithuania). The building with its square, as well as being a masterpiece of baroque architecture, is important for its historical vicissitudes and for the history of the Lithuanian people, because it was preceded by the presence of a mosque and a Tartar cemetery, both destroyed in Soviet times. State secularism did not spare the church, which was transformed into a storehouse. The square also saw the presence of a symbol of foreign domination, the headquarters of the KGB, the infamous secret service of the USSR. Once political religious freedom was regained, along with independence, the church was reconsecrated, and the square was the subject of a public competition for ideas for the reconfiguration of the square. If Rome and the Lazio reality are a case study of the coexistence of religious buildings of different confessions in space, Lukiškės square is an example of the same coexistence, but also on a temporal level and for a period of time Unfortunately, it lasted until the 1950s. The contest of ideas for the requalification has, therefore, introduced into the public space of the square the concept of memory, in particular that of the victims of dictatorship given the sad presence of the seat of the repressive hand of totalitarian domination, to which we will have to add, also because claimed, that of the already existing mosque with adjoining cemetery of the Tartar presence. Memory is one of the basic elements of cultural heritage, which can, thanks to new virtual and powered reality technologies, provide the material for the creation of a virtual public pizza, where knowledge is transmitted and the virtual reconstruction of historical traces, recreating the monuments that are no longer there, but that have left a trace, and are still present, in the culture of a people. These technologies are already in place also in the central archaeological area of Rome and beyond. Certainly, we cannot underestimate the virtual regeneration of spaces given by technology, now mature: from the point of view of dissemination for the mass, it is now to spread the points of connection on site and fill with cultural content and not only, Public spaces via the air. The theme of urban regeneration in relation to the buildings of worship and their adjacent spaces is also inserted into the reflections in a broad sense of different scholars. Jane Jacobs highlighted the role of urban elements, starting with the sidewalk in defining an urban space and more generally the public city [8]. On the contrary, Lewis Mumford has theorized the amenity of the city-garden and the rarefaction in front of the uninhabitable cities of the industrial revolution. From these two positions comes the third way to achieve the coexistence of life in a square worthy of a metropolis and with an oasis of tranquility and meditation given by the presence of a cult building. Henri Lefebvre, sociologist and philosopher, also analysed the concept of "right to the city" and "lived space", highlighting how people's daily practices and experiences shape spaces and places. Richard Sennett, sociologist, explored the link between public spaces and social interactions, encouraging interdisciplinarity with architect Pablo Sendra, highlighting the importance of designing squares that encourage reversibility to deal with "disorder" of social change.

Their work, using the tool of architectural design, to highlight the potential of the upper and lower levels of the earth line to be exploited thanks to the porosity of the pavement of public land in order to install technological infrastructures that give the possibility of generating ephemeral events, also and above all from below, to reconfigure the space at affordable costs [9].

This brings us closer to the contributions of computational sciences to redevelopment of public space. If, as already mentioned above, technology from the point of view of dissemination, fashionable can, and perhaps should, become a practice for learning and spreading memory, prodromic to attachment, of places, it, understood as the contribution of quantitative disciplines, what is summarily included in the term algorithm, has potential still to be put into practice in the design phase. Computational science offers tools, predictive models and simulations to assess the impact of different design solutions on user behavior and space use: an increasingly detailed analysis of the flows and precipitations by the citizen of space and the quality of life in it. The development of agent-based models (ABM) can simulate interactions between individuals and the urban environment, helping to predict how structural changes will affect social and cultural dynamics. Augmented and virtual reality technologies, metaverse and advanced renderings, allow a preview of proposed interventions, facilitating community participation, therefore a project process not only exclusive prerogative of the professionals or experts in the field in various capacities, in the decision-making process and verification with the citizenry of the project proposals and expected results. This inclusive approach ensures, or should encourage, that the solutions proposed and then adopted effectively respond to the needs of the different social groups involved in the urban project.

6   Places of the Bosphorus

The research is also directed to the Levant, where the term Bosphorus encapsulates in its original sense the movement of men and animals between continents. Just as the north and south of Europe are connected by the ancient Amber Road, the east and west are also joined by the Silk Road and the traveller Marco Polo. The metaphor of life as a journey is appropriate for the cosmopolitan man of the new millennium who is called to give meaning and significance to the buildings of worship and public spaces relevant to them, conferring an Odeporica image of human occurrences. This experience of travel also flows into the intangible heritage of places, for the memories and sensations that visiting these places evokes in the psyche of each one, whether inhabitant or traveller.

6.1   Şakirin Mosque and Courtyard

Şakirin Mosque is located within Karacaahmet Cemetery, one of the oldest and largest cemetery in Turkey, and was built by the Şakir family between 2005 and 2009 (Batuman 2018). Combining modern architecture with traditional Islamic art, the mosque was opened for worship in Istanbul in 2009. The architectural design of the structure was undertaken by Hüsrev Tayla, while the interior design was executed by Zeynep Fadıllıoğlu (Taşar & Düzenli 2020). The fact that the interior decoration was designed by a female designer constitutes a significant example in the context of gender roles and Islamic architecture, emphasizing the importance of women's presence in artistic and architectural fields within Islamic societies. Additionally, the mosque's design, which integrates modern aesthetics, adds a new dimension to the conventional perception of mosques. The architectural elements, technological integrations, social impact, and cultural significance of the Şakirin Mosque distinguish it as a contemporary religious space. Examining the mosque from these perspectives offers critical insights into the evolving role of religious architecture in the 21st century.

Şakirin Mosque harmonizes Ottoman and Seljuk architectural elements with contemporary architecture. While preserving the fundamental principles of Islamic architecture, the mosque's design incorporates modern materials and construction techniques. The integration of contemporary design principles reflects an aspiration to create a mosque that maintains its religious identity while also appealing to a modern audience. Although the main dome and minarets adhere to traditional design principles, the interior space adopts a minimalist and eclectic approach. The use of light and water elements within the mosque's interior enhances the spiritual dimension of the worship experience. Materials and ornamentation have been deliberately kept simple, a design choice aimed at fostering a focused and contemplative atmosphere for worshippers.

Modern construction technologies were employed in the design of the mosque, with an emphasis on environmentally friendly and sustainable materials. The structural system is reinforced concrete, with glass panels filling the voids. Floor-to-dome glass surfaces allow for the maximum penetration of natural light into the interior space. Additionally, the implementation of a rainwater harvesting system and energy-efficient lighting enhances the mosque's ecological sustainability. Acoustic systems and ventilation arrangements have been meticulously designed to optimize sound distribution within the mosque, ensuring an immersive and balanced auditory experience (Fig. 1).

Fig. 1. Şakirin Mosque, its courtyard area, and its ablution fountain (şadırvan). (Photo by Zeynep Fadıllıoğlu Design).

This small-scale mosque has a footprint of 500 m² (5,400 ft²) and is built on a platform covering 3,000 m² (32,300 ft²). The main prayer hall is covered by a freestanding dome that is supported only at four corner points where it meets the ground. This design enables the mosque to achieve an unprecedented level of transparency. The domed main structure is complemented by a 650 m² (7,000 ft²) courtyard, following the Ottoman tradition, and two separate minarets, each reaching a height of 35 m (115 ft) (Batuman, 2018). The courtyard is designed with sharply defined boundaries.

In Ottoman mosque architecture, the courtyard serves as a crucial transitional space leading to the prayer hall and is typically integrated with an ablution fountain (şadırvan).

While the courtyard of Şakirin Mosque follows this tradition, it also stands out as a spacious and open area shaped by modern architectural principles. It functions as a preparatory and social space before prayer. Unlike traditional Ottoman courtyards, which often feature colonnaded porticos (revak), the design of Şakirin Mosque prioritizes openness and transparency.

The ablution fountain of Şakirin Mosque differs from traditional Ottoman şadırvans, taking the form of a modern water sculpture. Traditional şadırvans are typically octagonal or circular in plan and covered by a dome. However, the şadırvan of Şakirin Mosque is a large stainless steel sphere positioned at the center of the courtyard, with water flowing over its surface, creating a mystical atmosphere within the mosque's courtyard. This design not only emphasizes the purifying qualities of water but also reinterprets traditional architectural elements in a contemporary manner. The minimalist design of the şadırvan integrates seamlessly with the overall aesthetic of the mosque, transforming it from a conventional functional element into a modern work of art.

Throughout history, mosque courtyards have served not only as spaces for ritual preparation but also as centers for social interaction. The courtyard of Şakirin Mosque continues this tradition, offering visitors a space for both physical and spiritual repose. The continuous flow of water from the şadırvan aligns with the Islamic concepts of purification and cleansing, reinforcing the symbolic significance of water in the mosque's architectural and spiritual composition.

According to Fadıllıoğlu, the structural simplicity of the dome in Şakirin Mosque stands out as an aesthetic feature, necessitating complementary elements that would "bring the project even closer to contemporary modern architecture." In line with this approach, the concrete dome was clad with aluminum panels featuring a fish-scale pattern. To reduce transparency and regulate daylight, a double-layered façade system was proposed. The outer layer consists of an inclined aluminum mesh curtain that conforms to the curved openings of the shell structure, while the inner layer is composed of frameless glass curtain walls (Batuman 2018). The mosque's roof is designed with a traditional approach, possessing a solid and substantial structure. The geometric-patterned glass panels extending from the pendentives to the dome continue seamlessly from the floor to the roof. As a whole, Şakirin Mosque features a design composed of inner and outer shells. The mosque, with its square floor plan, has an inner shell also enclosed by glass panels. The interior glass surfaces are adorned with Quranic verses and are designed with an aesthetic approach that allows light to filter through in a refined manner. Sunlight passes through the glass panels, casting intricate patterns that create a balanced interplay of brightness and shadow within the space (Akbulut & Erarslan 2017). The glass panels positioned at eye level for the congregation are designed to resemble the pages of the Quran. The spaces between the lines of text are embellished with gold gilding, producing a similar visual effect. Through this design, the interior space successfully integrates both traditional and contemporary aesthetic principles, fostering a unique architectural experience that bridges historical Islamic art with modern design sensibilities (Fig. 2).

The typical elements of a traditional mosque interior have been reinterpreted in unconventional forms. The mihrab, which indicates the qibla direction, has been designed as a freestanding element in the form of a turquoise crescent. In terms of design, this is

Fig. 2. Şakirin Mosque dome structure and glass details (Photo by Zeynep Fadıllıoğlu Design).

the first instance of a mihrab being presented in a semicircular shape. Its prominence is emphasized through the use of a niche, creating an inward-facing circular structure. As a distinct architectural feature in both form and material, the mihrab stands out as one of the most striking elements of the interior. While its outer circular form is made of turquoise metal, the inner section is gold-colored (Akbulut & Erarslan 2017). The minbar, from which the imam delivers sermons, has been designed as a sculptural object, inspired by the pendentives on the inner surface of the dome. The railings of the minbar's staircase extend from the floor and complete the structure in a crescent shape. The leaf motifs on the steps are arranged in a way that resembles Arabic letters when viewed from a distance. These motifs are said to symbolize the universe. The pulpit (kürsü), made from the same material as the minbar, also has a circular form similar to the mihrab. Additionally, the leaf motifs are incorporated into the design of the pulpit as well (Akbulut & Erarslan 2017). Finally, the chandelier design presents a modern reinterpretation of the traditional large circular iron-framed chandeliers that typically hold candles. In this case, three circular frames are fixed at different angles, forming a three-dimensional composition. Quranic verses are inscribed onto the frames, and glass droplets, which refract light, are suspended from them, enhancing the spiritual ambiance of the interior (Batuman 2018).

The integrated spatial design of the dome has allowed for a unique arrangement of the women's prayer area. In an unconventional approach, this section is positioned as a balcony on the entrance façade of the mosque, directly beneath the central dome, enabling women to fully experience the atmosphere of the main prayer hall. While balcony designs for women's sections are commonly preferred, the parapets used in this space are made from the same metal mesh material as the mosque's façade, ensuring a remarkable degree of transparency. As a result, the partition that visually separates the male and female congregations is as permeable and elegant as the aluminum curtain that delineates the mosque's interior from the external environment (Batuman 2018) (Fig. 3).

Fig. 3. Şakirin Mosque Interior Design: Mihrab, Minbar, and Chandelier Details. (Photo by Zeynep Fadıllıoğlu Design)

Following its inauguration, Şakirin Mosque has gained international recognition through promotional activities, establishing itself as a noteworthy architectural landmark. Interviews and documentaries featuring Zeynep Fadıllıoğlu in global media outlets have contributed to the mosque's worldwide visibility. Additionally, the Istanbul Directorate of Culture and Tourism has included Şakirin Mosque in tourist itineraries as a significant example of modern architecture. Frequently covered in both national and international media for its contemporary design and artistic details, the mosque has become an attractive destination for visitors with an interest in aesthetics and architecture (Taşar & Düzenli 2020). The high level of visitor interest has transformed the mosque into not only a place of worship but also a hub for artistic and cultural interaction.

Moreover, Şakirin Mosque functions as a social gathering space and a center for cultural exchange. Events such as iftar gatherings during Ramadan, charity campaigns, and donation drives contribute to strengthening social solidarity. By providing more visible and accessible prayer spaces for women, the mosque challenges traditional perceptions of mosque architecture and fosters stronger social connections among female congregants. Additionally, through courses, conferences, and seminars, Şakirin Mosque serves as an educational and informational hub that extends beyond its religious function.

In all these aspects, Şakirin Mosque makes a modern contribution to Istanbul's religious and cultural landscape, serving as a dynamic space for both local communities and international visitors.

7 Conclusions

Buildings of worship, as assembly buildings and places in the vicinity of public squares or spaces, are critical success factors in the process of urban regeneration. Computer science can and should be an aid to this process and the design process. Currently, they are used in electronic design and augmented or virtual reality computer programs, but their contribution to the analysis of data upstream and downstream of the urban project has yet to be developed and enhanced. This is what we might call the interpretation of data from sociological, anthropological, and logistical analysis of human capital flows. Computer science is also increasingly refining landscape modelling and project georeferencing, as well as the energy consumption of buildings, a next step in this direction, it would be to create intelligent maps where the results of social analysis are graficed, that is on the end users, the citizens. It is important, finally, their impact on the training of the designer and the schools of architecture and town planning. We often see a domination of the machine on man, whereas instead, it is essential to conceive the algorithm and the mathematical formula that makes augmented reality possible as a tool, not an illusory end, which can compensate for the lack of a project culture and knowledge of social dynamics. The case studies reported are significant precisely in showing a correct use of these new technological frontiers at the service of projects and works of quality, which have, in fact, led to a territorial regeneration.

References

1. Lynch, K.: The image of the city, Marsilio Editore, Padova (1960) (trans.)
2. Scatena D. (ed.): Poetically inhabit the earth. Gangemi, Rome (2008)
3. Scatena, D., Ercadi, M. (eds.): Paolo Portoghesi. Geoarchitecture, Skira, Milano (2005)
4. Portoghesi, P.: The Architecture of Listening in Portoghesi P., Gigliotti V., Mousawi S., The Mosque of Rome, Quaderno semestrale Demetra Spigolature, Alloro Editrice, Palermo (1993)
5. Scatena, D.: The cultural centre and the mosque of Rome between nature, geometry and history. In: DAr, n. 6, pp. 61–71 (2024)
6. Portoghesi, P.: Geomorphism, archetypes and symbols in architecture. In: Agathón, n. 2, pp. 11–24 (2017)
7. Portoghesi, P.: Church of SS. Cipriano e Cornelio at Calcata, Viterbo. In: Chiesa oggi: architettura e comunicazione, n. 88, p. 33–42 (2009)
8. Jacobs, J.: Life and death of big cities. Essay on American Metropolises, Einaudi (1961) (trans.)
9. Sennett, R., Sendra, P.: Designing disorder, Treccani (2024) (trans.)
10. Akbulut, N., Erarslan, A.: Türkiye'de Çağdaş Cami Mimarisi Tasarımında Yenilikçi Yaklaşımlar. İstanbul Aydın Üniversitesi Dergisi 9(3), 35–59 (2017)
11. Batuman, B.: Appropriating the masculine sacred: islamism, gender, and mosque architecture in contemporary Turkey. In: The routledge companion to modernity, space and gender, pp. 270–287. Routledge (2018)
12. Koolhaas, R.: Junkspace. Quodlibet (2006)
13. Lefebvre, H.: The right to the city. Marsilio (1970)
14. Scatena, D. (ed.): Communicating the landscape, FrancoAngeli, Milano (2016)
15. Taşar, E.S., Düzenlı, H.İ: Türkiye'de Cami Gündemi, Medya ve Mimarlık (2009–2013): Şakirin, Mimar Sinan, Çamlıca ve Sancaklar Camileri Üzerine. Milel ve Nihal 17(2), 299–332 (2020)

Geomatics for Resource Monitoring and Management (GRMM 2025)

Analysis of the Stability Conditions of the Grotte di Castellana (Apulia, Southern Italy)

Alessandro Reina[✉]

Politecnico di Bari, via Orabona 4, 70124 Bari, Italy
alessandro.reina@poliba.it

Abstract. The article describes the stability conditions of the rock mass of the summit part of the Grave in Grotte di Castellana (Puglia, southern Italy).

The geometric reconstruction, the geological, stratigraphic and mechanical characterization adopted for the safety status checks according to the NTC are illustrated, through 3D FEM modeling .

Direct (continuous core drilling) and indirect (seismic profiles and MASW) geognostic investigations were carried out. The surveys highlighted the presence of layers of variously fractured limestone rock with average RQD values equal to 55%. Rock samples were taken and subjected to laboratory tests for the recognition of physical and mechanical parameters (compression and traction). The quality of the rock mass was also assessed with Bieniawski (RMR), Burton (Q) and Hoeck & Marinos (GSI).

The reconstruction of all the geometric elements of the 3D CAD modeling was created starting from the point clouds, obtained from photographic survey and laser scanner, and used for the subsequent 3D FEM finite element modeling with the Midas FEA software.

Keywords: Castellana Caves · karst rocks · rock stability · 3D FEM modeling

1 Introduction

The karst complex of the Castellana Caves (Puglia, southern Italy) is an important tourist site: over 300,000 tourists visit each year. The Castellana Caves have been the subject of several publications [1, 2, 6], on the speleological, geological and stratigraphic characteristics of the site [3, 5]. For some representative sections, the safety conditions related to the stability of the rock mass have been analyzed in the past [4].

The following article proposes a structural model for the evaluation of deformations and safety factors through the FEM 3D finite element modeling of the rock mass that constitutes the karst complex of the Grave in the Castellana Caves (Fig. 1). For the first time, the geological, stratigraphic, mechanical characterization and the verification of the state of safety are illustrated by means of 3D FEM modeling. For the definition of rock mass, continuous core drilling and refraction seismic profiles were carried out with P waves and MASW.

© The Author(s), under exclusive license to Springer Nature Switzerland AG 2026
O. Gervasi et al. (Eds.): ICCSA 2025 Workshops, LNCS 15891, pp. 143–156, 2026.
https://doi.org/10.1007/978-3-031-97617-9_10

The reconstruction of all the geometric elements of the 3D CAD modeling was carried out starting from the point clouds (from laser scanner analysis) and used for the subsequent FEM 3D finite element modeling with the software Midas FEA.

The static conditions showed wide safety margins.

2   Geological Frameworks

The geological scheme of the Grotte di Castellana area is represented by a powerful calcareous-dolomitic substrate of the Cretaceous age (Fig. 2).

The calcareous layers that make up the karst complex can be traced back to the Upper Cretaceous [5] and outcrop extensively throughout the area of the south-eastern Murge with an overall thickness, underground, of several hundred meters. This succession is made up of limestones, dolomitic limestones and dolomites, well stratified with the presence of rudists, intensely fractured and affected by karst dissolution phenomena.

In relation to the state of fracturing and karst formation, limestone in general can present very different aspects both laterally and in depth.

The arrangement of the calcareous-dolomitic rocks is given by layers with weak inclinations (0–10°) linked to the presence of mild wide-ranging folds. The calcareous rocks are affected not only by the frequent fracturing mentioned above, but also by the presence of direct faults, with a prevalent NW-SE direction, which overall displace the sub-stratum in blocks, lowered proceeding from the internal areas of the Murgia towards sea.

The area of the Grotte di Castellana is characterized on the surface by a trend with a rather flat morphology, with more accentuated local slopes due to the presence of the surface hydrographic network and by depressions of karst origin (sinkholes). The entrance to the Grave is an evident example of sinking of the roof of the karst cavity (sinkhole). The remaining part of the roof of the cavity is represented by layers of calcareous rock which reach a minimum thickness of just 3 m. The Grave develops a very large underground cavity about 60 m deep, 50 m wide and 150 m long.

The calcareous-dolomitic rocks of the Cretaceous age of the Murge, permeable due to cracking and karst phenomena, host an extensive underground water table, characterized by considerable potential and thickness. The groundwater surface in static conditions is generally found at a depth of 280 m from the ground level and therefore at an altitude of about 40 m above sea level.

3   Metodology

To create a structural model for the evaluation of deformations and safety factors, it was necessary to carry out an internal survey of the Grave and a topographic survey of various points of the external areas. This chapter documents, with some images, the reconstruction of all the geometric elements of the 3D CAD modeling created starting from the point clouds and used for the subsequent 3D finite element modeling.

The relief was geo-referenced in such a way that it could be superimposable to that of the overlying area. Trattasi di rilievo di punti ausiliari, realizzato con strumentazione GPS GeoMax, mediante stazione con posizionamento cinematico, e più precisamente

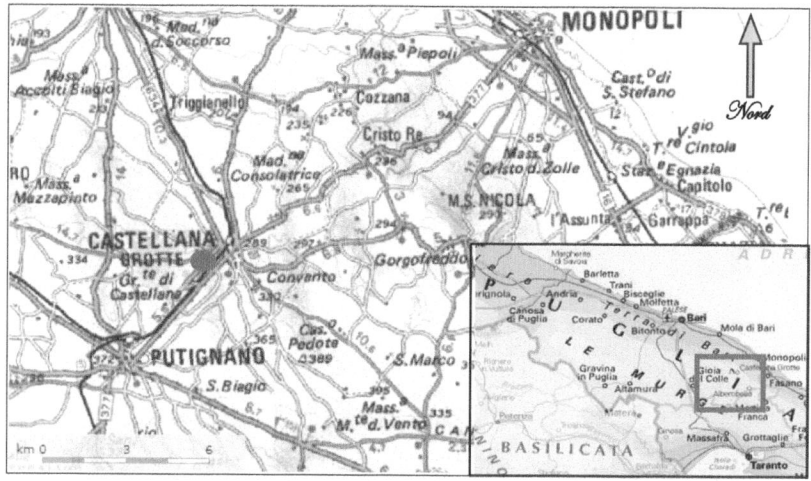

Fig. 1. Location of the karst complex of the Castellana Caves (Puglia, southern Italy)

le reti GNSS dinamiche sono stazioni GNSS statico: le reti GNSS statiche sono reti costituite da punti materializzati sul terreno e la tecnica impiegata è quella del RTK base-rover ovvero 2 ricevitori che registrano in maniera indipendente le osservazioni, il calcolo della posizione si effettua in post-processing. Il rilievo e stato geo-riferito in modo tale da poter essere sovrapponibile con quello del territorio sovrastante.

Due to the difficulty of reaching the places and the geological conformation of the cave, 3 small platforms were built to be able to arrange the necessary instrumentation for the survey.

The survey system was developed through the interpolation of two instrumental techniques: 3D laser scanning and photographic scanning (Fig. 3). The following instruments were used for the operations described above:

- Laser Scanner LEICAR DS3000;
- Macchina fotografica Canon EOS 6D Mark

The entire survey refers to a topographical support network previously prepared and created with a reference target to geo-reference the surface of the upper vault of the cave. All the tables necessary to understand the state of the places were then created. Furthermore, an interpolated three-dimensional model (mesh) with definition at 5 cm was developed for the plano-volumetric analysis of the entire area under examination. Subsequently, the upper part of the square was surveyed by developing a topographical grid and detecting some points in common with the surface of the underlying cave.

The following images illustrate the top and perspective views of the point cloud of the Grave area of interest (Fig. 4), the CAD model (Fig. 5) in which it is possible to observe the presence of the buildings, the upper layer of backfill and the underlying layer of limestones within which the cavity is modeled.

Fig. 2. a) The cave studied in this paper. **b)** Geomorphological map in which the dolines are in yellow, the impluvium lines in blue, the presumed faults in brown dotted lines, the red clay deposits in lightcyano and the Cretaceous limestones in green. The dashed blue line indicates the plan of the cave (Color figure online)

The geognostic investigations (Fig. 3) carried out concerned:

- 5 core boreholes at a depth of between 3 and 5 m with sampling;
- 2 points of geostructural measurements;
- two seismic profiles with P waves and Masw of 24 m;

• laboratory tests for physical and mechanical parameterization.

The stratigraphy of the boreholes has shown a perfect correspondence with the general stratigraphic framework of the territory. Below a short interval of soil there are layers of variously fractured limestone. The RQD values found are attributable on average to 55% which indicates a Mediocre quality of the rock mass according to the DEERE classification.

The MASW profiles both indicate $V_{s,eq}$ values higher than 800 m/s, indicating a soil category of type A as indicated by the NTC/2018.

The seismic profiles with P waves synthetically indicate two seismic events with average physical-elastic characteristics as indicated in the following Table 1.

Table 1. Physical-elastic characteristics

layer	thickness (m)	average speed (m/s)	volumetric weight (kN/m^3)	Young modulus (kg/cm^2)
1	1.0	440	20	15000–17000
2	5.0	1340	22	35000–55000

Table 2. Geometric characteristics of discontinuities

	dip	inclination
K1	65°	85°
K2	220°	85°
K3	300°	85°

The structural survey of the rock mass was carried out following the Bieniawski and Romana classifications which allow to satisfy the questions requested and the problems that arise. Two survey points were taken into consideration at the entrance to the grave.

The summary of the average positions of the main families of discontinuities obtained to which is added that of the sub-horizontal stratification with inclinations always lower than 5° indicates the following orientations and dips (Table 2):

The rock mass was classified according to Bieniawski (1989). The RMR Value is equal to 65 corresponding to a GOOD cluster (Table 3).

In the past [4], a stability analysis (two-dimensional finite element) was carried out on different stretches of the Castellana Caves than the one proposed in this work.

In relation to the importance of the site, linked to the presence of inhabited buildings and public roads and visitors, in addition to the uncertainties connected with the procedures adopted in the definition of the stratigraphy, the loads and the geotechnical parameters adopted, the minimum value to be guaranteed of a safety factor Fs ≥ 1.25 was set. Regarding actions, there are two types of loads, building loads and road loads. Below are illustrated the methods and regulatory references for their definition and application in the cases in question.

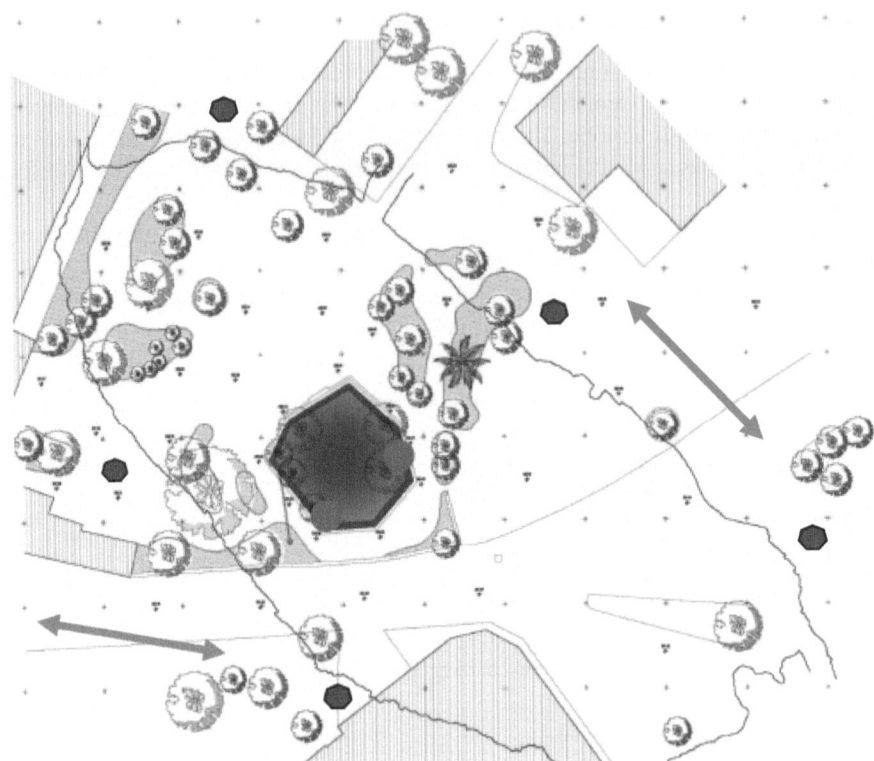

Fig. 3. Location of geognostic investigations: in red the geostructural measurements, in blue the boreholes, in green the profiles with P waves and MASW (Color figure online)

Since the dimensions of the buildings were possible to define from the surveys, it was decided to define the characteristic value of these loads depending on the plant dimension and height of the buildings reproducing solids with a certain specific weight (gamma). The solid of each building was reconstructed as a parallelepiped from point clouds and the load was therefore dependent on the plan geometries and proportional to the height of the parallelepipeds. To define the gamma, preliminary evaluations were made on 1, 2 or more floors typical buildings, finally, cautiously a value of 5 kPa per meter of building height (or 5 kN/m^3) was considered. To be amplified by 1.5 or 1.3, as a permanent load.

Road loads were considered as a variable load from traffic. The adopted regulatory reference is that of bridges, with the cautious value of 9 kPa of the first lane. In the following images are reported the FEM models (Fig. 3) in which it is possible to observe the buildings and, in evidence, the road loads.

The weight of the superficial soil layer present above the limestone layer, equal to about 1m, was modeled as a distributed load on the entire area, equal to 18 kN. Since it represents the weight of the soil, no factorizations were applied.

Since almost all buildings are higher than 6 m, the reference load was to be that of two-storey buildings, i.e. 5 kPa per metre of building height (i.e. 5 kN/m^3).

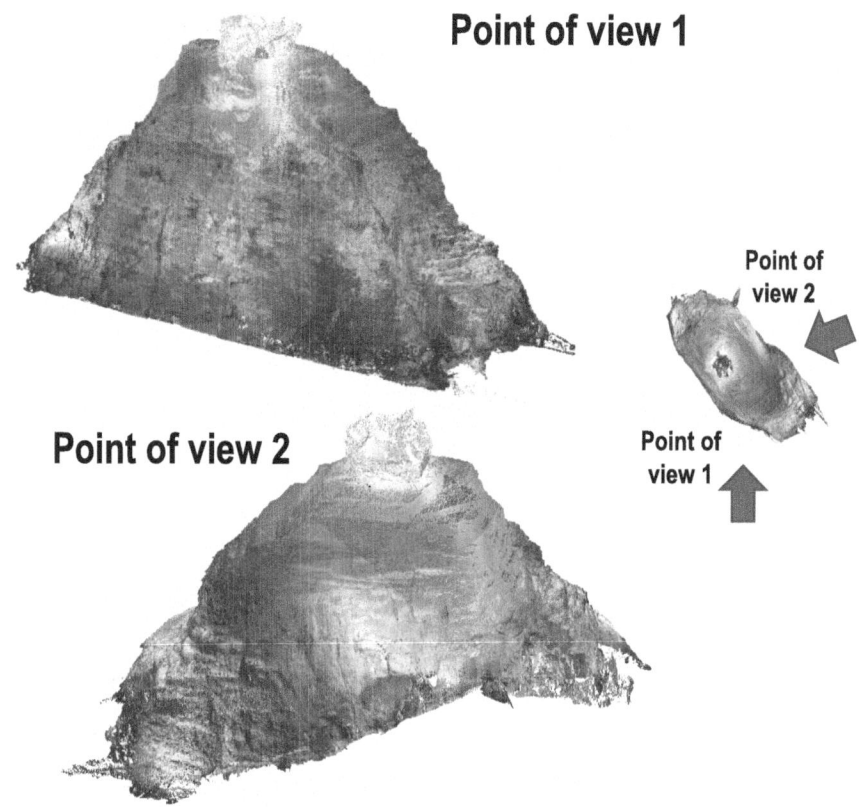

Fig. 4. Perspective views of the point cloud.

4   Mechanical Characterization

The mechanical characterization of the rock mass plays a fundamental role in the correct evaluation of safety conditions. Therefore, it is also essential to evaluate the uncertainties related to the variability of the results. In the study in question, and in the analysis of the results of laboratory tests (compression, tension) for mechanical characterization, a statistical approach was applied, as illustrated below.

The characteristic value of a parameter of a soil or rock must be chosen based on a cautious evaluation of the value that influences the occurrence of the limit state. The ultimate limit state of collapse is associated with a high level of deformation of the soil with the exceeding of the maximum mobilizable resistance. The serviceability limit state to a moderate level of deformation of the soil without exceeding the maximum mobilizable resistance. For the characteristic value of a geotechnical parameter, finally, it should be understood as a reasoned and cautious estimate of the value of the parameter in the limit state considered (Fig. 6).

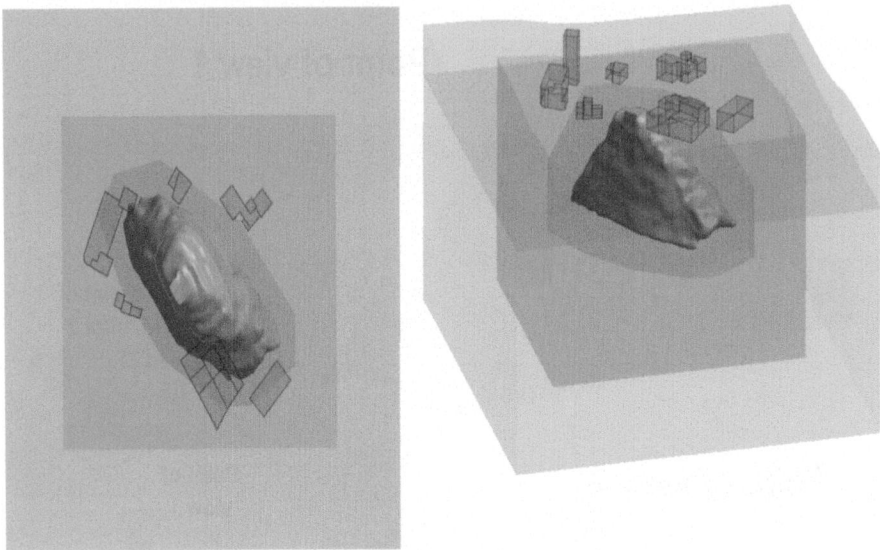

Fig. 5. Perspective views of the 3D CAD modeling including the solid around the entrance of the cave and the buildings above.

Table 3. Rock mass classification according to Bieniawski (Bieniawski 1989s)

RMR correscted	100 ÷ 81	80 ÷ 61	60 ÷ 41	40 ÷ 21	<20
Class	I	II	III	IV	V
description	Excellent	Good	Fair	Poor r	Very Poor
cohesion (kPa)	>400	300 ÷ 400	200 ÷ 300	100 ÷ 200	<100
friction angle (°)	>45	35÷ 45	25 ÷ 35	15 ÷ 25	<15

The summary of the statistical analysis carried out on the compression and tension tests for the determination of the characteristic parameters of the intact rock is reported.

The following tables (Tables 4 and 5) report the synthesis of the statistical analysis carried out on the compression and tensile tests for the determination of the characteristic parameters of the rock, the parameters and graphs of the Hoeck-Brwon constitutive model for the intact slope and for the mass (GSI = 60) and the corresponding linearization using the M-C model for the mechanical characterization to be adopted in the stability checks (Compensated resistances).

The characteristic value of the specific weight was determined as the average value of all the laboratory tests, equal to 24.6 kN/m^3. Similarly, stiffness has been adopted as the average value of the intact rock, as unlike resistance parameters, it has little impact on stability analyses. The same applies to the Poisson coefficient and from an analysis of the tests, the value of 0.31 was chosen. In the following table, the summary of the characteristic and design parameters to be adopted for global stability analysis

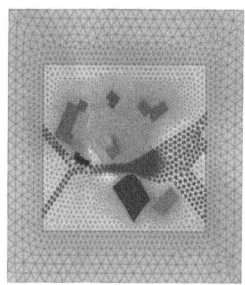

Fig. 6. FEM model. Perspective view and plan. Highlight buildings and road loads

is reported. As already described in previous chapters, it is reminded that the design parameters reported in the tables refer to static conditions.

Table 4. Summary of statistical analysis carried out on compression and tensile tests for determining characteristic parameters of intact rock.

		σc	E	σt
average	[MPa]	50.39	43803	9.24
Dev. standard	[MPa]	19.64	18767	2.96
Coeff. of variation	[–]	0.39	0.43	0.32
minimum	[MPa]	20.18	18605	4.00
Number of tests	[–]	13	13	13
Xk, medium	**[MPa]**	**40.68**		**7.78**
Xk, medium/average	[–]	0.81		0.84

Table 5. Summary of characteristic parameters

c	[kPa]	800
φ	[°]	49.3
Resist. To traction	[kPa]	300

Table 6. Summary of the results of the stability analysis

Condition	Status	FS
Static	Current	2.55

The results of the finite element model analysis to assess the level of safety in the current state of the rock mass are shown below.

Safety conditions are defined based on the global stability safety factor, which is calculated as the ratio between resisting stress and mobilized stress. In the numerical models, to calculate this ratio, the resistance parameters (in this example, the angle of friction and cohesion) are progressively reduced, identifying the reduction factor for which there is a loss of equilibrium in the system, that is, the one that starts under collapse conditions. This condition corresponds to the non-convergence of the numerical model. The reduction factor that determines collapse represents, therefore, the safety factor, as it corresponds to the ratio between the mobilized resistance parameters and the ultimate resistance parameters.

Graphically, this reduction is like what is done by the regulations with the factoring of the characteristic parameters, in static conditions, to determine the design parameters, as illustrated in the following figure. It is highlighted that the constitutive model for rocks adopted is bilinear, consisting of two linear segments: the Mohr-Coulomb line segment, linearization of the Hoeck-Brown constitutive model used for the characterization of rocks, and a vertical segment that limits the tensile strength. Therefore, the reduction of resistance parameters regards the angle, the cohesion of the Mohr-Coulomb line and the tensile strength.

To identify the most critical areas, the most plasticized areas have been analyzed, which indicates the areas where potential "failures" occur in the mass according to collapse kinematics determined by the reduction of resistance parameters as previously illustrated (Fig. 7).

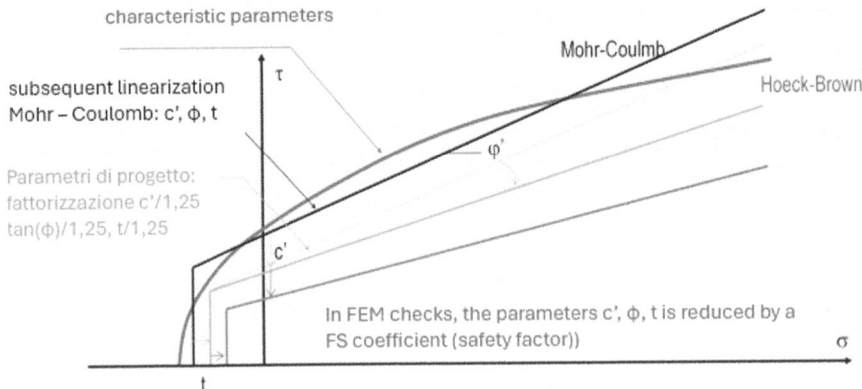

Fig. 7. Graphical illustration of the calculation of the safety factor of the bilinear constitute model adopted for calcarenite in FEM modelling

Plastic deformations in the intact rock begin for values of the order of 0.001. In the rock mass, due to a lower resistance, although in the presence of a lower stiffness, we expect that they occur for values of the order of 0.001–0.0003.

This analysis was carried out to define a criterion with which to identify the potentially most critical zones, that is, those that are most responsible for the potential collapse kinematics.

The results of the stability analysis in static conditions are reported (Table 6).

Based on a safety factor of 2.5, the current situation is considered safe. In the following figures, the results of the analyses carried out are illustrated. From the total displacements, the potential kinematics in the collapse limit conditions in the area around the edge emerges. Plasticization, on the other hand, indicates the most critical areas, the main cause of the limit conditions.

5 Result and Discussion

In the last year about 300.000 persons are visited the Grotte di Castellana: the static conditions showed wide safety margins, with factors greater than 2.5. This result is of great importance for the future management of the karst site.

The geometric reconstruction, geological, stratigraphic and mechanical characterization adopted for the verification of the state of safety are illustrated. For the definition of the rock mass, continuous core drilling and seismic profiles (with P waves and MASW) were carried out.

For the first time the reconstruction of all the geometric elements of the 3D CAD modeling was carried out starting from the point clouds (from laser scanner analysis) and used for the subsequent FEM 3D finite element modeling.

For first time with the classification of the rock mass with Beniawski and through the FEM analysis are describes the stability conditions of the rock mass of the Grotte di Castellana's Grave (Puglia, southern Italy): the results obtained are well comparable (Figs. 8 and 9).

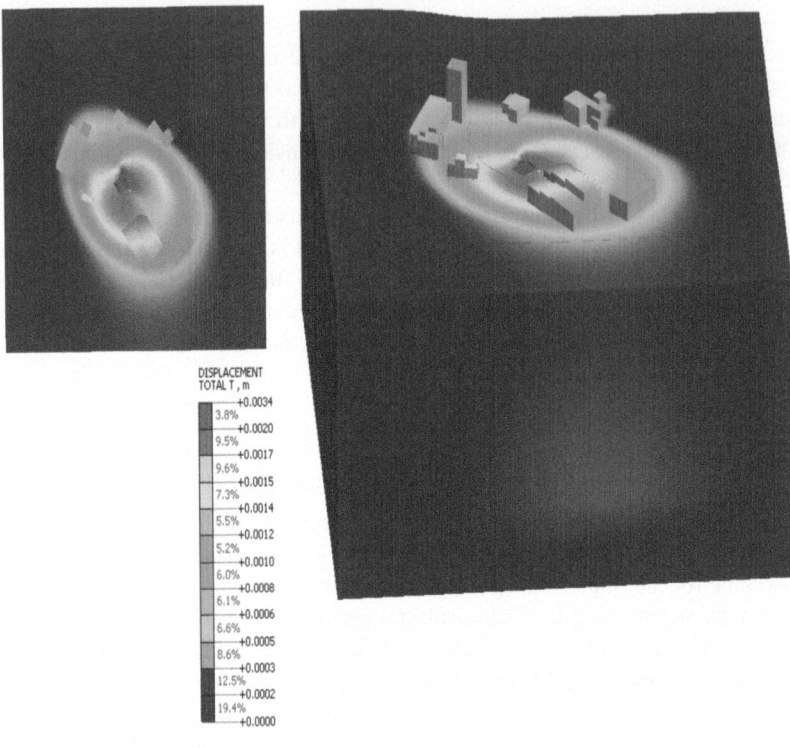

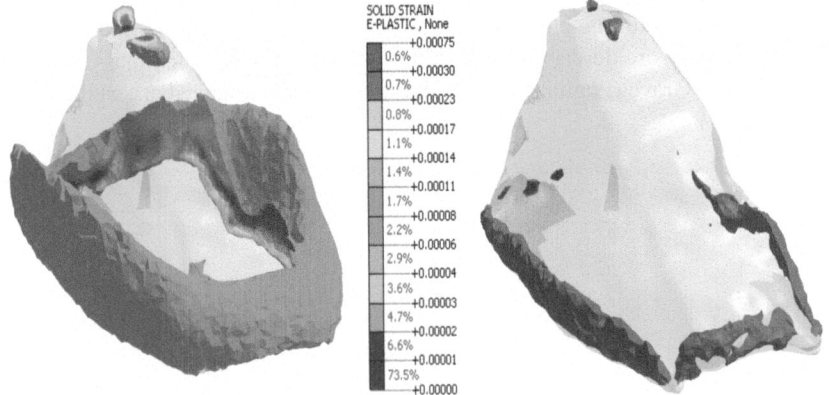

Fig. 8. Static conditions in the current state (FS of 2.55), at the top collapse kinematics (total displacements), at the bottom left plastic deformations > 0.001 and > 0.003 on the right.

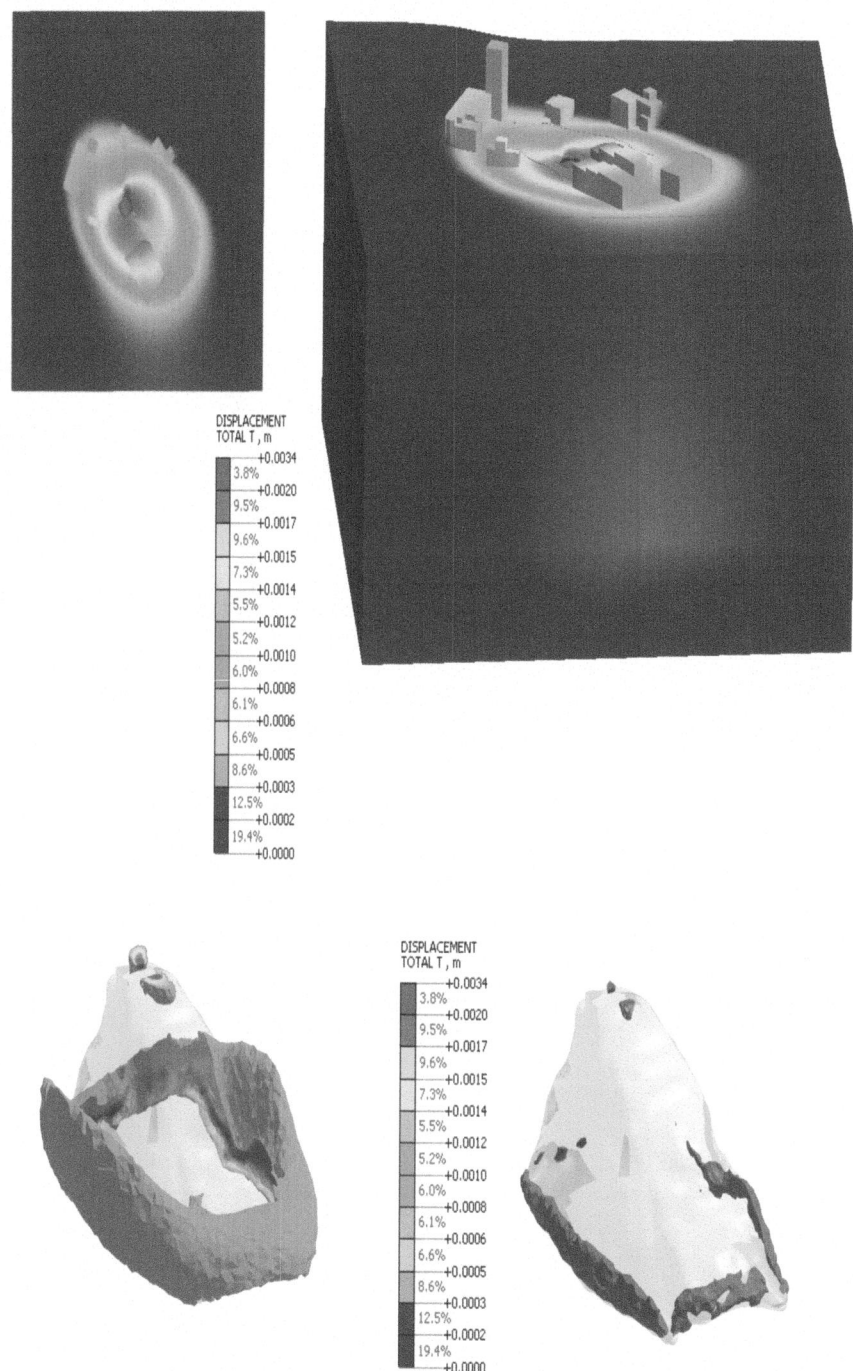

Fig. 9. Static conditions with intervention (FS of 2.55), at the top collapse kinematics (total displacements), at the bottom left plastic deformations > 0.001 and > 0.003 on the right.

Acknowledgments. We acknowledge the Grotte di Castellana srl for having permitted access to the Castellana Caves for this study.

References

1. Anelli, F.: Primo ricerche dell'Istituto Italiano di Speleologia nelle Murge di Bari. Le Grotte d'Italia **2**(3), 11–34 (1938)
2. Anelli, F.: Castellana. Arcano mondo sotterraneo in Terra di Bari. Comune di Castellana Grotte, ristampa del 1992, XI ed a76pp (1954)
3. Bruno, G., Pagliarulo, R.: Il controllo tettonico sulla genesi e conservazione dell'equilibrio carsico ipogeo delle Grotte di Castellana – Bari. Atti del I Cong. Naz. Giovani Ricercatori in Geologia Applicata, Gargnano, 22–23 ottobre, vol. 199, pp. 257–266 (1991)
4. Lollino, P., Parise, M., Reina, A.: Numerical analysis of the behaviors of carbonate rocks in the karst system of Castellana Grotte, Italy. In: First International UDEC/3DEC Symposium Sept.- Oct. 2004. Bochum, Germania (2004)
5. Reina, A., Parise, M.: – La successione stratigrafica delle Grotte di Castellana. Grotte e Dintorni **3**, 31–41 (2002)
6. Reina, A., Parise, M.: Speleologia delle Grotte di Castellana: ipotesi speleogenetiche. Geologi e Territorio 1/2004 pp. 3–14 (2004). www.geologipuglia.it. ISSN 1974-1189

Comparative Study of Different Constructions of Morphological Leveling Decompositions for Spatial Multi-scale Image Analysis

Nor El Houda Alioua[1]([⊠])📵, Samir L' Haddad[1]📵, Akila Kemmouche[1],
Alessandra Capolupo[2]📵, and Eufemia Tarantino[2]📵

[1] Laboratory of Image Processing and Radiation, Department of Telecommunication, Faculty of Electrical Engineering, University of Sciences and Technology Houari Boumediene, Algiers, Algeria
nalioua@usthb.dz

[2] Department of Civil, Environmental, Land, Construction and Chemistry (DICATECh), Politecnico di Bari, Bari, Italy

Abstract. Mathematical morphology is a powerful tool for analyzing the geometrical properties of land cover classes while mitigating spectral confusion in remote sensing data, particularly in hyperspectral images. Among various approaches for modeling spatial information, hierarchical image processing via morphological multi-scale decomposition is a prominent technique for structural image characterization. A key component of this decomposition is morphological leveling, which provides a robust framework for hierarchical image analysis. This study systematically investigates and compares different morphological leveling decomposition strategies using a hyperspectral image acquired in 2002 over the University of Pavia campus in Italy. Two experiments were conducted to assess the impact of different morphological leveling configurations on classification performance. The first experiment evaluated four morphological leveling constructions, each defined by distinct reference and marker parameters combined with three filtering techniques (Gaussian Convolution, Alternate Sequential Filter, and Averaged Alternate Sequential Filter). The second experiment assessed the effectiveness of residual leveling images derived from the results of the first experiment. Outputs from both experiments were integrated with the spectral information and used as input to a two-dimensional convolutional neural network to improve classification accuracy. The analysis of overall accuracy and agreement with ground truth data shows that incorporating morphological leveling significantly enhances classification performance. One configuration achieved nearly 99% accuracy with a very high level of agreement, highlighting the potential of multi-scale spectral–spatial feature extraction. These results offer valuable insights for future applications in remote sensing and environmental monitoring.

Keywords: Mathematical morphology · Morphological leveling · Multi-scale image analysis · Classification · 2D-CNN

© The Author(s), under exclusive license to Springer Nature Switzerland AG 2026
O. Gervasi et al. (Eds.): ICCSA 2025 Workshops, LNCS 15891, pp. 157–174, 2026.
https://doi.org/10.1007/978-3-031-97617-9_11

1   Introduction

Hyperspectral remote sensing employs sensors to capture images of a target area across numerous and contiguous spectral bands simultaneously [1]. Compared to multispectral imaging, HyperSpectral Imaging (HSI) provides richer spectral information, enhancing its ability to accurately identify ground features, particularly for land cover classification [2]. However, relying solely on spectral data presents numerous challenges in image classification. To improve this process, it is recommended to incorporate supplementary data in addition to the hyperspectral bands, like, for instance, spatial features [3]. Mathematical Morphology (MM) is a powerful tool for generating complementary spatial information about image structures.

Several techniques for obtaining spatial information exist, particularly morphological multi-scale decomposition methods, which provide hierarchical image representations by extracting structures at multiple scales. One of the earliest approaches, morphological granulometries and anti-granulometries [4–6], applied sequential openings and closings with Structuring Elements (SEs) of increasing size to analyze object structures. Granulometry utilizes a series of openings, whereas anti-granulometry employs closings to extract features at different scales.

Morphological leveling, introduced by F. Meyer [7–9], is another hierarchical decomposition method based on elementary dilation and erosion. This technique simultaneously decomposes bright and dark structures, ensuring spatial consistency and object contours across scales. Marker/reference images control the transition between scales, enabling hierarchical decomposition. A morphological scale-space representation based on leveling was used to create a fourth-dimensional dataset analyzed via Tensor Principal Components Analysis (TPCA) [10]. Similarly, an additive decomposition by leveling, integrating spatial information into the dimensionality reduction process was proposed [11].

More recently, hierarchical approaches include min-trees, max-trees, inclusion-trees (or tree of shapes), and Binary Partition Trees (BPTs) generate image decompositions based on connected component hierarchies were introduced [12–14]. These structures allow for efficient spatial characterization. On the contrary, the multi-scale image decomposition has also been performed through the Morphological Profiles (MPs) [15–17]. MPs decompose a greyscale image through sequential opening and closing by reconstruction with SEs of increasing size, extracting multi-scale structural features. To extend this approach, two categories of MPs were introduced to model both object length and width [17]: Additive Morphological Decomposition (AMD) and Extended Morphological Profiles (EMPs). The AMD method achieves morphological scale-space decomposition, producing residue images similar to MPs but incorporating an additional term related to image structures, allowing for a more refined representation of spatial features [18]. On the other hand, EMPs were specifically developed for hyperspectral and multispectral images by applying MPs to Principal Components (PCs) extracted via Principal Component Analysis (PCA) [19]. While EMPs enhance feature extraction by modeling shape at different scales, they only partially characterize objects, as they primarily focus on structural properties while neglecting other spatial attributes such as contrast and texture. To address this, morphological attribute operators were introduced, extracting geometric, textural, and contrast-based primitives [13,20]. Morphological Attribute Profiles (APs) refine MPs by filtering connected components based on morphological attributes rather than fixed SE sizes [21]. APs were further extended for multichannel data, resulting in Extended Attribute Profiles (EAPs), which apply APs to PCs or Feature Components (FCs), enhancing spatial feature extraction [21–23]. Additional hierarchical methods include Multiple Morphological Profiles (MMPs) [22], which integrate EMPs and EAPs from multiple base images, and AMD-based hierarchical representations [23], which model spatial information more effectively. Self-Dual Attribute Profiles (SDAPs) extend APs by simultaneously processing bright and dark structures [24], while Extended Self-Dual Attribute Profiles (ESDAPs) adapt SDAPs for multichannel data through dimensionality reduction techniques [25].

While those morphological approaches provide valuable spatial information, they often rely on predefined SEs and filtering criteria, which may limit their ability to capture complex spatial patterns in HSI. To overcome these limitations and further enhance spatial–spectral feature extraction, deep learning techniques, particularly Convolutional Neural Networks (CNNs), have gained significant interest in recent decades. CNNs have emerged as a promising solution for HIS classification, effectively extracting spectral–spatial features and making them a widely used algorithm for classification tasks [26]. The three common CNN architectures for hyperspectral image classification are one-dimensional (1D-CNN), two-dimensional (2D-CNN), and three-dimensional (3D-CNN). 1D-CNN models employ 1D convolution kernels to process spectral features, treating each pixel vector as 1D data. This approach enables deeper spectral analysis, but distinguishing between different land cover types can be challenging due to spectral mixing effects. 2D-CNN models utilize 2D convolution kernels to extract spatial features from 2D image representations, effectively capturing spatial relationships among neighboring pixels. While this enhances spatial feature extraction, it may overlook crucial spectral correlations. 3D-CNN models integrate both spatial and spectral information using 3D convolution kernels. Despite its effectiveness, the increased model complexity leads to higher computational costs [27].

HSI data typically encompasses various object categories, some of which exhibit distinct spatial features, while others are more easily distinguishable from spectral characteristics. Therefore, integrating spatial information derived from different morphological leveling decompositions with spectral data in CNNs can enhance classification accuracy and efficiency, particularly in multiclass classification tasks.

This paper aims to investigate and compare different constructions of morphological leveling decompositions from the literature to determine which approach yields the most discriminative features for spatial image analysis and achieves the highest classification accuracy using the 2D-CNN model. The proposed framework showcases its potential for advancing geospatial analysis in urban and environmental applications.

The paper is structured as follows: i) Sect. 2 provides the scientific background of the fundamental's concepts of PCA and morphological leveling; ii) Sect. 3 details the experiment, including a description of the dataset and the classification process; iii) Sect. 4 presents and discusses the results, comparing different approaches and evaluating their effectiveness; iv) finally, Sect. 5 concludes the study, summarizing key findings, limitations and outlines potential directions for future research.

2   Scientific Background

2.1   PCA

PCA is a widely used technique for feature extraction and dimensionality reduction in remote sensing applications, particularly for analyzing HSI [28]. Its objective is to preserve essential information while reducing data's dimensionality. By applying orthogonal transformations, PCA converts highly correlated HSI bands into a set of linearly uncorrelated variables, enabling the extraction of the most informative spectral features [29]. This is achieved by identifying PCs that maximize the variance within the data. In HSI, the data cube is first reshaped into a data matrix D of dimensions $B * A_{\text{Total}}$, where $A_{\text{Total}} = X * Y$ represents the total number of pixels and B is the number of spectral bands. Each spectral vector is denoted as:

$$\mathbf{x}_n = [x_{n1}, x_{n2}, \ldots, x_{nB}]^{\top}, \quad \text{with} \quad n \in [1, A_{\text{Total}}],$$

where T denotes the transpose operation. Next, the mean image vector is calculated as:

$$M = \frac{1}{A_{\text{Total}}} \sum_{n=1}^{A_{\text{Total}}} x_n \tag{1}$$

The mean-adjusted spectral vectors are: $I_n = x_n - M = [I_{n1}, I_{n2}, \ldots, I_{nB}]^{T}$, forming a zero-mean image: $I_n = [I_1, I_2, \ldots, I_B]^{T}$. The covariance matrix is then computed using:

$$C = \frac{1}{A_{\text{Total}}} I * I^{T} \tag{2}$$

Eigen-decomposition of C yields eigenvectors $(V_1, V_2, \ldots, V_F)$ and corresponding eigenvalues $(E_1, E_2, \ldots, E_F)$, expressed as:

$$C = V * E * V^{T} \tag{3}$$

The top k components are selected to construct a matrix w of size $B*k$, where k represents the dimensionality of the transformed feature space and satisfies $k \leq B$. Finally, the transformation matrix w is applied to project the original HSI data into the new feature space Y as follows:

$$Y = w^{T} * I \tag{4}$$

2.2 Morphological Leveling for Multi-scale Imaging Structure Decomposition

Morphological leveling is a powerful tool for multi-scale image decomposition, allowing the extraction of spatial information without distorting or replacing objects in the original data. It produces several levelings, denoted as Λ_i, each obtained by iterating Eq. (5) or Eq. (6) until convergence, where δ and ε represent morphological dilation and erosion, respectively, while "$\wedge$" and "$\vee$" denote the minimum (Infimum) and maximum (Supremum) operations:

$$\Lambda_i : \text{MarkFun}_i = (\text{RefFun} \wedge \delta(\text{MarkFun})) \vee \varepsilon(\text{MarkFun}) \qquad (5)$$

$$\Lambda_i : \text{MarkFun}_i = (\text{RefFun} \vee \varepsilon(\text{MarkFun})) \wedge \delta(\text{MarkFun}) \qquad (6)$$

The leveling process is completed when the marker function remains unchanged across two successive iterations. The final marker function from the last iteration represents the morphological leveling Λ_i at level i.

The construction of the morphological leveling is guided by the choice of "marker" and "reference" functions. Several approaches have been proposed in literature, among them:

– **Fixed reference function approach:** the reference function is set as the original grey scale across all levels [30,31].
– **Progressive reference function approach:** the reference function at level i is set as the leveling output for the previous level $(i-1)$ [7,9,31].

The marker function, considered as the second parameter of the morphological leveling, is typically derived using a simplification function ψ_i (defined by different filters) applied on the original image or the previous leveling Λ_{i-1}. The degree of simplification increases with each level. Different methods exist for computing marker functions:

– **Alternate Sequential Filters (ASF):** the marker functions are initialized with the original image (MarkFun_0 = original image) and evolve through ASF [9]. At the level i, it is given by:

$$\text{MarkFun}_i = \phi_i\gamma_i(\text{MarkFun}_{i-1}) \qquad (7)$$

where ϕ_i and γ_i are standard closings and openings with SE of size i. The simplification effect is controlled by the SE's size.
– **Averaged Alternate Sequential Filters (AASF):** the marker function is obtained by using the following equation [7]:

$$\text{MarkFun}_i = \frac{\text{ASF1}_{B_i} - \text{ASF2}_{B_i}}{2} \qquad (8)$$

where

$$\text{ASF1}_{B_i} = \phi_i\gamma_i \ldots \phi_2\gamma_2\phi_1\gamma_1 \,(f) \quad \text{and} \quad \text{ASF2}_{B_i} = \gamma_i\phi_i \ldots \gamma_2\phi_2\gamma_1\phi_1(f)$$

– **Gaussian Convolutions:** Gaussian kernel filters with standard deviations σ_i are applied at each level to produce a marker function [9,31]. The multi-scale leveling image decomposition is controlled by the standard deviation "σ" of the Gaussian kernel.

It is particularly useful to explore different morphological leveling constructions and compare the resulting multi-scale decompositions obtained using various marker/reference functions. To obtain multi-scale representation of image by morphological leveling, Λ_i, is based on the following functions (RefFun, Mark-Fun) applied at each level (lev (RefFun, MarkFun)).

– $\Lambda_i = \text{lev}(f, \psi_i(f))$
– $\Lambda_i = \text{lev}(f, \psi_i(\Lambda_{i-1}))$ with $\Lambda_0 = f$
– $\Lambda_i = \text{lev}(\Lambda_{i-1}, \psi_i(f))$ with $\Lambda_0 = f$
– $\Lambda_i = \text{lev}(\Lambda_{i-1}, \psi_i(\Lambda_{i-1}))$ with $\Lambda_0 = f$

where ψ_i is the filter transformation used to produce marker image at level i. ψ_i can be:

– Gaussian kernel (G_{σ_i}) of standard deviations σ_i;
– ASF_i of size i;
– AASF_i of size i.

For multichannel images, morphological leveling is applied independently to each spectral band. The final multi-scale decomposition consists of the leveling results from all image bands, which are then stacked with spectral responses for spectral-spatial classification. Residual leveling images can be computed to extract additional morphological descriptors which help in feature extraction. The several strategies exist for defining residual images are:

– Difference between the original and the leveling images:

$$R_i = |f - \Lambda_{i-1}| \tag{9}$$

– Differences between successive leveling [7,31]:

$$R_i = |\Lambda_i - \Lambda_{i-1}| \tag{10}$$

– Additive Decomposition by Leveling (ADL) [31]:

$$R_i = (\Lambda_i \times \Lambda_{i-1}) - (\Lambda_{i-1} \times \Lambda_{i-2}) \tag{11}$$

– Difference between leveling and filtered leveling images [9]:

$$R_i = |\Lambda_i - \psi_i(\Lambda_i)| \tag{12}$$

The effectiveness of different morphological leveling constructions and residual images in producing discriminative features for classification is evaluated in this study.

2.3   2D-Convolutional Neural Networks

CNNs have recently been demonstrated to significantly enhance the accuracy of land cover classification for hyperspectral images and efficiently acquire high-level representations of spatial and spectral features [32]. The main task of hyperspectral image processing using CNN architecture is to simultaneously handle spatial and spectral information through adjacent layers. Figure 1 illustrates the structure of the 2D-CNN classification framework with its specific parameters. The 2D-CNN architecture begins with a zero-padding preprocessing step to ensure spatial consistency when extracting patches from the hyperspectral image. This padding function expands the original image by adding a margin of zeros around the edges. Fixed-size patches of $5 * 5$ pixels, centered on each pixel, are then extracted, capturing both spectral and spatial information. The dataset was then split into training (70%), validation (20%), and test (10%) sets, ensuring class balance through stratified sampling. Oversampling was performed by replicating underrepresented samples to address class imbalance. Additionally, data augmentation was applied using random vertical flips, horizontal flips, and rotations (ranging from -180° to +180° in 30° increments) on the training patches to enhance model robustness and variability further.

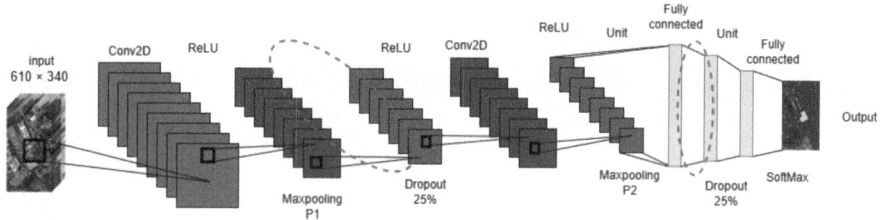

Fig. 1. 2D-CNN architecture.

Feature extraction phase consists of a two-layer convolutional network. The first convolutional layer extracts low level spatial features, while the second captures deeper spatial patterns. Both layers use the Rectified Linear Unit (ReLU) activation function, followed by 25% dropout layer to reduce overfitting and enhance the nonlinearity of the features [33]. The output of the convolutional layers was flattened and passed through a fully connected dense layer with 60 neurons, followed by another 25% dropout layer for regularization. The final classification layer consists of softmax-activated neurons, corresponding to the number of land cover classes. The model is optimized using the Adam optimizer and categorical cross-entropy loss for multi-class classification [34,35].

3   Experiments

This section presents experiments conducted to evaluate and compare different constructions of morphological leveling for enhancing HSI classification. The first experiment aimed to assess the classification performance of individual leveling constructions, while the second investigated the effectiveness of the possible residual image decompositions obtained from various leveling constructions for improving HSI classification. The methodology adopted in this work to obtain a classification map of the HSI from the Pavia University (PaviaU) dataset is illustrated in Fig. 2.

The PaviaU scene is a widely used dataset for land cover classification and remote sensing image analysis. Its high spatial and spectral resolution makes it particularly valuable for detailed studies of the Earth's surface, including urban land cover classification, vegetation monitoring, object recognition, and research in remote sensing image processing and computer vision.

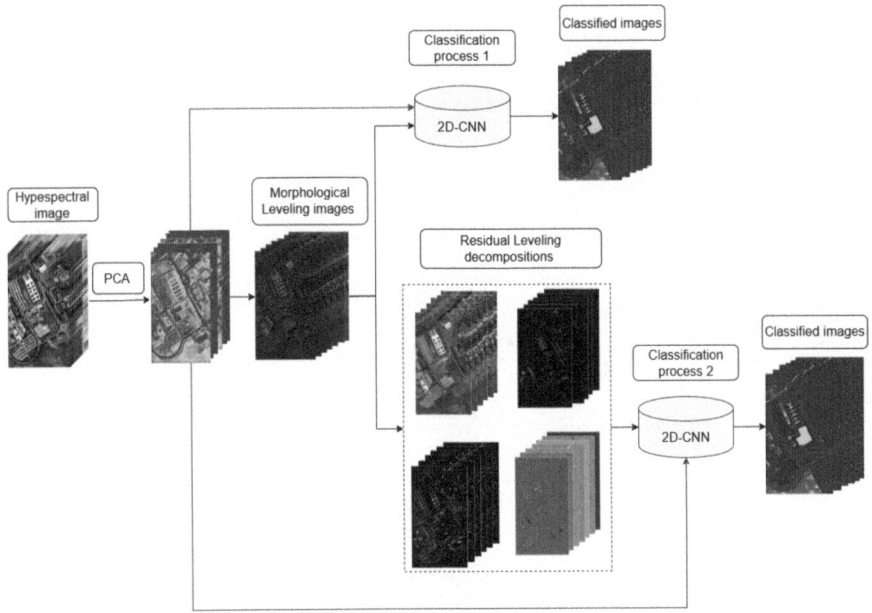

Fig. 2. Flowchart of the proposed spatial–spectral classification methodology.

The first experimental process consisted of three main stages. First, PCA was applied to the original HSI to reduce dimensionality by removing irrelevant and redundant spectral bands (i). During this first step, the number of spectral bands was reduced to 10, retaining the most significant components for subsequent processing. Subsequently, morphological leveling decomposition was performed on each selected PCA band (ii). The decomposition process generated a series of leveled images using different leveling configurations, each defined by distinct reference and marker functions as detailed in Sect 2.2. Specifically, 7 levels were chosen for each PCA image to capture a comprehensive range of spatial features across multiple leveling scales, balancing detail preservation with computational efficiency. These spatial descriptors were then combined with the PCA spectral bands and used as input features for the 2D-CNN classifier, with the classification rates serving as the evaluation metrics (iii). This experiment tested 12 alternative configurations, each representing a unique reference/marker function combination, yielding 12 classification settings.

In the second experiment, residual leveling images were computed to extract additional morphological descriptors using the strategies mentioned in Sect 2.2. These residuals were derived from the series of leveling images generated in the first experiment, resulting in four series of residual decompositions, each capturing unique spatial characteristics. For each residual decomposition strategy, 12 classification evaluations were performed, resulting in a total of 48 configurations for this experiment. These residual images were then added to the PCA spectral bands and used as input features for the 2D-CNN classifier to investigate their effectiveness in enhancing classification performance.

To assess the effectiveness of the 2D-CNN model, training was conducted over 20 epochs, using the validation set for performance monitoring. The suggested architecture's performance was quantitatively evaluated using the Overall Accuracy (OA) and Kappa coefficient (K) metrics. OA is the percentage of correctly classified pixels divided by the total number of classified pixels [36]. K reflects the consistency between the classified image and the ground truth image, ranging from -1 to 1, with values typically greater than 0 [37].

3.1 Dataset Description

The experiments were conducted on the PaviaU scene, captured in Pavia, Italy, in 2002 by the Reflective Optics System Imaging Spectrometer (ROSIS) sensor [38]. This image consists of 610×340 pixels, with a spatial resolution of $1.3\,\mathrm{m}/$ pixel. Initially, the number of data channels was 115, with a spectral range from 0.43 to $0.86\,\mathrm{\mu m}$. After removing low Signal-to-Noise Ratio (SNR) bands, 103 bands were retained for the experiments.

Table 1. Land use types listed in the ground truth map, as well as the amount of samples supplied for each of them.

#	Class	Samples
1	Asphalt	6631
2	Meadows	18649
3	Gravel	2099
4	Trees	3064
5	Metal sheets	1345
6	Bare Soil	5029
7	Bitumen	1330
8	Self-Blocking Bricks	3682
9	Shadows	947

The dataset is accompanied with a ground truth map that includes nine classes of interest, as shown in Table 1, as well as the number of training and test samples for each class (see Fig. 3). No further preprocessing was required, owing to the dataset's high-quality acquisition and comprehensive ground truth annotations.

This dataset is widely used as a standard dataset for the classification of urban structures in hyperspectral images.

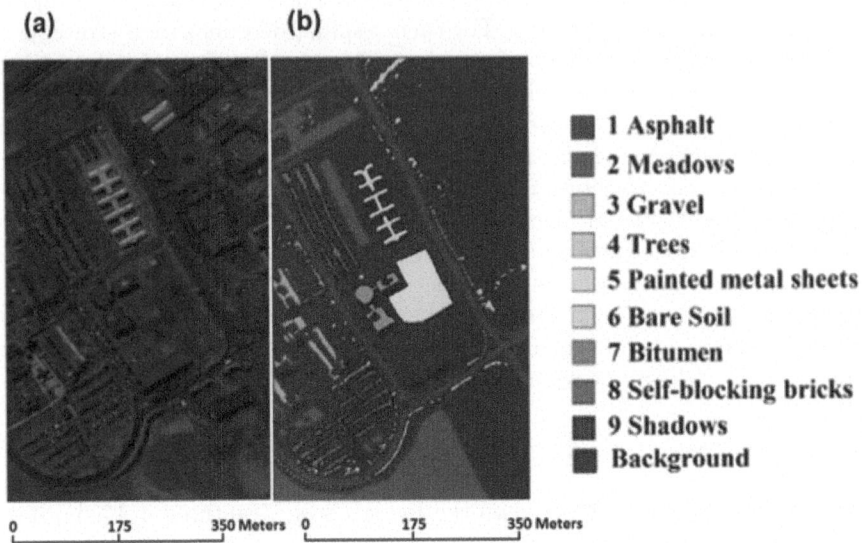

Fig. 3. PaviaU dataset: (a) false-color image, (b) ground-truth image.

4   Results and Discussion

To evaluate the performance of different leveling methods, two main tests were conducted in this study. The first aimed to assess the classification performance of various individual leveling families, using different reference/marker functions to determine how effectively each method preserves and enhances relevant spatial structures, thereby contributing to classification accuracy. Table 2 presents the classification performance of different morphological leveling methods based on OA and K metrics.

Among the tested methods, the highest classification performance was observed when the original spectral bands were used as the marker function $(f, \psi_i(f))$ in conjunction with G_{σ_i} filter, achieving an OA of 89.52% and K of 0.88. This combination preserved both spatial and spectral information, thus improving classification accuracy. Conversely, when the same configuration was applied using ASF_i and $AASF_i$ filters, lower classification performance was observed, indicating that these filters may not be effectively preserve relevant structural features in this context.

Table 2. Classification rates using Morphological Leveling images Λ_i

(RefFun, MarkFun)	ψ_i	OA (%)	K
$(f, \psi_i(f))$	ASF_i	84.89	0.83
	$AASF_i$	78.72	0.71
	$\mathbf{G}_{\sigma_i}$	**89.52**	**0.88**
$(f, \psi_i(\Lambda_{i-1}))$ with $\Lambda_0 = f$	ASF_i	**87.31**	**0.87**
	$AASF_i$	76.01	0.76
	G_{σ_i}	80.94	0.79
$(\Lambda_{i-1}, \psi_i(f))$ with $\Lambda_0 = f$	ASF_i	85.19	0.80
	$\mathbf{AASF_i}$	**88.19**	**0.85**
	G_{σ_i}	80.31	0.83
$(\Lambda_{i-1}, \psi_i(\Lambda_{i-1}))$ with $\Lambda_0 = f$	ASF_i	82.23	0.80
	$\mathbf{AASF_i}$	**86.07**	**0.84**
	G_{σ_i}	79.94	0.72

However, when the recursive marker function $\psi_i(\Lambda_{i-1})$ was used with $\Lambda_0 = f$, the ASF_i filter produced the best results, achieving an OA of 87.31% and K of 0.87. In this configuration, the $AASF_i$ and Gaussian-based leveling performed poorly, with significantly lower OA values of 76.01% and 80.94%, respectively.

Moreover, when a recursive reference function to the initial image was applied, the use of $AASF_i$ filter on the recursive mask function showed the best performance, achieving an OA of 88.19% and a K of 0.85. This suggests that the $AASF_i$ preserved meaningful spatial information while reducing noise. In the final leveling approach, where both the reference and marker functions were recursively applied, the $AASF_i$ filter performed well again, with an OA of 86.07% and a K of 0.84, while Gaussian-based leveling remained stable but did not reach the highest performance. These findings suggest that the ASF_i filter performs better when used with the recursive marker function on the original image, whereas the $AASF_i$ benefits most from a recursive reference function, and Gaussian-based leveling excels when applied directly to the original images. This highlights the importance of selecting the appropriate leveling method based on the desired balance between spectral and spatial feature preservation. Over-all, the results indicate that Gaussian-based leveling performs optimally when applied directly to spectral images.

In addition to the quantitative evaluation, a visual assessment of classification maps was performed to compare the leveling approaches. Figure 4 showcases the classification maps obtained by the best performing leveling configurations. As shown, $(f, \psi_i(f))$ with G_{σ_i} filter contained more homogeneous spatial structures and consistently outperformed other approaches. The classification maps produced by this configuration exhibited more clarity with some misclassified pixels, further demonstrating its ability to capture the complex spatial and spectral information present in the PaviaU dataset. The visually compelling results further reinforce the potential of the leveling methods in HSI classification tasks. Although integrating 2D-CNN with morphological leveling enhances spatial feature extraction, the results showed that it does not achieve optimal accuracy. While certain configurations improve classification outcomes, overall performance remains limited, suggesting the need for further refinements in the leveling process or the exploration of alternative feature extraction strategies to better exploit spatial and spectral information.

(a)   (b)   (c)   (d)

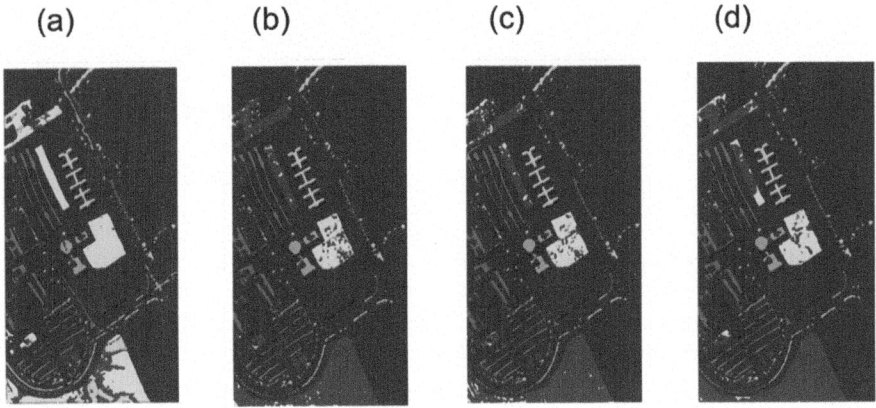

Fig. 4. G_{σ_i}.

The second test further analyzed the impact of morphological leveling on classification by investigating the performance of residual images generated by different leveling methods. These residual images captured the differences between consecutive levels of decomposition, highlighting fine-scale spatial structures and variations that provide additional discriminative features for classification. By computing multiple morphological leveling constructions with different reference and marker functions, the study assessed the impact of various spatial descriptors on classification performance. Finally, a comparative analysis was conducted to evaluate the efficiency of each approach, providing insights into the effectiveness of morphological leveling in enhancing classification accuracy and identifying the most suitable technique for HSI analysis.

Table 3 presents the classification accuracy rates obtained from different morphological leveling decompositions for HSI classification. Various decomposition strategies were evaluated based on their impact on 2D-CNN performance. The methods compared included level residual images $|\Lambda_i - \Lambda_{i-1}|$, ADL $(\Lambda_i \times \Lambda_{i-1}) - (\Lambda_{i-1} \times \Lambda_{i-2})$, residual images $|\text{MarkFun} - \Lambda_i|$, and difference images $|f - \Lambda_i|$. Each decomposition method was assessed across the different filter strategies.

Table 3. Classification rates using different residual image decompositions

Morphological leveling decompositions	ψ_i	$\|\Lambda_i - \Lambda_{i-1}\|$		$(\Lambda_i \times \Lambda_{i-1})- (\Lambda_{i-1} \times \Lambda_{i-2})$		$\|\text{MarkFun} - \Lambda_i\|$		$\|f - \Lambda_i\|$	
		OA (%)	K	OA (%)	K	OA (%)	K	OA (%)	K
$(f, \psi_i(f))$	ASF_i	**97.24**	**0.96**	73.98	0.67	**82.02**	**0.79**	81.67	0.67
	$AASF_i$	95.85	0.93	88.71	0.85	74.03	0.66	74.03	0.71
	G_{σ_i}	94.37	0.92	**94.37**	**0.92**	**87.05**	**0.83**	**87.05**	**0.88**
$(f, \psi_i(\Lambda_{i-1}))$ with $\Lambda_0 = f$	ASF_i	92.57	0.90	91.02	0.88	79.50	0.73	86.55	0.85
	$AASF_i$	89.25	0.86	91.77	0.89	79.78	0.72	88.05	0.84
	G_{σ_i}	**95.59**	**0.95**	**92.19**	**0.90**	**89.46**	**0.86**	**95.80**	**0.92**
$(\Lambda_{i-1}, \psi_i(f))$ with $\Lambda_0 = f$	ASF_i	90.51	0.88	**93.90**	**0.91**	76.25	0.68	76.04	0.68
	$AASF_i$	92.17	0.89	92.52	0.90	63.32	0.59	72.77	0.64
	G_{σ_i}	**95.21**	**0.93**	96.00	0.94	**77.33**	**0.70**	89.65	0.83
$(\Lambda_{i-1}, \psi_i(\Lambda_{i-1}))$ with $\Lambda_0 = f$	ASF_i	90.37	0.78	93.76	0.91	91.68	0.89	87.93	0.82
	$AASF_i$	**91.40**	**0.89**	**92.36**	**0.90**	79.62	0.74	79.05	0.88
	G_{σ_i}	90.81	0.89	94.92	**0.92**	**94.67**	**0.92**	**98.90**	**0.98**

The results indicate that the highest classification performance was achieved using the difference images $|f - \Lambda_i|$ decomposition, particularly when combined with the G_{σ_i} filter, resulting in an OA of 98.90% and a K of 0.98. This suggests that incorporating spectral and spatial information through morphological leveling significantly enhances classification accuracy. The results also demonstrate the effectiveness of ADL in capturing multi-scale texture components through successive leveling operations. This observation aligns with previous studies [10]. By utilizing three recursive levels of morphological leveling (Λ_i, Λ_{i-1}, and Λ_{i-2}), ADL effectively extracts discriminative spatial structures that improve classification accuracy.

Performance varied depending on the choice of reference and marker functions. The $(\Lambda_{i-1}, \psi_i(f))$ *with* $\Lambda_0 = f$ configuration consistently achieved the highest OA and K values across all configurations, reaching 96.00% OA and 0.94 K when using the G_{σ_i} filter. This demonstrates its effectiveness in preserving meaningful texture information across multiple scales. The results emphasize the importance of selecting an appropriate combination of reference/marker functions, with the consistent performance using G_{σ_i} filter across all configurations highlighting its robustness in extracting meaningful spatial features for classification.

Figure 5 illustrates the impact of different morphological leveling decompositions. The visual comparison indicates that hierarchical decomposition methods effectively enhance spatial feature extraction, leading to improved classification accuracy. The classification maps demonstrate a reduction in misclassified pixels, particularly in complex urban areas, where the preservation of spatial structures is evident. This suggests that morphological leveling contributes to improved class separability. Notably, the best-performing decomposition approach produces clearer and more homogeneous class regions, minimizing misclassifications. However, some residual noise remains in certain areas, particularly due to the classifier limitations, indicating that further feature extraction refinements could enhance classification performance. While the tested methods demonstrate significant improvements in HSI classification, they also have limitations that offer avenues for future research. Despite the integration of 2D-CNN layers to balance computational efficiency, the overall computational cost remains relatively high, with training and testing times reaching 1263.04 s and 84.25 s, respectively. This complexity poses challenges for scaling the model to applications involving large datasets. However, previous research has investigated the computational efficiency of different CNN architectures, 1D-CNN, 2D-CNN, 3D-CNN, and hybrid CNNs in hyperspectral image classification [27,39,40]. These studies indicate that 1D-CNNs offer the highest efficiency, 2D-CNNs balance accuracy and computational cost, and 3D-CNNs require most resources due to their use of 3D kernels, which significantly increase computational complexity and extend training and inference times. In future work, the impact of alternative deep learning architectures, such as 1D-CNN, 3D-CNN, and hybrid models, will be explored to provide a more comprehensive evaluation of their relative performance.

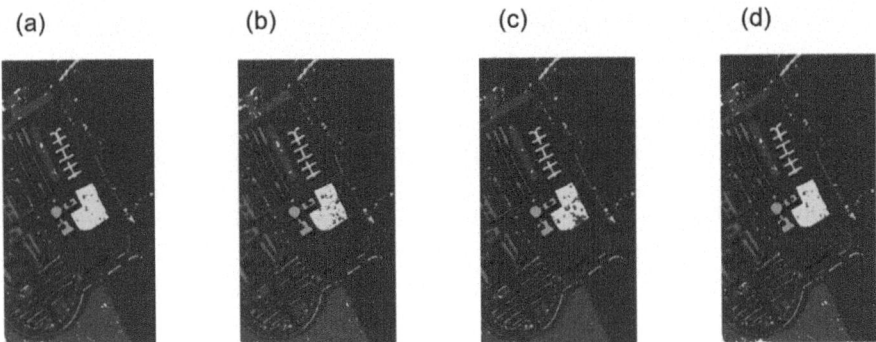

Fig. 5. (a) level residual images $|\Lambda_i - \Lambda_{i-1}|$, (b) ADL $(\Lambda_i \times \Lambda_{i-1}) - (\Lambda_{i-1} \times \Lambda_{i-2})$, (c) residual images $|\text{MarkFun} - \Lambda_i|$, and (d) difference images $|f - \Lambda_i|$.

Although the model generalizes well across the evaluated dataset, further validation on additional, more diverse datasets is necessary to confirm its adaptability to varying environments and spectral conditions. Expanding its application to domains, such as agriculture, environmental monitoring, and urban mapping, could further demonstrate its robustness and scalability in real-world scenarios. Finally, exploring optimization techniques could significantly enhance the model's scalability and suitability.

5   Conclusion

HSI classification is a vital task in remote sensing, with significant implications for agriculture, environmental, monitoring, and urban planning. Despite advancements in deep learning-based classification methods, achieving high accuracy remains challenging due to the complexity of hyperspectral data, its high dimensionality, and the need for effective spatial-spectral feature extraction. Traditional approaches often prioritize spectral information while overlooking valuable spatial structures that could enhance classification performance. Based on this perspective, this study compares and investigates the impact of morphological leveling decompositions on HSI classification by integrating multi-scale spatial features into a 2D-CNN framework. By systematically evaluating different leveling configurations using various reference and marker functions, the study demonstrates that morphological leveling effectively captures spatial structures while preserving object contours. The results highlight that although certain configurations improve classification accuracy, no single leveling approach is optimal overall. Instead, the effectiveness of each method depends on its ability to balance noise reduction and feature enhancement, underscoring the relevance of adopting optimization strategies for reference and marker functions to adaptively tune these parameters for different data characteristics and classification tasks.

Extensive experiments on the PaviaU dataset showed that integrating descriptors from morphological leveling enhances classification performance by highlighting the effectiveness of different constructions. However, the selection of the optimal configuration (reference/marker function combinations, filters, decomposition levels) requires manual tuning and experimentation, which could be time-consuming. Thus, an Auto-ML framework opens new perspectives to systematically automate the process of selecting these parameters.

Although 2D-CNN with leveling improves spatial feature representation, it does not achieve optimal accuracy, suggesting the need for further refinements in feature extraction strategies and deep learning architectures. Furthermore, while the morphological leveling methods enhances spatial feature, its computational cost remains a limiting factor, particularly for large-scale datasets. Future research could explore more efficient morphological decomposition strategies that maintain classification accuracy while reducing computational complexity. Another promising direction could involve the development of hybrid deep learning model to address data scarcity challenges.

Acknowledgments. This study was carried out within the Space It Up project funded by the Italian Space Agency, ASI, and the Ministry of University and Research, MUR, under contract n. 2024-5-E.0 - CUP n. I53D24000060005.

References

1. Liao, W., et al.: Classification of hyperspectral data over urban areas using directional morphological profiles and semi-supervised feature extraction. IEEE J. Sel. Top. Appl. Earth Obs. Remote Sens. **5**(4), 1177–1190 (2012)
2. Ferrato, L.J., Forsythe, K.W.: Comparing hyperspectral and multispectral imagery for land classification of the Lower Don River. Toronto. J. Geogr. Geol. **5**(1), 92–107 (2013)
3. Huang, X., et al.: Multiple morphological profiles from multicomponent-base images for hyperspectral image classification. IEEE J. Sel. Top. Appl. Earth Obs. Remote Sens. **7**(12), 4653–4669 (2014)
4. Fauvel, M., Tarabalka, Y., Benediktsson, J.A., Chanussot, J., Tilton, J.C.: Advances in spectral-spatial classification of hyperspectral images. Proc. IEEE **101**(3), 652–675 (2013)
5. Maragos, P.: Pattern spectrum and multiscale shape representation. IEEE Trans. Pattern Anal. Mach. Intell. **11**, 701–716 (1989)
6. Vincent, L.: Granulometries and opening trees. Fundam. Inform. **41**(1–2), 57–90 (2000)
7. Meyer, F.: The levelings. In: Heijmans, H., Roerdink, J. (eds.) Mathematical Morphology and Its Applications to Image and Signal Processing, pp. 199–206. Kluwer (1998)
8. Meyer, F., Maragos, P.: Nonlinear scale-space representation with morphological levelings. J. Vis. Commun. Image Represent. **11**(2), 245–265 (2000)
9. Meyer, F.: Levelings, image simplification filters for segmentation. J. Math. Imaging Vis. **20**, 59–72 (2004)
10. Velasco-Forero, S., Angulo, J.: Morphological scale-space for hyperspectral images and dimensionality exploration using tensor modeling. In: IEEE Workshop on Hyperspectral Image and Signal Processing: Emerging Remote Sensing (WHISPERS), pp. 1–4. IEEE (2009)
11. Velasco-Forero, S., Angulo, J.: Classification of hyperspectral images by tensor modeling and additive morphological decomposition. Pattern Recogn. **46**(2), 566–577 (2013)
12. Salembier, P., Oliveras, A., Garrido, L.: Antiextensive connected operators for image and sequence processing. IEEE Trans. Image Process. **7**(4), 555–570 (1998)
13. Salembier, P., Garrido, L.: Binary partition tree as an efficient representation for image processing, segmentation, and information retrieval. IEEE Trans. Image Process. **9**(4), 561–576 (2000)
14. Monasse, P., Guichard, F.: Fast computation of a contrast-invariant image representation. IEEE Trans. Image Process. **9**(5), 860–872 (2000)
15. Pesaresi, M., Benediktsson, J.: A new approach for the morphological segmentation of high-resolution satellite imagery. IEEE Trans. Geosci. Remote Sens. **39**(2), 309–320 (2001)
16. Plaza, A., et al.: Advanced processing of hyperspectral images. Remote Sens. Environ. **113**(1), S110–S122 (2009)

17. Dalla Mura, M., Benediktsson, J.A., Chanussot, J., Bruzzone, L.: The evolution of the morphological profile: from panchromatic to hyperspectral images. In: Optical Remote Sensing - Advances in Signal Processing and Exploitation Techniques. Springer, Cham (2011)
18. Bellens, R., et al.: Improved classification of VHR images of urban areas using directional morphological profiles. IEEE Trans. Geosci. Remote Sens. **46**(10), 2803–2813 (2008)
19. Benediktsson, J.A., Palmason, J.A., Sveinsson, J.R.: Classification of hyperspectral data from urban areas based on extended morphological profiles. IEEE Trans. Geosci. Remote Sens. **43**(3), 480–491 (2005)
20. Dalla Mura, M., et al.: Morphological attribute filters for the analysis of very high-resolution remote sensing images. In: IEEE International Geoscience and Remote Sensing Symposium (IGARSS), vol. 3, pp. III–97–III–100. IEEE (2009)
21. Breen, E.J., Jones, R.: Attribute openings, thinnings, and granulometries. Comput. Vis. Image Underst. **64**(3), 377–389 (1996)
22. Dalla Mura, M., et al.: Morphological attribute profiles for the analysis of very high-resolution images. IEEE Trans. Geosci. Remote Sens. **48**(10), 3747–3762 (2010)
23. Dalla Mura, M., et al.: Extended profiles with morphological attribute filters for the analysis of hyperspectral data. Int. J. Remote Sens. **31**(22), 5975–5991 (2010)
24. Dalla Mura, M., et al.: Self-dual attribute profiles for the analysis of remote sensing images. In: Mathematical Morphology and Its Applications to Image and Signal Processing, pp. 320–330. Springer, Cham (2011)
25. Cavallaro, G., et al.: Extended self-dual attribute profiles for the classification of hyperspectral images. IEEE Geosci. Remote Sens. Lett. (2015)
26. Mei, X., et al.: Spectral-spatial attention networks for hyperspectral image classification. Remote Sen. **11**(8), 963 (2019)
27. Liu, J., et al.: Integrated 1D, 2D, and 3D CNNs enable robust and efficient land cover classification from hyperspectral imagery. Remote Sens. **15**(19), 4797 (2023)
28. Rodarmel, C., Shan, J.: Principal component analysis for hyperspectral image classification. ACM Surv. Land Inf. Syst. **62**(2), 115–122 (2002)
29. Uddin, M.P., Mamun, M.A., Afjal, M.I., Hossain, M.A.: Information-theoretic feature selection with segmentation-based folded principal component analysis (PCA) for hyperspectral image classification. Int. J. Remote Sens. **42**(1), 286–321 (2021)
30. Gomila, C., Meyer, F.: Levelings in vector spaces. In: Proceedings of IEEE Conference on Image Processing, Kobe, Japan, 24–28 October 1999
31. Angulo, J., Velasco-Forero, S.: Structurally adaptive mathematical morphology on nonlinear scale-space representations. In: ICIP, vol. 17, 121–124 (2010)
32. Gao, Q., Lim, S., Jia, X.: Hyperspectral image classification using convolutional neural networks and multiple feature learning. Remote Sen. **10**(2), 299 (2018)
33. Srivastava, N., Hinton, G., Krizhevsky, A., Sutskever, I., Salakhutdinov, R.: Dropout: a simple way to prevent neural networks from overfitting. J. Mach. Learn. Res. **15**(1), 1929–1958 (2014)
34. Kingma, D.P., Ba, J.: Adam: a method for stochastic optimization. arXiv preprint arXiv:1412.6980 (2014)
35. Hui, L., Belkin, M.: Evaluation of neural architectures trained with square loss vs cross-entropy in classification tasks. arXiv preprint arXiv:2006.07322 (2020)
36. Yuan, D.: A simulation comparison of three marginal area estimators for image classification. Photogramm. Eng. Remote Sens. **53**(4) (1997)
37. Rwanga, S.S., Ndambuki, J.M.: Accuracy assessment of land use/land cover classification using remote sensing and GIS. Int. J. Geosci. **8**(4), 611 (2017)

38. Grupo de Inteligencia Computacional (GIC): Hyperspectral Remote Sensing Scenes. https://www.ehu.eus/ccwintco/index.php/HyperspectralRemoteSensing Scenes\PaviaCentreandUniversity. Accessed 26 Oct 2023
39. Roy, S.K., Krishna, G., Dubey, S.R., Chaudhuri, B.B.: HybridSN: exploring 3-D–2-D CNN feature hierarchy for hyperspectral image classification. IEEE Geosci. Remote Sens. Lett. **17**, 277–281 (2020)
40. Paoletti, M.E., Haut, J.M., Plaza, J., Plaza, A.: A new deep convolutional neural network for fast hyperspectral image classification. ISPRS J. Photogramm. Remote. Sens. **145**, 120–147 (2018)

Retro-Planning: A Time Machine for Cultural Heritage The Urban Gate S. Leonardo – Barletta (BAT)

Mongiello Giovanni[1]($\boxtimes$) (iD) and Cardo Grazia Dominique[2]

[1] Department DICATECh, Polytechnic University of Bari, Bari, Italy
giovanni.mongiello@poliba.it
[2] Engineer, Freelance 3D Modelling Expert, Bari, Italy

Abstract. The aim of this paper is to test the possibility of carrying out a backward design process, based on historical and iconographic data, to reconstruct an incomplete or destroyed heritage asset. By applying retro- planning, a reverse design process based on historical data, the gool is to restore the cultural asset studied to its original form, relocating it digitally, in the environment in which it stood when it was conceived by its designer. The technique was applied to the S. Leonardo gate in Barletta (BAT), which no longer exists today, but of which some artefacts are preserved. At the end of the reverse design, with digital modelling, it is possible to relocate the volumes of the architectural asset in the timeline to be passed on to future generations so that it will not be forgotten.

At the basis of the process, in addition to historical and iconographic research, it is necessary to investigate the construction techniques and materials in use at the time of the architectural asset to be redesigned, which is fundamental in order to create a model of the work as close as possible to the original. As will be seen, the expanded knowledge of those approaching this reconstruction process plays an important role, which most often starts with a few photographs and historical data that are not very representative of the real architectural form. For this reason, the intuitions of the operator are important in filling in the missing elements of the reconstruction process. The procedure has as its goal the representation of the cultural asset, elaborating in the drawings of the Mongiana representation the aspects proper to architectural speech in order to construct the idea initially elaborated by the creator of the work.

Keywords: Architecture · Retro - planning · Heritage

1 Introduction

Historical building heritage, in many aspects, is to be understood as a legacy of great value and necessarily to be protected, documented, studied and passed on. This represents a memory of the past of great importance, to be preserved in its place, recovering it for what it represented when it was created. The reading and knowledge of this building heritage that has been handed down to us or that has not come down to us because it has

O. Gervasi et al. (Eds.): ICCSA 2025 Workshops, LNCS 15891, pp. 175–189, 2026.
https://doi.org/10.1007/978-3-031-97617-9_12

been lost or unfinished, passes through the understanding of the original design intention, to be elaborated and generate the digital representation of the forms and volumes that represent it. Only by understanding the original idea of the designer, the construction technique and the materials in use at the time when the Cultural Heritage was conceived, will it be possible with the digital technique to represent the real design idea of the factory studied.

The goal of the paper is to apply retrospective design for the virtual reconstruction of the lost architectural heritage, in order to allow a complete understanding of the analysed architecture. This technique has already been successfully applied for the reconstruction of lost monuments or parts of architectural heritage, like the reconstruction of the Roman aqueduct Anio Novus, Castelmadama, Rome [2], the reconstruction of the wall where the tower of Cadì is located in l'Alhambra, Granada [22], the church of Santi Maria e Stefano in Arezzo [2], the reconstruction of the fortress of Montecastrese in Camaiore [2] and other sites [2, 23, 24]. Starting from the historical investigation and the collection of the documentary sources received, such as vintage images, historical drawings, and documents related to the works carried out on the artefact, the aim is to reconstruct the original architectural speech of a fundamental element of urban architecture such as an urban gate. The case study sees the application of retro-planning to the city gate S. Lorenzo, which no longer exists [1], one of the six city gates of the historic city of Barletta (BAT), inserted in the 16th century curtain wall, a crucial element for those who had to access the interior of the walls and an emblem of the city's magnificence.

The correct reading and interpretation of the data constitutes the starting point for the digital transposition of the case study, from which a predictive 3D model of the architecture can be extrapolated, so that the image obtained can establish a correct correspondence with the original architectural spatiality gate S. Leonardo, thus guaranteeing verification of the hypotheses formulated.

The interpretation of the collected data, the study of the site of the original building and the historical period made it possible to reconstruct a correct knowledge of the architecture. By using back-planning and tools for digital representation, it was possible to recreate a representative model of the original state of the cultural asset studied.

2   The Retro-Planning

The contribution of digital modelling, with increasingly powerful software and hardware, has become the usual equipment of the designer and academic in the field of Cultural Heritage. Using them for the documentation, design, restoration and reconstruction of architectural artefacts.

Using the techniques of digital representation, retro-planning (Fig. 1) expresses the intention to carry out a backward design of an artefact, starting from the tangible remains, if any, or from the available iconographic representations, and then going backwards through the process that led to its realisation, until it is possible to reconstruct its original layout.

Retro-planning, precisely because of its reconstructive procedure, is a process that is never complete and always capable of drawing new inspiration, from remains and clues to trace back by successive intuitions to the definition of the original project [2].

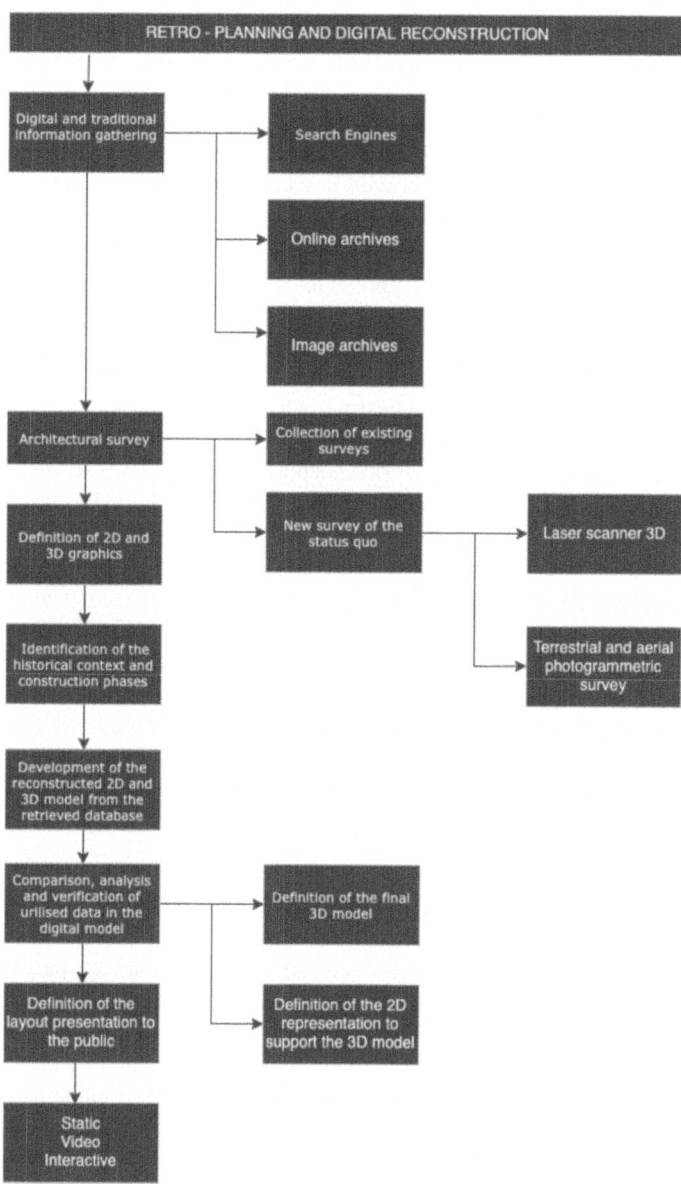

Fig. 1. General outline of the methodology of a retroproject

The scope of this process, not surprisingly, is the unbuilt, destroyed or unfinished works, whose original architectural spatiality is to be known.

The starting point is undoubtedly the collection of information, which must be certain and accurate, since it forms the basis for subsequent operations.

Essential is the historical investigation, necessary to understand the context of the building, the function it had and the reasons that forced it into its current state or the lack of or partial realisation. Researching works coeval to the one being studied is useful for tracing any construction and dimensional analogies.

Often, especially for the oldest artefacts, the collection of information does not lead to a total knowledge of the object, but only to a series of traces, of clues, so it will be the skill of the researcher to discretise the information and find the intuition capable of uniting the available data into a plausible reconstructive hypothesis, to allow the digital model to be elaborated to present the original appearance of the factory.

Reverse planning, in order to be done correctly, requires a thorough knowledge of the historical period in which the work was created, its technical and cultural aspects, because it is only by understanding this that it is possible to convey the intentions of the original project and attempt to reconstruct what is no longer there, filling the void created by its destruction or unfinished work.

The task of the designer who performs such a reverse design is to seek continuity between the concreteness of the property of the past and the hypotheses developed in the present, by which is meant a historical moment very different from the one in which the work originated, both in terms of the materials used and the construction methods.

This design process needs to assume what is missing, starting from what is available, be it artefacts, drawings, images or reproductions of the past, while at the same time reflecting on the evolution of history and the disintegrating power of time, which can erase even what may seem indestructible.

Retro-planning thus achieves its highest goal, no longer being limited to an action on the imagination of the recipients but allowing them to grasp the essence of the lost work, through direct observation of how it would have looked today in the place where it was intended if the structure had still existed.

3   The Case Study: Porta S. Leonardo in Barletta

Gate S. Leonardo was one of the six city gates of the city of Barletta, part of the 16th-century defensive curtain (Figs. 2 and 3). It was one of the first to be built and the last to be demolished. It takes its name from the nearby church belonging to the Templar order, which was later destroyed following the abolition of the same knightly order.

The structure, of remarkable historical and artistic value, was embellished in 1793 with two coats of arms of the city of Barletta and an inscription commemorating the restoration. These details, now housed in the city museum (Fig. 4), are the only elements to have been saved from demolition. The coats of arms and the inscription were placed on the east elevation, i.e. the elevation facing outside the city walls so as to be visible to those arriving in the city, amplifying the monumental character and image of the city gate. In 1899, with the demolition of the defensive wall curtain, the structure was isolated, remaining free on all sides. The building, built on a yielding and inconsistent terrain, is subject to severe instabilities that affect its stability. In 1925, the gate underwent several consolidation works that did not have the desired outcome due to the incompetence of the company in charge. In the same year, the municipality decreed that it was impossible to carry out the restoration and decreed the demolition of the structure [1]. The resulting material was to be used for the construction of the bell tower of the town church of the Holy Family, as can be read in the Municipal Council resolution of 26 August 1925.

Fig. 2. Palma Cannito. Reconstruction of the plan of Barletta in the 16th century.

4   Data Acquisition and Processing

A very important stage in the process of carrying out a retrospective is the collection of all data and information relating to the object of study.

For the case under study, the available elements are vintage images, representing the east (Fig. 5) and west elevations of the gate, sketches and drawings of some details with dimensions (Figs. 6 and 7), a site plan (Fig. 8), made during the preliminary surveys for the renovation work to be carried out, and documents related to the same work carried out during the year 1925, until its demolition.

Specifically, the drawings and documents were extremely helpful in understanding elements that were not clearly visible in the available images.

The documentary sources found have been objectively and directly verified, since the two coats of arms of the city and the inscription, dated 1793, that appeared on the east front of the St. Leonard's gate, as well as the elements in stone material behind the same coats of arms and present on the back of the finds, have been preserved in the Civic Museum of the Swabian Castle of Barletta.

This material, which became the property of the Barletta Civic Museum following the demolition of the gate, are the only remains of the monument still preserved today, in memory of what was once a symbol and an element of identity of the city.

Fig. 3. St. Leonard's gate position in the current road system

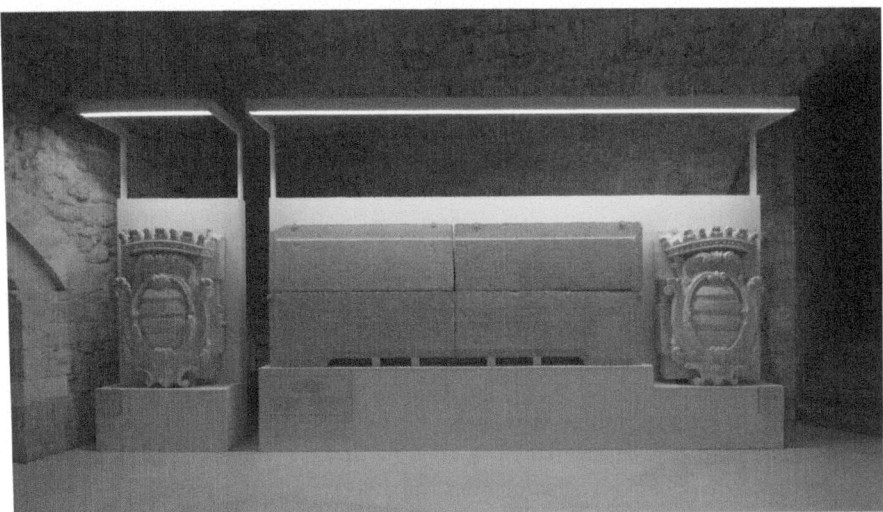

Fig. 4. Coats of arms of the city of Barletta and stone inscription, additions made in 1793 on the east front of Porta S. Leonardo, Museo Civico di Barletta.

With the survey carried out on the artefacts, it was possible to carry out a true-to-life measurement, in order to have the real and certain dimensions of certain elements belonging to the monument under study, which could later be compared with those in the drawings found. The opportunity to have the two coats of arms available made it

Fig. 5. East elevation of Porta S. Leonardo, Fotorudy archive.

possible to carry out a photogrammetric survey, for the reconstruction of the 3D digital model (Fig. 9) and maps showing the original urban layout.

The latter is almost unchanged today, as it usually is, barring wartime or social upheavals. From a comparative reading of the defensive wall perimeter and the existing urban grid, it was possible to understand how Porta S. Leonardo was placed approximately in the center of the present-day Via Cavour. Its position was not orthogonal with the axis of the road but inclined by five degrees. The gate, in fact, followed the same circular course as the city walls, as described in the rules for the construction of defensive walls [5, 6], where it is stated that access to the gates should not be perpendicular to the road, but inclined to the left, "because in this way the wall will face the right side of the attackers, which will not be covered by the shield" [5].

This planimetric layout is supported by the position of the buildings within the curtain wall that, even today, rise between Via Cavour and Via III Novembre and that, due to their location, make the sloping layout of the city gate obligatory. Another dimensional aspect verified is the depth of the building, comparing the dimensions read on some plans found with the numerical value obtained with the inverse perspective realised using the dimensions of the artefacts kept in the city's civic museum. Comparable values were obtained from the verifications, which made it possible to create a digital model realistic to what the original volume of the structure probably must have been. Otherwise, the vertical dimensions were well documented from the drawings found, so the dimensions of the missing friezes and decorations were obtained by photo-recording.

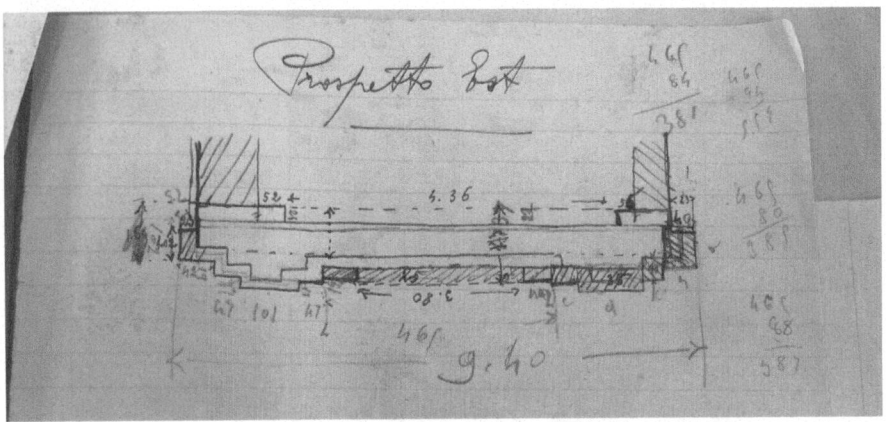

Fig. 6. Drawings of Porta S. Leonardo, Bari State Archives, Barletta section

5   The Digital Model of St. Leonard's Gate

Once the documentation has been completed, the next step is necessarily the creation of the drawings for the representation of the study subject, defining the graphical drawings necessary for the representation and modelling of the 3D digital model, of the architectural object (Fig. 10). This phase will be well thought out, as the choice of marks used, the drawing of lines for correct representation, will condition all subsequent steps in the processing of the digital model. A bad interpretation of the drawings found or the archive data on the materials used may compromise the representation and interpretation of the final model. The production of 2D drawings, the basis for processing the 3D digital model, involves knowledge of the rules of representation and the technique inherent in the use of CAD. The knowledge of the rules for representation are very important in

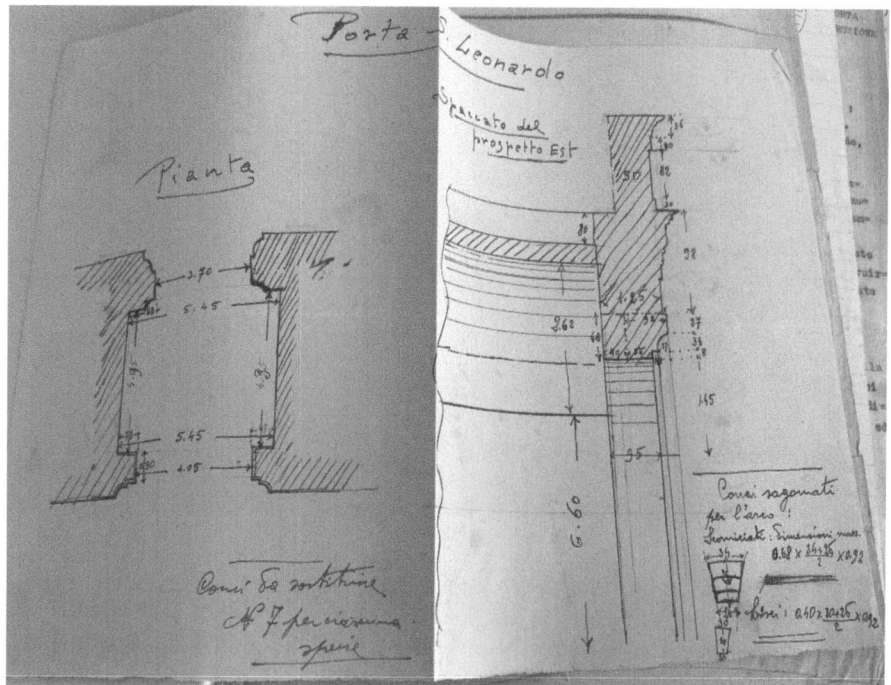

Fig. 7. Drawings of Porta S. Leonardo, Bari State Archives, Barletta section.

the retro-planning process, because it is in the representation that all the data collected converge, making them explicit in the graphic sign.

Extracting the drawing from historical data such as drawings, photographic representations or archaeological finds requires an uncommonly broad knowledge, which goes beyond that of the draughtsman. This phase, in fact, we can liken it to the phase in which the designer created the object of study. Thus, it is that phase in which there is the figuration of the design idea in the analogue drawing of the object on paper. Only later, thanks to the draughtsman's skill, can we make the transition from analogue to digital depiction to scale. The two-dimensional drawings produced for the retro-planning, "will not only have the purpose of producing drawings in accordance with some past style of drawing, but they are also in fact an important discretisation operation, they bring the spatial model back to historical forms of schematization, they bring thought back to the same steps of those who made that work" [2].

The need to represent traditional 2D drawings such as plans, elevations and sections, on which to base the digital model of the work, is a process of understanding the object being studied. Without the Mongiana representation drawings, it will not be possible to construct a three-dimensional model consistent with the information gathered. The 2D drawing elaborated with Monge's orthogonal projection theory involves further analysis to structure all the data collected, representing it in a homogeneous form that can be understood through drawing.

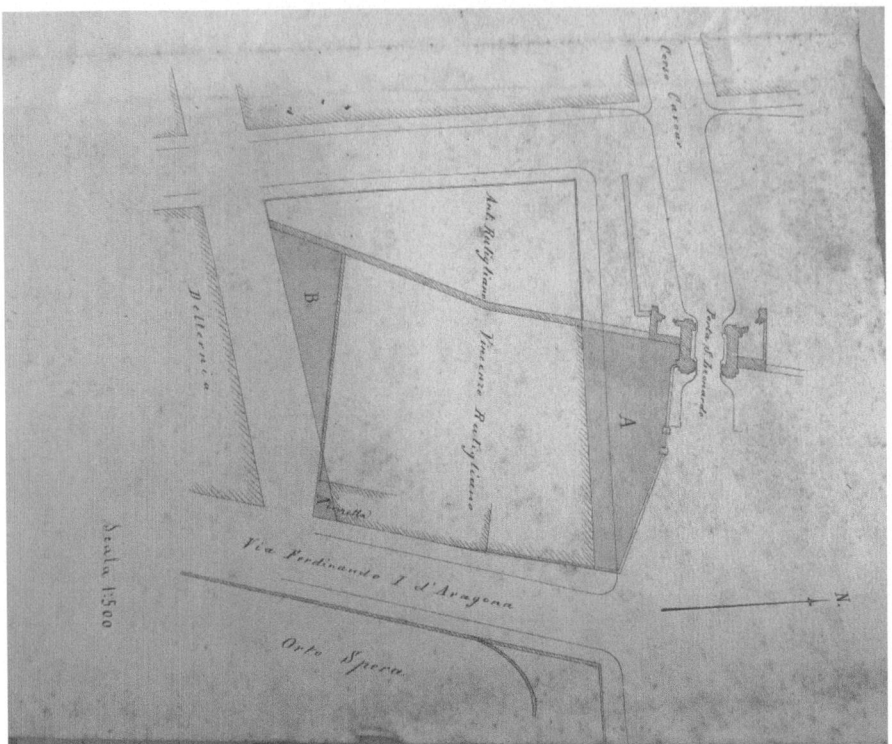

Fig. 8. Planimetry of the Porta S. Leonardo site, Bari State Archives, Barletta section.

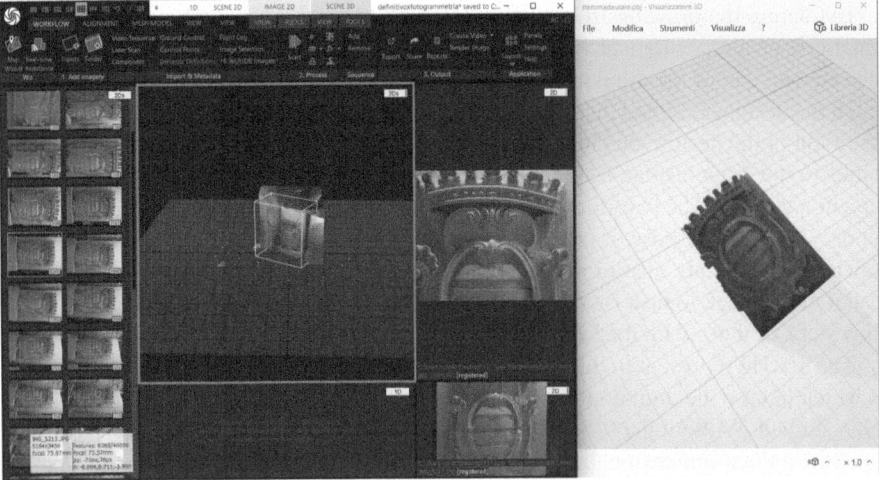

Fig. 9. Digital 3D model of the coat of arms of the city of Barletta using photogrammetry

As the entire S. Leonardo gate was destroyed, the only possible survey was carried out on the remains preserved at the museum in Barletta. Photogrammetry with *Realuty Capture* software was used to survey the coats of arms and the inscription preserved at the archaeological museum in Barletta. First, a series of photographs were shot with the camera, making a circular trajectory around each element to be surveyed, the images were taken with a fixed focal length of 35 mm. The focal length was determined by the need to include the entire element to be surveyed in the frame and for the layout of the exhibits within the museum. Subsequently, a few photographs were taken from a frontal position, varying the shooting height and keeping the focal length fixed.

The second step involves loading the images into the software, which automatically recognizes the correspondence of the various photograms in which the detected coat of arms or inscription is portrayed, superimposing them on each other to obtain, at the end of the processing, the 3D digital model of the detected element. Once the digital model of the coats of arms and the inscription was realized, the 3D digital model of the entire S. Leonardo gate was made, based on the 2D drawings processed using the historical data found. The models of the coats of arms and the inscription obtained from the photogrammetric survey were mounted on the 3D model, obtaining a photorealistic and true-to-life model of the gate (Figs. 11 and 12).

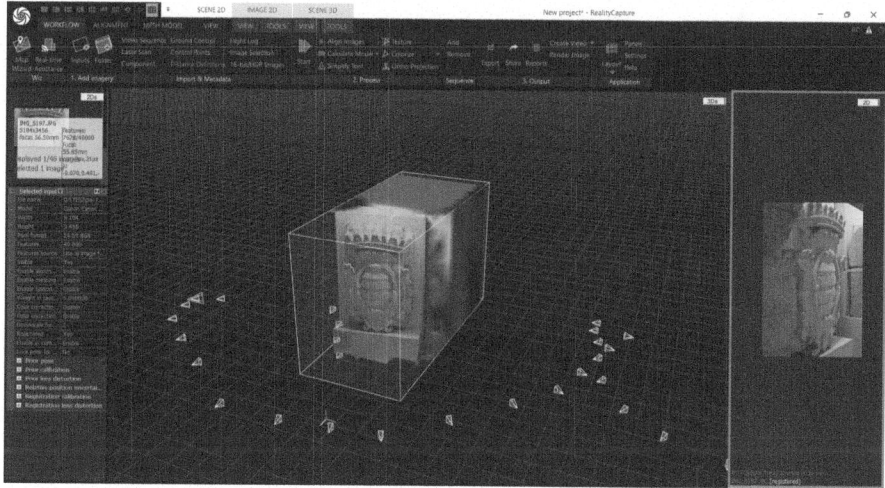

Fig. 10. Reality Capture. The photogrammetric survey reconstruction process.

Fig. 11. Barletta. Porta S. Leonardo. 3D rendering of the east elevation

Fig. 12. Barletta. Porta S. Leonardo. 3D rendering of the west elevation

6 Conclusions

The era we are living in is strongly influenced by new technologies and the spread of the Internet. Digital technologies have revolutionised the approach to the study and conservation of Cultural Heritage, changing the way we study, represent and visit them.

The computing power of today's computers makes it possible to represent what does not exist in a highly realistic manner. One only has to weigh the development that video games have undergone and how films have changed, which are increasingly being made using digital techniques to represent environments and scenarios that do not exist.

We can say that we are moving into an extended era, where digital representation is placed side by side with reality, creating digital worlds, even entire cities, with the metaverse, in which many large design studios and architects are engaged [3]. Inevitably, Cultural Heritage has also been touched by the innovations of digital technologies, enabling the reconstruction of works that no longer exist or are unfinished. The possibility of representing and showing all the features of a certain monument, building or statue has led to the development of specific solutions for different needs. Just think of 3D viewers to immerse and visit 3D digital models. All these new possibilities have given a boost to the knowledge, transmission and use of digitally depicted Cultural Heritage.

In normal design, the digital model is used to depict an artefact that does not exist. In back-planning, the digital model is used to visualise an architectural volume that was there but has now been lost, whose design has been fully or partially realised and which has already left its mark on time.

Retro-planning, requires a clear understanding of the new possibilities offered by digital technology, of the architectural language, of the technical and technological issues of the cultural asset being studied, but above all, it is essential to understand the thinking of the architects who conceived the work to be redesigned. This entails a significant abstraction to reach out and capture the philosophy and thinking of a period far removed from us. This mode of operation entails the need to reset all prior influences, rethinking from scratch the motive that drove the original designer of the good that is no longer present to make certain choices.

As we have seen, very often, the plans of the work have been lost, and reconstructing the history of the work studied is fundamental to its realisation but difficult to realise due to the lack of certain data that only a creative approach of the scholar will be able to deduce supported by his own cultural notions and the study of the oldest materials and construction techniques used at the time when the work was realised.

The reconstruction done on Porta S. Leonardo, compared with other similar experiences, reinforces the validity of the retro-design method. Among the various reconstructions already carried out, many started from the remains of architecture still present on the original site, such as the aforementioned Roman aqueduct Anio Novus, Castelmadama, Rome [2], or the walls of the tower of Cadì in l'Alhambra, Granada [22]. In the case study analysed here, there was no residual part of the architecture on which to base the reconstruction, this pushed the process to a higher level than previous ones, allowing this operative method to be taken to extremes, producing a 3D digital model based solely on research and historical analysis of the artefact.

A very difficult work where the use of computer technology becomes essential precisely because of its peculiarity of recreating virtual environments that can also be visited, so as to enjoy the reconstructed work. The cultural asset that has left its imprint in the passage of time, studied and reconstructed through retro-planning, is brought back to life in order to be placed again in the timeline, albeit in a digital manner, returning it to the cultural heritage as it was initially designed by its designer.

In this way, the digital model of the reconstructed work allows it to live on and be remembered forever.

Disclosure of Interests. The authors have no competing interests to declare that are relevant to the content of this article.

References

1. Resolution of the Municipal Council at its meeting on 12 August 1925
2. Verdiani, G.: Retroprogettazione. didapress, Firenze (2017)
3. Mongiello, G.: Metaverse: The architectural speech of digital representation. In: 20th World Heritage and Ecological Transition, pp. 384–389. Gangemi, Roma (2022)
4. Grellert, M., Pfarr-Harfest, M.: 25 Year virtual reconstruction, Currente Challenges and the comeback of physical model. In: Act of Digital Heritage Congres. Marsiglia (2013)
5. Pollione, M.V.: De Architettura. Edizioni Studio. Firenze (1999)
6. De Seta, C., Le Goff, J.: La città e le mura. Laterza, Bari (1989)
7. Ascani, V.: Il Trecento disegnato. Le basi progettuali dell'architettura gotica in Italia. Viella, Roma (1997)
8. Benevolo, L.: Storia della città: la città medievale. Laterza, Bari (1993)
9. Benevolo, L.: Storia dell'architettura del Rinascimento. Laterza, Bari (1968)
10. Bini, M., Bertocci, S.: Manuale di rilievo architettonico e urbano. Città studi, Torino (2012)
11. Cassandro, G.I.: Le pergamene della città di Barletta 1186–1507. Vecchi (1993)
12. Cassandro, G.I.: Barletta nella storia e nell'arte. Rizzi & Del Re, Barletta (1957)
13. Doronzo, G.: I borghi antichi di Barletta. CRSEC, Barletta (2003)
14. Musso, S.F.: Recupero e restauro degli edifici storici. EPC, Roma (2016)
15. Bitelli, G., Girelli, V., Vittuari, L.: The potential of 3D techniques for Cultural Heritage object documentation. In: Videometrics IX, Proceedings of electronic imaging science and technology. SPIE, USA (2007)
16. Cozzi, M.: Antonio da Sangallo il Vecchio e l'architettura del Cinquecento in Valdichiana. SAGEP, Genova (1992)
17. Docci, M., Maestri, D.: Manuale di rilevamento architettonico e urbano. Laterza, Bari (2009)
18. Grün, A., Remondino, F., Zhang, L.: Photogrammetric reconstruction of the great budha of Bamiyan, Afghanistan. In: The Photogrammetric Record n. 19 (107), pp. 177–199. Blackwell Publishing Ltd, UK (2004)
19. Guidi, G.: 3D visualization of cultural heritage artefacts with virtual reality devices. In: The International Archives of the Photogrammetry, Remote Sensing and Spatial Information Sciences, 25th International CIPA Symposium. Taipei, Taiwan (2015)
20. Le Goff, J.: L'immaginario medievale. Laterza, Bari (2011)
21. Verdiani, G.: I nuovi strumenti hanno compiuto quarantatré anni. In: La documentazione dei Beni Architettonici ed Ambientali, strumenti, indagini esperienze. Saffe, Firenze (2006)
22. Rodríguez-Navarro P., Cabezos-Bernal P.M.: Aplicaciones de la cámara Gopro para la toma de datos de arquitectura. In: APEGA 2014, XII Congreso Internacional Expresión Gráica aplicada a la Ediicación Graphic Expression applied to Building International Conference, Proceedings, Universidad Europea de Madrid (2014)
23. Belli, G., D'Andrea, S.: From Porta alla croce to piazza beccaria the evolution of florence from city to capital. In: Rodriguez-Navarro, P., Verdiani, G., Cornell, P. (eds.) Architecture, Archaeology and Contemporary City Planning "State of Knowledge in the Digital Age". Valencia, Spain, Lulu Press, USA, (2015)

24. Guidi G., et al.: 3D visualization of cultural heritage artefacts with virtual reality devices. In: The International Archives of the Photogrammetry, Remote Sensing and Spatial Information Sciences, Volume XL-5/W7, 2015 25th International CIPA Symposium. Taipei, Taiwan (2015)
25. Amico, N., Ronzino, P., Felicetti, A., Niccolucci, F.: Quality management of 3D cultural heritage replicas with CIDOC-CRM. In: CRMEX 2013 Practical Experiences with CIDOC CRM and its Extensions. Proceedings of the Workshop, Malta (2013)
26. Apollonio, F.I.: Classiication schemes and model validation of 3D digital reconstruction process. In: Börner, W., Uhlirz, S. (eds.) Proceedings of the 20th Cultural Heritage and New Technologies, Museen der Stadt Wien — Stadtarchäologie, Vienna (2016)
27. Kula, W.: Le misure e gli uomini dall'antichità a oggi, traduzione di Anna Salmon Vivanti, collana Storia e società, Laterza, Bari (1987)
28. Monti, C., Selvini, A.: Topograia, fotogrammetria e rappresentazione all'inizio del ventunesimo secolo, Maggioli Editore, Rimini (2015)
29. Rodríguez-Navarro, P.: Automated Digital Photogrammetry versus the systems based on active 3D sensors, «Revista EGA», n. 20, a. 17, Valencia (2012)

Monitoring Long-Term Trends in Aglianico Vineyards Using a Mann-Kendall Test Approach, Sen's Slope Estimator, and Sentinel-2 Time Series

Alessandra Capolupo[1]([⊠]) [iD], Raffaele Iannone[2] [iD], Pier Paolo Miglietta[3] [iD], and Eufemia Tarantino[1] [iD]

[1] Department of Civil, Environmental, Land, Construction and Chemistry (DICATECh), Politecnico di Bari, Via Orabona 4, 70125 Bari, Italy
`alessandra.capolupo@poliba.it`
[2] Department of Industrial Engineering, University of Salerno, Via Giovanni Paolo II, 132, 84084 Fisciano, SA, Italy
[3] Department of Biological and Environmental Sciences and Technologies, University of Salento, Complesso Ecotekne Via per Monteroni, 73100 Lecce, Italy

Abstract. The vineyard sector is a key economic driver in the Mediterranean Basin, particularly in Italy, requiring a scientifically sound management plan to optimize yield and quality. Geomatic techniques provide a fast, cost-effective, and non-destructive way to collect data, with remote sensing excelling in long-term grape monitoring. The Sentinel-2 mission, launched by the European Space Agency in 2015, captures multispectral images with spatial resolutions of 10 m, 20 m, and 60 m, depending on the spectral band. While this resolution does not allow for detailed analysis at the scale of individual grape rows or leaves, it enables vineyard monitoring at the field scale with medium spatial resolution. This study explores the potential of Sentinel-2 data for analysing long-term trends using two non-parametric statistical methods: the Mann-Kendall test and Sen's slope estimator. The former detects monotonic trends, while the latter quantifies the magnitude of change over time. A time series of Sentinel-2 imagery, comprising 1,348 images spanning a ten-year period (2015–2025), was collected and pre-processed. After cloud masking and resampling all bands to a 10m spatial resolution, four vegetation indices were computed and subjected to statistical analysis. The resulting maps served as input for the aforementioned non-parametric tests. Findings highlight the effectiveness of a well-structured management plan, though certain areas require closer attention. In particular, all statistical tests consistently indicate negative long-term trends in the lower portion of the field. These results emphasize the necessity of integrating geospatial big data to enhance decision-making, surpassing the limitations of management strategies based solely on farmers' experience.

Keywords: Geospatial Big Data · Google Earth Engine (GEE) · Cloud Computing Analysis

© The Author(s), under exclusive license to Springer Nature Switzerland AG 2026
O. Gervasi et al. (Eds.): ICCSA 2025 Workshops, LNCS 15891, pp. 190–206, 2026.
https://doi.org/10.1007/978-3-031-97617-9_13

1   Introduction

The vineyard sector is a key component of the Mediterranean Basin economy and has gained increasing attention in recent years [1]. Traditionally, vineyard management has relied on farmers' experience and expertise [2]. However, this approach alone is insufficient. To optimize both yield and quality, a scientifically based management plan, adaptable to grape characteristics at the field scale, is essential.

Geomatic techniques offer a viable solution, providing non-destructive methods for rapid and accurate data acquisition. Among these, remote sensing has been widely used since 1972 to assess plant health and monitor vegetation changes over time [3]. However, as noted by [4], four main challenges persist: (i) a limited number of usable images due to weather conditions; (ii) the low spatial resolution of many satellite platforms, making them unsuitable for detailed field-scale analyses; (iii) the need for efficient platforms to process large datasets; and (iv) the challenge of extracting meaningful information from both single images and time series.

The first issue can be mitigated by selecting satellite missions with high temporal resolution, ensuring frequent image acquisitions. Similarly, the second challenge can be addressed by choosing appropriate satellite platforms. Although freely available satellite imagery generally has low to medium spatial resolution, Landsat (NASA) and Sentinel-2 (ESA) provide viable alternatives, offering 30 m and 10 m spatial resolution in visible bands, respectively, with revisit times of 16 and 10 days [5]. However, analyzing long-term trends requires processing vast amounts of data, exceeding the computational capacity of standalone software [6]. This limitation can be overcome through cloud-based platforms like Google Earth Engine (GEE) [7], designed to handle geospatial big data using parallel computing [8]. Additionally, GEE integrates an extensive and continuously updated dataset catalog, facilitating data selection and import via its Application Programming Interface (API) [8]. It also provides numerous tools for processing geospatial data [10, 11], enabling the implementation of various analytical approaches.

A widely used method for extracting information from vegetation is the application of Vegetation Indices (VIs). Among the numerous indices developed, Normalized Difference Vegetation Index (NDVI) [12], Optimized Soil Adjusted Vegetation Index (OSAVI) [13], Green Normalized Difference Vegetation Index (GNDVI) [14] and Normalized Difference Red Edge Index (NDRE) [15] are particularly effective for vineyard monitoring [16]. However, while these indices capture plant characteristics at a specific moment, they do not provide insights into long-term vegetation dynamics.

To analyze gradual and abrupt vegetation changes over time, specific statistical approaches are required [17]. Both parametric and non-parametric methods can be used, although the former require assumptions that limit their applicability [18], such as data following a Gaussian distribution and being sensitive to outliers. Non-parametric techniques overcome these limitations as they do not require prior distribution assumptions and are resistant to outliers. Additionally, they can handle missing values and detection limits, making them widely used in remote sensing for long-term trend analysis. Among them, the Mann-Kendall trend test [19, 20] detects monotonic trends, while Sen's slope estimator [21] quantifies changes over time.

This study evaluates the potential of Sentinel-2 medium-resolution imagery for monitoring long-term trends in an Aglianico vineyard located in the Campania region

(Southern Italy). A Sentinel-2 time series spanning ten years was analyzed using these non-parametric approaches to assess vineyard dynamics over time.

2 Material and Methods

This section provides an overview of the datasets and methodology used to achieve the research objectives. A Sentinel-2 time series covering a vineyard field dedicated to Aglianico in Campania was collected over a 10-year period (2015–2025) and imported into the cloud-based GEE platform. The pre-processing phase was then carried out to remove cloud contamination and resample the spectral bands to ensure a consistent spatial resolution across all images.

Following pre-processing, the resulting images were averaged and used as input for the subsequent analytical steps: i) computation of VIs; ii) analysis of annual VIs distribution using basic statistical metrics; iii) comparison of VIs performance; and iv) assessment of VIs trends through non-parametric statistical tests.

Further details on the input datasets and processing methods are provided in the following sections.

2.1 Study Area

The experiment was conducted in a vineyard located in Avellino, a small town in the Campania Region (Southern Italy), provided by Cantina Di Prisco. The study area (41° 0'3.25"N; 15° 1'48.85"E) covers approximately 21000 m^2 and is dedicated to the cultivation of Aglianico grapes (Fig. 1). Aglianico is one of the most renowned wines produced in Southern Italy, particularly in the Campania and Basilicata regions. It comprises three distinct biotypes: Taurasi, Taburno, and Vulture [22]. However, the vineyard selected for this study exclusively cultivates the Taurasi variety.

Aglianico is a late-ripening grape variety that requires a long growing season to reach full maturity. Budburst typically occurs in early April, followed by flowering between late May and early June [22]. Veraison, the stage when grapes begin to change color and accumulate sugars, takes place between mid-August and early September. Due to its thick skin and high tannin content, Aglianico requires an extended ripening period, with harvest usually occurring between late October and early November. This prolonged maturation enhances the grape's deep color, firm structure, and high acidity, making it well-suited for aging [22].

The vineyard installation began in 2007 and was completed in 2015. Consequently, 2015 was considered the starting point for this research analysis. By Aglianico's phenological cycle, the growing season for this study was defined as spanning from April to October..

2.2 Data Collection and Pre-processing Analysis

GEE, the cloud-based platform developed by Google in 2017 for handling geospatial big data, was selected in this study as the most reliable environment for implementing customized code and overcoming the limitations of traditional standalone software [8, 9].

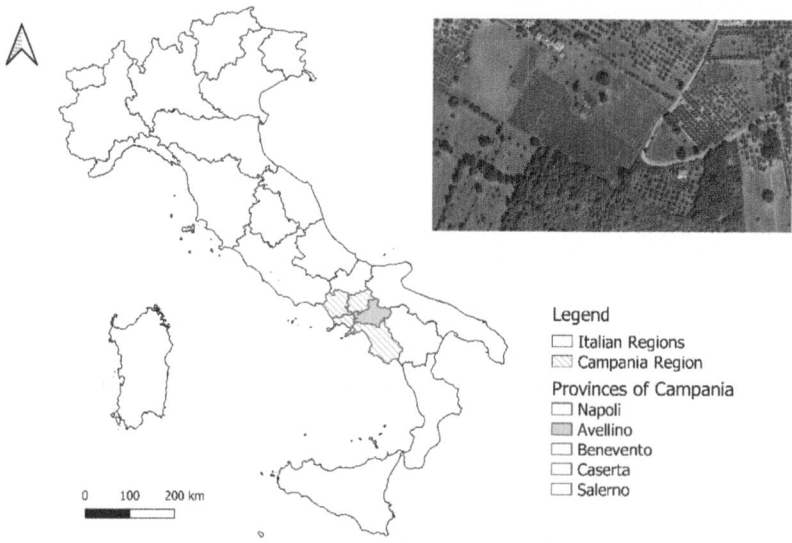

Fig. 1. Study area location.

Indeed, GEE offers innovative features that significantly accelerate both data acquisition and management processes.

Firstly, it leverages multiple processors working in parallel and provides access to an integrated data catalog, which is updated daily with 6,000 freely available scenes. These characteristics enable the processing of vast amounts of data in a relatively short time and reduce data collection efforts, as users can access raw and pre-processed datasets directly from a single platform. Additionally, users can import their own datasets. The platform also includes an integrated API that supports code development in both JavaScript and Python. In this study, customized scripts were implemented using JavaScript.

The integrated data catalog was used to select and import monthly Sentinel-2 images spanning the period from 2015 to 2025 into the GEE API. Sentinel-2 imagery consists of multiple spectral bands, each acquired at different spatial resolutions. Specifically, the four visible and Near-InfraRed bands (Blue, Green, Red, and NIR) have a native resolution of 10 m. The Red Edge (RE), ShortWave InfraRed (SWIR), and some additional bands are available at 20 m, while atmospheric and cirrus bands are provided at a coarser resolution of 60 m. The time frame was chosen to align with vineyard installation timelines. As mentioned in the previous section, the Aglianico grapevine plantation was completed in 2015. Therefore, this year was set as the starting point of the investigation to monitor the vineyard's development over time.

To maximize data availability, no cloud cover threshold was imposed during image selection. However, when necessary, images were corrected using a cloud-masking procedure based on the Quality Assessment (QA) band, as recommended by [23].

A total of 1,348 images, projected in the Universal Transverse Mercator (UTM) coordinate system and referenced to the World Geodetic System (WGS84) datum, were collected. Since their geometric accuracy was deemed satisfactory, no orthorectification was applied. Additionally, to enhance the usability of the RE band in vegetation index calculations, it was resampled from 20 m to 10 m.

Finally, the processed data were aggregated on a monthly basis by computing their mean values, and the resulting datasets were used as input for subsequent processing steps.

2.3 Index-Based Approach

The index-based approach relies on the mathematical combination of multiple spectral bands to extract information about various elements. Each object exhibits a characteristic spectral response across different wavelengths [24]. Based on these spectral signatures, specific indices have been developed to enhance the extraction of relevant features.

Indices designed for vegetation analysis are commonly referred to as VIs. Among these, the NDVI [12], OSAVI [13], GNDVI [14], and NDRE [15] have been recognized in the literature as particularly effective for monitoring vegetation in vineyards [16] (Eqs. 1–4).

$$NDVI = \frac{NIR - RED}{NIR + RED}, \tag{1}$$

$$OSAVI = \frac{NIR - RED}{NIR + RED + 0.16}, \tag{2}$$

$$GNDVI = \frac{NIR - GREEN}{NIR + GREEN} \tag{3}$$

$$NDRE = \frac{NIR - RE}{NIR + RE}. \tag{4}$$

These indices primarily combine RGB, NIR, and RE bands. RGB bands are useful for detecting pigments such as carotenoids and anthocyanins [25], while the inclusion of NIR allows for the estimation of biophysical parameters [26]. Additionally, integrating the RE band enables the assessment of chlorophyll concentration [27].

To compute these four vegetation indices within the GEE environment, a JavaScript script was developed. The computed indices were added as additional bands to each image. As with the other spectral bands, a monthly composite was generated by averaging all available images for each month.

2.4 Statistical Analysis of Spectral Indices Outcomes

Before analyzing VIs trends throughout the grapevine growing seasons using a non-parametric statistical approach, their annual variations were first assessed. This was done by computing the monthly mean, median, standard deviation (SD), minimum (min), and maximum (max) values. These statistical measures provide insights into the distribution, central tendency, and variability of the indices over time.

Additionally, the performance of different VIs was compared by calculating the Pearson correlation coefficient. This metric quantifies the strength and direction of the linear relationship between VIs, helping to identify which indices exhibit similar temporal patterns and how they relate to each other. A strong positive correlation suggests that two indices respond similarly to vegetation dynamics, while a weaker or negative correlation may indicate differences in their sensitivity to specific physiological or environmental factors.

2.5 Trend Analysis

Significant positive and negative trends in the annual VI time series can be identified using both parametric and non-parametric approaches. However, parametric methods require data to be independent and normally distributed, whereas non-parametric methods are more flexible and robust, as they only assume data independence [17].

For this reason, the Mann-Kendall test and Sen's slope estimator, two widely used non-parametric methods, were selected and combined to identify significant trends. Specifically, the Mann-Kendall test was applied to detect the presence of monotonic trends, while Sen's slope estimator quantified the rate of change over time. Both methods were applied just on vineyard growing seasons. A detailed description of both methods is provided in the following sections.

2.6 Mann-Kendall Test

The Mann-Kendall test, introduced by Mann (1945) and later expanded by Kendall [19, 20], is widely used for analyzing satellite time series due to its robustness against a small number of outliers, which have minimal impact on the results [28]. In this study, the test was applied to identify positive and negative trends in VI values at the pilot site. However, rather than considering the entire time series, the analysis was restricted to the Aglianico growing season, as previously explained. The test statistic S is computed using the following equation:

$$S = \sum_{i=1}^{n-1} \sum_{j=i+1}^{n} sgn(x_j - x_i), \tag{5}$$

where x_i and x_j represent valid observations at two different time points ($j > i$), and n is the total number of observations. The function sgn ($x_j - x_i$) is defined as follows:

$$sgn(x_j - x_i) = \begin{cases} 1, & \text{if } x_j - x_i > 0 \\ 0, & \text{if } x_j - x_i = 0 \\ -1, & \text{if } x_j - x_i < 0 \end{cases}, \tag{6}$$

This function detects increases and decreases in the time series: a positive value indicates an increasing trend, a negative value a decreasing trend, and zero signifies no change. The results were analyzed at both the local and overall levels to assess trends at specific points and their impact on the entire dataset [29]. Assuming the observations are independent, the expected value and variance of S are calculated as follows [30].

$$E(S) = 0. \tag{7}$$

$$VAR(S) = \frac{n * (n-1) * (2n+5)}{18}. \tag{8}$$

The test statistic S is then used to compute t, an estimator of Kendall's τ, which measures the probability of concordance between two observed variables:

$$t = \frac{2S}{n(n-1)}. \tag{9}$$

$$\tau = P\left(y_i < y_j | x_i < x_j\right) - P\left(y_i > |x_i < x_j\right). \tag{10}$$

The expected value and variance of t are given by:

$$E(t) = 0. \tag{11}$$

$$VAR(S) = \frac{2n * (2n+5)}{9n(n-1)}. \tag{12}$$

Finally, the standardized test statistic Z, which follows a normal distribution, is computed as follows:

$$Z = \begin{cases} \frac{S-1}{\sqrt{VAR(S)}}, & \text{if } S > 0 \\ 0, & \text{if } S = 0 \\ \frac{S+1}{\sqrt{VAR(S)}}, & \text{if } S < 0 \end{cases} \tag{13}$$

The test was conducted at a significance level of $\alpha = 0.05$. A trend is considered significant when $|Z| > Z_{1-\alpha/2}$, where $Z_{1-\alpha/2}$ is derived from the standard normal distribution table. In this study, a significant trend was identified when $|Z|$ exceeded 1.96.

2.7 Sen's Slope Estimator

The magnitude of statistically significant trends detected through the Mann-Kendall test was evaluated using Sen's slope estimator [21]. The slope (Q_i) was calculated by using the following formula:

$$Q_i = \frac{(X_j - X_k)}{j - k} \quad \text{for } i = 1, 2, \dots N. \tag{14}$$

where Xj and Xk are data values at times j and k ($j > k$), and N is the total number of observations in the time series. Sen's estimator B is then given by the median of all computed slopes:

$$B = \begin{cases} Q * \frac{N+1}{2}, & \text{if } N \text{ is odd} \\ \frac{1}{2}\left(Q * \frac{N}{2} + Q * \frac{N+1}{2}\right), & \text{if } N \text{ is even} \end{cases} \tag{15}$$

3 Results and Discussion

This study aims to analyze long-term trends in an Aglianico vineyard located in Avellino, a small municipality in the Campania Region, over a 10-year period (2015–2025). The starting year was chosen based on the vineyard's installation timeline. Although planting began in 2007, it was completed in 2015, making this the ideal starting point for a comprehensive analysis of vineyard development.

A Sentinel-2 time series covering the entire period was selected and processed within GEE, the cloud-based geospatial analysis platform developed by Google in 2017. Sentinel-2 imagery was preferred over other freely available datasets due to its higher spatial resolution. Likewise, GEE was chosen over traditional standalone software because of its ability to streamline data acquisition and processing. The platform benefits from an integrated data catalog, updated daily with 6,000 freely accessible scenes, which can be directly imported into its API without requiring manual downloads. Additionally, GEE's cloud computing infrastructure, leveraging multiple parallel processors, enables efficient storage and processing of large-scale geospatial datasets [8, 9].

A total of 1,348 Sentinel-2 images were collected and pre-processed. This included cloud removal where necessary and resampling of the RE band to 10 m to ensure consistency in spatial resolution and prevent errors in VI calculations. Four VIs, NDVI, OSAVI, GNDVI, and NDRE, were selected based on their proven effectiveness in vineyard monitoring [16]. These indices leverage different spectral combinations: NDVI, OSAVI, and GNDVI integrate NIR with RGB bands, allowing the estimation of biophysical parameters [26], while NDRE incorporates the RE band, making it particularly useful for assessing chlorophyll concentration [27].

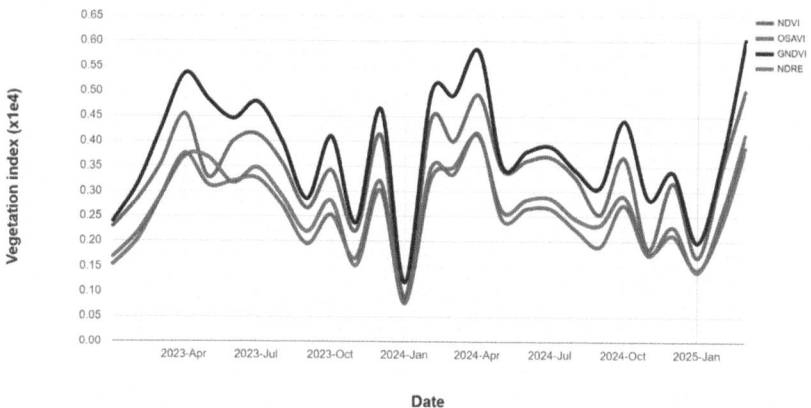

Fig. 2. Monthly mean of computed VIs over the 2015–2025 period.

Each index was computed for all available images, and basic statistical metrics (mean, median, standard deviation, minimum, and maximum) were extracted on a monthly basis to analyze their distribution over time. Figures 2, 3, 4, 5 and 6 illustrate the results.

The computed indices exhibit consistent seasonal trends across all statistical metrics, which aligns with the expected phenological cycle of grapevines. Vineyards typically

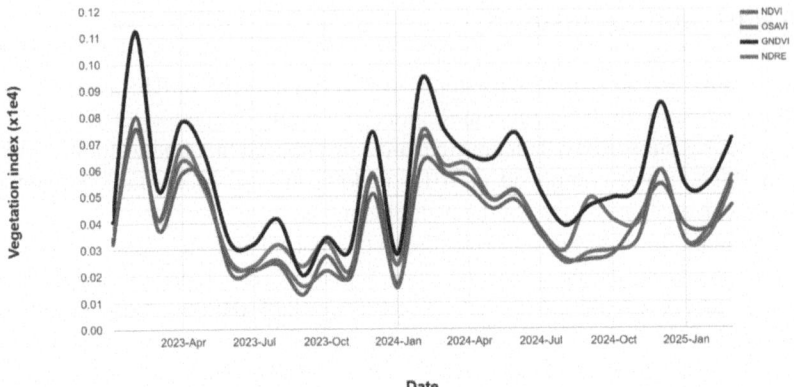

Fig. 3. Monthly standard deviation of computed VIs over the 2015–2025 period.

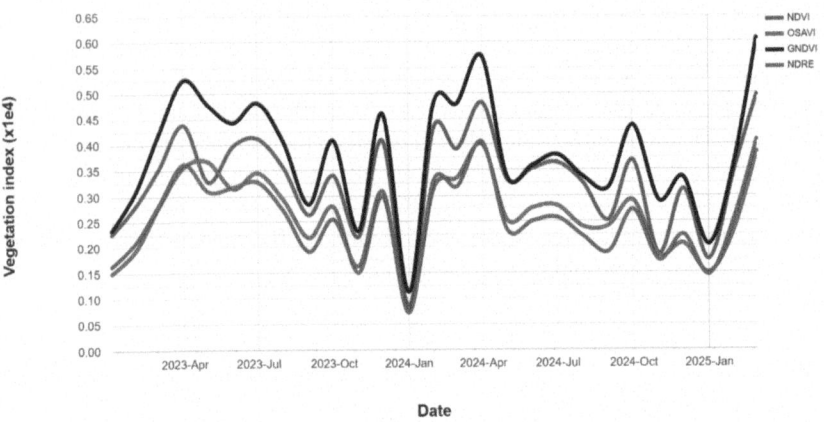

Fig. 4. Monthly median of computed VIs over the 2015–2025 period.

experience a progressive increase in vegetation indices from early spring to summer, corresponding to canopy development, followed by a decline in late summer and autumn due to senescence and harvest activities [16].

However, some notable differences emerge. OSAVI and NDRE display almost identical temporal patterns, with consistently lower values compared to NDVI and GNDVI. This suggests that these indices are more sensitive to soil background effects and canopy structure. OSAVI includes a correction factor (0.16) to minimize soil influence, which may explain its lower values [13], while NDRE incorporates the RE band, making it more responsive to subtle chlorophyll variations rather than overall vegetation cover [15]. GNDVI shows a distinct behavior, often diverging from the other indices. This could be attributed to its reliance on the green band, making it more responsive to variations in leaf pigment concentration, particularly chlorophyll content [14]. NDVI, widely recognized as a robust vegetation indicator, follows a trend similar to GNDVI but with slightly lower values, likely due to its greater sensitivity to overall vegetation density rather than specific leaf properties [25, 31].

These differences highlight the importance of selecting appropriate indices based on the specific characteristics of vineyard monitoring. The integration of RE-based indices (NDRE) and traditional NIR-based indices (NDVI, OSAVI, GNDVI) provides a more comprehensive understanding of vineyard health, balancing canopy vigor assessment with chlorophyll concentration analysis [32].

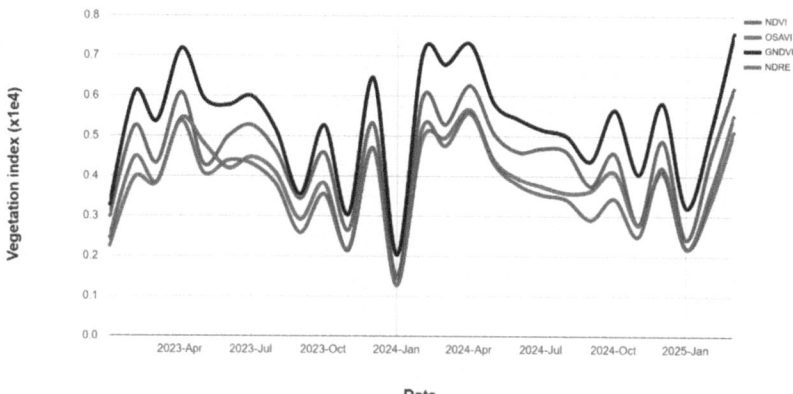

Fig. 5. Monthly maximum of computed VIs over the 2015–2025 period.

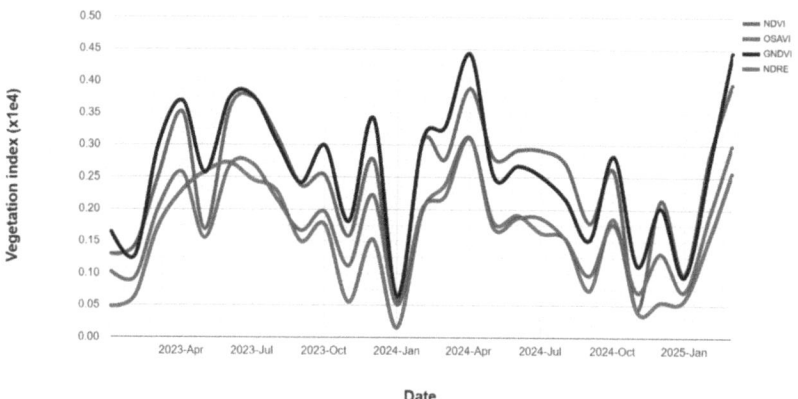

Fig. 6. Monthly minimum of computed VIs over the 2015–2025 period.

To gain deeper insight into the relationships among the four computed indices, the Pearson correlation coefficient was also calculated. The results are illustrated in Fig. 7, which presents a radial diagram depicting the strength and direction of the linear relationships between the indices over time.

A strong positive correlation (values close to $+1$) indicates that two indices follow similar temporal trends, suggesting that they respond similarly to vegetation changes.

Conversely, lower correlation values imply differences in sensitivity to specific vegetation properties. The high correlation between NDVI and OSAVI suggests that both indices are primarily influenced by vegetation density as they incorporate similar spectral bands in their formulation. On the other hand, NDRE shows a moderate correlation with the other indices, reflecting its unique sensitivity to chlorophyll content, which is particularly relevant in assessing plant health.

It is important to highlight that the Pearson coefficient measures the strength of linear relationships between two indices but does not describe their absolute values or distribution. While NDVI, OSAVI, GNDVI, and NDRE may exhibit different means, medians, minimum, and maximum values, their correlation coefficients remain high if they follow similar seasonal trends. This distinction is crucial: an index can have a lower or higher absolute value but still be strongly correlated with another if both increase and decrease in sync over time. Thus, correlation analysis complements the statistical metrics previously examined, providing a broader perspective on how these indices interact in vineyard monitoring.

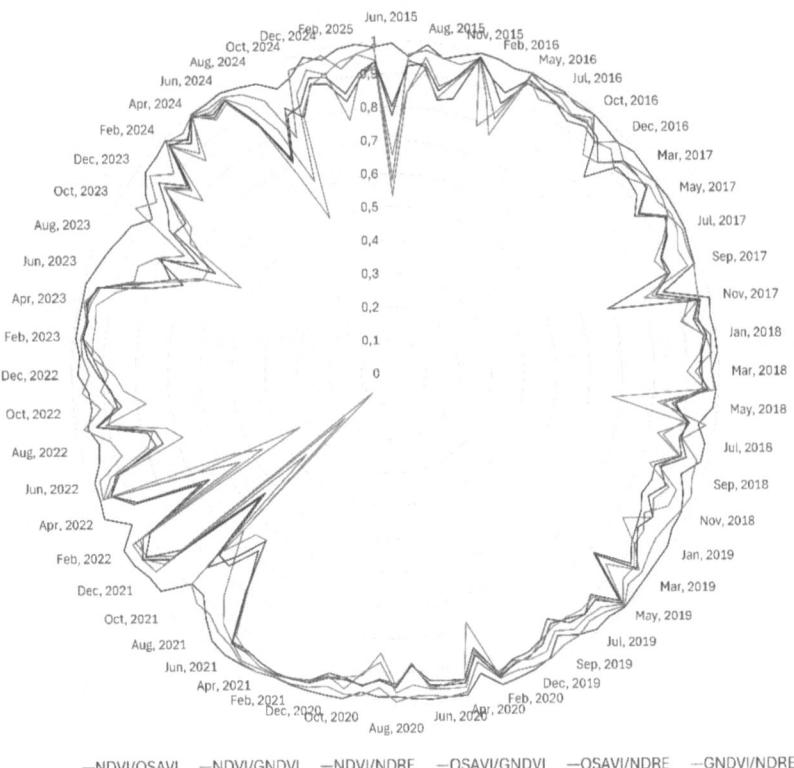

Fig. 7. Radial diagram of Pearson correlation coefficients among different vegetation indices.

However, these analyses do not provide direct insights into the long-term trends of the Aglianico vineyard. To address this, the non-parametric Mann-Kendall test and the

Sen's slope test were applied. The Mann-Kendall test was used to detect the presence of monotonic trends, while Sen's slope test quantified the rate of change over time. Both tests were performed on the results of the four computed vegetation indices.

Figures 8 and 9 present the results of the Mann-Kendall τ correlation and the Mann-Kendall Z-Test, respectively, applied to the four vegetation indices (NDVI, OSAVI, GNDVI, and NDRE) over the period 2015–2025. These analyses provide a comprehensive assessment of both the direction and statistical significance of the observed trends.

Figure 8 illustrates the Mann-Kendall τ correlation, which quantifies the strength and direction of monotonic trends in the computed vegetation indices. The τ values range from negative (blue tones) to positive (red tones), where: i) positive τ values indicate an increase in vegetation health or coverage over time; ii) negative τ values suggest a declining trend, though the intensity is generally low, with a minimum around -0.3.

The results reveal that most of the vineyard exhibits a positive trend, suggesting progressive improvement in vegetative conditions. This could be attributed to vine maturation, favorable environmental conditions, or effective agronomic practices. However, a localized area in the lower part of the field shows a weak negative trend, potentially indicating localized stress factors such as soil degradation, waterlogging, or nutrient deficiencies.

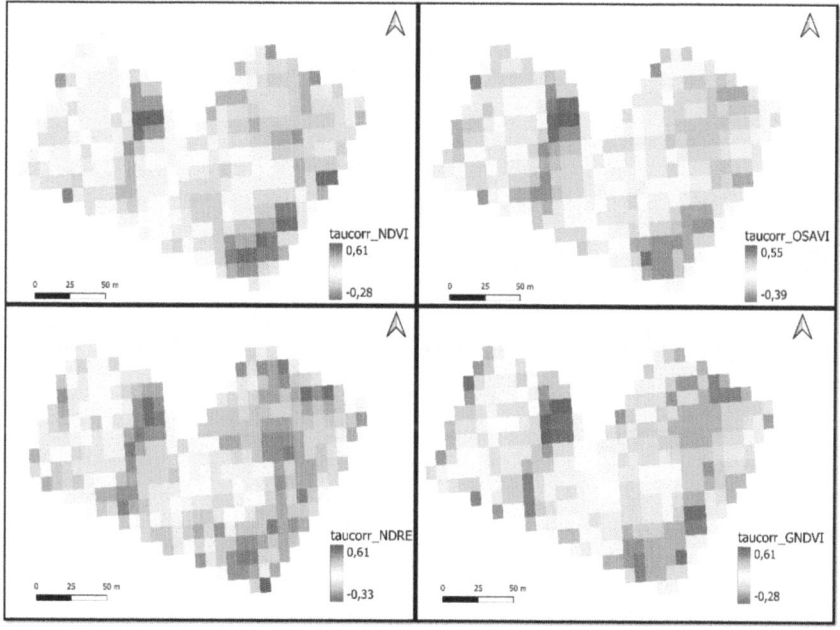

Fig. 8. Mann-Kendall's τ correlation of the four calculated vegetation indices (NDVI, OSAVI, GNDVI, and NDRE).

Figure 9 represents the results of the Mann-Kendall Z-Test, which evaluates the statistical significance of the trends identified in Fig. 8. The Z values range from -1.4

to 2.2, with: i) blue tones corresponding to negative trends, though limited in extent; ii) red tones indicating statistically significant positive trends across most of the vineyard.

The spatial pattern in Fig. 9 closely aligns with Fig. 8, confirming that the positive trends detected in the vineyard are statistically significant. Conversely, the negative values in the lower portion of the field remain relatively low, suggesting that while some declines are present, it is not severe.

The consistency between the two analyses reinforces the reliability of the detected trends. The general increase in vegetation indices supports the hypothesis of vineyard improvement, potentially due to i) canopy development and grapevine maturation over time; ii) sustainable management practices improving plant health; iii) favorable climatic conditions contributing to stable or increasing vegetation indices.

However, the localized negative trend observed in both figures suggests an area that may require further investigation. Potential causes could include soil degradation, water stress, or microclimatic variability. While the decline is not drastic, monitoring and targeted agronomic interventions may help mitigate any long-term impact.

By using the same color scale across both figures, the analysis ensures visual consistency, making it easier to compare the strength and statistical significance of detected trends. This reinforces the study's findings and provides valuable insights into the vineyard's long-term vegetation dynamics.

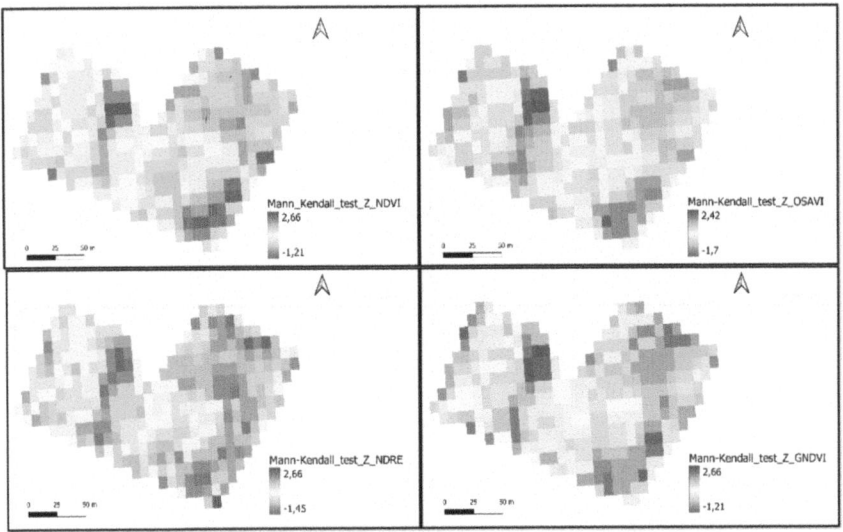

Fig. 9. Mann-Kendall's Z-Test of the four calculated vegetation indices (NDVI, OSAVI, GNDVI, and NDRE).

Unlike the Mann-Kendall τ correlation (Fig. 8) and Z-Test (Fig. 9), which identify the presence and significance of trends, Sen's Slope provides an estimate of their magnitude, indicating how rapidly vegetation indices are increasing or decreasing over time [21]. Sen's slope result is depicted in Fig. 10, which quantifies the rate of change in the four computed vegetation indices (NDVI, OSAVI, GNDVI, and NDRE) over the period

2015–2025. The color scale remains consistent with Figs. 8 and 9, ranging from blue (negative trends) to red (positive trends). This ensures visual coherence and facilitates comparison across analyses.

The findings confirm a predominant positive trend across most of the vineyard, suggesting an overall improvement in vegetation health and coverage. This trend is likely influenced by factors such as vine maturation, favorable climatic conditions, and effective agronomic management. However, a localized negative trend is evident in the lower portion of the vineyard, mirroring the patterns observed in the Mann-Kendall analyses. Although the magnitude of this decline remains relatively low, it indicates a gradual rather than abrupt deterioration, which may be linked to localized factors such as soil conditions, water stress, or microclimatic variability. Additionally, the asymmetry in the range, with a slightly higher maximum positive value than the minimum negative value, suggests that the overall trend is more inclined towards improvement rather than decline. However, the presence of negative slopes, even if limited, warrants attention to prevent further deterioration. This reinforces the importance of integrating statistical analyses with field observations to identify the underlying causes of such variations.

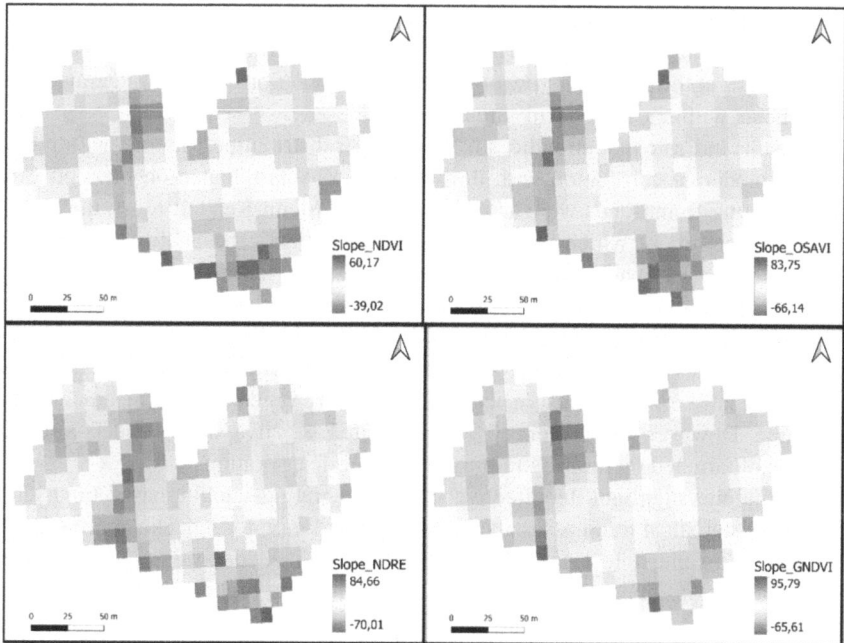

Fig. 10. Sen's slopes of the four calculated vegetation indices (NDVI, OSAVI, GNDVI, and NDRE).

The strong agreement among the results of the Mann-Kendall τ test, the Z-Test, and Sen's Slope strengthens the reliability of the observed trends. The overall positive trajectory suggests that the vineyard is experiencing stable or improving conditions, while the localized negative area highlights the need for further monitoring and potential intervention. Understanding the factors driving these trends can help optimize vineyard management strategies, ensuring long-term sustainability and productivity.

4 Conclusion

The vineyard ecosystem is a key component of the Mediterranean Basin, serving as a major economic driver, particularly in Italy, France, and Spain, which lead global wine production. In Italy, the Campania region is especially notable for its viticulture, with Aglianico standing out as one of its most renowned grape varieties. Given its economic and agricultural significance, the cultivation of Aglianico requires a precise and data-driven management approach that extends beyond traditional farming expertise. In this context, geospatial big data and remote sensing techniques play a crucial role in monitoring vine health and extracting valuable vineyard information.

This study aimed to detect long-term trends in Aglianico vineyards by analyzing a case study provided by Cantina Di Prisco. A 10-year Sentinel-2 time series was selected and processed using two non-parametric statistical methods: the Mann-Kendall test and Sen's slope estimator, applied to four spectral indices (NDVI, OSAVI, GNDVI, and NDRE). Sentinel-2 was chosen for its superior spatial resolution compared to other freely available satellite missions. However, despite its 10-m resolution, it does not capture changes at the grapevine row or leaf level but rather provides an integrated view of all elements within a 10×10 m^2 area.

The results indicate that all indices follow similar distribution patterns, with NDRE showing a moderate correlation with the others due to its reliance on the Red Edge (RE) band. Long-term trends were assessed using the Mann-Kendall τ test, the Z-Test, and Sen's Slope, all of which yielded consistent findings. The analysis reveals that most of the vineyard exhibits a positive trend, suggesting an overall improvement in vegetative conditions, while a small portion displays a negative trend, likely influenced by localized factors such as soil conditions, water stress, or microclimatic variability. Additionally, the asymmetry in the Sen's Slope range, with slightly higher positive values than negative ones, suggests a net tendency toward vegetation enhancement rather than decline. However, the presence of even limited negative slopes underscores the importance of targeted monitoring to prevent further deterioration.

These findings highlight the effectiveness of integrating satellite-based time series analysis with statistical trend assessments for vineyard monitoring. The approach provides valuable insights into vine health evolution over time, supporting more informed agronomic decisions. Future research could benefit from higher-resolution imagery and ground-based validation to refine the detection of fine-scale variations and better understand the driving factors behind vineyard dynamics.

Acknowledgments. This research was founded by the European Union – NextGenerationUE, Progetto PRIN-PNRR WIN-RIESCO (CUP Master: F53D23009390001 – CUP: D53D23017750001 - PNRR - Missione 4 "Istruzione e Ricerca" - Componente 2 "Dalla Ricerca all'Impresa" Investimento 1.1 "Fondo per il Programma Nazionale di Ricerca e Progetti di Rilevante Interesse Nazionale (PRIN)"). The authors sincerely thank Cantina Di Prisco (Contrada Rotole, 27, 83040 Fontanarosa AV, Italy) for their valuable support in providing the case study data for this research.

Disclosure of Interests. The authors declare that there are no conflicts of interest.

References

1. Costa, J.M., et al.: Modern viticulture in southern europe: vulnerabilities and strategies for adaptation to water scarcity. Agric. Water Manag. **164**, 5–18 (2016)
2. Hedley, C.B.: The role of precision agriculture for improved nutrient management on farms. J. Sci. Food Agric. **95**, 12–19 (2015)
3. Capolupo, A., Monterisi, C., Tarantino, E.: Landsat Images Classification Algorithm (LICA) to automatically extract land cover information in Google Earth Engine environment. Remote Sens. **12**(7), 1201 (2020)
4. Potapov, P., Turubanova, S., Hansen, M.C.: Regional-scale boreal forest cover and change mapping using Landsat data composites for European Russia. Remote Sens. Environ. **115**, 548–561 (2011)
5. Li, J., Roy, D.P.: A global analysis of Sentinel-2A, Sentinel-2B and Landsat-8 data revisit intervals and implications for terrestrial monitoring. Remote Sens. **9**(9), 902 (2017)
6. Hansen, M., et al.: Observing the forest and the trees: the first high resolution global maps of forest cover change. Science **342**, 850–853 (2013)
7. Capolupo, A., Santoro, P.M., Tarantino, E.: Exploiting medium-resolution sentinel data in google earth engine for burned area reflectance classification. In: Gervasi, O., Murgante, B., Garau, C., Taniar, D., C. Rocha, A.M.A., Faginas Lago, M.N. (eds.) Computational Science and Its Applications – ICCSA 2024 Workshops. ICCSA 2024. LNCS, vol. 14819. Springer, Cham. https://doi.org/10.1007/978-3-031-65282-0_13
8. Kumar LMutanga, O.: Google earth engine applications since inception: usage, trends, and potential. Remote Sens. **10**, 1509 (2018)
9. Gorelick, N., Hancher, M., Dixon, M., Ilyushchenko, S., Thau, D., Moore, R.: Google earth engine: planetary-scale geospatial analysis for everyone. Remote Sens. Environ. **202**, 18–27 (2017)
10. Barletta, C., Capolupo, A., Tarantino, E.: Estimating urban growth from landsat 8 data using post-classification and albedo change analysis in GEE environment. In: Gervasi, O., Murgante, B., Garau, C., Taniar, D.C., Rocha, A.M.A., Faginas Lago, M.N. (eds.) Computational Science and Its Applications – ICCSA 2024 Workshops. ICCSA 2024. LNCS, vol. 14819. Springer, Cham (2024). https://doi.org/10.1007/978-3-031-65282-0_12
11. Barletta, C., Capolupo, A., Tarantino, E.: Extracting land surface albedo from Landsat 9 data in GEE platform to support climate change analysis. Geomat. Environ. Eng. **17**(6) (2023)
12. Rouse, J., Jr., Haas, R.H., Schell, J.A., Deering, D.W.: Monitoring vegetation systems in the great plains with ERTS; NASA: Washington. DC, USA (1974)
13. Rondeaux, G., Steven, M., Baret, F.: Optimization of soil-adjusted vegetation indices. Remote Sens. Environ. **55**, 95–107 (1996)
14. Wu, W.: The generalized difference vegetation index (GDVI) for dryland characterization. Remote Sens. **6**, 1211–1233 (2014)
15. Boiarskii, B., Hasegawa, H.: Comparison of NDVI and NDRE indices to detect differences in vegetation and chlorophyll content. J. Mech. Contin. Math. Sci **4**, 20–29 (2019)
16. Giovos, R., Tassopoulos, D., Kalivas, D., Lougkos, N., Priovolou, A.: Remote sensing vegetation indices in viticulture: a critical review. Agriculture **11**(5), 457 (2021)
17. Maffei, C., Lindenbergh, R., Menenti, M.: Combining multi-spectral and thermal remote sensing to predict forest fire characteristics. ISPRS J. Photogramm. Remote Sens. **181**, 400–412 (2021)
18. Wang, F., et al.: Re-evaluation of the power of the mann-kendall test for detecting monotonic trends in hydrometeorological time series. Front. Earth Sci. **8**, 14 (2020)

19. Mann, H.B.: Nonparametric tests against trend. Econom. J. Econom. Soc. **13**, 245–259 (1945)
20. Kendall, M.G.: Rank correlation methods, 4th edn. Charles Griffin & Company Limited: London, UK (1984)
21. Sen, P.K.: Estimates of the regression coefficient based on Kendall's tau. J. Am. Stat. Assoc. **63**(324), 1379–1389 (1968)
22. Picariello, L., Rinaldi, A., Forino, M., Errichiello, F., Moio, L., Gambuti, A.: Effect of different enological tannins on oxygen consumption, phenolic compounds, color and astringency evolution of Aglianico wine. Molecules **25**(20), 4607 (2020)
23. Corbane, C., et al.: A global cloud free pixel-based image composite from Sentinel-2 data. Data Brief **31**, 105737 (2010)
24. Pal, M., Rasmussen, T., Porwal, A.: Optimized lithological mapping from multispectral and hyperspectral remote sensing images using fused multi-classifiers. Remote Sens. **12**, 177 (2020)
25. Zarco-Tejada, P.J., et al.: Assessing vineyard condition with hyperspectral indices: leaf and canopy reflectance simulation in a row-structured discontinuous canopy. Remote Sens. Environ. **99**, 271–287 (2005)
26. Weiser, R.L., Asrar, G., Millere, G.P., Kanemasu, T.: Assessing grassland biophysical characteristics from spectral measurements. Remote Sens. Environ. **20**, 141–152 (1986)
27. Munden, R., Curran, P.J., Catt, J.A.: The relationship between red edge and chlorophyll concentration in the Broadbalk winter wheat experiment at Rothamsted. Int. J. Remote Sens. **15**, 705–709 (1994)
28. Collaud Coen, M., et al.: Effects of the prewhitening method, the time granularity, and the time segmentation on the mann-kendall trend detection and the associated sen's slope. Atmos. Meas. Tech. **13**, 6945–6964 (2020)
29. Xu, H., Wang, Y., Guan, H., Shi, T., Hu, X.: Detecting ecological changes with a remote sensing Based Ecological Index (RSEI) produced time series and change vector analysis. Remote Sens. **11**, 2345 (2019)
30. Kendall, M.G.: Rank correlation methods. Griffin, London (1995)
31. Capolupo, A., Tarantino, E.: Landsat 9 Satellite images potentiality in extracting land cover classes in GEE environment using an index-based approach: the case study of savona city. In: Gervasi, O., et al. (eds.) Computational Science and Its Applications – ICCSA 2023 Workshops. ICCSA 2023. LNCS, vol. 14107. Springer, Cham (2023). https://doi.org/10.1007/978-3-031-37114-1_17
32. Capolupo, A., Monterisi, C., Caporusso, G., Tarantino, E.: Extracting land cover data using GEE: a review of the classification indices. In: Gervasi, O., et al. (eds.) Computational Science and Its Applications – ICCSA 2020. ICCSA 2020. LNCS, vol. 12252. Springer, Cham (2020). https://doi.org/10.1007/978-3-030-58811-3_56

SoilEye: An Interactive Web App Prototype for Soil Sealing Monitoring

Ahmad Asad[1,2] 🆔, Alessandra Capolupo[2](✉) 🆔, and Eufemia Tarantino[2] 🆔

[1] Department of Agricultural and Environmental Sciences,
University of Bari Aldo Moro, Bari, Italy
[2] Department of Civil, Environmental, Land, Construction and Chemistry (DICATECh),
Politecnico di Bari, Via Orabona 4, 70125 Bari, Italy
alessandra.capolupo@poliba.it

Abstract. Climate change problems are intensifying rapidly, making it essential to monitor environmental and geospatial issues in real time. With the advent of cloud computing, researchers and experts can develop more sustainable solutions in a shorter timeframe. In the geospatial field, the introduction of Google Earth Engine has been a game changer. As a powerful cloud computing platform, Google Earth Engine enables large-scale geospatial analysis by leveraging extensive public data and open-source geospatial datasets. One of the most impactful features introduced by such a tool is creating a web-based application, known as Google Earth Engine Apps. These Apps allow users to visualize, modify, share, and interact with their analysis, results, and outputs in real time. This paper focuses on the creation of "SoilEye", an innovative Google Earth Engine App designed to observe soil sealing patterns over the metropolitan area of Bari. It provides a detailed, step-by-step methodology for developing the app, highlighting its potential and functionality. This app tracks land use changes over approximately six years, from 2018 to 2024, by combining satellite images collected by the Sentinel 2 mission with other geospatial data. It identifies places that have been impacted by soil sealing and evaluates its trend over time. As a result, this App will serve as a valuable tool for policymakers, offering an interactive platform to monitor soil sealing dynamics continuously. This will aid the sustainable urban environment management and help planners make more informed decisions.

Keywords: Cloud Computing Platform · Google Earth Engine (GEE) · Urban Sustainability · Big Data for Environmental Monitoring · Impervious Surfaces

1 Introduction

Urbanization, by altering natural ecosystems, has become one of the biggest challenges and obstacles to sustainable development [1–3], contributing significantly to climate change and global warming. Indeed, the soil ecosystem plays a vital role in regulating temperature and providing resilience against climate change [4, 5]. However, the increasing spread of impervious surfaces, particularly in coastal areas where this phenomenon is more intense [6], has led to the degradation of natural habitats and soil properties [7].

© The Author(s), under exclusive license to Springer Nature Switzerland AG 2026
O. Gervasi et al. (Eds.): ICCSA 2025 Workshops, LNCS 15891, pp. 207–221, 2026.
https://doi.org/10.1007/978-3-031-97617-9_14

The United Nations' (UN) Sustainable Development Goal 13 enhances the urgent need for actions against climate change, advocating for increased awareness, and developing innovative solutions to mitigate and adapt to its effects [8]. Additionally, the UN is making a lot of effort to face the soil consumption issue, by defining many goals directly or indirectly linked with soil consumption, including SDG 2, 3, 11, 12, and 15. Indeed, protecting soil cover and creating a sustainable balance between natural habitats and anthropogenic activities are their main topics [9]. Therefore, it appears necessary to detect effective and efficient methods to extract land use/cover information and monitor its changes over time.

Recently, advancements in remote sensing technologies have revolutionized the way Earth's dynamics are observed, making large-scale monitoring more efficient and accurate [10]. Open-source satellite missions, such as Sentinel, Landsat, and Moderate Resolution Imaging Spectroradiometer (MODIS), continuously provide high-quality images of the Earth's surface and atmosphere [11–13]. However, tracking land changes requires processing vast amounts of data, which exceeds the computational capacity of traditional desktop systems. This constraint was recently overcome thanks to the introduction of cloud-based environments, like Google Earth Engine (GEE) (https://earthengine.google.org). This powerful tool, indeed, takes advantage of many processors in parallel to running custom algorithms, developed both in Python and JavaScript languages in its Application Programming Interface (API) [14]. Additionally, it allows speeding up the procedure thanks to the integrated data catalogue, daily updated with 6000 freely available datasets.

A new opportunity concerning App creation has recently been provided by the GEE environment. Such an App allows users to interactively showcase their analysis and results performed in the GEE API, and to disseminate them among policymakers and the public. Users can interact with simple front-end User Interface (UI) features, while the backend implementation is handled by a developer [15] using both JavaScript and Python coding in accordance with their expertise. Thus, the backend development is performed in the GEE code editor directly, where all possible analyses, from geospatial analysis and visualization up to UI design and dynamic text integration, are implemented. This approach enables customization of the UI based on specific needs, such as adding logos, tailored functions, and other elements to enhance its appeal and usability [16]. Additionally, visibility settings could be adjusted to restrict access to a Google group or make the app public. When GEE web app access is set to "public", anyone with the app's link can view it. GEE also provides "access without signing into Google," allowing any users to visit it without a Google account. This significantly saves time and reduces "login-barriers", making it easier for policymakers, researchers, and experts to go through the produced results included in the App. Although there are no widely known uses of the GEE platform for soil sealing, several apps cover related themes such as urban growth and impervious surface mapping. For instance, the UrbanWatch 1 m Land Cover and Land Use GEE app, in which developers used a fine-resolution, large-area Urban Thematic Information Extraction (FLUTE) framework, contains an extensive and large amount of data of 211 GB, which was reduced to 4.54 GB for GEE [17]. Another example closely linked to urban and non urban land monitoring using GEE is by [18], who used three decade Landsat data to monitor LULC in Brazil. Outside of GEE, few specialized WebGIS platforms visualize and detect soil sealing. For instance, the Urban Atlas and the Copernicus Land Monitoring Service (CLMS) provide high-resolution layers of artificial surfaces across Europe, as these platforms offer valuable insights into urban sprawl [19] and Copernicus created High Resolution Layer Imperviousness service providing different datasets on the imperviousness density and built-up areas [20].

This study aims to design and implement "SoilEye", a novel interactive application leveraging GEE as a cloud computing platform to detect and monitor soil sealing in the Puglia Region (Southern Italy). The SoilEye framework was built on a custom JavaScript code within the GEE environment, integrating remote sensing data, specifically Sentinel 2 images, with geospatial analysis tools. Crucially, the application has been carefully optimized for both desktop and mobile platforms, ensuring full functionality and a consistent, user-friendly experience across devices. This cross-platform compatibility greatly enhances accessibility, enabling users to access insights anytime and anywhere, whether from an office workstation or directly in the field. By detecting the temporal trend of soil sealing from 2018 up to 2024, this approach supports data-driven decision-making for sustainable land management.

The paper is structured as follows: i) Sect. 2 describes the methodology adopted to design and implement SoilEye app as well as the datasets and the analytical methods used to extract soil sealing information and evaluate its trend over time in the metropolitan area of Bari; ii) Sect. 3, instead, presents and discusses the outcomes, introducing the innovative, interactive App and detailing the findings concerning soil sealing trend; iii) lastly, SoilEye app strengths and weakness are outlined in the Conclusion Section.

2 Materials and Methods

This Section presents the dataset and techniques used to extract soil sealing information and assess its trends over time, as well as the approaches employed to develop the innovative, interactive "SoilEye" App. As previously mentioned, the cloud-based platform was chosen because of its capacity to handle geospatial big data and support web App creation [21–24]. Thus, GEE was used to select and process the input data, generate and visualize the findings, and create the app.

The entire workflow is summarized in Fig. 1. It consists of three primary phases: i) core GEE script development: implemented in JavaScript code editor, it involves importing freely available Sentinel 2A satellite dataset collected from the European Space Agency's (ESA), applying preprocessing techniques, and extracting soils sealing information through the integration of Sealed Urban Index (SUI) with Classification and Regression Tree (CART) Machine Learning (ML) algorithm; ii) SoilEye interface design: this phase is focused on two main steps: a) Wireframing and layout definition, aimed at defining App structural blueprint, which was useful in organizing the flow of user interaction; and, b) Optimization for multi-device compatibility, ensuring App visualization on different browsers and devices; and, lastly, iii) SoilEye App logic integration, focused on implementing the app's core functionality and optimizing its performance.

More details concerning the various steps are reported in the following paragraphs.

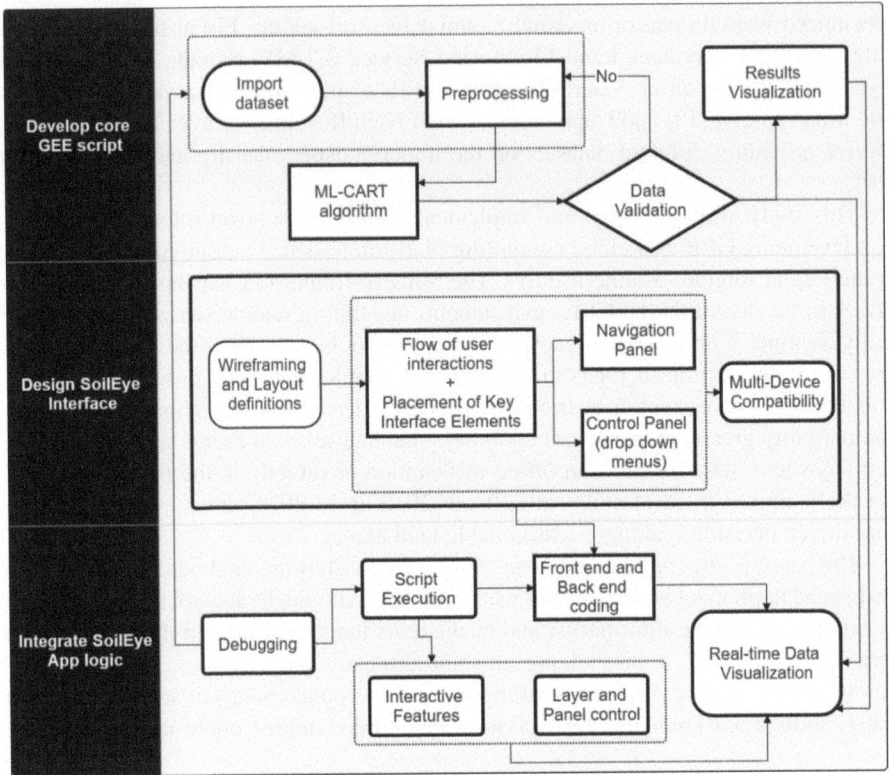

Fig. 1. GEE App creation workflow.

2.1 Development of Core GEE Script

The first step in the development of SoilEye App involved creating the core GEE script for generating soil sealing maps, essential to explore the trend of impervious surface in the metropolitan area of Bari (Fig. 2). To reach such a goal, the methodology proposed by [25] was adopted, which integrates the SUI with a ML algorithm, specifically the CART procedure. Indeed, as highlighted by [26], this combination has proved to be the most effective, yielding reliable results in investigating soil sealing dynamics from Sentinel 2A images This mission was preferred over other freely available satellite initiatives, such as Landsat and MODIS, because of its higher spatial resolution (10 m, 20 m, 60 m), frequent revisit time over the same area (5 days), and availability of more spectral bands (13).

Thus, to implement this approach, a custom JavaScript code was developed in the GEE environment to select the most appropriate dataset, compute SUI, and apply the CART algorithm.

A total of 28 Sentinel 2A images, covering the metropolitan area of Bari, were selected on the base of three primary criteria: i) study area (images had to fully cover the selected region); ii) cloud cover threshold (only images with a cloud coverage lower than 5 were considered. The only exception was reported by the image of May 2019 that features a cloud covered percentage equal to 18.34%); and, lastly, iii) timeframe (the selected images span from 2018 up to 2024 in order to ensure temporal consistency in the analysis). To satisfy these criteria, spatial, temporal, and cloud cover filters were carried out through the following instructions:

```
// Study area definition (Spatial Filter)
var studyArea = ee.FeatureCollection(bbari);
// Define the time periods for each year, specifically for February, May, July, and Oc-
tober
var years = [2018, 2019, 2020, 2021, 2022, 2023, 2024];
var months = ['02', '05', '07', '10'];
var timePeriods = [];
years.forEach(function(year) {
  months.forEach(function(month) {
    // Construct the start date
    var startDate = new Date(year, parseInt(month) - 1, 1);  // Months are 0-indexed in
JS Date

    // Get the last day of the month by moving to the next month and subtracting 1 day
    var endDate = new Date(year, parseInt(month), 0);

    // Format dates as 'YYYY-MM-DD'
    var startDateFormatted = startDate.toISOString().split('T')[0];
    var endDateFormatted = endDate.toISOString().split('T')[0];

    timePeriods.push([startDateFormatted, endDateFormatted]);
  });
});

console.log(timePeriods);
// Loop through each time period, filter Sentinel-2 data, and merge the results
var s2Collection = ee.ImageCollection([]);
timePeriods.forEach(function(period) {
  var tempCollection = ee.ImageCollection('COPERNICUS/S2_HARMONIZED')
    .filterBounds(studyArea)
    .filterDate(period[0], period[1]);
  // Function to filter images, compute indices, classify, and return classified image
  function classifyTimePeriod(startDate, endDate, classifier) {
    var filtered = s2.filter(ee.Filter.lt('CLOUDY_PIXEL_PERCENTAGE', 5))
      .filter(ee.Filter.date(startDate, endDate))
      .filterBounds(studyArea);
```

Nevertheless, when necessary, cloudy pixels were cleaned out by using the algorithm proposed by [27], which relies on metadata and the Quality Assurance band (Band QA60) of Sentinel 2A. On the contrary, both atmospheric and geometrical corrections were not applied since the selected images were already satisfying from those points of view. The main features of the 28 picked-up images are reported in Table 1.

Table 1. Sentinel 2A image details.

Year	Acquisition Dates	Cloud Cover Range (%)
2018	04 Feb, 25 May, 14 Jul, 12 Oct	0.23–3.36
2019	19 Feb, 05 May, 24 Jul, 12 Oct	0–18.34
2020	09 Feb, 04 May, 01 Jul, 01 Oct	0.04–3.55
2021	03 Feb, 09 May, 01 Jul, 04 Oct	0–0.01
2022	03 Feb, 12 May, 03 Jul, 04 Oct	0–4.06
2023	01 Feb, 07 May, 03 Jul, 01 Oct	0–4.19
2024	03 Feb, 01 May, 05 Jul, 13 Oct	0–3.92

After preprocessing the input dataset, the SUI and CART algorithms were implemented. SUI was calculated through Eq. 1:

$$SUI = \frac{(Green - SWIR1) \times (SWIR2 - Red)}{(Green + SWIR1) \times (SWIR2 + Red)} + 0.5. \tag{1}$$

Such an equation was implemented in GEE environment using the following JS code snippet: var SUI = singleImage.expression(

```
'(((Green - SWIR1) * (SWIR2 - Red)) / ((Green + SWIR1) * (SWIR2 + Red)))
+ 0.5', {
        'Green': singleImage.select('B3'),
        'Red': singleImage.select('B4'),
        'SWIR1': singleImage.select('B11'),
        'SWIR2': singleImage.select('B12')
});
```

Subsequently, a systematic procedure was adopted to implement the CART algorithm on the basis of SUI findings and ground truths. This algorithm was implemented to classify land use and land cover (LU/LC), with a particular focus on identifying soil sealing. The classification divided the territory into four main categories: sealed surfaces, vegetation, bare soil, and water bodies. Training data were derived from authoritative LU/LC maps provided by the Istituto Superiore per la Protezione e la Ricerca Ambientale (ISPRA), which include high-resolution shapefiles annotated according to national and European standards. A stratified random sampling approach was applied to extract representative samples across land cover types. To enhance class separability and reduce overlaps among the four categories, the Otsu's method, an image thresholding technique aimed at minimizing intra-class variance, was applied, along with adaptive thresholding based on mean (μ) and standard deviation (σ) values.

The dataset was split into 70% training and 30% testing data, enabling the CART algorithm to partition the input into increasingly homogeneous subsets recursively. The model's performance was evaluated using a confusion matrix, reporting metrics such as Overall Accuracy (OA), User's and Producer's Accuracy (UA and PA), and the Kappa coefficient (K). Validation was conducted using 487 ground truth points extracted from the ISPRA maps, confirming the reliability of the classification approach and supporting robust mapping of soil sealing patterns.

Findings were visualized by using the Map.addLayer() function, which enables visual interpretation by overlaying layers.

Lastly, to reduce the number of iterations and minimize handling time, batch processing procedure was applied. It was preferred to process each image individually to reduce analysis iterations. Comprehensive comments were added before each step to improve readability, facilitate debugging, and enhance error handling.

2.2 Designing SoilEye Interface

After implementing the core functionalities, the design of the SoilEye App interface started by taking into account the requirements of the target users. The main objective of this process was to create a user-friendly interface based on usability principles, ensuring accessibility, clarity, and efficiency in data visualization [28]. The interface was structured to facilitate user interaction with soil sealing analysis results, providing an intuitive experience across different devices.

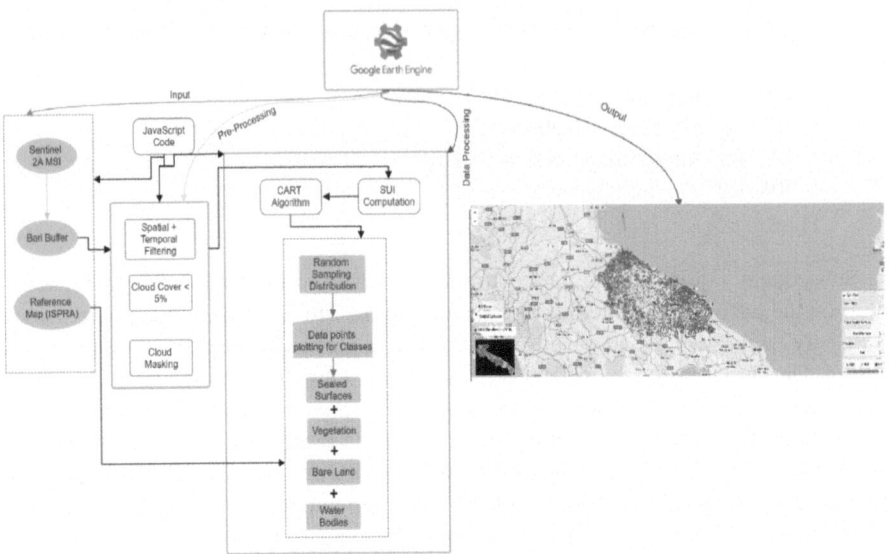

Fig. 2. Core GEE script development.

2.2.1 Wireframing and Layout Definition

The development of the GEE App followed a predefined wireframe, which was created to define the structural blueprint of the app. This served as a foundation for organizing the app's layout, ensuring that the interface components were logically placed for an intuitive user experience. In such a way, the wireframe establishes a clear structure, ensuring that Information Technology (IT) and non-IT skilled users can easily interact with the interface and allowing them to navigate the panel effortlessly and display information in the appropriate window [29].

Wireframe creation process consisted of several key aspects: i) investigating users' requirements and needs; ii) designing an initial UI layout by focusing on essential graphical and interactive tools; iii) ensuring consistency in spacing and responsiveness; and, lastly, iv) refining the design iteratively according to users' feedback [30]. Thus, this structured approach, based on the potential capabilities of integrating geospatial data processing with an intuitive user experience, was applied. According to both IT and non-IT skilled users requirements, three core elements were recognized as essential: i) visualization window (display area for maps); ii) navigation panel, allowing users to switch between functionalities; and, lastly, iii) Multi-device and multi-browser compatibility, ensuring accessibility across different platforms without structural limitations.

In the SoilEye app, the map window, strategically positioned at the center of the UI, displays real-time findings over a baseline map provided by OpenStreetMap. To its left, a control panel, with a drop-down button menu, supports users to filter data according to years and land use/cover classes, as well as to visualize accuracy metrics of the generated outcomes.

2.2.2 Optimization for Multi-device Compatibility

This step ensures GEE App compatibility across multiple devices and browsers, providing a seamless user experience. While desktop and laptop monitors offer large displays, the real challenge was optimizing the visualization on the smartphones' screens [31]. to address this, the app was built with flexible and scalable UI elements. Additionally, touch gesture support was implemented to ensure smooth interaction on touchscreens, increasing app usability on mobile devices.

Optimizing touch gesture support for multiple devices can be challenging, as key interactions, such as pinch-to-zoom, accessing panel features, and tap-to-select for feature identification, rely on precise touch input detection [32]. To provide seamless interaction, the size of the panel was adjusted to avoid obstructing the whole map while still allowing users to navigate efficiently.

2.3 Integrating SoilEye App Logic

This step is aimed at transforming SoilEye App's interface design into a fully functional interactive tool within the GEE platform, ensuring that user inputs were correctly processed and visualized. Its main objective was to run the core GEE script responsible for analysis and data processing [33], including the incorporation of datasets and the application of different filters. JS code was created for each step and analysis. The front and back-end coding facilitated the creation of the interactive interface (front-end) and handled the underlying logic and server communication (back-end) [34]. While implementing previous methods, debugging was consistently carried out to ensure the proper functioning of the GEE script, user interface, and app using the console log for troubleshooting. Thus, to prevent unexpected behaviors, such as crashes due to high memory consumption, and to ensure all steps functioned properly, a script execution was implemented [35].

To enhance usability, several interactive features were incorporated: i) real-time data visualization which immediately updates the map to the Bari study area, removing the need for users to search for it manually; ii) layer control allows users to enable or disable the different years and layers which are sealed surfaces, vegetation, bare land, and water; iii) accuracy assessment button containing OA and K values of each year which validate the results generated from each year.

2.3.1 Performance Optimization

The app was optimized by incorporating several performance optimization techniques, including asynchronous data loading. This step involved the use of asynchronous requests to fetch data from GEE, preventing UI elements from freezing during data retrieval. The optimal goal of any app is to reduce excessive computation that can cause unresponsiveness while ensuring smooth and fast responses for interactive functionalities [36, 37].

To minimize computation time, reduce memory load, and enhance responsiveness, instead of loading the entire satellite dataset, SoilEye applies strict spatial and temporal filters at the initial stage. This limits data size while maintaining results accuracy and enabling faster loading times across all devices. This optimization allows the app to efficiently retrieve and process only the necessary satellite data, preventing it from being overwhelmed by the full dataset.

Moreover, SoilEye defers index calculations and classification until they are explicitly requested by the user, for instance, when selecting options from the dropdown menu to display results on the map. The map interface is also optimized to load only essential layers initially, preventing clutter and ensuring smooth interactions.

2.3.2   Final Adjustments and Debugging

To optimize the app, results, like maps, were checked to verify their correct alignment with expectations. Additionally, after each step, error handling was performed by reviewing console logs, which directly pointed out the issues in the script. Syntax errors were debugged, and variable names were double-checked for consistency throughout the script.

3   Results and Discussion

This SoilEye App developed for this study provides an interactive platform for analyzing soil sealing changes, implementing the CART algorithm with the SUI calculation, and visualizing geospatial data over the study area of Bari in the Puglia region. This app integrates multi-temporal Sentinel-2 imageries spanning from 2018 up to 2024 and, when necessary, employs cloud masking techniques to ensure data accuracy. It was created in the GEE environment to leverage large-scale satellite data access, cloud-based processing capabilities, and the ability to handle multi-scale and multi-platform geospatial data, while also enabling the creation of a web-based application. Notably, accessing the SoilEye WebApp does not require users to create a Google account, allowing them to explore parameters and results simply by following a link.

Both desktop and smartphone interfaces of SoilEye (see Figs. 3 and 4) are composed of various key elements, including a visualization window, a control panel with buttons, and zoom in/out controls. The visualization window is centered in the UI while zoom in/out buttons as well as the control panel are located on the left.

Figure 3 shows the SoilEye interface with the legend, which displays class colors and labels and clearly highlights sealed surfaces. Users can select classes, navigate through years, select a province, and select K and OA statistics and export results.

Figure 5 provides a detailed view of the control panel, featuring a button-up menu allowing users to select years, land cover classes, and metrics on desktop and smartphone, respectively. As a result, scrolling through the year selection allows users to visualize the resulting classified maps, which are based on the composite from February, May, August, and October of each year. Similarly, scrolling land cover classes enables users to visualize the entire map or extract specific categories among sealed surfaces, vegetation, bare land, and water bodies. Lastly, the metrics button allows users to check the accuracy of the visualized layers through the K and OA values. Moreover, two additional buttons were placed on the top of the main window to zoom in and out.

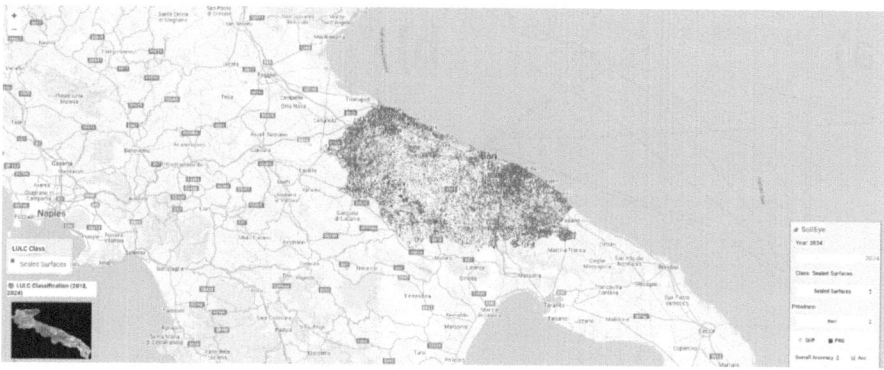

Fig. 3. SoilEye App interface visualized on desktop devices.

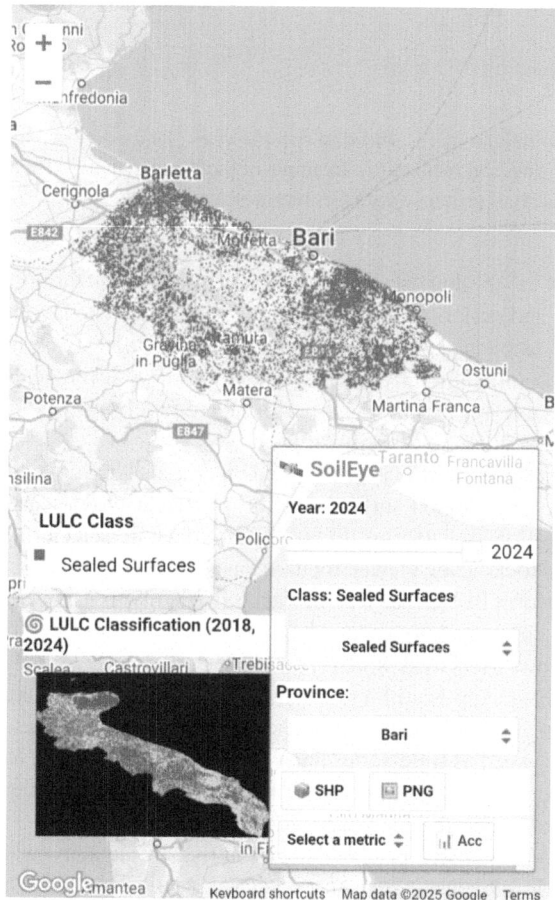

Fig. 4. SoilEye App interface visualized on smartphone devices.

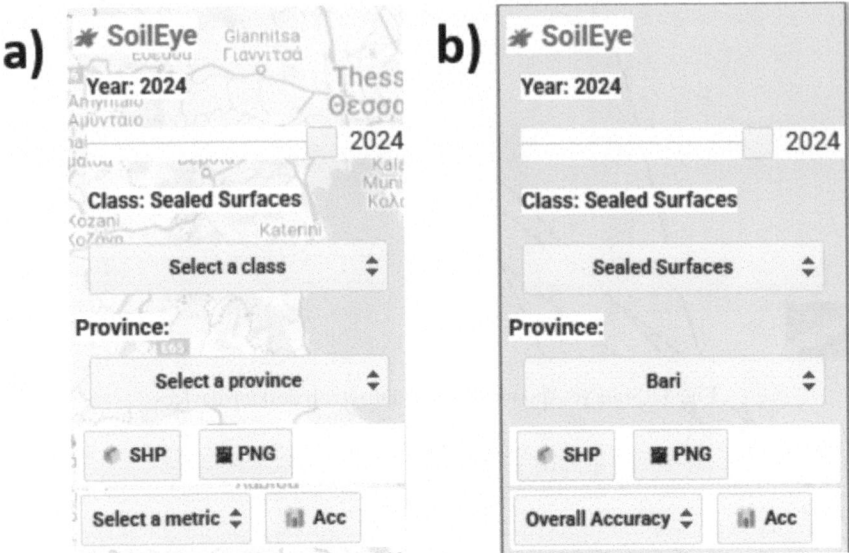

Fig. 5. Panel map with buttons for selecting specific years, land cover classes, province, export button for shapefile, png, and metrics (a). Example of the Panel map used for selecting the sealed surface class of 2024, Bari province with OA metric selection (b).

Figures 3 and 4 ensure that users can access and interact with the app seamlessly from both smartphones and desktops, regardless of their location. The layout is optimized for both screen types, allowing users to visualize results effortlessly, without unnecessary clicks. To handle computationally intensive tasks, SoilEye leverages GEE cloud computing, ensuring that heavy processing is performed remotely, preventing mobile devices from managing large computations directly.

There are several apps and platforms, like Copernicus Urban Atlas and CLMS, that provide static layers for sealed surfaces in Europe, but without using GEE. However, the previously mentioned platforms do not offer a dynamic selection of LULC classes and a province or local-level viewer focused on soil sealing trends. While apps built with the GEE platform like UrbanWatch, track urban growth using impervious surface data. The SoilEye app provides dynamic legends, class-wise selection to view each class separately, and allows users to explore urban sealing trends interactively with animation. However, the SoilEye App is still a prototype, and it has some limitations that need to be fixed. Enhancing interactivity is a key priority, which can be achieved by integrating additional features, such as time-series analysis and dynamic charts, to support users in investigating the findings more effectively. Furthermore, predictive solutions could be introduced to simulate future land cover scenarios.

Another aspect to be tested is related to its multi-scale capacity, which could expand its applicability. More features, such as a dedicated section for predicting land changes in Bari, could also be included. To further improve user interaction, a slider and auto-animation feature could be introduced, allowing users to visualize soil sealing changes dynamically within seconds. While the current app's version is ideally built for both mobile phone and desktop screens, adding new features will require careful optimization to maintain usability across different devices. The app also has the potential to scale up to a regional/national level without significantly increasing computational demands. Finally, a downloading option could be implemented to allow users to export results, requiring the development of extra code.

4 Conclusion

Monitoring soil sealing over the past years is essential for understanding its trends, assessing its impact on natural habitat and predicting future consequences. Two main challenges should be addressed to meet such a goal: developing an effective and efficient method able to extract this information and ensuring widespread dissemination to raise awareness among policymakers and the public.

This research is aimed at facing the second issue by introducing SoilEye, an innovative interactive app prototype designed to facilitate soil sealing monitoring. This app, indeed, provides policymakers and experts with a valuable tool to detect sealed surfaces, monitor land cover changes and inform the public. By bridging the gap between complex remote sensing workflows and user-friendly data exploration, SoilEye empowers researchers and policymakers to make data-driven decisions.

Through an intuitive and interactive interface, this app successfully delivers the required results. Its temporal analysis tool allows users to seamlessly explore changes over time, while the land cover classification feature enhances usability by enabling users to visualize each class separately. However, the app still lacks dynamic features like automatic scrolling animation that could give a quick overview of changes in Bari. Alongside the animation feature, a forecast for the next few years may include the use of predictive models. Other potential enhancements include dynamic charts, time-series visualizations, and interactive slides for annual comparisons.

Despite these limitations, this app offers a scalable and efficient solution for monitoring long/short-term changes. With further improvements, it has the potential to evolve into a powerful tool at provincial or even regional.

References

1. Güneralp, B., Reba, M., Hales, B.U., Wentz, E.A., Seto, K.C.: Trends in urban land expansion, density, and land transitions from 1970 to 2010: a global synthesis. Environ. Res. Lett. **15**(4), 044015 (2020)
2. Vogler, J.B., Vukomanovic, J.: Trends in united states human footprint revealed by new spatial metrics of urbanization and per capita land change. Sustainability **13**(22), 12852 (2021)
3. Shao, Z., Ahmad, M.N., Javed, A., Islam, F., Jahangir, Z., Ahmad, I.: Expansion of urban impervious surfaces in Lahore (1993–2022) based on gee and remote sensing data. Photogramm. Eng. Remote. Sens. **89**(8), 479–486 (2023)
4. Thomas, A., et al.: Topsoil porosity prediction across habitats at large scales using environmental variables. Sci. Total Environ. **922**, 171158 (2024)
5. Criado, M., Santos-Francés, F., Martínez-Graña, A., Sánchez, Y., Merchán, L.: Multitemporal analysis of soil sealing and land use changes linked to urban expansion of Salamanca (Spain) using landsat images and soil carbon management as a mitigating tool for climate change. Remote Sens. **12**(7), 1131 (2020)

6. Isinkaralar, O., Sharifi, A., Isinkaralar, K.: Assessing spatial thermal comfort and adaptation measures for the Antalya basin under climate change scenarios. Clim. Change **177**, 118 (2024)

7. Yu, J., et al.: Environmental threats induced heavy ecological burdens on the coastal zone of the Bohai Sea China. Sci. Total Environ. **765**(15), 142694 (2021)

8. Take urgent action to combat climate change and its impacts. https://sdgs.un.org/goals/goal13. Accessed 1 March 2025

9. Mikhailova, E.A., Post, C.J., Nelson, D.G.: Integrating united nations sustainable development goals in soil science education. Soil Syst. **8**(1), 29 (2024)

10. Lupi, V., Morretta, V., Zirulia, L.: Earth Observation data, innovation and economic performance: a study of the downstream sector in Italy. Eurasian Bus. Rev. **14**, 103–136 (2024)

11. Landsat Missions. https://www.usgs.gov/landsat-missions. Accessed 2 March 2025

12. The Sentinel missions. https://www.esa.int/Applications/Observ-ing_the_Earth/Copernicus/The_Sentinel_missions. Accessed 1 March 2025

13. MODIS. https://modis.gsfc.nasa.gov/about/index.php. Accessed 3 March 2025

14. Velastegui-Montoya, A., Montalván-Burbano, N., Carrión-Mero, P., Rivera-Torres, H., Sadeck, L., Adami, M.: Google earth engine: a global analysis and future trends. Remote Sens. **15**(14), 3675 (2023)

15. Stromann, O., Nascetti, A., Yousif, O., Ban, Y.: Dimensionality reduction and feature selection for object-based land cover classification based on sentinel-1 and sentinel-2 time series using google earth engine. Remote Sens. **12**, 76 (2019)

16. Earth Engine Apps. https://developers.google.com/earth-engine/guides/apps. Accessed 27 Feb 2025

17. Zhang, Y., et al.: UrbanWatch: a 1-meter resolution land cover and land use database for 22 major cities in the United States. Remote Sens. Environ. **278**, 113106 (2022)

18. Souza, C.M., et al.: Reconstructing three decades of land use and land cover changes in brazilian biomes with landsat archive and earth engine. Remote Sens. **12**(17), 2735 (2020)

19. Copernicus Land Monitoring Service – High Resolution Layer: Imperviousness. https://land.copernicus.eu/pan-european/high-resolution-layers/imperviousness. Accessed 5 May 2025

20. High Resolution Layer Imperviousness. https://land.copernicus.eu/en/products/high-resolution-layer-imperviousness. Accessed 5 May 2025

21. Capolupo, A., et al.: An interactive WebGIS framework for coastal erosion risk management. J. Marine Sci. Eng. **9**(6), 567 (2021)

22. Gorelick, N., Hancher, M., Dixon, M., Ilyushchenko, S., Thau, D., Moore, R.: Google Earth Engine: planetary-scale geospatial analysis for everyone. Remote Sens. Environ. **202**(1), 18–27 (2017)

23. Zhao, Q., Yu, L., Li, X., Peng, D., Zhang, Y., Gong, P.: Progress and trends in the application of google earth and google earth engine. Remote Sens. **13**(18), 3778 (2021)

24. Yang, L., Driscol, J., Sarigai, S., Wu, Q., Chen, H., Lippitt, C.D.: Google earth engine and Artificial Intelligence (AI): a comprehensive review. Remote Sens. **14**(14), 3253 (2022)

25. Asad, A., Capolupo, A., Tarantino, E.: Machine learning and index-based classification approaches for accurately evaluating sealed surfaces from medium-resolution Sentinel 2 data. In: 4th International Proceedings of Mediterranean Geosciences Union. Scopus, Barcelona (2025)

26. Asad, A., Capolupo, A., Tarantino, E.: Assessing soil sealing dynamics in the metropolitan area of Bari using sentinel-2, sealed surface index, and machine learning approaches. In: Computational Science and Its Applications–ICCSA 2025: 25th International Conference Proceedings, Springer International Publishing (2025)

27. Sola, I., et al.: Assessment of atmospheric correction methods for Sentinel-2 images in Mediterranean landscapes. Int. J. Appl. Earth Obs. Geoinf. **73**, 63–76 (2018)

28. Shamsujjoha, M., Grundy, J., Li, L., Khalajzadeh, H., Lu, Q.: Developing mobile applications via model driven development: a systematic literature review. Inf. Softw. Technol. **140**, 106693 (2021)
29. Gudoniene, D., Staneviciene, E., Buksnaitis, V., Daley, N.: The scenarios of artificial intelligence and wireframes implementation in engineering education. Sustainability **15**(8), 6850 (2023)
30. Gutierrez, C., Lara, R., Subauste, D.: Cloud application for the generation of static websites through the recognition of wireframes using artificial intelligence. In: Proceedings of the International Congress on Educational and Technology in Sciences 16–18 November 2021, Chiclayo, Peru (2021)
31. Saia, S.M., Nelson, N.G., Young, S.N., Parham, S., Vandegrift, M.: Ten simple rules for researchers who want to develop web apps. PLoS Comput. Biol. **18**(1), 1009663 (2022)
32. Setiyani, L., Tjandra, E.: UI/UX design model for student complaint handling application using design thinking method (Case Study: STMIK Rosma Karawang). Int. J. Sci. Technol. Manage. **18**(3), 690–702 (2022)
33. Capolupo, A., et al.: A WebGIS prototype for visualizing and monitoring the spatio-temporal changes in seawater quality. In: Gervasi, O., Murgante, B., Misra, S., Rocha, A.M.A.C., Garau, C. (eds) Computational Science and Its Applications – ICCSA 2022 Workshops. ICCSA 2022. LNCS, vol. 13379. Springer, Cham (2022). https://doi.org/10.1007/978-3-031-10545-6_24
34. Conti, G., Mercante, E., de Souza, G.E., Sobjak, R., Bazzi, L.C.: AGDATABOX-RS computational application: remote sensing data management. Software X. **23**, 101435 (2023)
35. Processing Environments. https://developers.google.com/earth-engine/guides/processing_environments. Accessed 5 March 2025
36. Capolupo, A., Monterisi, C., Tarantino, E.: Development of an open-source 3D webgis framework to promote cultural heritage dissemination. In: De Paolis, L.T., Arpaia, P., Sacco, M. (eds.) Extended Reality. XR Salento 2022. LNCS, vol. 13446. Springer, Cham (2022). https://doi.org/10.1007/978-3-031-15553-6_19
37. Mondejar, E.M., et al.: Digitalization to achieve sustainable development goals: steps towards a Smart Green Planet. Sci. Total Environ. **794**, 148539 (2021)

Earth Observation Big Data for Soil Moisture Estimation Techniques in Precision Viticulture

Alessandra Capolupo[1]([✉]) [ID], Andrea Gioia[1] [ID], Giulio Paolo Agnusdei[2] [ID],
Pier Paolo Miglietta[3] [ID], Raffaele Iannone[4] [ID], and Eufemia Tarantino[1] [ID]

[1] Department of Civil, Environmental, Land, Construction and Chemistry (DICATECh),
Politecnico di Bari, Via Orabona 4, 70125 Bari, Italy
alessandra.capolupo@poliba.it
[2] Department of Department of Psychology and Health Sciences, Pegaso University,
Centro Direzionale Isola F2, 80143 Napoli, Italy
[3] Department of Biological and Environmental Sciences and Technologies,
University of Salento, Complesso Ecotekne Via per Monteroni, 73100 Lecce, Italy
[4] Department of Industrial Engineering, University of Salerno,
Via Giovanni Paolo II, 132, 84084 Fisciano, SA, Italy

Abstract. Grapevine cultivation is one of the most relevant economic drivers of the Mediterranean basin, benefiting from favorable climate conditions, characterized by dry summers and wet winters. However, climate change poses new challenges that must be addressed and, thus, traditional farming expertise is no longer sufficient to ensure optimal wine productivity and quality. Among the key factors influencing grapevines, soil moisture plays a crucial role since it affects plant health, grape composition, and overall wine quality. Optimizing water management through advanced monitoring techniques is therefore essential for enhancing vineyard sustainability. The geomatic techniques, leveraging geospatial big data and information and communications technology, have emerged as powerful tools for monitoring vineyard health and optimizing wine productivity, quality, and sustainability. This paper presents the latest technological advancements in vineyard monitoring for soil moisture assessment, providing a comprehensive analysis of their strengths and weaknesses. The research methodology is structured into two key sections: the former focuses on monitoring technologies, while the latter describes the effectiveness and efficiency of these approaches, with particulat emphasis on machine learning applications and data fusion strategies to improve accuracy and decision-making in vineyard management. Up to now, most approaches have prioritized data acquisition and dissemination, leaving their full potential underexplored. This study outlines that integrating advanced earth observation techniques can lead to more data-driven, efficient, and sustainable viticulture.

Keywords: Precision Viticulture · Geomatics Techniques · Geospatial Big Data

© The Author(s), under exclusive license to Springer Nature Switzerland AG 2026
O. Gervasi et al. (Eds.): ICCSA 2025 Workshops, LNCS 15891, pp. 222–237, 2026.
https://doi.org/10.1007/978-3-031-97617-9_15

1 Introduction

Grapevine cultivation is widespread worldwide [1] and represents one of the most significant economic drivers, particularly in the Mediterranean Basin [2]. It is estimated that approximately 7.2 million hectares of land worldwide are dedicated to vineyards, with wine production reaching around 237 million hectoliters in 2023 [3, 4]. Thanks to their remarkable adaptability, grapevines can be cultivated in a wide range of environmental conditions. However, their quality and yield are influenced by a complex system of factors, including climate, soil, geography, variety, and terroir [5]. Among these, soil moisture and temperature are essential to optimizing the vineyard management system. Indeed, excessive water can stimulate plant growth and increase yield while, simultaneously, compromising quality by altering sugar content and acidity [6]. As a result, improving irrigation systems to optimize water efficiently and prevent the spread of plant diseases is essential [6]. Similarly, temperature significantly affects grape maturation and its sugar accumulation, consequently impacting the alcoholic content of the produced wine [5].

The Mediterranean climate provides an optimal substratum for enhancing grapevine quality, as its reproductive cycle is closely linked to temperature and water availability. Although weather patterns vary across the Mediterranean regions, the typical Mediterranean climate, characterized by wet winters and dry summers, favors grape maturation, enhancing both quality and yield [7, 8]. As a result, European countries, including Italy, Spain, and France, have long been recognized as leading contributors to this sector, benefiting from favorable climatic conditions. However, this privileged position is expected to change rapidly in the coming years due to climate change, as highlighted by the Intergovernmental Panel on Climate Change (IPCC) [9]. To address this challenge, the development of advanced monitoring approaches is essential for assessing vineyard conditions in real time in response to these evolving environmental challenges [10, 11].

Precision Agriculture (PA) has emerged as a transformative approach, encompassing a wide range of techniques and technologies for collecting both quantitative and qualitative data at field and sub-field scales, enabling precise estimation of crop parameters [12]. Recognized as one of the top ten developments in modern agriculture, PA allows farmers to "do the right thing, in the right place, at the right time" [13]. Although this discipline emerged in the mid-1980s, it has only recently begun to reach its full potential, driven by technological advancements that allow for precise, localized interventions. Unlike conventional agriculture, which assumes spatial homogeneity across fields, PA acknowledges intra-field variability and promotes tailored strategies that extend beyond traditional farmer expertise [14]. In such a way, the resulting management strategies optimize the use of site-specific resources, enhance product quality and yields, reduce environmental impacts, promote sustainability, improve plant health, and save costs while increasing benefits [15].

This process consists of three main steps: i) data collection through advanced geomatic techniques and sensors; ii) data manipulation and interpretation from an agronomic perspective; and, lastly, iii) execution of manual and/or automatic actions to preserve, correct, and mitigate potential issues. Data collection relies on various advanced technologies, including the Global Navigation Satellite System (GNSS)-based sensors for glocalization, proximal and remote sensors for extracting plant and soil parameters, and, lastly, wireless sensor networks for monitoring plant health and resource needs [16, 17]. These techniques are often used in combination to overcome individual limitations and enhance data accuracy and effectiveness [18]. This integrated approach supports targeted, effective decision-making for vineyard management. Data manipulation and interpretation are typically performed using specialized software designed to manage spatial data, with Geographic Information Systems (GIS) providing an optimal platform for this purpose. Finally, management strategies are implemented manually and/or automatically through the use of Variable Rate Technologies (VRT)/Variable Rate Application (VRA) machines. These tools are designed to optimize input rates of pesticides, fertilizers, etc., based on site-specific requirements.

When PA is implemented in viticulture, the discipline is tagged as Precision Viticulture (PV). Despite the significant socio-economic interest in this sector, PV only gained traction in the mid-2000s, primarily due to challenges in vineyard feature extraction. Grapevines are organized in rows with discontinuous canopies, requiring high-resolution images to distinguish the vineyard from the background and extract plants' biophysical and biochemical traits [19]. Additionally, until now, PV has not been focused on site-specific applications but rather on detecting features that are relatively homogeneous within a field. This information is usually generated using multi/hyperspectral [20] and thermal imagery [21], along with geolocated data [22], and integrating some of these [23].

Multiple approaches could be adopted to produce such data. Spectral indices, based on the mathematical combination of spectral bands, enable rapid classification of large areas and provide insights into plant physiology [24, 25]. However, although some indices have also been shown to be effective in indirectly determining water status [26, 27], their accuracy remains unsatisfactory [27]. As a result, Machine Learning (ML) approaches offer a viable solution to overcome these limits.

Given the pivotal role of soil moisture in vineyard management, this study aims to evaluate a range of estimation methodologies through an extensive and critical literature review. The objective is to identify the most effective approaches for supporting precision viticulture, with the ultimate goal of optimizing water use and improving vineyard management practices.

This paper is structured as follows: Sect. 2 reports the methodology adopted to extract the main information concerning soil moisture data from the literature. On the contrary, Sect. 3 explores the relevance of soil moisture parameters in vineyard management, reviews methodologies for their measurements and estimation, and highlights the strengths and weaknesses of each. Finally, Sect. 4 reports the main conclusion and future research directions.

2 Material and Methods

2.1 Meta-analysis of Literature

To ensure a rigorous and transparent evaluation of the existing scientific literature, this study employed a systematic review methodology inspired by the Preferred Reporting Items for Systematic Reviews and Meta-Analyses (PRISMA) framework (Fig. 1) [28]. This structured approach facilitated the identification, screening, and selection of relevant research focused on the application of geomatics technologies in viticulture for assessing surface soil moisture. The objective was to synthesize key advancements and highlight existing knowledge gaps pertinent to vineyard water status monitoring and sustainable management.

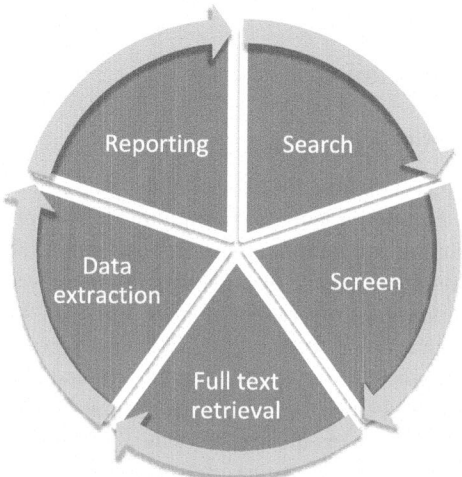

Fig. 1. Preferred Reporting Items for Systematic Reviews and Meta-Analyses (PRISMA) methodology adopted for the literature review.

The first step of the PRISMA approach involved a comprehensive search across leading academic databases, including Web of Science (WoS), Scopus, and Google Scholar, targeting publications released between 2000 and 2025. The search strategy employed a combination of relevant keywords and Boolean operators to refine the query, ensuring the retrieval of studies that aligned with the research focus. The primary keywords included: i) "Geomatics in viticulture", ii) "Precision agriculture", iii) "Grapevine water status monitoring", iv) "Surface soil moisture in viticulture", v) "Vineyard sustainability", and vi) "Earth Observation for assessing vineyard water status". Additional terms were included to account for emerging technological advancements, such as "machine learning", "microwave techniques", and "data fusion in precision viticulture". Filters were applied to limit the search to English-language articles and studies explicitly focused on geomatic approaches to vineyard water status analysis.

The screening process followed a two-step approach to refine the dataset. First, an initial screening was conducted by reviewing paper titles, keywords, and abstracts to exclude studies not directly related to viticulture or the application of geomatic technologies. Articles focusing on non-grapevine crops or non-geomatic methodologies were systematically removed. In the second step, the remaining articles underwent an in-depth assessment to evaluate their methodological rigor and relevance to vineyard water status assessment and monitoring. The inclusion criteria required studies to: i) investigate geomatic technologies in vineyard monitoring, such as vine vigor mapping or water stress detection; ii) focus on Mediterranean vineyards or regions with comparable climatic conditions; and iii) provide insights applicable to sustainable vineyard management and the development of advanced geospatial methodologies.

A total of 312 articles were selected and systematically analyzed to extract key findings relevant to the study objectives. The analysis emphasized methodologies such as spectral analysis, geospatial modeling, and machine learning-based extraction techniques.

3   Results and Discussion

3.1   EO-Based Approaches

Soil moisture monitoring is essential for balancing the grapevine reproductive cycle, as it regulates plant growth and pigment concentration [5]. This phenomenon influences several key factors, including evaporation, transpiration, biodiversity, and rainfall runoff, all of which affect ecosystem health. Specifically, excessive water levels can reduce grapevine quality by influencing sugar content and acidity [6], making the plants more susceptible to winter damage and diseases [6]. Conversely, water deficits may hinder proper plant growth, significantly lowering productivity and acidity while increasing sugar content [6]. Therefore, establishing an effective smart water management strategy is essential for improving grapevine quality and yield.

Traditionally, soil moisture has been measured using ground-based techniques, which offer several advantages, such as equipment portability, ease of installation, straightforward operation and maintenance, and methodological stability [30, 31]. However, these methods are not limitation-free. They tend to be expensive, often lack accuracy, and are difficult to scale due to their reliance on localized sensor data, which must be interpolated to obtain a broader spatial representation [32].

Thus, to go beyond these constraints, alternative methods have been developed to estimate soil moisture at various spatial and temporal scales [33]. Among them, EO-based approaches are currently recognized as the most efficient and cost-effective methods of assessing soil moisture variability within a field [34]. Instead of providing direct measurements, these methods estimate soil moisture by using spectral bands as input for physical and semi-empirical models, combined with inversion algorithms. Various algorithms have been developed for this purpose, each with own strengths and weaknesses [35]. Indeed, the first studies in soil moisture remote sensing started in the mid-1970s, just a few years after the introduction of satellite remote sensing. Over time, however, different parts of the electromagnetic spectrum, ranging from the optical to the microwave region, have been exploited. Previous studies have demonstrated the potential of near-infrared and thermal bands, as well as active and passive microwave remote sensing techniques [36], although the relationship between soil moisture content and sensor response varies depending on the spectral region. The benefits and constraints of each method are reported in Table 1.

Optical Remote Sensing

The potential of optical remote sensing has been explored since the early 20th century, albeit initial results were relatively coarse. In 1925, Angstrom observed an inverse relationship between reflectance and soil moisture content [37]. Later, Bowers and Smith [38]

Table 1. Advantages and challenges of EO-based approaches adopted for estimating soil moisture.

Spectral Domain	Key Observations	Advantages	Challenges
Optical	Surface reflectance	High spatial resolution, wide coverage	Limited penetration depth, affected by cloud cover and atmospheric noise
Thermal infrared	Surface temperature	Good spatial resolution, well-established methodology	Shallow penetration, influenced by meteorological conditions and vegetation
Passive microwave	Emitted radiation, dielectric properties	Less atmospheric interference, moderate soil penetration	Low spatial resolution, sensitive to surface roughness and vegetation cover
Active microwave	Backscatter signal, dielectric properties	High spatial resolution, moderate soil penetration, minimal atmospheric effects	Narrow imaging swath, influenced by surface roughness and vegetation density

established a linear relationship between water absorption bands and soil water content, while Dalal and Henry [39] used near-infrared absorbance values to estimate moisture levels. However, despite their potential, these approaches have proven inadequate for accurately assessing soil moisture, mainly due to optical bands' limited penetration depth and high sensitivity to atmospheric disturbances [40].

Recently, innovative spectral indices, derived from the mathematical integration of specific bands, have been introduced to estimate soil moisture. Although index-based approaches have been widely employed for land classification and biomass estimation, their application in viticulture remains limited. In fact, these indices have been used only nine times to assess and/or monitor water content in vine leaves [41]. Specifically, Normalized Difference Water Index (NDWI) [42], Global Vegetation Moisture Index (GVMI) [43], Moisture Stress Index (MSI) [43], and Shortwave Infrared Water Stress Index (SIWSI) [44]. The equations for these indices are summarized in Table 2. All of them rely on Near-Infrared (NIR) and Shortwave Infrared (SWIR) bands, as these are highly sensitive to water content, whereas Red, Green, and Blue (RGB) bands are ineffective for this purpose.

Previous studies have demonstrated the significant potential of spectral indices for estimating water content, although their accuracy ranges between 0.5 and 0.8. More sophisticated algorithms have been tested to improve the index-based method's performance.

Table 2. Summary of indices adopted to estimate water content.

Index	Equation	Equation number
Normalized Difference Water Index (NDWI)	$\frac{NIR-SWIR_2}{NIR+SWIR_2}$	(1)
Global Vegetation Moisture Index (GVMI)	$\frac{(NIR+0.1)-(SWIR+0.02)}{(NIR+0.1)+(SWIR+0.02)}$	(2)
Moisture Stress Index (MSI)	$\frac{SWIR}{NIR}$	(3)
Shortwave Infrared Water Stress Index (SIWSI)	$\frac{NIR-SWIR_1}{NIR+SWIR_1}$	(4)

Thermal Infrared Remote Sensing

Thermal infrared imagery can be used to estimate soil surface moisture either individually, as in the thermal inertia method, or in combination with other indices, as proposed by the thermal infrared index approach. The thermal inertia method, which is physically based, provides accurate soil moisture estimation; however, its reliability decreases in densely vegetated areas [45]. In this method, volumetric soil moisture (W_s) is calculated using the following equation:

$$W_s = a_0 * ATI + \alpha_1.$$

(5)

where α_0 and α_1 are the empirical parameter and ATI represents the Apparent Thermal Inertia, calculated as:

$$ATI = \frac{1-\alpha}{\Delta T}.$$

(6)

In this equation, ΔT denotes the diurnal temperature range, while α represents the surface albedo. ATI serves as an approximate measure of thermal inertia, which describes a material's ability to resist temperature fluctuations [46].

An alternative approach estimates W_s based on its relationship with the Normalized Difference Vegetation Index (NDVI) and Land Surface Temperature (LST) within a given area. This method, commonly referred to as the "Universal Triangle," is expressed as follows:

$$W_s = \sum_{i=0}^{n} \sum_{j=0}^{n} a_{ij} * NDVI^* * T^*.$$

(7)

where α_{ij} are the regression coefficients while T^* and $NDVI^*$ are the scaled LST and NDVI, respectively. These scaled values are computed as:

$$T^* = \frac{T-T_0}{T_s - T_0}.$$

(6)

$$NDVI^* = \frac{NDVI - NDVI_0}{NDVI_s - NDVI_0}.$$

(7)

where the subscripts 0 and s indicate the minimum and maximum values, respectively.

Due to the strong theoretical foundation and effectiveness of this approach, various modifications have been introduced over time, including Temperature-Vegetation conteXtual approach (TVX) [47], TemperatureVegetation Dryness Index (TVDI) [48], moisture index [49], and the VI/Trad relation [50].

Microwave Remote Sensing

Microwave remote sensing provides a direct method to measure soil moisture across the microwave band (0.5–100 cm), distinguishing itself from the other techniques discussed previously. In this portion of the electromagnetic spectrum, the atmosphere remains almost completely transparent, and the significant difference in dielectric properties, approximately 80 for water versus less than 4 for soil particles, greatly facilitates the retrieval of soil moisture data [51].

Depending on the sensor type and its operating mode, microwave remote sensing is classified into two main categories: active and passive. Active systems, such as Synthetic Aperture Radars (SAR), function by emitting microwave pulses and recording the energy that bounces back from the Earth's surface, whereas passive systems, like radiometers, measure the natural microwave emissions originating from the surface.

Microwave signals in the L-band (1–2 GHz), often termed the "water frequency channel," are particularly sensitive to moisture in the upper 5 cm of the soil and can effectively penetrate low to moderately dense vegetation covers [52]. In contrast, higher frequency bands, namely the C-band (4–8 GHz) and X-band (8–12.5 GHz), are responsive to very shallow soil layers and can only pass through sparse vegetation [53]. At the lower end of the spectrum, the P-band (<1 GHz) offers deeper soil penetration, making it particularly valuable for subsurface moisture estimation and biomass monitoring. However, its use is limited by Radio Frequency Interference (RFI) and stringent regulatory constraints.

Over recent decades, specialized inversion algorithms have been developed to estimate surface soil moisture, each tailored to specific frequencies, measurement principles, and the characteristics of various microwave sensors aboard satellites. This focused research effort has led to the development of a range of EO microwave soil moisture products, spanning from 1978 to the present.

Five quasi-operational satellite soil moisture products are currently available in Near Real-Time (NRT) or within a few days of acquisition:

- Soil Moisture and Ocean Salinity (SMOS), an Earth Explorer mission operational since January 2010, is expected to conclude by the end of 2025. It provides free, open-access data with a 35 km resolution [54];
- Advanced Microwave Scanning Radiometer 2 (AMSR2), aboard the Global Change Observation Mission for Water (GCOM-W), active since July 2012 and set to operate until late 2026. Its products offer a 10 km resolution [55];
- BEC L4, a soil moisture dataset derived from SMOS and refined using high-resolution MODIS (Aqua/Terra) data, has been in operation since January 2010. It currently provides 1 km resolution NRT soil moisture maps over the Iberian Peninsula [56];
- Sentinel-1 C-band Synthetic Aperture Radar Ground Range Detected (SAR GRD), launched in 2014 under the European Space Agency's Copernicus Program, delivers 10 m resolution images with a temporal revisit cycle of 6–12 days [57];

- NASA-ISRO SAR (NISAR), jointly developed by NASA and ISRO and launched in 2023, provides 7 m resolution data. Its L- and S-band capabilities enable precise global monitoring of above-ground biomass, which is particularly useful for vineyard health assessment and productivity analysis [58].

While these products enable large-scale soil moisture monitoring, their spatial resolution remains insufficient for field-scale applications in viticulture. To overcome these limitations, upcoming satellite missions, such as ESA Biomass, ROSE-L, HARMONY, TanDEM-L, ALOS-4, and Sentinel-1 C/D, will introduce improvements in spatial resolution, revisit frequency, and wavelength range. These advancements will enable more accurate and frequent moisture assessments, improving applications in environmental monitoring, precision agriculture, and hydrology. Further details on these missions are provided in Table 3.

Table 3. Summary of the main characteristics of new microwave missions.

Satellite Missions	Agency	Launch Date	Band	Frequency (GHz)	Revisit period (days)
ALOS-4	JAXA	1st July 2024	L	1.26	14
Sentinel-1C	ESA	5th December 2024	C	5.41	12
Biomass	ESA	2025 (planned)	P	0.44	25
Sentinel-1D	ESA	2025 (planned)	C	5.41	12
TanDEM-L	DLR	2028 (planned)	L	1.27	16
ROSE-L	ESA	2028 (planned)	L	1.26	6
Harmony	ESA	2029 (planned)	C	passive	12
Sentinel-1 NG	ESA	2032 (planned)	C	5.41	<6

Due to the limitations discussed above, these products have had limited application in vineyards, particularly for soil moisture estimation. In 2014, Ballester-Berman et al. [59] evaluated three different approaches for estimating soil moisture in vineyards using RADARSAT-2 polarimetric data and ground measurements: a two-component model, a classical three-component model enhanced with a physically constrained volume power, and a modified version of the latter incorporating the Integral Equation Model (IEM). While all three models yielded promising results, the IEM approach proved to be the most accurate.

Similarly, the C-SSM soil moisture product, derived from Sentinel-1 data and provided by the Copernicus Global Land Service for Europe at a 1 km resolution, demonstrated good performance. However, Bazzi et al. [60] found that it tends to overestimate soil moisture in forested and vineyard areas.

Other studies have explored the fusion of microwave data with optical remote sensing and terrain information to enhance soil moisture estimation. Further details on data fusion techniques using microwave data are discussed in the following section.

Data Fusion

To address the limitations of individual methodologies and enhance the accuracy of soil moisture estimation, several studies have explored the integration of multiple geomatics techniques [61]. This multidisciplinary approach is essential for improving water resource management and optimizing irrigation strategies in viticulture.

Thus, Lei et al. [62] investigated the fusion of high-resolution thermal infrared (TIR) data and Sentinel-1 SAR imagery within a soil–vegetation–atmosphere transfer (SVAT) model to refine soil moisture estimates in vineyards. Their study, based on a two-component polarimetric model using C-band radar data, demonstrated the potential of remote sensing and data assimilation techniques in monitoring evapotranspiration and soil moisture dynamics.

Similarly, Mendes et al. [63] analyzed the combined use of Sentinel-1 and Sentinel-2 data along with terrain parameters to identify low soil moisture areas in a drip-irrigated vineyard affected by agricultural drought. Their findings highlighted the cost-effectiveness of remote sensing for soil moisture monitoring and its ability to predict regions at risk of salinization, an issue that is expected to worsen with climate change. The study also emphasized the advantages of multi-sensor approaches, as different wavelengths exhibit varying sensitivities to environmental parameters, thereby improving the reliability of assessments. Conversely, Efremova et al. [64] explored the application of Sentinel-1 and Sentinel-2 Earth observation data for soil moisture prediction in vineyards using a cycle-consistent adversarial network (CycleGAN). They compared the performance of multiple ML algorithms, including linear regression, random forest, support vector regression, and neural networks. Among these, the random forest model yielded the most accurate results, while linear regression suffered from significant overfitting. Additionally, the study evaluated CycleGAN's effectiveness in translating imagery between Sentinel-1 and Sentinel-2, finding that, while the model could extract features from different spectral domains, its translation accuracy remained imperfect.

The Vineyard Data Assimilation (VIDA) system integrates remote sensing data with a soil water balance model to support vineyard irrigation decisions, demonstrating its ability to capture daily variations in soil moisture [65]. Effective soil moisture monitoring is crucial for optimizing irrigation strategies, including deficit irrigation. Technologies such as SAR and thermal-infrared sensing enable high-resolution soil moisture assessment. While VIDA has shown promise in improving irrigation efficiency, challenges remain, particularly in correcting biases in irrigation input data and accurately representing subsurface water flow processes.

3.2 Challenges in Soil Moisture Estimation in Vineyards Ecosystem

Accurately estimating soil moisture in vineyards using EO data presents several challenges, primarily due to the spatial and temporal resolution of currently available products. Soil moisture dynamics in viticultural environments occur at a fine scale, influenced by factors such as soil texture, vineyard management practices, and microclimatic variability [51]. However, EO-derived products often lack the necessary resolution to capture these variations effectively, limiting their applicability for irrigation management and hydrological modeling at the vineyard scale [51].

Another critical limitation is the penetration depth of EO signals, which affects the ability to retrieve soil moisture beyond the surface layer. Optical and infrared sensors, as well as certain microwave wavelengths, provide information only on the uppermost soil layer, resulting in an incomplete representation of soil moisture profiles. This is particularly problematic for vineyard applications, where deeper soil moisture measurements are essential for assessing irrigation needs. Moreover, the dense vine canopy during the growing season can introduce significant errors in soil moisture estimation, necessitating correction models that account for vegetation effects on soil reflectance and emissivity. Recent studies using L-band data have shown promising results in integrating soil moisture retrieval with vegetation index estimation [56].

Data acquisition conditions further complicate soil moisture estimation. Optical and thermal methods are ineffective under cloudy conditions, while microwave observations, although capable of providing all-weather measurements, are susceptible to Radio Frequency Interference (RFI), which can degrade data quality [66]. Additionally, the heterogeneous nature of vineyard parcels, often featuring alternating rows of bare soil, vegetation cover, or mulching, leads to significant spectral variability that can affect soil moisture retrieval accuracy. The presence of free-standing water within the sensor's footprint, particularly after heavy rainfall, can further distort measurements [66, 67].

Another major challenge is the frequency of data acquisition. Current microwave sensors operating in polar orbits provide observations only at specific times of the day, typically at dawn and dusk, limiting their usefulness for applications requiring sub-daily soil moisture monitoring [68]. A potential solution to this limitation could be the deployment of geostationary microwave sensors or the integration of polar-orbiting microwave data with geostationary optical and thermal observations [56].

Uncertainty in soil moisture estimates directly impacts irrigation management in vineyards, highlighting the need for a comprehensive characterization of errors associated with operational products. To enhance reliability and practical usability, increased validation efforts are required across different soil, climate, and vegetation conditions [29]. Incorporating sensitivity analyses into data verification processes could also help refine retrieval methodologies and reduce measurement uncertainties [69].

4   Conclusion

Soil moisture plays a fundamental role in vineyard management, directly influencing grapevine growth, yield, and quality. The precise assessment of soil moisture levels is essential for optimizing irrigation strategies, mitigating the risks of water stress, and ensuring sustainable viticulture practices. Traditional ground-based methods, while effective at local scales, present limitations in terms of spatial coverage, scalability, and cost. Consequently, Earth Observation-based approaches have emerged as a powerful alternative, enabling large-scale monitoring of soil moisture variability with enhanced efficiency and cost-effectiveness.

Among EO techniques, optical, thermal infrared, and microwave remote sensing methods have been widely investigated for their potential in soil moisture estimation. Optical and thermal sensors provide high spatial resolution and well-established methodologies but suffer from limitations such as shallow penetration depth and sensitivity to atmospheric conditions. Conversely, microwave techniques, both active and passive, offer greater penetration capabilities and reduced atmospheric interference, but often face challenges related to spatial resolution and surface roughness effects.

Recent advancements in remote sensing technology, including the development of spectral indices and machine learning algorithms, have significantly improved the accuracy of soil moisture estimation. While spectral indices provide a straightforward means of assessing water content, their application in viticulture remains limited. In contrast, machine learning approaches offer promising results by integrating multi-source data and capturing complex relationships between spectral signatures and soil moisture levels.

Despite the progress made, further research is needed to refine EO-based methodologies for vineyard-specific applications. Future studies should focus on integrating multiple remote sensing techniques, leveraging data fusion approaches, and improving algorithm robustness to enhance predictive accuracy. Additionally, the development of real-time monitoring systems and decision-support tools will be crucial for translating research findings into actionable vineyard management strategies.

Ultimately, the implementation of EO-based soil moisture assessment within the framework of precision viticulture represents a transformative step toward sustainable, resource-efficient, and climate-resilient grape production. By embracing these innovative technologies, vineyard managers can optimize water use, improve grape quality, and better adapt to the evolving challenges posed by climate change.

Acknowledgments. This research was founded by the European Union – NextGenerationUE, Progetto PRIN-PNRR WIN-RIESCO (CUP Master: F53D23009390001 – CUP: D53D23017750001 - PNRR - Missione 4 "Istruzione e Ricerca" - Componente 2 "Dalla Ricerca all'Impresa" Investimento 1.1 "Fondo per il Programma Nazionale di Ricerca e Progetti di Rilevante Interesse Nazionale (PRIN)").

Disclosure of Interests. The authors declare that there are no conflicts of interest.

References

1. Alston, J.M., Sambucci, O.: Grapes in the world economy. In: Cantu, D., Walker, M.A. (eds.) The Grape Genome, pp. 1–24. Springer International Publishing, Cham, Switzerland (2019). ISBN 978-3-030-18600-5. https://doi.org/10.1007/978-3-030-18601-2_1
2. Costa, J.M., et al.: Modern viticulture in southern europe: vulnerabilities and strategies for adaptation to water scarcity. Agric. Water Manag. **164**, 5–18 (2016)
3. FAO OIV. Non-alcoholic products of the vitivinicultural sector intended for human consumption. In: Table and Dried Grapes; FAO-OIV FOCUS. Rome, Italy. ISBN 978-92-5-109708-3 (2016)
4. OIV. State of the World Vine and Wine Sector in 2023. OIV, Paris, France (2024)
5. Baltazar, M., Castro, I., Gonçalves, B.: Adaptation to climate change in viticulture: the role of varietal selection—a review. Plants **14**(1), 104 (2025)
6. Van Leeuwen, C., Trégoat, O., Choné, X., Bois, B., Pernet, D., Gaudillère, J.P.: Vine water status is a key factor in grape ripening and vintage quality for red Bordeaux wine. How can it be assessed for vineyard management purposes?. Oeno One **43**(3), 121–134 (2009)
7. Kottek, M., Grieser, J., Beck, C., Rudolf, B., Rubel, F.: World map of the köppen-geiger climate classification updated. Meteorol. Z. **15**, 259–263 (2006)

8. Santos, J.A., Costa, R., Fraga, H.: New insights into thermal growing conditions of portuguese grapevine varieties under changing climates. Theor. Appl. Clim. **135**, 1215–1226 (2019)

9. IPCC. Climate change: impacts, adaptation and vulnerability. In: Contribution of Working Group II to the Sixth Assessment Report of the Intergovernmental Panel on Climate Change. Cambridge University Press, Cambridge, UK (2022)

10. Droulia, F., Charalampopoulos, I.: Future climate change impacts on european viticulture: a review on recent scientific advances. Atmosphere **12**, 495 (2021)

11. Santillán, D., Garrote, L., Iglesias, A., Sotes, V.: Climate change risks and adaptation: new indicators for mediterranean viticulture. Mitig. Adapt. Strateg. Glob. Change **25**, 881–899 (2020)

12. Crookston, R.K.: A top 10 list of developments and issues impacting crop management and ecology during the past 50 years. Crop Sci. **46**(5), 2253–2262 (2016)

13. Pierce, F.J., Novak, P.: Aspects of precision agriculture. Adv. Agron. **67**, 1–85 (1999)

14. Hedley, C.B.: The role of precision agriculture for improved nutrient management on farms. J. Sci. Food Agric. **95**, 12–19 (2015)

15. Gebbers, R., Adamchuk, V.: Precision agriculture and food security. Science 828–831 (2010)

16. Matese, A., Di Gennaro, S.F.: Technology in precision viticulture: a state of the art review. Int. J. Wine Res. **7**, 69–81 (2015)

17. Tisseyre, B., Taylor, J.A.: An overview of methodologies and technologies for implementing precision agriculture in viticulture, XII Congresso Brasileiro de Viticultura e Enologia—Anais. Patrícia Ritschel, Sandra de Souza Sebben, Bento Gonçalves, Brazil (2005)

18. Ammoniaci, M., Kartsiotis, S.P., Perria, R., Storchi, P.: State of the art of monitoring technologies and data processing for precision viticulture. Agriculture **11**(3), 201 (2021)

19. Matese, A., et al.: Intercomparison of UAV, aircraft and satellite remote sensing platforms for precision viticulture. Remote Sens. **7**(3), 2971–2990 (2015)

20. Bramley, R.G.V., Ouzman, J., Boss, P.K.: Variation in vine vigour, grape yield and vineyard soils and topography as indicators of variation in the chemical composition of grapes, wine and wine sensory attributes. Aust. J. Grape Wine Res. **17**(2), 217–229 (2011)

21. Santesteban, L.G., Di Gennaro, S.F., Herrero-Langreo, A., Miranda, C., Royo, J.B., Matese, A.: High-resolution UAV-based thermal imaging to estimate the instantaneous and seasonal variability of plant water status within a vineyard. Agric. Water Manag. **183**, 49–59 (2017)

22. Gras, J.P., Moinard, S., Valloo, Y., Girardot, R., Tisseyre, B.: Mapping grape production parameters with low-cost vehicle tracking devices. Prec. Agric. 1–18 (2024)

23. Urretavizcaya, I., Royo, J.B., Miranda, C., Tisseyre, B., Guillaume, S., Santesteban, L.G.: Relevance of sink-size estimation for within-field zone delineation in vineyards. Precision Agric. **18**, 133–144 (2017)

24. Capolupo, A., Kooistra, L., Berendonk, C., Boccia, L., Suomalainen, J.: Estimating plant traits of grasslands from UAV-acquired hyperspectral images: a comparison of statistical approaches. ISPRS Int. J. Geo Inf. **4**(4), 2792–2820 (2015)

25. Capolupo, A., Saponaro, M., Fratino, U., Tarantino, E.: Detection of spatio-temporal changes of vegetation in coastal areas subjected to soil erosion issue. Aquat. Ecosyst. Health Manage. **23**(4), 491–499 (2020)

26. Pôças, I., et al.: Predicting grapevine water status based on hyperspectral reflectance vegetation indices. Remote Sens. **7**(12), 16460–16479 (2015)

27. Capolupo, A., Monterisi, C., Saponaro, M., Tarantino, E.: Multi-temporal analysis of land cover changes using Landsat data through Google Earth Engine platform. In: Eighth International Conference on Remote Sensing and Geoinformation of the Environment (RSCy2020), vol. 11524, pp. 447–458. SPIE (2020)

28. Page, M.J., et al.: The PRISMA 2020 statement: an updated guideline for reporting systematic reviews. BMJ **372** (2021)

29. Romero, M., Luo, Y., Su, B., Fuentes, S.: Vineyard water status estimation using multispectral imagery from an UAV platform and machine learning algorithms for irrigation scheduling management. Comput. Electron. Agric. **147**, 109–117 (2018)

30. Crow, W.T., et al.: Upscaling sparse ground-based soil moisture observations for the validation of coarse-resolution satellite soil moisture products. Rev. Geophys. **50** (2012)

31. Palladino, M., Nasta, P., Capolupo, A., Romano, N.: Monitoring and modelling the role of phytoremediation to mitigate non-point source cadmium pollution and groundwater contamination at field scale. Ital. J. Agron. **13**, 59–68 (2018)

32. Petropoulos, G.P., Carlson, T.N., Griffiths, H.M.: Turbulent fluxes of heat and moisture at the earth's land surface: importance, controlling parameters and conventional measurement. In: Petropoulos, G.P., (ed.) Remote Sensing of Energy Fluxes and Soil Moisture Content, Chapter 1, pp. 3–28. Taylor and Francis, Oxford, UK (2013)

33. Tian, F., Qiu, G., Lü, Y., Yang, Y., Xiong, Y.: Use of high-resolution thermal infrared remote sensing and "three-temperature model" for transpiration monitoring in arid inland river catchment. J. Hydrol. **515**, 307–315 (2014)

34. Singh, S.K., Srivastava, P.K., Szabo, S., Petropoulos, G.P., Gupta, M., Islam, T.: Landscape transform and spatial metrics for mapping spatiotemporal land cover dynamics using Earth Observation datasets. Geocarto Int. **32**, 113–127 (2016)

35. Price, J.C.: The potential of remotely sensed thermal infrared data to infer surface soil moisture and evaporation. Water Resour. Res. **16**, 787–795 (1980)

36. de Troch F.P., Troch, P.A., Su, Z., Lin, D.S.: Chapter 9: Application of Remote Sensing for Hydrological Modelling. In: Abbott M B, Refsgaard J C, eds. Distributed Hydrological Modelling. Kluwer Academic Publishers, Dordrecht (1996)

37. Angstrom, A.: The albedo of various surfaces of ground. Geografiske Annales **7**, 323 (1925)

38. Bowers, S.A., Smith, S.J.: Spectrophotometric determination of soil water content. Soil Sci. Soc. Am. Proc. **36**, 978–980 (1972)

39. Dalal, H.: Simultaneous determination of moisture, organic carbon, and total nitrogen by infrared reflectance spectrometry. Soil Sci. Soc. Am. J. **50**, 120–123 (1986)

40. Wang, L., Qu, J.J.: Satellite remote sensing applications for surface soil moisture monitoring: a review. Front Earth Sci. China **3**, 237–247 (2009)

41. Giovos, R., Tassopoulos, D., Kalivas, D., Lougkos, N., Priovolou, A.: Remote sensing vegetation indices in viticulture: a critical review. Agriculture **11**(5), 457 (2021)

42. Borgogno-Mondino, E., Novello, V., Lessio, A., de Palma, L.: Describing the spatio-temporal variability of vines and soil by satellite-based spectral indices: a case study in Apulia (South Italy). Int. J. Appl. Earth Obs. Geoinform. **68**, 42–50 (2018)

43. Arango, R.B., Camposy, A.M., Combarro, E.F.: Identification of agricultural management zones through clustering algorithms with thermal and multispectral satellite imagery. Int. J. Uncertain. Fuzziness Knowl. Based Syst. **25**, 121–140 (2017)

44. Brook, A., et al.: A smart multiple spatial and temporal resolution system to support precision agriculture from satellite images: proof of concept on Aglianico vineyard. Remote Sens. Environ. **240**, 111679 (2020)

45. Xue, H., Ni, S.: Progress in the study on monitoring of soil moisture with thermal infrared remote sensing. Agric. Res. Arid Areas **24**, 168–172 (2006)

46. Verstraeten, W.W., Veroustraete, F., van der Sande, C.J., Grootaers, I., Feyen, J.: Soil moisture retrieval using thermal inertia, determined with visible and thermal spaceborne data, validated for European forests. Remote Sens. Environ. **101**, 299–314 (2006)

47. Czajkowski, K., Goward, S.N., Stadler, S.J., Waltz, A.: Thermal remote sensing of near surface environmental variables: application over the Oklahoma Mesonet. Profess. Geograph. **52**, 345–357 (2000)

48. Sandholt, I., Rasmussen, K., Andersen, J.: A simple interpretation of the surface temperature/vegetation index space for assessment of surface moisture status. Remote Sens. Environ. **79**, 213–224 (2002)

49. Dupigny-Giroux, L., Lewis, J.E.: A moisture index for surface characterization over a semiarid area. Photogram. Eng. Remote Sens. **65**, 937–946 (1999)

50. Kustas, W.P., Moran, M.S., Norman, J.M.: Evaluating the spatial distribution of evaporation. Chap. 26. In: Potter, T.D., Colman, B.R. (eds.) Handbook of Weather, Climate and Water: Atmospheric Chemistry, Hydrology and Societal Impacts, pp. 461–492. Wiley, Hoboken, N.J. (2003)

51. Petropoulos, G.P., Ireland, G., Barrett, B.: Surface soil moisture retrievals from remote sensing: current status, products & future trends. Phys. Chem. Earth (2015)

52. Wigneron, J.-P., et al.: Modelling the passive microwave signature from land surfaces: a review of recent results and application to the L-band SMOS and SMAP soil moisture retrieval algorithms. Remote Sens. Environ. **192**, 238–262 (2017)

53. Ulaby, F.T., Allen, C.T., Eger, G., Kanemasu, E.: Relating the microwave backscattering coefficient to leaf area index. Remote Sens. Environ. **14**, 113–133 (1984)

54. Kerr, Y.H., et al.: The SMOS soil moisture retrieval algorithm. IEEE Trans. Geosci. Remote Sens. **50**, 1384–1403 (2012)

55. Kim, S., Liu, Y.Y., Johnson, F.M., Parinussa, R.M., Sharma, A.: A global comparison of alternate AMSR2 soil moisture products: why do they differ? Remote Sens. Environ. **161**, 43–62 (2015)

56. Piles, M., et al.: On the synergy of SMOS and Terra/Aqua MODIS: High resolution soil moisture maps in near real-time. In: Proceedings of the International Geoscience and Remote Sensing Symposium (IGARSS), pp. 3423–3426. Melbourne, Australia, 21–26 July 2013

57. Paloscia, S., Pettinato, S., Santi, E., Notarnicola, C., Pasolli, L., Reppucci, A.: Soil moisture mapping using Sentinel-1 images: algorithm and preliminary validation. Remote Sens. Environ. **134**, 234–248 (2013)

58. Dinesh, D., Kumar, S., Saran, S.: Machine learning modelling for soil moisture retrieval from simulated NASA-ISRO SAR (NISAR) L-band data. Remote Sens. **16**(18), 3539 (2024)

59. Ballester-Berman, J.D., Jagdhuber, T., Lopez-Sanchez, J.M., Vicente-Guijalba, F.: Soil moisture estimation in vineyards by means of C-band radar measurements. In: Proceedings of the European Conference on Synthetic Aperture Radar, EUSAR 2014; 10th European Conference on Synthetic Aperture Radar, pp. 252–255. Berlin, Germany (2014)

60. Bazzi, H., Baghdadi, N., El Hajj, M., Zribi, M., Belhouchette, H.: A comparison of two soil moisture products S2MP and copernicus-SSM over southern France. IEEE J. Sel. Top. Appl. Earth Obs. Remote Sens. **12**, 3366–3375 (2019)

61. Bakon, M., et al.: Synthetic aperture radar in vineyard monitoring: examples, demonstrations, and future perspectives. Remote Sens. **16**(12), 2106 (2024)

62. Lei, F., et al.: Data assimilation of high-resolution thermal and radar remote sensing retrievals for soil moisture monitoring in a drip-irrigated vineyard. Remote Sens. Environ. **239**, 111622 (2020)

63. Mendes, M.P., Matias, M., Gomes, R.C., Falcão, A.P.: Delimitation of low topsoil moisture content areas in a vineyard using remote sensing imagery (Sentinel-1 and Sentinel-2) in a Mediterranean-climate region. Soil Water Res. **16**, 85–94 (2021)

64. Efremova, N., Seddik, M.E.A., Erten, E.: Soil Moisture estimation using sentinel-1/-2 imagery coupled with CycleGAN for time-series gap filing. IEEE Trans. Geosci. Remote Sens. **60**, 4705111 (2022)

65. Chen, F., et al.: Application of the vineyard data assimilation (VIDA) system to vineyard root-zone soil moisture monitoring in the California Central Valley. Irrig. Sci. **40**, 779–799 (2022)

66. Kerr, Y.H., Wigneron, J.P., Al Bitar, A., Mialon, A., Srivastava, P.K.: Soil moisture from space: techniques and limitations, Chapter 1, pp. 3–27. Satellite Soil Moisture Retrieval. Elsevier, Amsterdam, The Netherlands (2016)

67. Gruber, A., Su, C., Crow, W., Zwieback, S., Dorigo, W., Wagner, W.: Estimating error cross-correlations in soil moisture data sets using extended collocation analysis. J. Geophys. Res. Atmos. **121**, 1208–1219 (2016)

68. Srivastava, P.K.: Satellite soil moisture: Review of theory and applications in water resources. Water Resour. Manag. **31**, 3161–3176 (2017)

69. Lee, L., Srivastava, P.K., Petropoulos, G.P.: Overview of sensitivity analysis methods in earth observation modelling. In: Petropoulos, G.P., Srivastava, P.K., (eds.) Sensitivity Analysis in Earth Observation, Chapter 1, pp. 4–18. Elsevier, Amsterdam, The Netherlands (2016)

Assessing Soil Sealing Dynamics in the Metropolitan Area of Bari Using Sentinel-2, Sealed Surface Index, and Machine Learning Approaches

Ahmad Asad[1,2] ⓘ, Alessandra Capolupo[2](✉) ⓘ, and Eufemia Tarantino[2] ⓘ

[1] Department of Agricultural and Environmental Sciences, University of
Bari Aldo Moro, Bari, Italy
[2] Department of Civil, Environmental, Land, Construction and Chemistry (DICATECh),
Politecnico di Bari, Via Orabona 4, 70125 Bari, Italy
alessandra.capolupo@poliba.it

Abstract. Soil sealing, the irreversible covering of natural soil with imperme-able material, impacts environmental sustainability by degrading ecosystems and reducing water quality and infiltration capacity. Advanced geospatial detecting and monitoring approaches are, thus, needed to face this critical environmen-tal challenge. This study assesses the effectiveness of two advanced geomatics approaches in detecting the dynamics of sealed surfaces in the metropolitan area of Bari from 2018 to 2024 using Sentinel-2 satellite imageries processed in Google Earth Engine: the sealed surface index and the machine learning-based Classifica-tion and Regression Trees algorithm. Twenty-eight Sentinel-2 imageries, acquired during February, May, July, and October, were analyzed. When necessary, a cloud cover masking process was employed before classification. After that, the fil-tered maps were classified with the two above-mentioned techniques generating four land cover classes: sealed surfaces, vegetation, bare land, and water bodies. Their accuracy was assessed against the training data gathered from the land use map provided by ISPRA. The outcomes demonstrated that incorporating machine learning significantly improved classification accuracy. The sealed surface class exhibited the highest classification accuracy, with Producer's and User's Accuracy consistently exceeding 90% and 85%, respectively. Conversely, bare soil proved more challenging to classify, leading to slightly lower accuracy values. These find-ings highlight the annual variations in sealed surfaces and their correlation with seasonal land-use dynamics. A notable increase in urban sealing, exceeding 2%, was observed between February 2018 and October 2024. This study underscores the importance of continuous monitoring of soil sealing for sustainable urban planning and environmental management.

Keywords: Soil Sealing · SUI · CART algorithm · Sustainability · Urbanization

© The Author(s), under exclusive license to Springer Nature Switzerland AG 2026
O. Gervasi et al. (Eds.): ICCSA 2025 Workshops, LNCS 15891, pp. 238–255, 2026.
https://doi.org/10.1007/978-3-031-97617-9_16

1 Introduction

Soil is a finite, essential, and crucial nonrenewable resource that has been abruptly covered with impermeable materials and excessive agricultural activities. This has led to the degradation of natural habitats and ecosystems, as well as a decline in water quality and infiltration capacity [1–3]. Such a phenomenon, commonly named "soil sealing", has been particularly evident in coastal areas worldwide over the past century [4, 5]. This is partly due to the historical oversight of urban planners regarding the environmental consequences of infrastructure expansion and the removal of soil cover, resulting in significant habitat loss [6].

Given its environmental impact, soil sealing analysis and monitoring have become a top priority of the European Union [7], resulting in the development of various methods to track and monitor Land Use/Land Cover (LU/LC) changes [8]. Advances in technology have significantly enhanced the observation of soil sealing patterns, with Remote Sensing (RS) emerging as a key tool in this field [9]. Indeed, it continuously provides multiscale information, offering, with time, a vital resource of global geospatial information without the need for direct field studies [10, 11]. However, RS has limitations, including the effects of weather conditions, particularly cloud cover and dust particles, that can distort imagery [12, 13] as well as limitations in spatial and temporal resolution [14]. In contrast, Remotely Piloted Aircraft Systems Services (RPAS) provide high-resolution, fine-scaled data making them particularly useful for local analysis [15, 16]. However, they are less suitable for large-scale studies due to the increased time and resources required for comprehensive data collection [17, 18].

Among the various satellite initiatives providing free open-source imagery, the Landsat mission, launched in 1972 by NASA/USGS, is the longest-running program [19]. Although it is particularly useful for long-term monitoring, its spatial resolution (30 m) is too coarse to detect LU/LC changes accurately. Thus, more recently, the Sentinel initiative, launched by the European Space Agency (ESA) in 2014, offers higher spatial resolution imagery (10 m) [20]. Nevertheless, both programs are widely used by researchers due to their accessibility and superior spatial resolution compared to the Moderate Resolution Imaging Spectroradiometer (MODIS) satellite, which has provided coarse resolution imagery of 250 m, 500 m, and 1 km at 36 spectral bands since 1999 [21]. Additionally, both Landsat and Sentinel imageries are adopted to extract LU/LC categories [22–25].

These LU/LC categories can be extracted using various approaches. Traditional pixel-based classification methods analyze individual entities based on spectral characteristics but fail to account for spatial relationships between neighboring pixels, limiting their effectiveness in higher-resolution datasets [26]. Nevertheless, among them, the index-based approach is suitable for quickly classifying the largest areas. Thus, proper indices were designed to monitor and detect impervious surfaces [27–30] but without considering the sealing of soil by agricultural activities, except the Sealed Urban Index (SUI), developed for Sentinel 2 satellite characteristics [31].

Object-Based Image Analysis (OBIA), on the other hand, is particularly suited for high-resolution imagery, as it differentiates shapes, sizes, and textures of spatial objects, making it ideal for heterogeneous and complex landscapes [32, 33]. However, OBIA requires significant computational power and processing time, especially for the larger study areas [34], and it is not suited to handle coarse resolution satellite images [35]. Machine Learning (ML) algorithms, like Classification and Regression Tree (CART), offer an alternative approach by leveraging statistical and computational models to reduce classification errors and inconsistencies in LU/LC data. These algorithms excel in processing both medium and high-resolution imagery, and handling non-linear, large, and complex datasets [36]. However, their primary drawback is the need for extensive training and careful calibration of threshold parameters to achieve optimal results [37].

The primary aim of this study is to analyze the dynamics of soil sealing in the Bari metropolitan area, within the Puglia region, using advanced methodologies to detect, quantify, and monitor LU/LC based on Sentinel-2 satellite data over a period of about 6 years (2018–2024). To meet such a purpose, a temporal trend of soil sealing was analyzed for specific months (February, May, July, and October) to identify seasonal and long-term changes. Both pixel-based and machine learning techniques were employed, using the SU index and CART classifier to detect soil sealing and other LU/LC categories such as vegetation, bare soil, and water.

2 Materials and Methods

For this research, proper Sentinel 2 satellite images covering the metropolitan area of Bari were selected and handled within the Google Earth Engine (GEE) environment using a custom-developed JavaScript code. Before employing two different classification approaches, index-based and ML, a cloud masking procedure was applied, when necessary. The accuracy of the resulting maps was assessed by computing the confusion matrix, based on training data collected from the LU/LC map provided by Istituto Superiore per la Protezione e la Ricerca Ambientale (ISPRA). The entire process is summarized in the workflow reported in Fig. 1, while each step is detailed in the following subparagraphs.

2.1 Geodatabase and Pre-processing

The Sentinel satellite Level-2A (surface reflectance) dataset was picked up to achieve the research goal. The Level 2A product was first introduced on March 26, 2018, as the initial baseline and was subsequently refined based on quality control reports embedded in the product. Sentinel 2A is equipped with a MultiSpectral Instrument (MSI) that captures data across 13 bands at 10 m, 20 m, and 60 m spatial resolution. Specifically, four bands (Red (R), Green (G), Blue (B), Near-InfraRed (NIR)) operate at 10m resolution; six bands, including four narrow bands in Visible Near Infra-Red (VNIR) for vegetation red-edge spectral domain and two wider bands in Shortwave Infra-Red (SWIR), work at 20m resolution; and, the remaining three bands (Coastal Aerosol, Water Vapor, and SWIR-Cirrus), dedicated to atmospheric and aerosol monitoring, operate at 60m.

The ESA provides temporal offset values between bands [38] to ensure data consistency and minimize information loss. A significant offset can reduce the suitability of certain bands for direct combination in indices without mathematical corrections. Table 1 reports these values, highlighting that Bands 9 and 2 have an offset of 2.59s,

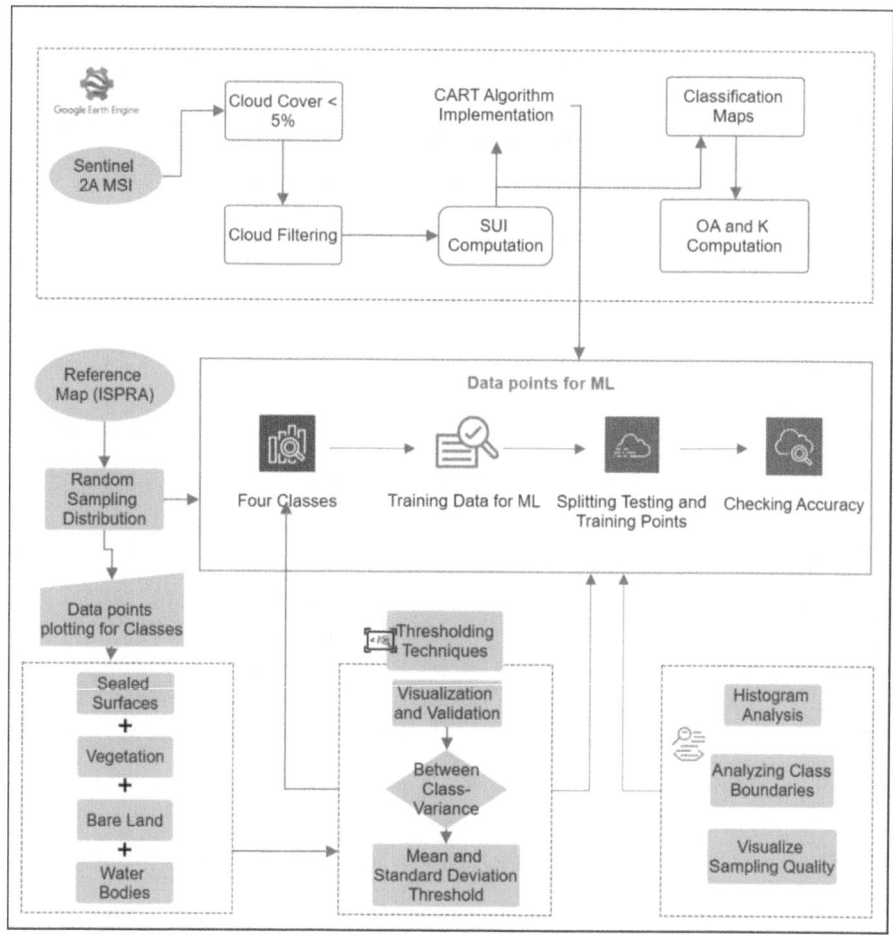

Fig. 1. Research workflow.

making them unsuitable for direct use together without appropriate adjustments. This parameter is crucial for identifying the optimal indices to extract LU/LC information.

As a result, Sentinel 2A images were selected as input data for this study. Specifically, 28 images, covering four different months (February, May, June, and October) from 2018 up to 2024, were gathered and processed in the GEE environment (https://earthengine. google.com/). These months were chosen to analyze seasonal trends in urban sprawl over the years, helping to minimize misclassifications caused by seasonal variations. Additionally, a cloud cover threshold (5%) was set to reduce clouds and shadow effects, ensuring high-quality data. The only exception was the May 2019 image, which exhibited a cloud cover of 18.34% due to generally high cloud cover in the Bari region during that month. Further details of the collected data are provided in Table 2.

Table 1. Wavelengths and temporal offset between bands in Sentinel 2.

Band Pair	Temporal Offset (s)	Band 1 Wavelength (nm)	Band 2 Wavelength (nm)
B08 / B02	0.264	842	490
B03 / B08	0.264	560	842
B03 / B02	0.527	560	490
B10 / B03	0.324	1375	560
B10 / B02	0.851	1375	490
B04 / B10	0.154	665	1375
B04 / B02	1.005	665	490
B05 / B04	0.264	705	665
B05 / B02	1.269	705	490
B11 / B05	0.199	1610	705
B11 / B02	1.468	1610	490
B06 / B11	0.057	740	1610
B06 / B02	1.525	740	490
B07 / B06	0.265	783	740
B07 / B02	1.790	783	490
B8a / B07	0.265	865	783
B8a / B02	2.055	865	490
B12 / B8a	0.030	2190	865
B12 / B02	2.085	2190	490
B01 / B12	0.229	443	2190
B01 / B02	2.314	443	490
B09 / B01	0.271	945	443
B09 / B02	2.586	945	490

Before starting the processing phase, the data were atmospherically corrected, and the clouds were masked using the approach proposed by [39]. However, geometric correction was not performed, as the data provided by USGS was already deemed satisfactory.

2.2 Processing Steps

Two approaches were adopted to extract LU/LC classes: a pixel-based analysis relying on the computation of the SUI and a ML-based approach utilizing the CART algorithm. Both methods are described in detail in the following sub-sections.

Table 2. Sentinel 2A image details.

Image IDs	Acquisition Date	Cloud Cover (%)
20180204T094159_20180204T094518_T33TXF	04/02/2018	3.36
20180525T094029_20180525T094824_T33TXF	25/05/2018	0.49
20180714T094029_20180714T094337_T33TXF	14/07/2018	0.23
20181012T094029_20181012T094403_T33TXF	12/10/2018	1.79
20190219T094039_20190219T094304_T33TXF	19/02/2019	0
20190505T094041_20190505T094230_T33TXF	05/05/2019	18.34
20190724T094041_20190724T094126_T33TXF	24/07/2019	0
20191012T094031_20191012T094345_T33TXF	12/10/2019	0.18
20200209T094131_20200209T094333_T33TXF	09/02/2020	0.04
20200207T095059_20200207T095055_T33TXF	07/02/2020	3.55
20200504T094029_20200504T094809_T33TXF	04/05/2020	0.44
20200701T095031_20200701T095501_T33TXF	01/07/2020	1.02
20201001T094039_20201001T094320_T33TXF	01/10/2020	2
20210203T094211_20210203T094345_T33TXF	03/02/2021	0
20210509T094029_20210509T094028_T33TXF	09/05/2021	0
20210701T095029_20210701T095030_T33TXF	01/07/2021	0
20211004T095031_20211004T095403_T33TXF	04/10/2021	0.01
20220203T094109_20220203T094111_T33TXF	03/02/2022	0.19
20220512T095031_20220512T095033_T33TXF	12/05/2022	4.06
20220703T094039_20220703T094036_T33TXF	03/07/2022	0
20221004T095029_20221004T095027_T33TXF	04/10/2022	0
20230201T095129_20230201T095130_T33TXF	01/02/2023	1.23
20230507T095031_20230507T095028_T33TXF	07/05/2023	0
20230703T094041_20230703T094035_T33TXF	03/07/2023	1.18
20231001T094031_20231001T094348_T33TXF	01/10/2023	4.19
20240203T094119_20240203T094116_T33TXF	03/02/2024	3.61
20240501T095031_20240501T095031_T33TXF	01/05/2024	3.92
20240705T094549_20240705T094718_T33TXF	05/07/2024	0.014
20241013T095029_20241013T095746_T33TXF	13/10/2024	0

Sealed Urban Index

Traditional pixel-based methods rely on the principle that different materials exhibit unique spectral reflectance signatures due to variations in the absorption and reflection of electromagnetic radiation. This approach enables the rapid classification of large areas. However, most existing indices were developed using Landsat data, making them less suitable for Sentinel imagery. Additionally, many of these indices focus primarily on urban areas, limiting their applicability to broader land cover classifications. On the other hand, the SUI, specifically designed for Sentinel images, not only detects impervious surfaces (asphalt, concrete, buildings, roads) but also identifies overused agricultural land, where water infiltration is significantly reduced. SUI is calculated using Eq. 1:

$$SUI = \frac{(Green - SWIR1) \times (SWIR2 - Red)}{(Green + SWIR1) \times (SWIR2 + Red)} + 0.5. \tag{1}$$

However, as reported in a previous study [31], SUI alone does not yield highly accurate results. When combined with ML techniques, its efficiency improves significantly. Moreover, the integration of ML not only enhances the detection of sealed surfaces but also facilitates the identification of other land cover types, enabling a more effective differentiation among classes.

Classification Using the CART Algorithm

CART is a decision tree ML algorithm used for both classification and regression tasks [40]. It works by recursively partitioning the dataset into smaller, more homogeneous subsets. In this study, the CART model was employed to classify soil sealing and other LU/LC categories, dividing them into four distinct classes: sealed surfaces, vegetation, bare land, and water bodies. This partitioning process improved the accuracy of the model by making the classification more precise for the trained data. Indeed, training data are crucial for ML models, as inaccurate training can lead to misclassification and unreliable results. In this study, the training data were sourced from the ISPRA LU/LC map [41].

To remove the overlapping of the four data classes, the Otsu thresholding techniques were applied. Otsu's method, which minimizes intra-class variance, helped improve the separability between classes. Additionally, standard deviation (σ) and mean (μ) values were used for adaptive image thresholding. These techniques effectively removed redundancies and ensured clearer results in the testing phase.

To evaluate the performance of the model, the truth data collected on the ISPRA maps were split into 70% training data and 30% testing data. This split was performed automatically by the CART algorithm, and the final accuracy was calculated using the testing data. Because of the diverse LU/LC features, a random sampling distribution method was selected for the data points.

2.3 Accuracy Assessment

To evaluate the performance of the two applied approaches, a testing dataset was selected from the ISPRA map applying the random sampling techniques, used as ground truth. These points served as the input data for computing the confusion matrix and extracting the following statistical metrics: Overall Accuracy (OA), Producer accuracy (PA), User accuracy (UA), and Kappa coefficient (K). OA was used to check whether the pixels classified into the four different LU/LC classes were correctly assigned, while K was calculated to evaluate the reliability of the classification, as it accounts for chance agreements [42]. PA and UA were measured to determine whether classification results for each category fell within the acceptable accuracy thresholds [43].

2.4 Case Study of Bari

The study focuses on the Metropolitan City of Bari and its surrounding areas located in the Puglia region (Southern Italy) (Fig. 2). It is over 116 square kilometers, and it was selected as a pilot case since it was characterized by a significant urban and agricultural expansion over the last few decades. Indeed, Bari has experienced the most extensive urban sprawl in the entire Puglia region.

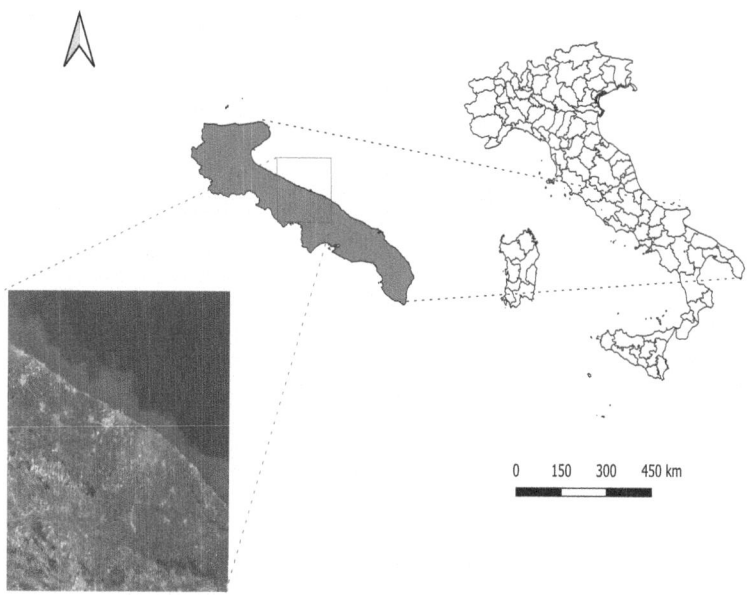

Fig. 2. Study area of Bari.

The urban sprawl along the Adriatic Sea coast of Bari city is one of the causes of the rapid expansion since the 21st century. Therefore, it was selected as pilot site.

3   Results and Discussion

This paper evaluates the effectiveness of the SU index for detecting sealed surfaces, both as a standalone method and when integrated with ML techniques. Its performance was tested over about six years, spanning from 2018 up to 2024, using a total of 28 images collected by Sentinel 2A.

The spatial distribution map of SUI results is depicted in Fig. 3, which presents a composite panel of classification maps corresponding to the selected months and years. Figure 3, a), b), c), d) represents 2018 images of February, May, July, and October respectively, while e), f), g), h) are February, May, July, and October of 2019 and so on.

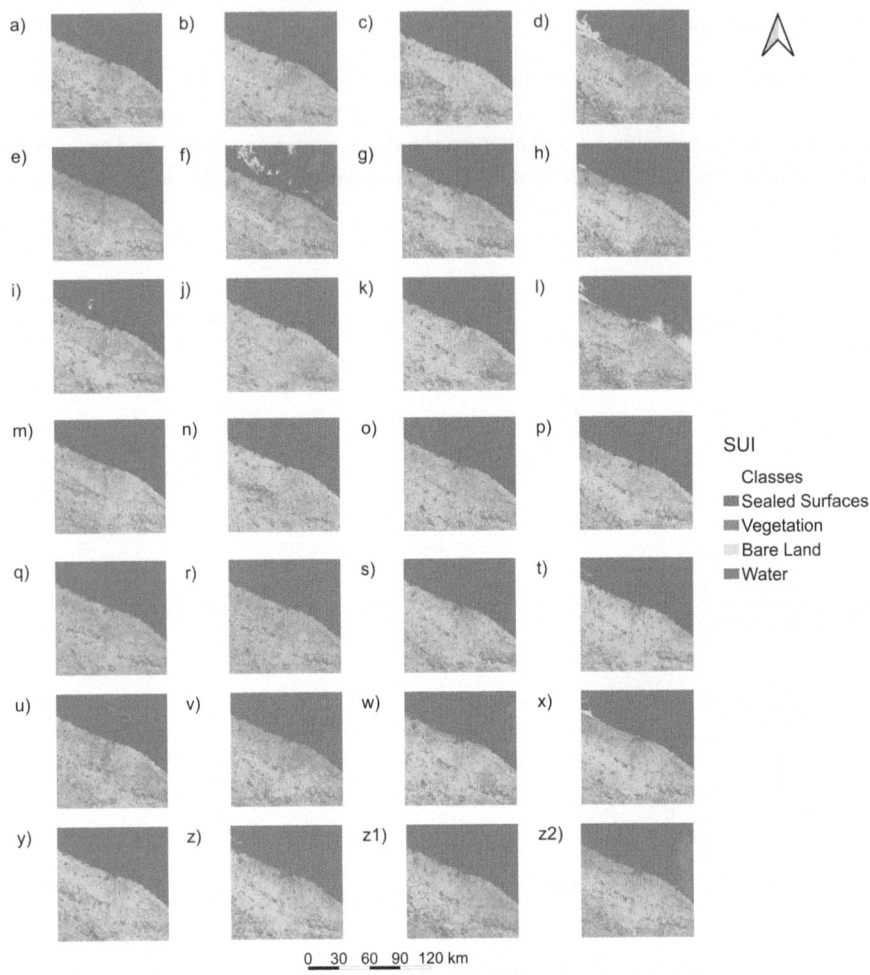

Fig. 3. Spatial representation of SUI.

Nonetheless, substantial cloud cover in the May 2019 image significantly affected outputs quality, as observed in Fig. 3 (f). This finding is also confirmed by the accuracy metrics reported at the end of this section. The analysis of the spatial LU/LC distribution around the metropolitan area of Bari indicates that SUI successfully detected overused agricultural lands, with and without the implementation of the ML algorithm. However, Fig. 4, which compares SUI results obtained with and without ML, suggests that incorporating ML enhances class differentiation.

The left panel (a) of Fig. 4, representing SUI outcome, primarily identifies impervious surfaces and a limited extent of overused agricultural land based on an image from February 2022. In contrast, the right panel (b) of Fig. 4, incorporating ML, clearly identifies all sealed surfaces, including overused agricultural land, with only minor misclassification of bare soil. Sealed surfaces are represented in red, frequently appearing

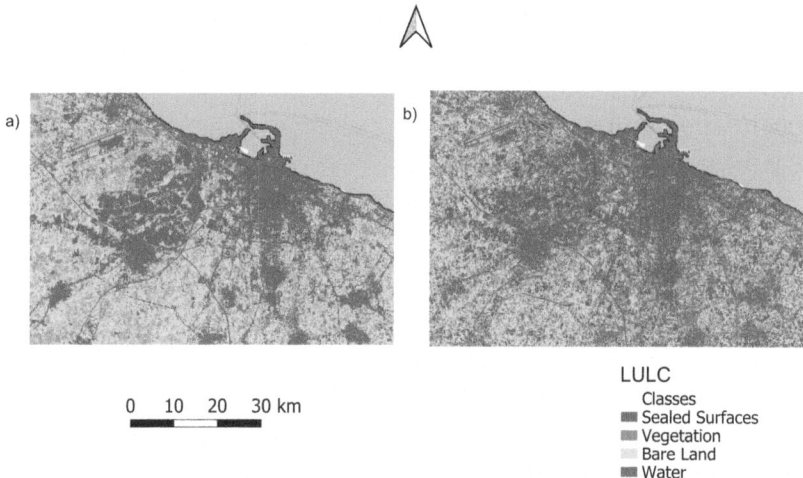

a)   b)

0   10   20   30 km

LULC
Classes
■ Sealed Surfaces
■ Vegetation
▨ Bare Land
■ Water

Fig. 4. Spatial representation of SUI (left) and ML outcomes (right).

along the coastal zone across all selected months and years. Seasonal variations were also observed, with sealed surfaces being more prevalent in the elevated areas opposite Bari and the Adriatic Sea during February and October, regions characterized by extensive agricultural activities.

An interesting finding pertains to the classification results of 2020, where a significant increase in the detection of abundant vegetation was observed. This trend is likely associated with the COVID-19 lockdown period, during which reduced human activities such as traffic and urbanization contributed to the enhancement of vegetation growth. Despite the persistence of urban sprawl, these findings suggest that decreased anthropogenic pressure may have positive ecological effects. The other three classes are vegetation, bare land, and water, which are represented in green, yellow, and blue, respectively. Bare soil has been slightly misclassified, as it was one of the most difficult classes to identify.

Table 3 depicts the OA and K for each image analyzed after applying ML. The results indicate consistently high classification accuracy, with OA exceeding 90% in most cases. K values greater than 0.81 indicate that the results from the supervised classification produced reliable results. However, the image collected in May 2019 exhibited lower accuracy ($< 90\%$) and a K value of 0.8008 due to excessive cloud cover, which introduced distortions into the classification process. In contrast, the metrics generated by using the SU index standalone showed slightly lower OA and K values (Table 4). Nevertheless, although OA is lower than 90%, K values remain above 0.80, suggesting that even SUI still produces promising results. The May 2019 image also yielded the lowest results for SUI, with a K value of 0.7826, again due to cloud cover.

Simultaneously, Tables 4 and 5 describe the PA and UA generated from the CART algorithm and SUI, respectively. The former shows that PA and UA consistently exceeded 90% and 85%, respectively, across all images. In contrast, the bare land class exhibited the lowest accuracy, with PA and UA values mostly falling below 90%, while the vegetation

Table 3. Kappa coefficient (K) and Overall Accuracy (OA) of the CART algorithm.

Image IDs	K	OA (%)
20180204T094159_20180204T094518_T33TXF	0.86	91
20180525T094029_20180525T094824_T33TXF	0.86	91
20180714T094029_20180714T094337_T33TXF	0.89	93
20181012T094029_20181012T094403_T33TXF	0.86	92
20190219T094039_20190219T094304_T33TXF	0.86	92
20190505T094041_20190505T094230_T33TXF	0.80	88
20190724T094041_20190724T094126_T33TXF	0.86	92
20191012T094031_20191012T094345_T33TXF	0.90	93
20200209T094131_20200209T094333_T33TXF	0.86	91
20200207T095059_20200207T095055_T33TXF	0.86	91
20200504T094029_20200504T094809_T33TXF	0.85	92
20200701T095031_20200701T095501_T33TXF	0.94	97
20201001T094039_20201001T094320_T33TXF	0.91	94
20210203T094211_20210203T094345_T33TXF	0.89	93
20210509T094029_20210509T094028_T33TXF	0.90	94
20210701T095029_20210701T095030_T33TXF	0.86	92
20211004T095031_20211004T095403_T33TXF	0.86	94
20220203T094109_20220203T094111_T33TXF	0.88	93
20220512T095031_20220512T095033_T33TXF	0.92	95
20220703T094039_20220703T094036_T33TXF	0.85	90
20221004T095029_20221004T095027_T33TXF	0.85	90
20230201T095129_20230201T095130_T33TXF	0.89	93
20230507T095031_20230507T095028_T33TXF	0.91	94
20230703T094041_20230703T094035_T33TXF	0.90	93
20231001T094031_20231001T094348_T33TXF	0.92	95
20240203T094119_20240203T094116_T33TXF	0.89	92
20240501T095031_20240501T095031_T33TXF	0.86	92
20240705T094549_20240705T094718_T33TXF	0.89	93
20241013T095029_20241013T095746_T33TXF	0.86	91

class maintained excellent accuracy, surpassing 90%. It is noteworthy that the sealed surface class achieved higher PA and UA values in most winter images, whereas bare land tended to perform worse during the summer months. As shown in Table 3, images captured in July over the years yielded excellent results, with OA above 90% and K

Table 4. Kappa coefficient (K) and Overall Accuracy (OA) of SUI.

Image IDs	K	OA (%)
20180204T094159_20180204T094518_T33TXF	0.82	90
20180525T094029_20180525T094824_T33TXF	0.81	90
20180714T094029_20180714T094337_T33TXF	0.84	91
20181012T094029_20181012T094403_T33TXF	0.83	90
20190219T094039_20190219T094304_T33TXF	0.83	91
20190505T094041_20190505T094230_T33TXF	0.78	86
20190724T094041_20190724T094126_T33TXF	0.82	90
20191012T094031_20191012T094345_T33TXF	0.84	92
20200209T094131_20200209T094333_T33TXF	0.81	80
20200207T095059_20200207T095055_T33TXF	0.82	90
20200504T094029_20200504T094809_T33TXF	0.81	90
20200701T095031_20200701T095501_T33TXF	0.85	93
20201001T094039_20201001T094320_T33TXF	0.83	91
20210203T094211_20210203T094345_T33TXF	0.83	91
20210509T094029_20210509T094028_T33TXF	0.84	91
20210701T095029_20210701T095030_T33TXF	0.83	90
20211004T095031_20211004T095403_T33TXF	0.81	91
20220203T094109_20220203T094111_T33TXF	0.82	91
20220512T095031_20220512T095033_T33TXF	0.85	92
20220703T094039_20220703T094036_T33TXF	0.81	90
20221004T095029_20221004T095027_T33TXF	0.80	89
20230201T095129_20230201T095130_T33TXF	0.82	91
20230507T095031_20230507T095028_T33TXF	0.83	91
20230703T094041_20230703T094035_T33TXF	0.85	93
20231001T094031_20231001T094348_T33TXF	0.83	91
20240203T094119_20240203T094116_T33TXF	0.83	91
20240501T095031_20240501T095031_T33TXF	0.82	90
20240705T094549_20240705T094718_T33TXF	0.85	92
20241013T095029_20241013T095746_T33TXF	0.83	91

values greater than 0.85. This is likely due to the favorable weather conditions in July, when minimal rainfall results in less distorted satellite imagery.

Tables 4 and 6, which present the results of SUI, show lower accuracy across all images compared to those processed with ML. Specifically, UA and PA values for all classes were somewhat reduced when ML was not employed, as detailed in Table 6.

Table 5. PA and UA obtained from CART algorithm.

Acquisition Date	PA - Sealed Surfaces	PA - Vegetation Class	PA - Bare Land	PA - Water	UA - Sealed Surfaces	UA - Vegetation Class	UA - Bare Land	UA - Water
02/04/18	85	94	89	100	92	95	80	100
05/25/18	90	94	83	100	95	96	76	100
07/14/18	89	94	94	100	97	98	80	100
10/12/18	88	98	79	100	91	92	88	80
02/19/19	99	77	88	100	97	100	73	75
05/05/19	95	86	80	75	88	92	81	75
07/24/19	91	91	84	100	85	97	84	100
10/12/19	98	98	74	100	96	97	85	100
02/09/20	86	93	89	100	92	93	81	100
05/09/20	97	94	74	100	91	95	77	100
07/23/20	93	92	86	100	93	90	83	100
10/21/20	92	98	98	100	98	98	88	100
02/03/21	98	92	96	100	95	99	83	100
05/09/21	93	98	81	100	89	94	93	100
07/23/21	96	97	86	100	96	100	87	100
10/21/21	92	91	87	100	89	94	90	100
02/03/22	98	88	88	67	97	97	97	67
05/14/22	95	90	88	100	90	98	88	100
07/23/22	96	99	85	100	90	98	91	100
10/16/22	87	94	88	100	90	90	87	100
02/18/23	91	91	84	100	89	96	79	100
05/29/23	94	90	83	100	90	96	86	100
07/18/23	90	97	89	100	90	90	92	100
10/11/23	90	93	87	100	97	93	83	100
02/08/24	98	93	97	75	93	99	88	100
05/23/24	90	96	90	100	93	98	83	100
07/17/24	88	91	80	100	89	95	78	100
10/15/24	94	90	88	100	94	98	79	100

Notably, even in the May 2019 image, despite a higher cloud cover percentage, the accuracy for sealed surfaces remained high, demonstrating the robustness of this index under challenging conditions.

Table 6. PA and UA generated from SUI.

Acquisition Date	PA - Sealed Surfaces	PA - Vegetation Class	PA - Bare Land	PA - Water	UA - Sealed Surfaces	UA - Vegetation Class	UA - Bare Land	UA - Water
02/04/18	84	92	88	100	90	92	77	100
05/25/18	90	94	80	100	93	94	73	100
07/14/18	88	93	92	100	96	98	78	100
10/12/18	87	98	78	100	90	91	86	80
02/19/19	98	75	86	100	96	100	71	75
05/05/19	90	86	78	75	87	90	78	75
07/24/19	89	90	81	100	84	96	82	100
10/12/19	97	97	72	100	94	96	82	100
02/09/20	83	92	87	100	91	93	79	100
05/09/20	96	93	73	100	90	94	76	100
07/23/20	92	91	84	100	93	89	81	100
10/21/20	91	97	96	100	97	97	85	100
02/03/21	97	91	94	100	95	97	82	100
05/09/21	91	97	79	100	89	93	91	100
07/23/21	95	95	85	100	95	99	85	100
10/21/21	91	90	80	100	88	94	88	100
02/03/22	96	86	86	70	96	96	95	70
05/14/22	94	88	87	100	89	95	87	100
07/23/22	95	97	83	100	89	96	90	100
10/16/22	85	92	86	100	90	90	86	100
02/18/23	91	90	84	100	88	96	78	100
05/29/23	94	89	81	100	89	94	83	100
07/18/23	89	95	87	100	89	88	91	100
10/11/23	89	92	86	100	97	92	82	100
02/08/24	91	93	90	75	91	96	85	100
05/23/24	90	95	88	100	90	97	81	100
07/17/24	87	91	78	100	88	94	76	100
10/15/24	93	89	86	100	91	97	78	100

4 Conclusion

This study assesses the performance of the SU index standalone and integrated into the CART algorithm for mapping sealed surfaces and detecting their changes over about 6 years (2018–2024). The two techniques were tested on 28 Sentinel 2A images collected over the metropolitan area of Bari in order to analyze the sealed surface variations across seasons and years.

Study results highlight the effectiveness of SUI in detecting and mapping sealed surfaces, particularly when combined with machine learning techniques. Indeed, the integration of SUI with CART significantly enhances classification accuracy, facilitating a more precise differentiation of sealed surfaces with vegetation and bare land, as enhanced in the confusion matrix. Despite minor misclassifications, the high accuracy levels observed in this study underscore the reliability of SUI for large-scale land monitoring applications. However, the challenge of accurately classifying bare soil slightly reduced the OA. Despite this, the classification still achieved satisfying results, with OA consistently exceeding 90% for all tested images captured in February, May, July, and October from 2018 to 2024. The only exception was affected by a higher percentage of cloud cover, which significantly reduced accuracy.

These findings support the analysis of annual variations in sealed surfaces. In the metropolitan area of Bari, sealed surfaces increased by more than 2%. Specifically, the sealed surface class measured 10 m^2 in February 2018 and reached 15 m^2 in October 2024. SU index and the outcomes of this research will assist urban planners in developing more effective sustainable solutions, as the identification of different classes is crucial. Furthermore, this research will also provide insights into monitoring changes in different geospatial features, supporting urban planners and policymakers to develop new sustainable cities.

References

1. Fini, A., Frangi, P., Mori, J., Donzelli, D., Ferrini, F.: Nature based solutions to mitigate soil sealing in urban areas: Results from a 4-year study comparing permeable, porous, and impermeable pavements. Environ. Res. **156**, 443–454 (2017)
2. Capolupo, A., Barletta, C., Esposito, D., Tarantino, E.: Earth observation data for sustainable management of water resources to inform spatial planning strategies. In: Marucci, A., Zullo, F., Fiorini, L., Saganeiti, L. (eds.) Innovation in Urban and Regional Planning. INPUT 2023. Lecture Notes in Civil Engineering, vol. 467, pp. 24–35. Springer, Cham (2024). https://doi.org/10.1007/978-3-031-54118-6_3
3. Morabito, M., et al.: The impact of built-up surfaces on land surface temperatures in Italian urban areas. Sci. Total. Environ. **551–552**(1), 317–326 (2016)
4. Mannucci, S., Kwakkel, H., Morganti, M., Ferrero, M.: From past to future: understanding urban development in flood-prone coastal Rome. J. Urban Des., 1–32 (2024)
5. Smiraglia, D., Cavalli, A., Giuliani, C., Assennato, F.: The increasing coastal urbanization in the mediterranean environment: the state of the art in Italy. Land **12**(5), 1017 (2023)
6. Hamilton, B., Coops, C.N., Lokman, K.: Time series monitoring of impervious surfaces and runoff impacts in Metro Vancouver. Sci. Total. Environ. **760**(15), 143873 (2021)
7. Tombolini, I., Rodrigo-Comino, J., Salvati, L.: Toward a sustainable use of land: urbanization, policies and (mis)understanding of degradation processes. In: Land Quality and Sustainable Urban Forms. Springer Geography, pp. 17–74. Springer, Cham (2022). https://doi.org/10.1007/978-3-030-94732-3_2
8. Peroni, F., et al.: How to map soil sealing, land take and impervious surfaces? A systematic review. Environ. Res. Lett. **17**, 053005 (2022)

9. Säurich, A., Möller, M., Gerighausen, H.: A novel remote sensing-based approach to determine loss of agricultural soils due to soil sealing — a case study in Germany. Environ. Monit. Assess. **196**, 510 (2024)

10. Mastrorosa, S., Crespi, M., Congedo, L., Munafò, M.: Land consumption classification using sentinel 1 data: a systematic review. Land **12**, 932 (2023)

11. Barletta, C., Capolupo, A., Tarantino, E.: Copernicus geodatabase for investigating land cover changes at the European scale. In: Marucci, A., Zullo, F., Fiorini, L., Saganeiti, L. (eds.) Innovation in Urban and Regional Planning. INPUT 2023. Lecture Notes in Civil Engineering, vol. 467, pp. 12–23. Springer, Cham (2024). https://doi.org/10.1007/978-3-031-54118-6_2

12. Shen, H., Li, H., Qian, Y., Zhang, L., Yuan, Q.: An effective thin cloud removal procedure for visible remote sensing images. ISPRS J. Photogramm. Remote Sens. **96**, 224–235 (2014)

13. Lan, X., Zhang, L., Shen, H., Yuan, Q., Li, H.: Single image haze removal considering sensor blur and noise. EURASIP J. Adv. Sign. Proces., 1–13 (2013)

14. Wang, Q., Tang, Y., Ge, Y., Xie, H., Tong, X., Atkinson, M.P.: A comprehensive review of spatial-temporal-spectral information reconstruction techniques. Sci. Remote Sens. **8**, 100102 (2023)

15. Pour, T., Miřijovský, J., Purket, T.: Airborne thermal remote sensing: the case of the city of Olomouc, Czech Republic. Eur. J. Remote Sens. **52**(sup1), 209–218 (2019)

16. Pepe, M., Fregonese, L., Scaioni, M.: Planning airborne photogrammetry and remote-sensing missions with modern platforms and sensors. Eur. J. Remote Sens. **51**(1), 412–436 (2018)

17. Saponaro, M., Tarantino, E.: LULC classification performance of supervised and unsupervised algorithms on UAV-Orthomosaics. In: Gervasi, O., Murgante, B., Misra, S., Rocha, A.M.A.C., Garau, C. (eds.) Computational Science and Its Applications – ICCSA 2022 Workshops. ICCSA 2022. Lecture Notes in Computer Science, vol. 13379, pp. 311–326. Springer, Cham (2022). https://doi.org/10.1007/978-3-031-10545-6_22

18. Saponaro, M., Capolupo, A., Tarantino, E., Fratino, U.: Comparative analysis of different UAV-based photogrammetric processes to improve product accuracies. In: Misra, S., et al. Computational Science and Its Applications – ICCSA 2019. ICCSA 2019. Lecture Notes in Computer Science, vol. 11622, pp. 225–238. Springer, Cham (2019). https://doi.org/10.1007/978-3-030-24305-0_18

19. Landsat Missions. https://www.usgs.gov/landsat-missions. Accessed 2 Feb 2025

20. The Sentinel missions. https://www.esa.int/Applications/Observing_the_Earth/Copernicus/The_Sentinel_missions. Accessed 1 Feb 2025

21. MODIS. https://modis.gsfc.nasa.gov/about/index.php. Accessed 13 Feb 2025

22. Capolupo, A., Tarantino, E.: Landsat 9 satellite images potentiality in extracting land cover classes in GEE environment using an index-based approach: the case study of Savona City. In: Gervasi, O., et al. Computational Science and Its Applications – ICCSA 2023 Workshops. ICCSA 2023. Lecture Notes in Computer Science, vol. 14107, pp. 251–265. Springer, Cham (2023). https://doi.org/10.1007/978-3-031-37114-1_17

23. Capolupo, A., Monterisi, C., Saponaro, M., Tarantino, E.: Multi-temporal analysis of land cover changes using Landsat data through Google Earth Engine platform. In: Proceedings of the Eighth International Conference on Remote Sensing and Geoinformation of the Environment (RSCy2020), vol. 11524, pp. 447–458. SPIE (2020)

24. Aguilar, M.A., Jiménez-Lao, R., Ladisa, C., Aguilar, F.J., Tarantino, E.: Comparison of spectral indices extracted from Sentinel-2 images to map plastic covered greenhouses through an object-based approach. GIScience Remote Sens. **59**(1), 822–842 (2022)

25. Capolupo, A., Santoro, P.M., Tarantino, E.: Exploiting medium-resolution sentinel data in google earth engine for burned area reflectance classification. In: Gervasi, O., Murgante, B., Garau, C., Taniar, D., C. Rocha, A.M.A., Faginas Lago, M.N. (eds.) Computational Science and Its Applications – ICCSA 2024 Workshops. ICCSA 2024. Lecture Notes in Computer Science, vol. 14819, pp. 201–216. Springer, Cham (2024). https://doi.org/10.1007/978-3-031-65282-0_13

26. Misra, I., Rohil, M.K., Manthira Moorthi, S., Dhar, D.: Feature based remote sensing image registration techniques: a comprehensive and comparative review. Int. J. Remote Sens. **43**(12), 4477–4516 (2022)

27. Tian, Y., Chen, H., Song, Q., Zheng, K.: A novel index for impervious surface area mapping: development and validation. Remote Sensimh **10**, 1521 (2018)

28. Sun, G., Chen, X., Jia, X., Yao, Y., Wang, Z.: Combinational Build-up Index (CBI) for effective impervious surface mapping in urban areas. IEEE J. Sel. Top. Appl. Earth Observations Remote Sens. **9**(5), 2081–2092 (2016)

29. Bouhennache, R., Bouden, T., Taleb-Ahmed, A., Cheddad, A.: A new spectral index for the extraction of built-up land features from Landsat 8 satellite imagery. Geocartography Int. **34**(14), 1531–1551 (2019)

30. Zhang, L., Tian, Y., Liu, Q.: A novel urban composition index based on water-impervious surface-pervious surface (W-I-P) model for urban compositions mapping using landsat imagery. Remote Sens. **13**, 3 (2021)

31. Asad, A., Capolupo, A., Tarantino, E.: Machine learning and index-based classification approaches for accurately evaluating sealed surfaces from medium-resolution Sentinel 2 data. In: Proceedings of the 4th International Proceedings of Mediterranean Geosciences Union. Scopus, Barcelona (2025)

32. Sarzana, T., Maltese, A., Capolupo, A., Tarantino, E.: Post-processing of pixel and object-based land cover classifications of very high spatial resolution images. In: Gervasi, O., et al. Computational Science and Its Applications – ICCSA 2020. ICCSA 2020. Lecture Notes in Computer Science, vol. 12252, pp. 797–812. Springer, Cham (2020). https://doi.org/10.1007/978-3-030-58811-3_57

33. Blaschke, T.: Object based image analysis for remote sensing. ISPRS J. Photogramm. Remote Sens. **65**(1), 2–16 (2010)

34. Liu, D., Xia, F.: Assessing object-based classification: advantages and limitations. Remote Sens. Lett. **1**(4), 187–194 (2010)

35. Johnson, A.B., Ma, L.: Image segmentation and object-based image analysis for environmental monitoring: recent areas of interest, researchers' views on the future priorities. Remore Sens. **12**(11), 1772 (2020)

36. Waghela, H., Patel, S., Sudesan, P., Raorane, S., Borgalli, R.: Land use land cover classification using machine learning. In: Proceedings of the 2022 International Conference on Automation, Computing and Renewable Systems (ICACRS), Pudukkottai, India, pp. 708–711 (2022)

37. Milojevic-Dupont, N., Creutzig, F.: Machine learning for geographically differentiated climate change mitigation in urban areas. Sustain. Cities Soc. **64**, 102526 (2021)

38. Binet, R., Bergsma, E., Poulain, V.: Accurate Sentinel-2 inter-band time delays. ISPRS Annals of the Photogrammetry, Remote Sensing and Spatial Information Sciences, vol. V-1–2022 XXIV ISPRS Congress (2022 edition), Nice, France (2022)

39. Sola, I., et al.: Assessment of atmospheric correction methods for Sentinel-2 images in Mediterranean landscapes. Int. J. Appl. Earth Obs. Geoinf. **73**, 63–76 (2018)

40. Sarker, H.I.: Machine learning: algorithms, real-world applications and research directions. SN Comput. Sci. **2**, 160 (2021)

41. Geological and Geotematics Map. https://www.isprambiente.gov.it/en/databases/data-base-collection/soil-and-territory/geological-and-geotematics-map. Accessed 13 Jan 2025
42. Moody, M.G.: Explaining the unsuitability of the kappa coefficient in the assessment and comparison of the accuracy of thematic maps obtained by image classification. Remote Sens. Environ. **239**, 111630 (2020)
43. Nicolau, A.P., Dyson, K., Saah, D., Clinton, N.: Accuracy assessment: quantifying classification quality. In: Cardille, J.A., Crowley, M.A., Saah, D., Clinton, N.E. (eds.) Cloud-Based Remote Sensing with Google Earth Engine, pp. 135–145. Springer, Cham (2024). https://doi.org/10.1007/978-3-031-26588-4_7

TLS Radiometric Analysis for Monitoring Plant Diseases in Apulia's Olive Groves

Noemi Pagano$^{(\boxtimes)}$ (iD), Eufemia Tarantino(iD), and Alberico Sonnessa(iD)

Department of Civil, Environmental, Land, Construction and Chemistry (DICATECh),
Politecnico di Bari, Via Orabona 4, 70125 Bari, Italy
n.pagano@phd.poliba.it, {eufemia.tarantino,
alberico.sonnessa}@poliba.it

Abstract. Threats to agricultural environments are constantly rising due to global trade, dangerous infections, harmful pathogens, anthropogenic pressure, and climate change. Simultaneously, the world's population is increasing at a rate of approximately 70 million people per year, driving the demand for food and emphasizing the need for effective crop health monitoring strategies.

In Southern Italy, the Apulia region is famous for its centuries-old olive groves, recognized by UNESCO for their cultural and landscape significance. However, this vital resource is seriously threatened by the *Xylella fastidiosa* (Xf) bacterium, which was first identified in Apulia in 2013. Over the past decade, the infection has spread rapidly in Salento, causing irreversible damage and gradually extending throughout the region.

To control this pathogen, the Apulia region has created a geodatabase of areas affected by Xf (i.e., infected, containment, and buffer zones), which is available through web mapping services. Various techniques, including non-invasive geomatics and remote sensing methods, have been employed to monitor the progression of the disease. This study presents preliminary results from the analysis of high-resolution three-dimensional point clouds acquired in the Gorgognolo area using a terrestrial Light Detection and Ranging (LiDAR) sensor.

To identify the impact of Xf on olive trees and to monitor the development of the infection, the work focuses on radiometric metrics, i.e. intensity. The results demonstrate how remote sensing technologies can be used to track plant diseases and assess the progression of infection.

Keywords: *Xylella fastidiosa* · LiDAR · Apulia Region · LiDAR intensity · plant disease monitoring

1 Introduction

The agricultural environment has deteriorated rapidly in recent decades due to multiple factors, including increasing anthropogenic pressure, pollution, the reckless use of agricultural land and water resources, the expansion of global trade and the evident and catastrophic effects of climate change. The world population is growing at a rate of 70

O. Gervasi et al. (Eds.): ICCSA 2025 Workshops, LNCS 15891, pp. 256–267, 2026.
https://doi.org/10.1007/978-3-031-97617-9_17

million per year [1], thus exacerbating the demand for food supply and posing new challenges for sustainable agricultural production and global food security [2]. Agricultural ecosystems in the Mediterranean area are also threatened and the protection of biodiversity, which is essential to ensure the stability of local ecosystems and agricultural production, has become a recognized priority and endorsed by the United Nations in Agenda 2030 in different Sustainable Development Goals(https://unric.org/it/agenda-2030/).

In Italy, the Apulia region, located in the south of the peninsula, is an emblematic example of this challenge. Well-known for its centuries-old olive groves, which constitute not only an economic resource but also a distinctive element of its cultural heritage and landscape [3, 4], Apulia has suffered the effects of climate change [5, 6], alongside the effects related to the spread of the bacterium *Xylella fastidiosa* (Xf). First identified in 2013 in the Salento district, Xf has rapidly proliferated, causing a significant drop in agricultural productivity, with tremendous economic impacts at a local and national scale. Infected areas cover more than 200.000 hectares, amounting to around 21 million trees and the associated huge financial losses.

The impact of this plant disease has irreversibly transformed the Apulian landscape, leading to the loss of productive olive trees and forcing farmers to shift cultivation practices, reducing agricultural biodiversity. However, countering the Xf pathogen has set new challenges, focused on increasing resilience to these potentially catastrophic events.

As a result, the crisis caused by *Xylella* is no longer an isolated issue in the phytosanitary sphere, but affects the entire economic, social and environmental context. On this side, the public awareness of Xf and effective communication on the related risk can help the public in fully understanding the problem, and lead policymakers in their management and prevention plans, as demonstrated in different research fields [7–9]. *Xylella*, initially confined to the olive groves of Salento, has now expanded to new crops, including almonds, cherries and vines, through its aggressive variants, thus raising the economic implications of its spread. For instance, almond production in Apulia covers about a third of the national requirement and is particularly vulnerable to infection. To cope with its spread, local and regional authorities have adopted a series of containment measures, set out in multiple decrees [10], which include the felling of infected plants and the continuous monitoring of hazardous areas. Since a way to permanently eradicate such epidemics is still under study, despite numerous scientific efforts and encouraging discoveries [11]. Monitoring is the only action that can be carried out to better understand this phenomenon. To fulfill these obligations and provide up-to-date and official information, the Apulia Region has set up a constantly updated database containing the perimeter of infected, containment and buffer zones, available via web platform at (https://webapps.sit.puglia.it/freewebapps/DatiFasceXF/index.html), in a user-friendly layout.

In the domain of environmental monitoring, and particularly for precision agriculture, geomatics is the discipline that assumes a cornerstone role [12]. Light Detection and Ranging (LiDAR) is one of the most promising non-invasive geomatic technologies [13–15]. When used with terrestrial devices like Terrestrial Laser Scanners (TLS), it constitutes an essential tool for obtaining precise dimensional information in both agricultural and forestry contexts [16]. Recent studies have demonstrated the potential of intensity-based segmentation techniques for vegetation analysis and classification [17]. These approaches exploit the radiometric response of LiDAR to improve the detection of physiological changes, providing a valuable complement to traditional and consolidated spectral data. This paper reports the results of an in-depth analysis of high-resolution three-dimensional point clouds, acquired by a TLS, on a set of olive trees located in the area of Gorgognolo (BR). The analysis focused on the understanding of the intensity parameter of the laser returns to distinguish the specific characteristics of the two main components of the tree: the trunk and the leaf canopy. Afterward, a detailed investigation of the progression of the *Xylella fastidiosa* infection, which seriously challenges the survival of the olive groves, has been carried out.

2 The Case Study

The Gorgognolo area, an agricultural territory near the town of Ostuni (BR), belongs to the Salento peninsula and is in the infected zone.

The investigated location, covering an area of approximately $8250\,m^2$, was surveyed for the first time in August 2023, referred to as T_0. Two additional measurements have been carried out in January 2024 (T_1) and May 2024 (T_2).

The Apulia Region's Phytosanitary Observatory has revised the extension of affected areas, now including Triggiano and Santeramo in Colle, and detected a new outbreak of the multiplex and pauca subspecies, recently identified respectively, near the southern township of Santeramo and Bari. Following an extensive monitoring activity, the Observatory published four official determinations (n. 91, 92, 93 and 94) [18], which provides an update of the classification of the areas bounded by subspecies and displays revised maps illustrating the location of the sampled plants and the corresponding laboratory results. In addition, through the decree of the Director of the Phytosanitary Observatory Section dated 23 August 2024, additional phytosanitary measures have been addressed and new subspecies (i.e. fastidiosa, multiplex and pauca) have been identified. The informations are regularly uploaded on the official website of the Apulia Region (www.eme rgenzaxylella.it). In order to address the increasingly critical situation, despite considerable efforts over the past decade, Resolution No. 1593 – 25 November 2024 [19] was issued, introducing an updated classification of infected areas. To give a visual idea of the progress of the pathogen, maps (Fig. 1) illustrating the situation in April 2024 and its latest update in November 2024 are shown.

3 Methodology Employed

In forestry, TLS technology is increasingly used to evaluate the geometric properties of plants [20]. By shooting laser pulses that rebound off neighbouring objects, the TLS measures the distance by timing the beam's return to the instrument. Along with the spatial coordinates, the collected data, which are visualized as point clouds, contain information on the intensity of the reflected signal [21, 22], which can be used to investigate the physical characteristics of the surface deep [23]. It should be noted that the

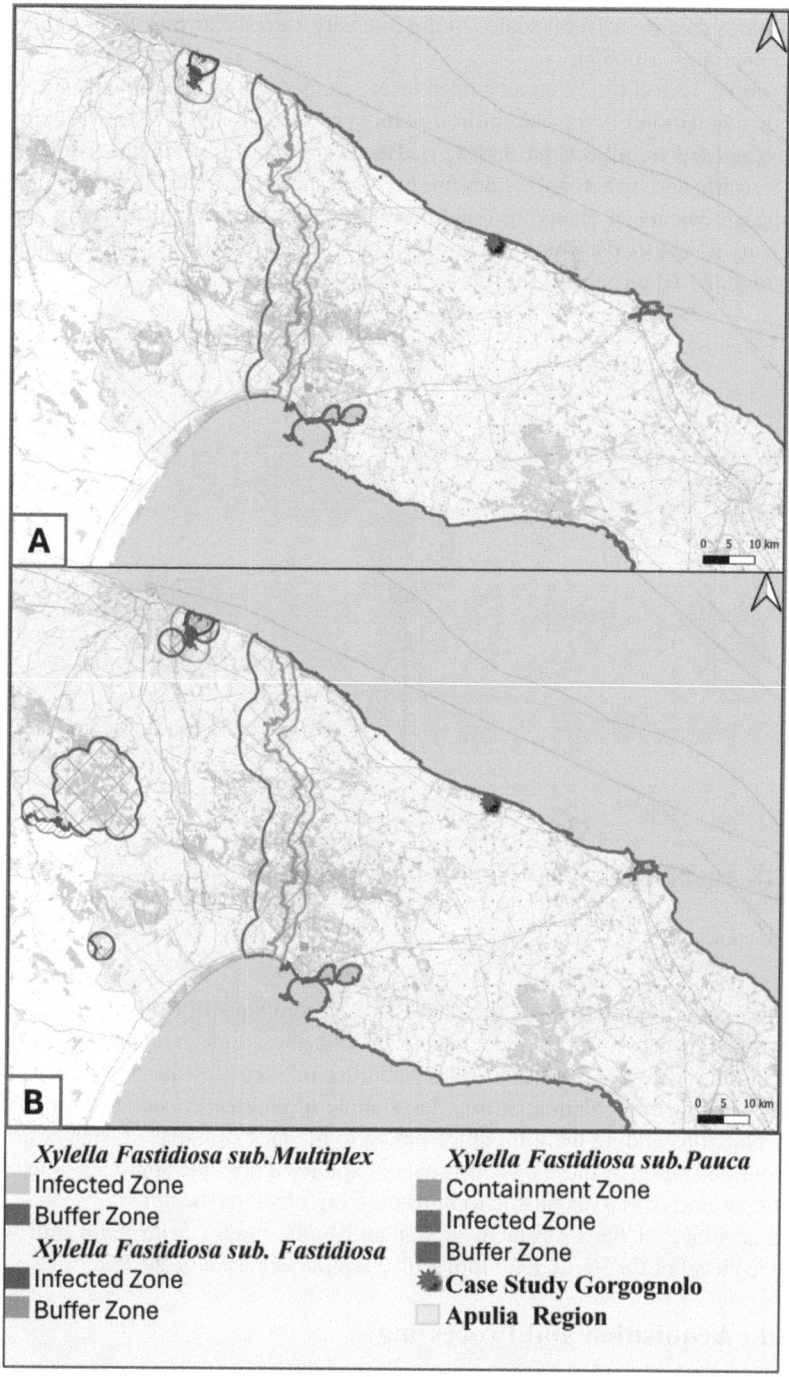

Fig. 1. Boundaries of the areas affected by *Xylella fastidiosa* (Apulia Region web map service) in April 2024 (A) and November 2024 (B). The study area is marked with a red star.

TLS provides data on a 16-bit scale, so the intensity values can vary from a minimum of 0 to a maximum of 65535.

A Trimble TX8 (Fig. 2), an advanced laser scanner with a maximum range of 300 m and an acquisition rate of one million points per second, and a laser wavelength of 1.5μm, was used to collect the data [24]. Because of the wavelengths available, the laser is less affected by aerosols and humidity than shorter wavelengths, ensuring more stable measurements in changing conditions [25]. The instrument produces precise, high-density point clouds, which can be enriched with colour (RGB) information thanks to the integrated 10 megapixel full-field camera.

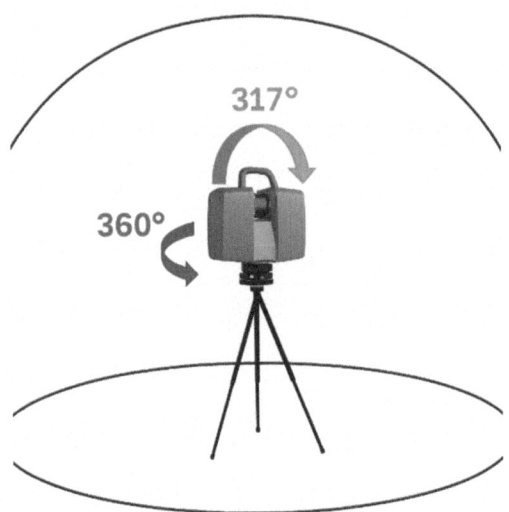

Fig. 2. The TLS used in Gorgognolo is characterized by a 34 mm beam diameter at 100 m, a 317° vertical field of view (FOV), limited below the laser scanner, and a horizontal 360° FOV, 80 μrad angular accuracy.

Determining the intensity of the data is a key component of this analysis, as this information may prove useful in identifying specific alterations in infected plants. Their interpretation, however, requires careful handling of variables that may affect signal intensity, such as triangulation, sitting, laser angle of incidence, and atmospheric conditions. Notwithstanding the difficulties linked to the lack of universal standardization for the normalization of these data, this paper explores a possible approach to using the intensity parameter as a diagnostic tool in assessing olive tree health.

The accuracy of the instrument in standard mode ranges from ±2.8 mm with a confidence level of 68.3% to ±8.5 mm with a confidence level of 99.7%.

4 Data Acquisition and Processing

The present work is framed in a monitoring campaign started in August 2023 and constitute a refinement of the analyses carried out previously and presented in [26]. In keeping with the expectations of reliable monitoring, scan positions, recorded by a geodetic

GNSS receiver, and operating modes have been set out in the first measurement and maintained through the whole period (Fig. 3). The complete single scan of the study area of approximately 8,250 m^2 took approximately five hours to complete, including positioning of the TLS stations, data acquisition and field control.

Fig. 3. Data acquisition in August 2023, January 2024, and May 2024, (T_0, T_1 and T_2).

The preliminary point cloud co-registration has been performed via Trimble Real-Works software (Trimble Navigation Limited, USA). The pairwise scan recording reached an average accuracy of 12mm, by using targets mounted on tripods as a reference (Fig. 4).

The point clouds were then processed using CloudCompare (https://www.cloudc ompare.org/) to remove noise and outliers, such as spikes or anomalous reflections. One of the filters used in the field was the SOR (Statistical Outlier Removal) algorithm, applied with default parameter settings to ensure the consistency and reliability of the dataset.

The analysis was performed targeting four olive trees, exemplary of the conditions in the study area, as they are characterized by different degrees of desiccation. The targeted trees are named as F,23,24,25 (Fig. 5).

Fig. 4. Raw point cloud acquired in the survey of May 2024, as displayed in Trimble Real Works.

5   Intensity Parameter Analysis

The opportunity of using the intensity radiometric parameter collected during TLS surveys to discriminate between different surface types has been investigated. By understanding and processing the data, it is possible to separate a tree into its main constitutive elements, namely leaves and trunk. However, the susceptibility of the intensity parameter to numerous factors such as environmental conditions (temperature, humidity and pressure), acquisition geometry (distance to the surveyed object, angle of incidence) and scanning mode can considerably affect the analysis [26]. The meteorological conditions during the three surveys ranged from a very summery climate, with peaks of 40 °C during the T_0 measurement to 10 °C in T_1, while the T_2 survey has been carried out in May 2024 in intermediate conditions with a temperature of about 25 °C. To account for this variability, the area containing the objects of interest was extracted, and the related intensity values were normalized on a scale from 0 to 10.

A cloud-to-cloud estimation was also carried out to evaluate changes in the geometry of the trees. Detected differences resulted in values comparable with the instrument sensitivity along the canopy surface, thus ensuring that at least the structural degradation of the wood has not occurred.

A sample of 4 trees, representative of the disease and its effects at different stages, was first segmented by building two macro classes containing trunk and leaves. The average intensity values and the associated standard deviation were then calculated for each class in T0 (Table 1). Once identified, these values were used as references in subsequent scans. Assuming that dry leaves behave as wood, the intervals useful to classify points as trunk or leaf were calculated considering an uncertainty equal to 2σ, thus generating a negligible overlapping zone equal to 0.03%, on the normalized intensity scale (the overlap interval is between 5.03 and 5.33).

Fig. 5. Basemap of the study area. Location of target trees is indicated by triangles and numbered (source: Google Earth Pro).

Table 1. Intensity value recorded in T_0

	Trunk (T_0)	Leaf (T_0)
Average Intensity	7.7	3.3
Std. dev.	1.34	0.98

The ranges obtained have been used to characterize the remaining scans, leading to the results shown in the following tables (Figs. 6 and 7).

The pictures are displayed in conjunction with the analyses carried out on the intensity parameter to emphasize how much this parameter closely mirrors the reality recorded during the three monitoring campaigns (T_0, T_1 and T_2).

The results' analysis shows that the tree identified as 23 is the most seriously damaged by the pathogen, with an increasing predominance of the class comparable to wood.

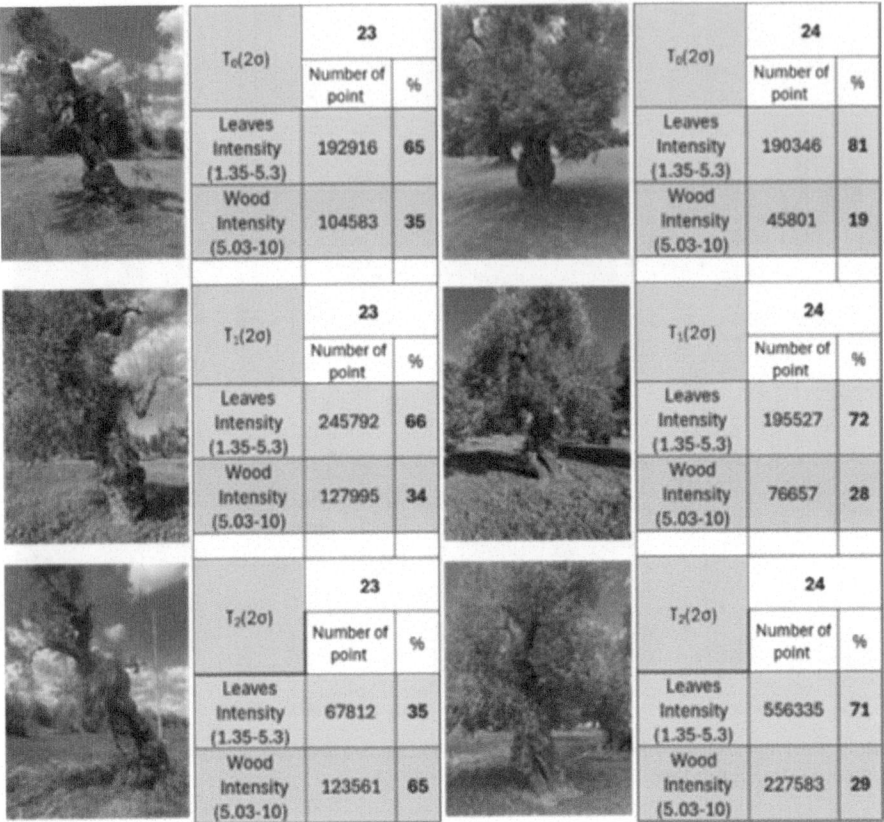

Fig. 6. Classification intensity value collected for every single year for 23 and 24. Pictures and percentage of leaves and wood in T_0, T_1 and T_2, obtained by classifying the point cloud by the intensity value, related to collected for every single year for 23 and 24. The corresponding pictures evidence the evolution of the infection

Over the same monitoring period, tree 25 showed a more uniform trend, with a gradual decrease of the number of points which intensity correspond to leaf between T_0, to T_2 (80%, 75%, 64%) and a simultaneous increase of the points classified as wood, indicating the onset of desiccation.

The least affected tree overall turns prominently out to be 24, as it shows percentages of healthy leaves ranging between 80 and 71%. Although the trend is negative, the tree is still relatively far from the final stage of infection. While tree F initially showed the same trend as tree 24 for T_0 and T_1, it progressed significantly in the last survey and reached a green leaf percentage of 34%.

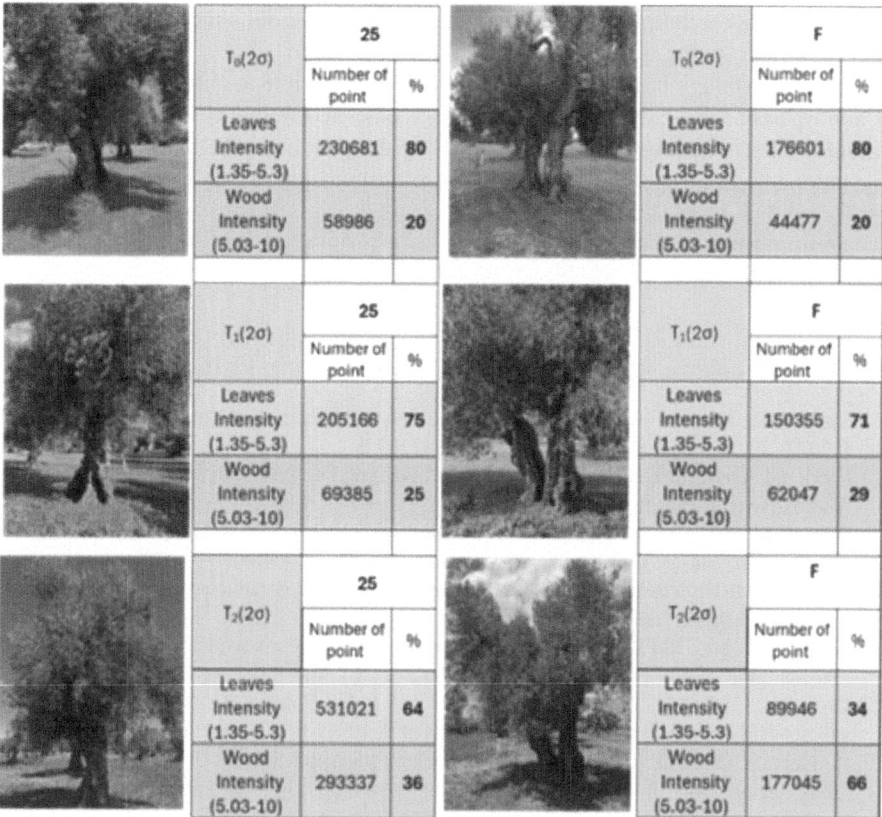

Fig. 7. Percentage of leaves and wood in T_0, T_1 and T_2, obtained by classifying the point cloud by the intensity value, related to 25 and F. The corresponding pictures evidence the evolution of the infection.

6 Conclusions, Remarks and Further Developments

The potential of adopting laser scanning technology to monitor the damages to olive trees caused by the *Xylella fastidiosa* was confirmed by the results obtained from the analysis of the laser intensity data. This is consistent with preliminary visual and qualitative analysis and confirms that laser intensity is a good proxy for detecting and controlling the progress of the Xf infection on olive trees. The classification between leaf and wood using the radiometric parameter of intensity at different time intervals provided the opportunity to show the progress of drying in the four targets, highlighting which trees are at an early stage of infection and the ones already severely affected by the disease.

However, due to the operator's experience in performing and processing the survey and the time required (approximately 1000 m^2/hour), static TLS is not the most cost-effective option for crops larger than one hectare. This problem could be overcome by using drone-mounted laser sensors, which can cover large areas in a relatively short time and with reduced operating costs. On the other hand, the accuracy of the observations collected by this technique is lower than an analogous dataset collected using a static TLS, so further testing is needed to verify its effectiveness.

The methodology proposed in the study makes it possible to operate independently of atmospheric and/or solar conditions, unlike other technologies such as NIR (Near Infrared), which, although a more than established solution in the field of monitoring vegetation and its physiological state, do not allow penetration inside the canopy.

Acknowledgments. The authors want to thank Dr. Pietro Sumeraro at ARIF PUGLIA (Agenzia Regionale Attività Irrigue e Forestali) for supporting the logistics.

References

1. Sadigov, R.: Rapid growth of the world population and its socioeconomic results. Sci. World J. **2022** (2022). https://doi.org/10.1155/2022/8110229
2. Food and Agriculture Organization of United Nation: The future of food and agriculture – Alternative pathways to 2050 (2018)
3. Acciani, C., de Gennaro, B.C., Fucilli, V., Roselli, L.: Valutazione dell'impatto economico e paesaggistico causato da *Xylella fastidiosa* sull'olivicoltura del Salento (2015)
4. Ciervo, M.: Il disseccamento degli olivi in Puglia, evidenze, contraddizioni, anomalie, scenari. Società Geografica Italiana (2020)
5. Gioia, A., Bruno, M.F., Totaro, V., Iacobellis, V.: Parametric assessment of trend test power in a changing environment. Sustain. (Switz.) **12** (2020). https://doi.org/10.3390/su12093889
6. Gioia, A., Totaro, V., Bonelli, R., Esposito, A.A.M.G., Balacco, G., Iacobellis, V.: Flood susceptibility evaluation on ephemeral streams of Southern Italy: a case study of Lama Balice. In: Gervasi, O., et al. Computational Science and Its Applications – ICCSA 2018. ICCSA 2018. Lecture Notes in Computer Science, vol. 10964, pp. 334–348. Springer, Cham (2018). https://doi.org/10.1007/978-3-319-95174-4_27
7. Wang, P., Li, Y., Zhang, Y.: An urban system perspective on urban flood resilience using SEM: evidence from Nanjing city, China. Nat. Hazards **109**, 2575–2599 (2021). https://doi.org/10.1007/s11069-021-04933-0
8. Santoro, S., Lovreglio, R., Totaro, V., Camarda, D., Iacobellis, V., Fratino, U.: Community risk perception for flood management: a structural equation modelling approach. Int. J. Disaster Risk Reduction **97**, 104012 (2023). https://doi.org/10.1016/j.ijdrr.2023.104012
9. Schweiger, E.W., Grace, J.B., Cooper, D., Bobowski, B., Britten, M.: Using structural equation modeling to link human activities to wetland ecological integrity. Ecosphere **7** (2016). https://doi.org/10.1002/ecs2.1548
10. DET_494_20_12_2023
11. Latino, M.E., Menegoli, M., Signore, F., Corallo, A., De Devitiis, B., Viscecchia, R.: Micro knowledge as a driver for systemic emergencies management: the case of Xylella in Italy. J. Knowl. Econ. (2024). https://doi.org/10.1007/s13132-024-02210-6
12. Escandón-Panchana, P., Herrera-Franco, G., Jaya-Montalvo, M., Martínez-Cuevas, S.: Geomatic tools used in the management of agricultural activities: a systematic review (2024). https://doi.org/10.1007/s10668-024-04576-8
13. Voegtle, T., Schwab, I., Landes, T.: Influences of different materials on the measurements of a terrestrial laser scanner (TLS). Int. Arch. Photogrammetry Remote Sens. Spat. Inf. Sci. (2008)
14. Baiocchi, V., et al.: First geomatic restitution of the sinkhole known as 'Pozzo del Merro' (Italy), with the integration and comparison of 'classic' and innovative geomatic techniques. Environ. Earth Sci. **77** (2018). https://doi.org/10.1007/s12665-018-7244-6

15. Fascia, R., Barbieri, F., Gaspari, F., Ioli, F., Pinto, L.: From 3D survey to digital reality of a complex architecture: a digital workflow for cultural heritage promotion. In: International Archives of the Photogrammetry, Remote Sensing and Spatial Information Sciences - ISPRS Archives, pp. 205–212. International Society for Photogrammetry and Remote Sensing (2024). https://doi.org/10.5194/isprs-Archives-XLVIII-2-W4-2024-205-2024

16. Spadavecchia, C., Campos, M.B., Piras, M., Puttonen, E., Shcherbacheva, A.: Wood-leaf unsupervised classification of silver birch trees for biomass assessment using oblique point clouds. In: International Archives of the Photogrammetry, Remote Sensing and Spatial Information Sciences - ISPRS Archives, pp. 1795–1802. International Society for Photogrammetry and Remote Sensing (2023). https://doi.org/10.5194/isprs-archives-XLVIII-1-W2-2023-1795-2023

17. Miao, Y., Wang, L., Peng, C., Li, H., Zhang, M.: Single plant segmentation and growth parameters measurement of maize seedling stage based on point cloud intensity. Smart Agric. Technol. **9** (2024). https://doi.org/10.1016/j.atech.2024.100665

18. ATTO DIRIGENZIALE, N. 00109 del 23/08/2024 del Registro delle Determinazioni della AOO 1810

19. DEL_1593_2024

20. Spadavecchia, C., Belcore, E., Grasso, N., Piras, M.: A fully automatic forest parameters extraction at single-tree level: a comparison of MLS and TLS applications. In: International Archives of the Photogrammetry, Remote Sensing and Spatial Information Sciences - ISPRS Archives. pp. 457–463. International Society for Photogrammetry and Remote Sensing (2023). https://doi.org/10.5194/isprs-archives-XLVIII-1-W1-2023-457-2023

21. Tan, K., Zhang, W., Shen, F., Cheng, X.: Investigation of TLS intensity data and distance measurement errors from target specular reflections. Remote Sens. (Basel) **10**, 1077 (2018). https://doi.org/10.3390/rs10071077

22. Kaasalainen, S., Krooks, A., Kukko, A., Kaartinen, H.: Radiometric calibration of terrestrial laser scanners with external reference targets. Remote Sens. (Basel) **1**, 144–158 (2009). https://doi.org/10.3390/rs1030144

23. Peppe, P.J., et al.: High-resolution geomatic and geophysical techniques integrated with chemical analyses for the characterization of a Roman wall. J. Cult. Herit. **17**, 141–150 (2016). https://doi.org/10.1016/j.culher.2015.06.005

24. Almukhtar, A., Saeed, Z.O., Abanda, H., Tah, J.H.M.: Reality capture of buildings using 3D laser scanners. Civil Eng. **2**, 214–235 (2021). https://doi.org/10.3390/civileng2010012

25. SCHEDA TECNICA Caratteristiche principali Trimble TX8 (2013)

26. Pagano, N.: Using the intensity values obtained from terrestrial laser scanner for monitoring the effects of plant disease: the case study of Gorgognolo (Italy). In: Gervasi, O., et al. (eds.) Computational Science and Its Applications – ICCSA 2024. LNCS, vol. 14226, pp. 245–259. Springer, Cham (2024). https://doi.org/10.1007/978-3-031-65282-0_16

GIS-Based Approach to Evaluate the Photovoltaic Potential of a Territory: The Case Study of the Municipality of San Severo in the Apulia Region

Alberico Sonnessa[1]($\boxtimes$) (iD), Michele Vomero[2], Antonio Leone[3] (iD), Nicolina Ripa[2] (iD), and Micaela Falcone[1] (iD)

[1] Department of Civil, Environmental, Land, Construction and Chemistry (DICATECh), Politecnico di Bari, Via Orabona 4, 70125 Bari, Italy
{alberico.sonnessa,micaela.falcone}@poliba.it
[2] Università degli Studi della Tuscia, Via S.M. in Gradi n.4, 01100 Viterbo, Italy
{michele.vomero,nripa}@unitus.it
[3] Università del Salento, Piazza Tancredi, 7, 73100 Lecce, Italy
antonio.leone@unisalento.it

Abstract. This study explores a Geographic Information Systems (GIS)-based approach to assess the photovoltaic (PV) potential of a specific territory, focusing on the municipality of San Severo in the Apulia Region, Italy. The research highlights the growing need for renewable energy sources (RES) in response to climate change and the global energy transition. Using GIS, the study evaluates solar radiation, land use, and technical constraints to identify suitable locations for PV installations, including agrivoltaic systems that integrate agriculture and solar energy production. The methodology combines spatial analysis and environmental data to optimize energy planning while considering landscape and policy constraints. The results demonstrate the effectiveness of GIS tools in supporting sustainable energy development and local decision-making processes. This case study provides a replicable model for assessing solar energy potential in other regions with similar climatic and geographical characteristics.

Keywords: Renewable Energy Sources (RES) · GIS · photovoltaic systems · agrivoltaics · climate change · energy transition

1 Introduction

Critical long-term phenomena, such as climate change, have a direct impact on the cities, their pollution and rainfall levels, the aging of buildings and the relative energy consumption [1–3]. In the light of this, the ongoing climate emergency requires an integrated approach that must encompass the energy transition towards renewable sources [4, 5], in order to speed up the decarbonization process.

Renewable Energy Sources (RES) have the potential to produce clean and low-cost energy, being a driver for the enhancement and development of the territory by

O. Gervasi et al. (Eds.): ICCSA 2025 Workshops, LNCS 15891, pp. 268–284, 2026.
https://doi.org/10.1007/978-3-031-97617-9_18

sharing locally generated energy through models called Renewable Energy Communities (RECs) [6, 7]. In this scenario, photovoltaic (PV) technology plays a leading role for the achievement of the 2050 decarbonization targets, provided by European Union (EU) [8, 9], and national legislation through the Integrated National Energy and Climate Plan (Piano Nazionale Integrato per l'Energia il Clima – PNIEC) [10, 11]. Since ground-based PV farms compete with food production for land allocation, solutions as agrivoltaic systems (APV), namely the shared use of land for food and energy production, allow to implement PV minimizing the related land use [12, 13]. As European, national and regional policies related to RES, in particular the above-mentioned models of energy production and consumption with low environmental impact, require to consider the impact on the agricultural sector, the location of electricity production plants in areas classified as agricultural must take into account this indication, with particular reference to the enhancement of local agri-food traditions, the protection of biodiversity, as well as the cultural heritage and the rural landscape. RECs and agri/photovoltaic systems can help to achieve the objectives within the framework of energy and climate policies at EU and national level and are also a promising solution to grow clean energy in an integrated way with the territory, in a systemic vision that holds together ecology, energy, landscape, with a view to the multifunctionality to which the agricultural systems should tend.

To this end, this research work wants to explore in a GIS environment, built through the Quantum GIS (QGIS) open suite [14], the energy potential, connected with the extensive use of photovoltaic systems installed on existing buildings and agricultural areas, of the Municipality of San Severo belonging to the Apulia Region and located in the southern of Italy, where, as the average irradiation values are among the highest in the Italian peninsula, these plants are generally characterized by high performances [15]. GIS tools have been extensively used to evaluate the economics of utility-scale photovoltaic system [16], to identify the optimal sites for PV power plants [17–19] and assess the photovoltaic potential of particular areas [20, 21]. The specialization of a part of rural areas towards this this form of energy production could represent an effective response to climate change and a reduction in dependence on fossil fuels to mitigate related economic and environmental impacts [22].

2 The Study Area

San Severo is an Italian municipality of about 50000 inhabitants located in the northern part of the Apulian territory close to the borders with Molise region. The economy of this area, based on mercantile and agricultural traditions, it is essentially focused on the tertiary sector. The municipality, positioned at the center of a road network in the northern part of the Tavoliere delle Puglie, which is the second largest plain in the peninsular Italy after the Po Valley, extends between the Dauni Mountains to the west, the Gargano promontory and the Adriatic Sea to the east, the Fortore river to the north and the Ofanto river to the south (Fig. 1).

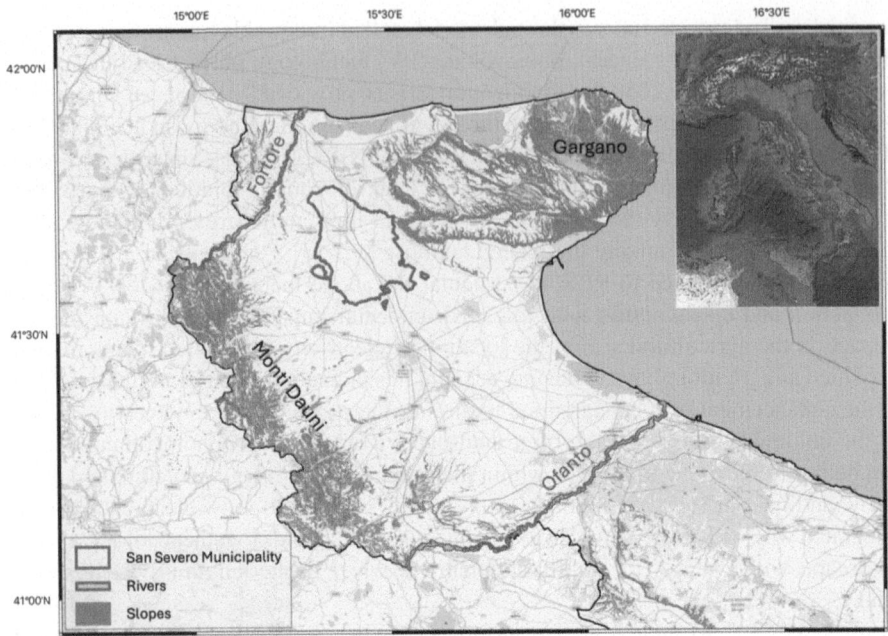

Fig. 1. The municipality of San Severo (highlighted in red), located in the Tavoliere delle Puglie plain (base layer: OpenStreetMap).

3 Methodology of Investigation

The proposed methodological approach aims to create a prototype for a dynamic database easily accessible through a GIS environment and useful for territorial planning purposes, from which retrieving the diffusion of the RES already present in urban and rural areas, as well as the determination of the areas suitable for the installation of plants and the related potential to cover the energy needs of the local community, obtainable from a photovoltaic source.

The investigation has been based on the following steps:

1. the definition of the GIS model, entailing the delimitation of the boundaries and the size of the study area, the choice of the datum and the basic information layers;
2. the acquisition of a vector cartography at an adequate scale (i.e. 1:5000) so as to be able to build a digital model capable of representing the elements of interest (buildings, sites, existing plants, etc.), the complex morphology of the built urban space and the rural one. Specifically, the technical and thematic maps made available through the Sistema Informativo Territoriale (S.I.T.) - Puglia portal [23] (namely digital orthophoto and Regional Technical Map (CTR) were used as base informative layer). The cadastral database has been also added into the system to retrieve information on the surfaces available for hosting photovoltaic modules;
3. the computation of the energy demand at municipal level retrieved by analyzing public databases;

4. the area potentially available for agrivoltaics plants, according to the legislative requirements;
5. the set-up of a quantitative indicator useful to evidence the solar energetic potential at urban and rural scale, to quantify the efficiency of a possible massive use of RES on the study area;
6. as conclusive step, the analysis of locally available energy resources by deriving the potential annual total amount of energy production from RES, in GWh.

Since energy planning cannot disregard the available resources of the territory, the possible location of new production plants has been optimized according to the criteria established for the identification of surfaces and areas suitable (or not suitable) for the installation of renewable energy plants. In this phase of the work, the guidelines and regulatory instruments on renewable energy sources specified in the following sections were taken into consideration. On this basis, the photovoltaic potential of plants located in rural areas and on buildings have been derived following the provisions dictated by technical standards and legislative instruments.

4   Energy Balance at Municipal Level

4.1   Quantitative Analysis of Current Energy Consumption

To properly plan the actions to be taken for sustainable development with a view to energy transition, it is essential to consider the data relating to the energy demand for electricity. To this end, publicly accessible databases have been analyzed, and specifically:

1. as regards the demographic development, the National Statistical Institute (ISTAT) database containing the number of families, inhabitants and production activities;
2. for electricity consumption, the information provided by Terna S.p.A, manager of the national electrical distribution network, albeit as aggregate values at a provincial level.

Starting from the energy consumption at provincial level, the electricity consumed by the municipality of San Severo has been estimated based on the value per inhabitant available for the province of Foggia, as well as the distribution of local consumption in the sectors of agriculture, domestic industry and services, obtaining a total amount of 152.70 GWh for the year 2022. Table 1 and Fig. 2 show the energy requirements for the reference year in the study area, with a focus on the domestic and agricultural consumption.

The domestic consumption amounts to 29%, while the agricultural sector covers 7% of the total electricity demand. The share of energy consumption of the agricultural and domestic sectors, as equivalent CO_2 emissions, according to the respective emission factor for national gross thermal production, with an estimated average value of 415.5 g CO_2/kWh, results into 227153.9 tons of CO_2 equivalent of greenhouse gas emissions in one year (Tables 2 and 3).

Table 1. Average electric consumption, municipality of San Severo (FG).

PROVINCE OF FOGGIA				
ELECTRICITY CONSUMPTION (GWh per Year) – source Terna S.p.A. 2022				
YEAR	AGRICULTURE	HOUSEHOLD	INDUSTRY	SERVICES	TOT.
2022	118.46	545.31	537.05	649.77	1848.59
MUNICIPALITY OF SAN SEVERO				
ELECTRICITY CONSUMPTION (GWh per Year)				
YEAR	AGRICULTURE	HOUSEHOLD	INDUSTRY	SERVICES	TOT.
2022	9.79	44.88	44.36	53.67	152.70

DEMOGRAPHIC DATA (Istat 2022)		
	Population	N. of families
Prov. of Foggia	599028.00	
Mun. of San Severo	49481.00	20446.00

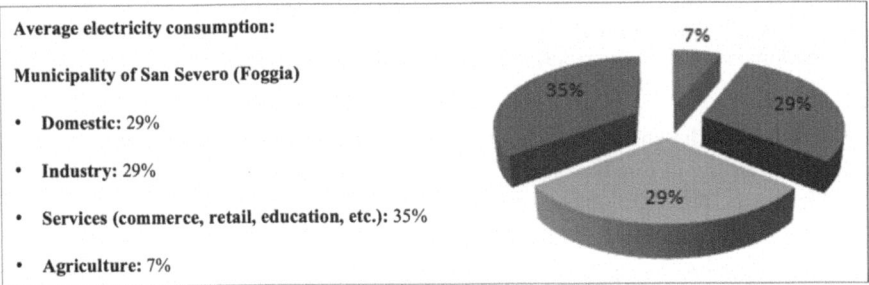

Average electricity consumption:

Municipality of San Severo (Foggia)

- **Domestic: 29%**
- **Industry: 29%**
- **Services (commerce, retail, education, etc.): 35%**
- **Agriculture: 7%**

Fig. 2. Average electric consumption of each category, municipality of San Severo (FG).

Table 2. CO_2 emissions by the agricultural and domestic sectors.

CO$_2$ EMISSIONS (tons)			
Year	AGRICULTURE	DOMESTIC	TOT.
2022	40677.50	186476.40	227153.90

4.2 Energy Plants in the Study Area and Annual Energy Needs

The renewable energies plants, whether from photovoltaics or wind, are by their nature scattered throughout the territory. It is then fundamental to evaluate the impact of already existing plants on the decision-making process. In the following table, the energetic balance of the municipality is analyzed, with a focus on the electricity consumption in the above-mentioned sectors, and the corresponding RES production. A geographic database, containing the main information on renewable energy production plants, has been built starting from the information made available by the Italian Energy Services Manager (Gestore Servizi Energetici – GSE) through the Atlaimpianti Webgis [24], and integrated with the CTR and the cadastral map (Fig. 3).

Table 3. RES energy balance at municipal level.

Energy balance – Municipality of San Severo (GWh/year)					
Sector	AGRICULTURE	DOMESTIC	INDUSTRY	SERVICES	TOT.
Total demand	9.79	44.88	44.36	53.67	152.70
Total production	4.75	1.63	0.08	0.23	6.69
Deficit	-5.04	-43.25	-44.28	-53.44	-146.01

5 Assessment of the Agrivoltaic Potential

The potential of agrivoltaic of the San Severo territory has been then explored, by identifying the areas with compatibility and sustainability characteristics according to the legislative requirements. Aside of the inevitable land consumption, these infrastructures impact on the surrounding environment also in terms of landscape. Therefore, the relation between areas suitable and not suitable to host these plants has been explored in the GIS environment, to quickly deduce the presence and territorial diffusion of photovoltaic technologies in urban areas and agrivoltaics technologies in rural areas, with the aim of supporting future planning operations.

5.1 Relationship with Energy Planning Tools

The identification of areas suitable for the installation of renewable energy plants, functional to the achievement of the objectives set by the PNIEC, followed the indications in the Legislative Decree no. 199/2021 (par.8) and the Ministerial Decree of 21 June 2024, "Regulations for the identification of surfaces and areas suitable for the installation of renewable infantry plants", according to the context of the Municipality of San Severo (Table 4). The identified areas are shown in Fig. 4.

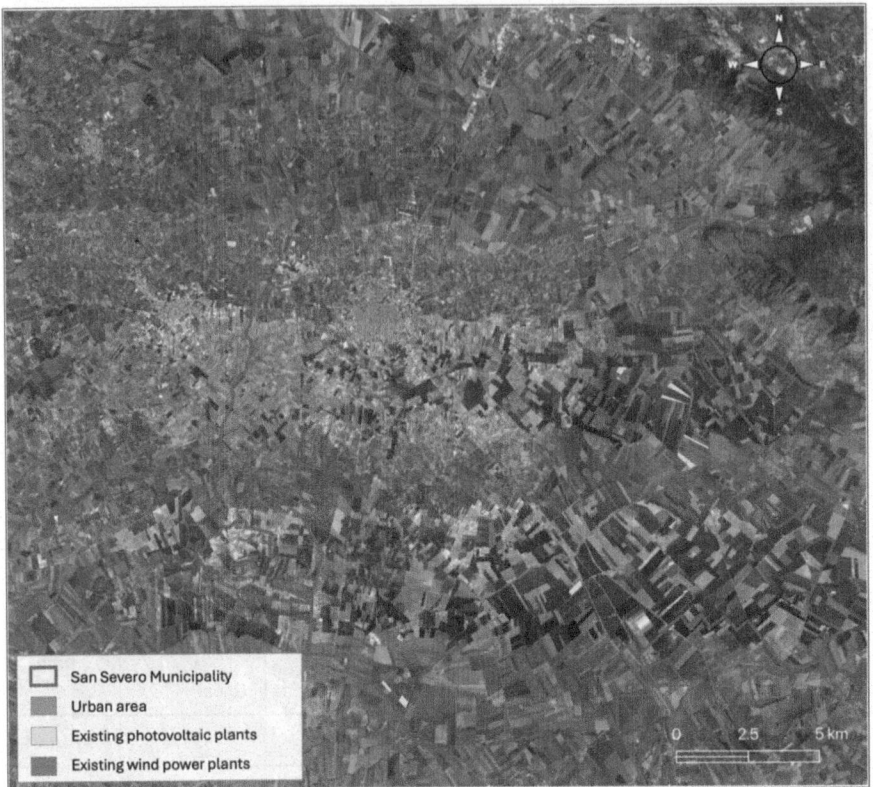

San Severo Municipality
Urban area
Existing photovoltaic plants
Existing wind power plants

Fig. 3. Existing power plants using renewable resources (base layer:Ortophoto 2019).

5.2 Relationship with the Objectives of Protection

Environmental and landscape requirements have been considered according to the provisions of the current national legislation regarding unsuitable areas and the related planning tools at regional and local level, as follow:

- Ministerial Decree 10–09-2010 National Guidelines for the procedure referred to in Article 12 of Legislative Decree no. 387 of 29 December 2003 for the authorization of the construction and operation of plants for the production of electricity from renewable sources;
- Legislative Decree no. 42 of 22 January 2004, Code of Cultural Heritage and Landscape, pursuant to Article 10 of Law no. 137 of 6 July 2002;
- Puglia Region, R.R. 24/2010, "Guidelines for the authorization of plants powered by renewable sources";
- Regional Territorial Landscape Plan (P.P.T.R.) of Puglia;
- P.U.G. of the Municipality of San Severo;
- Hydrogeological Asset Plan (P.A.I.).

The corresponding areas and their extension are shown in Table 5 and Fig. 5.

Table 4. Area suitable for agrivoltaic system according to the Italian regulatory framework.

	Suitable areas, *ex lege*	Area (m²)
	Existing plants where modification interventions, are carried out for refurbishment, enhancement or complete reconstruction, and do not involve a change in the occupied area of more than 20% (rural areas)	1047888.00
★	Areas subject to remediation identified pursuant to Title V, Part IV, of Legislative Decree No. 152 of 3 April 2006 (Environmental Code)	65860.00
	Sites and facilities available to Italian State Railways group and railway infrastructure managers as well as motorway concessionaires	114890.00
	Agricultural areas enclosed in a perimeter within 500 meters from areas for industrial/artisanal/commercial use, including sites of national interest, quarries and mines	116218051.00
	Areas inside industrial plants and plants, the latter as defined by Article 268, paragraph 1, letter h) of Legislative Decree no. 152 of 3 April 2006	2929174.00
	Areas adjacent to the motorway network within 300 metres	12698667.00

5.3 Net Area Usable for Agrivoltaic Plants

The net available area has been first computed in the GIS environment by corelating the planning tools and the regulatory prescription (Fig. 6 and Table 6).

6 Potential of Solar Energy

As part of the methods of using RES for production purposes, photovoltaics, unlike other renewable sources, can be integrated into existing building structures, with an improvement in the energy performance of buildings both in terms of reducing consumption and increasing the use of renewable sources.

Thanks to the favorable location, the municipality of San Severo has an annual global radiation of 1894.00 kWh/m², with an annual production of energy from PV of 1462.00 kWh for 1 kWp of photovoltaic installed.

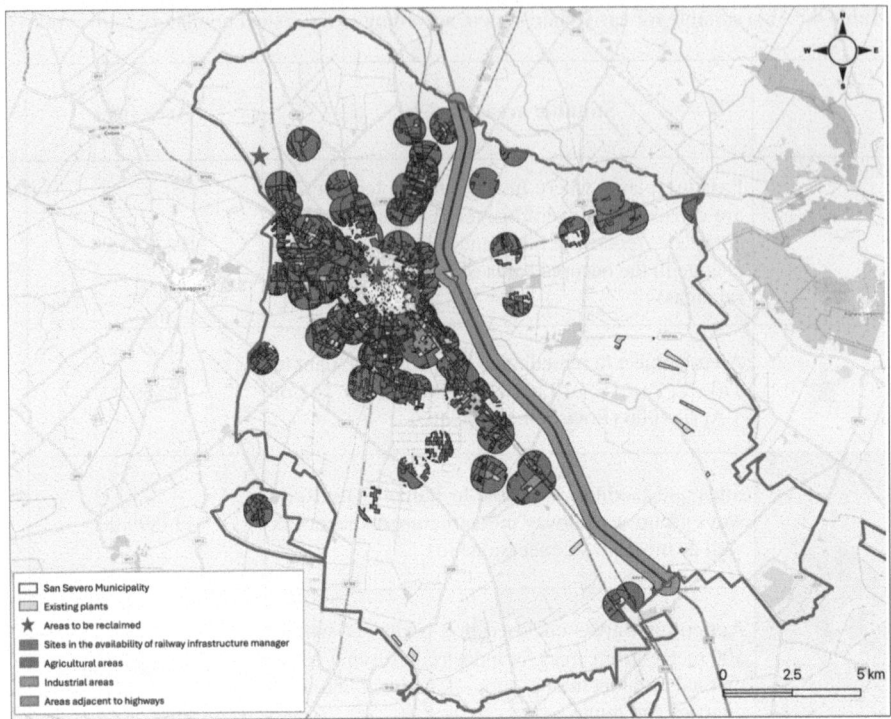

Fig. 4. Area suitable for agrivoltaic system in the municipality of San Severo (base layer:OpenStreetMap).

With the aim of quantifying the efficiency of a possible massive use of RES on the study area, quantitative indicators have been set up to analyze the energetic potential at urban and rural scale.

6.1 Photovoltaic Potential Indicator – Agrivoltaics Plants

To infer an indicator of the producibility of an agrivoltaic plant, reference was made to national and European technical and legislative regulations, summarized by the following indications:

- Minimum area to be dedicated to cultivation (agricultural area - Aa) $\geq 0,7$ of the total available area (Taa), to consider the need of preserving areas dedicated exclusively to the cultivation, in compliance with Good Agricultural Practices (Buone Pratiche Agricole – BPA) [25];
- Level of shading generated by the plant on the ground, expressed as the maximum acceptable percentage of total area covered by modules (LAOR- Land Area Occupation Ratio), computed as the ratio between the total overall area of the agrivoltaic system (Toa) and the total available area (Taa), and set on 40%;

To estimate the production potential of the plant, the use of a standard monocrystalline photovoltaic module, with half-cut technology cells and integrated power optimizer,

Table 5. Area unsuitable for agrivoltaic system.

	AGRIVOLTAIC SYSTEMS – Unsuitable areas		
	Protection bond	**PPTR/PUG**	**Area (m²)**
	Areas located near **archaeological parks** and in **areas bordering emergencies of particular cultural, historical and/or religious interest**	*Area of respect for cultural and settlement components (100m-30m). (sheep track network)*	24327312.00
		Area of respect for cultural and settlement components (100m-30m). (historical and cultural sites)	
		Area of respect for cultural and settlement components (100m-30m) (areas of archaeological interest)	
	Wetlands of international importance designated under the Ramsar Convention	*Wetlands*	6200.00
	Areas characterized by **situations of hydrogeological instability and/or risk** delimited in the **Hydrogeological Asset Plans (P.A.I.)** adopted by the competent Basin Authorities pursuant to Legislative Decree 180/98 and subsequent amendments.	*Hydrographic network connecting the Regional Ecological Network. (100m)*	28290742.00
		Rivers, streams, watercourses registered in the lists of public waters (150m).	11317914.00
		Areas subject to hydrogeological constraints	31777152.00
	Areas identified pursuant to Article 142 of Legislative Decree 42 of 2004 by assessing the existence of characteristics incompatible with the construction of the plants.	*Consolidated city*	2492415.00
		Woods	17175.00

sizing 1.80x1.15, and characterized by 360W (0.36 kW) of power and 23.5% of efficiency (European average value of plant productivity) has been assumed.

The PV annual production has been calculated using the Photovoltaic Geographical Information System (PVGIS) [26], a free web application developed by the Energy Efficiency and Renewables Unit of the European Commission's Joint Research Centre, that allows the user to get data on solar radiation and PV system energy production, at any place in most parts of the world [27]. The photovoltaic potential of an agrivoltaic plant (PVAGRI), located in the Municipality of San Severo, resulted in 0.236 GWh/ha/year (Table 7).

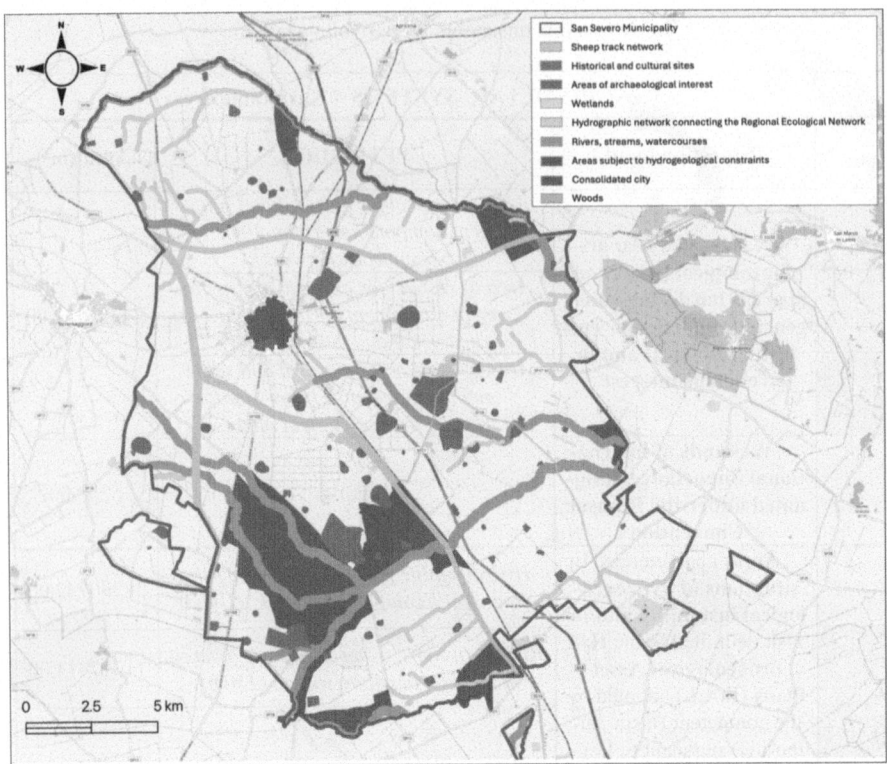

Fig. 5. Unsuitable areas for agrivoltaic system in the municipality of San Severo.

Table 6. Area usable for agrivoltaics plants.

Usable area (m^2)	Usable area (Ha)
12698668.00	1269.87

6.2 Photovoltaic Potential Indicator – Plants on Buildings

The estimation of the production potential of building roofs has been carried out assuming the use of the same standard type of monocrystalline photovoltaic module, while two classes of building roofing have been identified. In order to assess the space required for the installation of the photovoltaic generator with a reference power of 1 kWp, according to the provisions of the Italian Electrotechnical Committee (CEI) 82-25 standard [28], two fundamental cases were distinguished: (a) photovoltaic generator placed on a suitably inclined surface (e.g. pitched roof); – and on a horizontal surface (flat roof, terrace, etc.). The coverage ratio, computed using the mean latitude of the municipality of San Severo (41°41′23′), and following the CEI 82-25 (3.22, 4.3.1 a/b) standards, is equal to 51,42%. For both types of roofing, through PVGIS, the net production of electricity referred to the installation of a photovoltaic system with a power of 1 kWp was

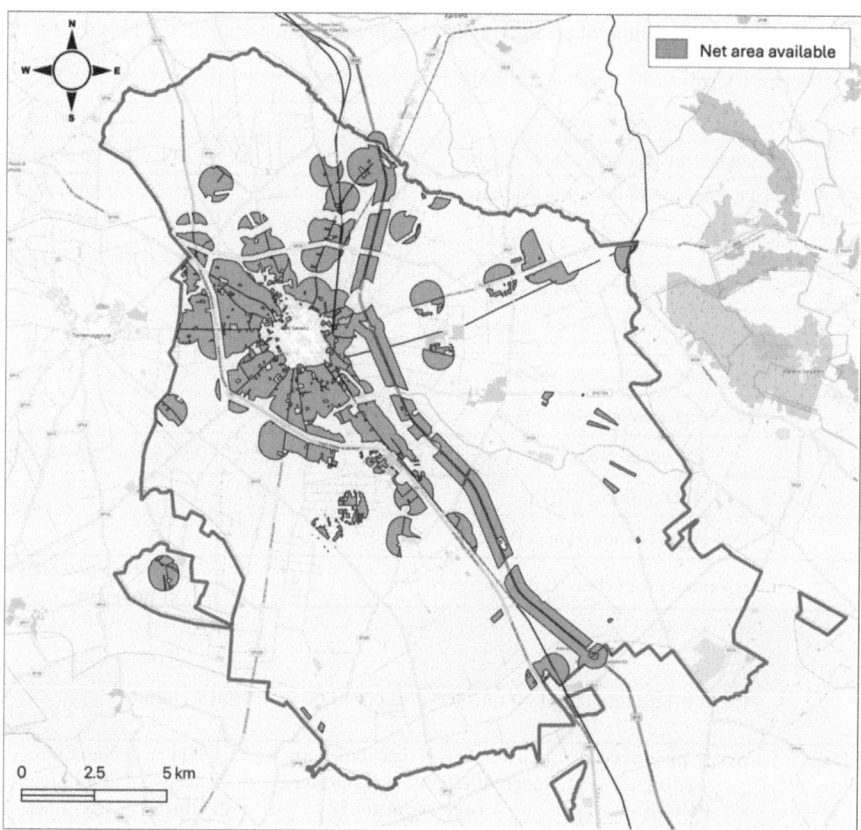

Fig. 6. Net area available for agrivoltaic plants (base layer: OpenStreetMap).

calculated and related to the net coverage available for the installation in the two cases (Tables 8, 9 and 10).

7 Analysis of Locally Available Energy Resources

Following the estimate of the surface area potentially available for the installation of photovoltaic systems and related assumptions on the photovoltaic power potentially installable, and using the indicator derived in the previous section, the potential annual total amount of energy production from RES, in GWh, has been computed. Several factors can affect the surface available for new PV systems, such as chimneys, air conditioning systems, shading from construction elements or nearby buildings.

JRC estimates that the percentage of roofs suitable for hosting plants can vary, at urban level, between 49 and 64%. A further 60% reduction is due to the distance between the panels to allow maintenance [29] (Table 11).

Additional power coming from agrivoltaics that could be installed in rural areas, without increasing land consumption, and would lead to an electricity production of about 46.00 GW (Table 12).

Table 7. PV potential of an agrivoltaic plant in the municipality of San Seevro

		Ha	m^2
Total available area	Taa	1	10000.00
Minimum area for agricultural activity	Aa ≥ 0,7 Taa		7000.00
Total overall area of the agrivoltaic system	Toa		3000.00
Max. acceptable percentage of area covered by modules	LAOR = 40 %		1200.00
Area covered by modules (%)	LAOR (≤40 %)		30%
Single monocrystalline photovoltaic module size			2.07
Number of implantable modules	435		
Total peak power x hectare (kWp)	**156.600**		
PV annual production	302563.51	Derived through PVGIS	
Total loss (%) -22.15	67017.82		
Net annual production (kWh)	**235545.69**		
PV Net annual production (GWh/ha/year)	**0.24**	**Agrivoltaic potential indicator**	

Table 8. Energy supplied into the grid based on the PVGIS output.

Peak Power 1 kWp	Energy produced, according to PVGIS	Power losses (incidence angle, spectral effects, low temperature/radiation)	Net Energy Produced	Net Energy Produced (GWh)
Tot.kWh	1456.21	-307.55	1148.66	0.00115

Table 9. Photovoltaic system placed on an inclined surface.

Standard CEI 82-25 (4.3.1.a)		Photovoltaic potential indicator (kWh/m^2)
(Kw/module efficiency=23,5%)		
Minimum usable surface area for 1kWp generator installation (m^2)	Number of panels	
4.26	2	269.93

Thus, the potential annual total amount (urban PV and agrivoltaic) of energy production from RES, equal to **365.49 GWh**, would be sufficient to entirely cover the needs municipality of San Severo, while generating a surplus of energy.

Table 10. Photovoltaic system placed on a horizontal surface.

Standard CEI 82-25 (4.3.1.b)		Photovoltaic potential indicator (kWh/m²)
Coverage ratio=51,42%.		
Minimum usable surface area for 1kWp generator installation (m²)	Number of panels	
4.26*1.51=6.44	3	178.27

Table 11. Urban area: surface potentially available for the installation of PV on roofs and associate annual production.

Existing plants			
Urban built area	Total area (m²)	Nominal power installed (kWp)	Annual production (GWh)
	438375.00	2306.84	1.94
Potentially available areas			
Roofs	Surface (m²)	Suitable roofs (64%)	Reduction rate for maintenance (60%)	Net surface (m²)
	1439668.00	21388.00	-552832.00	368555.00
Photovoltaic potential indicator (kWh/m²)			178.27
		kWh	65702301.28
	Annual production (GWh)		65.70

Table 12. Rural area: surface potentially available for the installation of agrivoltaic plants and associate production.

	Usable area (m²)	Usable area (Ha)
Agrivoltaics	12698668.00	1269.87
Agrivoltaic potential indicator (GWh/Ha)		0.24
Annual production (GWh)		299.69

8 Discussion and Final Remarks

The presented work was aimed at investigating the potential photovoltaic production capacity of the municipality of San Severo, located in the south of Italy, by corelating different spatial data in a GIS environment. To this purpose, digital cartography, cadastral data, geo-located information about the existing plants built from the database provided by the Italian Energy Services Manager and models assessing the annual production of photovoltaic plants installed on edifices and agricultural areas have been jointly analyzed. This allowed the production of reasoned maps and quantitative results describing the examined area, useful to highlight its energy potential and the issues related to the correct location of photovoltaic technologies as well as their compatibility with the urban and rural space. The outcomes show how, in principle, the municipality of San Severo could entirely satisfy its energy needs using only renewable energy and generate an energetic surplus.

As highlighted in [30], this methodology evidence some critical aspects, as the identification of the input parameters derived from low-precision databases, or the general lack in the evaluation of the panel degradation throughout its life cycle. Also, the daily variable productivity is often not considered, and geomatics data availability/resolution represents a discriminating factor. Therefore, the building typology analyzed has been standardized to simplify the study.

Nevertheless, even simplified, this study evidences once again the importance of a GIS-based approach in the evaluation and management of energy systems and as a support territorial planning, as it allows to quantify in advance the photovoltaic potential in territorial contexts, however, heterogeneous and complex. The advantage of this methodology is also linked to its high flexibility and scalability, which allows the automatic extension of the assessment of production potential from the single site of specific interest to an entire municipal area, since the workflow analyzed in this study could be easily replied. This certainly can support the planning activities required by the municipalities within the objectives set at national and European level in the energetic field, playing a key role in the growing shift towards renewable energy sources.

References

1. Sonnessa, A., Cantatore, E., Esposito, D., Fiorito, F.: A multidisciplinary approach for multi-risk analysis and monitoring of influence of SODs and RODs on historic centres: the ResCUDE project. In: Gervasi, O., et al. Computational Science and Its Applications – ICCSA 2020. ICCSA 2020. Lecture Notes in Computer Science, vol. 12252, pp. 752–766. Springer, Cham (2020). https://doi.org/10.1007/978-3-030-58811-3_54
2. Cantatore, E., Esposito, D., Sonnessa, A.: Mapping the multi-vulnerabilities of outdoor places to enhance the resilience of historic urban districts: the case of the apulian region exposed to slow and rapid-onset disasters. Sustain. (Switz.) **15** (2023). https://doi.org/10.3390/su1519 14248
3. Mascitelli, A., et al.: Cultural heritage resilience in the face of extreme weather: lessons from the UNESCO site of Alberobello. Sustain. (Switz.) **15** (2023). https://doi.org/10.3390/su1521 15556
4. Hassan, Q., et al.: A comprehensive review of international renewable energy growth (2024). https://doi.org/10.1016/j.enbenv.2023.12.002
5. Danish, Ulucak, R., Khan, S.U.D.: Determinants of the ecological footprint: role of renewable energy, natural resources, and urbanization. Sustain. Cities Soc. **54** (2020). https://doi.org/10.1016/j.scs.2019.101996
6. Gruber, L., Bachhiesl, U., Wogrin, S.: The current state of research on energy communities. Elektrotechnik und Informationstechnik **138** (2021). https://doi.org/10.1007/s00502-021-009 43-9

7. de São José, D., Faria, P., Vale, Z.: Smart energy community: a systematic review with metanalysis. Energy Strategy Rev. **36** (2021). https://doi.org/10.1016/j.esr.2021.100678
8. European Union: EU 2050 long-term strategy. https://climate.ec.europa.eu/eu-action/climate-strategies-targets/2050-long-term-strategy_en. Accessed 15 Jan 2025
9. Golombek, R., Lind, A., Ringkjøb, H.K., Seljom, P.: The role of transmission and energy storage in European decarbonization towards 2050. Energy **239** (2022). https://doi.org/10.1016/j.energy.2021.122159
10. Ministero dello Sviluppo Economico, Ministero dell'Ambiente e della Tutela del Territorio e del Mare, Ministero delle Infrastrutture e dei Trasporti: Piano Nazionale Integrato per l'Energia e il Clima (2020)
11. Dell'Anna, F.: Green jobs and energy efficiency as strategies for economic growth and the reduction of environmental impacts. Energy Policy **149** (2021). https://doi.org/10.1016/j.enpol.2020.112031
12. Toledo, C., Scognamiglio, A.: Agrivoltaic systems design and assessment: a critical review, and a descriptive model towards a sustainable landscape vision (three-dimensional agrivoltaic patterns) (2021). https://doi.org/10.3390/su13126871
13. Di Francia, G., Cupo, P.: A cost–benefit analysis for utility-scale agrivoltaic implementation in Italy. Energies (Basel) **16** (2023). https://doi.org/10.3390/en16072991
14. QGIS.org: QGIS geographic information system. QGIS Association (2022)
15. Monarca, U., Cassetta, E., Pozzi, C., Dileo, I.: Tariff revisions and the impact of variability of solar irradiation on PV policy support: the case of Italy. Energy Policy **119** (2018). https://doi.org/10.1016/j.enpol.2018.04.058
16. Benalcazar, P., Komorowska, A., Kamiński, J.: A GIS-based method for assessing the economics of utility-scale photovoltaic systems. Appl. Energy **353** (2024). https://doi.org/10.1016/j.apenergy.2023.122044
17. Adjiski, V., Serafimovski, D.: GIS-and AHP-based decision systems for evaluating optimal locations of photovoltaic power plants: case study of republic of North Macedonia. Geomatics Environ. Eng. **18** (2024). https://doi.org/10.7494/geom.2024.18.1.51
18. Gao, J., Wang, Y., Guo, F., Chen, J.: A two-stage decision framework for GIS-based site selection of wind-photovoltaic-hybrid energy storage project using LSGDM method. Renew. Energy **222** (2024). https://doi.org/10.1016/j.renene.2023.119912
19. Rane, N.L., et al.: GIS-based multi-influencing factor (MIF) application for optimal site selection of solar photovoltaic power plant in Nashik, India. Environ. Sci. Eur. **36** (2024). https://doi.org/10.1186/s12302-023-00832-2
20. Borfecchia, F., Caiaffa, E., Pollino, M., De Cecco, L., Martini, S., La Porta, L., Marucci, A.: Remote sensing and GIS in planning photovoltaic potential of urban areas. Eur. J. Remote Sens. **47** (2014). https://doi.org/10.5721/EuJRS20144713
21. Kalyan, S., Sun, Q.: Interrogating the installation gap and potential of solar photovoltaic systems using GIS and deep learning. Energies (Basel) **15** (2022). https://doi.org/10.3390/en15103740
22. Gallo, A., De Simone, C.S.: Agrovoltaic as an answer to the difficult relationship between land use and photovoltaics. a case study from Apulia Region. In: Gervasi, O., et al. Computational Science and Its Applications – ICCSA 2023 Workshops. ICCSA 2023. Lecture Notes in Computer Science, vol. 14107, pp. 547–559. Springer, Cham (2023). https://doi.org/10.1007/978-3-031-37114-1_38
23. Regione Puglia: S.I.T. Puglia. https://www.sit.puglia.it/. Accessed 15 Mar 2025
24. Gestore Servizi Energetici (GSE): Atlaimpianti. https://www.gse.it/dati-e-scenari/atlaimpianti. Accessed 14 Jan 2025
25. Ministero delle Transizione Ecologica (MITE): Linee guida in materia di impianti agrivoltaici (2022)

26. European Commission, J.R.C.E.E. and R.U.: PWGIS. https://re.jrc.ec.europa.eu/pvg_too ls/en/. Accessed 17 Mar 2025
27. European Commission, J.R.C.E.E. and R.U.: PWGIS user manual. https://joint-research-cen tre.ec.europa.eu/photovoltaic-geographical-information-system-pvgis/getting-started-pvgis/ pvgis-user-manual_en. Accessed 17 Mar 2025
28. Comitato Elettrotecnico Italiano: Guida alla realizzazione di sistemi di generazione foto-voltaica collegati alle reti elettriche di Media e Bassa Tensione. https://mycatalogo.ceinorme. it/cei/item/000008704?lang=en. Accessed 17 Mar 2025
29. Bódis, K., Kougias, I., Jäger-Waldau, A., Taylor, N., Szabó, S.: A high-resolution geospatial assessment of the rooftop solar photovoltaic potential in the European Union. Renew. Sustain. Energy Rev. **114** (2019). https://doi.org/10.1016/j.rser.2019.109309
30. Anselmo, S., Ferrara, M.: Trends and evolution of the GIS-based photovoltaic potential calculation (2023). https://doi.org/10.3390/en16237760

Environmental Processes Related to Soil Temperature: Problems and Analysis Methodologies

Francesca Miccoli$^{(\boxtimes)}$ ⓘ and Antonio Leone ⓘ

University of Salento, 73100 Lecce, Italy
francesca.miccoli@unisalento.it

Abstract. This article investigates specific environmental degradation processes driven by climate and land use changes. These changes significantly influence the surface energy balance, leading to increased aridity in rural environments and the urban heat island (UHI) effect in urban areas. Land Surface Temperature (LST), a key variable influencing the surface energy balance, serves as a crucial indicator for monitoring these degradation phenomena.

Aridity represents a significant risk in Italy, with the National Atlas of areas at risk of desertification reporting 51.8% of the territory as potentially vulnerable, particularly the Southern and Central Italian regions. A primary consequence is reduced soil fertility due to the loss of organic matter and carbon. This degradation can lead to desertification, consequently increasing the demand for nutrients and irrigation to sustain agricultural productivity, thus exerting greater pressure on natural resources.

The UHI effect is a major challenge in contemporary urban planning, negatively affecting the comfort and health of city dwellers. Since LST is a key indicator for both aridity/desertification and UHI, this article focuses on methods for its estimation and application. A significant advantage of LST is its relatively inexpensive determination over vast areas (land-scape scale) using remote sensing. The article provides a critical review of methodologies for LST retrieval from satellite data. The contribution of this paper is twofold: it underscores the importance of the integrated analysis of urban and rural landscapes through climate-related processes, unified by the LST indicator, which can be determined efficiently via remote sensing, particularly using imagery from Landsat Thematic Mapper (TM) and Moderate Resolution Imaging Spectroradiometer (MODIS).

Furthermore, while the scientific literature offers numerous solutions addressing the impacts of climate change on soils or urban climates separately, the potential for integrated analysis of these interconnected processes is less investigated. This paper aims to contribute to filling this gap.

Consequently, the research seeks to advance the integrated and holistic planning of urban and rural landscapes.

Keywords: Land Surface Temperature (LST) · Climate change and aridity · Remote Sensing

O. Gervasi et al. (Eds.): ICCSA 2025 Workshops, LNCS 15891, pp. 285–301, 2026.
https://doi.org/10.1007/978-3-031-97617-9_19

1 Introduction

The topics addressed in this paper are the risk of desertification of most of the soils of arid climates and the phenomenon of the urban heat island. These two processes are usually studied separately, but they have in common the climate issue, exacerbated by global change and the increase, both in air and surface land temperatures.

Land Surface Temperature (LST), which derives from the energy balance at the Earth's surface (absorption and partitioning of solar radiation), is strongly correlated with land use. This correlation makes LST analysis a crucial component for sustainable land planning. LST influences numerous environmental processes and reflects significant environmental impacts related to land use. Considering the two main macro-categories of land use (rural and urban), the key environmental processes influenced by LST or which LST itself can indicate include:

a. Soil aridity and desertification risk in rural environments.
b. The urban heat island (UHI) affects urban environments.

These two phenomena, although manifesting in different contexts and ways, share the commonality of unsustainable land management, the effects of which are exacerbated by global warming. Such management includes both soil artificialization and sealing linked to urban development, and unsustainable agricultural practices leading to the degradation of rural lands. In both cases, the analysis of LST distribution serves as a fundamental parameter for understanding and monitoring both processes [1, 2].

The scientific literature is very rich on both processes, while a lack has been found in their integrated analysis, which is instead important, especially for planning. This paper wants to give a contribution to this last aspect, for a more holistic approach.

The bibliography has been selected based on the specific contents regarding the desertification risk and the urban heat island, with particular attention to the influence of land use on them and their integrated treatment. In the face of the enormous cases on the two separate processes, the lack in their integration has emerged. In the face of the enormous case history of the two separation processes, the lack of their integration emerged. Consequently, this paper has drawn from the consulted bibliography what was the most effective approach, which turned out to be the assessment of the LST indicator.

1.1 Aridity and Soil Desertification Risk in Rural Environments

Desertification, defined as land degradation in arid, semi-arid, and dry sub-humid areas, results from factors including climate variations and human activities, particularly land use. The Intergovernmental Panel on Climate Change (IPCC) reports that desertification has intensified in some dryland areas in recent decades, posing significant threats to food security and ecosystem services [3].

This phenomenon is expanding, now covering approximately 40% of the planet's land surface and contributing to reduced agricultural productivity. This change has caused significant economic losses, particularly in Africa, where GDP decreased by 12% from 1990 to 2015 due to increased aridity [4].

In Europe, Italy is significantly affected by these problems, as can be observed in the National Atlas of areas at risk of desertification, the map of which is shown in

Fig. 1[1]. Based on climatic and soil analyses, 51.8% of Italian territory has been considered potentially at risk, particularly the entire southern region and parts of the regions of Central Italy. Specifically, within these potentially at-risk areas: 4.3% (1.3 million hectares) exhibit characteristics of functional sterility; 4.7% (1.4 million hectares) are susceptible to desertification processes; and 12.3% (3.7 million hectares) are considered vulnerable [5].

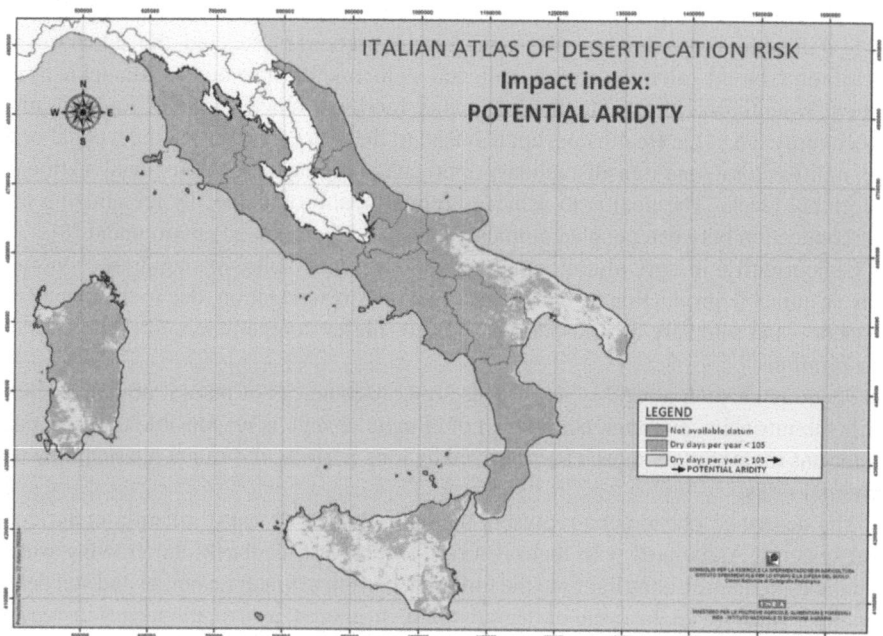

Fig. 1. Desertification risk for Italy (from Costantini et al., 2007).

Although direct measurement of the complex dynamics of desertification on a large scale presents challenges, LST serves as a valuable indirect indicator for monitoring land surface conditions related to aridity and degradation. Indeed, several scientific studies have explored the relationship between LST and desertification, focusing particularly on the degradation of soil organic matter and its impact on agricultural productivity.

Yuan et al. highlight that rising temperatures disturb soil organic carbon stocks, which poses threats to fertility and biodiversity and can exacerbate soil salinization problems [4]. Similarly, Peplau et al. indicate that deforestation for agriculture leads to soil warming, which increases organic matter decomposition [6]. This suggests that land use changes contributing to increased soil temperatures can accelerate the degradation of soil organic matter [4].

Soil degradation represents one of the main threats to environmental sustainability, negatively impacting not only agricultural productivity but also the balance of natural

---

[1] The desertification index used is the number of days of "dry soil". A soil is "dry" when water is absent in the layer between the level reached by a rainfall of 25 mm and one of 75 mm.

ecosystems. The loss of fertility, caused by phenomena such as erosion, salinization, and depletion of organic matter, increases dependence on chemical fertilizers to ensure adequate agricultural yields. However, the intensive use of such products generates a significant environmental impact, risking the contamination of surface and groundwater resources through leaching and runoff processes. Nitrates and phosphates, in particular, can cause eutrophication of water bodies, compromising aquatic biodiversity and water potability. Furthermore, the high sensitivity of groundwater bodies to nitrate contamination resulting from leaching from agricultural soils is well-known [7].

Soil health, the reduction of fertilizer and pesticide use, and the adoption of microbiome-based solutions are fundamental elements for promoting sustainable agriculture, essential for the production of quality food and other resources for a circular bioeconomy. The One Health concept is linked to these needs, representing a collaborative, multisectoral, and transdisciplinary approach operating at local, regional, national, and global levels. The goal is to achieve optimal health outcomes by recognizing the interconnection between people, animals, plants, and their shared environment [8].

Concurrently, in agricultural contexts with degraded soils, maintaining economically sustainable production levels increasingly requires irrigation, due to the increased frequency and intensity of arid periods. Indeed, higher temperatures intensify evapotranspiration.

Phenomena such as aridity and floods are consequences of natural climate cycles, while the intrinsic environmental impact of climate change is responsible for profound alterations in rainfall regimes, characterized by long periods of drought alternating with torrential rains.

The described phenomena represent the main drivers of transformation in agricultural systems. Associated with them is a risk of negative feedback: the growing water demand for irrigation contributes to the further depletion of water resources and soil deterioration. Thus, a vicious cycle of degradation is triggered, as irrigation itself increases the risk of uncontrolled runoff, soil erosion (including organic matter), and the leaching of agrochemicals.

In light of these challenges to sustainability, integrating advanced technologies into agricultural systems is fundamental. In particular, the adoption of machine learning techniques, combined with the analysis of high-resolution satellite imagery, allows for real-time monitoring of crop health status, early detection of water stress, and optimization of irrigation practices. Such tools support informed decisions based on objective data, improving water use efficiency and contributing to food security within the framework of sustainability and climate change adaptation.

1.2 The Urban Heat Island (UHI)

The urban heat island (UHI) is characterized by significantly higher temperatures in urban areas compared to surrounding rural zones, a phenomenon particularly pronounced during the night, whereas during the day the difference may be less marked. In urban areas, inadequately planned urbanization processes induce significant changes in land cover, replacing natural permeable and vegetated surfaces with predominantly impermeable artificial materials. Such surfaces, besides reducing rainwater absorption capacity, possess a high capacity to retain heat from solar radiation, contributing to the effect known as UHI.

In summary, two main phenomena contribute to the intensification of the UHI: the increase in temperatures due to the absorption of solar radiation and, indirectly, the reduced heat dissipation through evaporation (latent heat of evaporation) owing to the lower presence of vegetated and evaporating surfaces [9].

This phenomenon has significant implications for public health, exposing the urban population to a greater risk of heatstroke. Concurrently, it increases the energy demand for building cooling, which contributes to further greenhouse gas emissions and intensifies the UHI itself through anthropogenic heat release from buildings into the external environment.

Land cover and land use play a key role in influencing the intensity and distribution of the UHI effect; it is therefore essential that urban planners consider this factor. Numerous studies show that anthropogenic activities have modified between one-third and one-half of the global land surfaces, with significant impacts on local and global climate [10].

The UHI phenomenon is a central topic in urban climatology studies. Its considerable complexity derives from the multiple interacting processes that contribute to it, often characterized by complex feedback dynamics that can amplify its effects. Consequently, it is necessary to employ synthetic indicators capable of effectively representing the entirety of these processes. Land Surface Temperature (LST) proves to be a suitable indicator for this purpose, as it reflects the spatio-temporal variations associated with these dynamics [11]. Land use significantly influences the UHI through variations in surface cover and materials, leading to higher land surface temperatures (LST) in urban areas compared to surrounding rural areas [12].

The study of UHI requires a multitude of processes to be analysed, first of all land use/land cover change, which can increase the extent of impermeable surfaces, thus intensifying the UHI effect and the consequent higher temperatures in cities compared to surrounding rural areas. The UHI effect has significant implications, including contributing to increased energy demand (e.g. for air conditioning), which in turn increases greenhouse gas emissions in urban centers, already hubs for major emissive activities [13]. For example, the summer UHI drives air conditioning use in buildings, leading to approximately 12% higher energy consumption [14].

2 Materials and Methods

In line with the objectives stated so far, remote sensing has been considered to increase knowledge of aridity and UHI.

In the analysis, preference was given to other review articles because they allow access to "third-party" analyses by other authors and are therefore themselves a demonstration of the thesis underlying this paper: the notable quantity of studies on individual topics, compared to the limitations of integrated analyses.

Aridity and Desertification

Drought and water stress significantly affect plant physiology, leading to changes aimed at improving water efficiency and survival. To combat soil degradation, sustainable land management practices are essential. For example, bare soils exacerbate the tendency

Fig. 2. Evaluation of the maximum urban heat island according to the Oke model (from Leone et al., 2020).

towards desertification due to the loss of organic matter [6]. At the same time, irrigation is now almost structural, in order to support agricultural production and its economic return [18].

The reviewed literature suggests a strong interest in utilizing satellite-based spectral information to update soil maps, particularly for soils that are bare during satellite image acquisition. Satellite imagery contributes to improving the management of cultivated areas in the following ways [16]:

- Need for Updated Soil Mapping: for monitoring Soil Organic Carbon (SOC) within the upper soil horizons across both temporal and spatial dimensions. Such initiatives are essential to underpin sustainable land management practices, aligning with global policy frameworks including the United Nations Sustainable Development Goals and the European Commission's "Caring for Soil" mission.
- Digital Soil Mapping (DSM): over recent decades, the practice of DSM has conventionally relied upon georeferenced soil samples subjected to laboratory chemical analysis. These techniques integrate morphometric data and indices derived from Earth observation, such as the Normalized Difference Vegetation Index (NDVI).
- Challenges of soil sampling: the direct collection of soil samples is difficult and expensive; therefore, data acquired via Earth observation platforms is strategic.
- Spectral characteristics of SOC: SOC exhibits specific spectral features across various wavelength bands. These spectral signatures enable the development of predictive models that correlate soil reflectance data with SOC content.
- Historical context: since the early stages of satellite remote sensing, pedologists began establishing correlations between Landsat Thematic Mapper (TM) radiance values

and soil properties. However, the direct linkage between image reflectance and surface soil SOC content remained less prevalent until the advent of satellite time series offering high revisit frequency (e.g., weekly). Consequently, this research domain has witnessed a significant increase in attention over the past decade.

Irrigation is essential for achieving sufficient yields and quality in agricultural products, especially in semi-arid environments like the Mediterranean basin, which faces growing water scarcity. Efficient irrigation scheduling requires determining the water and physiological status of plants to prevent water stress and water waste. Traditional methods for monitoring plant status are often burdensome in terms of time and cost for field operations. Remote sensing is an efficient technology and is therefore increasingly employed to supplement traditional monitoring methods [17].

Remote sensing technologies offer detailed and high-frequency information on crop water status. This allows for the identification of areas subject to water stress and the optimization of irrigation both temporally and spatially.

A further technological advantage lies in the possibility of integrating remote sensing data with Geographic Information Systems (GIS). This approach, for example, supports precision irrigation, enabling the delivery of water to different field zones based on their specific needs, potentially modulated via local sensors that complement satellite data. Furthermore, machine learning algorithms and IoT solutions applied to remote sensing data have recently been tested with the aim of predicting irrigation needs based on current crop conditions and weather forecasts [18].

Urban Heat Island

Urban heat islands (UHIs) are characterized by higher surface and atmospheric temperatures compared to surrounding rural areas, resulting primarily from the alteration of the land surface energy balance in densely built environments. UHI research utilizes remote sensing data to monitor land cover changes and quantify key UHI characteristics, such as intensity and spatial extent, often derived from Land Surface Temperature (LST). Studies demonstrate that urbanization significantly affects the local climate, influencing surface temperature and energy exchange with the atmosphere. The literature highlights the importance of developing methods to assess the physical and spatial indicators of urban heat islands [9].

Land Surface Temperatures

The processes described so far are significantly different, as are the territories involved: the rural one in the first case, the urban one in the second. But the analysis carried out shows that they have in the LST the fundamental common thread, with the further advantage of the relative ease of surveying the LST. Consequently, it satisfies the objective of carrying out the integrated analysis of the territories, being, moreover, modified by land use.

LST is commonly measured using remote sensing techniques, particularly through the acquisition of satellite thermal imagery. Several satellite sensors acquire data in the thermal infrared range, which are subsequently processed to estimate LST over broad spatial coverage. Among the sensors employed are:

- Landsat TM/ETM+ (Thematic Mapper/Enhanced Thematic Mapper Plus): widely used for detailed spatial analyses of LST.

- MODIS (Moderate Resolution Imaging Spectroradiometer): provides data with high temporal resolution, suitable for global and daily LST analyses.
- ASTER (Advanced Spaceborne Thermal Emission and Reflection Radiometer): acquires both daytime and nighttime thermal data.

The following sections will discuss the main physical parameters influencing LST and the advantages offered by Landsat 8 data, as an illustration of techniques possible through remote sensing; however, this does not diminish the importance of other satellites. LST corresponds to the radiative temperature emitted by the land surface, distinguishing it from the air temperature measured at standard height, and is influenced by multiple factors, such as land use, vegetation cover, intrinsic soil properties, and atmospheric conditions [19].

The Landsat program, jointly managed by NASA and the U.S. Geological Survey (USGS), offers a historical archive of multispectral data spanning over four decades, specifically in terms of temporal coverage, spatial resolution, sensor quality, and data accessibility. In particular, the Landsat 8 satellite is equipped with two main sensors: the Operational Land Imager (OLI) and the Thermal Infrared Sensor (TIRS). These instruments acquire data in various spectral bands, including those in the thermal infrared necessary for LST estimation. This estimation typically relies on determining three key parameters: surface emissivity, atmospheric transmittance, and effective mean atmospheric temperature [20].

The main advantages offered by Landsat data include the relatively high spatial resolution, free accessibility (open access), temporal continuity of the archive, and high radiometric quality of the sensors. The Landsat program thus constitutes a fundamental tool for environmental monitoring and the study of climatic and territorial dynamics, holding particular importance for LST estimation. Indeed, an accurate estimation of the mentioned parameters (emissivity, transmittance, atmospheric temperature) allows for deriving LST.

The essential characteristics of Landsat 8 include [21, 22]:

- Accessibility: Landsat 8 adheres to an open access policy, allowing researchers and public and private entities free access to the data. This availability promotes the replicability of studies, supports environmental planning, and informs management decisions in urban and natural contexts.
- Temporal Coverage: The satellite ensures global coverage with a 16-day revisit cycle. This permits the analysis of LST variations on both seasonal and multi-year time scales, useful for monitoring phenomena such as urban heat islands or the effects of land use changes.
- Spatial Resolution: The Visible and Near-Infrared (VNIR) bands acquired by the OLI sensor possess a native spatial resolution of 30 m. The thermal bands of the TIRS sensor have a native resolution of 100 m, but LST products are commonly made available at 30 m through resampling. Such resolution proves adequate for detailed analyses, such as mapping soil organic carbon (SOC) content or urban thermal zoning.
- Data Quality: The OLI and TIRS sensors ensure high radiometric performance and superior data quality compared to previous Landsat missions, factors that contribute to improving accuracy in LST estimation.

Overall, Landsat 8's advanced features and data quality significantly contribute to the effectiveness and accuracy of the research on surface urban heat island intensity and land cover changes.

Deriving Land Surface Temperature (LST) from thermal sensor data, such as that acquired by Landsat satellites or comparable instruments, necessitates a multi-stage computational procedure. This process begins with the conversion of raw digital numbers (DN) into at-satellite brightness temperatures, followed by the estimation of the actual land surface temperature. The principal stages involved in this calculation, drawing upon methodologies outlined by researchers like Liu and Zhang [23],Convert the digital number (DN) into spectral radiance:

1. Transformation of Digital Numbers (DN) to spectral radiance

The initial computational step involves converting the sensor-recorded digital numbers (DN) for each pixel into at-sensor spectral radiance (L_i). This transformation utilizes sensor-specific parameters representing maximum and minimum radiance and DN values, as expressed in Eq. (1):

$$L_i = (L_{max} - L_{min}) Q_{dn} / Q_{max} \tag{1}$$

where L_i denotes the at-sensor spectral radiance ($MW \times cm^{-2} \times sr^{-1} \times \mu m^{-1}$); L_{max} is the maximum at-sensor spectral radiance; L_{min} is the minimum at-sensor spectral radiance; Q_{max} represents the maximum DN value of pixels and Q_{dn} represents the DN value of pixel.

Frequently, particularly for sensors like Landsat, this relationship is simplified in metadata or technical documentation to a linear equation involving sensor- and band-dependent coefficients (a, b), as shown in Eq. (2):

$$L_i = a + b Q_{dn} \tag{2}$$

2. Conversion of the spectral radiance to at-sensor brightness temperature

Following the calculation of spectral radiance, the next stage converts this value into an equivalent at-sensor brightness temperature (T_i). This conversion is typically achieved by inverting Planck's radiation law, using established physical constants (C_1, C_2) and the central wavelength (λ_i) of the specific thermal band, as formulated in Eq. (3):

$$T_i = C_2 \Big/ \{\lambda_i \times \ln[1 + C_1/(\lambda_i^5 \times L_i)]\} \tag{3}$$

$$C_1 = 1.19104356 \times 10^{-16} W \cdot m^2 \tag{4}$$

$$C_2 = 1.4387685 \times 10^4 \mu m \cdot K \tag{5}$$

where T_i represents the at-sensor brightness temperature in Kelvin (K); C_1 and C_2 are Plank constants; λ_i is the central wavelength and L_i is the previously calculated at-sensor spectral radiance (from Eq. 1).

3. Estimation of Land Surface Emissivity

Determining the land surface emissivity (ε_i), a crucial parameter representing the efficiency of thermal energy emission by the surface, is often accomplished indirectly. A common approach utilizes the Normalized Difference Vegetation Index (NDVI), a widely adopted indicator derived from the contrast between near-infrared (NIR) and red (R) reflectance measurements (Eq. 6), which enhances the vegetation signal [24]:

$$NDVI = (NIR - R)/(NIR + R) \qquad (6)$$

The calculated NDVI value is then employed to estimate emissivity. For instance, Van De Griend and Owe [24] proposed an empirical relationship applicable within a specific NDVI range (0.157 to 0.727), as shown in Eq. (7):

$$\varepsilon = 1.0094 + 0.047 \ln(NDVI) \qquad (7)$$

Comprehensive formulas for estimating land surface emissivity based on different NDVI value ranges, adapted from Liu and Zhang [23], are presented in Table 1.

Table 1. Estimation of emissivity by NDVI (from Liu and Zhang, 2011)

NDVI	Land surface emissivity (ε_i)
NDVI < −0.185	0.995
−0.185 ≤ NDVI < 0.157	0.970
0.157 ≤ NDVI < 0.727	$1.0094 + 0.047\ln(NDVI)$
NDVI > 0.727	0.990

4. Determination of atmospheric transmittance

Accounting for the atmosphere's influence on the thermal signal requires estimating atmospheric transmittance (τ_i) for the thermal band. This typically involves two substeps:

a. Estimation of water vapor content (w_i)

Atmospheric water vapor content (w_i, in g/cm2) is frequently estimated using empirical equations that rely on near-surface air temperature (T_0, in K) and relative humidity (RH) data, typically sourced from local meteorological stations (Eq. 8):

$$w_i = 0.0981 \times \left\{ 10 \times 0.6108 \times exp\left[\frac{17.27 \times (T_0 - 273.15)}{237.3 \times (T_0 - 273.15)} \right] \times RH \right\} + 0.1697 \qquad (8)$$

where w_i is the water vapor content (g/cm^2); T_0 is the near-surface air temperature in K and RH represents the relative humidity. The water vapor content, near-surface air temperature and relative humidity are all from local meteorological stations.

b. Calculation of atmospheric transmittance

The estimated water vapor content (w_i) is then used to calculate the atmospheric transmittance (τ_i) for the specific band 'i', often via a linear relationship with sensor- and band-dependent empirical coefficients (a, b), as shown in Eq. (9):

$$\tau_i = a - b \times w_i \tag{9}$$

5. Calculation of effective mean atmospheric temperature (T_a)

An estimate of the effective mean atmospheric temperature (T_a) is also required for atmospheric correction in some LST retrieval algorithms. This parameter can be approximated from the more readily available near-surface air temperature (T_0, in K) using empirical linear relationships that may vary depending on factors like season and latitude. Examples for mid-latitude conditions include:

– For mid-latitude summer: $T_a = 16.01 + 0.93 \times T_0$
– For mid-latitude winter: $T_a = 19.27 + 0.93 \times T_0$

6. Land Surface Temperature (LST) retrieval

The final step involves retrieving the Land Surface Temperature (LST) by integrating the previously calculated parameters. Using a mono-window algorithm as an illustrative example, LST (in Kelvin) can be computed as a function incorporating the at-sensor brightness temperature (T_i), land surface emissivity (ε_i), atmospheric transmittance (τ_i), and the effective mean atmospheric temperature (T_a). The specific formulation involves intermediate terms (a, b, C, D) as defined in Eqs. (10) through (14):

$$LST = \frac{\{a(1 - C - D) + [b(1 - C - D) + C + D]T_i - DT_a\}}{C} \tag{10}$$

$$a = -67.355351 \tag{11}$$

$$b = 0.458606 \tag{12}$$

$$C = \varepsilon_i \times \tau_i \tag{13}$$

$$D = (1 - \tau_i)[1 + (1 - \varepsilon_i) \times \tau_i] \tag{14}$$

where LST is the final Land Surface Temperature in Kelvin, T_i is the at-sensor brightness temperature, ε_i is the land surface emissivity, τ_i is the atmospheric transmittance, and T_a is the effective mean atmospheric temperature.

Figure 3 shows an application of this LST retrieval procedure to the area identified as having the highest risk in Fig. 2, adapted from Scarano [25].

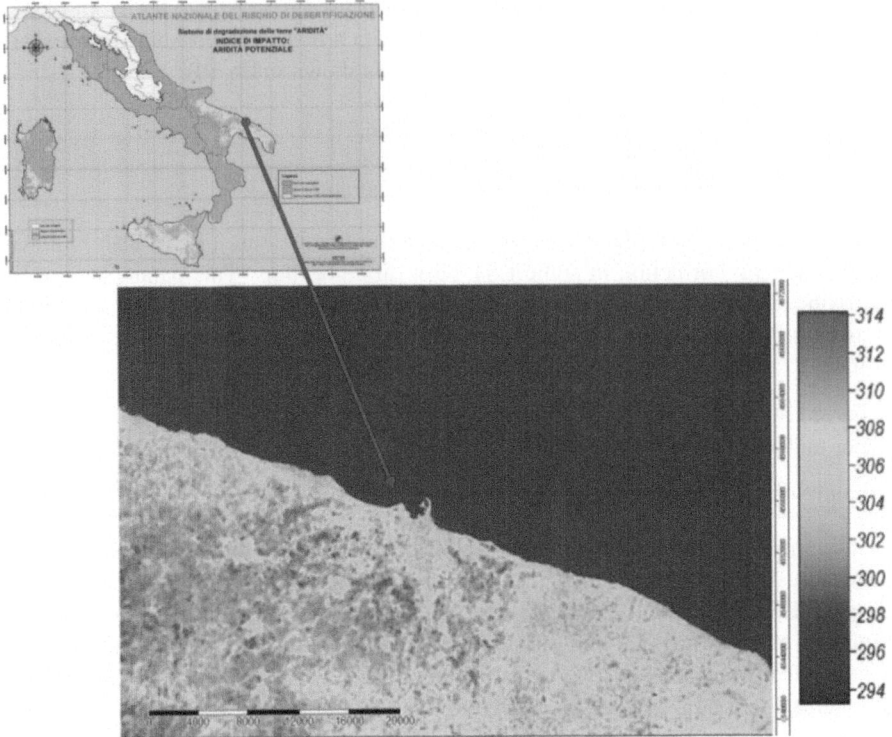

Fig. 3. Example of LST obtained using applying explained algorithms at Landsat-8 daytime image from September 24, 2013.

3 Discussion

The following three main key points emerge:

1. Desertification and sustainable soil management
- Desertification affects drylands, which cover very significant areas, both globally and in Italy, impacting approximately 500 million people [3].
- The causes of desertification include climate variability, anthropogenic climate change, and human activities such as cropland expansion and unsustainable land management practices.
- Socio-economic responses and sustainable land management are essential to prevent degradation and restore degraded drylands. Policies include improving market access, empowering women, expanding agricultural extension services, strengthening land tenure security, payments for ecosystem services, decentralized natural resource management, and investments in modern renewable energy sources [2, 32].
- Imperative for contemporary soil data: there exists a pressing imperative to generate contemporary soil maps and consistently track SOC levels within superficial soil layers. This effort is crucial for enhancing decision support systems in land management and ensuring alignment with major international directives, including the UN

Sustainable Development Goals and the European Commission's i.e. the 'Caring for Soil' mission [33].

- Spatio-temporal SOC assessment: the assessment of Soil Organic Carbon encompasses monitoring its variations across both geographical space and time. Initiatives like '4 per 1000' prominently highlight the significance of large-scale SOC storage quantification as a prerequisite for reliable estimation and cartographic representation of its distribution [16].
- Sampling constraints and alternatives: traditional soil sampling demands significant resources, primarily time and labour. Consequently, an alternative methodology for obtaining SOC information involves combining data from Earth observation platforms and proximal sensors, thereby reducing the reliance on extensive field sample collection [16].
- SOC spectral signatures: Soil Organic Carbon demonstrates distinct spectral responses within multiple wavelength bands spanning the Visible, Near-Infrared, and Shortwave Infrared spectrum (VNIR-SWIR; 400–2500 nm). These characteristic spectral features provide the basis for developing quantitative models designed to correlate measured soil reflectance with SOC concentrations [3].
- Historical perspective on remote SOC sensing: following the advent of satellite-based Earth observation, soil scientists established initial connections between Landsat Thematic Mapper (TM) radiance data and various soil characteristics. However, the direct quantification of surface SOC using image reflectance data remained relatively infrequent until the emergence of satellite time series offering high temporal resolution, such as weekly revisits. This technological advance has spurred a renewed and intensified research focus in this area over the last ten years [3, 16].
- Time-consuming and labour-intensive: Collecting soil samples and performing laboratory analyses are both processes that are time-consuming and labour-intensive.
- Spatial and temporal monitoring: Regular monitoring of soil properties is necessary to support decision-making and land management but requires extensive resources and coordination.
- Variability in soil properties: SOC and other soil properties exhibit spatial variability at multiple scales, from national to regional to field levels, complicating the mapping process.

These challenges highlight the need for innovative approaches and technologies to improve the accuracy and efficiency of soil map updates.

2. Impact of climate change on agricultural production
- Global warming and the increased frequency and intensity of extreme weather events negatively impact agricultural production. The increase in average temperatures has reduced the growing season duration for many crops and, together with a higher incidence of water stress, negatively affects their life cycle and nutrient assimilation [18]. More pronounced temperature fluctuations further compromise the quality and quantity of harvests.
- Increased evapotranspiration rates contribute to greater soil aridity, leading to increasing water requirements for crops and significantly reducing their yield [17].
- The increased frequency and intensity of extreme weather events, particularly floods and heatwaves, besides causing direct damage to crops, can intensify soil erosion,

compromising the SOC content, one of the main carbon storage and sequestration compartments in the biosphere.

• The destabilization of SOC, fundamental for soil fertility and biodiversity, combined with salinization problems, exacerbates difficulties for farmers, threatening the sustainability, including economic sustainability, of production [7].

These phenomena highlight the interconnections between climate change, land management, and agricultural production. It is therefore fundamental to adopt sustainable and locally adapted policies and practices such as precision agriculture, regenerative soil agriculture, crop rotation, and the use of advanced technologies, to mitigate negative impacts and ensure global food security.

Challenges in Water Management in Agriculture

Water management in agriculture faces numerous challenges requiring innovative and sustainable solutions. Climate change, through rising temperatures and altered rainfall regimes (greater variability and alternation between drought and floods), makes water availability for crops increasingly unpredictable. This further complicates the management of water resources. In many agricultural regions, especially in semi-arid areas like those in Southern Italy, water scarcity is a frequent condition that also impacts the management of artificial reservoirs. A further management challenge arises from the considerable spatial heterogeneity of soils, both in terms of SOC content and regarding hydrological properties (water retention capacity, drainage). Such variability requires site-specific irrigation interventions, often over large areas. This results in operational difficulties and high costs for implementing advanced irrigation systems (e.g., precision irrigation, [18]), which can represent a significant barrier, especially for the small farms prevalent in many Italian areas. To address these issues, research has long focused on precision agriculture, an approach where satellite remote sensing represents a key enabling technology [26]. Remote sensing finds application in multiple areas related to environmental sustainability, to which the agricultural sector can provide relevant contributions. An example is represented by the emerging mechanisms of 'carbon farming', also incentivized at the European level (e.g., through the Common Agricultural Policy – CAP or other initiatives), which involve forms of remuneration for farmers adopting practices capable of increasing soil carbon sequestration, thus contributing to climate neutrality objectives. These mechanisms can foster the development of a market for agricultural carbon credits, whose effectiveness, however, requires rigorous Monitoring, Reporting, and Verification (MRV) systems. In this context, as discussed in the present work, analysis via remote sensing can assume a priority role. Carbon farming can be framed within the principles of the Circular Economy applied to agriculture [2]. Similarly, water saving represents another crucial sustainability objective, for which technologies like remote sensing provide essential information for better planning and management of irrigation interventions [17].

3. Urban Heat Island

It is clear that ground temperature measurements are a powerful indicator of UHI. Furthermore, having maps of the different thermal areas at the landscape scale is an essential tool/element for ensuring the sustainability of the urban microclimate and, therefore, for effective urban planning [13, 14].

4 Conclusion

Satellite Survey and Soil Quality in Relation to Aridity and Desertification Issues

Satellite remote sensing represents a fundamental tool for monitoring soil quality and studying the phenomena of aridity and desertification. Spectral data acquired by satellites such as Landsat, MODIS, or Sentinel allow for estimating Soil Organic Carbon (SOC) content and other fundamental soil properties. Such data are essential for updating pedological mapping, identifying areas at risk of desertification, and implementing sustainable land management practices, with particular reference to agricultural areas. Monitoring SOC levels and soil moisture via remote sensing supports decision-making processes aimed at mitigating soil degradation, optimizing irrigation, and improving agricultural productivity.

Satellite Detection of Urban Heat Islands

The urban environment significantly alters numerous natural processes, primarily the local hydrological cycle and the surface energy balance. In the former case, the cause is the substantial impermeability of urban soils; in the latter, the causes are multiple and derive from a combination of factors, including the thermal and optical properties of building materials, urban morphology (e.g., street canyons), and anthropogenic heat release.

The urban heat island (UHI) phenomenon is complex and highly site-specific; its manifestations and consequences are therefore neither unambiguous nor easily generalizable.

Given the complexity and local specificity of the UHI phenomenon, mitigation strategies require detailed case-by-case analyses. However, the integration of vegetation into urban spaces (green infrastructure) is recognized as a fundamental and effective measure to counteract the increase in temperatures. The general objective should be to integrate natural elements into the built environment in a planned manner, based on an understanding of the underlying physical processes. To this end, multi-parametric environmental analysis is crucial. In this context, Land Surface Temperature (LST), as a synthetic indicator of surface thermal conditions, assumes a fundamental role. Its availability on a large scale, thanks to satellite remote sensing, makes it a valuable tool for the diagnosis, monitoring, and evaluation of UHI mitigation strategies. These data help to understand the impact of urbanization on the local climate, identify hotspots, and develop strategies to mitigate the UHI effect. The ability to compare LST data from different times and locations improves the accuracy of UHI studies and supports urban planning efforts to enhance thermal comfort and reduce energy consumption.

Importance of measuring Land Surface Temperature

The measurement of LST is of fundamental importance as it serves as a key indicator for both aridity and desertification processes and the UHI. Elevated LST values can contribute to the degradation of soil organic matter, reducing its fertility and increasing the risk of desertification. In urban areas, the spatial distribution of LST highlights the intensity of the UHI effect, with direct implications for thermal comfort and the health of the resident population. Remote sensing techniques, predominantly based on the analysis of satellite imagery, offer wide spatial coverage and provide essential data for LST analysis. These data allow researchers and territorial planners (planners) to monitor environmental dynamics, assess the impact of land use changes, and develop sustainable strategies aimed at mitigating the negative effects associated with both aridity/desertification in rural environments and the UHI in urban contexts.

Acknowledgments. This study was funded by PRIN_EO4DES Earth Observation for Desertification, Italian University Ministry.

Disclosure of Interests. The authors have no competing interests to declare that they are relevant to the content of this article.

References

1. Roth, M., Oke, T.R., Emery, W.J.: Satellite-derived urban heat islands from three coastal cities and the utilization of such data in urban climatology. Int. J. Remote Sens. **10**, 1699–1720 (1989)
2. Climate change, heat stress and labour productivity: a cost methodology for city economies
3. Desertification. https://www.ipcc.ch/site/assets/uploads/sites/4/2019/11/06_Chapter-3.pdf. Accessed 26 Mar 2025
4. Yuan, X., et al.: Impacts of global climate change on agricultural production: a comprehensive review. Agronomy **14**(7), 1360 (2024)
5. Atlante nazionale delle aree a rischio di desertificazione. https://www.researchgate.net/pub lication/260065322_Atlante_nazionale_delle_aree_a_rischio_di_desertificazione. Accessed 26 Mar 2025
6. Peplau, T., Poeplau, C., Gregorich, E., Schroeder, J.: Deforestation for agriculture leads to soil warming and enhanced litter decomposition in subarctic soils. Biogeosciences **20**, 1063–1074 (2023)
7. Garnier, M., Recanatesi, F., Ripa, M.N., Leone, A.: Agricultural nitrate monitoring in a lake basin in Central Italy: a further step ahead towards an integrated nutrient management aimed at controlling water pollution. Environ. Monit. Assess. **170**(1), 273–286 (2009)
8. Health Joint Plan of Action (2022–2026): Working together for the health of humans, animals, plants and the environment. https://openknowledge.fao.org/items/fddae6a2-e7ef-4a2a-ad54-2463dbbb0b32. Accessed 26 Mar 2025
9. Cooling our communities: a guidebook on tree planting and light-colored surfacing. https://escholarship.org/content/qt98z8p10x/qt98z8p10x.pdf. Accessed 26 Mar 2025
10. Li, X., Zhou, Y., Hejazi, M., et al.: Global urban growth between 1870 and 2100 from integrated high resolution mapped data and urban dynamic modeling. Commun. Earth Environ. **2**, 201 (2021)
11. Reducing urban heat islands: Compendium of strategies. https://www.epa.gov/heat-islands/heat-island-compendium. Accessed 26 Mar 2025
12. Oke, T.R.: Canyon geometry and the nocturnal urban heat island: comparison of scale model and field observations. J. Climatol. **1**(3), 237–254 (1981)
13. Pelorosso, R., Gobattoni, F., Leone, A.: The low-entropy city: a thermodynamic approach to reconnect urban systems with nature. Landsc. Urban Plan. **168**, 22–30 (2017)
14. Landsberg, H.E.: The Urban Climate. Academic Press, New York (1981)
15. Leone, A., Balena, P., Pelorosso, R.: Take advantage of the black swan to improve the urban environment. TeMA – J. Land Use Mobility Environ., 247–259 (2020)
16. Vaudour, E., et al.: Satellite imagery to map topsoil organic carbon content over cultivated areas: an overview. Remote Sens. **14**(12), 2917 (2022)

17. Abioye, E.A., et al.: A review on monitoring and advanced control strategies for precision irrigation. Comput. Electron. Agric. **173**, 105441 (2020)
18. Severino, G., D'Urso, G., Scarfato, M., Toraldo, G.: The IoT as a tool to combine the scheduling of the irrigation with the geostatistics of the soils. Futur. Gener. Comput. Syst. **82**, 268–273 (2018)
19. Li, Z.-L., et al.: Satellite-derived land surface temperature: current status and perspectives. Remote Sens. Environ. **131**, 14–37 (2013)
20. Landsat 8 Data Users Handbook. https://www.usgs.gov/landsat-missions/landsat-8-data-users-handbook. Accessed 26 Mar 2025
21. Sobrino, J.A., Jiménez-Muñoz, J.C., Paolini, L.: Land surface temperature retrieval from LANDSAT TM 5. Remote Sens. Environ. **90**(4), 434–440 (2004)
22. Weng, Q., Lu, D., Schubring, J.: Estimation of land surface temperature–vegetation abundance relationship for urban heat island studies. Remote Sens. Environ. **89**(4), 467–483 (2004)
23. Liu, L., Zhang, Y.: Urban heat island analysis using the landsat TM Data and ASTER data: a case study in Hong Kong. Remote Sens. **3**(7), 1535–1552 (2011)
24. Van de Griend, A.A., Owe, M.: On the relationship between thermal emissivity and the normalized difference vegetation index for natural surfaces. Int. J. Remote Sens. **14**, 1119–1131 (2003)
25. Scarano, M., Sobrino, J.A.: On the relationship between the sky view factor and the land surface temperature derived by Landsat-8 images in Bari, Italy. Int. J. Remote Sens. **36**(19–20), 4820–4835 (2015)
26. Berger, K., et al.: Evaluation of the PROSAIL model capabilities for future hyperspectral model environments: a review study. Remote Sens. **10**(1), 85 (2018)
27. Van de Griend, A.A., Owe, M.: On the relationship between thermal emissivity and the normalized difference vegetation index for natural surfaces. Int. J. Remote Sens. **14**(6), 1119–1131 (1993)
28. Stewart, I.D.: A systematic review and scientific critique of methodology in modern urban heat island literature. Int. J. Climatol. **31**(2), 200–217 (2011)
29. Nichol, J.: Remote sensing of urban heat islands by day and night. Photogramm. Eng. Remote Sens. **71**(5), 613–621 (2005)
30. Moran, M., Jackson, R., Slater, P., Teillet, P.: Evaluation of simplified procedures for retrieval of land surface reflectance factors from satellite sensor output. Remote Sens. Environ. **41**, 169–184 (1992)
31. Mallick, J., Singh, C.K., Shashtri, S., Rahman, A., Mukherjee, S.: Land surface emissivity retrieval based on moisture index from LANDSAT TM satellite data over heterogeneous surfaces of Delhi city. Int. J. Appl. Earth Obs. Geoinf. **19**, 348–358 (2012)
32. https://www.lse.ac.uk/GranthamInstitute/wp-content/uploads/2016/07/Working-Paper-248-Costa-et-al.pdf. Accessed 26 Mar 2025
33. European Commission: Directorate-General for Research and Innovation, Veerman, C., Pinto Correia, T., Bastioli, C., Biro, B., et al.: Caring for soil is caring for life – Ensure 75% of soils are healthy by 2030 for food, people, nature and climate – Report of the Mission board for Soil health and food, Publications Office (2020). https://data.europa.eu/doi/https://doi.org/10.2777/821504

EU Regulatory Framework and Funding to Combat Desertification

Micaela Falcone(✉) 🆔

Polytechnic University of Bari, Bari, Italy
micaela.falcone@poliba.it

Abstract. Due to the lack of a univocal organic approach to the desertification within the EU regulatory framework, this latter is critically examined in this paper by illustrating the strategies that guide the Member States towards an integrated solution as well as to environmental, agricultural, climatic and financial policies contributing to the management of the phenomenon. The legal implications of the regulatory gap at European level are also investigated, evaluating the effectiveness of the existing discipline, the limits and the prospects for improvement, aiming at an integrated regulatory strategy that can respond in a coordinated and sustainable way to combat the desertification.

Keywords: Desertification · Environment · Finance · European Union Law

1 Introduction

In 2009 the Commission held jointly by The Lancet and University College of London stated that *"Climate change is the biggest global health threat of the 21st century"* [1]. Soil desertification stems directly from climate change, representing one of the most urgent environmental challenges of our time, with heavy consequences on soil, bio-diversity and living communities. The term "desertification" is commonly used to describe processes linked mainly to human activities and to climate that increase problems in arid zones such as reduced food production, soil infertility, decreasing land natural resilience and worsening water quality. degradation is not limited to desert areas, affecting wide vulnerable ecosystems in mediterranean region.

Although it is not among world's regions most severely affected by desertification, EU is facing severe impacts, especially in southern regions suffering from soil degradation, water scarcity and loss of agriculture productivity, with repercussion on local economies and natural systems. About 23% of the EU territory is classified as "moderately vulnerable" and 8% as "highly vulnerable" to desertification, particularly in Italy, Hungary, Bulgaria, Spain [2].

The causes of desertification can be anthropogenic, such as improper use of water resources, fires, poor agricultural and livestock practices, urbanization and extractive activities, or natural, such as climate change, droughts and rain erosive action. Most harmful is the intensive agriculture, which causes erosion, salinization, soil compaction,

O. Gervasi et al. (Eds.): ICCSA 2025 Workshops, LNCS 15891, pp. 302–318, 2026.
https://doi.org/10.1007/978-3-031-97617-9_20

overexploitation of water resources and excessive use of fertilizers that deteriorate water quality.

The EU does not have yet a specific legal framework dedicated to desertification, but in recent years the efforts to address it were most intensified. There are currently various directives and regulations that, while not focused on this problem, contribute indirectly to mitigating desertification through the protection of soil, water resources and ecosystems. Those EU instruments apply to various sectors, ranging from rural development and reforestation up to the Common Agricultural Policy (CAP) and European policy on biodiversity, converging in a broad strategy for sustainability and climate adaptation. Under the increasing challenges on the issue, in October 2024 the EU Council adopted conclusions urging a more decided action against desertification, land degradation and drought.

Among the Member States most exposed to the risk of desertification, Italy stands out with about 28% of the national territory classified as highly vulnerable [3].

This paper illustrates the strategies that guide member states towards an integrated and coordinated approach against desertification as well as the related binding legal instruments such as sector-specific regulations and directives. The research methodology adopted follows a holistic perspective, integrating legal, environmental, agricultural, climate, and financial dimensions to fully understand the complexity of the phenomenon. The legal implications of the current regulatory framework are then illustrated, investigating the causes and effects of the regulatory gap at the European level, to assess its effectiveness, limitations, and prospects for improvement.

2 European Strategies and Regulations on Desertification

2.1 International Framework: UNCCD Convention and Agenda 2030

As mentioned, the EU does not have specific legislation on desertification, while the contrast to this phenomenon is part of a broader legal framework involving environmental, climate, agricultural and financial policies. The commitments made by the EU are also framed within the international context outlined by the United Nations Convention for Combating Desertification (UNCCD), that imposes the prevention and management of soil degradation [4]. Signed in 1994 after the Environment and Development Summit held in Rio de Janeiro in 1992 and ratified by the EU in 1998, the UNCCD represents the main instrument for international cooperation to contrasting the desertification globally, promoting an integrated approach through measures of sustainable land management, support to local communities and integration of environmental and economic strategies. The signatory parties of the UNCCD can voluntarily declare themselves "affected by desertification," obliged to define and implement *National Action Programmes* (NAPs) to prevent, mitigate and reverse the process. Based on their self-assessment, 13 EU Member States stated such declaration. However, so far their NAPs resulted poorly effective, being scarcely integrated into national planning processes and lacking the technical and financial resources needed for implementation.

Within the EU, the Council has set up a Working Party on Desertification (WPD), the only regular forum to discuss UNCCD and desertification related issues at EU level. Furthermore, jointly with the Council and other Commission services, the European

Commission's Directorate-General for Environment (DG ENV) coordinates the EU's position for UNCCD events such as the *Conferences of Parties* (COP), which take place every second year. In addition, Ispra's Joint Research Centre (JRC) is instrumental to providing scientific background and participants in the UNCCD roster of experts.

In 2015 the UN adopted the 2030 Agenda for Sustainable Development, setting 17 sustainability goals (SDGs) to be achieved by 2030, with SDG No.15 explicitly dedicated to desertification [5–8]. By reference to it, The European Commission's Directorate-General for Statistics (DG ESTAT) issues an annual report on progresses along the SDGs, including assessment of indicators on land degradation under SDG No.15.

To implement the commitments made under Agenda 2030, in 2017 UNCCD adopted the 2018–2030 Strategic Framework, focused on achieving target No.15.3 of SDGs [9]. According to The UN 2021 Global Sustainable Development Report (GSDR) and to the most recent ASviS 2024 Report, however, at the current rate only 17% of global targets may be achieved by 2030, while $1/3^{rd}$ shows no progress or even regression.

In addition, the objectives set by the actions to combat desertification agree with more recent international initiatives on climate, renewed after the momentum created by the Paris Agreement (2016) which, signed at COP 21 on Climate (UNFCCC) [10–14], also stressed the negative interaction between climate change and desertification. The recent COP 16 (Our Land. Our Future, 2024) proposed new strategies for sustainable land management, promoting greater dialogue among UNCCD Member States on the opportunity to increase political and financial commitments for the soil protection and restoration.

2.2   European Coordination Strategies

Lacking an integrated strategy within the EU, the governance of the phenomenon of desertification relies on transversal regulatory instruments, strategies and policy guidelines aimed at orienting sectoral interventions. Indeed, the Soil Protection Strategy adopted by the Commission in 2016 failed to achieve the legislative objective of an *ad hoc* directive and was withdrawn after 8 years due to the lack of sufficient majorities for approval.

Of particular relevance is the Special Report No.33/2018 of the European Court of Auditors entitled "Combating desertification in the EU: a growing threat in need of more action". It underscores the absence of a long-term vision, criticizes the fragmented approach of EU policies on the subject and highlights the factors confirming its seriousness and urgency: on one hand, the prolonged period of high temperatures and low rainfall culminated in summer 2018; on the other hand, studies conducted by the European Environment Agency (in 2008 and in 2017) and a comprehensive audit launched by the Court to monitor soil condition indicators.

A few years later, similar indications can be found in the Conclusions of the EU Council (October 2024) [15] where Member States reiterated the need to strengthen EU's action against desertification, soil degradation and drought. The Council recognized the limited progress in this area and emphasized the urgency of a more coordinated approach among existing regulatory and financial instruments. In particular, the Council recalled the objectives of the European Green Deal (EGD) and the need to enhance soil protection measures under the Common Agricultural Policy (CAP) which reaffirmed the necessity of improving monitoring and evaluation mechanisms for soil degradation and strengthening the indicators used under Directive 2000/60/EC on water resource management and Directive 2001/42/EC on strategic environmental assessment.

Another significant aspect, in line with the cross-cutting approach introduced by the 8th Environmental Action Programme (2022) [16], concerns the reinforcement of financial resources allocated to combat desertification, to be achieved through greater synergy between EU structural funds, the LIFE Programme, the Rural Development Fund and other forms of innovative financing. Although lacking legal force, the Council Conclusions represent an important political signal, paving the way for the adoption of future and more effective regulatory instruments in this area. In this direction, the EU Soil Strategy for 2030 (2021) represents a first step toward greater coherence in the EU action. Its implementation will depend on the adoption of binding legislative instruments, including the Soil Monitoring Law [17], currently under discussion, which is part of the Strategy and aims to regulate soil monitoring and resilience.

One of the most critical issues remains the persistent lack of common and uniform indicators to map the extent of desertification and soil degradation within the EU in a coherent and comprehensive framework. Given the complexity of those phenomena, influenced by numerous interdependent factors, there is no scientific consensus on how to quantify them. Additionally, some countries, such as Italy, Spain and Romania so far, have monitored factors associated with desertification through their own self-assessment systems, providing useful data on soil conditions, but diverging from EU data collection procedures.

2.3 The European Green Deal, the EU Soil Strategy for 2030, the Biodiversity Strategy for 2030 and the EU Strategy for Climate Change

In the broader and more current framework related to the *European Green Deal*, since 2019 the *Commission* has implemented several initiatives to achieve ecological transition and climate neutrality by 2050, which, indirectly, also address the phenomenon of desertification [18–23].

An integral part of the EGD is the EU Soil Strategy for 2030 [24] and the EU Biodiversity Strategy for 2030 [25], complementary and synergistic strategies that provide political and programmatic guidelines, steering the legislative action of the EU and its Member States. These strategies are based on existing legal instruments but also propose new legislative initiatives. The Soil Strategy, adopted in November 2021, is currently the main instrument to address soil degradation, including desertification and loss of soil fertility. It is linked to the objectives set by the Biodiversity Strategy, sharing the aim of preserving ecosystems and ensuring their environmental sustainability. However, while Biodiversity Strategy takes a general approach to nature conservation, the Soil Strategy focuses specifically on the quality and functionality of soils. The current legal framework for biodiversity is based on established legal instruments, such as the Habitats Directive (92/43/EEC) and the Birds Directive (2009/147/EC), while soil protection remains without a unitary and binding regulation at European level. To fill this gap, within the numerous initiatives promoted, the Soil Strategy foresees the adoption of a binding legislative proposal on soils by 2025, which aims to fill the void left by the withdrawal of the 2006 Soil Framework Directive proposal. This represents an intermediate step towards a potential regulatory intervention that would more comprehensively regulate soil protection, establishing obligations for the prevention of degradation and for the restoration of the most compromised areas. A key element of the Strategy is the recommendation to adopt conservative agricultural practices that limit soil loss and protect its ability to absorb water and nutrients.

The Biodiversity Strategy, which aims to restore 30% of degraded ecosystems by 2030, promotes in particular the restoration of peatlands and wetlands, crucial for soil protection by maintaining moisture in arid soils, thus preventing erosion and biodiversity loss. To this end, actions such as reforestation, protection of vulnerable agricultural lands and the enhancement of natural resources are planned. Additionally, this Strategy aims at reducing land consumption by 2050 to halt the progressive loss of agricultural and natural lands in favor of urbanization and other economic activities. Monitoring soil degradation is another central objective, with obligations for Member States to collect data on soil wealth and to adopt corrective measures against degradation.

Finally, within the framework of the EGD, it is important to mention the EU Strategy on adaptation to climate change (2021) [26] which, although indirectly, pursues objectives that align with the fight against desertification through the European Law on Climate (EU Regulation, 2021/1119).

Table 1. European green deal framework

Year	Document	Regulation	Content
2019	*European Green Deal*	COM/2019/640	Ecological transition and climate neutrality by 2050
2020	*EU Biodiversity Strategy for 2030*	COM/2020/380	Aims to restore 30% of degraded ecosystems by 2030, promoting soil protection
2021	*EU Soil Strategy for 2030*	COM/2021/699	Main instrument to address soil degradation, including desertification and loss of soil fertility
2021	*EU Strategy on adaptation to climate change*	COM/2021/82	Pursues objectives aligned with the fight against desertification
2021	*European Law on Climate change*	Regulation (EU) 2021/1119	Sets climate neutrality objective by 2050

2.4 The Common Agricultural Policy (CAP) and Measures to Combat Desertification

CAP, established since the Treaty of Rome (1957), is one of EU's main policies, accounting for approximately 39% of its budget. It introduced measures to promote sustainable agriculture by encouraging practices that reduce the risk of erosion and soil degradation, with the aim of supporting farmers, ensuring food security, promoting rural development and, most important, addressing environment challenge to agriculture. Although it was not originally structured to directly combat desertification, in recent decades CAP has undergone significant evolution in terms of environmental sustainability and soil protection, becoming a crucial policy in the fight against land degradation and desertification. Its recent reform (CAP 2023–2027) puts strong emphasis on results and performance (establishing a common set of indicators) and grants member states greater flexibility in adapting measures to local conditions. The reformed CAP covers 3 regulations, started from 1st January 2023: Regulation (EU) 2021/2115 (Strategic Plans), Regulation (EU) 2021/2116 (Financing, management and monitoring) and Regulation (EU) 2021/2117, which amends previous sectoral regulations [27, 28].

With the new National Strategic Plans (NSP), all CAP measures are consolidated into a single plan for each member State. Each country's NSP should include direct payments to farmers, market measures (e.g., support for sectors in crisis) and rural development, previously managed through *Rural Development Programs* (RDPs), less flexible [29]. Although the NSP is national, in some countries (such as Italy) the management of rural development remains at the regional level.

Through the NSPs, CAP aims at contributing better to the objectives of the EGD and the Farm to Fork Strategy [30], whose goal is to promote more sustainable and environmentally friendly agriculture. Regulatory changes and income-support measures, as well as market regulation introduced by the NSPs, significantly contribute to reducing soil fertility loss, erosion and unsustainable management of natural resources through incentives for sustainable agricultural practices such as crop rotation, permanent vegetation cover and soil protection.

The new basic income support system for sustainability has replaced the previous basic payment scheme, linked to historical entitlements, by introducing stricter criteria related to environmental sustainability, social conditionality and redistribution of support to farmers. Redistributive payments for small farms and coupled payments for specific agricultural sectors are foreseen. The main goal is to ensure greater sustainability and equity by reducing disparities among farmers and encouraging more responsible agricultural practices [31]. With the 2023–2027 CAP reform, eco-schemes have also been introduced, offering additional voluntary payments to farmers who adopt more sustainable practices compared to the minimum requirements set by conditionality. Responsible use of fertilizers, conservation agriculture systems and sustainable irrigation techniques are examples of actions promoted by the CAP that help to strengthen soil's resilience to climate stress. Another key aspect is the integration of climate change policy within the CAP, of which desertification is one of the most direct consequences. To that end, CAP provides major support for adaptation to evolving climatic conditions and promotes the introduction of drought-resistant crops and the adoption of conservation farming techniques that improve agricultural resilience and also help to preserve soil and to limit its degradation.

Despite the progress made, CAP still faces challenges in combating desertification. In particular, the difficulty in applying effective measures across all EU regions, especially in the most vulnerable areas of Southern Europe, remains one of the main issues. Disparities among regions, slow implementation of policies and limited dissemination of sustainable agricultural technologies are obstacles that must be overcome to ensure effective protection of soils at risk. The success of such measures depends on the ability of Member States to adapt interventions to specific territorial conditions, allocating more resources to areas at higher risk of desertification. Furthermore, the fragmentation of funding programs and the need to improve coordination among CAP and other EU policies, such as those related to the environment and climate, remain central themes. To this end, greater synergy among CAP, EGD and the Biodiversity Strategy could be crucial to creating a more integrated and coherent network of policies. Despite significant progress, further efforts seem necessary to improve the effectiveness of these measures and to ensure their wider application in most vulnerable regions of the EU [32].

According to the Council Conclusions (2024), the transformation of agriculture and food systems towards sustainability should be guided by 13 principles of agroecology defined by the FAO High-Level Panel of Experts on Food Security and Nutrition [33]. CAP undoubtedly has the potential to make a substantial contribution to soil protection and desertification prevention. However, CAP faces significant political, regulatory, economic and territorial challenges like the rift recently emerged between a part of the agricultural sector seeing EGD as a threat to their economic sustainability and another part that believes these policies necessary to address the environmental and structural crises affecting EU agriculture. Recently (February 19, 2025), the European Commission presented a Vision Document for Agriculture by 2040, which does not seem to resolve the situation.

Table 2. Common agricultural policy (CAP)

Year	Document	Regulation	Content
2021	CAP Strategic Plans	Regulation (EU) 2021/2115	Consolidated plan for each member state to promote sustainable agriculture
2021	CAP Financing, management and monitoring	Regulation (EU) 2021/2116	Rules for CAP financing and management
2021	CAP amendment	Regulation (EU) 2021/2117	Amends previous sectoral regulations
2023-2027	CAP reform	COM/2017/713	Emphasizes results and performance, granting flexibility to member States
2025	A Vision for Agriculture and Food	COM/2025/75	Promotes an attractive, competitive, resilient, future-oriented and equitable agri-food system

2.5 Other Environmental Regulations on Natural Resource Management

Even if not explicitly addressed to desertification, the regulations for the protection and sustainable management of water resources are crucial for preventing soil degradation and the loss of agricultural productivity by creating a protective framework that helps combat drought phenomena that cause desertification. The Water Framework Directive (2000/60/EC) aims at protecting EU's water resources, including rivers lakes groundwater and coastal waters [34]. The Floods Directive (2007/60/EC) also indirectly contributes to the prevention of desertification through soil protection and careful management of water resources [35]. Water is an essential resource for maintaining soil fertility and the protection of watersheds is crucial for ensuring sustainable water supply in areas vulnerable to desertification. The measures to address periods of drought and to improve water quality included in the directive contribute directly to mitigating the effects of desertification. However, it should be noted that, despite regulatory efforts, the situation of water resources in the EU remains critical. Recent reports highlight that only 39.5% of EU's surface waters are in good ecological status and 26.8% in good chemical status, with significant issues related to contamination and climate change [36].

The European Commission emphasizes the need for more sustainable and integrated management of water resources to effectively address desertification and other related environmental issues [37]. An interesting case study is represented by the recent RAINS project, a European initiative launched in January 2025 that aims to improve the resilience of the agricultural sector to water scarcity. Coordinated by 16 institutions from six European countries, the project focuses on finding practical solutions to increase the efficiency of water and nutrient management in agriculture. Through the testing of ten innovative solutions, including new irrigation techniques and advanced technologies, the RAINS project aims to improve water efficiency by 50% on a test area of 12,700 hectares across over 20 EU regions. The project involves more than 500 farmers in the transition to more sustainable irrigation practices and expects significant economic and environmental benefits, with an estimated saving of 6.1 billion euros and 244.3 million liters of water by 2050 [38].

The Directive on ambient air quality and cleaner air for Europe (Air Directive) (2008/50/EC) [39] and the Directive on the conservation of natural habitats and of wild fauna and flora (Habitat Directive) (92/43/EEC) [40] also provide useful regulatory tools against desertification. The Air Directive has an indirect impact on soil protection as it limits the emission of air pollutants responsible for acidification processes and the deposition of harmful substances. In particular, the reduction of particulate matter and NOx helps mitigate chemical degradation of soil, preserving its fertility and reducing the risk of erosion. Furthermore, improving air quality promotes vegetation growth, essential for stabilizing soils in areas at risk of desertification.

The Habitat Directive, on the other hand, plays a more direct role in preventing soil degradation through protection of natural ecosystems. The establishment of the Natura 2000 Network requires Member States to adopt specific conservation measures for sensitive habitats, many of which address the fight against soil loss and desertification.

While not explicitly addressing desertification as such, Air and Habitat directives provide essential regulatory tools to counteract its main triggering factors. The reduction of air pollution and the protection of natural ecosystems represent complementary strategies to agricultural and climate policies, helping to strengthen the European territory's ability to adapt to environmental challenges.

Also relevant is EU Regulation No.2018/841, which contributes to EU climate goals by requiring Member States to monitor and report greenhouse gas emissions from land use and deforestation [41]. It establishes rules that account for emissions resulting from land use, land use change and forestry. Another relevant aspect of this regulation is the focus on reforestation and sustainable forest management, which play a crucial role in moisture retention and soil protection against erosion, closely linked to desertification. In this regard, the recent Regulation (EU) 2023/1115 - EUDR (*European Deforestation-free Products Regulation*) also contributes to combat global deforestation and forest degradation resulting from unsustainable production and consuption patterns within the EU [42, 43].

Finally, Regulation (EU) 2024/1991 on the restoration of nature, which entered into force on August 18, 2024 [44], represents a significant step towards reversing biodiversity loss and increasing EU resilience to the effects of climate change.

Table 3. Other environmental regulations and documents

Year	Document	Regulation	Content
1992	*Habitats Directive*	Dir. 92/43/EEC	Protects natural habitats and species
2000	*Water Framework Directive*	Dir. 2000/60/EC	Protects EU's water resources
2007	*Floods Directive*	Dir. 2007/60/EC	Prevents and manages flood risks
2008	*Air Directive*	Dir. 2008/50/EC	Limits air pollutant emissions
2009	*Birds Directive*	Dir. 2009/147/EC	Protects wild birds and their habitats
2018	*EU Regulation on greenhouse gas emissions*	Reg. (EU) 2018/841	Requires monitoring and reporting of greenhouse gas emissions from land use
2023	*European Deforestation-free Products Regulation (EUDR)*	Reg. (EU) 2023/1115	Combats global deforestation and forest degradation
2024	*Regulation on the restoration of nature*	Reg. (EU) 2024/1991	Reverse biodiversity loss and increase EU resilience to climate change
2025	*Report on Water Directive*	SWD (2025)34	Water Framework Directive Report
2025	*Report on Implementation*	COM/2025/2	Report on the Implementation of the Water Framework Directive and the Floods Directive

2.6 Financial Measures

The EU has not established a fund dedicated exclusively to combating desertification, but it has developed a series of cross-cutting financial instruments contributing, directly or not, to soil protection. These instruments operate in different regulatory areas, reflecting EU integrated approach to environmental protection by the intersection of agricultural, climate, cohesion and research policies. Among the main funding mechanisms is the LIFE Program, adopted by Regulation (EU) No. 2021/783, which represents the EU's primary tool for financing environmental projects (a package of investments totaling over €290 million, mobilizing an overall investment of approximately €560 million, with projects in almost all Member States) [45]. Under the subprogram "Mitigation and Adaptation to Climate Change", LIFE finances interventions aimed at combating the effects of desertification, with particular attention to the sustainable management of water resources and the restoration of degraded ecosystems.

In addition to LIFE, a key role is played by the European Agricultural Fund for Rural Development (EAFRD) (established by Regulation EU No. 1305/2013 and later governed by Regulation EU No. 2021/2115), which introduces "eco-schemes" as tools to stimulate environment friendly farming practices. Specifically, the financial support provided by EAFRD is aimed at promoting conservative agricultural techniques, reforestation actions and sustainable soil management practices, key measures to prevent land degradation in the most vulnerable areas. In this context, EAFRD sets eligibility criteria for projects and investments such as those related to irrigation and reforestation, including conditions aimed at ensuring the sustainability of these initiatives.

Further resources are allocated through the European Structural and Investment Funds, including the European Regional Development Fund (ERDF) and the Cohesion Fund (CF), governed by Regulation (EU) 2021/1058 [46]. Both funds can provide essential support for infrastructure projects aimed at preventing soil erosion and managing water resources, particularly with regard to the southern regions of the EU, more exposed to soil desertification.

In parallel, the InvestEU Program, established by Regulation (EU) 2021/523, provides guarantees for private investments in the environmental sector, promoting the development of innovative solutions for land management [47]. Horizon Europe, EU main research and innovation program, also plays an important role in funding studies and projects aimed at combating desertification by promoting the development of advanced technologies for water management and the restoration of degraded soils [48].

In this perspective, a significant contribution also comes from the *Innovation Fund*, financed through the EU Emissions Trading System (ETS) and aimed at supporting advanced technologies for climate change adaptation, with potential applications in the regeneration of degraded soils.

Moreover, the role of funding linked to the Next Generation EU (NGEU) programming should not be overlooked. This economic recovery package, introduced in response to the COVID-19 pandemic crisis, foresees significant investments in the ecological transition: 8 billion euros allocated to the FEASR for the period 2021–2027 [49]. These additional funds help to support rural areas in implementing structural changes necessary to achieve the objectives of the EGD and to foster the transition.

Satellite remote sensing, intelligent water resource management systems and conservation agriculture techniques are essential tools for preventing soil degradation, but their implementation requires significant investments and specialized skills, which are not always evenly distributed among Member States. Further opportunities may arise from intensifying monitoring and prevention measures by using digital technologies and GIS systems to map vulnerable areas and respond promptly, avoiding costly and delayed interventions. Other financial instruments can be complementary. For instance, although primarily aimed at sustainable management of marine resources, the European Maritime and Fisheries Fund (EMFF), regulated by Regulation (EU) 2021/1139, includes specific measures for protecting coastal ecosystems and combating erosion, a phenomenon often linked to desertification in some Mediterranean regions. The EU Solidarity Fund (EUSF), established by Regulation (EC) 2012/2002, can also provide resources for emergency interventions in cases of extreme drought, although its scope is limited to natural disaster situations.

The EU's commitment to combating desertification is not limited to the European territory, it extends to international actions. Through the new Neighbourhood, Development and International Cooperation Instrument (NDICI – Global Europe) [50] (which under the Multiannual Financial Framework 2021–2027 has incorporated the former European

Development Fund, EDF), EU contributes to supporting projects in third countries, particularly in Africa and Mediterranean areas, to combat land degradation and promote the sustainable management of natural resources.

Particular attention should be given to the support for the outermost regions of the EU (i.e., France: Guadeloupe, French Guiana, Martinique, Réunion, Saint Martin and Mayotte; Spain: Canary Islands; Portugal: Azores and Madeira) [51] which, due to the limits linked to isolation, insularity and particular environmental vulnerability, benefit from specific measures through the POSEI Program. This program provides financial resources for the protection of local ecosystems and for adaptation to climate change, addressing the specific needs of territories highly exposed to land degradation phenomena.

Although the EU spending programmes make funding available for projects addressing desertification, the global amount of EU funds planned and used to that aim is not available, due to the multiplicity of funding and the variety of initiatives that prevent a precise mapping.

Table 4. Financial measures

Year	Financial Instrument	Regulation	Description
2002	EU Solidarity Fund (EUSF)	Reg. (EC) 2012/2002	Provides resources for emergency interventions in case of extreme drought
2013	European Agricultural Fund for Rural Development	Reg. (EU) 1305/2013	Promotes sustainable agricultural practices and soil management
2021	LIFE Program	Reg. (EU) 2021/783	Financing environmental projects, including interventions against desertification
2021	European Structural and Investment Funds	Reg. (EU) 2021/1058	Support for infrastructure projects to prevent soil erosion and manage water resources
2021	InvestEU Program	Reg. (EU) 2021/523	Guarantees for private investments in the environmental sector
2021	Horizon Europe	Reg. (EU) 2021/695	Funding studies and projects on desertification and water resource management
2021	Next Generation EU (NGEU)	Reg.(EU) 2020/2094	Investments in ecological transition and support for rural areas
2021	European Maritime and Fisheries Fund (EMFF)	Reg. (EU) 2021/1139	Protection of coastal ecosystems and combating erosion
2021	POSEI Program	COM/2016/797	Financial support for protecting local ecosystems and adapting to climate change in outermost regions
2021	Neighbourhood, Development and International Cooperation Instrument (NDICI)	Reg. (EU) 2021/947	Support for projects in third countries to combat land degradation
2024	Innovation Fund	C/2024/8011	Support for advanced technologies for climate change

3   Regulatory Gaps and Legal Implications

The lack of specific legislation on desertification at the European level raises several legal issues concerning key aspects of EU law. First, the implementation of international obligations arising from the UNCCD, as the EU's fragmented regulatory framework on the matter complicates the alignment of international commitments with the Union's internal policies. The difficulty in harmonizing these obligations results in a lack of coherence in national and regional policies, potentially causing conflicts between the international commitments undertaken and the measures adopted at the national level. This scenario entails the risk of a lack of coordination, which could undermine the overall effectiveness of global and regional efforts to combat desertification.

Another issue concerns the absence of clear unambiguous regulation creates uncertainty regarding the division of competences among the EU and the Member States, particularly in a context were managing the factors responsible for desertification affects multiple intervention sectors falling under both exclusive and shared competences of the Union. In the absence of dedicated sectoral EU legislation, Member States have a certain degree of autonomy in adopting measures against desertification, but the resulting fragmentation of national regulations could lead to an inconsistent application of countermeasures, undermining the overall effectiveness of EU action and distorting competition conditions among States with different levels of regulation.

The heterogeneity of the measures adopted so far also limits the full application of the Principle of Solidarity (Articles 2 and 3 TEU) [52–54], which obliges Member States to cooperate in addressing common challenges and, from an environmental perspective, to ensure the necessary support to the most vulnerable regions. The absence of binding legislation on desertification hinders the concrete application of this principle, leading to fragmented interventions. Integrating the fight against desertification - which affects European regions unevenly - into the Cohesion Policy (Articles 174 -178 TFEU) could facilitate the development of targeted regional strategies, contributing to the effective and sustainable management of soil through a fair distribution of resources and adaptation measures.

Another issue, concerning a different aspect of protection, relates to the direct implications of desertification on human rights, such as the right to a healthy environment and food security, protected by the Charter of Fundamental Rights of the European Union (Articles 35, 37 and 38) [55]. The absence of a precise legal framework obstructs the establishment of clear legal responsibilities for the protection of these rights in cases of environmental damage resulting from desertification.

The lack of specific legislation on desertification also complicates the consistent application of the Environmental Liability Regime established by Directive 2004/35/EC which, in application of the Polluter pays Principle (Article 191 TFEU), sets out the principles of prevention and remediation of environmental damage [56]. Desertification, as a phenomenon affecting large areas and involving complex impacts, could fall within the scope of environmental damage. However, the absence of sectoral legislation, the lack of a uniform EU definition of "soil degradation," and the ambiguity of the concept of "environmental damage" when applied to cumulative phenomena - such as desertification, which often occurs on a large scale with long-term effects - risk weakening its enforcement, resulting in difficulties in obtaining compensation for damages and ensuring environmental restoration.

Furthermore, the absence of a clear legal framework inevitably reduces the possibility of resorting to the Court of Justice of the European Union (CJEU), which plays a central role in the interpretation and application of EU's law. Through its case law, the Court could effectively contribute to resolving issues related to Member States' responsibilities in implementing environmental policies about desertification and ensuring that the law is applied uniformly and consistently, thereby enhancing environmental protection and safeguarding citizens' rights.

Finally, the lack of a coherent legal framework risks to undermine the effectiveness of European environmental governance and to limit the access to funding, creating disparities among Member States, particularly those most vulnerable to desertification. The absence of a robust legal framework to address this phenomenon also makes it difficult to monitor and assess progress, thereby impairing the EU's ability to respond to environmental challenges in a cohesive and strategic manner.

In this context, the legal implications of desertification provide numerous points for meditation, both in terms of regulatory gaps and regarding the possibility of greater involvement of the CJEU in monitoring and enforcing EU policies to prevent desertification and soil degradation. The absence of norms explicitly addressing desertification as an autonomous phenomenon - merely regulating related aspects - thus raises a series of complex legal questions that range from systemic levels to practical aspects, weakening its ability to respond in a coherent and integrated manner to one of the most pressing environmental challenges of our time.

4   Conclusions

Despite the lack of specific legislation, the EU has progressively developed a complex indirect regulatory framework to combat desertification and soil degradation. The results, however, remain uneven, particularly in the most vulnerable areas such as the southern regions. Although the European regulatory approach - through integrated policies and financial instruments - has laid the foundations for addressing this phenomenon, significant challenges persist. One main limitation of the current system lies in the difficulty of reconciling the need for unified regulation with the necessity of specific provisions for different environmental sectors. Soil management is closely interconnected with water resource protection, biodiversity conservation and climate change mitigation, yet each sector presents technical and regulatory peculiarities requiring tailored measures. The plurality of legal instruments and their partial overlap reflect not only a coordination issue, but also the complexity of a phenomenon that encompasses environmental economic and social dimensions.

Moreover, beyond legal aspects, the effectiveness of desertification countermeasures is influenced by numerous technical, institutional and social factors. Disparities in access to advanced technologies and modern environmental monitoring systems affect the ability to prevent soil degradation, determining the success or failure of the adopted policies. Social awareness and local community involvement also play a crucial role. However, economic pressures related to intensive agricultural expansion, real estate speculation and increasing competition for natural resources can hinder the adoption of long-term soil conservation strategies. Gender-related factors are also significant, as in the most under-developed rural areas, inequalities persist among genders in access to land ownership, financing and technical training.

At the institutional level, multilevel governance and the fragmentation of compe-tences among the EU governance, the Member States, and local administrations add further complexity. Additionally, the availability of funding and economic incentives varies significantly across Member States, creating disparity in the implementation of soil protection strategies.

The absence of a unified legal framework and the lack of integration among policies at national, regional and European levels are main obstacles to establishing an effec-tive strategy against desertification. Improved coordination between European financial instruments and national and local environmental policies could allow more rational use of resources, ensuring timely interventions and avoiding late and fragmented measures.

In this context, the recent call by the EU Council for the Commission to develop a comprehensive action plan to combat desertification represents a significant step towards greater coordination. For this plan to yield tangible results it will be necessary to strengthen the governance of financial resources and to ensure that European policies on desertification are more effectively integrated into the Union's environmental and climate objectives.

Lastly, the second Report on zero pollution monitoring and outlook, published on March 2025 by the European Commission and the European Environment Agency, highlights that, despite progress in reducing air pollution, more decisive actions are needed to achieve the zero pollution targets by 2030 [57].

In summary, although progress has been made, the lack of effective coordination among various measures and the persistence of sectoral approaches limit the ability to structurally combat the phenomenon of soil desertification. Future opportunities lie in strengthening cooperation across different levels of government, increasing commit-ment to soil protection and promoting sustainable development models that integrate environmental, agricultural and climate policies. The harmonization of European rules to contrast desertification, while desirable, must necessarily contend with the plurality of interests and regulatory domains involved as well as with the need to maintain a bal-ance between regulatory specialization and institutional coordination. Only through an integrated and multidimensional approach will it be possible to develop truly effective strategies for soil protection and desertification prevention.

Acknowledgments. This study was carried out within the PRIN 2022 RESEARCH PROJECTS OF RELEVANT NATIONAL INTEREST funded by the Ministry of University and Research (MUR) (Grant Assignment Decree n. 20437 adopted on 06.11.2024 - CUP n. D53C24004290006).

References

1. The Lancet Commission, Managing the health effects of climate change, vol. 373, 16 May 2009. www.thelancet.com

2. Report UNCCD, The Global Threat of Drying Lands, 2025 and World Drought Atlas UNCCD (2024)
3. Report SNPA n. 43/2024. https://www.snpambiente.it/temi/suolo/consumo-di-suolo-dinami che-territoriali-e-servizi-ecosistemici-edizione-2024/
4. Convention to Combat Desertification in those Countries Experiencing Serious Drought and/or Desertification, particularly in Africa, UNCCD-UN (1994(
5. Agenda 2030 for Sustainable Development, UN (2015)
6. Diaz Barrado, C.M.: Sustainable development goals: a principle and several dimension. In: Duràn y Lalaguna-Dìaz Barrado-Fernandez Liesa (eds.), International Society and Sustainable Development Goals, Thomson Reuters-Aranzadi, Cizur Menor (2016)
7. French, D., Kotzè, L. (eds.): Governing Through Goals: Sustainable Development Goals as Governance Innovation. Edward Elgar, Cheltenham (2018)
8. Montini, M.: L'interazione tra gli SDGs ed il principio dello sviluppo sostenibile per l'attuazione del diritto internazionale dell'ambiente. In: federalismi.it, fasc. 9 (2019)
9. Chiussi, L.: The UN 2030 Agenda on Sustainable Development: Talking the Talk, Walking the Walk? In: La Comunità internazionale, 49 ss. (2016)
10. The UNCCD 2018–2030 Strategic Framework. Document ICCD/COP(13)/L.18
11. Bodansky, D.: The Paris climate change agreement: a new hope? Am. J. Int. Law, 288 ss. (2016)
12. Savaresi, A.: The Paris agreement: a new beginning? J. Energy Natural Resour. Law, 16 ss. (2016)
13. Montini, M.: Riflessioni critiche sull'Accordo di Parigi sui cambiamenti climatici. In: Rivista di diritto internazionale, p. 719 ss. (2017)
14. Ingravallo, I.: Lineamenti del nuovo diritto internazionale dello sviluppo sostenibile. In: Buonfrate, A., Uricchio, A. (eds.), Trattato breve di diritto dello sviluppo sostenibile, pp. 275–306. Kluwer (2023)
15. Council Conclusions n.14146/24(2024)
16. Decision (EU) 2022/591 on a General Union Environment Action Programme to 2030
17. COM/2023/416 final, proposal for a directive of the European Parliament and of the Council on Soil Monitoring and Resilience (Soil Monitoring Law)
18. The European Green Deal, COM/2019/640 final
19. Falcone, M.: Il Green Deal europeo per un continente a impatto climatico zero: la nuova strategia europea per la crescita tra sfide, responsabilità e opportunità. In: Studi sull'integrazione europea, pp. 379–394 (2020)
20. Rifkin, J.: Green New Deal, Mondadori (2021)
21. Chiti, E.: Managing the ecological transition of the EU: the European green deal as a regulatory process. In: Common Market Law Review, p. 19 ss. (2022)
22. Perrotto, G.: Il finanziamento del Green Deal europeo: fra risorse proprie e la creazione di una capacità fiscale europea. In: Quaderni AISDUE, p. 424 ss. (2022)
23. Bonomo, A.: Green Deal europeo e misure attuative nella prospettiva della transizione ecologica. In: Buonfrate, A., Uricchio, A. (eds.), Trattato breve di diritto dello sviluppo sostenibile, pp. 349–375. Kluwer (2023)
24. COM/2021/699 final, EU Soil Strategy for 2030
25. COM/2020/380 final, EU Biodiversity Strategy for 2030
26. COM/2021/82 final
27. EC, Common Agricultural Policy For 2023–2027 (2022). https://agriculture.ec.europa.eu/common-agricultural-policy/cap-overview/cap-2023-27_en
28. Sotte, F.: La politica agricola europea. Storia e analisi. Firenze University Press, Firenze, 209 ss. (2023)
29. EC, Agriculture and rural development. https://agriculture.ec.europa.eu/cap-my-country/cap-strategic-plans_it

30. COM 381, final. Farm to Fork Strategy for a fair, healthy and environmentally friendly food system (2020)
31. EU, Agriculture and rural development. https://agriculture.ec.europa.eu/common-agricultu ral-policy/income-support/income-support-explained_it
32. European Parliament resolution of 13 December 2022 on a long-term vision for the EU's rural areas - Towards stronger, connected, resilient and prosperous rural areas by 2040 (2021/2254(INI))
33. Agroecology Europe. https://www.agroecology-europe.org/the-13-principles-of-agroec ology/
34. Directive 2000/60/EC of the European Parliament and of the Council of 23 October 2000 establishing a framework for Community action in the field of water policy
35. Directive 2007/60/EC of the European Parliament and of the Council of 23 October 2007 on the assessment and management of flood risks
36. EC, Water Framework Directive Report, SWD 34 final (2025)
37. COM/2025/2, final, Report on the Implementation of the Water Framework Directive (2000/60/Ec) And the Floods Directive (2007/60/EC)
38. Resilient Agricultural IrrigatioN systems for water Scarcity in Europe (RAINS). https://doi. org/10.3030/101181890
39. Directive 2008/50/EC of the European Parliament and of the Council of 21 May 2008 on ambient air quality and cleaner air for Europe
40. Directive 92/43/EEC of 21 May 1992 on the conservation of natural habitats and of wild fauna and flora, Habitat Directive
41. Regulation (EU) 2018/841 of The European Parliament and of The Council on The Inclusion of Greenhouse Gas Emissions and Removals from Land Use, Land Use Change and Forestry in the 2030 Climate and Energy Framework and Amending Regulation (EU) n. 525/2013 and Decision n. 529/2013/EU
42. Regulation (EU) 2023/1115 of 31 May 2023 on the making available on the Union market and the export from the Union of certain commodities and products associated with deforestation and forest degradation and repealing Regulation (EU) No. 995/2010
43. Pastorino, L.F.: Comercio internacional y responsabilidad ambiental y climática. A propósito del Reglamento (UE) 2023/1115 contra la desforestación. In: rivista.eurojus.it, fasc. 3 (2024)
44. Regulation (EU) 2024/1991 of 24 June 2024 on nature restoration and amending Regulation (EU) 2022/869
45. https://cinea.ec.europa.eu/programmes/life_en
46. Regulation (EU) 2021/1058 of 24 June 2021on the European Regional Development Fund and on the Cohesion Fund
47. www.investeu.eu.it
48. Regulation (EU) 2021/695 of the European Parliament and of the Council of 28 April 2021 establishing Horizon Europe – the Framework Programme for Research and Innovation, laying down its rules for participation and dissemination (2021)
49. Fabbrini, F.: Next Generation EU. Il futuro di Europa ed Italia dopo la Pandemia. Il Mulino, Bologna (2022)
50. Regulation (EU) 2021/947 of the European Parliament and of the Council of 9 June 2021 establishing the Neighbourhood, Development and International Cooperation Instrument – Global Europe (2021)
51. COM/2016/0797 final, Report from the Commission to the European Parliament and the Council on the Implementation of the Scheme of Specific Measures for Agriculture in Favour of the Outermost Regions of the Union (POSEI) (2016)
52. Asaro, G.: Prime considerazioni sulla natura dell'obbligo di solidarietà tra gli Stati membri dell'Unione europea. In: Fogli di lavoro per il diritto internazionale (2018)

53. Mengozzi, P.: L'idea di solidarietà nel diritto dell'Unione europea, Bologna (2022)
54. Morgese, G.: Il nuovo meccanismo di solidarietà volontaria, il gattopardismo degli Stati membri e la lezione non appresa della crisi ucraina. In: Quaderni AISDUE, p. 289 (2022)
55. Charter of Fundamental Rights of the European Union, OJ C 202, 7.6.2016, pp. 389–405 (2016)
56. Directive 2004/35/EC of the European Parliament and of the Council of 21 April 2004 on environmental liability with regard to the prevention and remedying of environmental damage (2004)
57. EEA – JRC Report 13/2024, 3.3.2025

Simulating Dissolved Oxygen Concentrations at the Watershed Scale: A Machine Learning Approach with Physical Constraints

Pedro Pertusso[1] , Martina Pou[2] , Federico Vilaseca[2] , Alberto Castro[1,3] , and Angela Gorgoglione[2(✉)]

[1] Department of Computer Science, School of Engineering, Universidad de la República, Montevideo 11300, Uruguay
[2] Department of Fluid Mechanics and Environmental Engineering, School of Engineering, Universidad de la República, Montevideo 11300, Uruguay
agorgoglione@fing.edu.uy
[3] Department of Electrical Engineering, School of Engineering, Universidad de la República, Montevideo 11300, Uruguay

Abstract. This study focuses on simulating dissolved oxygen (DO) concentrations at the watershed scale using machine learning (ML) models, with an emphasis on incorporating domain constraints to improve prediction accuracy. The main objectives are to evaluate the performance of different ML models, assess the impact of physical and spatial dependencies, and identify the most critical features influencing DO simulation. Random Forest (RF), Extra Trees (ET), and Histogram-based Gradient Boosting (HGB) were selected for this study and trained using a set of input variables, including water and air temperature, and other hydrological information. Model performance was assessed by calculating Mean Square Error (MSE), Mean Absolute Error (MAE), and Nash-Sutcliffe Efficiency (NSE). The best model-metric combination was selected for each station, and the results were satisfactory for most monitoring stations in the basin. The feature selection analysis, run with SHapley Additive exPlanations (SHAP), was designed to capture spatial, temporal, and physical dependencies, ensuring that the models remained accurate and aligned with established physical principles. Temperature-related variables were found to be the most significant predictors of DO levels. These outcomes demonstrate the potential of ML approaches with physical constraints to effectively predict DO concentrations and contribute to better-informed water quality management in natural watersheds.

Keywords: Water quality · Dissolved oxygen · Machine learning models · Hydroinformatics

1 Introduction

Water quality management in urban watersheds is a critical component of sustainable development. Urbanization increases impervious surfaces, alters hydrological cycles, and intensifies pollutant loads entering aquatic systems, often leading to degraded water quality [1]. Effective monitoring and predictive modeling

O. Gervasi et al. (Eds.): ICCSA 2025 Workshops, LNCS 15891, pp. 319–334, 2026.
https://doi.org/10.1007/978-3-031-97617-9_21

of water quality are essential for supporting decision-making processes that aim to protect public health, maintain ecosystem services, and ensure the resilience of urban water supplies [2]. In the context of global sustainability goals, managing urban water quality contributes directly to achieving clean water and sanitation (SDG 6), sustainable cities and communities (SDG 11), and climate action (SDG 13), emphasizing the need for robust, data-driven tools like those developed in this study.

Dissolved oxygen (DO) is a crucial indicator of water quality, and it plays a key role in maintaining the health of the aquatic ecosystem and sustainable biodiversity [3]. In fact, adequate DO levels are essential for the survival of fish, invertebrates, and microbial communities that contribute to ecosystem functioning. On the other side, low DO concentrations can lead to hypoxic or even anoxic conditions, causing fish death, modifying biogeochemical cycles, and decreasing overall water usability for human consumption, industry, and recreation [4].

In watersheds like the Santa Lucía one, located in Uruguay (South America), which serves as the primary drinking water source for more than half of the Uruguayan population, understanding and predicting DO dynamics is essential for the sustainability of water resource management [5]. This is particularly important due to the increasing pressures from agricultural runoff, wastewater discharge, and climate variability, which contribute to DO concentration variations within the Santa Lucía watershed [6].

However, DO concentrations are influenced by a complex interaction of physical, chemical, and biological processes rather than a single influencing factor [7]. Hydrological processes, such as streamflow variability and groundwater exchanges, impact oxygen diffusion and dilution capacity. Temperature significantly affects the amount of oxygen that can dissolve in water and the rates at which microbes respire. At the same time, nutrient inputs, especially nitrogen and phosphorus from agricultural and urban activities, can cause eutrophication. This process results in a reduction in oxygen levels due to algal blooms and their subsequent decomposition. Furthermore, human activities like deforestation, land use and land cover alterations, and industrial waste discharges influence these processes, creating difficulties for managing water quality [8,9]. Considering this complexity, the capacity to accurately model DO levels is crucial for evaluating water quality threats, identifying the most significant sources of pollution, and guiding policy decisions.

Recent advances in machine learning (ML) have demonstrated very good performance in modeling water quality parameters, including DO [10,11]. In contrast to conventional physically-based models, machine learning techniques leverage large datasets to achieve high predictive performance by capturing complex relationships between environmental variables and DO levels [12]. Studies have applied various ML techniques, such as artificial neural networks (ANNs), random forests (RF), and support vector machines (SVMs), demonstrating their potential to improve predictive precision [13,14]. Furthermore, physics-informed ML methods, which integrate domain knowledge into data-driven models, have gained attention to improve interpretability and reliability in environmental applications [15]. Despite these advances, there are still challenges in defining the optimal model structure, selecting relevant input features, and incorporating physical constraints to improve generalizability.

A major limitation in current research is the lack of in-depth evaluations of ML-based DO simulations at the watershed scale. While many studies focus on localized or site-specific modeling [16,17], relatively few have investigated large-scale applications that incorporate spatial variability and different environmental conditions. Furthermore, the influence of domain constraints on ML performance remains underexplored, particularly in the context of integrating hydrological and biogeochemical principles into data-driven approaches. Addressing these gaps is crucial for improving the robustness and applicability of ML techniques in water quality assessments.

To bridge this gap, this study focuses on the Santa Lucía River basin and aims to (1) simulate DO concentrations at the watershed scale using different ML models, (2) evaluate the impact of domain constraints on simulation results, and (3) identify and quantify the key variables influencing model performance. By addressing these objectives, this research will contribute to advancing ML applications in water quality modeling by demonstrating the effectiveness of domain-informed feature selection and assessing the performance of multiple algorithms across varied water quality targets.

2   Materials and Methods

2.1   Study Site

The Santa Lucía River Basin is a strategically important watershed in Uruguay, providing raw water for drinking and supplying over half of the country's population (Fig. 1). It also holds substantial economic value, concentrating 32% of the national rural population and serving as one of the main food production hubs. Additionally, the basin supports significant industrial activity [18,19].

However, human activities have led to notable water quality degradation. According to the Action Plan [20], diffuse pollution sources, primarily from agriculture (crop production, horticulture, forage crops, dairy farming, feedlot operations, and pig and poultry farms), account for approximately 75% of the total nitrogen load and 62% of the total phosphorus load. The remaining pollution originates from point sources, including industrial activities (meatpacking, dairy, and leather industries), agroindustry, and domestic wastewater discharges due to inadequate sanitation [21].

The basin under study spans $13,376\,km^2$, with a perimeter of $1,014\,km$ and a compactness index of 2.46 (Fig. 1). It is distributed across six departments: Florida (35%), San José (25%), Canelones (17%), Lavalleja (16%), Flores (6%), and Montevideo (1%). Elevation ranges from $390.5\,m$ in Lavalleja to $-1.20\,m$ near the basin's outlet, with an average slope of 1.92%. The climate is temperate, with four distinct seasons, annual precipitation between $1,000\,mm$ and $1,500\,mm$, and temperatures varying from $3\,°C$ to $30\,°C$ [5].

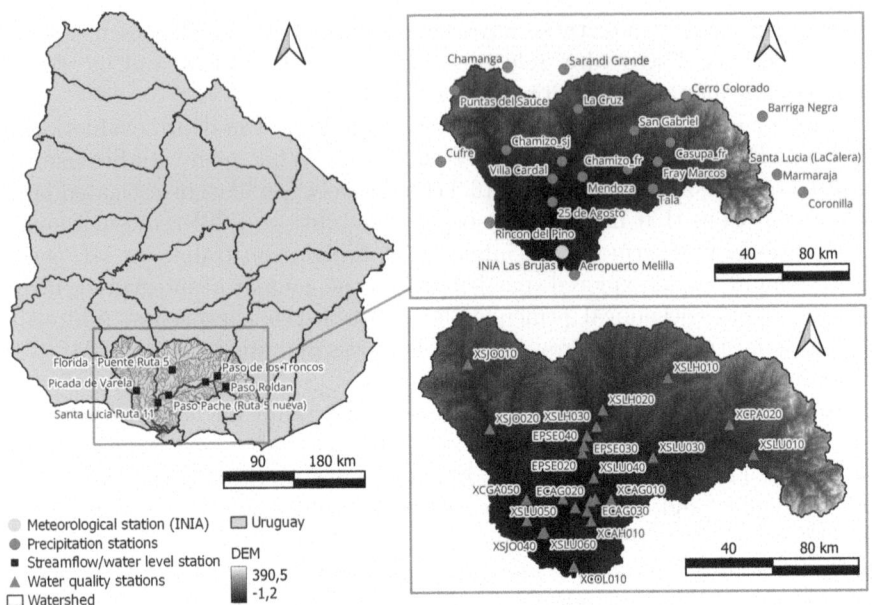

Fig. 1. Study area and location of measurement stations.

2.2 Dataset

This study utilizes hydrometric, meteorological, and water quality data obtained from national monitoring networks.

Hydrometric data consist of streamflow and water level, recorded by the Uruguayan National Water Board from January 1, 1980, to July 4, 2023. Measurements were taken at 8 monitoring stations, represented by black squares in Fig. 1.

Meteorological data were gathered from two institutions: the National Institute of Agricultural Research and the Uruguayan Institute of Meteorology. The Las Brujas station provided daily records of Penman evapotranspiration, relative humidity, mean air temperature, maximum air temperature, minimum air temperature, and wind speed, covering the period from January 1, 1980, to July 4, 2023. Additionally, precipitation was recorded daily by 21 conventional rain gauges between January 1, 1980, and June 27, 2023. The meteorological stations are represented in green and yellow dots in Fig. 1.

Water quality data were collected by the National Board for Quality and Environmental Assessment between January 18, 2011, and December 23, 2022, at 25 monitoring stations (orange triangles in Fig. 1). From the initial 25 water quality monitoring stations, we selected nine for this study based on the availability of concurrent water quality and streamflow data, as well as their strategic locations within the basin. The selected stations are XSLH020 (Florida, Puente Ruta 5), XSLU040 (Paso Pache, Ruta 5 nueva), XSLU050 (Santa Lucía,

Ruta 11), XCPA020 (Paso de los Troncos), XSLU010 (Paso Roldán), EPSE020, XSJO010, XSJO020, and XSLH010. EPSE020 was included due to its critical position at the lake's outlet, serving as a key control point for water dynamics, while XSJO010, XSJO020, and XSLH010 were chosen to represent the upstream sections of the watershed. This selection ensures comprehensive spatial representation and reliable hydrological and water quality data for robust model development. The dataset includes key physicochemical and biological parameters: total phosphorus, total nitrogen, nitrate, nitrite, ammonium, phosphate, total solids, total suspended solids, turbidity, water temperature, dissolved oxygen, biochemical oxygen demand, chlorophyll-a, glyphosate, pH, and conductivity. This dataset is publicly accessible through the National Environmental Observatory.

Due to significant missing data, this dataset was previously imputed in our earlier work [15], and the resulting monthly dataset was used for this study.

2.3   Modeling

In this study, three machine learning models were implemented and compared to simulate DO concentrations in the Santa Lucía River Basin. Each model has different strengths in terms of accuracy, computational efficiency, and ability to capture complex environmental relationships.

Random Forest (RF). RF is an ensemble learning method based on decision trees, where multiple trees are trained using different subsets of the data, and their predictions are averaged to improve accuracy and reduce overfitting. RF has the ability to detect nonlinear correlations and handle noisy data, making it an adequate tool for environmental modeling [22].

Extra Trees Regressor (ET). ET is a variation of RF that adds more randomness to the decision tree building process. On the one hand, RF determines the optimal split points using information gain. On the other hand, ET randomly selects the split points, increasing the variance and helping to reduce the overfitting. This approach enhances computational efficiency compared to RF and is effective with high-dimensional datasets, making it a valuable tool for water quality modeling [23].

Histogram-Based Gradient Boosting Regressor (HGB). HGB is an optimized version of Gradient Boosting. It improves computational efficiency by discretizing continuous features into discrete bins before training. This approach makes the training process much faster and reduces memory consumption, allowing scalability for large datasets. HGB also has the advantage of handling missing data effectively [24]. However, a very careful hyperparameter tuning is required to avoid overfitting, and it may be less interpretable than tree-based models like RF and ET.

2.4   Model Training and Testing

To ensure robust model performance, we adopted a 5-fold cross-validation approach for hyperparameter optimization. This method divides the dataset into
five subsets, using four for training and one for validation in each iteration,
ensuring that every instance contributes to both training and validation sets.
By averaging the outcomes from each fold, cross-validation assesses the model's
performance, helping to decrease overfitting and enhance generalization while
reducing data loss.

Furthermore, an "all-against-all" evaluation framework was applied, considering three different machine learning models (RF, ET, and HGB) and three
different objective functions (Nash-Sutcliffe Efficiency (NSE), Mean Absolute
Error (MAE), and Mean Squared Error (MSE)). This approach ensured that
the best model-metric combination was selected at each station, providing an
in-depth assessment of predictive accuracy and robustness.

Once the optimal hyperparameters were selected, each model was trained
with the complete training set and evaluated using the NSE as the primary
performance metric. The final selection of the best-performing model for each
target variable was based on the highest NSE value in the test set.

2.5   Model Performance Evaluation

Three objective functions were considered for model optimization: NSE, MAE,
and MSE. A rigorous "all-against-all" approach was applied, where each model
was evaluated using all three metrics. The best-performing model-metric pair
was then selected individually for each monitoring station.

Nash-Sutcliffe Efficiency (NSE). NSE measures how well the simulated values match observed data, with values closer to 1 indicating better performance.
It is defined as:

$$NSE = 1 - \frac{\sum_{i=1}^{n}(O_i - P_i)^2}{\sum_{i=1}^{n}(O_i - \bar{O})^2} \tag{1}$$

where O_i and P_i are observed and predicted values, respectively, and $\overline{O}$ is the
mean of observed values.

Mean Absolute Error (MAE). MAE quantifies the average magnitude of
errors without considering their direction. A lower MAE indicates better model
accuracy. It is given by:

$$MAE = \frac{1}{n} \sum_{i=1}^{n} |O_i - P_i| \tag{2}$$

Mean Squared Error (MSE). MSE penalizes larger errors more heavily than MAE by squaring the residuals. It is defined as:

$$MSE = \frac{1}{n} \sum_{i=1}^{n} (O_i - P_i)^2 \tag{3}$$

Kling-Gupta Efficiency (KGE). The KGE metric was also employed to verify the robustness of the model predictions. KGE combines correlation, bias, and variability components into a single efficiency score, providing a more holistic assessment of model performance. It is defined as:

$$KGE = 1 - \sqrt{(r-1)^2 + (\alpha - 1)^2 + (\beta - 1)^2} \tag{4}$$

where r is the Pearson correlation coefficient between observed and predicted values, $\alpha = \frac{\sigma_p}{\sigma_o}$ is the ratio of the standard deviation of predicted (σ_p) to observed values (σ_o), and $\beta = \frac{\mu_p}{\mu_o}$ is the bias ratio between the mean of predicted (μ_p) and observed values (μ_o) [25]. A KGE value closer to 1 indicates better agreement between observed and predicted data, accounting for both precision and bias in the simulation.

This selection process ensured that the final model configuration for each station maximized predictive accuracy while maintaining robustness.

It is important to clarify that in this study, the MSE was employed as the loss function for training the three machine learning models (RF, ET, and HGB). During the hyperparameter optimization process, the three performance metrics were utilized as objective functions in an "all-against-all" approach to identify the best model-metric combination for each station. Finally, the evaluation of the models on the testing set was conducted using NSE and KGE to assess their predictive accuracy and reliability.

2.6   Physical Constraints Applied to Machine Learning Models

The process begins with the calculation of the correlation matrix for the input variables using Pearson, Spearman, and Kendall methods. Variables with a median correlation coefficient lower than 0.5 with the target variable are discarded to ensure that only the most relevant predictors are considered.

Next, both spatial and physical dependencies are taken into account. Spatial dependencies evaluate the location of monitoring stations, discarding those situated downstream of the target station to avoid information leakage. Physical dependencies consider the inherent physical relationships between variables. This means that even if a variable exhibits a correlation lower than 0.5 with the target variable, it may still be included in the model if a strong physical relationship exists. For example, water temperature (WT) is highly dependent on air temperature (AT). Therefore, even if the correlation between WT and AT is below 0.5, AT is included as an input variable in the WT prediction model due to their known physical connection [15].

Since all target variables have a monthly frequency, variables with a daily frequency are resampled to capture their monthly evolution. This is done by calculating their monthly average.

Many variables exhibit high autocorrelation. For instance, water temperature measured at a downstream station is often strongly correlated with measurements from an upstream station. To prevent information leakage and ensure model independence, input variables that contain direct or derived information about the target variable are excluded from the training process, ensuring that the models remain independent of the target variable.

Finally, additional techniques are applied to better reflect spatial and temporal relationships. The Inverse Distance Weighting (IDW) method is used to assign higher weights to observations from nearby sites, effectively reflecting spatial relationships. To address variability over time, the Exponentially Weighted Moving Average (EWMA) is implemented, assigning more importance to recent data points. These methods enhance the model's ability to identify significant patterns while ensuring physical consistency in the simulation of DO levels. A thorough description of such methods is reported in [15].

2.7 Feature Importance Analysis

In this study, we adopted the SHapley Additive exPlanations (SHAP) method to compute the contribution of each input feature for each ML model considered [26]. SHAP values provide an in-depth understanding of the impact that each feature has on model predictions, delivering deeper insights into how the model makes its decisions and behaves under different environmental conditions.

This analysis helps to identify not only the most influential variables but also to determine whether the model is able to capture the underlying physical processes that govern DO dynamics. By quantifying each variable's impact, SHAP enhances model interpretability and allows us to be sure that the predictions align with the real environmental processes.

3 Results and Discussion

3.1 Hyperparameter Optimization

To ensure optimal performance, we conducted hyperparameter optimization for the three different ML models (RF, ET, HGB). Each model was trained and evaluated using the three distinct performance metrics (NSE, MAE, MSE), resulting in a total of nine different trained models.

The optimization was performed using Optuna with a 5-fold cross-validation strategy to enhance model generalization and prevent overfitting. Table 1 summarizes the optimal hyperparameters obtained for the best models after the tuning process.

Table 1. Optimal hyperparameters for the best trained model at each station.

Station	Trained Model	Hyperparameters
EPSE020	RF (MSE)	max_depth = 22 min_samples_leaf = 5 min_samples_split = 6
XCPA020	RF (NSE)	max_depth = 25 min_samples_leaf = 3 min_samples_split = 8
XSJO010	HGB (NSE)	l2_regularization = 0.1997 learning_rate = 0.0233 max_leaf_nodes = 97
XSJO020	ET (MSE)	max_depth = 25 min_samples_leaf = 7
XSLH010	ET (MSE)	max_depth = 7 min_samples_leaf = 2 min_samples_split = 9
XSLH020	ET (NSE)	max_depth = 6 min_samples_leaf = 6 min_samples_split = 12
XSLU010	RF (MSE)	max_depth = 11 min_samples_leaf = 3 min_samples_split = 7
XSLU040	HGB (MAE)	l2_regularization = 0.6274 learning_rate = 0.0168 max_leaf_nodes = 106
XSLU050	HGB (MSE)	l2_regularization = 0.6538 learning_rate = 0.0358 max_leaf_nodes = 103

3.2   Simulation Results

Once the optimal hyperparameters were identified, the models were evaluated using the best configurations obtained during the optimization process. Each model was tested under different performance metrics (NSE, MAE, and MSE) in an exhaustive pairwise evaluation approach, where all models were assessed using each metric. This allowed for a comprehensive comparison of their predictive capabilities.

After evaluating the results, the best model-metric combination was selected based on overall performance across different stations. Table 2 summarizes the final results, detailing the best-performing model, the optimal metric, and the NSE values for both training and testing at each monitoring station. Figure 2 presents boxplots comparing predicted and observed OD values across all stations, while Fig. 3 presents two plots comparing simulated and observed OD time series at two stations (XSLU050 and XSLH010) as examples.

Table 2. NSE and KGE values for training and testing of the best-trained model at each station.

Station	Best Model (Metric)	Train NSE	Train KGE	Test NSE	Test KGE
EPSE020	RF (MSE)	0.81	0.77	0.44	0.46
XCPA020	RF (NSE)	0.82	0.80	0.81	0.90
XSJO010	HGB (NSE)	0.80	0.76	0.51	0.74
XSJO020	ET (MSE)	0.82	0.83	0.66	0.84
XSLH010	ET (MSE)	0.92	0.89	0.84	0.88
XSLH020	ET (NSE)	0.82	0.83	0.88	0.93
XSLU010	RF (MSE)	0.87	0.83	0.66	0.84
XSLU040	HGB (MAE)	0.31	0.27	−0.05	−0.15
XSLU050	HGB (MSE)	0.83	0.81	−0.02	0.43

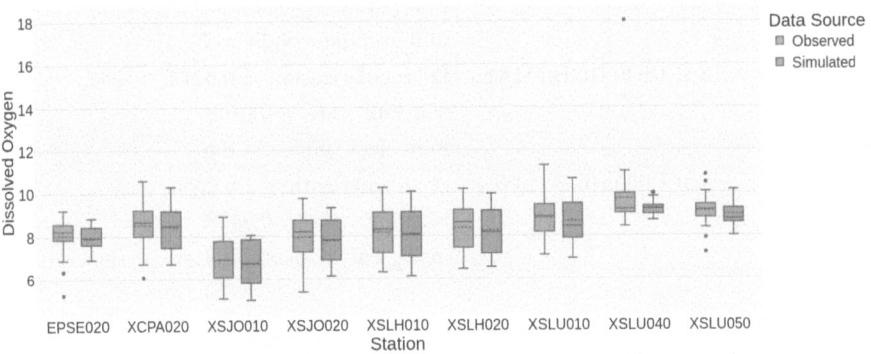

Fig. 2. Simulated and observed DO levels across monitoring stations. Green boxplots represent observed values, while red boxplots represent simulated values. (Color figure online)

The overall model performance across the study area was satisfactory in most cases, with 7 out of 9 stations achieving an NSE value above 0.4, indicating that the models were able to capture the variability of DO dynamics reasonably well. Among these, five stations demonstrated particularly strong performance ($NSE > 0.65$), suggesting that the chosen input variables and model configurations were well-suited for those locations.

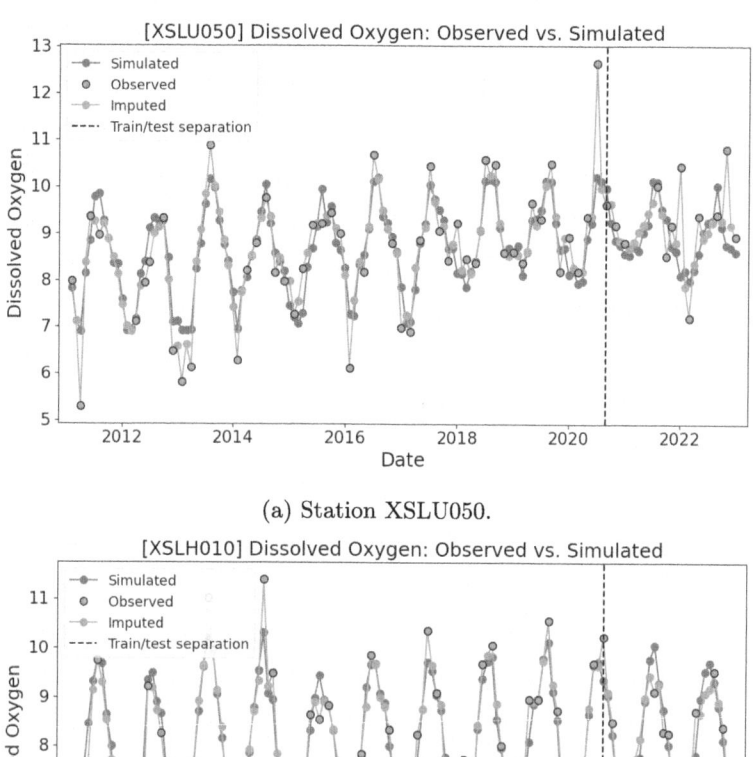

(a) Station XSLU050.

(b) Station XSLH010.

Fig. 3. Comparison of simulated and observed DO time series at stations (a) XSLU050 and (b) XSLH010.

However, two stations, XSLU040 and XSLU050, exhibited unsatisfactory results. This could be attributed to several factors, including data quality issues or unaccounted local hydrodynamic processes.

Figure 4 shows the number of times each model and each performance metric were selected as the optimal choice across all stations.

The results indicate that no single model consistently outperformed the others, as each of the three models was selected three times. This suggests that model performance is highly dependent on the specific characteristics of each

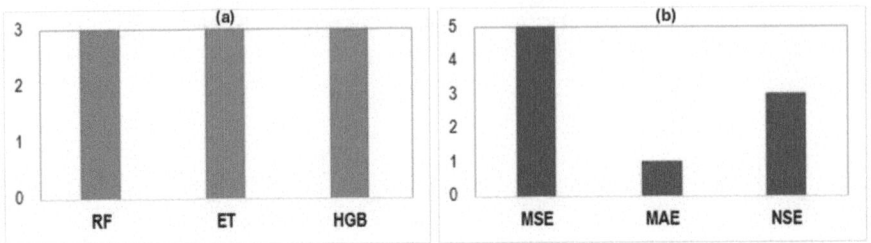

Fig. 4. Number of times each model (a) and each performance metric (b) was selected as the best.

station and dataset rather than on the intrinsic superiority of one algorithm over the others. Factors such as local hydrodynamic conditions, data distribution and availability, and the influence of different input variables likely played a role in determining which model was best suited for each case. Additionally, the differences in how each algorithm handles feature interactions and nonlinearity may have contributed to this even distribution.

Regarding the performance metrics, MSE was selected as the best metric five times, compared to the MAE, which was chosen only once, and the NSE, which was selected three times. This preference for MSE may be explained by its sensitivity to large errors, which makes it more effective in optimizing models that aim to minimize extreme deviations in DO predictions. Since water quality data can exhibit occasional high variability due to sudden changes in environmental conditions (e.g., rainfall events, pollution discharges), MSE's emphasis on penalizing larger errors likely led to better model selection in most cases. In contrast, MAE gives equal weight to all errors, which may not be ideal for capturing the nuances of DO fluctuations. Meanwhile, NSE, though widely used in hydrological modeling, balances both variance and bias, but its performance may have been influenced by the characteristics of the dataset at specific stations.

3.3   Feature Importance Results

The feature importance analysis was conducted using SHAP values, which were calculated based on the best-performing model at each station. This approach allowed for a detailed assessment of the contribution of each input variable to the DO predictions. For each monitoring station, the most influential variables were ranked, providing insights into the dominant drivers of DO variability across the watershed. In Fig. 5, the SHAP results for the stations XSLH020 and XCPA020 are reported as an example.

The SHAP analysis revealed that the most influential variables for DO simulation were water temperature at the target station and at the nearest upstream station, along with air temperature (minimum, average, and maximum). These findings align with well-established physical and biochemical processes governing DO dynamics in freshwater systems [5].

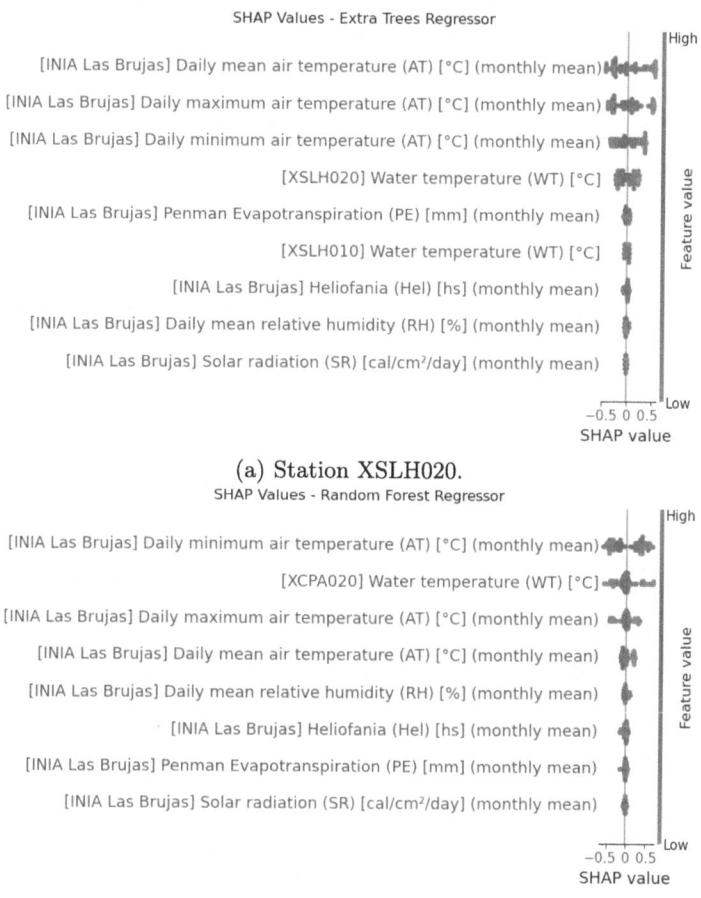

(a) Station XSLH020.

(b) Station XCPA020.

Fig. 5. SHAP values for the best-performing models at stations XSLH020 and XCPA020.

Water temperature plays a key role in predicting DO concentration due to its direct effect on oxygen solubility and biological activity. As temperature increases, oxygen solubility decreases, leading to lower DO concentrations. Moreover, higher temperatures accelerate microbial and biochemical oxygen demand, further reducing available oxygen. The strong impact of water temperature at the target station is expected, as it directly influences local DO conditions. The importance of upstream water temperature, instead, suggests that thermal conditions propagate downstream, impacting DO levels at the target monitoring station.

Air temperature, particularly its minimum, average, and maximum values, also emerged as a key predictor. This is consistent with its role in controlling water temperature through heat exchange processes [5]. The inclusion of multiple air temperature statistics suggests that both short-term (daily variations) and long-term (monthly trends) thermal dynamics affect DO fluctuations.

The dominance of temperature-related variables in DO predictions indicates that the model successfully captures the thermal dependency of DO dynamics.

4   Conclusions

This study aimed to simulate DO concentrations at the watershed scale using ML models, assess the impact of physical constraints on the simulation results, and identify the key variables driving model performance. By incorporating domain knowledge through physical constraints, the models were able to capture essential environmental relationships, improving the realism and accuracy of DO predictions.

The models were optimized using hyperparameter tuning, and performance was evaluated through a rigorous "all-against-all" approach, selecting the best model-metric pair for each station. The results revealed no clear preference for any single model, as RF, ET, and HGB were each chosen three times. Among the evaluation metrics, MSE was selected more frequently than the other metrics, highlighting its greater sensitivity to large errors during model training.

The models performed satisfactorily in most stations, with seven out of nine stations achieving NSE values above 0.4 and five stations yielding very good results. However, two stations (XSLU040 and XSLU050) exhibited unsatisfactory performance, possibly due to data limitations or the absence of key predictors.

The feature importance analysis shows that water temperature, both at the target station and an upstream station, along with air temperature, were the most influential variables in the DO simulations. These results align with the known physical processes governing DO dynamics, where temperature plays a crucial role in oxygen solubility and biological activity.

In conclusion, the study demonstrates the effectiveness of applying ML models with physical constraints to simulate DO concentrations at the watershed scale. The results emphasize the importance of incorporating domain-specific knowledge into model design while also pointing to the potential for future improvements by expanding the range of input variables and refining the model's physical assumptions.

Acknowledgments. This work was supported by the National Research and Innovation Agency (ANII) [grant numbers FMV-3-2022-1-172720].

Disclosure of Interests. The authors have no competing interests to declare that are relevant to the content of this article.

References

1. Gorgoglione, A., Russo, C., Gioia, A., Iacobellis, V., Castro, A.: Comparing neural network architectures for simulating pollutant loads and first flush events in urban watersheds: balancing specialization and generalization. Chemosphere **379**, 144395 (2025). https://doi.org/10.1016/j.chemosphere.2025.144395
2. Boratto, T.H., et al.: Hybridized machine learning models for phosphate pollution modeling in water systems for multiple uses. J. Water Process Eng. **64**, 105598 (2024). https://doi.org/10.1016/j.jwpe.2024.105598
3. Banerjee, A., Chakrabarty, M., Rakshit, N., Bhowmick, A.R., Ray, S.: Environmental factors as indicators of dissolved oxygen concentration and zooplankton abundance: deep learning versus traditional regression approach. Ecol. Indicat. **100**, 99–117 (2019). https://doi.org/10.1016/j.ecolind.2018.09.051
4. Lucas, C., et al.: Nutrient levels, trophic status and land-use influences on streams, rivers and lakes in a protected floodplain of Uruguay. Limnologica **94**, 125966 (2022). https://doi.org/10.1016/j.limno.2022.125966
5. Gorgoglione, A., Gregorio, J., Ríos, A., Alonso, J., Chreties, C., Fossati, M.: Influence of land use/land cover on surface-water quality of Santa Lucía river, Uruguay. Sustainability **12**(10), 4692 (2020). https://doi.org/10.3390/su12114692
6. Aubriot, L.E., Delbene, L., Haakonsson, S., Somma, A., Hirsch, F., Bonilla, S.: Evolución de la eutrofización en el Río Santa Lucía: Influencia de la intensificación productiva y perspectivas. INNOTEC (14 jul-dic), 07–16 (2017)
7. Cox, B.A.: A review of dissolved oxygen modelling techniques for lowland rivers. Sci. Total Environ. **314–316**, 303–334 (2003)
8. Greig, S.M., Sear, D.A., Carling, P.A.: A review of factors influencing the availability of dissolved oxygen to incubating salmonid embryos. Hydrol. Process. **21**(3), 323–334 (2006)
9. Peña, M.A., Katsev, S., Oguz, T., Gilbert, D.: Modeling dissolved oxygen dynamics and hypoxia. Biogeosciences **7**(3), 933–957 (2010)
10. Valera, M., Walter, R.K., Bailey, B.A., Castillo, J.E.: Machine learning based predictions of dissolved oxygen in a small coastal embayment. J. Marine Sci. Eng. **8**(12), 1007 (2020). https://doi.org/10.3390/jmse8121007
11. Ziyad Sami, B.F., et al.: Machine learning algorithm as a sustainable tool for dissolved oxygen prediction: a case study of Feitsui Reservoir, Taiwan. Sci. Rep. **12**, 3649 (2022). https://doi.org/10.1038/s41598-022-06969-z
12. Pou, M., Pastorini, M., Alonso, J., Gorgoglione, A.: Exploring the nexus between water quality and land use/land cover change in an urban watershed in Uruguay: a machine learning approach. Environ. Sci. Pollut. Res. **31**, 48687-48705 (2024). https://doi.org/10.1007/s11356-024-34414-3
13. Russo, C., Castro, A., Gioia, A., Iacobellis, V., Gorgoglione, A.: Improving the sediment and nutrient first-flush prediction and ranking its influencing factors: an integrated machine-learning framework. J. Hydrol. **616**, 128842 (2023)
14. Vilaseca, F., Castro, A., Chreties, C., Gorgoglione, A.: Assessing influential rainfall-runoff variables to simulate daily streamflow using random forest. Hydrol. Sci. J. **68**(12), 1738—1753 (2023). https://doi.org/10.1080/02626667.2023.2232356
15. Pastorini, M., Rodríguez, R., Etcheverry, L., Castro, A., Gorgoglione, A.: Enhancing environmental data imputation: a physically-constrained machine learning framework. Sci. Total Environ. **926**, 171773 (2024)
16. Barreto, P., Dogliotti, S., Perdomo, C.: Surface water quality of intensive farming areas within the Santa Lucia river basin of Uruguay. Air Soil Water Res. **10** (2017). https://doi.org/10.1177/1178622117715446

17. Díaz, I., et al.: Empirical modeling of stream nutrients for countries without robust water quality monitoring systems. Environments **8**(11), 129 (2021). https://doi.org/10.3390/environments8110129

18. DINOT/MVOTMA. Atlas de la cuenca del río santa lucía (2015). https://www.gub.uy/ministerio-vivienda-ordenamiento-territorial/comunicacion/publicaciones/atlas-cuenca-del-rio-santa-lucia. Accessed 11 Feb 2025

19. MVOTMA. Plan Nacional de Aguas (2017). www.gub.uy/inisterio-ambiente/politicas-y-gestion/planes/plan-nacional-aguas. Accessed 11 Feb 2025

20. SNAAC. Plan de acción para la protección de la calidad ambiental de la cuenca del río Santa Lucía. Medidas de segunda generación (2018). https://www.gub.uy/ministerio-ambiente/sites/ministerio-ambiente/files/documentos/publicaciones/PLAN_DE_ACCION_RIO_SANTA_LUCIA_MEDIDAS_DE_2da_GENERACION.pdf. Accessed 11 Feb 2025

21. Navas, R., Alonso, J., Gorgoglione, A., Vervoort, R.W.: Identifying climate and human impact trends in streamflow: a case study in Uruguay. Water **11**(7), 1433 (2019). https://doi.org/10.3390/w11071433

22. Breiman, L.: Random forests. Mach. Learn. **45**(1), 5–32 (2001). https://doi.org/10.1023/A:1010933404324

23. Geurts, P., Ernst, D., Wehenkel, L.: Extremely randomized trees. Mach. Learn. **63**(1), 3–42 (2006). https://doi.org/10.1007/s10994-006-6226-1

24. Ke, G., et al.: LightGBM: a highly efficient gradient boosting decision tree. In: Advances in Neural Information Processing Systems (NIPS 2017), vol. 30, pp. 3149–3157 (2017)

25. Izzaddin, A., Langousis, A., Totaro, V., Yaseen, M., Iacobellis, V.: A new diagram for performance evaluation of complex models. Stoch. Env. Res. Risk Assess. **38**(6), 2261–2281 (2024)

26. Lundberg, S.M., Lee, S.-I.: A unified approach to interpreting model predictions. In: Advances in Neural Information Processing Systems, pp. 4768–4777 (2017)

International Workshop on Information and Knowledge in the Internet of Things (IKIT 2025)

Determinants of University Dropout and Educational Quality Improvement

Alicia Andrade Vera[1]([✉]) [iD], Juan Martinez[2], and Anthony Pachay Espinoza[1] [iD]

[1] Universidad Estatal Península de Santa Elena, Santa Elena, Ecuador
{aandrade,aespinoza}@upse.edu.ec
[2] Universidad Internacional De La Rioja, La Rioja, Spain
juanpedromartinezramon@um.es

Abstract. University dropout is a multifaceted phenomenon that affects students, educational institutions, and society. This study systematically analyzes the factors contributing to this phenomenon and their connection to educational quality through a multidisciplinary approach that includes educational, psychological, and sociological theories. Through a systematic mapping of recent literature, the main internal and external factors influencing dropout, as well as the strategies implemented to mitigate it, were identified. The results highlight factors such as lack of belonging, low academic performance, and economic difficulties, and propose retention strategies based on institutional strengthening and comprehensive support. This work aims to provide practical and sustainable solutions to reduce university dropout rates and improve educational quality.

Keywords: Educational quality · university dropout · retention strategies · systematic mapping

1 Introduction

University dropout is a significant issue that negatively impacts students' academic trajectories, institutional performance, and the social and economic development of communities. This phenomenon, defined as the definitive or temporary interruption of higher education studies, has multifactorial causes, including academic, personal, socioeconomic, and institutional aspects. According to recent studies, approximately 30% of university students in Latin America abandon their studies during the first year of training [1].

The effects of dropout are not limited to the individual; they also impact on the reputation of educational institutions, tuition revenue, and the overall efficiency of the education system. Additionally, dropout perpetuates social inequalities, as students from disadvantaged socioeconomic backgrounds face greater barriers to completing their studies [2]. In Europe, [3] pointed out that factors such as migrant background and parental education also influence the sense of belonging, exacerbating challenges for these groups. In the case of France, [4] found that the combination of work and study, rather than being a support mechanism, can hinder academic success. On the other hand, research in Ireland and Scotland highlights that inclusive admission policies can significantly improve retention rates, promoting greater equity [5]. This study aims to identify and analyze the factors influencing university dropout and its relationship with educational quality through a systematic literature review and a critical analysis of effective student retention strategies. The findings are expected to support the design of evidence-based interventions to reduce dropout and improve educational quality in higher education institutions.

2 Theoretical Foundations

2.1 University Dropout

University dropout is defined as the abandonment of studies before completing an academic program, representing one of the major challenges in higher education [6]. This phenomenon results from multiple academic, personal, economic, and institutional factors and can be classified as early or late dropout. Among the main influencing factors are financial difficulties, low academic performance, lack of institutional support, and mental health issues, whose interaction can determine student retention [7].

Educational quality in the university context encompasses teaching performance, infrastructure, program relevance, and academic support. The competence and adaptability of teachers play a crucial role in learning quality, while student satisfaction and the effectiveness of retention programs are key indicators of educational quality [8]. In Ecuador, educational quality has been a priority in educational policies, although scientific production on this topic has significantly declined (-85.71%) in the Web of Science. Recent research has focused on management strategies, educational assessment, and curricular adaptation, highlighting the need to strengthen studies aimed at improving the country's educational system [9].

2.2 Educational Quality Models

Tinto's Integration Model [6] is one of the most recognized approaches in the study of university dropout. This model suggests that students leave university due to a lack of both academic and social integration. Academic integration includes performance and satisfaction with study programs, while social integration relates to student life and the ability to form relationships within the university. Students who fail to integrate in these aspects are more likely to drop out. On the other hand, the Higher Education Quality Model [10] defines educational quality through five dimensions: exceptionality, consistency, fitness for purpose, transformation, and added value. This model emphasizes that educational quality is not limited to academic performance but also includes the institution's ability to transform students by providing support services, adapting to their needs, and continuously improving educational processes.

2.3 Relationship Between Factors and University Dropout

Economic factors are one of the main determinants of university dropout, as low-income students face difficulties in covering education costs. This often forces them to work while studying, negatively impacting their academic performance and increasing the likelihood of dropping out [4]. [11] highlight that financial difficulties account for a significant proportion of dropout cases, particularly in the early years of university education.

Academic performance also influences dropout rates. Students who struggle to meet academic demands or lack adequate support often become demotivated and leave their studies [7]. However, access to tutoring and mentoring programs can significantly reduce this risk by providing students with the tools needed to overcome academic challenges.

Mental health has become a crucial factor in university dropouts. Stress, anxiety, and depression increase the likelihood of students abandoning their studies, especially if they lack psychological support networks [3]. Institutions that offer student wellness programs can significantly improve retention by creating a supportive and caring environment. Institutional support and retention policies play a key role in student retention. Strategies such as personalized tutoring, academic advising, and career counseling have proven effective in keeping students enrolled [12].However, a lack of coordination and resources in some universities limits the impact of these strategies, highlighting the need for reevaluation of retention policies to better address student needs.

A lack of financial, academic, and psychological support negatively affects students' perception of educational quality. Universities that fail to address these issues are often seen as lower quality, further reinforcing dropout rates. Conversely, institutions that implement comprehensive retention and student support strategies not only improve student retention rates but also enhance student satisfaction and academic commitment.

2.4 Factors Influencing University Student Dropout

Table 1 presents a structured classification of the primary factors associated with university dropout, organized into six comprehensive categories: socioeconomic, academic, personal, institutional, technological, and social. These categories emerged from a synthesis of the most recurrent themes identified in the reviewed literature, reflecting the multifactorial and systemic nature of student attrition in higher education. Each category encompasses specific variables that have shown significant influence on dropout decisions across diverse contexts. The factors are not only interconnected but also often cumulative, meaning that students affected by multiple vulnerabilities are at even greater risk of abandoning their studies. For each factor, a concise description is provided to clarify its impact, alongside bibliographic references that substantiate its inclusion. This classification aims to provide a holistic overview of the complexity surrounding the university dropout and serves as a foundation for designing targeted retention strategies and institutional policies.

3 Methods

This study was conducted using a systematic mapping review of scientific literature, applying the PRISMA 2020 (Preferred Reporting Items for Systematic Reviews and Meta-Analyses) guidelines to ensure transparency and reproducibility in the search, selection, and analysis of sources. The review aimed to identify the main determinants

Table 1. Factors Influencing University Dropout

Category	Factor	Description	References
Socioeconomic	Financial difficulties	Economic difficulties affect academic performance and can lead to dropout	[2, 4, 7, 11, 13–15]
	Need to work	Many students must work while studying, affecting their performance	[2, 4, 5, 16–19]
	Lack of scholarships or financial support	The lack of scholarships and financial support limits student retention	[1, 2, 4, 5, 16–18]
	Family socioeconomic inequality	Students from low-income families have less access to educational resources	[3, 20]
Academic	Low academic performance	Students with low academic performance tend to become demotivated and drop out	[2, 7, 11, 14, 16, 21–24]
	Dissatisfaction with the study program	Lack of interest in the study program can lead to dropout	[7, 16, 17, 21, 22]
	Lack of tutoring	The absence of tutoring and academic support affects student retention	[5, 11, 14]
	Wrong vocational choice	The lack of adequate vocational guidance leads to early dropout	[4, 13, 16, 25]

(*continued*)

of university dropout, and the strategies implemented to improve educational quality, based on empirical and theoretical academic research. Searches were performed in three

Table 1. (*continued*)

Category	Factor	Description	References
	Excessive academic workload	An excessive academic workload can cause stress and dropout	[4, 7, 13, 16, 24–26]
Personal	Mental health problems (stress, anxiety, depression)	Stress, anxiety, and depression increase the likelihood of dropout	[1, 3, 16, 19, 24, 26, 27]
	Lack of motivation	Lack of interest and motivation contributes to university dropout	[16–18, 22, 28, 29]
	Low self-efficacy	Students with low confidence in their abilities tend to drop out	[16–18, 30]
Institutional	Lack of institutional support	The lack of tutoring, academic guidance, and counseling increases dropout rates	[5, 7, 11, 16, 31, 32]
	Deficient admission policies	Inadequate admission policies can lead to early dropout	[5, 23]
	Dissatisfaction with the university	A negative perception of the university influences the decision to drop out	[2, 16, 22, 33, 34]
	Inadequate infrastructure	Poor infrastructure affects educational quality and student retention	[2, 23, 31]
Technological	Difficulties with virtual education	Difficulties in virtual education can increase dropout rates	[19, 22, 25, 27, 33, 35, 36]

(*continued*)

major academic databases: Scopus, ERIC, and ProQuest, focusing on studies published between 2021 and 2024.

Table 1. (*continued*)

Category	Factor	Description	References
	Lack of access to adequate technology	Lack of access to technology affects learning and student retention	[7, 14, 19, 22, 27]
Social	Social isolation	Social isolation increases the risk of dropout	[3, 14, 16, 37]
	Lack of integration into the university community	Lack of academic and social integration increases dropout rates	[3, 7, 15, 23, 30]
	Mismatch between university life and personal life	The imbalance between university and personal life leads to dropout	[26, 38]

Source: Own elaboration.

3.1 Materials

The selected material consisted of peer-reviewed articles published in English or Spanish from 2021 to 2024, addressing factors related to university dropout, retention, and educational quality. Articles were managed with Mendeley for reference organization and processed using Microsoft Excel for thematic categorization.

The inclusion criteria for this review required articles to be focused on university-level dropout, student retention, or academic quality; they had to be peer-reviewed, published between 2021 and 2024, written in either English or Spanish, and available in full-text format. Studies were excluded if they constituted gray literature—such as these, reports, or editorials—or if they did not pertain to higher education, were duplicate records, or were inaccessible at the time of review.

There was no direct human intervention. However, the reviewed studies included diverse samples such as undergraduate students, faculty members, and academic authorities from various countries and regions, including Latin America, Europe, and Asia. All selected studies adhered to their own ethical protocols regarding participant protection.

3.2 Search and Analysis Procedures

The methodology employed in this study involved a rigorous, multi-stage process designed to ensure a comprehensive and transparent examination of the available literature on university dropout and educational quality improvement. This process followed the PRISMA 2020 guidelines and was divided into three main phases: data collection, thematic analysis, and evidence synthesis. Data Collection the initial phase consisted of a systematic search of academic literature using three high-impact databases: Scopus, ERIC, and ProQuest. The search strategy was developed based on a combination of relevant keywords, including "university dropout," "student retention," "educational quality," and "higher education." Boolean operators (AND, OR) were used to refine results, and filters were applied to restrict the time range to publications from 2021 to 2024, and to peer-reviewed articles written in English or Spanish.

The selection process followed the four standard PRISMA phases: identification, screening, eligibility, and inclusion. A total of 493 records were initially identified across the databases. After removing duplicates, 430 unique titles and abstracts were screened for relevance. Of these, 65 full-text articles were reviewed in detail, and 12 studies met all eligibility criteria and were selected for the final synthesis.

Each article was analyzed in detail and coded according to these dimensions, allowing for the identification of cross-cutting themes, points of convergence, and divergences across cultural and geographic contexts. Patterns such as the prevalence of financial stress in Latin America, or the impact of social belonging in European universities, were systematically compared to understanding both global and regional challenges. Each study was categorized using a predefined codebook that included thematic tags (e.g., "financial strain," "academic integration," "self-efficacy," "institutional policy") and methodological dimensions (qualitative, quantitative, mixed). Additionally, effectiveness ratings were assigned based on the clarity of the intervention described, the presence of measurable outcomes, and statistical significance when reported.

This approach allowed for cross-contextual comparison while maintaining analytical consistency. In the final phase, the extracted data were synthesized through a narrative and comparative approach, combining qualitative insights and quantitative indicators where available. Studies were assessed in terms of the dropout-related variables they addressed, the methodology used (qualitative, quantitative, or mixed), and the effectiveness of the interventions proposed. Particular attention was paid to studies that included: Longitudinal tracking of student performance and persistence, evaluation of institutional programs aimed at increasing retention and predictive modeling using machine learning or survival analysis techniques.

This comparative summary supports methodological transparency and highlights the diversity of contexts and approaches present in the current literature. Figure 1 presents the PRISMA 2020 flow diagram illustrating this selection process, ensuring transparency and traceability in the methodology.

To contextualize the findings, impact indicators such as reported dropout rates, institutional satisfaction, or policy outcomes were used. For example, study [11] demonstrated that perceived institutional support had a statistically significant effect on the intention to remain enrolled, highlighting the importance of non-academic variables in student persistence. A comprehensive overview of the studies included in the review, detailing authorship, methodology, country, and thematic focus, is presented in Table 2.

3.3 Limitations of the Method

While this systematic review provides a comprehensive overview of the determinants of university dropout and educational quality, it is not without limitations. First, the

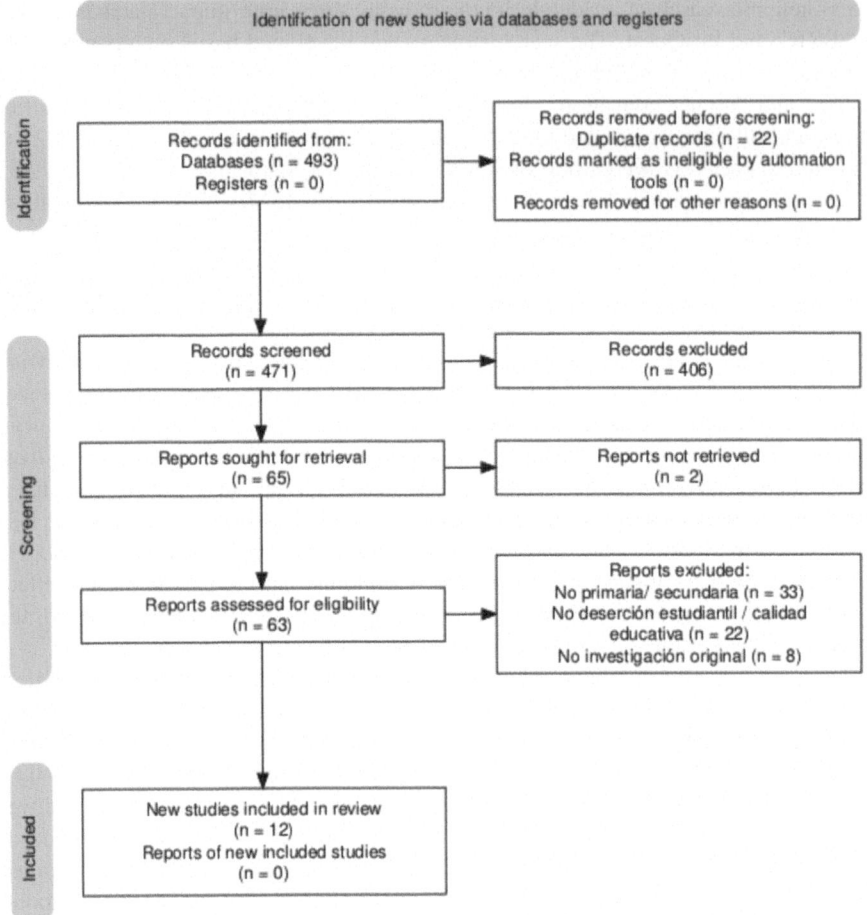

Fig. 1. Prisma Flow Diagram

heterogeneity of the studies included—in terms of methodology, geographical scope, and target populations—limits direct comparability and generalizability of the findings.

Second, most of the included studies are cross-sectional, which restricts the ability to identify long-term trends or causal relationships between the variables examined. The lack of longitudinal or experimental designs is a limitation frequently noted in literature itself.

Third, although a robust search strategy was implemented using high-quality academic databases, some relevant studies may have been excluded due to language restrictions, limited access to full texts, or publication outside the 2021–2024-time frame. Finally, due to the diversity in research designs and variables, no statistical meta-analysis was conducted. As a result, the synthesis was primarily qualitative, which,

Table 2. Summary of Selected Studies.

Ref.	Authors	Year	Country	Type & Design	Objective	Limitations	Results
[11]	Barrientos-Illanes et al.	2021	Chile	Quant., Path analysis	Autonomy & self-efficacy	Single private university	Satisfaction mediates
[4]	Béduwé & Giret	2021	France	Quant., Regression	Student employment impact	French context only	Work during exams raises failure risk
[3]	Janke et al.	2024	Germany	Quant., Survey	Migration and social ostracism	Cross-sectional design	Minorities show lower belonging
[40]	Llauró et al.	2023	Spain	Quant., Statistical analysis	Dropout-related variables	No personal/family data	Perf. And satisfaction affect dropout
[25]	Vega-Martínez et al.	2023	Spain	Quant., Exploratory	Learning patterns and stress	Single institution	Patterns link to stress and performance
[2]	Valencia-Arias et al.	2023	Colombia	Quant., Predictive model	Dropout prediction model	Not generalizable globally	Identifies key dropout factors
[18]	Morelli et al.	2023	Italy	Quant., Moderation analysis	Self-efficacy and friendships	Italian-only sample	Friendships affect dropout intention
[41]	Galve-González et al.	2024	Spain	Quant., Longitudinal	Transitions and uncertainty	Early years focus only	Career doubts lead to dropout
[5]	Iannelli et al.	2024	Ireland & Scotland	Quant., Comparative	Admission policy effects	Two-country scope	Inclusive policies boost retention
[39]	Cobo-Rendón et al.	2023	Chile	Quant., Cross-sectional	Academic emotions	No longitudinal data	Positive emotions reduce dropout
[31]	Bernardo et al.	2022	Switzerland	Quant., Path model	Satisfaction and engagement	Regional sample	Both reduce dropout
[1]	Reyes-González & Meneses-Báez	2024	Colombia	Qual., Systematic review	Psychosocial adjustment	Possible study omissions	Support and motivation aid retention

Source: Own elaboration.

while rich in contextual interpretation, may reduce statistical precision. These limitations should be considered when interpreting the results and their implications for institutional decision-making and policy development.

4 Discussion and Interpretation of Results

4.1 Main Patterns and Cross-Contextual Findings

This study has analyzed the key factors influencing university dropout and its relationship with educational quality, contributing to the understanding of a complex and multifaceted phenomenon. The obtained results confirm and expand upon previous research findings, highlighting common patterns and discrepancies across different contexts. Findings indicate that factors such as lack of belonging, economic difficulties, and dissatisfaction with the study program are key elements that increase the risk of dropout. Additionally, self-regulation strategies and institutional support emerge as protective variables that promote student retention. These results align with the conclusions of [1], who emphasized that learning self-regulation and institutional commitment are essential for improving student persistence.

[11] demonstrated that perceived autonomy support, self-efficacy, and academic satisfaction are crucial factors in students' intention to persist. These findings coincide with the results of this study, which underscores the importance of educational environments that foster satisfaction and intrinsic motivation as key measures to reduce dropout rates.

Similarly, the findings of [28]in Italy reinforce this relationship, showing that students with high self-efficacy exhibit lower dropout intentions, highlighting the value of academic empowerment.

[4] argued that intensive work during studies hinders academic success, increasing dropout rates and extending graduation times in France. This finding is also reflected in the analysis by [37], who studied cases in South Africa, observing that economic and work-related pressures disproportionately affect students from disadvantaged backgrounds, limiting their ability to meet academic demands.

[31] identified that academic commitment, and the use of self-regulated learning strategies are key predictors of dropout intention. This resonates with the findings of [39], who analyzed the impact of a peer mentoring program and found that such approaches significantly reduce dropout rates by fostering social and academic engagement in the early years of university.

[40] emphasized that positive emotions such as hope, and enjoyment facilitate adaptation to the university environment and reduce dropout intention. This result is consistent with the study by [17], who analyzed how the pandemic affected students' mental health and concluded that negative emotions, such as stress, exacerbate dropout risks among students with prior vulnerabilities.

[5] in Ireland and Scotland highlighted that inclusive admission systems improve retention and reduce social inequalities. Similarly, [24] observed that, in Chile, equitable access and institutional support are critical to ensuring educational continuity, especially for students from rural regions.

[29] addressed course transitions and how uncertainty during the early years affects student retention. This complemented the findings of [16], who demonstrated that appropriate workload distribution per course in STEM programs improves academic outcomes and reduces dropout rates. This study presents some important limitations. The systematic review methodology may exclude relevant studies not included in the selected

databases. Additionally, the absence of longitudinal analysis limits the ability to observe how risk and protective factors evolve over time.

Given these considerations, future research should conduct longitudinal studies to examine the temporal dynamics of dropout factors, as well as experimental investigations to evaluate the effectiveness of specific interventions. Moreover, it would be valuable to explore how cultural and contextual differences impact the effectiveness of retention strategies.

The results highlight that:

1. Internal factors, such as low academic performance, lack of self-regulation, and mental health difficulties, are directly related to university dropout [31]. These factors affect students' ability to meet academic demands and adapt to the university environment.
2. External factors, such as economic difficulties and limited institutional support, worsen dropout rates, especially among students from disadvantaged socioeconomic backgrounds [2]. [25] found that surface learning patterns are linked to higher academic stress and lower performance.
3. The most effective retention strategies include mentoring programs, financial support, and the creation of inclusive environments that foster a sense of belonging [40]. In a related study, [29] highlighted that academic engagement mediates the relationship between self-regulation strategies and students' intention to persist.
4. Dropout prediction models based on data analysis have proven to be valuable tools for identifying students at risk and developing personalized interventions. In countries like Spain and Colombia, these models have enabled better management of institutional resources [5].
5. The perception of social and academic support also plays a crucial role in student retention [18]. Found that students with broader support networks exhibit lower dropout intention rates, even in contexts of low self-efficacy.
6. The interaction between institutional policies and student profiles is key to designing effective interventions. For example, inclusive admission policies in Scotland have significantly reduced dropout gaps among students from different socioeconomic backgrounds [5].
7. Finally, emotional factors such as anxiety and intrinsic motivation are related to academic performance and students' intention to continue their studies, as evidenced [40]. These variables highlight the need for a comprehensive approach that considers both academic and emotional aspects in retention strategies.

4.2 Evidence-Based Strategies for Student Retention

The analysis of the selected studies reveals a wide range of strategies aimed at improving student retention and mitigating university dropouts. These strategies vary not only in their focus—academic, psychosocial, institutional, and economic—but also in their contextual effectiveness depending on region, discipline, and student demographics.

Academic strategies are among the most common and effective interventions. These include learning skills workshops, tutoring programs, and the implementation of adaptive curricula. Several studies [18] emphasize the importance of self-regulated learning, academic self-efficacy, and performance monitoring systems. In STEM fields, restructuring course loads to balance academic demand has shown positive effects on reducing stress and dropout intentions [1]. Moreover, early warning systems based on performance indicators, such as grades or attendance, have been successfully deployed to identify at-risk students and provide targeted academic support [29, 31].

Psychosocial Strategies are interventions that address the emotional, motivational, and relational dimensions of the student experience. Peer mentoring, counseling services, and initiatives that strengthen the sense of belonging are fundamental components in this area. Studies such as [31] show that students who feel emotionally supported and connected to their peers are significantly more likely to persist in their studies. This is especially important for minority and first-generation college students [3], who often report feelings of isolation. The promotion of mental health awareness, combined with access to professional psychological support, is also crucial, especially considering the rising prevalence of anxiety and depression among university students [15].

Institutional strategies that promote student engagement, community building, and meaningful interactions with faculty have a proven impact on retention. These include structured onboarding programs, co-curricular learning communities, and student-centered pedagogical models. In contexts like Ireland and Scotland, as shown by [31] inclusive admissions policies that consider non-academic factors have improved retention among disadvantaged groups. In Latin America, holistic retention programs that combine tutoring, financial support, and academic advising—such as those analyzed by [2] demonstrate the value of integrated institutional responses.

Economic Support Strategies are consistently identified as critical contributors to student attrition, particularly in developing countries. Strategies such as merit-based scholarships, need-based grants, and flexible part-time study options are essential for supporting economically vulnerable students. Several studies [15] highlight that students who receive sustained financial support show higher persistence rates. However, the mere existence of aid is not sufficient; its continuity and alignment with students' real costs of living and studying are essential.

It is important to note that the effectiveness of retention strategies is highly context dependent. For example, while early alert systems are widely effective in technologically advanced environments, in rural or resource-limited settings, the focus should shift toward personalized academic support and socio-economic assistance. Cultural attitudes toward failure, help-seeking, and university identity also influence how interventions are received. Therefore, a one-size-fits-all model is not feasible. Instead, universities should adopt evidence-based, yet adaptable retention frameworks tailored to the specific needs and vulnerabilities of their student populations.

Effective student retention is not the result of isolated interventions, but rather the outcome of coherent, multidimensional strategies embedded in institutional culture. The literature affirms that when academic, emotional, economic, and structural supports align, the likelihood of persistence increases significantly, especially for students at the greatest risk of dropout.

4.3   Implications for Institutional and Policy Development

The evidence gathered in this review has substantial implications for the design and implementation of institutional practices and higher education policies aimed at improving student retention and educational quality. While much research focuses on individual-level predictors of dropout, a key contribution of this synthesis is its emphasis on the need for systemic and structural responses that transcend individual responsibility. First, universities must move from reactive to preventive approaches. This implies developing early warning systems that use real-time data to identify students at risk of dropout before academic failure becomes irreversible. Institutions should also implement comprehensive onboarding and mentoring programs for first-year students, which are especially beneficial for vulnerable populations, such as first-generation students or those with limited social support networks.

Second, curricular flexibility and relevance are critical. Academic policies that allow students to explore different disciplines before formal specialization, or to personalize their learning paths based on interests and aptitudes, have been associated with lower dropout rates in systems such as those in Ireland, the Netherlands, and Canada. This is particularly important for students who experience vocational dissonance, those who feel misaligned with their chosen field of study, one of the most frequently cited predictors of dropout in the reviewed literature.

From a governance perspective, institutions must recognize that student wellbeing and mental health are not peripheral issues but central pillars of academic success. Investment in counseling services, peer support structures, and mental health literacy campaigns should be institutional priorities. Furthermore, policies must ensure that psychological support is accessible, non-stigmatizing, and proactive, rather than merely reactive to crises.

Third, policy makers at the national and regional levels should address the structural inequalities that exacerbate dropout risk. This includes guaranteeing financial aid continuity throughout the entire academic journey—not just at the point of entry—and aligning support with actual living and study costs. In countries where economic hardship is a dominant cause of attrition, such as in Latin America and parts of Eastern Europe, targeted need-based grants and work-study programs can serve as effective buffers.

At the intersection of institutional autonomy and state oversight, policy frameworks must incentivize retention as a quality indicator. This includes accountability mechanisms that go beyond completion rates to assess student satisfaction, engagement, and development. National quality assurance systems can integrate retention-based indicators into funding formulas or accreditation processes, thus aligning incentives with student-centered outcomes.

At the policy level, governments should integrate student retention as a core indicator of educational quality. National accreditation systems can incorporate dropout rates, student satisfaction, and psychological wellbeing as evaluative metrics. Furthermore, funding formulas could be aligned with student-centered outcomes to incentivize institutions to invest in early detection systems and holistic support structures. Collaborative networks among universities, especially in Latin America and underserved regions, should be encouraged to facilitate the sharing of effective retention practices.

These initiatives would contribute to reducing educational inequalities and promoting sustainable academic success across diverse populations.

4.4 Limitations and Future Research

While this review offers a comprehensive synthesis of the factors influencing university dropouts and the strategies used to promote student retention, several limitations must be acknowledged. These constraints also provide fertile ground for future research that can extend and deepen the understanding of this critical issue in higher education.

One notable limitation is the heterogeneity of the selected studies. The research included span of diverse countries, academic disciplines, and methodological approaches. While this enriches the comparative perspective, it also complicates direct comparability and weakens the ability to generalize findings universally. Additionally, many of the studies relied on self-reported data, which can be subject to bias and limitations in accuracy.

A second limitation is the prevalence of cross-sectional designs among the reviewed articles. Although useful for identifying correlations, such studies lack the longitudinal perspective required to assess how dropout risk and protective factors evolve over time. Consequently, the causal pathways between variables—such as academic stress, institutional support, or financial strain—and student attrition remain insufficiently understood.

Third, due to the diversity in study objectives and outcomes, a meta-analytical synthesis was not feasible. While this review provides a rich thematic overview, future work should aim to quantify effect sizes and statistical relationships across comparable contexts through meta-analysis or longitudinal modeling.

Additionally, the geographic distribution of the literature reveals a concentration of research in Europe and Latin America, with fewer studies emerging from African or Southeast Asian contexts. Given the cultural and systemic differences in those regions, there is a clear need for more inclusive, globally representative research.

Future investigations should also explore institutional and cultural mediators of dropout and retention. For example, how organizational climate, pedagogical models, or faculty engagement influence student persistence remains underexplored. Moreover, qualitative research can provide deeper insight into student narratives and lived experiences, particularly for marginalized or underrepresented populations.

Finally, as educational systems increasingly adopt digital and hybrid learning environments, future research must address how online modality, digital infrastructure, and remote student engagement affect retention. This includes evaluating how interventions that are effective in face-to-face settings translate (or fail to translate) into virtual contexts. By addressing these limitations and building on the foundations laid by existing literature, future research can inform more nuanced, context-sensitive, and effective strategies to support student success and reduce attrition in higher education.

Future research should focus on the development of longitudinal studies that trace students' trajectories from enrollment to graduation, to capture causal relationships between dropout determinants and protective factors. Mixed-method designs combining quantitative indicators with in-depth qualitative interviews can provide richer insights, especially into vulnerable populations. Additionally, exploring how interventions operate across cultural contexts—such as indigenous communities, remote rural areas, and online universities—remains an urgent research gap. Lastly, the integration of AI-driven predictive models should be investigated not only for early alerts, but also for adaptive resource allocation and personalized academic guidance.

5 Conclusions

University dropout is a complex challenge that negatively impacts both students and higher education institutions. This study has addressed the key factors influencing this phenomenon, analyzing their relationship with educational quality.

The research objective, which was to identify and analyze the key factors determining university dropout and their connection to educational quality, has been successfully met. This was achieved through a systematic review of recent literature and a critical analysis of the strategies implemented to address this issue.

The theoretical framework has been relevant and appropriate, integrating educational, psychological, sociological, and management theories. This multidisciplinary approach has allowed for a comprehensive understanding of the problem from various perspectives, providing a solid foundation for the conclusions.

The systematic literature review, based on qualitative and quantitative approaches, enabled the identification of key variables associated with dropout and the evaluation of the effectiveness of retention strategies. Limitations such as the heterogeneity of the included studies do not compromise the overall validity of the findings.

The results reveal that internal factors such as motivation, self-efficacy, and learning regulation, along with external factors such as socioeconomic background, lack of institutional support, and admission policies, are key determinants of university dropout. Academic support programs, financial aid, and the promotion of inclusive environments have proven effective in reducing dropout rates and improving educational quality.

Among the study's limitations, the lack of longitudinal analysis prevents the establishment of more robust causal relationships. Future research should explore in greater depth the impact of specific interventions and their adaptability to different educational and cultural contexts. Additionally, it would be valuable to develop predictive models to identify students at risk of dropout at an early stage.

This study contributes to academic discourse by offering a multidimensional framework that links university dropout to educational quality. It advocates for evidence-based interventions that address both structural and emotional determinants of student attrition. By implementing comprehensive retention strategies that are grounded in research and sensitive to local realities, higher education institutions can fulfill their role as agents of personal and social transformation.

References

1. Reyes-González, N., Meneses-Báez, A.L.: Psychosocial factors associated with dropout, performance and adjustment in university first year: a systematic review of reviews. Revista Electrónica Educare **28**(2), 1–23 (2024). https://doi.org/10.15359/ree.28-2.18435

2. Valencia-Arias, A., Chalela, S., Cadavid-Orrego, M., Gallegos, A., Benjumea-Arias, M., Rodríguez-Salazar, D.Y.: University dropout model for developing countries: a Colombian context approach. Behav. Sci. **13**(5), May 2023. https://doi.org/10.3390/bs13050382

3. Janke, S., Messerer, L.A.S., Merkle, B., Rudert, S.C.: Why do minority students feel they don't fit in? Migration background and parental education differentially predict social ostracism and belongingness. Group Process. Intergroup Relat. **27**(2), 278–299 (2024). https://doi.org/10.1177/13684302221142781

4. Béduwé, C., Giret, J.F.: Student employment in France: hindrance rather than help for higher educational success? J. Educ. Work. **34**(1), 95–109 (2021). https://doi.org/10.1080/13639080.2021.1875127

5. Iannelli, C., McMullin, P., Smyth, E.: Higher education retention in Ireland and Scotland: the role of admissions policies. High Educ. (Dordr) (2024). https://doi.org/10.1007/s10734-024-01259-1

6. Tinto John Cullen, V.: Filmed from best available copy dropout di higher education: a review and theoretical suirmis of recent research this document has seen reproduced exactly as received from the person or organization originating it. points of view or opinions stated 00 not necessarily repre (1973)

7. Llauró, A., Fonseca, D., Villegas, E., Aláez, M., Romero, S.: Improvement of academic analytics processes through the identification of the main variables affecting early dropout of first-year students in technical degrees. A case study. Int. J. Interact. Multimedia Artif. Intell. In Press, p. 1 (2023). https://doi.org/10.9781/ijimai.2023.06.002

8. Ccoto Tacusi, T.F.: Desempeño docente en la calidad educativa. Horizontes. Revista de Investigación en Ciencias de la Educación **7**(29), 1361–1373, April (2023). https://doi.org/10.33996/revistahorizontes.v7i29.597

9. Bonilla Carchi, S.M., de J. Barbecho Quizhpe, N., Coronel Rosero, C.X.: Calidad educativa en el Ecuador: un estudio bibliométrico. Trascender, Contabilidad Y Gestión **7**(21sept-dic), 126–142, September 2022. https://doi.org/10.36791/tcg.v7i21sept-dic.184

10. Harvey, L., Green, D.: Defining quality. Assess. Eval. High. Educ. **18**(1), 9–34 (1993). https://doi.org/10.1080/0260293930180102

11. Barrientos-Illanes, P., Pérez-Villalobos, M.V., Vergara-Morales, J., Díaz-Mujica, A.: Influence of the perceived autonomy support, self-efficacy, and academic satisfaction in the intentions of permanence of university students. Revista Electronica Educare **25**(2), August 2021. https://doi.org/10.15359/ree.25-2.5

12. Guzmán Rincón, A., Sotomayor Soloaga, P.A., Carrillo Barbosa, R.L., Barragán-Moreno, S.P.: Satisfaction with the institution as a predictor of the intention to drop out in online higher education. Cogent Educ. **11**(1) (2024). https://doi.org/10.1080/2331186X.2024.2351282

13. Fouarge, D., Heß, P.: Preference-Choice Mismatch and University Dropout (2023). www.iza.org

14. Guzmán Rincón, A., Barragán Moreno, S., Cala-Vitery, F.: Rural population and COVID-19: a model for assessing the economic effects of drop-out in higher education. Front Educ. (Lausanne) **6**, December 2021. https://doi.org/10.3389/feduc.2021.812114

15. Helland, H., Strømme, T.B.: Social inequality in completion rates in higher education: heterogeneity in educational fields. Br. J. Sociol. **75**(2), 201–218 (2024). https://doi.org/10.1111/1468-4446.13075

16. Aina, C., Aktaş, K., Casalone, G.: Effects of workload allocation per course on students' academic outcomes: evidence from STEM degrees. Labour Econ. **90**, October 2024. https://doi.org/10.1016/j.labeco.2024.102559

17. Cage, E., McManemy, E.: Burnt out and dropping out: a comparison of the experiences of autistic and non-autistic students during the COVID-19 pandemic. Front Psychol. **12**, January 2022. https://doi.org/10.3389/fpsyg.2021.792945

18. Morelli, M., Chirumbolo, A., Baiocco, R., Cattelino, E.: Self-regulated learning self-efficacy, motivation, and intention to drop-out: the moderating role of friendships at University. Curr. Psychol. **42**(18), 15589–15599 (2023). https://doi.org/10.1007/s12144-022-02834-4
19. Segovia-García, N., Said-Hung, E., Aguilera, F.J.G.: Virtual higher education in Colombia: Factors associated with dropping out. Educacion XX1 **25**(1), 197–218, January 2022. https://doi.org/10.5944/educxx1.30455
20. Di Paola Naranjo, A., Sánchez, S., Pereno, G.L.: Factores sociodemográficos que inciden en la retención de ingresantes a la universidad: un estudio exploratorio en la Licenciatura en Psicología de la Universidad Nacional de Córdoba (UNC). Revista Educación, June 2022. https://doi.org/10.15517/revedu.v46i2.47784
21. Fernandez-Garcia, A.J., Preciado, J.C., Melchor, F., Rodriguez-Echeverria, R., Conejero, J.M., Sanchez-Figueroa, F.: A real-life machine learning experience for predicting university dropout at different stages using academic data. IEEE Access **9**, 133076–133090 (2021). https://doi.org/10.1109/ACCESS.2021.3115851
22. Guzmán, A., Barragán, S., Cala Vitery, F.: Dropout in rural higher education: a systematic review. Frontiers Media S.A., 08 September 2021. https://doi.org/10.3389/feduc.2021.727833
23. Kocsis, Á., Molnár, G.: Factors influencing academic performance and dropout rates in higher education. Oxf. Rev. Educ. (2024). https://doi.org/10.1080/03054985.2024.2316616
24. Maluenda-Albornoz, J., Berríos-Riquelme, J., Zamorano-Veragua, M.: Abandono universitario: predictores y mediadores en estudiantes universitarios chilenos de primer año. Revista Costarricense de Psicología **42**(1), 45–64 (2023). https://doi.org/10.22544/rcps.v42i01.03
25. Vega-Martínez, A., Martínez-Fernández, J.R., Coiduras-Rodríguez, J.L.: Learning patterns, academic stress and performance in first year university students: an exploratory study. Educar **59**(1), 163–178 (2023). https://doi.org/10.5565/rev/educar.1527
26. Turhan, D., et al.: University students' profiles of burnout symptoms amid the COVID-19 pandemic in Germany and their relation to concurrent study behavior and experiences. Int. J. Educ. Res. **116**, January 2022. https://doi.org/10.1016/j.ijer.2022.102081
27. Leow, T., Li, W.W., Miller, D.J., McDermott, B.: Prevalence of University Non-Continuation and Mental Health Conditions, and Effect of Mental Health Conditions on Non-Continuation: a Systematic Review and Meta-Analysis. Taylor and Francis Ltd. (2024). https://doi.org/10.1080/09638237.2024.2332812
28. Buizza, C., Cela, H., Sbravati, G., Bornatici, S., Rainieri, G., Ghilardi, A.: The role of self-efficacy, motivation, and connectedness in dropout intention in a sample of Italian college students. Educ. Sci. (Basel) **14**(1), January 2024. https://doi.org/10.3390/educsci14010067
29. Galve-González, C., Bernardo, A.B., Carlos Núñez, J.: Academic trajectories: The role of engagement as a mediator in the decision of university dropout or persistence. Revista de Psicodidactica **29**(2), 130–138, July 2024. https://doi.org/10.1016/j.psicod.2024.04.002
30. Dinh, N.B.K., Zhu, C., Caliskan, A.: Perceived effectiveness of academic leadership development training: the contribution of motivational factors and peer interaction. Res. Educ. Admin. Leader. **7**(3), 633–678 (2022). https://doi.org/10.30828/real.1159480
31. Bernardo, A.B., Galve-González, C., Núñez, J.C., Almeida, L.S.: A path model of university dropout predictors: the role of satisfaction, the use of self-regulation learning strategies and students' engagement. Sustainability (Switzerland) **14**(3), February 2022. https://doi.org/10.3390/su14031057
32. Buenaño, E., Beletanga, M.J., Mancheno, M.: What factors are relevant to understanding dropout? analysis at a co-financed university in Ecuador and policy implications, using survival cox models. J. Lat. Educ. (2023). https://doi.org/10.1080/15348431.2023.2271570
33. Maluenda-Albornoz, J., Infante-Villagrán, V., Galve-González, C., Flores-Oyarzo, G., Berríos-Riquelme, J.: Early and dynamic socio-academic variables related to dropout intention: a predictive model made during the pandemic. Sustainability (Switzerland), **14**(2), January 2022. https://doi.org/10.3390/su14020831

34. Segura, M., Mello, J., Hernández, A.: Machine learning prediction of university student dropout: does preference play a key role?. Mathematics **10**(18), September 2022. https://doi.org/10.3390/math10183359

35. Brem, A., Viardot, E., Nylund, P.A.: Implications of the coronavirus (COVID-19) outbreak for innovation: which technologies will improve our lives? Technol. Forecast Soc. Change **163**, 120451 (2021). https://doi.org/10.1016/j.techfore.2020.120451

36. Ebadi, S., Ebadijalal, M.: The effect of Google Expeditions virtual reality on EFL learners' willingness to communicate and oral proficiency. Comput. Assist. Lang. Learn. **35**(8), 1975–2000 (2022). https://doi.org/10.1080/09588221.2020.1854311

37. Bayaga, A., Lekena, L.L., Selepe, C., du Plessis, A., Blignaut, S., Morar, T.: Academic, social and economic experiences of first-year students: case study. South Afr. J. High. Educ. **36**(2) (2022). https://doi.org/10.20853/36-2-4592

38. Constante-Amores, A., Martínez, E.F., Asencio, E.N., Fernández-Mellizo, M.: Factors associated with university dropout. Educacion XX1 **24**(1), 17–44 (2021). https://doi.org/10.5944/educXX1.26889

39. Alonso, M.A., González-Ortiz-de-Zárate, A., Gómez-Flechoso, M.Á., Castrillón, M.: Effectiveness of a peer mentoring on university dropout and academic performance. Psicol Educ. (Madr) **30**(1), 29–37 (2024). https://doi.org/10.5093/psed2024a5

40. Cobo-Rendón, R., Hojman, V., García-Álvarez, D., Cobo Rendon, R.: Academic emotions, college adjustment, and dropout intention in university students. Front Educ. (Lausanne) **8** (2023). https://doi.org/10.3389/feduc.2023.1303765

Comprehensive Home Monitoring System for Cardiovascular Health Management

Marcia M. Bayas⑩, Mario Alomoto Tomalá⑩, Manuel Montaño Blacio⑩, Oscar W. Gomez$^{(\boxtimes)}$ ⑩, and Ronald H. Rovira Jurado⑩

Universidad Estatal Península de Santa Elena, FACSISTEL, grupo de investigación
TECED, La Libertad, Ecuador
{mbayas,oscargomez}@upse.edu.ec

Abstract. Monitoring devices and systems are indispensable tools for patients with cardiovascular health issues. These tools are typically operated by trained personnel in healthcare institutions. However, the need to monitor patients' vital signs at home remains a significant challenge. To address this, we propose the design of a non-invasive, autonomous IoT (Internet of Things.) device capable of recording heart rate, blood oxygen levels, and body temperature. The proposed device integrates with monitoring and data control platforms using IoT protocols. For validation, the data collected by the proposed device was compared with that of a smartwatch using statistical methods based on mean, median, and mode determination. The prototype demonstrated results comparable to those of a smartwatch, with measurements of 77.49 bpm (heart rate), 98.79% (S_pO_2), and 37.37 °C (body temperature). In contrast, the smartwatch recorded 75.38 bpm, 98%, and 37.4 °C, respectively. The proposed predictive model serves as an analytical framework for the study variables, consisting of three layers that can be adapted to wearable monitoring devices with the proposed architecture. The model achieved an RMSE of 0.470 for blood oxygen, 5.769 for heart rate, and 1.534 for body temperature. The developed algorithm is intelligent enough to provide accurate predictions, helping to prevent major cardiovascular health complications in patients.

Keywords: IoT device · cardiovascular health · machine learning · SPO2

1 Introduction

Cardiovascular diseases are one of the leading causes of morbidity and mortality worldwide. According to statistics from the OPS[1], 2 million people died from cardiovascular diseases inhad elevated blood pressure without a diagnosis, the year 2019 [1].

---

[1] Pan American Health Organization.

O. Gervasi et al. (Eds.): ICCSA 2025 Workshops, LNCS 15891, pp. 355–369, 2026.
https://doi.org/10.1007/978-3-031-97617-9_23

According to a STEPS survey conducted by the MSP[2] and the INEC[3] in 2018, data on cardiovascular health among individuals aged 18 to 69 years revealed that 45.2% had elevated blood pressure without a diagnosis, 12.6% had elevated blood pressure with a diagnosis but without any treatment, 16.2% had diagnosed hypertension with treatment but remained uncontrolled, and 26% had elevated blood pressure with treatment and was controlled [2].

Despite technological advances, there are still limitations in access to continuous medical care and the early detection of health problems. The current health monitoring system, especially for patients with chronic diseases or at risk, presents significant limitations that affect the quality of medical care, ranging from appointment scheduling to the shortage of human resources in the healthcare sector [3].

Among the limitations, we find that medical visits and laboratory tests are conducted infrequently, and access to specialized medical care, particularly cardiology, is restricted for some patients, especially those with reduced mobility. Likewise, healthcare professionals do not always have access to up-to-date patient data, making it difficult to make informed treatment decisions [4].

Therefore, the main objective of this project is to develop a technological solution aimed at individuals with cardiovascular diseases, in order to monitor their vital signs in real time using low-cost technology and the integration of IoT protocols. The study variables considered in this proposal are heart rate, blood oxygen level, and body temperature.

To complement the proposal, a model based on recurrent neural networks (RNN) is proposed. This approach allows for the analysis of sequential data, facilitating the learning of the behavior of the study variables, and, of course, enabling timely prediction of abnormalities [5]. This enables early assistance, improving the response capability in critical patient situations.

This document is structured as follows: Sect. 2 describes related work focused on continuous monitoring and machine learning techniques; Sect. 3 describes the materials and methods used, which are based on an IoT-based technological architecture; Sect. 4 presents the results and discussion. Finally, Sect. 5 concludes the study.

2   Related Work

In [6], a device is presented for measuring blood oxygen levels non-invasively, using the MAX30100 sensor and an Arduino Uno microcontroller. The device includes an alarm that is triggered when oxygen levels drop below 95%, making it a valuable tool for health monitoring. Additionally, it integrates an alarm to alert the user when S_pO_2 levels are below normal, allowing for quick intervention in case of hypoxemia. Furthermore, the device features an LCD screen that clearly and simply displays the S_pO_2 Omeasurement results. The tests conducted

---

[2] Ministry of Health.
[3] National Institute of Statistics and Censuses.

showed that the device's measurements are comparable to those of calibrated tools, with a mean error of only 0.0123%.

In [7], a home telemedicine system is presented, which involves the remote monitoring of patients. The system uses IoT devices and the cloud to securely and efficiently collect, analyze, and share health data. Users wear an affordable wristband that measures their heart rate and oxygen saturation. This data is transmitted via Bluetooth to a mobile application running on an Android TV. The application sends the data to the cloud, where it is analyzed by healthcare professionals. Based on the data analysis, professionals can issue medical prescriptions that are sent to the user through the app. The system also provides professionals with tools to track the patient's progress and manage their healthcare. A survey conducted with healthcare professionals yielded positive results. The majority of respondents (88.5%) expressed their willingness to implement the system in their practice, recognizing the importance of the collected data (92.4%) and the usefulness of the system's tools for medical care (76.9%).

In [8], a proposal is presented for the development of a monitoring system, which is specifically designed for the care of patients at home, providing a compact and affordable solution that offers timely medical information. The system has been designed with the perspective of incorporating cloud computing and IoT technologies in the future, enabling remote monitoring of the patient's data. The article describes in detail the design and implementation of the system's main board, the selection of biomedical sensors, the creation of the supports, and the programming of the system.

In their research work [9], an automated monitoring system is presented to ensure remote access and efficient data capture. This research used both qualitative and quantitative approaches. User tests were conducted to gather feedback on the proposed interface, and a comparative method was employed to assess the system's effectiveness in comparison to equipment available on the market. The information transmission phase sends data obtained from the sensors to the ThingSpeak IoT platform, while simultaneously using a local area connection through the VNC Viewer platform to ensure dual communication in case the ThingSpeak servers fail. Although the proposed system can measure basic parameters such as heart rate, temperature, and electrocardiogram (ECG), it is not suitable for providing definitive medical analysis. However, it is useful for obtaining basic data in educational settings, such as at the Instituto Superior Tecnológico Luis Tello in the province of Esmeraldas, Ecuador.

This article [10] presents a system based on Long Short-Term Memory (LSTM) neural networks for the detection and classification of cardiac arrhythmias. LSTM networks are a variant of recurrent neural networks (RNNs) that allow for the analysis of data sequences of variable length, making them particularly useful for processing temporal signals such as electrocardiograms (ECG). The proposed system uses an LSTM network to classify ECG signals as normal or with arrhythmias, based on prior training with labeled data.

In [11], a portable device is proposed that detects arrhythmias. The methodology is based on developing a simplified Convolutional Neural Network (CNN) classifier capable of identifying multiple types of arrhythmias using real-time two-dimensional images of ECG waves. The proposed model achieves an accuracy of 99.23%, outperforming most existing solutions and demonstrating its potential for low-power portable devices.

Despite advances in IoT technologies, their implementation in healthcare faces challenges that limit their integration, especially in the design of portable devices for continuous monitoring of vital signs. One of the main challenges is ensuring the reliability in measuring parameters such as heart rate, blood oxygen levels, and body temperature, which are interrelated variables [12].

In addition, it is essential to maintain low energy consumption and continuous communication of health-related devices. To achieve this, it is necessary to integrate IoT technologies with lighter connection protocols, such as MQTT servers, which ensure continuous real-time data transmission and monitoring [13].

3   Materials and Methods

The technological proposal presented is aimed at patients with cardiovascular diseases, whether in hospital, clinical, or home settings. This is achieved through the development of a portable IoT device designed to facilitate continuous and non-invasive monitoring of vital signs. To carry out this proposal, a phase-based model has been designed [14], following the technological architecture proposed in Fig. 1.

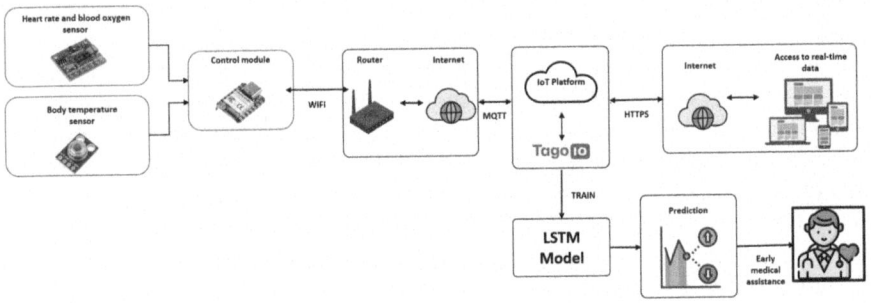

Fig. 1. Technological architecture.

The first phase consists of developing the IoT-based electronic prototype by integrating open-source hardware and software components. The component selection is primarily based on their dimensions, as the proposed device is designed to be portable.

The second phase focuses on collecting heart rate and blood oxygen level data using the MAX30100 sensor, with values recorded in beats per minute (bpm) and percentages (%), respectively. For measuring body temperature in degrees Celsius (°C), the MLX90614 sensor was used. The main control unit is the Xiao ESP32C3 development board, chosen for being a microcontroller that supports low-power IoT communication protocols. The connection diagram of the proposal is shown in Fig. 2.

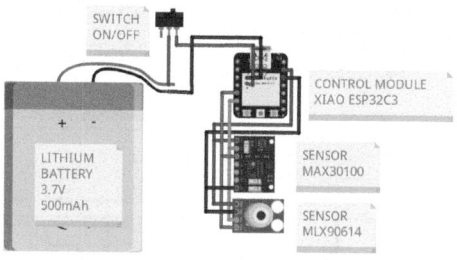

Fig. 2. Electronic diagram of the proposed components.

The third phase focuses on the design and 3D printing of a casing intended to integrate the electronic components in a way that makes the device compact, ergonomic, and non-invasive for the patient. Considering non-invasive aspects is important, especially for devices that require constant use, as it promotes user acceptance and satisfaction, increasing the likelihood of continuous use [15]. The dimensions of the casing are shown in Fig. 3.

The fourth phase focuses on validating the data collected by the proposed device, which are compared with data from a smartwatch. For the validation, the Xiaomi S1 Pro smartwatch was chosen, as it complies with European Union (EU) standards [16]. By applying statistical methods such as calculating the mean, median, and mode, an error margin is obtained. Below are the equations that define the mean (1), median (2), and mode (3) for heart rate, blood oxygen level, and body temperature.

$$\bar{FC} = \frac{\sum_{i=1}^{n} X_i}{n_{\text{val}}} \tag{1}$$

where:

- $\bar{X}$ represents the mean of the variable.
- X_i represents all recorded values of the variable.
- n_{val} is the number of non-null values of the variable.

$$\tilde{X} = \begin{cases} X_{\frac{n+1}{2}}, & \text{if } n \text{ it is odd} \\ \frac{X_{\frac{n}{2}} + X_{\frac{n}{2}+1}}{2}, & \text{if } n \text{ is even} \end{cases} \tag{2}$$

where:

- $\tilde{X}$ represents the median of the variable.
- X_i represents the recorded values of the variable.

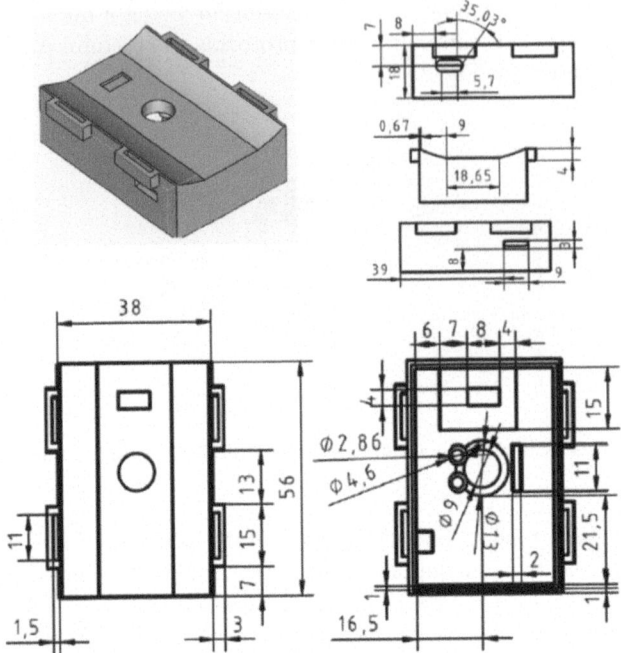

Fig. 3. 3D-printed PLA casing with its dimensions from various perspectives.

– n is the total number of values of the variable.

$$\hat{X} = \{X_i \mid f(X_i) = \max f(X)\} \tag{3}$$

where:

– $\hat{X}$ represents the mode of the variable.
– X_i represents the recorded values of the variable.
– $f(X_i)$ is the absolute value.
– $\max f(X)$ is the maximum observed value.

The fifth phase consists of presenting the data collected by the device on the TagoIO IoT platform. Communication between the device and TagoIO is established via the MQTT communication protocol. One of the most relevant features of TagoIO is its tool for defining threshold values, allowing the platform to send a notification if a received data point falls outside the established range. Figure 4 shows the TagoIO interface that monitors the study variables.

The final phase focuses on the development of a machine learning algorithm as in [17], which is based on training an LSTM model [18]. The model consists of 3 layers as in [19], divided into: a long short-term memory (LSTM) layer, a hidden dense layer with 100 neurons, and an output layer. The model runs a

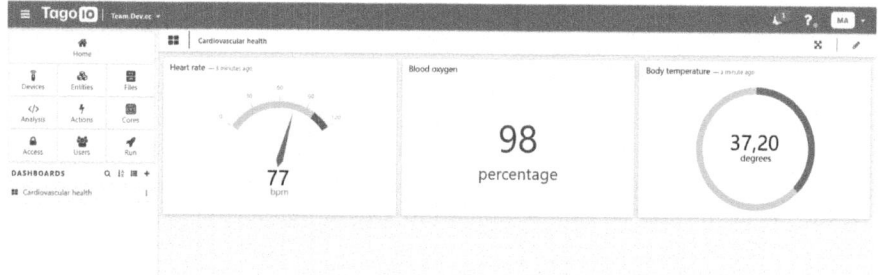

Fig. 4. Data monitoring from the TagoIO platform.

training loop for N epochs, during which it calculates the training and validation loss. The forward propagation is performed as follows:

$$\hat{y} = f(X; \theta) \tag{4}$$

– where: θ are the model parameters.

The loss function measures the difference between prediction and actual value:

$$L = \frac{1}{n} \sum_{i=1}^{n} \ell(\hat{y}_i, y_i) \tag{5}$$

Backpropagation is used and the weights are updated with:

$$\theta \leftarrow \theta - \eta \nabla L \tag{6}$$

The RMSE[4] is also calculated between the actual values and the predictions using the formula:

$$\text{RMSE} = \sqrt{\frac{1}{n} \sum_{i=1}^{n} (y_i - \hat{y}_i)^2} \tag{7}$$

This model is developed using the Google Colaboratory tool and libraries such as TensorFlow and Torch [20,21]. In this way, the algorithm predicts unusual values in the data obtained from the device, playing an important role in the timely assistance of the patient to avoid potential cardiovascular health risks.

Although this study prioritizes LSTM due to its strength in temporal data modeling, future research will explore alternative models such as Gated Recurrent Units (GRUs), Random Forest Regression, and hybrid CNN-LSTM architectures to improve performance across all measured variables.

---

[4] Root Mean Square Error.

4   Results

4.1   Device Implementation

Figure 5 shows the installation of the device, which is placed on the index finger, as the sensors are located on the upper part. Adjustable Velcro straps are used to secure it, allowing it to be comfortably and safely fitted to any user. In this way, the device meets the goal of a non-invasive design for the patient.

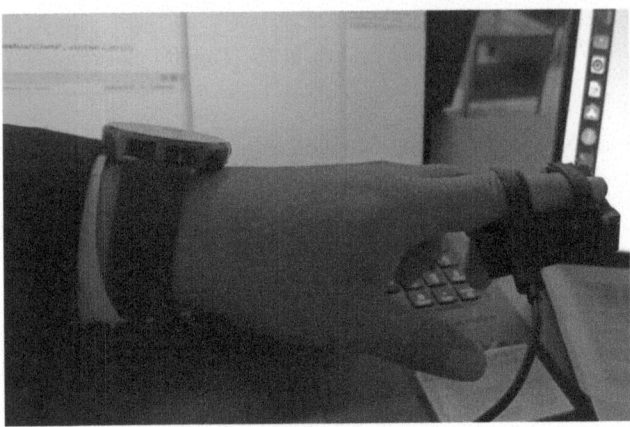

Fig. 5. Device implementation.

4.2   Device Autonomy

Table 1 presents the individual power consumption of the ESP32C3 control unit and the sensors integrated into the electronic device. Additionally, the total consumption in milliamperes is shown.

Table 1. Shows the consumption of each component and the total consumption of the proposed device.

Component	Power Consumption
Xiao ESP32C3	75 [mA]
MLX90614	0.17 [mA]
MAX30100	1.2 [mA]
Total Consumption	76.37 [mA]

According to the characteristics of the lithium battery, which are 3.7 [V] and 500 mAh, the device's autonomy in hours is:

$$\text{Autonomy} = \frac{\text{Battery Capacity}}{\text{Device Consumption}} \tag{8}$$

$$\text{Autonomy} = \frac{500\,[\text{mAh}]}{76.37\,[\text{mA}]} \tag{9}$$

$$\text{Autonomy} = \frac{500\,[\text{mAh}]}{76.37\,[\text{mA}]} \tag{10}$$

$$\text{Autonomy} \approx 6.54\,[\text{h}] \tag{11}$$

Although the validation was conducted using the Xiaomi S1 Pro smartwatch, which complies with European Union standards—such as CE marking and the Radio Equipment Directive (RED)—ensuring consumer safety and wireless communication compliance, the study acknowledges the limitation of relying on a single commercial-grade device that is not medically certified. Future iterations will include comparisons against multiple certified medical-grade instruments to enhance the generalizability, statistical robustness, and clinical relevance of the findings.

4.3   Body Temperature Data Analysis

The scatter plot presented in Fig. 6 shows the temperature of a person without hypertension, comparing the readings of the proposed prototype (in blue) with those of the Xiaomi S1 Pro smartwatch (in red). The red dots (Xiaomi S1 Pro) are more evenly distributed around the 37.4 °C line, matching their statistical measures: a mean, median, and mode of 37.4 °C. On the other hand, the blue dots (proposed prototype) show greater variability, with temperatures fluctuating more widely, although its mean is 37.374 °C, the median is 37.37 °C, and the mode is 37.35 °C. Therefore, the proposed prototype may have slightly greater variability in its temperature readings compared to the Xiaomi S1 Pro smartwatch.

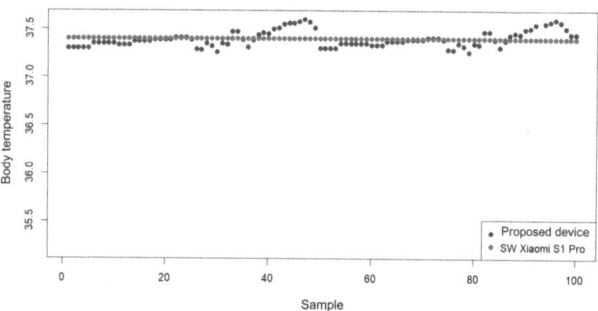

Fig. 6. Scatter plot of body temperature in a person without hypertension. (Color figure online)

The scatter plot presented in Fig. 7 shows the temperature of a person with hypertension, comparing the readings of the proposed prototype (in blue) with those of the Xiaomi S1 Pro smartwatch (in red). The red dots from the Xiaomi S1 Pro are grouped around 36.4 °C, which aligns with its mean and median of 36.496 °C and 36.4 °C respectively, showing a uniform and consistent distribution. In contrast, the blue dots from the proposed prototype show greater variability, with some significantly high values and more dispersed statistics: a mean of 37.1055 °C, a median of 36.29 °C, and multiple modes (6.81, 36.84, 36.87). This suggests that the prototype has greater dispersion in measurements, with several outliers, compared to the stability of the Xiaomi S1 Pro.

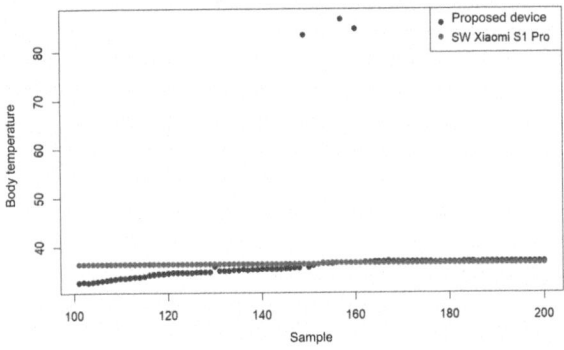

Fig. 7. Scatter plot of body temperature in a person with hypertension. (Color figure online)

Both compared devices have very similar means, medians, and modes (the prototype with a mean of 37.374 °C, a median of 37.37 °C, and a mode of 37.35 °C, and the smartwatch with 37.4 °C in all measures), but the prototype shows greater variability in its temperature readings. The red dots from the Xiaomi S1 Pro smartwatch are uniformly distributed around the 37.4 °C line, indicating more consistent stability compared to the blue dots from the prototype, which fluctuate more widely. This greater variability suggests that the prototype has slightly lower precision. Nevertheless, due to the proximity of the central measures, the reliability of the prototype can be estimated at 92%.

4.4   Machine Learning Model: LSTM Neural Networks

Figure 8 presents the prediction analysis of SPO2 using an LSTM model. SPO2 values range between 60% and 100%, and the predicted values by the model are compared with the actual values. The evaluation metrics indicate solid model performance: the Root Mean Square Error (RMSE) is 0.470, the Coefficient of Determination (R^2) is 0.733, meaning the model explains a significant portion of the data variability, and the Mean Absolute Error (MAE) is 0.241. These results

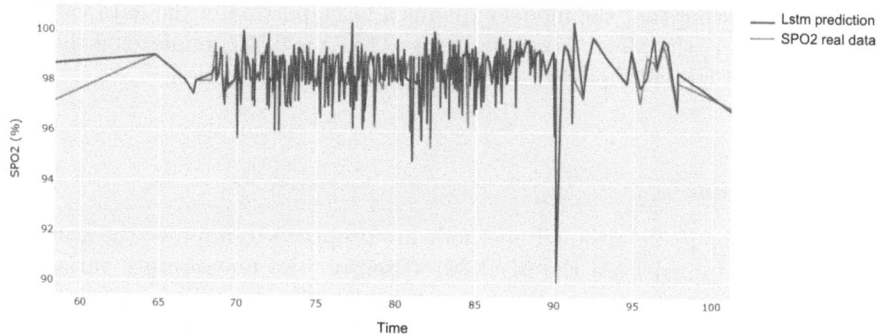

Fig. 8. Graph obtained from the LSTM model for SPO2.

show that the LSTM model has adequate predictive capability for estimating SPO2 levels.

Figure 9 presents an analysis of heart rate prediction using an LSTM model. The predicted values by the model are compared with the actual values, and evaluation metrics are presented to assess the model's performance. The Root Mean Square Error (RMSE) is 0.569, indicating a significant deviation between the predicted and actual values. The Coefficient of Determination (R^2) is 0.797, suggesting that the model explains only a small portion of the variability in the data. Additionally, the Mean Absolute Error (MAE) is 0.346, reinforcing the idea that the model has limited performance in predicting heart rate.

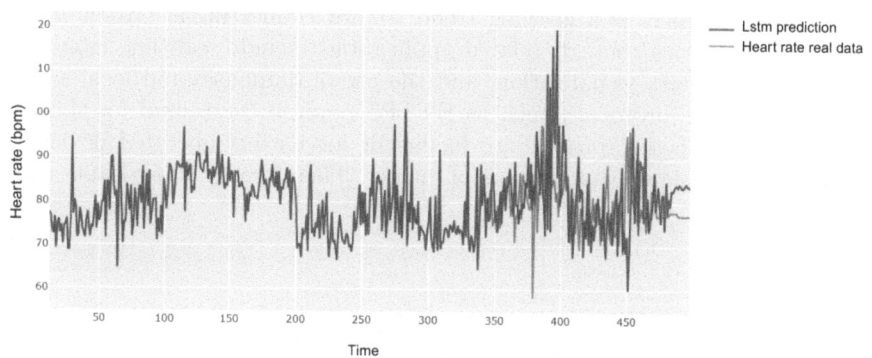

Fig. 9. Graph obtained from the LSTM model for heart rate.

Figure 10 describes the analysis of temperature prediction using an LSTM model. The predicted values by the model are compared with the actual values, and evaluation metrics are presented to assess the model's performance. The Root Mean Square Error (RMSE) is 1.534, indicating a relatively low deviation between the predicted and actual values. The Coefficient of Determination (R^2)

is 0.847, suggesting that the model explains a large portion of the data variability. Furthermore, the Mean Absolute Error (MAE) is 0.527, reinforcing the idea that the model has solid performance in temperature prediction.

4.5   Discussion

In the studies by [6–9], although methods are proposed to improve the accuracy of the data obtained from the MAX30100 sensor, the temperature variable is not considered. According to the present study, this variable is important in monitoring patients with hypertension problems, as it is directly related to blood pressure. Based on these findings, the importance of including temperature in the analysis is highlighted to ensure a more comprehensive follow-up of the patient's condition.

Regarding the prototypes analyzed in the reviewed works, there is a lack of design for devices that are ergonomic and non-invasive for the patient. To overcome these limitations, an innovative prototype has been developed that is placed solely on the finger, allowing measurement of heart rate, blood oxygenation, and body temperature. This compact and portable device includes a battery that ensures its autonomous operation, offering an efficient solution for continuous patient monitoring. Unlike existing commercial devices that are often costly and require professional calibration or frequent replacement parts, the proposed prototype offers affordability (<$50), full open-source compatibility, and simplified maintenance. Its ergonomic design, using 3D-printed PLA and minimal electronic components, ensures both portability and comfort—attributes not always prioritized in current market options.

In addition, there is a growing trend toward connecting electronic devices to the cloud. In this context, related applications include real-time monitoring screens, remote data visualization, and the use of databases and local servers. Conventional IoT protocols, such as HTTPS requests[5], are used for this purpose. However, these protocols are inefficient for battery-operated devices, as they consume a significant amount of energy. Therefore, it is advisable to use

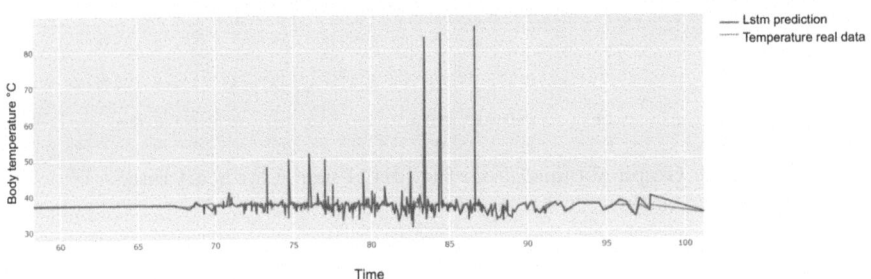

Fig. 10. Graph obtained from the LSTM model for body temperature.

---

[5] Hypertext Transfer Protocol Secure.

lighter and more specific protocols, such as MQTT[6]. In this sense, the present proposal opts for the use of the MQTT protocol, which offers significant advantages by allowing the management of multiple simultaneous connections without compromising device performance, ensuring continuous operation.

Despite promising results, the prototype has not yet undergone formal clinical validation. Future deployments will include trials in collaboration with certified medical institutions to assess diagnostic reliability in real-world scenarios and under diverse patient conditions.

Finally, regarding the predictions of the study variables, it is important to highlight the need to design health devices that not only focus on controlling and monitoring data through IoT but also integrate learning models using current technology. These models serve as essential tools for preventing cardiovascular health issues, allowing healthcare professionals to intervene in a timely manner before complications arise.

5   Conclusions

This work presents the design and development of a non-invasive device for people with a history of cardiovascular diseases. The proposed device aims to collect and monitor signals of heart rate, blood oxygen levels, and body temperature. The signals are collected using sensor modules integrated with a microcontroller, and the data are transmitted using IoT protocols such as MQTT to the TagoIO platform.

According to the data analysis and comparison with the smartwatch, the following results were obtained: the proposed device showed results similar to those of a smartwatch, with measurements of 77.49 bpm for heart rate, 98.79% for SpO2, and 37.37 °C for body temperature. In comparison, the smartwatch recorded 75.38 bpm, 98%, and 37.4 °C, respectively.

The work also focused on the implementation of a prediction model based on artificial neural networks. We introduced a three-layer process with 100 neurons. The algorithm was applied to the three study variables, calculating the Root Mean Square Error (RMSE), the Mean Absolute Error (MAE), and the Coefficient of Determination (R). These values are essential for evaluating the learning performance and improving prediction accuracy. This prediction method is crucial for triggering early alerts in case of unusual signal values from the patient, enabling timely medical assistance.

Compared to conventional wrist-worn smartwatches, the proposed device achieves a similar level of signal reliability while significantly reducing manufacturing costs. The simplified design also eliminates dependency on proprietary platforms, making it a scalable solution for low-resource healthcare environments.

As future research, the integration of additional modules such as an electrocardiograph (ECG) is proposed to enhance the robustness of the system and

---

[6] Message Queuing Telemetry Transport.

enable more comprehensive cardiovascular monitoring, while preserving the non-invasive and portable nature of the device. Furthermore, to improve the predictive accuracy across all vital signs, future work will explore alternative machine learning models beyond LSTM, including Gated Recurrent Units (GRUs), Random Forest Regression, and hybrid CNN-LSTM architectures, aiming to optimize performance and adaptability in diverse health monitoring scenarios.

References

1. Pan American Health Organization: https://www.paho.org/es/enlace/carga-enfermedades-cardiovasculares. Accessed 16 Nov 2024
2. Ecuador Report: https://www.paho.org/es/noticias/16-5-2023-informe-ecuador-mejorando-salud-cardiovascular-desde-comunidades-locales-hasta. Accessed 16 Nov 2024
3. Naranjo, N.: Teleconsultation: Analysis of the virtual medical consultation tool in the public health system. J. Sci. Res. **1**, 23–26 (2022). https://doi.org/10.26910/issn.2528-8083vol1iss2.2016pp23-26
4. Vaccaro, G., Jurado, M., Gonzabay, E., Witt, P.: Challenges and problems of public health in Ecuador. Reciamuc **7**, 10–21 (2023). https://doi.org/10.26820/reciamuc/7.(2).abril.2023.10-21
5. Ascenzo, F., Filippo, O.D., Gallone, G., Mittone, D., Agostino, M., Iannaccone, M.: Machine learning-based prediction of adverse events following an acute coronary syndrome (PRAISE): a modeling study of pooled datasets. Lancet **397**, 199–207 (2021). https://doi.org/10.1016/s0140-6736(20)32519-8
6. Lukman, A., Wahyuni, R.: DRANCANG BANGUN ALAT PENGUKUR KADAR OKSIGEN NON INVASIVE MENGGUNAKAN SENSOR MAX3010. Jurnal Ilmiah Elektrokrisna **8** (2020). https://journal.teknikunkris.ac.id/index.php/elektro
7. Garcés, A., Manzano, S., Núñez, C., Pallo, J., Jurado, M., García, M.: Low-cost IoT platform for telemedicine applications. RISTI Revista Ibérica de Sistemas e Tecnologias de Informação, 153–166 (2021). https://www.proquest.com/scholarly-journals/plataforma-iot-de-bajo-coste-para-aplicaciones/docview/2562270453/se-2
8. Bejarano, M., Manzano, E.: Implementation of a prototype-level monitoring system for vital signs: pulse, temperature, and oxygen saturation for patients. Revista Interfases **14**, 17–40 (2021). https://doi.org/10.26439/interfases2021.n014.5168
9. Vela, J., Mera, E., Palacios, E.: Proposal of a health indicator monitoring system through IoT for vital signs measurement. Revista Social Fronteriza **4** (2021). https://doi.org/10.59814/resofro.2024.4(1)16
10. Rivera, I., Hernández, M., Pérez, P.: System for the detection of cardiac arrhythmias based on LSTM neural networks. Revista Electrónica Ciencia tecnología y humanidades **12** (2020). https://bit.ly/3QbSeCA
11. Wasimuddin, M., Elleithy, K., Abuzneid, A., Faezipour, M., Abuzaghleh, O.: Multiclass ECG signal analysis using global average-based 2-D convolutional neural network modeling. Electronics **10**, 170 (2021). https://doi.org/10.3390/electronics10020170
12. Graff, B., et al.: Relationship between heart rate variability, blood pressure and arterial wall properties during air and oxygen breathing in healthy subjects. Auton. Neurosci. **178**, 60–66 (2013). https://doi.org/10.1016/j.autneu.2013.04.009

13. Alomoto, M.: Design and implementation of a home monitoring system for comprehensive cardiovascular health management. Universidad Estatal Península de Santa Elena (2024). https://repositorio.upse.edu.ec/handle/46000/12242
14. Montaño, M., González, J., Jiménez, Ó., Mingo, L., Carrion, C.: Design and deployment of an IoT-based monitoring system for hydroponic crops. Ingenius, 9–18 (2023)
15. Santoyo, I., Avilés, C., Zúñiga, A.: Portable non-invasive system for monitoring and displaying vital signs of patients in emergency rooms on a mobile device. Res. Comput. Sci. **149**, 157–172 (2020)
16. Xiaomi: Xiaomi Watch S1 Pro Smart Watch Manual. Manuals+ (n.d.). https://manuals.plus/xiaomi/watch-s1-pro-smart-watch-manual.pdf
17. Chowdhury, M.H., et al.: Estimating blood pressure from the photoplethysmogram signal and demographic features using machine learning techniques. Sensors (Switzerland) **20**(11) (2020)
18. Kłosowski, G., Rymarczyk, T., Wójcik, D., Skowron, S., Cieplak, T., Adamkiewicz, P.: The use of time-frequency moments as inputs of LSTM network for ECG signal classification. Electronics **9**, 1452 (2020)
19. LeCun, Y., Bengio, Y., Hinton, G.: Deep learning. Nature **521**, 436–444 (2015)
20. Sanabria, N., Cymberknop, L., Monzon, J.: Application of neural networks for the prediction of cardiovascular signals. In: AJEA (Proceedings of Academic Conferences and Events of UTN) (2024). https://doi.org/10.33414/ajea.1695.2024
21. Gil, A.: Modern tools in neural networks: Google's TensorFlow library. Repository of Universidad Autónoma de Madrid (2017)

Contrasting Neural Network Techniques for Enhanced Natural Language Understanding in Conversational Agents – CoN²LUC

Arnulfo Alanis[1]([⊠]), J. Ascención Guerrero-Viramontes[2], Gulliermo Daniel Prieto[1], and Bogart Yail Marquez[1]

[1] Systems and Computer Department, National Technology of México, Campus Tijuana, Calzada del Tecnológico S/N, Fraccionamiento Tomas Aquino, Baja California, C.P. 22414, Tijuana, B.C, México
{alanis,gulliermo.prieto17,Bogart}@tectijuana.edu.mx
[2] Division of Postgraduate Studies and Research, Tecnológico Nacional de México, Campus Aguascalientes, Aguascalientes, Mexico
jaguerrero@aguascalientes.tecnm.mx

Abstract. Language is one of the processes that human beings use to be able to communicate effectively, this helps to share not only information, but elements of everyday life, to process all kinds of situations, ranging from instructions for a certain event to show and identify and express emotional states. With the passage of time when individuals have an inter-relationship with other people, through various elements, such as work and educational environments, the factors of collaboration and exchange of ideas become more important, since as more communication takes place, emotional processes can be identified, as these end up becoming factors. With the above, it can be assumed and indicated that emotional intelligence takes a greater relevance, since it contributes in a very important way to the way in which individuals process and manage emotions in various social contexts. In this article, a development using machine learning is presented, the main objective is to be able to have a simple and easy understanding, based on natural language. Contemplating a DataSet that contains conversational elements, for this study two strategies will be applied to classify and predict the intentions and emotions of users, the study seeks to determine which of these two approaches, have better performance to support the understanding of natural language.

This type of research work, contemplating neural networks, is intended that the creation of tools such as conversational agents, can have a better response, be more accurate and supported by various techniques to be empathetic to user conversations.

Keywords: Convolutional Neural Networks (CNN) · Recurrent Neural Networks (RNN) · LSTM (Long Short-Term Memory) LSTM

O. Gervasi et al. (Eds.): ICCSA 2025 Workshops, LNCS 15891, pp. 370–380, 2026.
https://doi.org/10.1007/978-3-031-97617-9_24

1   Introduction

Currently in many applications that have AI, the PLN has a very important relevance, as this ranges from personal assistants, attention assistants to text analysis [1]. The PLN has the main function of classifying text entered by users, ranging from short instructions to complex commands (i.e., e.g., user intentions and sentiments).

In order to determine and find complex elements and to be able to learn the representation of complex data without the need for very complex requirement analysis processes, neural networks support these processes as well as others[2].

Initially, convolutional neural networks (CNN) were proposed to solve problems and situations of pattern identification in the area of computer vision, because they take advantage of two-dimensional convolution operations in images.

However, for text classification, one-dimensional (1D) convolution can be applied to token embedding sequences. This 1D approach mitigates the noise that could arise from forcing text into a 2D structure, while preserving the advantages of CNN in local feature extraction [3].

There are also the recurrent neural networks (RNN), and in particular those that have an improvement with the LSTM, these are of great relevance in those processes of the capture that contemplates long term dependencies [4]. Something to consider is that when performing sequential processing of tokens, this type of neural networks can maintain those hidden states that have longer text information.

A development in Python is presented, with the objective of making a comparison of the deep learning models: CNN 1D and RNN, which perform text classification, which will be in an application known as "chabot". Each of the models has its strengths, for example: CNN 1D performs the data capture efficiently, and with them identifies the patterns, and on the other hand the RNN contains the information and uses it in the context of the work, to be used in the long term. This article will show what considerations should be taken into account in the design of the models, reviewing the data preprocessing and, as in all model development, reviewing the evaluation metrics.

After that, the development of the data preprocessing, its architectures and training will be presented, once the processes are indicated, the performance comparison and an analysis of the results will be made. As a result, the results will be indicated, highlighting the best numbers as well as the advantages and disadvantages.

2   Network Structure

The analysis for this development is based on having text inputs, contemplating two different neural architectures, which were developed in Python, TensorFlow/Keras. In each of the models' different strategies are applied in order to identify the patterns of the word sequences, and ultimately having a prediction.

2.1   Evolutionary Neural Network (CNN)

The CNN had its highest point of disclosure, in environments of pattern and image recognition [2], these networks, have the peculiarity that they can adapt to natural language, being able to apply one-dimensional filters, in an environment of temporal dimension for the use of tokens [3].

Some characteristics, per layer:

- Convolutional: In these layers are applied different filters, also called "Kernels", which are used to detect features.
- Activation: Their function is to add nonlinearity.
- Pooling: These layers are designed to reduce the dimensionality and to have a low computational cost.
- Fully connected: These layers are designed for the process of performing the qualification, which is based on the extracted features [6].

This model has an uncomplicated but not simple implementation for those who are starting, the model is composed: First, by an embedding layer, whose task is to assign each token index to a vector. Second, by a 1D convolutional layer (Conv1D) which has the task of scanning the embedding vectors, and captures the features as well as n-gram patterns. Third, it performs an operation called "GlobalMaxPooling1D", which is responsible for selecting the activations, thereby merging the maps into a single vector. Fourth, in the dense layers, it performs the transformation of the vector into an output distribution over the class labels:

$$Y(i,j) = \sum_m \cdot \sum_n .K(m,n) \cdot X(i+m,j+n) + b \tag{1}$$

Its efficiency and very low computational cost performance position it as one of the most useful models in tasks such as voice recognition, sentiment identification, biometric data, and power electronics [7].

2.2 Recurrent Neural Network (RNN) with LSTM

RNNs are a type of network that are applicable to sequential data, this because they can have a hidden state that is maintained through temporal processes [4]. The layer that is in charge of embedding is to convert the indexes of each token into embedding vectors, that is why an LSTM layer can process the vectors in order, considering the relationships across multiple.

LSTM, being a variant of RNNs, use gate structures that help them to control and regulate the information and, moreover, a very important feature is the ability to retain the information "dependencies" in the long term.

This type of network, with the passage of time has helped the problem of the weakness of the gradient, which allows the RNN to have long-term dependencies in those data sequences that can be considered complicated [8].

2.3 Model Compilation and Trainingdebilidad

Both the CNN and RNN, the Adam optimizer is used, which is a good tool as it supports adaptivity and training efficiency. A cross-entropy is used to analyze the loss, which is considered to be highly efficient when the labels are encoded with integers [2]. A callback called "EarlyStopping" is implemented which function is to monitor the loss that occurs in the training when a high point is reached, this will help to mitigate the overfitting.

3 Comparison of Architectures

3.1 CNN

It focuses on the extraction of features in the text, for this, convolutional filters are used. By applying the 1D filter, the training minimizes the noise of the additional dimensions, this is very convenient as it makes it an accurate method, and strong enough to identify textual patterns [3].

3.2 RNN (LSTM)

Its main feature is the sequentiality of the language, turning token contexts into easily identifiable values, and thus with them, being able to better interpret subsequent words [4]. Another feature is to be able to identify long term dependencies, this gives developers a point to consider, as support in queries or statements, regardless of whether they depend on contextual clues.

Since the 2 models will be trained and the dataset will be the same, it will be possible to better visualize the performance of both, and thus evaluate which method has a more robust prediction for a given application. From the literature it could be indicated that the CNN can be efficient, the RNN having the characteristic of visualizing the context in a wider way can also be a good prediction. In the end, to determine which one would be the correct one, several factors should be considered such as: the size of the data set, the length of the words and phrases, the analysis of speed and accuracy.

3.3 Summary

A summary of both models is made, as show in Table 1.

Table 1. Comparation RNN with LSTM and CNN [4, 6, 9, 10]

Characteristics	RNN with LSTM (Recurrent Neural Network with Long-Term Memory)	CNN (Convolutional Neural Network)
Architecture	It has cells that regulate the information in its sequence	It has convolutional and pooling layers that are used to extract characteristics
Data	Are sequential or temporal, for example: audio, text, etc	Structured, e.g. images
Previous data memory	Can store relevant information	It does not store information, so it has no memory of previous data
Training	Its processing is sequential	It is parallelizable
Long-term dependency	Can model long-term dependencies	Not suggested for long term dependencies
Use	PLN, for time series	Clasificacion de imágenes, detencccion de objetos, etc
Advantages	Can capture context and temporal dependency	Learns spatial patterns

4 Algorithms

This paper presents two deep learning approaches, (CNN) and (LSTM) to identify and classify user data in a chatbot environment [2–4]. Each of the models are prohramed and trained using tools such as: TensorFlow/Keras, this is to take advantage of working with embedded word vectors and specialized layers.

Onsidering NumPy and Pandas, supports the work of numerical operations and therefore the management of data, while NumPy allows to have efficient calculations, pandas help to have the data and help in the preprocessing of the data, such as CSV files.

In the training and evaluation process, the use of TensorFlow/Keras provides a high level of functionality to support the conversion of token indices into vectors, "EarlyStopping" in order to have the ability to automatically stop training when the loss is too high or no longer improves. On the other hand, the Conv1D and GlobalMaxPooling1D, analyze and take the patterns for the CNN model, the LSTM layer is in charge of processing the sequential data for the RNN. It is contemplated to have tools such as "scikit-learn" to help split the data into training and test sets.

In the FrondEnd environment, "matplotlib" is worked with to plot the training metrics and confusion matrices, this supports the developed to have a clearer view of the performance of each model. For the graphical user interface (GUI) we have "tkinter", which is integrated with the "speech_recognition" library, in order to have voice input and produce real-time transcriptions.

A helpful point is that by separating tasks such as data processing, model building, training, evaluation and user interaction, the system is intended to remain flexible and adaptable to other situations and scenarios.

5 Definition of Model Architectures

This paper generates and analyzes two different deep learning designs for text-based classification: (CNN) and (RNN), both using LSTM. Both CNN and RNN are TensorFlow/Keras implementations, for each an embedding layer is contemplated to transform integer encoded inputs [2–4].

5.1 CNN Model

CNN has as first an embedding layer, second a Conv1D layer that slides a kernel over the sequence of embedding vectors, it is worth mentioning that it focuses on text patterns, third, it has the operation "GlobalMaxPooling1D", which has the function of selecting the maximum value of each feature map, to condense the extracted patterns in a single vector.

Algorithm 1

```
1.   def create_cnn_model(vocab_size, embedding_dim, input_length,
2.       num_classes):
3.         model = Sequential([
4.         Embedding(input_dim=vocab_size, output_dim=embedding_dim, in
5.         put_length=input_length),
6.         Conv1D(filters=128, kernel_size=5, activation='relu'),
7.         GlobalMaxPooling1D(),
8.         Dense(64, activation='relu'),
9.         Dense(num_classes, activation='softmax')
10.   ])
11.       model.compile(optimizer='adam', loss='sparse_categorical_crossentro
12.       py', metrics=['accuracy'])
13.   return model
```

One thing to note is that compared to typical 2D convolutions applicable to image processing, the 1D architecture used here is adapted to sequential data. It is good to point out that by restricting the convolutions to a single dimension, the evolution of the model thus avoids noise, which can be generated and focuses on the detection of critical n-gram type features [3].

5.2 RNN Model (LSTM)

On the other hand, the LSTM based model which is responsible for processing the input tokens. And after the embedding layer, the data is fed into a 64-unit LSTM layer, this helps the network to propagate hidden states over time and capture long-range dependencies. A final dense layer generates class probabilities:

LSTMs have a feature that gives them their value, which is being able to retain the relevant context in long sequences [4]. This positions them as a good choice and more so when the order and relationship of tokens are important.

Algorithm 2

```
1.   def create_rnn_model(vocab_size, embedding_dim, input_length,
2.       num_classes):
3.         model = Sequential([
4.         Embedding(input_dim=vocab_size, output_dim=embedding_dim, in
5.         put_length=input_length),
6.         LSTM(64),
7.         Dense(64, activation='relu'),
8.         Dense(num_classes, activation='softmax')
9.   ])
10.       model.compile(optimizer='adam', loss='sparse_categorical_crossen
11.       tropy', metrics=['accuracy'])
12.   return model
```

5.3 Comparison of Models

While, one may think that both models fulfill the same goal i.e. classification, it would not have much relevance to perform this strategy time, but their differences may generate different performance results. That is, while CNNs quickly extract salient and localized features [3]. For LSTM models, additional computations are required per token [4]. Trying to do this exercise time and stealing these two strategies, tending the same dataset, gives a guideline to be able to identify which method provides higher accuracy or generalization for a particular application, be it speed-sensitive chatbot interactions or more context-aware tasks that require deeper sequential understanding.

6 DataSet

The DataSet that was used, at the beginning was very small, and contained some predefined intents coming from Kaggle [5]. It contemplated some intents such as: greeting, farewell, creator and hours. Upon analysis and observing that it could not satisfy the work, as it did not generate the interlocution intents, nor did it generate enough variability in user expressions, the new approach focused on orienting it towards a wider and more adaptable JSON based scenario, which allowed the incorporation of additional tags (to mention a few: weather, time, joke, news) along with a significantly larger list of possible user inputs.

The new DataSet is composed of several patterns for each intent, with various phrases that users might employ in real conversations. Each of the elements will be processed with the features of the text preprocessing routines, i.e. lower case, punctuation removal, which will be enhanced prior to model training. By doing this, consistency can be guaranteed and noise can be reduced, plus one can integrate user-generated text, which can come from a variety of sources. Also, the new DataSet has a series of response lists for each intent, allowing for more natural and varied responses.

The DataSet, by having a wider range of intentions, and examples, will be able to improve the chatbot's ability to have the dialog, by being more robust, will be able to support evaluating and contrasting CNN and LSTM architectures.

7 Model Comparison and Reporting

The proposal shown in this paper demonstrates a simple methodology for comparing CNN and RNN (LSTM) architectures, with a wide variety of training conditions. This active function prompts the user to train each model, considering the different epochs: 20, 30, 40 and 50, and the data are divided into separate training and test sets. For each configuration, the following steps are performed, accuracy values: Each training a graph is generated showing the accuracy, accuracy values of the tests: Once the training was performed, confusion matrices: Each of the best performing CNN and RNN models generates its confusion matrix.

The results, are compared based on the above items, and this gives a clearer picture of the performance of the CNN and RNN architectures under different training conditions as shown in Table 2.

8 Result

8.1 CNN Model Results

The ROC curves show that almost all predictions are correct. The CNN model is relevant for its ability to extract correctly the localized features of the text, this supports the conditions could be controlled DataSet, and thus with them generate a classification that could be considered of very high value. However, it should be noted that, during the tests that were performed with real users, it should also be noted that in some occasions it classified erroneously, such as: some ambiguous greetings or some text-dependent queries, as shown in Figs. 1 and 2.

Table 2. Classification Report for Best CNN Model:

Class	Precision	Recall	F1-Score	Support
Goodbye	1	1	1	147
Greeting	1	1	1	163
Help	1	1	1	147
Joke	1	1	1	148
Name	1	1	1	132
News	1	1	1	138
programmer	1	1	1	155
Thanks	1	1	1	150
Time	1	1	1	156
Weather	1	1	1	164
Overall Accuracy	1			1500
Macro Avg	1	1	1	1500
Weighted Avg	1	1	1	1500

8.2 Results of the RNN Model (LSTM)

In this proposal the RNN model, which is based on a LSTM architecture, generates and processes data sequentially, and keeps its states hidden throughout the token work. The design of this architecture is planned to check and have the dependencies and context in the user inputs. At the point when the model was analyzed and trained under the same conditions, i.e., 20 epochs at a learning rate of 0.001, it achieved 100% accuracy on the controlled test set, as shown in Table 3.

When the LSTM processes the complete sequence of words, it allows you to control the sentence structures that are considered more complex. But, however, like CNN, its environment is also controlled and is good, which shows that the DataSet is adequate.

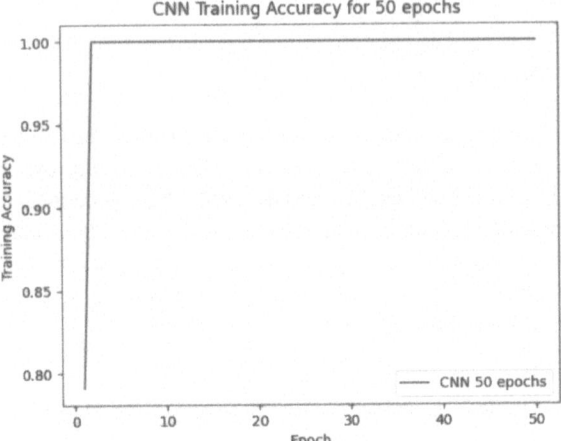

Fig. 1. ROC Curve of CNN accuracy, with 50 epochs

Table 3. Classification Report for Best RNN Model:

Class	Precision	Recall	F1-Score	Support
Goodbye	1	1	1	147
Greeting	1	1	1	163
Help	1	1	1	147
Joke	1	1	1	148
Name	1	1	1	132
News	1	1	1	138
programmer	1	1	1	155
Thanks	1	1	1	150
Time	1	1	1	156
Weather	1	1	1	164
Overall Accuracy	1			1500
Macro Avg	1	1	1	1500
Weighted Avg	1	1	1	1500

When testing with real users, RNN a at times maintains the context better than CNN, but also has challenges with inputs that deviated from the observed values (patterns) that were visualized in it during training. This indicates as a final point, that both models are very accurate in the test DataSet, but when generalized they have some problems, but this can be analyzed.

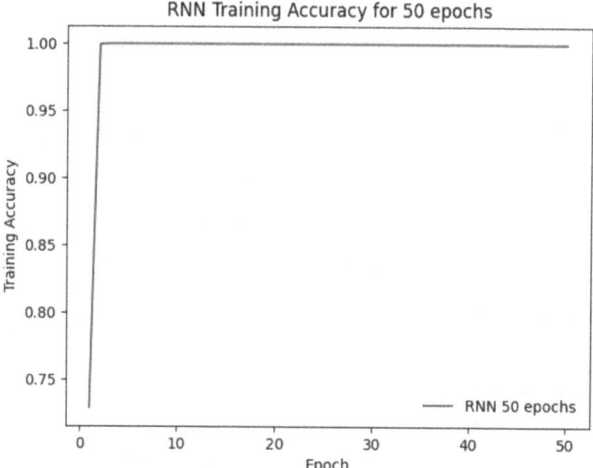

Fig. 2. ROC Curve of RNN accuracy, with 50 epochs

8.3 Model Comparison and Analysis

The following is a list of the results of both models.

The CNN model, by focusing on local patterns, has a high identification of phrases and words, which supports the identification of specific intentions in the context. Being a very efficient architecture, it can respond quickly during the question-answer process. But it can miss some circumstances where some words do not match in order and context, and this is not good because it can change the meaning of the expressions. However, the RNN model (LSTM), whose functionality is designed to maintain the context throughout a sequence, is more appropriate. This makes it more robust in scenarios where language structures are complex or ambiguous.

Both models obtained 100% accuracy in the controlled tests, indicating that the DataSet is consistent with very little inconsistency. But, in real-time user testing, the CNN misclassified some entries. The RNN can be identified as a more accurate model at long dependencies, indicating that the DataSet may not fully reflect the diversity of natural language.

Experiments performed with different numbers of epochs indicated that learning tended to a point where it no longer had growth after a certain point, between 20 and 100 epochs. This may indicate that both models can have convergence in very tight times, this when you have a well selected DataSet. But if you indicate the performance metrics this is high.

Both models show that classification errors are minimal under controlled conditions. When generating the ROC curves, they indicate in each model a good performance, but it was observed that there is a slight better performance in the CNN model versus the RNN in terms of AUC values.

The overall conclusion of the proposal, it can be indicated that for both models, it is identified that they have a very good performance in the control DataSet. If we consider values such as speed and efficiency in feature extraction in CNN model places it as a good choice for where this is of utmost importance, and in relation to the ability of the RNN to capture elements of the context it may be ineffective in more complex situations.

9 Future Work

The controlled environments, and more when you have a performance considered good, not in all cases, is a point that can be considered equivalent in real environments.
  Listed are some solutions that could be part of the proposal.

- To have a wider and more varied Dataset, contemplating real world examples,
- Having a larger DataSet could support having more arguments in the conversation.
- Consider using pre-trained models.
- To have a wider and more varied Dataset, contemplating real world examples,
- To analyze possible improvements in data preprocessing, considering: tokenization, case sensitivity, punctuation marks, to mention a few points.
- Review whether cross validation helps the final results.
- To analyze methods of regularization and argumentation.

For this proposal, the use of controlled tests was proposed to analyze performance, which was positive. In future studies we will perform tests and scenarios applicable to the real world, where the scenarios could be acoustic and analyze how the CNN and RNN models are applicable, but for this as a hypothesis it is proposed that the phases and diversify the training data should be broad and clean. The pipeline should be revised to make the work more transparent and thus achieve a considerable improvement.

References

1. Hirschberg, J., Manning, C.D.: Advances in natural language processing. Science **349**(6245), 261–266 (2015)
2. LeCun, Y., Bengio, Y., Hinton, G.: Deep learning. Nature **521**(7553), 436–444 (2015)
3. Kim, Y.: Convolutional neural networks for sentence classification. In: Proceedings of 2014 Conference on Empirical Methods Natural Language Processing (EMNLP), pp. 1746–1751 (2014)
4. Hochreiter, S., Schmidhuber, J.: Long short-term memory. Neural Comput. **9**(8), 1735–1780 (1997)
5. Vaghani, N.: "Chatbot Dataset," Kaggle (2023). https://www.kaggle.com/datasets/niraliiva ghani/chatbot-dataset. Accessed 01 March 2025
6. Krizhevsky, A., Sutskever, I., Hinton, G.E.: ImageNet classification with deep convolutional neural networks. Adv. Neural. Inf. Process. Syst. **25**, 1097–1105 (2012)
7. Li, Z., Yang, W., Peng y F. Liu, S.: A survey of convolutional neural networks: analysis, applications, and prospects. Mech. Syst. Signal Process. **151**, 107398 (2021). https://doi.org/10.1016/j.ymssp.2020.107398
8. Ghojogh y A. Ghodsi, B.: Redes Neuronales Recurrentes y Redes de Memoria a Largo Corto Plazo: Tutorial y Revisión. arXiv preprint arXiv:2304.11461 (2023)
9. Goodfellow, I., Bengio, Y., Courville, A.: Deep Learning. MIT Press (2016). https://www.deeplearningbook.org/
10. Ghojogh, B., Ghodsi, A.: Recurrent neural networks and long short-term memory: a tutorial and review. arXiv preprint arXiv:2304.11461 (2023). https://arxiv.org/abs/2304.11461

A Lightweight FPGA-Based Steganography Accelerator Core for Edge Platforms

Cuong Pham-Quoc[1,2(✉)] 🆔

[1] Ho Chi Minh City University of Technology (HCMUT), 268 Ly Thuong Kiet
Street, District 10, Ho Chi Minh City, Vietnam
cuongpham@hcmut.edu.vn
[2] Vietnam National University - Ho Chi Minh City (VNU-HCM), Thu Duc, Ho Chi
Minh City, Vietnam

Abstract. In the era of edge computing, where IoT devices are increasingly connected to the Internet, data security and privacy have become critical concerns. Steganography, a technique for embedding hidden information within digital media, offers a lightweight security measure that complements traditional cryptographic methods. However, implementing steganographic techniques efficiently in edge devices poses challenges related to computational overhead, power consumption, and real-time performance. This paper introduces a lightweight FPGA-based steganography accelerator core designed for edge computing platforms. Our design optimizes resource efficiency, low latency, and adaptability while ensuring robust data hiding and retrieval capabilities. The proposed system is evaluated with respect to hardware utilization, power efficiency, and embedding performance. We evaluated our system on the Xilinx Kria KV260 edge computing platform, analyzing hardware utilization, execution time, power consumption, and throughput across different image sizes. Experimental results demonstrate that our FPGA-based accelerator outperforms a traditional ARM processor-based software implementation, achieving up to 2.42× speed-up with dual-core configurations. Furthermore, power efficiency analysis shows that the system effectively minimizes energy consumption, making it suitable for power-sensitive edge applications. The proposed solution is highly adaptable and can be integrated with other hardware accelerators, such as video encoding or network security modules, to enhance processing capabilities in IoT environments.

Keywords: FPGA · Hardware accelerator · DCT · Steganography · Edge Computing · IoTs

1 Introduction

In the era of edge computing, while more and more IoT devices are connected to the Internet [16], data security and privacy have become critical concerns

O. Gervasi et al. (Eds.): ICCSA 2025 Workshops, LNCS 15891, pp. 381–392, 2026.
https://doi.org/10.1007/978-3-031-97617-9_25

due to the increasing reliance on distributed devices and resources restricted [7]. Steganography, a technique for concealing information within digital media, has gained attention as a lightweight security measure that complements traditional cryptographic methods. However, implementing steganographic techniques efficiently in edge devices presents challenges related to computational overhead, power consumption, and real-time performance.

Field-Programmable Gate Arrays (FPGAs) offer an attractive solution to address these challenges by providing hardware acceleration with low power consumption and high processing efficiency. In this paper, we propose a lightweight FPGA-based steganography core optimized for edge computing platforms. Our design prioritizes resource efficiency, low latency, and adaptability to various edge applications while ensuring robust data hiding and retrieval capabilities.

The proposed steganography core is evaluated in terms of hardware utilization, power efficiency, and embedding performance. The results demonstrate its suitability for security-sensitive applications in edge environments, such as IoT networks, industrial automation, and smart surveillance systems. Using FPGA-based acceleration, this work contributes to the development of secure and efficient data hiding techniques tailored for edge computing platforms.

The main contributions of our paper can be summarized in three folds.

1. We introduced our lightweight FPGA-based Steganography accelerator core targeting IoT platforms for embedded hidden messages into containers such as images or videos.
2. We illustrate our proposed system with the prototype on the Xilinx Kria KV260 edge computing platform to evaluate performance and throughput.
3. We analyze our experimental results with the prototype platform and different image sizes for comparison of future studies.

The remainder of the paper is organized as follows. Section 2 shows the background on the work related to steganography and FPGA-based systems. We introduce our proposed FPGA-based steganography accelerator core in Sect. 3. Section 4 shows our prototype with Xilinx Kria KV260 edge computing. Experiments with various image sizes and the prototype platform are analyzed in Sect. 5. Finally, Sect. 6 concludes our paper.

2   Preliminaries and Related Work

In this section, we first present the background of steganography in data security. We then analyzed related work in the literature that targets the implementation of FPGA-based steganography.

2.1   Steganography

Steganography is the practice of concealing information within a carrier medium in a way that prevents detection by unauthorized parties [5,8,9]. Unlike cryptography, which focuses on encrypting data to make it unreadable without a decryption key, steganography aims to hide the existence of the communication itself. This covert approach makes steganography an effective tool for secure data transmission, digital watermarking, and anti-forensic applications.

Traditional steganographic techniques embed information into various digital media such as images, audio files, videos, and text. Common methods include Least Significant Bit (LSB) substitution, transform domain techniques, and adaptive steganography, each offering different trade-offs between security, capacity, and imperceptibility. With the rise of modern communication systems and digital forensics, researchers continue to develop advanced steganographic approaches that enhance robustness against detection while maintaining efficiency.

The growing adoption of edge computing and resource-constrained devices has introduced new challenges and opportunities for steganography. Efficient and lightweight steganographic solutions are increasingly required to ensure secure data exchange in environments with limited processing power and storage. As a result, hardware-based steganography, particularly FPGA and ASIC implementations, has gained attention for its ability to accelerate steganographic processes while minimizing power consumption and latency.

2.2 FPGA-Based Steganography Related Work

FPGA-based steganography cores are specialized hardware implementations designed to enhance the performance and efficiency of steganography techniques that involve hiding secret data within digital media. These cores leverage the reconfigurability and parallel processing capabilities of Field Programmable Gate Arrays (FPGAs) to achieve high-speed data embedding and extraction, making them suitable for real-time applications.

FPGA-based implementations of steganography algorithms, such as the Exploiting Modification Direction (EMD) and Least Significant Bit (LSB) methods, offer significant advantages in terms of speed and flexibility. These architectures are designed to handle variable image resolutions and pixel group sizes, allowing real-time processing at high frame rates. For example, EMD-based systems can embed secret messages in images with resolutions up to 512×512 pixels at 549 frames per second [15]. Similarly, LSB-based systems achieve high throughput by incorporating pipelining and parallel operations, processing data at rates of 183.48 frames per second [13].

The use of FPGAs in steganography provides several benefits, including reduced computational delay, increased throughput, and lower power consumption. These systems are capable of real-time data processing, which is crucial for applications requiring immediate data embedding and extraction [2]. Furthermore, FPGA implementations are cost-effective and offer flexibility to adapt to different steganography algorithms and cover media types, such as images, audio, and video [6].

Despite the advantages, FPGA-based steganography systems face challenges such as the complexity of algorithm implementation and the need for efficient resource utilization. Future research may focus on optimizing these systems for even higher performance and exploring new algorithms that can be effectively implemented on FPGAs. There is also potential for integrating cryptographic techniques to improve the security of the steganographic process [1, 14].

3   Proposed FPGA-Based Steganography Core Architecture

In this section, we introduce our FPGA-based steganography accelerator core. We design the core according to the hardware accelerator paradigm [11] so that the core can be integrated with different hardwired or soft general-purpose processors to develop applications.

3.1   Overview Architecture

Figure 1 illustrates the overview architecture of our steganography core. The core communicates with the host processor through a communication infrastructure (bus, shared memory, etc.) for transferring input data (parameters, messages, images/videos, etc.) and output results. Exchange registers and two buffers (one for Discrete Cosine Transform - DCT, and one for Steganography) are used for these purposes.

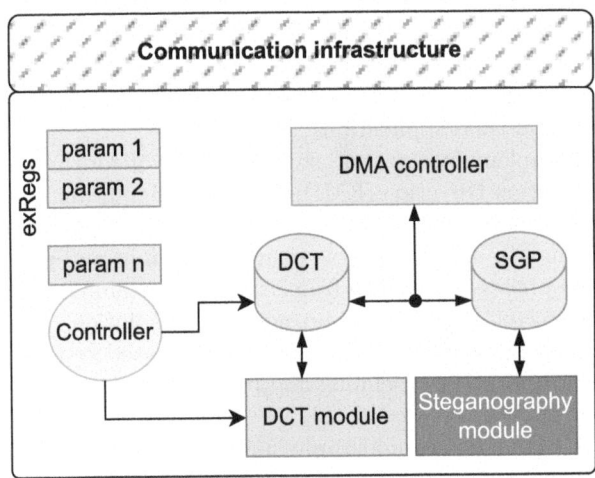

Fig. 1. The overview of the lightweight FPGA-based steganography accelerator core for IoT platforms

The core components of the accelerated steganography engine consist of two main modules: the discrete cosine transform (DCT) computation module and the steganography module. The DCT module performs discrete cosine transform operations on input data matrices extracted from background image frames. The

DCT-transformed data are then transferred to the buffer of the steganography module, where the hidden messages are embedded using steganographic techniques. The final output is transmitted to the processor via DMA. The details of the two modules are discussed in the following subsections.

3.2   DCT Module

The 2D discrete cosine transform (DCT) is formed by two consecutive steps of the 1D discrete cosine transform, connected by a transposition step. Initially, the 1D DCT reads data from the input matrix row by row, then a series of computations is performed, and the results are stored in an intermediate matrix column by column. Once the input matrix has been fully processed and the intermediate matrix is completely filled, the second 1D DCT begins, repeating the same process with the intermediate matrix as input, and reading the transposed results from the first 1D DCT. The final results are then stored in the output matrix. This process is illustrated in Fig. 2. Since this work focuses on the 8×8 DCT for images, two 1D DCTs with 8-point computations are used to perform the 2D DCT.

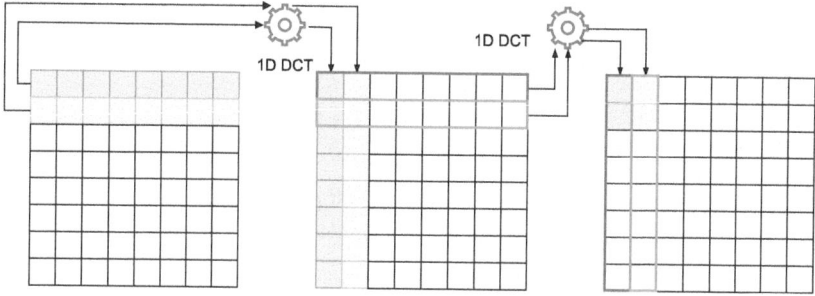

Fig. 2. 2D-DCT computation based on $2\times$ 1D-DCT

Based on the DCT principle mentioned above, we designed the architecture of the DCT calculation module using a pipelined processing model to improve performance, as shown in Fig. 3. The processing of a DCT matrix consists of four stages, where the last two stages repeat the first two. These stages include butterfly computations, multiply-accumulate (MAC) operations, and transpose map.

The task of the Butterfly unit is to compute the sum and difference of each pair of numbers from the input matrix data. The input data is an 8×8 matrix, where each row is processed sequentially and fed into the Butterfly unit for computation. The output of this unit for each row produces eight values, with four values being the result of addition and the other four being the result of subtraction for each pair of numbers in the corresponding row of the input matrix.

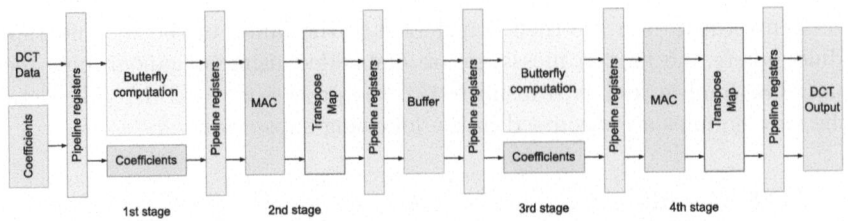

Fig. 3. The pipeline architecture for 2D DCT computation

The `MAC` unit performs multiplication and accumulation on the output values of the `Butterfly` unit to compute the DCT coefficient values. The summed values from the `Butterfly` unit is multiplied by the coefficients of the matrix, which are retrieved from the memory block (buffer), and the accumulated results produce the DCT coefficients. The same process is applied to the difference values from the Butterfly unit. The computed results from the MAC unit are stored in RAM to be used in subsequent computation stages.

The Transpose map block plays a crucial role in the DCT acceleration module. Due to the nature of the algorithm, the output data from the MAC unit does not follow a specific order. The Transpose Map block is responsible for transposing the matrix and mapping the output results from the MAC unit to their correct memory addresses in storage.

3.3 Steganography Module

Based on the steganography algorithms developed, the steganography system utilizes the Fully Exploiting Modification Direction (EMD-3) algorithm. According to the EMD-3 algorithm, we choose $n = 3$, which means that for every three values of the cover data, we can embed hidden information with a maximum value of $3^3 = 27$. For each byte of hidden information, the system uses six values of the cover data for embedding. Figure 4 illustrates the architecture of the Steganography module with three functional groups: "steganography algorithm implementation," "data read/write," and "control."

To implement the steganography algorithm, the `Extract`, `Decision`, and `Embedding` blocks perform tasks based on the algorithm. The `Extract` block functions in two modes: embedding and extracting hidden information from input data. In embedding mode, it handles data preprocessing and computes the extract function. The output of the Extract block consists of cover data (or carrier data) and the result of the extract function. The `Decision` block is responsible for computing the decision function based on the output of the extract function and the hidden information value. Using these inputs, the Decision block determines whether modifications to the cover data values are necessary. The `Embedding` block is the most critical component, responsible for comparing and embedding hidden information into the cover data. It uses the output of the extract function of the `Extract` block and the decision function of

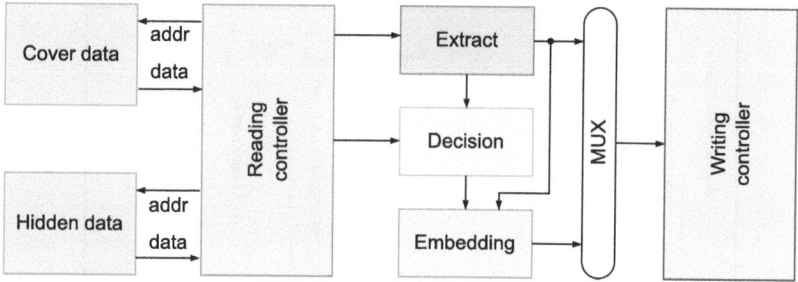

Fig. 4. The architecture for the steganography module

the `Decision` block. Based on the comparison result of the `Decision` block, the `Embedding` block calculates values and decides whether to increase or decrease each cover data value by 1.

To read/write data, we build the `Reading` and `Writing` controllers. The `Reading Controller` block performs the task of reading data values from external memory and splitting these data into individual data units. Then it loads them into the Input Register block for data packaging. The `Writing Controller` block operates similarly to the Reading Controller block, verifying output data and segmenting the result data into individual units suitable for storage in external memory.

Finally, for handling operations of data read/write and steganography, the `Control unit` checks the parameters configured by the user and the system's operating mode to manage and regulate the output data appropriately. It also controls the stages in the pipeline of the Steganography accelerator system. Additionally, the Control block monitors the completion of the data hiding or extraction process to configure registers and notify the software.

4   FPGA Edge Computing Prototype

This section presents our prototype FPGA-based edge computing platform with our integrated steganography accelerator core[1]. In this work, we use the Xilinx Kria KV260 edge computing system [3] to deploy our prototype. The platform contains a Xilinx Zynq UltraScale+ MPSoC ZU5CG with 256K logic cells, 144 Block RAM (36 Kbits/block), and other components. The core modules are described by Verilog HDL and synthesized with Xilinx Vivado [4]. Along with the reconfigurable logic for building the Steganography accelerator core, the Zynq FPGA chip also contains a hardwired dual-core ARM Cortex-A53 processor for executing software. One of the use-cases is to embed a signature into images/videos for certifying that the images/videos are generated from trust devices.

---

[1] The author thanks Mr. Le Phu Thuan for describing the core with Verilog-HDL.

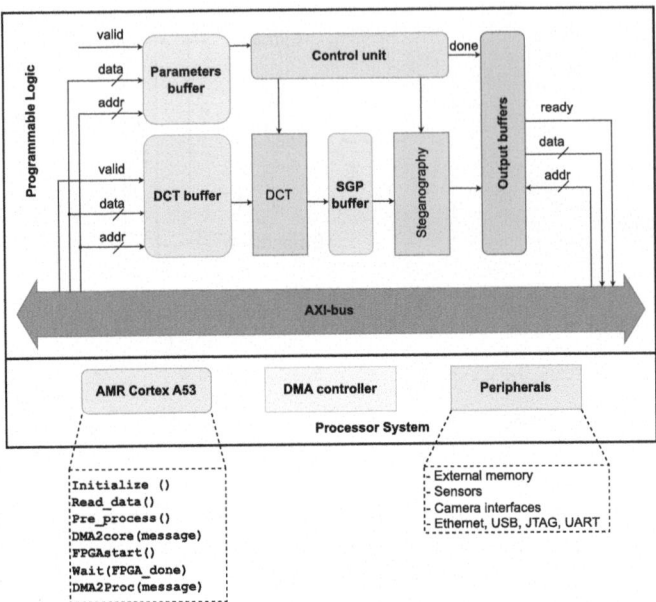

Fig. 5. The prototype system with Xilinx Kria KV260 board

Figure 5 presents an overview of our prototype system. In this prototype, the hardwired ARM processor is a host processor to control and collect data from peripherals such as sensors and cameras and to communicate with the cloud through the Ethernet interface. To certify the images, videos, the host processor starts transferring data to our Steganography core by Direct Memory Access (DMA) through the AXI bus interface for the signing process. During this interval, the host processor can wait or perform other tasks. Images/videos after embedded message or signature are transferred back from the accelerator core for sending to the cloud.

5   Experiments

This section presents experiments to evaluate the effectiveness of the Steganography accelerator core and the FPGA-based prototype systems. The experiment results are then examined, comparing the system's performance with the accelerator against using only software on the ARM processor. In addition, power consumption will be evaluated, analyzed, and compared.

5.1   Synthesis Results

The Steganography accelerator core, developed by Verilog-HDL, and the entire system are synthesized and configured on the Kria board by Xilinx Vivado 2023.2. For testing purposes, we synthesize the system that consists of one

DCT & one Steganography modules and two modules of each (two DCT and two Steganography), respectively. The results of the synthesis reveal that with two DCT & Steganography modules, the system can operate at 150 MHz and requires 2.973 W of total power consumption. Table 1 presents the usage of hardware resources for the system with one and two DCT & Steganography modules, respectively.

Table 1. Hardware resources usage for the proposed system with one or two DCT & Steganography modules

Resources	2 cores		1 core		Available
	Amount	Percentage	Amount	Percentage	
Look-up tables (LUTs)	50,109	42%	24,670	21%	117,120
Flip-flop (FFs)	28,693	24%	14,597	12%	234,240
DSP	58	4%	29	2%	1,248
Block RAMs (BRAMs)	176	50%	176	50%	352

As presented in the table, our system uses up to 42% of the hardware resources of the FPGA, indicating the potential to integrate additional modules DCT and Steganography to further enhance performance. Using the hardware accelerator computing model, the system also enables the incorporation of specialized cores for specific tasks, such as video encoding/decoding [10] or attack detection [12], thereby improving processing efficiency and overall performance in IoT edge computing environments.

5.2 Simulation Results

Figure 6 illustrates how the DCT module operates as a pipeline. When the module begins the computation, each output value corresponds to a mapped address. For the DCT module, in each cycle, it computes two output values. Thus, it only takes 32 clock cycles to write the entire 8 × 8 DCT matrix (containing 64 DCT coefficients).

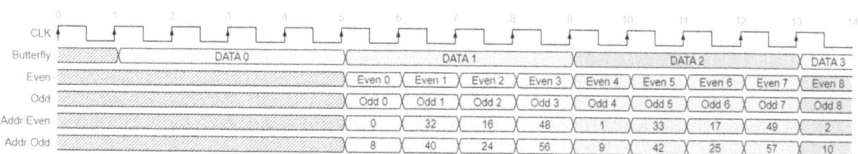

Fig. 6. The waveform for simulation the DCT module

For the Steganography module, the data hiding process requires four cycles from the start to package the first data block to embed the file. Similarly, at the system's output, the data packet must be split into smaller subpackets and written into BRAM. Figure 7 illustrates the process of segmenting the read data from BRAM into subfiles and packaging the data every three subdata units. Data packets are read every three cycles to ensure continuous processing of the entire dataset.

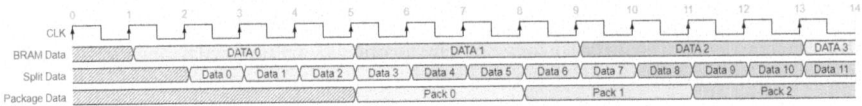

Fig. 7. The waveform for simulation the Steganography module

5.3   Performance Evaluation and Comparison

We evaluate the processor performance using one and two DCT & Steganography modules with different image sizes: 512×512, 256×256, and 128×128 pixels. The data hiding process is performed using: (1) A hardwired ARM core operating at 1.5 GHz, call software; and (2) Our accelerated system, which utilizes a dedicated Steganography accelerator core.

Table 2 shows the execution time of our accelerator system (with one and two DCT & Steganography modules) and of ARM processor only. As shown in the table, when one DCT & Steganography modules are deployed, we manage to achieve speed-ups by up to 1.54× compared to the ARM processor functioning at 1.5 GHz. When two of the modules are integrated, our system outperforms the ARM processor by up to 2.42×.

Table 2. Execution time (s) with different image sizes

Image	2 cores		1 core		Software
	Exec. time	Speed-up	Exec. Time	Speed-up	
512×512	3.12	2.17×	4.58	1.48×	6.80
256×256	0.91	1.97×	1.61	1.53×	1.78
128×128	0.19	2.42×	0.30	1.54×	0.46

In addition to comparing execution time, we also evaluated processing bandwidth using the parameters pixels per second (pixel/s) and hidden data size per second (bit/s). Furthermore, we assess the system's energy consumption using the micro-joule metrics per Byte (mJ/byte) and micro-joules per Pixel (mJ/pixel) to measure energy usage based on the amount of hidden information or image size. Table 3 compares throughput and energy efficiency between different hidden data and image sizes. As shown in the table, the system functions well with small-size images in terms of throughput bit/s and energy consumption per hidden byte. This characteristic is suitable for edge computing systems where energy is a critical issue.

Table 3. Throughput and energy consumption

Image	Data (byte)	pixel/s	bit/s	mJ/byte	mJ/pixel
128×128	124	54,631	413	16.99	0.127
256×256	375	56,415	322	22.39	0.128
512×512	975	57,169	212	33.98	0.126

6 Conclusion

This paper presented a lightweight FPGA-based steganography accelerator core optimized for edge computing environments. The proposed system efficiently embeds hidden messages within digital media while maintaining low power consumption and high processing performance. Through synthesis and experimental evaluation on the Xilinx Kria KV260 platform, we demonstrated that our design effectively accelerates steganographic operations compared to software-based implementations. The results highlight significant improvements in execution time, throughput, and energy efficiency, making the accelerator a viable solution for IoT and edge AI applications.

Future work will explore further optimizations, including the integration of advanced compression techniques and the extension of support for additional media types such as audio and video. Additionally, we aim to enhance the security robustness of the system against steganalysis attacks, ensuring its applicability in diverse real-world scenarios requiring covert communication and data protection.

Acknowledgement. We acknowledge Ho Chi Minh City University of Technology (HCMUT), VNU-HCM for supporting this study.

References

1. FPGA based data hiding through steganography. Int. J. Recent Technol. Eng. (2020). https://doi.org/10.35940/ijrte.a2751.059120
2. Al-Ashwal, A.Y., Al-Arashi, W.H., Saad, A., Al-Shadadi, M.M.: Comprehensive survey of image steganography systems based on FPGA implementation. Univ. Sci. Technol. J. Eng. Technol. **2**(1), 35–70 (2024)
3. AMD Xilinx: Kria KV260 vision AI starter kit user guide (UG1089) (2022). https://docs.amd.com/r/en-US/ug1089-kv260-starter-kit. Accessed 31 Jan 2024

4. AMD Xilinx: Xilinx vivado design suite 2023.2 (2023). https://www.xilinx.com/products/design-tools/vivado.html. Accessed 31 Jan 2024

5. Cox, I., Miller, M., Bloom, J., Fridrich, J., Kalker, T.: Digital Watermarking and Steganography. Morgan Kaufmann (2007)

6. He, J., Sun, W., Jiang, H.: Implementation and verification of steganography IP core based on HLS and openCV. J. Phys. Conf. Ser. **2245**, 012010 (2022)

7. Hossain, M.M., Fotouhi, M., Hasan, R.: Towards an analysis of security issues, challenges, and open problems in the internet of things. In: 2015 IEEE World Congress on Services, pp. 21–28. IEEE (2015)

8. Hussain, M., Wahab, A., Idris, Y., Ho, A.T., Jung, K.H.: Image steganography in spatial domain: a survey. Signal Process. Image Commun. **65**, 46–66 (2018)

9. Kadhim, I.J., Premaratne, P., Vial, P.J., Halloran, B.: Comprehensive survey of image steganography: techniques, evaluations, and trends in future research. Neurocomputing **335**, 299–326 (2019)

10. Pham-Quoc, C.: FPGA-based hardware/software codesign for video encoder on IoT edge platforms. In: International Conference on Computational Science and Its Applications, pp. 82–96. Springer (2023)

11. Pham-Quoc, C., Heisswolf, J., Werner, S., Al-Ars, Z., Becker, J., Bertels, K.: Hybrid interconnect design for heterogeneous hardware accelerators. In: 2013 Design, Automation & Test in Europe Conference & Exhibition (DATE), pp. 843–846. IEEE (2013)

12. Pham-Quoc, C., Thinh, T.N.: FPGA-enabled efficient framework for high-performance intrusion prevention systems. In: International Conference on Computational Science and Its Applications, pp. 83–98. Springer (2023)

13. Sathish Shet, K., Aswath, A., Hanumantharaju, M., Gao, X.Z.: Design and development of new reconfigurable architectures for LSB/multi-bit image steganography system. Multimedia Tools Appl. **76**, 13197–13219 (2017)

14. Savani, V., Mecwan, A., Gajjar, V.: Design and implementation of audio steganography on FPGA. STM J. **1**, 1–6 (2021). https://doi.org/10.37591/JOEDT.V1I1-3.4951

15. Shet, K.S., Aswath, A., Hanumantharaju, M., Gao, X.Z.: Novel high-speed reconfigurable FPGA architectures for EMD-based image steganography. Multimedia Tools Appl. **78**(13), 18309–18338 (2019)

16. Statista Research Department: Internet of things - number of connected devices worldwide 2015-2025 (2016). https://www.statista.com/statistics/471264/iot-number-of-connected-devices-worldwide/. Accessed 01 Apr 2023

Experimental Evaluation of LoRa RSSI Performance in Educational IoT Deployments

Anabel Pineda-Briseño[1,5]([✉]) [iD], Rosario Baltazar[2],
Rodrigo Cadena Martínez[3] [iD], Eduardo Eloy Loza Pacheco[4] [iD],
and Daniel Gonzalo Galván Rodríguez[1] [iD]

[1] TecNM/Instituto Tecnológico de Matamoros, H. Matamoros, Tamps., Mexico
{anabel.pb,daniel.gr}@matamoros.tecnm.mx
[2] TecNM/Instituto Tecnológico de León, Guanajuato, Mexico
rosario.baltazar@leon.tecnm.mx
[3] Universidad Americana de Europa, Cancún, Mexico
rodrigo.cadena@aulagrupo.es
[4] Universidad Nacional Autónoma de México, Estado de México, Mexico
eduardo.loza@acatlan.unam.mx
[5] Ubicomp Technologies, H. Matamoros, Tamps., Mexico
apineda@ubicomp.mx
https://ubicomp.mx

Abstract. In this work LoRa RSSI performance under five critical parameters pertinent to educational IoT settings: distance variation, physical barriers, wireless interference, elevation, and multinode setups is presented. The results suggest that RSSI exhibits a logarithmic decay with distance, with a substantial decline beyond 100 m. The intensity of the signal is proportional to the density of the material with physical obstructions, with composite panels resulting in the highest attenuation. RSSI remains stable in spread-spectrum environments but appears to have moderate interference from Wi-Fi, Bluetooth, and additional LoRa transmissions, illustrating LoRa's resilience. Multi-node transmission has a minimal effect on RSSI, while elevation offers minimal enhancement. These results underscore the resilience of LoRa and offer valuable insights for the optimization of IoT deployments.

Keywords: LoRa · RSSI · wireless communication · network performance · environmental impact · IoT environmental

1 Introduction

The Internet of Things (IoT) has emerged as an essential foundation of technological advancement, its development through a multitude of sectors, including healthcare, agriculture, smart urban environments, and education. Within this technological framework, LoRa (Long Range) technology is particularly valued for its capacity to facilitate long-range communication while utilizing minimal power, rendering it exceptionally appropriate for environments characterized by hard constraints [17,22,26]. A variety of measurements can assess the functionality of a LoRa network, and RSSI (Received Signal Strength Indicator) is notably significant for its practical implications. It has a direct impact on the reliability of the connection, the distance the signal can cover, and the overall efficiency of the network [15,25].

Some research has already explored how LoRa RSSI performs in industrial and farming environments, especially under tough conditions like high humidity [11,16]. But when it comes to educational settings, there's still a noticeable gap. These places aren't simple to work with—they often involve tricky building layouts, lots of signal interference, and the need to keep wireless communication reliable over long distances, which makes them a unique challenge for IoT deployment. Current research predominantly emphasizes predictive modeling approaches, including neural networks, for estimating LoRa performance, rather than conducting thorough experimental assessments. Nevertheless, theoretical predictions alone inadequately address the complexities associated with real-world deployments, especially in the context of smart campus initiatives.

The present research empirically examines the behavior of LoRa RSSI in five key scenarios relevant to educational IoT networks: distance variations, physical barriers, wireless interference, elevation differences, and multi-node transmissions. This study presents a reproducible experimental framework that focuses solely on the empirical acquisition of RSSI data across diverse environmental and network contexts, in contrast to previous research that emphasizes performance estimation via machine learning methods. In this work, we draw from both theoretical foundations and practical fieldwork to better understand and improve the implementation of LoRa networks within educational environments. Rather than relying solely on simulations or models, our approach includes real-world testing and observation. The sections that follow describe in detail the methodology we used, how measurements were taken, and the analytical techniques applied to assess performance across different use cases.

2   Related Work

Multiple studies on LoRa networks have delved into core performance metrics, with a particular emphasis on RSSI characteristics, data transmission reliability, and system optimization across diverse operational environments, including industrial, agricultural, and urban contexts. One example is the study by [26], where machine learning was applied to improve RSSI prediction accuracy in industrial contexts. They found that working with real-world data actually led to better performance. Even so, many of these studies don't take into account the unique hurdles that schools and universities face. The mix of complicated building layouts, interference from other networks, and the need for reliable long-distance communication makes deploying IoT solutions in these settings far from straightforward. In a similar way, [2] examined propagation models in campus environments; although their focus remained mostly on outdoor spaces, they included important considerations such as indoor signal variability and multiple classroom designs. In [14], LoRa networks in subway systems revealed the structural complexity and how it can lead to signal degradation, interference, and packet loss challenges that, don't fully reflect the realities of IoT used in educational buildings.

Additionally, in [1], Effective Signal Power (ESP) was suggested as a better option than RSSI to make networks more reliable in places with many changes, which could help educational IoT networks but hasn't been widely studied in this area. Other research efforts have focused on optimizing LoRa networks for high-density deployments, such as the work of [29], who analyzed the impact of transmission rates and large data packets on LoRa efficiency, emphasizing the need for optimized communication in applications like IoT enabled classrooms. In [4], the authors looked at how the height of transmission affects network performance, but their results are mostly relevant to suburban areas instead of indoor classrooms, where materials can weaken signals and there are other wireless networks nearby.

Most studies rely on predictive modeling or generalized propagation assessments without capturing the real-world deployment challenges in smart campuses. This study addresses these gaps by conducting a systematic experimental evaluation of LoRa RSSI under five key conditions: distance variation, physical obstructions, wireless interference, elevation, and multi-node transmissions.

3 Methodology

3.1 Experimental Setup

The study was carried out in the laboratory of the Instituto Tecnológico de Matamoros (ITM), this campus spreads over 22 ha and includes open fields, structures, and vegetated areas. This platform offered a controlled yet realistic setting for assessing IoT communication performance in various propagation conditions.

The testbed is comprising of six E220-900T22D LoRa modules from Ebyte, and was set up with one module assigned as the receiver and five as transmitters. The modules operate in the 915 MHz ISM band, and have a fixed transmission power of 22 dBm, a packet transmission period of 3 s, and a payload size of 32 bytes.

The spreading factor was analized, the bandwidth was setup for an adequate assessing performance across five experimental conditions: distance variation, obstacle interference, external radio interference, elevation impact, and multinode communication. RSSI value retrieval from the LoRa modules was done using the Ebyte E220 library and configuration parameters supplied by Mischianti's online documentation, hence guaranteeing consistency in RSSI readings throughout all tests. The experimental setups were designed to explore how environmental conditions and network-related variables impact the reliability and performance of LoRa communication in educational settings.

Each LoRa module was connected to the ESP-WROOM-32 microcontroller, which comes equipped with a dual-core processor running at 240 MHz and has 520 KB of SRAM. Including a UART connection, for packet transmission, and performed local data logging. Each configuration included a DS3231 RTC module linked to the ESP32. The module checked that the timestamps on sent and received packets were exactly the same by using correct Unix timestamps. To keep timing differences between devices to a minimum, some synchronization timestamps were sent out by a different reference node before each experiment.

The environmental parameters, including temperature, humidity, and potential interference sources, where recorded at the beginning of each experiment to reach their influence on signal performance. The receiver node was powered by a portable supply battery o make easy the measurements of the signal in various locations on campus to simulate different propagation conditions, including open fields, structural obstructions, and interference areas [15,17,25].

The Node-Red system was used for manage real-time data, and the MySQL Workbench was used for efficient database management. We kept track of several details during each test—like the experiment and node IDs, the exact timestamp, and the RSSI. Having that information on hand made it easier to follow what happened in each transmission and helped us make sense of the results later on. Figure 1 includes photos of both the transmitter and receiver modules used, plus some notes on how they were set up.

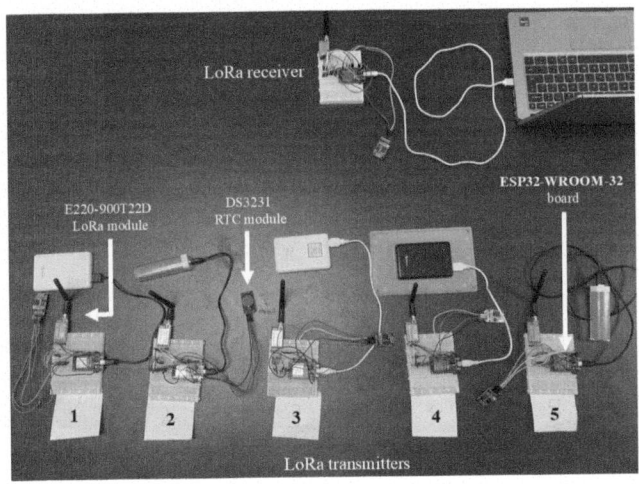

Fig. 1. Hardware components used in the experimental setup.

3.2   Experimental Scenarios

Each experiment was designed to analyze a specific factor of LoRa RSSI performance, ensuring controlled conditions to minimize external variables that affect the measurements.

EXP-01: Distance Variation in Line of Sight. This experiment evaluated the effect of distance on RSSI in an outdoor structured environment. The receiver was positioned in the main outdoor corridor of the ITM, while the transmitters were sequentially placed along the corridor at distances of 10 m, 50 m, and 100 m from the receiver to evaluate the impact of increasing separation on signal strength.

The receiver and transmitter nodes were placed on benches with a height of 70 cm to maintain a consistent elevation throughout the experiment, minimizing variations due to reflections and obstructions of the ground.

Data collection was made between 12:00 PM and 4:00 PM under environmental conditions of 28 °C and 97% humidity. During the experiment, the students was moving in the corridor, occasionally obstructing the transmission path, and it could affect the signal propagation due to human absorption and reflection effects.

Figure 2 provides a visual representation of the experimental setup, showing the placement of the receiver and transmitter devices at the specified distances.

Fig. 2. Experimental setup for RSSI distance variation in outdoor corridor.

EXP-02: Obstructed Environments (Concrete, Glass/Metal, and Composite Material Panel). This experiment evaluated how RSSI is affected by different physical barriers in an indoor structured environment. The test consisted of four distinct scenarios:

1. Line-of-Sight (LoS) reference experiment. The transmitter and receiver were positioned 10 m apart in an unobstructed environment to establish a baseline measurement.
2. Concrete wall experiment. A 30 cm thick concrete wall was placed between the transmitter and receiver, which were positioned 5 m apart on opposite sides of the barrier, to assess signal attenuation through dense structural material.
3. Glass/Metal door experiment. The signal was transmitted through a double-leaf aluminum frame with large transparent glass panels, with the door remaining closed to evaluate its impact on RSSI. The transmitter and receiver were again placed 5 m apart on opposite sides.

4. Composite material panel experiment. A non-load-bearing partition made of an aluminum frame, polyurethane-based sponge panel, and fabric upholstery (10 cm thick) was used to assess attenuation caused by common office and classroom partition materials, with the devices positioned 5 m apart.

These four experimental conditions allowed for a comparative analysis of how different materials impact LoRa signal propagation, with the LoS scenario serving as a reference for evaluating attenuation levels in obstructed environments.

To ensure consistent elevation over all the experiments, the transmitter and receiver were placed on tables of different heights depending on the test. For tests 1, 2, and 3 (LoS reference, concrete wall, and glass/metal door tests), the devices were located on tables measuring 75.5 cm in height. These tests were conducted on the first day, with data collection taking place between 2:00 PM and 5:30 PM, under indoor environmental conditions of 8 °C and 94% humidity.

For experiment 4 (composite material panel), the transmitter and receiver were placed on a table measuring 75.8 cm in height to match the test conditions. This experiment was carried out on the second day, with measurements recorded between 5:30 PM and 6:30 PM, under an ambient temperature of 22 °C and 68% humidity.

Figure 3 illustrates the positioning of the transmitter and receiver for the four tested scenarios.

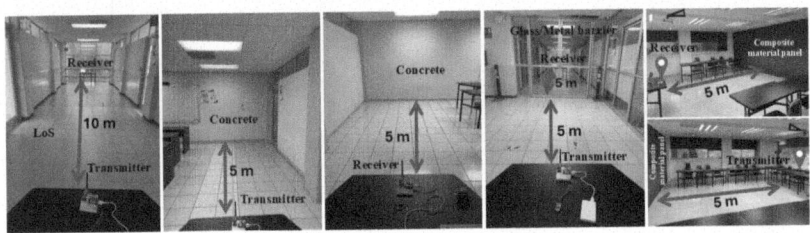

Fig. 3. Experimental setup for RSSI analysis with concrete, glass/metal, and composite panel obstructions.

EXP-03: Multi-source Wireless Interference (Wi-Fi, Bluetooth, and LoRa). This experiment evaluated LoRa performance in the presence of simultaneous wireless technologies, including Wi-Fi, Bluetooth, and an additional LoRa network. The tests were conducted in a library setting under two experimental conditions:

1. Baseline scenario: A single LoRa transmitter and receiver operated without interference from other wireless devices.

2. High-interference scenario: Forty students actively used laptops and smartphones connected to Wi-Fi, streamed music via Bluetooth, and an additional network of four LoRa transmitters operated simultaneously.

The experiments were carried out between 3:00 PM and 5:00 PM under indoor environmental conditions of 31 °C and 61% humidity. The LoRa transmitter and receiver were placed on tables measuring 77 cm in height to ensure consistent elevation across tests.

To ensure interference conditions, the devices were activated before RSSI measurements. Wi-Fi traffic was generated through instant messaging platforms, and Bluetooth interference was introduced by streaming music. The additional LoRa nodes transmitted at fixed intervals, synchronized with the primary LoRa transmitter, ensuring simultaneous operation during the RSSI measurement period.

Figure 4 illustrates the experimental setup for both scenarios, depicting the placement of the LoRa transmitter and receiver within the library environment and students using Wi-Fi and Bluetooth devices.

Fig. 4. Experimental setup for LoRa performance evaluation in a library environment under Wi-Fi, Bluetooth, and LoRa interference.

EXP-04: Elevation Variation and Multi-level Transmission. This experiment analyzed RSSI behavior at different heights in a multi-story educational environment. The receiver was positioned on the ground floor, placed directly on the floor in one of its corners. The transmitter was first placed on the second level at a height of 3.36 m and subsequently relocated to the third level at a height of 6.10 m.

Data collection was done between 4:00 PM and 6:00 PM under environmental conditions of 26 °C and 74% humidity. These measurements allowed for an assessment of how elevation differences impact signal strength, particularly in an outdoor multi-level setting where structural elements and height variations may influence LoRa signal propagation.

To ensure measurement consistency, the transmitter and receiver remained in a fixed orientation throughout the experiment. RSSI readings were recorded at predefined intervals of 3 s, maintaining uniform data collection.

Figure 5 represents the transmitter positions at different elevations, along with the receiver's position on the ground floor. Illustrates the vertical transmission path, offering insight into potential signal attenuation and structural interference effects.

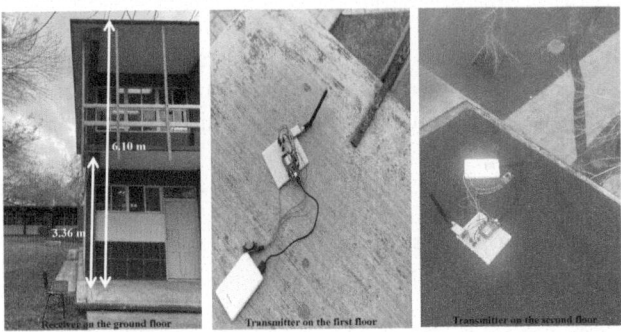

Fig. 5. Vertical transmitter-receiver placement for multi-level RSSI evaluation.

EXP-05: LoRa RSSI Performance in a Multi-node Network Simulation. This experiment evaluated LoRa RSSI performance in a simulated multi-node network at Technological and Business Innovation Node (NITE). Two test conditions were analyzed to assess the impact of multiple concurrent transmitters on signal strength and network behavior:

1. Baseline scenario: A single LoRa transmitter and receiver operated in isolation, serving as a control condition.
2. Multi-node scenario: Four additional LoRa transmitters operated simultaneously, introducing potential interference and testing network scalability.

The experiments were made between 1:30 PM and 3:30 PM under indoor environmental conditions of 24 °C and 72% humidity. All LoRa devices were placed on tables measuring 75.5 cm in height to ensure consistent positioning across tests.

To prevent uncontrolled packet collisions, the LoRa transmitters were incorporated into the network in a staggered manner, ensuring that multiple nodes did not transmit simultaneously. All devices were operated with the default spread factor and bandwidth settings provided by the LoRa modules used in the experiments, ensuring consistency in RSSI comparisons.

The experimental setups, objectives, configurations, and execution times are summarized in Table 1.

Table 1. Summary of the proposed experimental scenarios

Id	Objective	Details of the Configuration	Execution Time
EXP-01	Analyze RSSI based on varying distances.	**Distance Variation (Line of Sight).** The receiver was placed in an open corridor. Transmitters were positioned at 10 m, 50 m, and 100 m distances in a clear line-of-sight (LoS) environment. Three distance conditions were tested.	135 min (3 tests × 45 min)
EXP-02	Evaluate RSSI degradation caused by obstacles.	**Obstructed Environments (Concrete, Glass/Metal, and Composite Material Panel).** The receiver was placed indoors. Transmitters were placed 5 m away behind three types of barriers: concrete wall (30 cm thick), glass/metal door, and composite material panel (aluminum frame, polyurethane sponge, and fabric upholstery). A 10 m LoS reference test was also conducted.	180 min (4 tests × 45 min)
EXP-03	Measure RSSI under active interference.	**Multi-Source Wireless Interference (Wi-Fi, Bluetooth, LoRa).** The receiver was placed in a library. Two scenarios were tested: (1) baseline (no interference), and (2) high interference with 40 students using Wi-Fi and Bluetooth devices, plus an additional LoRa network with four transmitters.	90 min (2 tests × 45 min)
EXP-04	Evaluate RSSI at different node heights.	**Elevation Variation and Multi-Level Transmission.** The receiver was on the ground floor. The transmitter was placed at 3.36 m (second level) and 6.10 m (third level) to evaluate the impact of height on signal propagation.	90 min (2 tests × 45 min)
EXP-05	Evaluate RSSI in a multi-node network.	**LoRa RSSI Performance in a Multi-Node Network Simulation.** Tests conducted at NITE with two conditions: (1) a single transmitter and receiver, and (2) a multi-node network with four additional transmitters operating simultaneously.	90 min (2 tests × 45 min)

4   Experimental Results

LoRa performance was tested under five conditions to analyze their effect on RSSI, offering practical insights for optimizing IoT use in education.

4.1   Results for EXP-01: Distance Variation in Line of Sight

The first experiment evaluated how RSSI degrades as the distance between the transmitter and receiver increases in a line-of-sight (LoS) scenario. The objective was to quantify signal attenuation over increasing separation and evaluates the feasibility of long-range LoRa communication in an open environment.

Figure 6 illustrates the variation of RSSI as a function of distance. The recorded values indicate a clear decline in signal strength as the transmitter-receiver separation increased.

The results show an expected inverse correlation between distance and RSSI, where signal strength weakened progressively as the separation increased. A decrease of approximately 24.25 dB in RSSI was observed when the distance increased from 10 m to 100 m, aligning with theoretical free-space path loss models. Specifically, at 10 m, the RSSI measured −67.27 dBm, whereas at 100 m, it dropped to −91.52 dBm, confirming significant signal attenuation.

Despite the open environment, RSSI fluctuations varied across different distances, with standard deviations of ±1.49 dB at 10 m, ±0.92 dB at 50 m, and ±0.49 dB at 100 m. At 10 m, RSSI exhibited the highest variability, likely due to small-scale multipath effects and sporadic student movement momentarily obstructing the line-of-sight (LoS) path. At 50 m, RSSI fluctuations were lower, suggesting reduced environmental influence, while occasional deviations were observed, potentially caused by transient obstructions. At 100 m, RSSI showed the lowest variability, indicating a relatively stable signal despite increased attenuation. The reduced fluctuations at longer distances suggest minimal external interference and a dominant free-space path loss effect.

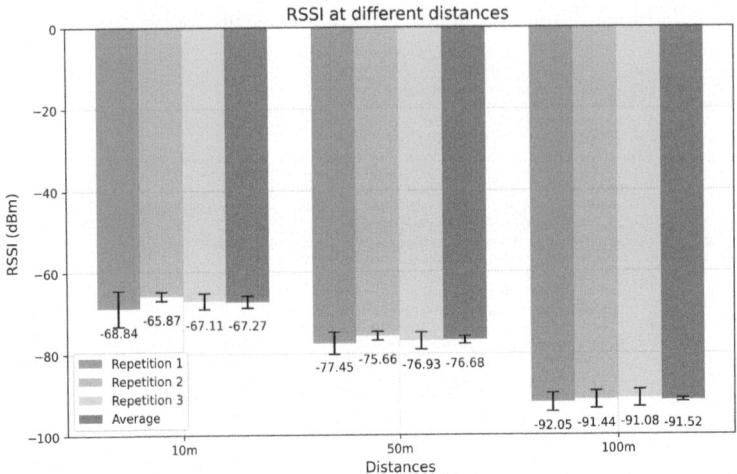

Fig. 6. RSSI attenuation as a function of distance in a Line-of-Sight environment.

These findings align with theoretical models predicting logarithmic signal attenuation over distance, as described in [3,13,19]. The results are consistent with the free-space path loss equation and empirical studies on signal degradation in LoRa networks [13,19]. The slight variability in RSSI measurements at intermediate distances suggests potential multi-path effects and environmental factors, which have been identified in prior studies analyzing RSSI fluctuations and their dependence on propagation conditions [3,19]. Despite the absence of major obstructions, the observed deviations may be influenced by uneven measurement distribution and minor reflections, factors previously discussed in path loss modeling research [3].

The results indicate that LoRa devices can maintain communication at moderate distances, but beyond 100 m, signal degradation is present. The importance of strategic node placement in large-scale IoT deployments to ensure optimal coverage and reliability in real-world environments.

4.2 Results for EXP-02: Obstructed Environments

This experiment analyzed the impact of physical obstructions on LoRa signal strength by comparing RSSI values in four different propagation environments: free space, concrete wall, glass/metal door, and a composite material panel. The objective was to quantify the signal degradation caused by each barrier type and evaluate how different materials influence LoRa communication.

Figure 7 presents the measured RSSI values for each propagation environment, showing a clear reduction in signal strength as obstacles were introduced. In the free-space scenario, the average RSSI was −40.22 dBm, indicating minimal signal attenuation. When a concrete wall was introduced, the RSSI dropped to −51.96 dBm, representing an attenuation of 11.74 dB. The glass/metal door

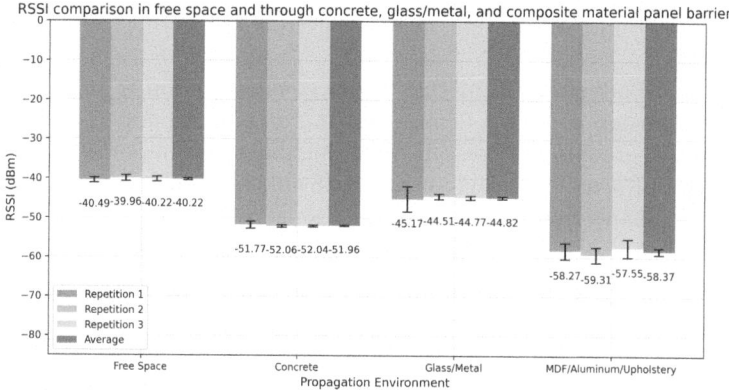

Fig. 7. RSSI variation across different propagation environments: free space, concrete, glass/metal, and composite material panel (aluminum frame, polyurethane sponge, and fabric upholstery).

caused a lower attenuation effect, with an average RSSI of -44.82 dBm, which is 4.60 dB weaker than free space but still higher than concrete. The composite material panel, consisting of an aluminum frame, polyurethane-based sponge panel, and fabric upholstery, exhibited the highest signal loss, with an average RSSI of -58.37 dBm, marking an attenuation of 18.15 dB relative to free space. These results confirm that denser and multi-layered materials cause greater signal degradation, reinforcing the importance of material-aware node deployment in indoor LoRa networks.

These results are consistent with established signal propagation behaviors, where denser materials introduce greater attenuation due to increased absorption and reflection effects. Concrete, with its high density and composition, led to significant RSSI reduction, aligning with prior empirical studies on LoRa signal degradation in urban environments [12]. The glass/metal barrier exhibited moderate attenuation, likely due to the partial penetration of glass, while the metal frame contributed to signal reflection and absorption [28]. The composite material panel resulted in the highest attenuation, suggesting that the combination of metallic elements, dense polyurethane padding, and fabric upholstery creates strong multi-path interference and absorption effects, severely impacting signal propagation [21,28]. These findings highlight the critical influence of material properties on LoRa communication and emphasize the importance of selecting optimal deployment locations in obstructed environments.

These results align with expected signal propagation behaviors, where denser materials introduce greater attenuation. Concrete, due to its higher density, led to significant RSSI reduction [12], while the glass/metal barrier showed moderate attenuation, likely because glass allows partial signal penetration while the metal frame contributes to reflections and absorption [28]. The composite material panel caused the highest attenuation, suggesting that the combination of metallic elements, dense polyurethane padding, and fabric covering creates strong reflection and absorption effects, severely impacting signal propagation [21,28].

Overall, the findings confirm that LoRa communication is highly sensitive to physical obstructions, with denser and more complex materials leading to greater signal degradation. These insights highlight the importance of careful placement of LoRa nodes in indoor environments to minimize signal loss and ensure reliable connectivity.

4.3   Results for EXP-03: Multi-source Wireless Interference

This experiment evaluated the impact of simultaneous wireless interference from Wi-Fi, Bluetooth, and an additional LoRa network on RSSI performance. The objective was to determine whether the presence of multiple active communication technologies in the 915 MHz ISM band would cause significant signal degradation in LoRa transmissions. Two scenarios were tested: one without interference (baseline) and one with active interference sources.

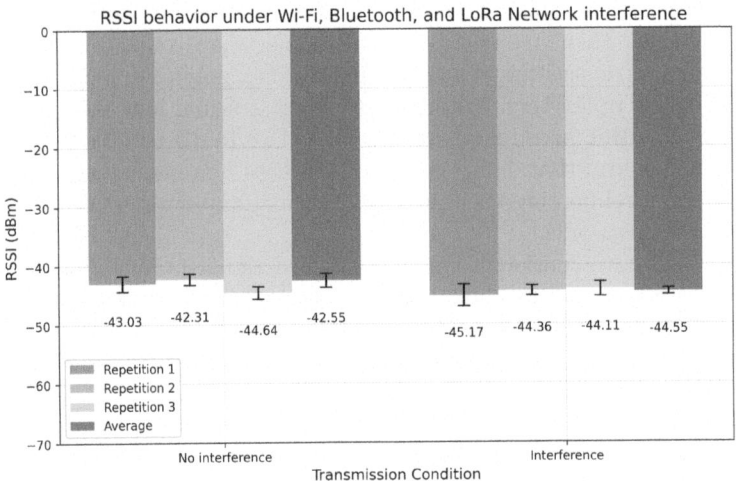

Fig. 8. RSSI behavior under Wi-Fi, Bluetooth, and LoRa network interference.

Figure 8 presents the measured RSSI values in both transmission conditions. In the no-interference scenario, the average RSSI was −42.55 dBm, with minor fluctuations between repetitions. When interference was introduced, the average RSSI decreased slightly to −44.55 dBm, representing a 2 dB drop in signal strength. This suggests that the presence of Wi-Fi, Bluetooth, and LoRa network transmissions introduced a moderate but measurable impact on LoRa signal reception.

The relatively small decrease in RSSI indicates that LoRa communication remains robust under moderate levels of interference from coexisting wireless technologies. Previous studies have demonstrated LoRa's high resilience to co-channel interference, particularly against Bluetooth operating in the 2.4 GHz band, with its performance being highly dependent on system configuration [20].

Regarding Wi-Fi interference, research suggests that LoRa can experience communication failures when operating in the 2.4 GHz spectrum, but proposed solutions such as exploiting signal demodulation correlations have been effective in significantly reducing packet error rates [24]. Although the LoRa network in this experiment operates at 915 MHz, harmonics and sideband emissions from nearby Wi-Fi and Bluetooth transmissions could still contribute to minor disruptions in the LoRa spectrum [20, 24].

Moreover, in-band interference from multiple LoRa nodes transmitting simultaneously is a challenge, as the network capacity is influenced by the number of end-devices and their transmission settings [10]. The presence of additional LoRa nodes in this experiment can introduce low levels of self-interference, affecting overall signal consistency. However, staggered transmission intervals were employed to minimize collisions, ensuring stable RSSI despite concurrent transmissions. Studies have shown that optimizing LoRa parameters can enhance signal robustness, even under interference conditions, with machine learning models being used to predict and adjust RSSI to improve network performance [26].

These findings support the notion that LoRa networks can coexist with other wireless technologies with minimal degradation in RSSI, reinforcing its suitability for dense communication environments. However, further research is needed to evaluate packet delivery rates and signal-to-noise ratios (SNRs) to comprehensively assess network performance under varying interference conditions.

4.4   Results for EXP-04: Elevation Variation

This experiment evaluated the impact of elevation variation on RSSI by comparing signal strength at two different transmission heights: first floor (ground level) and second floor (elevated position). The objective was to determine whether increased elevation improves signal stability and reception in an indoor environment.

Figure 9 presents the RSSI measurements recorded at both transmission positions. The experiment was conducted in an outdoor environment, where the transmitter was placed at two different elevations to evaluate the impact of height on RSSI stability. At ground level (first floor), the average RSSI was -63.12 dBm, with minor variations among repetitions. On the second floor, the average RSSI improved slightly to -61.40 dBm, representing an increase of approximately 1.72 dB in signal strength.

The relationship between transmission height and RSSI in outdoor environments is influenced by multiple factors, including signal propagation, environmental interference, and the physical setup of the communication system. Increasing the transmission height generally leads to improved RSSI due to reduced ground-level obstructions and lower signal absorption by surrounding structures. This effect is particularly relevant in outdoor settings, where line-of-sight (LoS) conditions can be more easily achieved, minimizing signal degradation [8, 9].

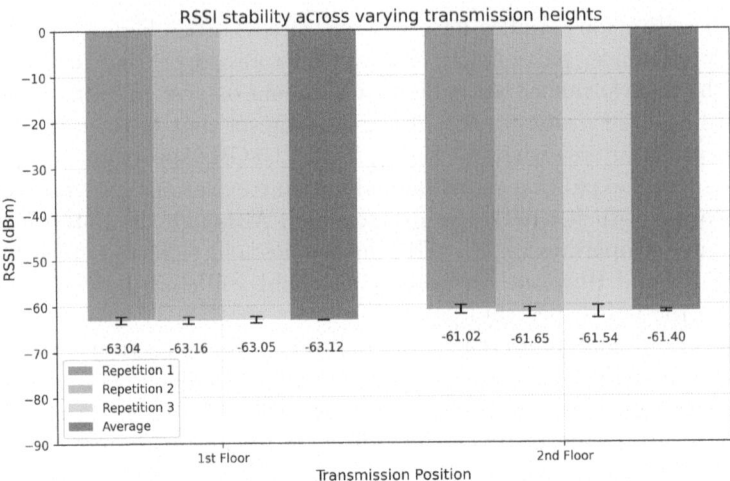

Fig. 9. RSSI stability across varying transmission heights.

A key factor contributing to improved RSSI at higher elevations is enhanced LoS visibility. The reduction of ground-level obstructions such as buildings and vegetation allows for a more stable communication link, decreasing attenuation and improving signal consistency [8,9]. Additionally, higher elevations reduce the likelihood of signal absorption and reflection by nearby structures, mitigating multipath fading and interference, which are common challenges in wireless communication [7].

Furthermore, research indicates that averaging RSSI over multiple heights can significantly reduce signal strength variation, improving localization precision in outdoor environments [18]. Implementing a height-only strategy has proven effective in stabilizing RSSI by minimizing the influence of ground-level interferences and reflections. Moreover, even small variations in transmission height can impact the path loss index, leading to measurable deviations in RSSI values. This further supports the idea that higher transmission heights help mitigate path loss effects, ensuring more stable and reliable LoRa communication in outdoor environments. Empirical path-loss models have shown that increasing transmission height improves signal coverage and reduces shading effects, which is essential for maintaining a stable connection in environments with varying topography and vegetation [4].

4.5 Results for EXP-05: Multi-node Network Performance

This experiment evaluated the impact of multinode LoRa transmission on RSSI performance by comparing two transmission conditions: a single transmitting node versus multiple transmitting nodes operating simultaneously. The objective was increase the network load, and concurrent transmissions introduced significant variations in signal strength, potentially affecting communication stability.

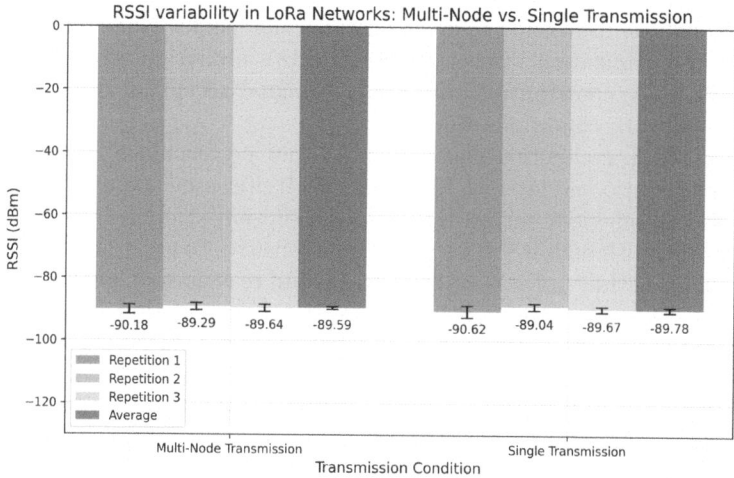

Fig. 10. RSSI variability in LoRa networks: Multi-node vs. single transmission.

Figure 10 presents the measured RSSI values under both transmission conditions. In the multi-node scenario, the average RSSI was −89.59 dBm, while in the single transmission scenario, the average RSSI was −89.78 dBm. The difference of 0.19 dB between the two conditions is minimal, it suggests that simultaneous transmissions from multiple LoRa nodes had a negligible impact on overall signal strength.

The relatively stable RSSI values across both scenarios indicate that LoRa communication is resistant to network congestion in terms of received signal power, a claim supported by multiple studies on LoRa's robustness under varying network conditions [5,6]. The small variations in RSSI observed in this experiment can be attributed to adaptive transmission schemes, which mitigate interference by dynamically adjusting transmission parameters such as spreading factor and transmission power. This adaptability, enabled by LoRa's Adaptive Data Rate (ADR) mechanism, helps maintain stable communication quality even in congested networks [23,27].

LoRa's strong anti-interference capability further contributes to signal stability, as it allows communication to remain reliable despite external sources of interference such as Wi-Fi networks. Studies have shown that techniques leveraging signal demodulation correlations significantly reduce packet error rates, reinforcing the stability of RSSI values across different network conditions [24]. Additionally, empirical research comparing simulated and real-world RSSI data confirms that LoRa networks maintain consistent signal strength across various deployment environments, highlighting their resilience to network congestion [5,6].

Furthermore, dynamic configuration techniques within enhanced ADR algorithms have been shown to improve packet delivery rates while reducing in-band interference, ensuring that transmission timing among nodes is efficiently distributed [23,27]. Emerging machine learning models for RSSI prediction and transmission optimization further support LoRa's ability to adapt to environmental variations, contributing to consistent signal reception strength despite fluctuating network conditions [26].

While network contention can influence other performance metrics such as packet delivery ratio and latency, LoRa's network efficiency and capacity to manage multiple end-devices ensure that signal reception strength remains largely unaffected [10]. Although RSSI is known to be sensitive to environmental factors, research confirms that LoRa networks can sustain reasonable signal levels across different environments, reinforcing their resilience in congested scenarios [5].

These findings support the conclusion that LoRa networks can maintain stable RSSI values under increased network load, ensuring reliable communication even in dense IoT deployments. However, while signal reception remains stable, other network performance aspects, such as latency and packet loss, may still require further optimization to maximize overall efficiency in congested environments.

5   Conclusion and Future Work

This study examined LoRa signal strength (RSSI) through five applied experiments in an educational IoT setting. As expected, signal quality diminished with distance, and physical obstacles—especially dense materials—caused notable attenuation. Interference from other wireless technologies showed minimal disruption, and changes in elevation had only a minor effect. Even under simultaneous activity from multiple nodes, the system remained stable, suggesting that LoRa can reliably support more dynamic configurations. These observations mark the starting point of a larger effort focused on designing adaptable IoT networks for real-world use in academic environments.

At this stage, the analysis was based solely on RSSI. Future phases will expand the evaluation by incorporating additional metrics such as Signal-to-Noise Ratio (SNR), Packet Error Rate (PER), and Effective Signal Power (ESP). Although the current implementation does not yet include full data transmission or network interconnection, its modular architecture was conceived with scalability in mind. It is worth noting that three of the five experiments were conducted indoors, including those involving signal obstruction and interference. Further tests across varied building types and indoor layouts will be necessary to broaden the relevance and reliability of the findings.

Acknowledgements. We sincerely acknowledge the partial financial support from TecNM/Instituto Tecnológico de Matamoros, Instituto Tecnológico de León, the Secretaría de Ciencia, Humanidades, Tecnología e Innovación (SeCiHTI), and Ubicomp Technologies. Their contributions in funding, infrastructure, and technical expertise were essential to the development and advancement of this research on IoT technologies in educational environments.

References

1. Abdelghany, A., Uguen, B., Moy, C., Lemur, D.: On superior reliability of effective signal power versus RSSI in LoRaWAN. Wirel. Netw. **27**(12), 4545–4560 (2021)
2. Anisah, N., K.A., Basri, S.: Experimental results of LoRa network radio propagation modeling in campus area. J. Wirel. Commun. Netw. **29**(3), 235–245 (2023)
3. Azevedo, J.A., Mendonça, F.: A critical review of the propagation models employed in LoRa systems. Sensors **24**(12), 3877 (2024)
4. Batalha, I.d.S., et al.: Large-scale modeling and analysis of uplink and downlink channels for LoRa technology in suburban environments. IEEE Internet Things J. **9**(23), 24477–24491 (2022)
5. Boonsong, W., Inthasuth, T., Kannan, U.: The quality of RF signal communication performance of LoRa-RSSI analysis based on various environments tests (2023)
6. Dinev, D., Haka, A., Aleksieva, V., Valchanov, H.: Analysis of LoRa RSSI data using simulations and real devices. In: 2023 18th Conference on Electrical Machines, Drives and Power Systems (ELMA), pp. 1–4. IEEE (2023)
7. Dong, Q., et al.: Study of RSSI accuracy for outdoor sensor localization. J. Circuits Syst. Comput. **31**(06), 2250115 (2022)
8. Dong, Q., Zhu, F., Cai, Y., Fang, L., Lu, M.: Analysis of RSSI feasibility for sensor positioning in exterior environment. In: 2021 Wireless Telecommunications Symposium (WTS), pp. 1–7. IEEE (2021)
9. Gao, J., Liu, Z., Guo, L., Hu, S., Zhong, Z., Nan, Z.: Design and analysis of outdoor multipath measurement system. In: 2024 Photonics & Electromagnetics Research Symposium (PIERS), pp. 1–6. IEEE (2024)
10. Gkotsiopoulos, P., Zorbas, D., Douligeris, C.: Performance determinants in LoRa networks: a literature review. IEEE Commun. Surv. Tutor. **23**(3), 1721–1758 (2021)
11. Irianto, K.D.: Performance evaluation of LoRa in farm irrigation system with internet of things. Kinet. Game Technol. Inf. Syst. Comput. Netw. Comput. Electron. Control **4**(1), 81–90 (2022)
12. Jörke, P., Böcker, S., Liedmann, F., Wietfeld, C.: Urban channel models for smart city IoT-networks based on empirical measurements of LoRa-links at 433 and 868 mhz. In: 2017 IEEE 28th Annual International Symposium on Personal, Indoor, and Mobile Radio Communications (PIMRC), pp. 1–6. IEEE (2017)
13. Karttunen, A., Molisch, A.F., Wang, R., Hur, S., Zhang, J., Park, J.: Distance dependence of path loss models with weighted fitting. In: 2016 IEEE International Conference on Communications (ICC), pp. 1–6. IEEE (2016)
14. Liu, J., et al.: Measurement and analysis of LoRa transmission performance in subway station. IEEE Trans. Wirel. Commun. **21**(7), 5201–5210 (2022)
15. Lopez, J., Kim, M., Nakamura, H.: Performance evaluation of LoRa communications in harsh industrial environments. Sens. Actuators, A **320**, 210–225 (2024)
16. Moradbeikie, A., Zare, M., Keshavarz, A., Lopes, S.I.: RSSI-based Lorawan dataset collected in a dynamic and harsh industrial environment with high humidity. Data Brief **53**, 110120 (2024)
17. Nguyen, P., Zhang, L., Singh, Y.: Performance evaluation and comprehensive analysis of LoRa network planning for IoT deployment scenarios. J. IoT Appl. **12**(4), 320–335 (2023)
18. Obeidat, H., Al-Sadoon, M., Zebiri, C., Obeidat, O., Elfergani, I., Abd-Alhameed, R.: Reduction of the received signal strength variation with distance using averaging over multiple heights and frequencies. Telecommun. Syst. **86**(1), 201–211 (2024)

19. Onykiienko, Y., Popovych, P., Yaroshenko, R., Mitsukova, A., Beldyagina, A., Makarenko, Y.: Using RSSI data for LoRa network path loss modeling. In: 2022 IEEE 41st International Conference on Electronics and Nanotechnology (ELNANO), pp. 576–580. IEEE (2022)

20. Polak, L., Paul, F., Simka, M., Zedka, R., Kufa, J., Sotner, R.: On the interference between LoRa and bluetooth in the 2.4 ghz unlicensed band. In: 2022 32nd International Conference Radioelektronika (RADIOELEKTRONIKA), pp. 1–4. IEEE (2022)

21. Ren, Y., Liu, L., Li, C., Cao, Z., Chen, S.: Is LoRaWAN really wide? Fine-grained LoRa link-level measurement in an urban environment. In: 2022 IEEE 30th International Conference on Network Protocols (ICNP), pp. 1–12. IEEE (2022)

22. Rifki, M.I., Ikhwan, A., Muhammad, F.: Performance evaluation of RSSI prediction methods in wireless communication networks. ZERO Jurnal Sains Matematika dan Terapan 8(1), 14–25 (2024)

23. Sanou, F.d., Hamadoun, T., Yelemou, T.: Dynamic adaptation of the modulation in a LoRa channel according to the link quality. In: 2024 IEEE Multi-conference on Natural and Engineering Sciences for Sahel's Sustainable Development (MNE3SD), pp. 1–8. IEEE (2024)

24. Shao, C., Tsukamoto, K., Ma, Y.W.: Toward resilient LoRa communication under Wi-Fi interference. In: 2024 International Conference on Consumer Electronics-Taiwan (ICCE-Taiwan), pp. 249–250. IEEE (2024)

25. Syed Taha, S.N., Abu Talip, M.S., Mohamad, M., Azizul Hasan, Z.H., Tengku Mohmed Noor Izam, T.F.: Evaluation of LoRa network performance for water quality monitoring systems. Appl. Sci. 14(16), 7136 (2024)

26. Tabaa, M., Hachimi, H., et al.: RSSI prediction for improved LoRa communications performance. In: 2024 IEEE 12th International Symposium on Signal, Image, Video and Communications (ISIVC), pp. 1–7. IEEE (2024)

27. Wang, H., Zhao, B., Liu, X., Pan, R., Pang, S., Song, J.: An adaptive data rate algorithm for power-constrained end devices in long range networks. Mathematics 12(21), 3371 (2024)

28. Wu, Z., Shen, Q., Wang, J.: Researching on signal transmission performance of LoRa technology in urban environment. In: 2023 IEEE 12th Data Driven Control and Learning Systems Conference (DDCLS), pp. 1056–1061. IEEE (2023)

29. Zhang, Z., Zhang, B., Zhang, X.: Performance research of LoRa at high transmission rate. J. Phys: Conf. Ser. 1544, 012177 (2020)

Pedagogical Challenges of Generative AI in Academic Writing

Teresa Guarda[1,2,3]([⊠]) [iD], Luis Chuquimarca[1,2] [iD], and Maria Fernanda Augusto[4] [iD]

[1] Universidad Estatal Península de Santa Elena, La Libertad, Ecuador
tguarda@gmail.com
[2] Facultad de Sistemas y Telecomunicaciones, La Libertad, Ecuador
[3] Algoritmi Centre, Minho University, Guimarães, Portugal
[4] BiTrum Research Group, Leon, Spain

Abstract. This review looks at the challenges and methods for using generative AI in academic writing across many subjects. Recent studies (2023–2024) that used mixed methods, case studies, and theory show many ways AI is used in schools. Students use AI tools for brainstorming, creating ideas, and check-ng their work [1]. There are problems with academic honesty, basic learning, and grading methods [2]. In science and tech, AI-written text can sometimes match or even be better than student work. In subjects like history and literature, it is hard to keep a student's unique voice and style [3]. Students and teachers see AI very differently. This gap grows because schools do not give enough training and the rules are not clear [4]. Studies show that AI affects each sub-ject in its own way. There are concerns about keeping work real and helping students think clearly [5].

Keywords: Generative AI · Academic Writing · Academic Integrity

1 Introduction

Generative AI tools in higher education have changed the usual ways of teaching academic writing. This change brings new chances and challenges in how teachers work. As these tools get better and easier to use, schools must decide how to use them in college teaching [6].

These tools help with everything from coming up with ideas to organizing work and fixing grammar mistakes [1]. Even though AI makes writing easier, it also brings up real concerns. Educators worry about keeping academic standards high and making sure students truly learn, not just rely on AI.

The issues go beyond technical matters and raise questions about how we should teach writing when AI plays such a big role in education. Teachers and schools are working to balance using these tools while keeping the main goal of writing education [8].

Students and teachers see AI in writing very differently. Students are mostly positive about these tools and see them as a helpful part of writing [4]. They like that AI can help with coming up with ideas, creating drafts, and checking work [3].

O. Gervasi et al. (Eds.): ICCSA 2025 Workshops, LNCS 15891, pp. 411–421, 2026.
https://doi.org/10.1007/978-3-031-97617-9_27

Teachers worry about AI in their classes. They fear cheating, the loss of proper writing skills, and that students may depend too much on AI [4]. The issue is harder because many schools do not have clear rules for using AI.

Teachers do not get enough training on these tools, and there is no standard way to grade writing when AI is used [6]. This difference in how students and teachers view AI makes it hard to develop teaching methods that work for everyone.

AI affects college subjects in different ways, bringing both issues and benefits to each field. In technical subjects like computer science and engineering, AI can sometimes write papers that match or even surpass the quality of student work [8]. This leads to questions about how to grade student work and what the true goal of teaching in these subjects should be [5].

Humanities courses face clear challenges. They must keep each student's own voice, grow creative work, and keep the realness of student work [2]. Writing classes have trouble balancing help from AI with the basic goal of building students' own writing skills [5].

Each subject has its own issues that need special plans for using AI. These plans must fit different teaching needs and learning goals. Research shows we need clear rules for ethics, grading work, and teaching changes [9].

Studies list key parts for success: clear school rules on AI, strong teacher training, classes to build AI skills, grading methods that include AI, and firm ethical rules [6]. Making these plans takes care to match what the technology can do with how teaching works.

AI helps students learn without lowering the quality of education. Recent studies show that to succeed, we must set clear limits on using AI and teach students to think and write on their own [1].

This study examines the challenges that AI tools bring to college writing classes. It considers ten recent studies that use different methods and cover various subjects.

The work focuses on key areas: finding good ways to use these tools, noting differences in AI use among subjects, setting clear rules for fair use, and testing new teaching ideas.

This review collects results from several studies. It shows clear ways to keep school work honest when using AI for writing in class. It brings together findings from many studies and explains how to keep learning fair while using AI's benefits.

The study stresses a balanced approach to builds critical thinking, keeps student choice, and changes old tests to include AI tools [5]. This review of current evidence aims to guide school rules and teaching methods in a world with more AI.

2 Generative AI in Academic Writing

Generative AI is a new tool that changes how college students write. It brings both help and problems for students and teachers. These tools work well for tasks like brainstorming, coming up with ideas, and handling basic writing tasks [10, 11].

This AI uses models such as Generative Adversarial Networks (GANs) and Variational Autoencoders (VAEs) to study large sets of data and produce similar content [12].

It is used in many areas like healthcare, movies, and education [13]. Unlike older AI systems that follow set tasks, this tool makes new data on its own.

It is changing work and how we talk to each other [14]. It may also improve search tools and the way we create information in the metaverse era [15]. At the same time, it raises issues about privacy and fairness [13].

Generative AI has grown a lot. Key changes include neural networks, language models, and ways to create images [16]. New tools like ChatGPT and DALL-E let anyone use strong language tech, which helps people make work that sounds very human [1].

These tools work in many areas. They help computers read images and text and assist in health care and business decisions. This technology is exciting, but it also brings up serious ethical issues, such as fake content and the safe use of these tools [6].

As AI gets better, it affects many fields. We must think about the new tools and the ethical risks [5]. In schools, tools like ChatGPT change how students write and do research. They help students work faster, spark new ideas, and let them share their thoughts clearly [2], but they also bring challenges for both teachers and students [4].

The goal is to use AI as a tool that supports learning while keeping true academic work and real understanding [3]. Using AI tools raises concerns about academic honesty and the truth of scholarly work [17, 18].

Generative AI may ease some academic work but can also make current problems in higher education worse [19]. Universities are handling this by enforcing rules on academic honesty, teaching those involved, and finding ways to use AI responsibly [20]. In tourism and hospitality research, AI tools can change how data is collected and studied while raising ethical issues.

As the landscape evolves, there is a need for ongoing discussions about the ethical use of AI in academia, emphasizing human intelligence and critical [21].

3   Methodology

The method used in this study was shaped by the research question: "What are the specific pedagogical challenges introduced by generative AI technologies in undergraduate academic writing across different disciplines?".

To explore this, we carried out a systematic review of current researches following the PRISMA approach to ensuring the transparency and rigor of this process.

3.1   Review Strategy

The review adhered to the four standard stages outlined by the PRISMA model: identification, screening, eligibility, and inclusion. These procedures facilitated the acquisition of recent and pertinent studies that investigate the application of generative AI in academic writing.

3.2   Data Sources and Search Terms

We used two well-known academic databases, Scopus and Web of Science (WoS), because they offer a wide range of peer-reviewed studies in education and technology. The search used combinations of these keywords:

- "generative AI" OR "artificial intelligence"
- "academic writing" OR "undergraduate writing"
- "higher education" OR "undergraduate education"
- "pedagogy" OR "teaching" OR "instruction"

These keywords were chosen to focus the search on how generative AI is being used in writing courses in higher education and to identify studies that explore teaching and learning impacts.

3.3 Inclusion and Exclusion Criteria

In this step, we used strict inclusion and exclusion criteria for publication date, context, scope, study type, and educational setting to guarantee the relevance and quality of the studies in this review.

Inclusion Criteria

- Published between 2023 and 2024;
- Focus on undergraduate academic writing;
- Address pedagogical challenges, implementations, or experiences with generative AI;
- Include empirical research, theoretical analysis, systematic reviews, or case studies;
- Context: higher education;
- Language: English.
- Exclusion Criteria:
- Solely technical studies without pedagogical relevance;
- Focused on K-12 or postgraduate education;
- Published before 2023;
- Provided insufficient methodological detail or only preliminary findings.

Exclusion Criteria

- Solely technical studies without pedagogical relevance;
- Focused on K-12 or postgraduate education;
- Published before 2023;
- Provided insufficient methodological detail or only preliminary findings.

3.4 Selection Process

A total of 148 studies were found through database searches. After removing duplicates, 63 studies were left for full-text review. From these, 28 articles did not meet the eligibility criteria and were excluded. The final review was based on 10 peer-reviewed studies. This process is shown in the PRISMA flow diagram below. (Fig. 1).

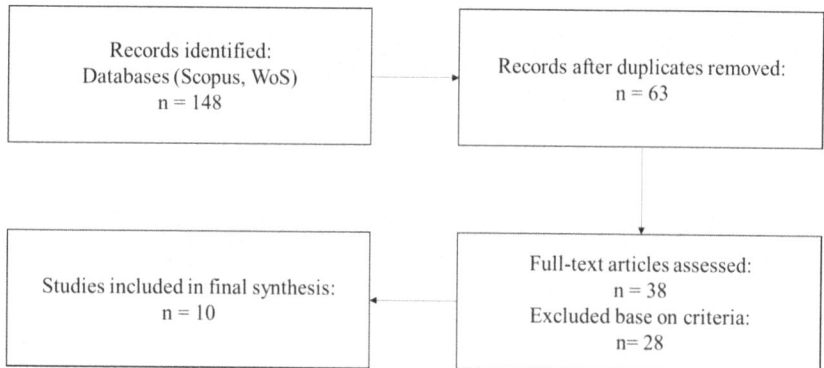

Fig. 1. PRISMA Flow Diagram, Integration of Generative AI in Academic Writing.

3.5 Quality Assessment

The included studies were evaluated based on:

- Methodological rigor;
- Relevance to the research question;
- Clarity of findings;
- Contribution to understanding pedagogical challenges;
- Applicability across disciplines.

3.6 Data Synthesis

A thematic synthesis approach was applied to analyze the diverse methodologies. The main themes that emerged were:

- Barriers to pedagogical integration of AI;
- Disciplinary differences in AI usage and challenges;
- Divergent student-teacher perceptions;
- Emerging pedagogical frameworks and implementation models.

We removed all studies that met the exclusion criteria we had set. This part of the process involved carefully reading the full texts of papers that seemed relevant and reviewing the quality of those that moved forward.

We assessed each study's quality by looking at five key points: how solid the methods were, how closely the study matched our research question, how clearly the findings were explained, whether it helped us understand the pedagogical challenges of AI, and if its conclusions could apply to more than one field.

These steps helped us keep the review focused on the topic while making sure we included research that was recent and relevant to how generative AI is affecting undergraduate academic writing.

In the end, we worked with 10 studies. The methods they used were diverse: we included 2 mixed-methods studies, 2 case studies, 2 theoretical or conceptual papers, and one each of a cross-sectional study, an action research project, a scoping review, and a phenomenological study.

The studies covered a range of subjects. Three looked at multiple disciplines, two focused directly on academic writing, and the rest explored areas like English composition, first-year writing, teacher education, and fields in science, economics, and higher education.

The pedagogical settings included first-year writing programs (3 studies), general undergraduate writing contexts (2 studies), and individual studies in workshops, teacher training programs, bachelor's degrees, and higher education settings.

We read and analyzed all the full-text studies included in the review. Our analysis was guided by recurring themes across the research. These included how AI is being used in writing tasks, what makes it difficult for educators to apply in practice, how these issues vary between disciplines, and the differences in how students and teachers experience and understand AI. We also looked at how new teaching approaches are starting to take shape in response to these changes.

4   Discussion: Pedagogical Implications and Future Directions

The synthesis of findings reveals several critical implications for the integration of generative AI in undergraduate writing. The persistent tension between technological assistance and authentic learning emerges as a central challenge, with multiple studies indicating that while AI tools can enhance idea generation and reduce cognitive load [1], they simultaneously raise concerns about skill development and academic integrity [8].

A significant finding warranting further discussion is the notable disconnect between student and faculty perspectives. While students generally demonstrate greater acceptance of AI tools [4], instructors express more substantial reservations about their impact on learning outcomes. This gap suggests a critical need for institutional dialogue and policy development to bridge these divergent viewpoints.

The cross-disciplinary analysis reveals that challenges manifest differently across academic fields. Technical disciplines face unique challenges in maintaining academic integrity when AI-generated content can match or exceed student work quality [8], while humanities-focused courses struggle more with preserving individual voice and creative expression [2].

Several key implications for practice emerge highlighting: the need for institutional framework development; faculty development requirements; and the assessment reform (Table 1).

The future research directions highlight:

(1) The investigation of effective assessment strategies in an AI-enabled environment.
(2) Realize longitudinal studies on the impact of AI integration on writing skill development.
(3) The evaluation of various pedagogical frameworks for AI integration.

As limitation, the current analysis primarily reflects early-stage implementation experiences and may not fully capture long-term implications or successful adaptation strategies.

This discussion framework contextualizes the findings within broader educational practice while highlighting critical areas for future investigation and development.

Table 1. Emerged key implications.

Key Implications	Description
Need for institutional framework development	Current findings suggest that institutions must develop comprehensive policies that address both ethical concerns and practical implementation guidelines [5]
Faculty development requirements	The identified gap in faculty preparedness indicates a pressing need for systematic professional development programs [7]
Assessment reform	Traditional assessment methods require significant revision to account for AI capabilities while maintaining educational integrity [8]

5 Results

The systematic review analyzed 10 studies that met the inclusion criteria. The methodological approaches varied considerably, comprising two mixed methods studies, two case studies, two theoretical/conceptual analyses, and individual studies using quantitative cross-sectional, action research, scoping review, and phenomenological approaches. The disciplinary distribution showed three studies focused on various disciplines, two on academic writing, and individual studies examining English composition, first-year writing, teacher education, scientific/economic disciplines, and higher education.

5.1 Primary Findings

The analysis revealed consistent patterns regarding AI tool utility across studies. Researchers found that AI tools provided significant benefits for brainstorming and idea generation [1], while also proving valuable for mechanical checks and proofreading tasks [7].

Students reported reduced cognitive load when utilizing these tools [3]. In terms of academic performance, a notable finding emerged showing that AI-generated papers scored higher than student-written work in certain disciplines [8], though students often expressed a preference for developing their own voice despite AI capabilities [2].

5.2 Thematic Analysis Results

The integration of AI into the writing process revealed several significant challenges. Primary concerns centered around balancing AI support with independent skill development [1], maintaining authenticity in student work [3], and adapting assessment methods to account for AI capabilities [8].

A notable divergence emerged between student and faculty perspectives, with students generally showing greater acceptance of AI tools [4], while faculty expressed more significant concerns about academic integrity and skill development [6].

Cross-disciplinary analysis revealed distinct patterns across academic fields. Technical disciplines reported higher performance of AI-generated content and faced specific challenges in maintaining academic integrity [8]. In contrast, humanities-focused courses emphasized preserving student voice [2] and developing critical thinking skills [5].

5.3 Implementation Frameworks

The analysis identified five essential components for institutional guidelines: clear institutional policies, faculty training programs, AI literacy curriculum, adaptive assessment methods, and ethical use frameworks. Successful pedagogical implementation required self-regulated learning approaches [5], development of critical AI literacy [5], and modified assessment strategies [8].

Faculty development emerged as a crucial factor, with studies highlighting the need for training in AI tool integration [7] and understanding of ethical implications [9]. Implementation barriers manifested at both institutional and classroom levels.

At the institutional level, studies identified a lack of clear policies and guidelines [4] and insufficient faculty training resources [7].

Classroom-level challenges included difficulties in detecting AI-generated content, maintaining academic integrity, and adapting assessment methods to account for AI capabilities (Table 2).

Table 2. Key Components, Pedagogical Factors, and Implementation Barriers for Integrating Generative AI in Undergraduate Academic Writing.

Dimension	Component/Factor	References
Institutional Guidelines	Clear institutional policies	[3]
	Faculty training programs	[22]
	AI literacy curriculum	[4]
	Adaptive assessment methods	[6]
	Ethical use frameworks	[23]
Pedagogical Implementation	Self-regulated learning approaches	[4]
	Critical AI literacy	[4]
	Modified assessment strategies	[6]
Faculty Development	Training in AI tool integration	[22]
	Understanding ethical implications	[23]
Implementation Barriers	Lack of clear policies and guidelines (institutional)	[22]
	Insufficient faculty training resources (institutional)	
	Difficulty detecting AI-generated content (classroom)	
	Maintaining academic integrity (classroom)	
	Adapting assessment methods for AI (classroom)	

The findings collectively suggest that successful integration of generative AI in undergraduate academic writing requires a comprehensive approach addressing both institutional policy development and classroom-level implementation strategies. The evidence indicates that while AI tools offer significant potential benefits, their effective integration demands careful consideration of pedagogical implications and systematic support structures.

6 Conclusions and Future Perspectives

The systematic review of recent studies reveals several crucial insights about the integration of generative AI in undergraduate academic writing. First, while AI tools demonstrate clear benefits for brainstorming and mechanical aspects of writing [1], their implementation presents significant challenges for maintaining academic integrity and developing authentic writing skills [6].

A notable finding is the persistent gap between student and faculty perspectives on AI use. Students generally show greater acceptance and appreciation for AI tools, while faculty members express more concerns about academic integrity and skill development [4]. This disconnect is exacerbated by insufficient institutional guidelines and inadequate faculty training [7].

The cross-disciplinary analysis reveals that while challenges vary across fields, common threads emerge regarding the need for balanced integration approaches. Technical disciplines face particular challenges in maintaining academic integrity [8], while humanities-focused courses emphasize preserving student voice and critical thinking [2].

The emerging pedagogical framework, incorporating clear institutional policies, faculty training, AI literacy curriculum, adaptive assessment methods, and ethical guidelines, provides a comprehensive approach to addressing these challenges [5]. However, successful implementation requires institutional commitment and systematic faculty development.

Respecting to the future perspectives, several key areas require further investigation and development: assessment innovation; faculty development; ethical framework evolution; cross-disciplinary applications; and student skill development. The following Table 3 gives detailed information.

Table 3. Key areas require further investigation and development.

Key areas	Description
Assessment Innovation	Development and validation of new assessment methods that effectively evaluate AI-assisted work Creation of rubrics that balance technological integration with skill development Research on the long-term impact of AI-integrated assessment approaches [6]

(continued)

Table 3. (*continued*)

Key areas	Description
Faculty Development	Design and evaluation of comprehensive faculty training programs Investigation of effective methods for building faculty confidence in AI integration Development of support systems for ongoing pedagogical adaptation [3]
Ethical Framework Evolution	Research on emerging ethical considerations as AI technology advances Development of more sophisticated plagiarism detection methods Investigation of best practices for maintaining academic integrity [5]
Cross-disciplinary Applications	Further study of discipline-specific challenges and solutions Investigation of transferable practices across fields Research on discipline-specific assessment adaptations [4]
Student Skill Development	Long-term studies on the impact of AI integration on writing skill development Research on effective methods for fostering critical thinking alongside AI use Investigation of strategies for maintaining student autonomy and creativity [1]

For future research, it would be important to examine the long-term impacts of AI integration on student learning outcomes and writing skill development. Additionally, attention should be paid to developing more sophisticated frameworks for ethical AI use that can adapt to rapidly evolving technology while maintaining academic integrity and educational quality.

References

1. Wang, C.: Exploring students' generative AI-assisted writing processes: perceptions and experiences from native and nonnative English speakers. Technol. Knowl. Learn. 1–22 (2024). https://doi.org/10.1007/s10758-024-09744-3
2. Cummings, R.E., Monroe, S.M., Watkins, M.: Generative AI in first-year writing: an early analysis of affordances, limitations, and a framework for the future. Comput. Compos. **71**, 1–11 (2024). https://doi.org/10.1016/j.compcom.2024.102827
3. Gabriel, S.: Generative AI in writing workshops: a path to AI literacy. In: Proceedings of the International Conference on AI Research, ICAIR 2024, vol. 4, no. 1, pp. 126–132 (2024). https://doi.org/10.34190/icair.4.1.3022
4. Barrett, A., Pack, A.: Not quite eye to A.I.: student and teacher perspectives on the use of generative artificial intelligence in the writing process. Int. J. Educ. Technol. High Educ. **20**(59), 1–24 (2023). https://doi.org/10.1186/s41239-023-00427-0

5. Kong, S.C., Lee, J.C., Tsang, O.: A pedagogical design for self-regulated learning in academic writing using text-based generative artificial intelligence tools: 6-P pedagogy of plan, prompt, preview, produce, peer-review, portfolio-tracking. Res. Pract. Technol. Enhanced Learn. **19**, 1–18 (2024). https://doi.org/10.58459/rptel.2024.19030

6. Moya, B.A., Eaton, S.E.: A rapid scoping review on academic integrity and algorithmic writing technologies. Can. Symp. Acad. Integr. **6**(1), pp. 1–5 (2023). https://doi.org/10.55016/ojs/cpai.v6i1.76882

7. Cirstea, A.: Pedagogical uses of AI tools: reflection on a case study. J. Learn. Dev. High. Educ. **32**, 1–7 (2024). https://doi.org/10.47408/jldhe.vi32.1402

8. Molinari, A., Molinari, E.: The added value of academic writing instruction in the age of large language models: a critical analysis. Int. J. WWW/Internet **22**(1), 44–58 (2024)

9. Oravec, J.A.: Artificial intelligence implications for academic cheating: expanding the dimensions of responsible human-AI collaboration with ChatGPT and bard. J. Interact. Learn. Res. **34**(2), 213–237 (2023). Obtenido de. https://www.learntechlib.org/primary/p/222340/

10. Ramdurai, B., Adhithya, P.: The impact, advancements and applications of generative AI. Int. J. Comput. Sci. Eng. **10**(6), 1–8 (2023). https://doi.org/10.14445/23488387/ijcse-v10i6p101

11. Kar, S., Roy, C., Das, M., Mullick, S., Saha, R.: AI Horizons: unveiling the future of generative. Int. J. Adv. Res. Sci. Commun. Techno. (IJARSCT) **3**(1), 1–5 (2023). https://doi.org/10.48175/ijarsct-12969

12. Leslie, D., Rossi, F.: ACM TechBrief: generative artificial intelligence. ACM (2023). https://doi.org/10.1145/3626110

13. Warankar, M., Patil, R.: Generative artificial intelligence. Int. J. Sci. Res. Eng. Manag. (IJSREM) **8**(4), 1–7 (2024). https://doi.org/10.55041/IJSREM31146

14. Feuerriegel, S., Hartmann, J., Janiesch, C.: Generative AI. Bus Inf. Syst. Eng. **66**, 111–126 (2024). https://doi.org/10.1007/s12599-023-00834-7

15. Zhihan, L.: Generative artificial intelligence in the metaverse era. Cogn. Robot. **3**, 1 (2023). https://doi.org/10.1016/j.cogr.2023.06.001

16. Balasubramaniam, S., et al.: The road ahead: emerging trends, unresolved issues, and concluding remarks in generative AI—a comprehensive review. Int. J. Intell. Syst. 1–38 (2024). https://doi.org/10.1155/2024/4013195

17. Eke, D.O.: ChatGPT and the rise of generative AI: threat to academic integrity? J. Respon. Technol. **13**, 1–4 (2023). https://doi.org/10.1016/j.jrt.2023.100060

18. Dergaa, I., Chamari, K., Zmijewski, P., Saad, H.B.: From human writing to artificial intelligence generated text: examining the prospects and potential threats of ChatGPT in academic writing. Biol. Sport **40**(2), 615–622 (2023). https://doi.org/10.5114/biolsport.2023.125623

19. Watermeyer, R., Phipps, L., Lanclos, D., Knight, C.: Generative AI and the automating of academia. Postdigital Sci. Educ. **6**(2), 446–466 (2024). https://doi.org/10.1007/s42438-023-00440-6

20. Plata, S.D.: Emerging research and policy themes on academic integrity in the age of chat GPT and generative AI. Asian J. Univ. Educ. **19**(4), 743–758 (2023). https://doi.org/10.24191/ajue.v19i4.24697

21. Grimes, M., Von Krogh, G., Feuerriegel, S., Rink, F., Gruber, M.: From scarcity to abundance: scholars and scholarship in an age of generative artificial intelligence. Acad. Manag. J. **66**(6), 1617–1624 (2023). https://doi.org/10.5465/amj.2023.4006

22. Luk, M.: Generative AI: overview, economic impact, and applications in asset management. Econ. Impact Appl. Asset Manag. (2023). https://doi.org/10.2139/ssrn.4574814

23. Batchu, C., Satya, V.: Generative AI: evolution and its future. Int. J. Multidisciplinary Res. **6**(1), 1–6 (2024). https://doi.org/10.36948/ijfmr.2024.v06i01.12046

Author Index

O. Gervasi et al. (Eds.): ICCSA 2025 Workshops, LNCS 15891, pp. 423–424, 2026.
https://doi.org/10.1007/978-3-031-97617-9

The manufacturer's authorised representative in the EU is Springer
Nature Customer Service Centre GmbH, Europaplatz 3, 69115 Heidelberg,
Germany. If you have any concerns regarding our products, please
contact ProductSafety@springernature.com

Printed and bound by CPI Group (UK) Ltd, Croydon, CR0 4YY
29/04/2026
02099458-0011